A Practical Review
of German Grammar

GERDA DIPPMANN

Central College, Pella, Iowa

A PRACTICAL REVIEW
OF GERMAN GRAMMAR

PRENTICE HALL, Englewood Cliffs, New Jersey 07632

Library of Congress Cataloging-in-Publication Data

Dippmann, Gerda.
  A practical review of German grammar / Gerda Dippmann.
    p.   cm.
  Originally published: New York : Macmillan, 1987.
  Includes index.
  ISBN 0-13-690090-9
  1. German language--Grammar--1950- 2. German language--Textbooks
for foreign speakers--English.   I. Title.
PF3112.D56 1992
438.2'421--dc20   92-30238
                                                        CIP

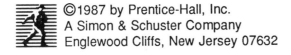 ©1987 by Prentice-Hall, Inc.
A Simon & Schuster Company
Englewood Cliffs, New Jersey 07632

Printed in the United States of America
10 9 8 7 6 5 4 3 2

ISBN 0-13-690090-9

Prentice-Hall International (UK) Limited, *London*
Prentice-Hall of Australia Pty. Limited, *Sydney*
Prentice-Hall Canada Inc., *Toronto*
Prentice-Hall Hispanoamericana, S.A., *Mexico*
Prentice-Hall of India Private Limited, *New Delhi*
Prentice-Hall of Japan, Inc., *Tokyo*
Simon & Schuster Asia Pte. Ltd., *Singapore*
Editora Prentice-Hall do Brasil, Ltda., *Rio de Janeiro*

Preface

College students enrolled in second-year German courses usually vary greatly in their grasp of German grammar. They need a solid grammar foundation if they are to continue their language learning; however, class time that may be devoted to grammar is limited.

A Practical Review of German Grammar is arranged so that the instructor can assign the major portion as homework. Sequence and treatment of the grammatical features are based on an empirical approach. The foremost consideration has been to facilitate comprehension by the students. Most explanations are simple enough that even students with little formal knowledge of grammar will be able to understand them. Each explanation is followed immediately by exercises to allow students to check their ability to apply what they have just read. Summarizing exercises at the end of a section or chapter review larger units. Students with deficient backgrounds will appreciate the detailed treatment; those with strong backgrounds will be able to work through the review rapidly.

The exercises are in natural German, frequently in conversational form. Words presumed to be unknown are footnoted for quick reference. In order to give the instructor the freedom to assign chapters in any sequence, the vocabulary for each chapter is largely self-contained. (This accounts for some duplication in the glossed words.)

SUPPLEMENTS

1. A taped key to all exercises: 10 dual-track cassettes (total running time approximately 12 hours). So that students may use the cassettes wherever and whenever they do their homework, schools may wish to make multiple copies that can be checked out in the language lab, department, or audio-visual section of the library. In addition, copies may be made on cassettes provided by the students.

2. An *Instructor's Key* with the answers to all exercises (transcripts of the cassettes). Thus by reading the *Key* instructors can easily check what the students heard without listening to the cassettes themselves.

SUGGESTIONS FOR APPROACHING THE GRAMMAR REVIEW

The three general steps below outline how the grammar review may be approached.

1. The instructor makes assignments. Because of the detailed treatment of the grammatical features in the book, the instructor may need to provide only very brief explanations before assigning material. Many assignments may be made with no prior explanations.

2. Students complete the assignments. They note features they do not understand completely. The taped key to the exercises will prove especially useful for students who have difficulty grasping grammatical concepts.

3. Class time is devoted to answering questions the students may have, checking homework assignments, and administering tests. If instructors require all students to use the taped key, they may choose to check only selected exercises that address the problems of their students.

Acknowledgments

I would like to thank friends, colleagues, and students for their suggestions and assistance. My special thanks go to: Leo Connolly (Memphis State University), G. Thomas Mann (Graceland College, Lamoni, Iowa), Ellin Feld (Columbia University), Maxine Fish Huffman (Central College, Pella, Iowa), Eckhard Kuhn-Osius (Hunter College, CUNY), Gina Sauer (Luther College, Decorah, Iowa); and to the students of Central College and Graceland College who worked with a manuscript version of this text.

G.D.

Contents

Appendix   A-1

1

Preliminary Remarks about German Word Order

KEY TO THE EXERCISES ON CASSETTE 1.
RUNNING TIME: APPROX. 15 MIN.

This chapter deals with some basic aspects of German word order. Other aspects will be treated in subsequent chapters.

Word Order in Statements

§1 NORMAL WORD ORDER: SUBJECT – INFLECTED VERB

The inflected (conjugated) verb is the form with the personal endings.

> **Wir** **wiederholen** die Grammatik.   *We are reviewing grammar.*
> | | |
> **SUBJECT**   **VERB**   **DIRECT OBJECT**

Adding an adverb:

> Wir wiederholen **oft** die Grammatik. We **often** review grammar.

In English an adverb may be placed between the subject and the verb. This cannot be done in German. The verb must be the second element.

§2 INVERTED WORD ORDER: INFLECTED VERB – SUBJECT

For emphasis or stylistic reasons an element other than the subject may be in first position.

> Heute **wiederholen** **wir** die Grammatik.
> | | |
>   **VERB**   **SUBJ.** **DIR. OBJ.**

The verb remains in second position; the subject follows the inflected verb. Thus the normal subject-verb sequence is inverted.

PRACTICE 1   *Restate the following sentences, placing the boldface elements first.*

Model: Ich gehe **heute abend** mit Hans ins Kino.
            Heute abend gehe ich mit Hans ins Kino.

1. Du glaubst das **natürlich** nicht.
2. Sie verstehen mich **vielleicht**[1] nicht.
3. Wir spielen **am Montag** Tennis.
4. Mein Kassettenrecorder funktioniert **leider**[2] nicht.
5. Ich fahre nicht wieder **mit dir** in die Stadt.
6. Michael sagt **hoffentlich**[3] die Wahrheit.[4]
7. Wir spielen **manchmal**[5] Karten.
8. Es war **gestern** sehr kalt.
9. Helga ist **jetzt** nicht zu Hause.
10. Viele Leute wissen **das** nicht.

Elements with no effect on word order

The most common elements that do not affect word order are listed below.

a. Set off by a comma:

ja	Ja, **ich verstehe** Sie.
nein	Nein, **ich verstehe** Sie nicht.
(form of address)	Frau Böhme, **ich verstehe** Sie nicht.

b. Not set off by a comma:

aber (*but*)   Aber
denn (*for*)   Denn
oder (*or*)   Oder ⟩ **viele Leute wissen** das nicht.
und (*and*)   Und

Aber, denn, oder, und are coordinating conjunctions that usually connect two clauses (cf. Chap. 12, §1).

Das Postamt ist heute geschlossen, aber viele Leute wissen das nicht.
The post office is closed today, but many people don't know that.

§3   DEPENDENT WORD ORDER: INFLECTED VERB STANDS LAST

Dependent word order occurs in dependent clauses. Such clauses cannot stand alone; they are dependent upon other clauses. They are introduced by subordinating conjunctions, such as **daß, weil** (*because*), **wenn** (*when, if*). (Cf. Chap. 12, §2)

1 **vielleicht**	perhaps
2 **leider**	unfortunately
3 **hoffentlich**	*lit.* hopefully, *generally used in the sense of* I hope
4 **die Wahrheit sagen**	to tell the truth
5 **manchmal**	sometimes

Es ist möglich,   daß **wir** heute die Grammatik **wiederholen**.

└─MAIN CLAUSE─┘   └──────────DEPENDENT CLAUSE──────────┘

It is possible   that we'll review grammar today.

The subject usually follows the subordinating conjunction immediately. The inflected verb is in final position.

PRACTICE 2   *Convert the following sentences to dependent clauses by beginning with* **Es ist möglich, daß . . .**

Model: Das ist ein Fehler.
Es ist möglich, daß das ein Fehler ist.

1. Das ist Peters Freundin.
2. Müllers[1] sind jetzt zu Hause.
3. Herr Schmidt arbeitet heute nicht.
4. Andreas und Barbara heiraten[2] im Juni.
5. Frau Braun sagt die Wahrheit.
6. Die Hausaufgaben[3] sind zu schwer.
7. Karin hat heute keine Zeit.
8. Es wird morgen kälter.
9. Wir besuchen Sie am Sonntag.
10. Ich bin nicht tolerant genug.

Word order without *daß*

When **daß** is omitted, normal or inverted word order is used.

Ich weiß, **Müllers sind** jetzt nicht zu Hause.
Ich glaube, jetzt **sind Müllers** nicht zu Hause.

The dependent clause preceding the main clause

Wir gehen heute abend nicht ins Kino, weil wir kein Geld haben.
Weil wir kein Geld haben, **gehen wir** heute abend nicht ins Kino.

└── DEPENDENT CLAUSE──┘ └────────── MAIN CLAUSE──────────┘

The main clause has inverted word order when it is preceded by a dependent clause. The latter is treated as the first element of the main clause. Compare:

Wir	**gehen**	heute abend nicht ins Kino.
SUBJ.	VERB	
Heute abend	**gehen**	**wir** nicht ins Kino.
	VERB	SUBJ.
Weil wir kein Geld haben,	**gehen**	**wir** heute abend nicht ins Kino.
	VERB	SUBJ.

1 **Müllers**   *the* Müllers (in German without article)
2 **heiraten**   to marry, get married
3 **die Hausaufgaben** (*pl.*) homework

PRACTICE 3 *Restate the following sentences, beginning with the dependent clause.*
Model: Wir kaufen ein neues Auto, wenn wir genug Geld haben.
    Wenn wir genug Geld haben, kaufen wir ein neues Auto.

1. Ich schreibe dir, wenn ich mehr Zeit habe.
2. Er geht heute nicht in die Vorlesung, weil er Fieber hat.
3. Ich werde sehr böse,[1] wenn du nicht pünktlich bist.[2]
4. Inge hat schlechte Laune,[3] weil Heinz nicht anruft.
5. Ich nehme zwei Aspirintabletten,[4] wenn ich Kopfschmerzen habe.

Word Order in Questions

§4 DIRECT QUESTIONS

Direct questions have inverted word order: the inflected verb is in first or second position. Compare the following two types of questions:

Wann **wiederholen wir** die Grammatik?
        | |
     VERB   SUBJ.

Wiederholen wir heute die Grammatik?
    | |
  VERB   SUBJ.

The verb is in second position when the question begins with a question word, such as **wann** (*when*), **warum** (*why*), **wo** (*where*), **wieviel** (*how much*).

When there is no question word, the verb is in first position.

Note that there is no German equivalent for the English auxiliary *do* in questions:

Do you understand me?
Verstehen Sie mich?

PRACTICE 4 *Convert the following statements to questions.*
    A. *Begin with the verb.*
    Model: Das ist ein Fehler.
        Ist das ein Fehler?

1. Elke hat einen Job.
2. Andreas sagt die Wahrheit.
3. Neumanns sind nicht zu Hause.

---

1 **böse werden**	to become angry
2 **pünktlich sein**	to be on time
3 **die Laune**	mood
gute/schlechte Laune haben	to be in a good/bad mood
4 **die Aspirintablette, -n**	aspirin

4. Es wird morgen kälter.
5. Der Kassettenrecorder funktioniert nicht.
6. Ich bin nicht tolerant genug.

B. *Begin with the indicated question word.*
Model: Das ist ein Fehler. (warum)
Warum ist das ein Fehler?

1. Schmidts sind zu Hause. (wann)
2. Anita fährt in die Stadt. (wann)
3. Andreas hat schlechte Laune. (warum)
4. Du glaubst das nicht. (warum)
5. Dieter und Elke heiraten. (wann)
6. Monika und Renate spielen Tennis. (wo)

§5   INDIRECT QUESTIONS

Indirect questions have dependent word order: the inflected verb stands last. They depend on an introductory clause, such as **Ich weiß nicht** . . . , **Ich möchte wissen** . . . (*I would* or *I'd like to know* . . .). Compare the following two types of indirect questions:

Wann wiederholen wir die Grammatik?
Ich möchte wissen,
  wann wir die Grammatik **wiederholen.**
*I would like to know **when** we"ll review the grammar.*

In an indirect question the question word functions as a subordinating conjunction, hence the dependent word order.

Wiederholen wir heute die Grammatik?
Ich möchte wissen,
  ob wir heute die Grammatik **wiederholen.**
*I'd like to know **whether** (**if**) we'll review grammar today.*

If the direct question has no question word, the subordinating conjunction **ob** (*whether, if*) is used to introduce the indirect question.

PRACTICE 5   *Convert the following direct questions to indirect questions using the introductory clause of the model.*
A. **Direct questions with question word**
Model: Was ist das?
    Ich weiß nicht, was das ist.

1. Wo wohnen Bergers?
2. Wo ist die Toilette?[1]
3. Warum lachen die Leute?

1 **die Toilette, -n**   toilet (*commonly used as the equivalent of ladies' room, men's room, lavatory*)

4. Wann kommt Klaus nach Hause?
5. Wieviel kostet dieser Ring?
6. Warum ist Frau Köhler so schockiert?[1]
7. Wo sind die Autoschlüssel?[2]
8. Was kostet das?

B. **Direct questions without a question word**
Model: Hat Andreas eine Freundin?
   Ich möchte wissen, ob Andreas eine Freundin hat.

1. Sind Schmidts jetzt zu Hause?
2. Ist das ein Fehler?
3. Sagt Rita die Wahrheit?
4. Bin ich tolerant genug?
5. Hat der Chef[3] gute oder schlechte Laune?
6. Ist die Chefin in ihrem Büro?[4]
7. Liebst du mich wirklich?[5]

The introductory clause may be a question, such as **Weißt du . . . ?**, **Wissen Sie . . . ?**, **Können Sie mir sagen . . . ?**, **Kannst du mir sagen . . . ?**

DIRECT QUESTION	INDIRECT QUESTION
Was ist das?	**Weißt du, was das ist?**
	Do you know what that is?
Sind Schmidts zu Hause?	**Wissen Sie, ob Schmidts zu Hause sind?**
	Do you know whether the Schmidts are at home?
Wo wohnen Bergers?	**Können Sie mir sagen, wo Bergers wohnen?**
	Can you tell me where the Bergers live?

Remember:

> An indirect question depends on an introductory clause (statement or question) and may be regarded as a "dependent question" requiring dependent word order.

PRACTICE 6   *The following questions begin with or without a question word. Convert them to indirect questions, using the indicated introductory clauses.*
Model: Wo ist der Bahnhof? (Können Sie mir sagen)
   Können Sie mir sagen, wo der Bahnhof ist?

1	**schockiert sein**	to be shocked
2	**der Autoschlüssel, -**	car key
3	**der Chef, -s**	male boss
	die Chefin, -nen	female boss
4	**das Büro, -s**	office
5	**wirklich**	real(ly)

1. Wo ist die nächste Tankstelle?[1] (Können Sie mir sagen)
2. Wann beginnt das Konzert? (Wissen Sie)
3. Wieviel kostet dieser Kassettenrecorder? (Weißt du)
4. Wo wohnt Helga? (Wissen Sie)
5. Wohnt Helga bei ihren Eltern? (Wissen Sie)
6. Hat Andreas einen Job? (Weißt du)
7. Ist Professor Wagner jetzt in seinem Büro? (Wissen Sie)
8. Wo ist sein Büro? (Können Sie mir sagen)
9. Hat Renate die Grippe?[2] (Weißt du)
10. Was bedeutet[3] dieses Wort? (Kannst du mir sagen)

§6   SUMMARY

The following patterns illustrate the normal word order, the inverted word order, and the dependent word order.

		INFLECTED VERB	
a. NORMAL WORD ORDER	Wir	**wiederholen**	die Grammatik.
b. INVERTED WORD ORDER			
STATEMENT	Heute	**wiederholen**	**wir** die Grammatik.
DIRECT QUESTION			
WITH QUESTION WORD	Wann	**wiederholen**	**wir** die Grammatik?
WITHOUT QUESTION WORD		**Wiederholen**	**wir** die Grammatik?

The inflected verb is in second position except in direct questions that do not begin with a question word, in which case it is in first position.

			INFLECTED VERB
c. DEPENDENT WORD ORDER			
STATEMENT	Es ist möglich,	**daß** wir die Grammatik	**wiederholen.**
INDIRECT QUESTION	Ich weiß nicht,	**wann** wir die Grammatik	**wiederholen.**
	Ich weiß nicht,	**ob** wir die Grammatik	**wiederholen.**
	Weißt du,	**wann** wir die Grammatik	**wiederholen?**

The inflected verb is in final position.

1 **die Tankstelle, -n**   gas station
2 **die Grippe, -n**   flu
3 **bedeuten**   to mean

PRACTICE 7   *Translate into German.*

Model: a. She is in a good mood.   **Sie hat gute Laune.**
b. I hope she's in a good mood.   **Hoffentlich hat sie gute**
                                      Laune.

c. Is she in a good mood?   **Hat sie gute Laune?**
d. Do you (**du**) know whether she   **Weißt du, ob sie gute**
   is in a good mood?   **Laune hat?**

1. a. He has a car.   **Er hat einen Wagen.**
   b. I hope he has a car.
   c. Does he have a car?
   d. Do you (**du**) know whether he has a car?
2. a. She believes that.   **Sie glaubt das.**
   b. I hope she believes that.
   c. Does she believe that?
   d. I don't know whether she believes that.
3. a. She is Dieter's girlfriend.   **Sie ist Dieters Freundin.**
   b. Perhaps she is Dieter's girlfriend.
   c. Is she Dieter's girlfriend?
   d. I'd like to know whether she is Dieter's girlfriend.
   e. It is possible that she is Dieter's girlfriend.
4. a. I am not tolerant enough.   **Ich bin nicht tolerant genug.**
   b. Perhaps I am not tolerant enough.
   c. Am I not tolerant enough?
   d. It is possible that I am not tolerant enough.
5. a. The Neumanns live in Munich.   **Neumanns wohnen in**
      München.
   b. Do the Neumanns live in Munich?
   c. Where do the Neumanns live?
   d. I'd like to know where the Neumanns live.
6. a. She is not at home.   **Sie ist nicht zu Hause.**
   b. Is she not at home?
   c. Why isn't she at home?
   d. I don't know why she isn't at home.
7. a. He's in a bad mood.   **Er hat schlechte Laune.**
   b. Perhaps he's in a bad mood.
   c. Why is he in a bad mood?
   d. Do you (**Sie**) know why he is in a bad mood?

The Position of *nicht*

A distinction has to be made between normally accented negation and strong negation of a particular element.

§7   NORMALLY ACCENTED NEGATION

Nicht follows the inflected verb, pronoun objects, and most noun objects.

INFLECTED VERB	Sein Bruder raucht **nicht**.
PRONOUN OBJECT	Ich kenne ihn **nicht**.
NOUN OBJECT	Ich kenne seinen Bruder **nicht**.

Nicht precedes most other elements.

a. predicate adjectives and predicate nouns
    (they follow the main verbs **sein, werden, heißen**):

> Ich bin **nicht** nervös.
> Ich werde **nicht** nervös.
> Sabine wird **nicht** Lehrerin.
> Er heißt **nicht** Martin.

b. most adverbs:

> Sie sprechen **nicht** laut genug.
> Wir fahren **nicht** zu schnell.

but **nicht** follows most adverbs of time:

> Er kommt heute **nicht**.
> Ich arbeite abends **nicht**.

c. most prepositional phrases:

> Dieser Brief ist **nicht** für mich.
> Susanne wohnt **nicht** bei ihren Eltern.

If several of the above elements occur in a sentence, **nicht** usually precedes the first one:

> Sie ist **nicht** freundlich zu mir.
> Schmidts fliegen **nicht** mit uns nach Europa.

The position of **nicht** is the same in questions:

> Ist sie **nicht** freundlich zu dir?
> Warum fliegen Schmidts **nicht** mit uns nach Europa?

When negating dependent clauses, keep in mind that the inflected verb stands last. Compare:

> Frau Weber kennt meinen Vater **nicht**.
> Es ist möglich, daß Frau Weber meinen Vater **nicht** kennt.

Otherwise the position of **nicht** follows the same rules that are valid for main clauses.

§8   STRONG NEGATION OF A PARTICULAR ELEMENT

If one element is strongly negated, **nicht** precedes that particular element. Such an emphatic negation is often part of a contrast.

> Ulrich kauft **nicht diesen Wagen**; er kauft einen anderen.
>
> **Nicht Mathias** kauft diesen Wagen; seine Schwester kauft ihn.

PRACTICE 8   A. *Explain the position of* **nicht** *in the following sentences.*

> **Model:** Sie ist nicht nett[1] zu mir.
>
> ***Nicht** precedes the predicate adjective *nett*.*

1. Helga ist nicht meine Freundin.
2. Dieser Ring gefällt mir nicht.
3. Klaus weiß, daß der Ring Annette nicht gefällt.
4. Ich verstehe die Hausaufgaben nicht.
5. Warum fragen Sie ihn nicht?
6. Ich möchte wissen, warum Sie ihn nicht fragen.
7. Das ist nicht mein Hobby.
8. Martin fliegt nicht mit seinen Eltern nach Florida.
9. Ich gehe mit Peter nicht ins Kino; wir gehen in die Disko.
10. Fräulein Schiller arbeitet nicht bei dieser Firma.
11. Warum glauben Sie mir nicht?
12. Nicht Schmidts, sondern (*but rather*) Bergers besuchen uns morgen.
13. Schmidts besuchen uns morgen nicht.
14. Es ist schade,[2] daß sie uns morgen nicht besuchen.
15. Hoffentlich wird es nicht kälter.
16. Monikas Freund heißt nicht Thomas.

B. *Negate the following sentences according to the rules for normally accented negation. (Do not negate the boldface introductory clauses.)*

1. Meine Eltern fliegen nach Paris.
2. Margot ist meine Freundin.
3. Ich bezahle diese Rechnung.[3]
4. **Es ist möglich**, daß er die Rechnung bezahlt.
5. Peter arbeitet in der Bibliothek.
6. Meine Noten[4] werden besser.
7. Arbeiten Sie heute?
8. Sind Zimmermanns zu Hause?
9. **Ich weiß**, daß Zimmermanns heute zu Hause sind.
10. Der italienische Film gefällt meiner Freundin.
11. **Es ist möglich**, daß der italienische Film meiner Freundin gefällt.
12. Vielleicht weiß Astrid seinen Namen.
13. **Es ist möglich**, daß unsere Fußballmannschaft[5] morgen gewinnt.

---

1 **nett**	nice
2 **es ist schade**	it is a pity
3 **die Rechnung, -en**	bill
4 **die Note, -n**	grade
5 **die Fußballmannschaft, -en**	soccer team

14. Das ist gut für die Nerven.
15. **Wissen Sie**, daß das gut für die Nerven ist?
16. Verstehen Sie mich?
17. **Ich weiß**, daß er mich versteht.

(For the position of **nicht** in sentences that contain verb complements, see Chap. 19, §4 [Note].)

§9   USING *nicht wahr?*

Du hast eine Schwester, **nicht wahr?**
*You have a sister, **don't you?***

Du hast keinen Bruder, **nicht wahr?**
*You don't have a brother, **do you?***

Hans und Margot haben geheiratet, **nicht wahr?**
*Hans and Margot got married, **didn't they?***

Du kannst mich verstehen, **nicht wahr?**
*You can understand me, **can't you?***

Nicht wahr? (lit. *not true?*) is used like English *don't you?*, *do you?*, *didn't they?*, *can't you?*, and the like, to seek confirmation of what was just said. **Nicht wahr?** is often shortened to **nicht?**

Du hast eine Schwester, **nicht?**

PRACTICE 9   *Translate into English.*

1. Helga ist deine Freundin, nicht wahr?
2. Sie hat einen Wagen, nicht wahr?
3. Du verstehst mich, nicht wahr?
4. Renate und Frank spielen Tennis, nicht?

2

Verbs in the Present Tense
The Imperative

KEY TO THE EXERCISES ON CASSETTE 1.
RUNNING TIME: APPROX. 40 MIN.

Verbs in the Present Tense

§1   BASIC FORMS OF THE PRESENT TENSE

The infinitive is the form of the verb you will find in a dictionary. It usually has the ending **-en**. A small group of verbs has the ending **-n**, such as **sammeln** (*to collect*), **bewundern** (*to admire*), **tun** (*to do*). The verb stem may be obtained by dropping the ending **-en** or **-n**.

INFINITIVE:	gehen	STEM:	geh-
	studier**en**		**studier-**
	sammel**n**		**sammel-**
	bewunder**n**		**bewunder-**
	tu**n**		**tu-**

The inflectional endings of the present tense are added to the stem. They are as follows:

infinitive ending *-en*

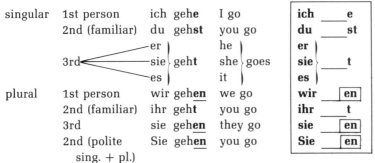

singular	1st person	ich geh**e**	I go	**ich** ___ **e**		
	2nd (familiar)	du geh**st**	you go	**du** ___ **st**		
	3rd	er / sie / es geh**t**	he / she / it goes	**er / sie / es** ___ **t**		
plural	1st person	wir geh**en**	we go	**wir** [**en**]		
	2nd (familiar)	ihr geh**t**	you go	**ihr** ___ **t**		
	3rd	sie geh**en**	they go	**sie** [**en**]		
	2nd (polite sing. + pl.)	Sie geh**en**	you go	**Sie** [**en**]		

Note that the three marked forms have the same endings as the infinitive.

infinitive ending -*n*

The three marked forms add -**n** instead of -**en**, making them identical to the infinitive.

ich samm(e)le*	ich bewund(e)re*	ich tue	ich ____ e
du sammelst	du bewunderst	du tust	du ____ st
er ⎫	er ⎫	er ⎫	er ⎫
sie ⎬ sammelt	sie ⎬ bewundert	sie ⎬ tut	sie ⎬ ____ t
es ⎭	es ⎭	es ⎭	es ⎭
wir sammeln	wir bewundern	wir tun	wir ____ n
ihr sammelt	ihr bewundert	ihr tut	ihr ____ t
sie sammeln	sie bewundern	sie tun	sie ____ n
Sie sammeln	Sie bewundern	Sie tun	Sie ____ n

* Verbs ending in -**eln** or -**ern** often omit the **e** before **l** or **r** when an inflectional **e** is added.

There are three German equivalents to the English *you*:

you ⎯⎯ **du** familiar address singular
⎯⎯ **ihr** familiar address plural
⎯⎯ **Sie** formal address singular and plural

The familiar form **du** and its plural counterpart **ihr** are used when addressing relatives, close friends, children up to about the age of 15, pets, or deity. Young people usually also say **du** to one another. Otherwise **Sie** is used.

PRACTICE 1   A. *Substitute the appropriate forms of the verbs in parentheses.*

Model: Helga lernt es nicht. (studieren, tun).
Helga studiert es nicht.
Helga tut es nicht.

1. Frank sagt das nicht. (glauben, sammeln, bewundern, tun, organisieren)
2. Warum glaubst du das nicht? (lernen, studieren, tun)
3. Warum raucht ihr? (lachen, lächeln,[1] applaudieren)
4. Warum verstehen Sie das nicht? (glauben, korrigieren, tun)
5. Ich frage ihn. (lieben, bewundern, kritisieren, manipulieren, irritieren)

B. *Restate the following sentences, using the subjects in parentheses.*

1. Wir lernen Deutsch. (ich, sie [she], sie [they])
2. Meine Schwester studiert in Bonn. (ich, wir)
3. Warum lachen Sie? (du, er, ihr)

1 **lächeln**   to smile

4. Warum applaudieren Sie? (du, ihr)
5. Er bewundert Sie. (ich, wir)
6. Meine Freundin sammelt Briefmarken.[1] (ich, wir, sie [they])
7. Ich tue das nicht. (er, wir, viele Leute)
8. Warum tun Sie das nicht? (du, ihr)
9. Diese Musik irritiert mich. (diese Kinder)
10. Thomas sagt nichts, er lächelt nur. (ich, wir, sie [they])

A note on the German equivalents of *to study*

Studieren is used
a. to refer to enrollment at a college or university:

> Klaus studiert an der Universität Bonn.
> or: Klaus studiert in Bonn.

b. to indicate a student's major:

> Anita studiert Chemie. (Meaning: *Anita's major is chemistry.*)

c. to mean "gaze at intently":

> Ich studiere den Fahrplan.   *I'm studying the time table.*
> Wir studieren die Speisekarte.   *We're studying the menu.*

Lernen is used to render *to study* in the sense of studying for a test, an exam, or of learning something:

> *I'm studying for an exam.*   Ich **lerne** für eine Prüfung.
> *Barbara studies German and*   Barbara **lernt** Deutsch und Spanisch.
> *Spanish.*   Meaning: *Barbara is taking German and Spanish courses.* (Neither German nor Spanish is her major.)

§2   VERBS WITH STEMS ENDING IN *-d. -t*, OR CONSONANT CLUSTERS

To facilitate pronunciation, an **e** is inserted between the stem and the endings of the 3rd pers. sing. and the **du** and **ihr**-forms of:

a. verbs whose stems end in **-d** or **-t**, such as **antworten**, (*to answer*), **arbeiten** (*to work*), **bedeuten** (*to mean*), **beneiden** (*to envy*), **finden** (*to find*), **heiraten** (*to marry*), **reden** (*to talk*);

b. verbs whose stems end in certain consonant clusters, i.e.

> a single **m** or **n** that is preceded by a consonant other than **l** or **r**.

Few verbs belong to this group. Some common ones are **atmen** (*to breathe*), **öffnen** (*to open*), **regnen** (*to rain*), **zeichnen** (*to draw*).

---

1 **die Briefmarke, -n**   stamp

PRACTICE 2   A. *Supply the appropriate forms of the verbs in parentheses.*

Model: Barbara _____. (reden, zeichnen)
Barbara redet.
Barbara zeichnet.

1. Rainer _____ nicht. (arbeiten, antworten, warten)
2. _____ du mich? (beneiden, heiraten, bitten)
3. Warum _____ ihr nicht? (warten, antworten, reden, zeichnen)
4. _____ du den Brief nicht? (finden, öffnen)
5. Es _____ viel. (regnen, kosten, bedeuten)

B. *Restate the following sentences, using the subjects in parentheses.*

1. Wir arbeiten zuviel. (du)
2. Sie atmen nicht tief genug. (der Patient)
3. Warten Sie auf mich? (du)
4. Ich rede zuviel. (meine Freundin)
5. Warum beneiden Sie mich? (ihr)
6. Ich bitte um Verzeihung.[1] (Klaus)
7. Ich zeichne gern.[2] (Helga)
8. Finden Sie diesen Film wirklich interessant? (du)

§3   VERBS WITH STEMS ENDING IN -*s*, -*ss*, -*ß*, -*tz*, or -*z*

These verbs add only **-t** to the stem of the **du**-form; thus the 2nd and 3rd person singular are identical.

Some common verbs that belong to this group are **hassen** (*to hate*), **heißen** (*to be called*), **reisen** (*to travel*), **schließen** (*to close*), **schwänzen** (*to skip class*), **sitzen** (*to sit*), **tanzen** (*to dance*), **übersetzen** (*to translate*).

---

1 **um Verzeihung bitten**   to apologize
2 **etwas gern tun**   to like doing something

reisen	hassen	heißen	sitzen	schwänzen
ich reise	ich hasse	ich heiße	ich sitze	ich schwänze
du reist	du haßt*	du heißt	du sitzt	du schwänzt

er }
sie } reist
es }

er }
sie } haßt
es }

er }
sie } heißt
es }

er }
sie } sitzt
es }

er }
sie } schwänzt
es }

* Note that **ss** becomes **ß** when followed by a consonant (cf. Appendix, §1).

PRACTICE 3   *Restate the following sentences using* **du** *as the subject.*

1. Sitzen Sie immer in der ersten Reihe?[1]
2. Reisen Sie viel?
3. Warum hassen Sie diese Frau?
4. Warum übersetzen Sie diesen Satz nicht?
5. Warum schließen Sie die Tür nicht?
6. Wie heißen Sie?
7. Monika schwänzt jeden Freitag.
8. Susanne tanzt sehr gut.

§4   VERBS WITH STEM CHANGES

Many strong verbs (cf. chap. 3, §5) change their stem vowels in the 2nd and 3rd pers. sing. In addition, the verbs **nehmen** and **treten** also change stem consonants.

1. **Change from** *e* **to** *ie* **or** *i*

sehen	lesen	essen	geben	nehmen (to take)
ich sehe	ich lese	ich esse	ich gebe	ich nehme
du **siehst**	du **liest**	du **ißt**	du **gibst**	du **nimmst**

er }
sie } **sieht**
es }

er }
sie } **liest**
es }

er }
sie } **ißt**
es }

er }
sie } **gibt**
es }

er }
sie } **nimmt**
es }

wir sehen	wir lesen	wir essen	wir geben	wir nehmen
ihr seht	ihr lest	ihr eßt	ihr gebt	ihr nehmt
sie sehen	sie lesen	sie essen	sie geben	sie nehmen
Sie sehen	Sie lesen	Sie essen	Sie geben	Sie nehmen

Note that the forms **du liest** and **du ißt** add **-t,** rather than **-st,** because of the stem ending in **s** or **ß.**

1 **die Reihe, -n**   row

2. Change from *a, au, o* to *ä, äu, ö*

fahren	schlafen	laufen (*to run*)	stoßen (*to push*)
ich fahre	ich schlafe	ich laufe	ich stoße
du **fährst**	du **schläfst**	du **läufst**	du **stößt**
er ⎫	er ⎫	er ⎫	er ⎫
sie ⎬ **fährt**	sie ⎬ **schläft**	sie ⎬ **läuft**	sie ⎬ **stößt**
es ⎭	es ⎭	es ⎭	es ⎭
wir fahren	wir schlafen	wir laufen	wir stoßen
etc.	etc.	etc.	etc.

Verbs whose stems end in **-d** or **-t** do not add the usual **e** when the vowel changes:

laden (*to load*)	halten (*to hold, stop*)	raten (*to advise*)	treten (*to step*)
ich lade	ich halte	ich rate	ich trete
du **lädst**	du **hältst**	du **rätst**	du **trittst**
er ⎫	er ⎫	er ⎫	er ⎫
sie ⎬ **lädt**	sie ⎬ **hält**	sie ⎬ **rät**	sie ⎬ **tritt**
es ⎭	es ⎭	es ⎭	es ⎭
wir laden	wir halten	wir raten	wir treten
ihr lad_e_t	ihr halt_e_t	ihr rat_e_t	ihr tret_e_t
sie laden	sie halten	sie raten	sie treten
Sie laden	Sie halten	Sie raten	Sie treten

Note that **halten** and **raten** do not add an ending in the 3rd pers. sing.

Verbs with a stem change in the singular are listed in this book showing their 3rd pers. sing. form as follows:

helfen (hilft)	*to help*
sprechen (spricht)	*to speak*
vergessen (vergißt)	*to forget*

PRACTICE 4   *Restate the following sentences, using the subjects in parentheses.*

1. Wir laufen sehr schnell. (du, ihr, Anita)
2. Sehen Sie den Fehler nicht? (du, er, ihr)
3. Essen Sie gern Eis?[1] (du, deine Freundin, ihr)
4. Ich vergesse das vielleicht. (Karin, du, ihr)
5. Lesen Sie deutsche Zeitungen? (du, ihr)
6. Sie sprechen zu schnell. (du, er)
7. Warum fahren Sie nicht mit dem Bus? (ihr, du)
8. Die Busse halten hier nicht. (der Bus)
9. Warum nehmen Sie kein Taxi? (du, ihr, Astrid)

---

1 **das Eis**   ice, ice cream

10. Warum laden Sie das Gepäck[1] nicht ins Auto? (er, du, ihr)
11. Warum treten Sie nicht auf die Bremse?[2] (du)
12. Was raten Sie mir? (du, ihr)
13. Warum stoßen Sie mich? (du)
14. Schlafen die Kinder? (das Baby)
15. Helfen Sie mir bei den Hausaufgaben? (du)
16. Ich gebe Monika einen Kuß. (er)

§5   IRREGULAR CONJUGATION OF *haben, sein, werden*

haben (*to have*)   **sein** (*to be*)   **werden** (*to become, get*)

ich **habe**	ich **bin**	ich **werde**
du **hast**	du **bist**	du **wirst**
er	er	er
sie ⟩ **hat**	sie ⟩ **ist**	sie ⟩ **wird**
es	es	es
wir **haben**	wir **sind**	wir **werden**
ihr **habt**	ihr **seid**	ihr **werdet**
sie **haben**	sie **sind**	sie **werden**
Sie **haben**	Sie **sind**	Sie **werden**

§6   IRREGULAR CONJUGATION OF *wissen*

wissen (*to know*)

ich **weiß**
du **weißt**
er
sie ⟩ **weiß**
es
wir **wissen**
ihr **wißt**
sie **wissen**
Sie **wissen**

Note: The stem vowel changes throughout the singular to **ei**; the 1st and 3rd pers. sing. do not have an inflectional ending.

PRACTICE 5   *Restate the following sentences, using the subjects in parentheses.*

1. Andreas ist sehr nervös. (ich, Sie, du, ihr)
2. Warum werden Sie so nervös? (du, ihr)
3. Sie haben recht.[3] (du, Anita, ich)

---

1 **das Gepäck**   luggage
2 **die Bremse, -n**   brake
3 **recht haben**   to be right

4. Wissen Sie das nicht? (er, du, ihr)
5. Ich werde zu dick.[1] (das Baby, die Kinder)
6. Sie haben es immer eilig.[2] (du, er, ihr)
7. Warum sind Sie so unfreundlich? (du, ihr)
8. Klaus ist ein Miesepeter.[3] (ich, sie [she])

§7   USES OF THE PRESENT TENSE

1. Since German has neither a progressive nor an emphatic form, a single present tense form may have any of three English equivalents:

Sie raucht.   *She smokes.*
            She is smoking. (progressive form)
            She does smoke. (emphatic form)

The context generally indicates which meaning is applicable. If it is necessary to make absolutely clear in German that an action is in progress, an abverb is added or the sentence is paraphrased.

Er kommt gerade.   *He is (just now) coming.*
Ich bin gerade dabei, einen Brief zu schreiben.   *I am writing a letter.*
                                            (I am in the process of
                                            writing a letter.)

Emphasis may be expressed by intonation or by adding the flavoring particle **doch** (cf. Appendix, §4).

Er weiß das doch.   *He does know that.*

2. The present tense often has future meaning, particularly when the sentence contains a future-time element, such as **morgen, nächste Woche, bald** (*soon*).

Ich glaube, morgen schneit es.   *I think it will snow tomorrow.*
                        or: *I think it is going to snow tomorrow.*

PRACTICE 6   *Translate into German, using the present tense.*

1. I am going home.
2. Are they going to the movies?
3. Is he sleeping?
4. What are you eating? (fam. sing.)
5. Renate will visit us next week.
6. I won't work tomorrow.
7. We are going to buy the house in Waldheim.

---

1 **dick werden**   to get fat
2 **es eilig haben**   to be in a hurry
3 **ein Miesepeter sein** to be a grouch, sourpuss
                        (*lit.* grouchy Peter; *also used for*
                        a female: **Sie ist ein Miesepeter.**)

3. The present tense is also used to express a stretch of time that began in the past and continues into the present. English uses the present perfect in such instances, as the following examples illustrate.

Wie lange lernen Sie schon Deutsch?	*How long have you been studying German?*
Ich lerne seit einem Jahr Deutsch.	*I have been studying German for a year.*
Wie lange kennen Sie Herrn Berger schon?	*How long have you known Mr. Berger?*
Ich kenne ihn schon seit Oktober.	*I have known him since October.*

This use of the present tense can easily be recognized by time expressions introduced with **schon** (*already*), **seit** (*since*), or **schon seit. Schon** usually remains untranslated. Note that in German the time element generally precedes the place element.

Wir wohnen **schon fünf Jahre** in Hamburg.
*We have been living in Hamburg **for five years.***

Ich arbeite **schon seit April** dort.
*I've been working there **since April.***

PRACTICE 7   *Translate the following questions and answers into English.*

1.   X: Wie lange arbeiten Sie schon im Supermarkt?
      Y: Ich arbeite schon ein Jahr dort.
2.   X: Seit wann lernt Barbara Deutsch?
      Y: Sie lernt es schon seit drei Jahren.
3.   X: Seit wann studiert Frank an der Universität Heidelberg?
      Y: Er studiert seit November dort.
4.   X: Wohnen Sie schon lange in Bremen?
      Y: Wir wohnen schon viele Jahre dort.
5. a. X: Wie lange ist Herr Köhler schon im Krankenhaus?[1]
      Y: Er ist seit Sonntag dort.
   b. X: Wie lange weißt du das schon?
      Y: Ich weiß das schon seit Montag.

Verbs with Prefixes

There are two basic types of verb prefixes: inseparable and separable prefixes.

§8   VERBS WITH INSEPARABLE PREFIXES

These verbs pose few problems. Some of the verbs have already appeared in the exercises. The following prefixes always remain attached to the verb:

---

1 **das Krankenhaus, ⸚er**   hospital

be-	bekommen	*to get, receive*
emp-	empfehlen (empfiehlt)	*to recommend*
ent-	entlassen (entläßt)	*to dismiss, fire*
er-	erklären	*to explain*
ge-	gewinnen	*to win*
miß-	mißverstehen	*to misunderstand*
ver-	verkaufen	*to sell*
zer-	zereißen	*to tear up*

These prefixes always remain unstressed with the exception of **miß-** where the stress varies. It carries the stress in **míßverstehen** whereas the verb **mißáchten** (*to disregard*) may be pronounced **mißáchten** or **míßachten**.

PRACTICE 8   *Supply the appropriate forms of the verbs in parentheses.*

1. Warum _____ Bergmanns ihr schönes Haus? (verkaufen)
2. Dr. Winkler _____ diese Hautcreme.[1] (empfehlen)
3. Vielleicht _____ du diese Geste.[2] (mißverstehen)
4. Unsere Nachbarn _____ alle Warnungen.[3] (mißachten)
5. Wir _____ zu wenig Geld für unsere Arbeit. (bekommen)
6. Wann _____ Sie uns dieses Experiment? (erklären)
7. Wir alle hoffen, daß du den ersten Preis _____. (gewinnen)
8. Ich verstehe nicht, warum du Peters Brief _____. (zerreißen)
9. Ich glaube nicht,[4] daß er seine Sekretärin _____. (entlassen)
10. Herr Schulze, Sie _____ uns. (beleidigen[5])

The following verbs are often confused:

verkaufen *to sell*	**bekommen** *to get,* in the sense of *to receive*
kaufen *to buy*	**werden** *to get,* in the sense of *to become*

PRACTICE 9   *Insert in the blanks provided the German equivalents of the English verb forms.*

1. Mr. Zimmermann is selling his car.
   Herr Zimmermann _____ seinen Wagen.
2. Why are you not buying his car?
   Warum _____ du seinen Wagen nicht?
3. Mrs. Schulze buys and sells stamps.
   Frau Schulze _____ Briefmarken.

1 **die Hautcreme**	skin cream
2 **die Geste, -n**	gesture
3 **die Warnung, -en**	warning
4 **ich glaube nicht**	I don't believe ... *frequently used as the German equivalent of* I don't think ...
5 **beleidigen**	to insult

4. The days are getting longer.
Die Tage _____ länger.
5. I hope I'll get a scholarship.
Hoffentlich _____ ich ein Stipendium.
6. How often do you get mail from home?
Wie oft _____ du Post von zu Hause?
7. The matter is getting complicated.
Die Sache _____ kompliziert.
8. This term I am getting better grades.
In diesem Semester _____ ich bessere Noten.
9. My grades are getting better.
Meine Noten _____ besser.

§9   VERBS WITH SEPARABLE PREFIXES

In English there are a number of verbs that complete their meanings by using complements:

> *to give:*   *to give up, give in*
> *to turn:*   *to turn on, turn off, turn down, turn in, turn out*

The position of these complements may vary:

> *They turned down our offer.*
> or: *They turned our offer down.*

In German such a complement is attached to the front of the infinitive:

> **nach.geben**   *to give in, yield*
> **auf.geben**   *to give up*
> **an.geben**   *to show off, brag*

These complements are called *separable prefixes* because they are separated from the verb under certain conditions. (The dot is not part of the spelling of the infinitive; it is used in this book to identify separable prefixes.) The separable prefix is always accented: **nách.geben, aúf.geben, án.geben.**

Use of verbs with separable prefixes in main clauses and questions

The prefix stands last.

a. Peter gibt **an.**   *Peter is showing off.*
b. Peter gibt **an.**   *Peter is showing off today.*
    heute

c. Peter gibt **an.**   *Peter is showing off today with his new motorcycle.*

heute mit seinem neuen Motorrad

Sentence *a* consists of the bare minimum of words. The additions in sentences *b* and *c* are not tacked on at the end, as in English, but are inserted between the verb and the prefix.

This also applies to questions:

> Warum gibt Peter heute so sehr **an**?

These common verbs with separable prefixes occur in the exercises:

ab.holen	*to pick up*
ab.nehmen (nimmt ab)	*to decrease; lose weight*
an.fangen (fängt an)	*to begin, start*
an.geben (gibt an)	*to show off, brag, put on airs*
an.nehmen (nimmt an)	*to accept; assume*
an.rufen	*to phone, call*
auf.geben (gibt auf)	*to give up*
auf.hören	*to stop, end, cease*
auf.machen	*to open*
auf.passen	*to pay attention, watch, keep an eye on*
aus.gehen	*to go out*
aus.sehen (sieht aus)	*to appear, look*
ein.laden (lädt ein)	*to invite (lit. to load in)*
mit.bringen	*to bring along*
mit.kommen	*to come along*
mit.nehmen (nimmt mit)	*to take along*
nach.geben (gibt nach)	*to give in, yield*
übel.nehmen (nimmt übel)	*to take amiss, resent, take offense*
vor.haben	*to plan, have plans*
weiter.lesen (liest weiter)	*to continue reading, go on reading*
weiter.machen	*to continue (doing something)*
weiter.sprechen (spricht weiter)	*to continue talking, go on talking*
zu.hören	*to listen*
zu.machen	*to close*
zu.nehmen (nimmt zu)	*to increase; gain weight*
zurück.bringen	*to bring back, take back, return*
zurück.fahren (fährt zurück)	*to drive back, return*
zurück.geben (gibt zurück)	*to give back, return*
zurück.gehen	*to go back, return*

Note that verbs with prefixes have the same stem changes as their unprefixed forms.

PRACTICE 10   A. *Restate the following sentences, using the subjects indicated in parentheses.*

1. Sie sehen müde aus. (du, er)
2. Paßt du auf meine Sachen auf?[1] (Sie, ihr)
3. Ich gebe zuviel an. (du, ihr, Renate)

---

1 **auf meine Sachen auf.passen**   to keep an eye on my things

4. Ich gebe die Hoffnung noch nicht[1] auf. (wir, er)
5. Hoffentlich geben Sie nicht nach. (du, Margot)
6. Ich nehme das übel. (Dieter, wir)
7. Nehmen Sie mich mit? (du, ihr)
8. Hoffentlich nehme ich nicht zu. (du, Andreas)
9. Wann geben Sie mir das Geld zurück? (du, ihr)
10. Haben Sie heute abend etwas vor? (du, ihr)
11. Warum sprechen Sie nicht weiter? (du)

B. *Supply the appropriate forms of the verbs in parentheses.*

Model: Monika _____ heute abend mit Volker _____ .
(aus.gehen)
   Monika geht heute abend mit Volker aus.

1. Herr Kaufmann _____ mich um 7 Uhr _____ . (ab.holen)
2. Margot _____ nächsten Monat nach Wien _____ . (zurück.fahren)
3. Michael _____ auf meine Sachen _____ . (auf.passen)
4. Ellen _____ heute ein bißchen _____ . (an.geben)
5. Ich _____ dich vielleicht heute nachmittag _____ . (an.rufen)
6. Dein neuer Wagen _____ sehr schick _____ . (aus.sehen)
7. Frau Krause _____ mich in ihrem Wagen _____ . (mit.nehmen)
8. Hoffentlich _____ ich etwas _____ . (ab.nehmen)
9. Vielleicht _____ Gisela diese Bemerkung[2] _____ . (übel.nehmen)
10. Wann _____ das Postamt _____ ? (auf.machen)
11. Warum _____ ihr nicht _____ ? (mit.kommen)
12. Warum _____ du nicht _____ ? (weiter.lesen)
13. Wann _____ das neue Semester _____ ? (an.fangen)
14. Hoffentlich _____ er mich wieder _____ . (ein.laden)
15. Warum _____ du ihn nicht _____ ? (ein.laden)
16. _____ ihr mich auch _____ ? (ein.laden)
17. _____ Sie mir _____ ? (zu.hören)
18. _____ du schon wieder[3] _____ ? (zu.nehmen)
19. Was _____ Sie morgen abend _____ ? (vor.haben)
20. Warum _____ du Peters Einladung nicht _____ ? (an.nehmen)
21. Er weiß es nicht genau;[4] er _____ es nur _____ . (an.nehmen)

1 **noch nicht**   not yet
2 **die Bemerkung, -en**   remark
3 **schon wieder**   again (*emphatic*)
4 **genau**   exact(ly), precise(ly)
   etwas genau wissen to know something for sure

Verbs with separable prefixes in dependent clauses

Compare:

> Karin **kommt** nicht **mit.**
> Es ist schade, daß Karin nicht **mitkommt.**

In dependent clauses the inflected verb is at the end and is attached to the prefix.

PRACTICE 11   *Restate the following sentences, using the indicated introductory clauses.*

> **Model:** Ich rufe Markus heute abend an.
> **Ich weiß noch nicht, ob ich Markus heute abend anrufe.**

1. Elke bringt ihren Freund mit.
   Ich glaube nicht, daß ...
2. Sie gibt mir das Geld zurück.
   Ich nehme an, daß ...
3. Er lädt mich nicht wieder ein.
   Es ist möglich, daß ...
4. Margot hat heute abend etwas vor.
   Ich habe keine Ahnung,[1] ob ...
5. Herr Schumann geht nicht zu seiner Familie zurück.
   Es ist schade,[2] daß ...
6. Die Bank macht schon um 4 Uhr zu.
   Schade,[3] daß ...
7. Jörg und Elke gehen heute abend aus.
   Ich weiß nicht, ob ...
8. Er bringt ein paar Bücher zur Bibliothek zurück.
   Ich nehme an, daß ...
9. Du siehst etwas müde aus.
   Ich finde, daß ...

§10   THE USE OF *her* AND *hin* AS SEPARABLE PREFIXES

Her suggests "this way, here" and **hin** suggests "that way, there."

her.kommen *to come here*	**hin.gehen** *to go there*
(motion toward the speaker or the perspective of the narrator)	(motion away from the speaker or the perspective of the narrator)
Er **kommt** zu mir **her.**	Ich **gehe** zu ihm **hin.**

Her and **hin** are frequently combined with other adverbs and prepositions:

herauf.kommen *to come up* (here)	**hinunter.gehen** *to go down* (there)
Sie **kommt** die Treppe **herauf.**	Sie **geht** die Treppe **hinunter.**

---

1 **keine Ahnung haben**   to have no idea
2 **es ist schade**   it is a pity
3 **schade**   too bad

herein•kommen *to come in (here)*	**hinein•gehen** *to go in (there)*
Warum **kommen** Sie nicht **herein**?	Warum **gehen** Sie nicht **hinein**?
Idiom: **Herein!** *Come in.*	

Remember:

> **her** denotes **coming**, motion toward the speaker
> **hin** denotes **going**, motion away from the speaker

PRACTICE 12   *Insert* **her-** *or* **hin-** *according to context.*

1. Das Wasser im Schwimmbad ist heute zu kalt. Da geht niemand _____ ein.
2. Bauers sind unsere Nachbarn. Wir gehen oft zu ihnen _____ über, und sie kommen oft zu uns _____ über.
3. Ich mache ein Fenster auf und hänge eine Fahne[1] _____ aus.
4. Der Ball liegt auf dem Dach.[2] Klaus holt[3] eine Leiter[4] und steigt _____ auf. Ich habe Angst, daß Klaus _____ unterfällt.
5. Diese Autotür schließt nicht gut. Hoffentlich falle ich nicht _____ aus.

Her and **hin** are also used in several idioms in which the directional distinction does not apply.

Examples:

herein•fallen	*to be taken in*
hinein•ziehen	*to drag in, involve, implicate*
hin•richten	*to execute*

Wo ... hin? Wo ... her?

In spoken German, the question words **wohin** and **woher** are often separated: **wo** is placed at the start of the question, while **hin** and **her** are treated as separable prefixes.

> **Wohin** geht Renate? ⎫
> or: **Wo** geht Renate **hin**? ⎬ *Where is Renate going?*

> Ich weiß nicht, **wohin** Renate geht. ⎫
> or: Ich weiß nicht, **wo** Renate **hingeht**. ⎬ *I don't know where Renate is going.*

> **Woher** kommt Andreas? ⎫
> or: **Wo** kommt Andreas **her**? ⎬ *Where is Andreas coming from?*

> Ich weiß nicht, **woher** Andreas kommt. ⎫
> or: Ich weiß nicht, **wo** Andreas **herkommt**. ⎬ *I don't know where Andreas is coming from.*

1	**die Fahne, -n**	flag
2	**das Dach, ̈er**	roof
3	**holen**	to fetch, (go and) get
4	**die Leiter, -n**	ladder

§11   PREFIXES THAT ARE USED SEPARABLY AND INSEPARABLY

Some prefixes, such as **durch-, über-, um-, wieder-,** are used both separably and inseparably with different meanings. The verb with the separable prefix is usually used in its literal sense, whereas its counterpart with the inseparable prefix often has a figurative meaning.

SEPARABLE	INSEPARABLE
durch-	
dúrch•fahren *to go nonstop*	**durchfáhren** *to run through, go through*
Der Zug **fährt** bis Hamburg **durch.**	Ein großer Schreck **durchfährt** die Menge.
The train goes nonstop (through) to Hamburg.	*A (feeling of) great horror is running through the crowd.*
über-	
über•setzen *to ferry across*	**übersétzen** *to translate*
Hier ist keine Brücke. Ein Boot **setzt** die Leute **über.**	Wie **übersetzt** man das?
There is no bridge here. A boat ferries the people across.	*How does one translate that?*
um-	
úm•gehen *to go around, circulate*	**umgéhen** *to circumvent, dodge, evade, bypass*
Dumme Gerüchte **gehen um.**	Sie **umgehen** meine Frage.
Stupid rumors are circulating.	*You are dodging my question.*
wieder-	
wíeder•holen *to (go and) get (something or someone) back*	**wiederhólen** *to repeat, to review*
Die Zeitung ist im Mülleimer. Ich **hole** sie **wieder.**	Ich **wiederhole** meine Frage.
The newspaper is in the garbage can. I'll (go and) get it back.	*I will repeat my question.*
	Wir **wiederholen** die Grammatik.
	We are reviewing the grammer.

When in doubt about the use of a prefix, consult a good dictionary. It will indicate possible uses and meanings.

PRACTICE 13   Summarizing exercises.

A. *Supply the appropriate forms of the verbs in parentheses.*

1. X: _____ du an dieser Tankstelle? (halten)
    Y: Nein. Wir _____ bis München _____. (durch•fahren)
2. X: Wo _____ dein Kassettenrecorder? (sein)
    Y: In Barbaras Zimmer. Ich _____ ihn gleich _____.
    (wieder•holen)

3. X: _____ du mir bei den Hausaufgaben? (helfen)

   Y: Natürlich. Vielleicht _____ wir zuerst[1] die Grammatik. (wiederholen)

4. X: Die ganze Familie Baumann _____ die Grippe. (haben)

   Y: Kein Wunder. Die Grippe _____ jetzt _____. (um.gehen)

5. X: Herr Schubert _____ keine Steuern.[2] (bezahlen)

   Y: Wie _____ er das Gesetz?[3] (umgehen)

6. X: Helga _____ einen netten Freund. (haben)

   Y: _____ du sie? (beneiden)

7. X: _____ ihr es eilig? (haben)

   Y: Wir _____ es immer eilig. (haben)

8. X: _____ du schlechte Laune? (haben)

   Y: Nein, aber meine Nachbarin _____ mich. (irritieren)

9. X: _____ du heute abend etwas _____? (vor.haben)

   Y: Bis jetzt[4] _____ ich noch nichts _____. (vor.haben)

10. X: Warum _____ du so schnell? (laufen)

   Y: Weil es sehr spät _____. (sein)

11. X: Hoffentlich _____ du uns nicht, wenn du in Europa _____. (vergessen; sein)

   Y: Und ihr? Hoffentlich _____ ihr mich nicht. (vergessen)

12. X: Rainer _____ nicht gut _____. (aus.sehen) Hoffentlich _____ er nicht krank. (werden)

   Y: Er _____ zuviel und _____ zu wenig. (arbeiten; schlafen)

13. X: Du _____ nie _____, wenn man mit dir _____. (zu.hören; sprechen)

   Y: Es ist nicht wahr, daß ich nie _____. (zu.hören)

14. a. X: Wann _____ ihr? (heiraten)

     Y: Wir _____ vielleicht im Juni. (heiraten)

   b. X: _____ ihr mich zur Hochzeit _____? (ein.laden)

     Y: Natürlich _____ wir dich _____. (ein.laden)

15. a. X: Heinz _____ zuviel. (reden)

     Y: Du _____ auch manchmal zuviel. (reden)

   b. X: Du _____ sehr unhöflich.[5] (sein)

     Y: Ich _____ nur die Wahrheit. (sagen)

16. a. X: Dietmar _____ oft frech. (werden)

     Y: Du _____ auch manchmal frech. (werden)

   b. X: Du _____ mich. (beleidigen)

     Y: Ich _____ um Verzeihung. (bitten)

17. a. X: Warum _____ du soviel? (essen)

     Y: Weil ich zu dünn[6] _____. (sein)

1	**zuerst**	first
2	**die Steuer, -n**	tax
3	**das Gesetz, -e**	law
4	**bis jetzt**	so far
5	**unhöflich (höflich)**	impolite (polite)
6	**dünn**	thin

b. X: Zu dünn? Du _____ zu dick. (meinen[1])

Y: Warum _____ du mir immer so nette Komplimente? (machen)

c. X: Weil ich ...

Y: Warum _____ du nicht _____? (weiter.sprechen)

d. X: Ich fürchte, die Sache _____ zu kompliziert. (werden)

B. *Translate into German.* (Use **Ich glaube nicht** for *I don't think*)

1. a. Helga is going back to the dormitory. **Helga geht ins Studentenheim zurück.**

b. Why is she going back to the dormitory?

c. I have no idea why she is going back to the dormitory.

2. a. That is impolite. **Das ist unhöflich.**

b. Why are you so impolite? (fam. sing., fam. pl., formal)

c. Too bad that they are so impolite.

3. a. He is picking me up. **Er holt mich ab.**

b. Are you picking me up? (fam. sing.)

c. I don't think that they are picking me up.

4. a. I apologize. **Ich bitte um Verzeihung.**

b. Why are you apologizing? (fam. sing., formal)

c. It is not necessary[2] that she apologize.

5. a. She is not right. **Sie hat nicht recht.**

b. You are not right. (fam. sing., fam. pl.)

c. You know that you are not right. (formal)

6. a. They are getting nervous. **Sie werden nervös.**

b. Are you getting nervous? (fam. sing., formal)

c. I am not getting nervous, I am already nervous.

7. a. He often skips class. **Er schwänzt oft.**

b. Why do you skip class so often? (fam. sing.)

c. I'd like to know why you skip class so often. (formal)

8. a. I envy Andreas. **Ich beneide Andreas.**

b. Why do you envy Andreas? (fam. sing., fam. pl.)

c. I don't understand why you envy Andreas. (formal)

9. a. I am not inviting Helga. **Ich lade Helga nicht ein.**

b. Are you inviting Karin? (fam. sing.)

c. Frank is inviting Karin.

d. I don't think that he is inviting Karin.

10. a. She is always in a hurry. **Sie hat es immer eilig.**

b. You are always in a hurry. (fam. sing., fam. pl.)

c. Too bad that you are always in a hurry. (formal)

11. a. I don't know it for sure. **Ich weiß es nicht genau.**

b. We don't know it for sure.

c. Do you know it for sure? (fam. sing., formal)

---

1 **meinen**   to mean

2 **nötig**   necessary

12. a. I am only assuming it. **Ich nehme es nur an.**
    b. She is only assuming it.
    c. Are you only assuming it? (fam. sing.)
    d. Do you know it for sure or are you only assuming it? (fam. sing., formal)

The Imperative

Imperatives express commands, requests, or directives. German has three imperative forms corresponding to the three words for *you*:

1. **Sie**-address **Bitte kommen Sie!**
2. **du**-address **Bitte komm(e)!** ⟶ *Please come.*
3. **ihr**-address **Bitte kommt!**

Imperative sentences end with an exclamation mark or, if there is no special emphasis, with a period.

§12 BASIC PATTERN OF THE IMPERATIVE

1. The **formal (*Sie*-address) imperative** is identical to the present tense **Sie**-form except that it has inverted word order.

PRESENT TENSE	IMPERATIVE	
Sie stören	**Stören Sie** mich nicht!	*Don't disturb me.*
Sie tun	**Tun Sie** das nicht!	*Don't do that.*
Sie haben	**Haben Sie** keine Angst!	*Don't be afraid.*
Sie rufen an	**Rufen Sie** Herrn Köhler **an!**	*Phone Mr. Köhler.*

2. **The familiar singular (*du*-address) imperative** consists of the stem of the verb with the optional ending **-e**. The pronoun **du** is omitted.

   Stör(e) mich nicht!
   Tu(e) das nicht!
   Hab(e) keine Angst!
   Ruf(e) Herrn Köhler an!

The final **-e** is added if the stem ends in

a. **-d, -t,** or certain consonant clusters (cf. §2):

   Bade nicht zu lange!
   Arbeite schneller!
   Öffne die Tür!

b. **-ig,** as in **erledigen** (*to take care of, settle*), **beleidigen** (*to insult*) **entschuldigen** (*to excuse*):

   Erledige das sofort! *Take care of that immediately.*
   Beleidige mich nicht! *Don't insult me.*
   Entschuldige! *Excuse me. (me added in English)*

3. **The familiar plural (*ihr*-address) imperative** is identical to the **ihr**-form of the present tense except that **ihr** is omitted.

PRESENT TENSE	IMPERATIVE
ihr stört	**Stört** mich nicht!
ihr tut	**Tut** das nicht!
ihr habt	**Habt** keine Angst!
ihr ruft an	**Ruft** Herrn Köhler an!
ihr wartet	**Wartet** hier!

The use of *doch* or *doch mal* in imperatives

Doch is frequently added for emphasis:

> Komm doch mit! *Do come along. Do join us.*

When **doch** is followed by **mal,** it has a more casual tone:

> Komm doch mal mit!

A note on the position of *bitte*

> **Bitte** rufen Sie mich an.
> Rufen Sie mich an, **bitte.**

When final, **bitte** is set off by a comma except after very short sentences, such as:

> **Warten Sie bitte. Warte bitte.**

Bitte may also be placed in the middle of the sentence. It then generally follows pronoun objects but precedes all other elements.

> Rufen Sie mich **bitte** an.
> Rufen Sie **bitte** Frau Krause an.

PRACTICE 14   *Add the two familiar forms to the following formal imperatives.*

> **Model:** Kommen Sie bitte herein!
> **Komm(e) bitte herein!**
> **Kommt bitte herein!**

1. Hören Sie bitte zu!
2. Gehen Sie doch zum Arzt!
3. Besuchen Sie uns doch mal!
4. Bitte tun Sie das nicht!
5. Bitte warten Sie einen Augenblick![1]
6. Beleidigen Sie mich nicht!
7. Entschuldigen Sie bitte.
8. Machen Sie ein Fenster auf, bitte.
9. Rufen Sie doch mal an!
10. Bitte stören Sie uns nicht!

---

1 **einen Augenblick warten**   to wait a moment *or* a minute

11. Bitte erledigen Sie das sofort!
12. Sagen Sie doch nicht immer nein zu mir!

§13 VARIATIONS AND IRREGULARITIES IN IMPERATIVE FORMS

1. **The familiar singular form of verbs with vowel change from *e* to *i* or *ie***

helfen (hilft)	Helfen Sie mir!
	Hilf mir! ⟶ Help me.
	Helft mir!

essen (ißt)	Essen Sie das nicht!
	Iß das nicht! ⟶ Don't eat that.
	Eßt das nicht!

übel•nehmen	Nehmen Sie es nicht übel!
(nimmt übel)	**Nimm** es nicht übel! ⟶ Don't take offense.
	Nehmt es nicht übel!

The familiar singular form has the same stem changes that occur in the present tense singular. The ending **-e** is never added.

Exception:

werden (wird)	Werden Sie nicht krank!
	Werde nicht krank! ⟶ Don't get sick.
	Werdet nicht krank!

The fam. sing. form has no vowel change and adds the ending **-e**.

Note that the changes from **a** to **ä**, **au** to **äu**, and **o** to **ö** in the present tense do not occur in the imperative:

schlafen (schläft)	**Schlaf(e)** gut!
ein•laden (lädt ein)	**Lade** auch Margot **ein**!
laufen (läuft)	**Lauf(e)** doch nicht so schnell!
stoßen (stößt)	**Stoß(e)** mich doch nicht so!

2. **The imperative forms of *sein***

formal	**Seien Sie** still!
fam. sing.	**Sei** still! ⟶ Be quiet.
fam. pl.	**Seid** still!

In the formal address the ending **-en** is added to the stem **sei-**.
The fam. sing. address never has the ending **-e**.
The fam. pl. address ends in **-d**; it is identical to the **ihr**-form of the present tense: **(ihr) seid.**

PRACTICE 15   *Add the two familiar forms to the following formal imperatives.*

1. Seien Sie vorsichtig![1]
2. Werden Sie nicht frech!

1 **vorsichtig**   careful

3. Sprechen Sie etwas lauter, bitte!
4. Schlafen Sie gut!
5. Fahren Sie doch nicht so schnell!
6. Bitte laden Sie auch meinen Freund ein!
7. Essen Sie doch nicht so viel!
8. Vergessen Sie das nicht!
9. Nehmen Sie mich bitte mit!
10. Halten Sie bitte an der nächsten Tankstelle!
11. Seien Sie doch ein bißchen nett zu mir!

§14   THE GERMAN EQUIVALENT OF ENGLISH *Let's* ...

Let's go home.	**Gehen wir** nach Hause.
Let's begin.	**Fangen wir an.**
Let's stop (come to an end).	**Hören wir auf.** *or:* **Machen wir Schluß.**
Let's be fair.	**Seien wir** doch fair.

Note the inverted word order of the present tense **wir**-form and the use of **seien wir.**

PRACTICE 16   *Answer in German.*

Model: Wollen wir es noch einmal versuchen? *OK, let's try it again.*
O.K., versuchen wir es noch einmal.

1. Wollen wir in die Disko gehen?	*OK, let's go to the disco.*
2. Wollen wir im Juni heiraten?	*OK, let's get married in June.*
3. Wollen wir eine Pause machen?[1]	*OK, let's take a break.*
4. Wollen wir die Sache begraben?[2]	*OK, let's bury the matter.*
5. Wollen wir mal vernünftig[3] sein?	*OK, let's be sensible.*
6. Wollen wir aufhören?	*OK, let's stop.*

§15   USING INFINITIVES

Commands directed to the public are often expressed with the infinitive.

Bitte **weitergehen!**	*Please keep moving.*
(instead of: Bitte gehen Sie weiter!)	
Bitte **einsteigen!**	*All aboard, please.*
(instead of: Bitte steigen Sie ein!)	
Bitte nicht **rauchen!**	*Please don't smoke.*
(instead of: Bitte rauchen Sie nicht!)	

1	**die Pause, -n**	recess, break
	eine Pause machen	to take a break
2	**begraben (begräbt)**	to bury
3	**vernünftig**	sensible, reasonable

PRACTICE 17   Summarizing exercise for the imperative.

Translate into German.

1. Please come in. (formal, fam. sing., pl)
2. Drive carefully. (formal, fam. sing., pl.)
3. Please don't disturb me. (formal, fam. sing., pl.)
4. Please be quiet. (formal, fam. sing., pl.)
5. Don't get nervous. (formal, fam. sing., pl.)
6. Let's begin.
7. Let's bury the matter.
8. Excuse me please. (formal, fam. sing.)
9. Please help me. (formal, fam. sing.)
10. Don't be afraid. (fam. sing., pl.)
11. Don't eat so much. (fam. sing., pl.)
12. Don't forget that. (fam. sing., formal)
13. Please don't take offense. (formal, fam. sing.)
14. Please take care of that. (fam. sing.)
15. Please wait a minute. (fam. sing.)
16. Let's be fair.
17. Let's take a break.
18. Let's stop.

3

Verbs in the Past and Future Tenses

KEY TO THE EXERCISES ON CASSETTE 2.
RUNNING TIME: APPROX. 60 MIN.

Introduction

There are six tenses in English:

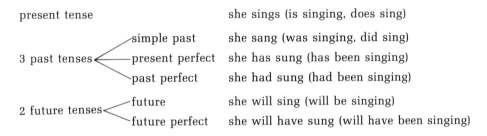

present tense		she sings (is singing, does sing)
3 past tenses	simple past	she sang (was singing, did sing)
	present perfect	she has sung (has been singing)
	past perfect	she had sung (had been singing)
2 future tenses	future	she will sing (will be singing)
	future perfect	she will have sung (will have been singing)

These tenses can be derived from three basic verb forms, the so-called "principal parts" of a verb:

	INFINITIVE	PAST	PAST PARTICIPLE
regular verb	to ask	asked	asked
irregular verb	to sing	sang	sung

Ordinarily, the principal parts are stated only for irregular verbs, because the forms of the regular verbs are predictable and need not be learned.

As in English, there are six tenses in German, but they do not have progressive or emphatic forms (cf. Chap. 2, §7, 1). German distinguishes between weak verbs (corresponding to English regular verbs) and strong verbs (corresponding to English irregular verbs). In addition, there is a third group of verbs that fit neither pattern; they are called *irregular*.

The Simple Past and Present Perfect of Weak Verbs

§1   THE SIMPLE PAST TENSE

Formation

The personal endings are added to the stem as shown here:

infinitive **lachen**	ich lach**te** *I laughed*	ich ____ **te**
	du lach**test**	du ____ **test**
	er ⎫	er ⎫
	sie ⎬ lach**te**	sie ⎬ ____ **te**
	es ⎭	es ⎭
	wir lach**ten**	wir ____ **ten**
	ihr lach**tet**	ihr ____ **tet**
	sie lach**ten**	sie ____ **ten**
	Sie lach**ten**	sie ____ **ten**

PRACTICE 1   *Substitute the appropriate past-tense forms of the verbs in parentheses.*

1. Helga glaubte es nicht. (erklären, lernen, sammeln, studieren)
2. Die Leute fragten nicht. (rauchen, lachen, lächeln, kritisieren)
3. Er haßte mich. (lieben, bewundern, irritieren, ignorieren)

Verbs with stems ending in -*d*, -*t*, or certain consonant clusters (cf. Chap. 2, §2) insert an **e** between the stem and the personal endings:

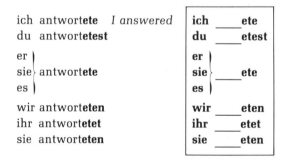

ich antwort**ete** *I answered*	ich ____ **ete**
du antwort**etest**	du ____ **etest**
er ⎫	er ⎫
sie ⎬ antwort**ete**	sie ⎬ ____ **ete**
es ⎭	es ⎭
wir antwort**eten**	wir ____ **eten**
ihr antwort**etet**	ihr ____ **etet**
sie antwort**eten**	sie ____ **eten**

PRACTICE 2   *Substitute the appropriate past-tense forms of the verbs in parentheses.*

1. Ich antwortete nicht. (arbeiten, warten, reden)
2. Sie zeichneten es. (öffnen, landen)
3. Es regnete viel. (kosten, bedeuten)

PRACTICE 3   *Supply the appropriate forms of the simple past tense.*

1. Wir _____ viel, aber leider _____ wir nicht viel Geld.
       (arbeiten)   (verdienen)[1]
2. Martin _____ die Verkäuferin[2], aber sie _____ ihm nicht.
         (fragen)   (antworten)
3. Alle _____ , aber der Redner _____ es nicht.
       (gähnen)[3]   (merken)[4]
4. Frau Zimmermann _____ , und das _____ den Chef.
                 (lachen)   (irritieren)
5. Ich _____ Gisela und _____ sie auch ein wenig.
       (bewundern)   (beneiden)
6. Bergers _____ ihr Haus und_____ eine Wohnung.[6]
       (verkaufen)   (mieten)[5]
7. Mathias _____ einen Ring und _____ ihn seiner Freundin.
       (kaufen)   (schenken)[7]

Use of the simple past

In German the simple past tense commonly expresses connected past actions. It is used mainly in descriptions and narratives and is therefore also called *narrative past*. Thus we might read in a report of a meeting:

> „Der Redner merkte nicht, daß die Zuhörer gähnten. Er redete und redete. Als er endlich aufhörte, applaudierten nur seine höflichen Freunde."

> *"The speaker did not notice that the audience was yawning. He talked and talked. When he finally stopped, only his polite friends applauded."*

§2   THE PRESENT PERFECT TENSE

The basic difference between the English and German use of the present perfect

Compare the following two sentences:

> **I paid** the bill yesterday.
> **I haven't paid** the bill yet.

The first sentence expresses an act completed at a point of time in the past, i.e. yesterday. There is no relation to the present; the simple past is used. The second sentence relates to the present and is expressed in the present perfect.

1 **verdienen**	to earn (*make money*)
2 **die Verkäuferin, -nen**	saleslady
3 **gähnen**	to yawn
4 **merken**	to notice
5 **mieten**	to rent
6 **die Wohnung, -en**	apartment
7 **schenken**	to give (*as a gift*)

The German equivalents of the two sentences above are:

> **Ich habe** die Rechnung gestern **bezahlt.**
> **Ich habe** die Rechnung noch nicht **bezahlt.**

In contrast to English, the first sentence is expressed in the present perfect. As mentioned in §1, in German the simple past is used to relate connected past acts in descriptions and narratives. The first sentence refers to an individual act that does not form part of a series of happenings. It is therefore not expressed in the simple past but in the present perfect.

Keep in mind:

> Unlike English, German expresses single past acts in the present perfect tense.

In conversation, with its interrupted dialogue, most past events are considered as isolated and thus are in the present perfect tense. They are rendered into English by the simple past tense.

Was hast du gestern gemacht?	*What did you do yesterday?*
Ich habe Tennis gespielt.	*I played tennis.*

Because it is so frequent in conversation, the German present perfect tense is also called *conversational past.*

Formation of the present perfect

The present perfect is formed with an auxiliary verb (in most cases **haben**) and the past participle of the main verb.

Conjugation: ich **habe** gefragt
du **hast** gefragt

er
sie } **hat** gefragt
es

wir **haben** gefragt
ihr **habt** gefragt
sie **haben** gefragt
Sie **haben** gefragt

The auxiliary verb **haben** is inflected. The past participle **gefragt** remains unchanged. It is formed as follows:

1. The prefix **ge-** and the ending **-t** are added to the stem of the verb.

lernen	**gelernt**	wandern	**gewandert**
lachen	**gelacht**	schneien[1]	**geschneit**
lächeln	**gelächelt**		

1 schneien   to snow

2. Past participles of verbs whose stems end in **-d, -t,** or certain consonant clusters add **-et** to the stem.

antworten	**geantwortet**	öffnen	**geöffnet**
kosten	**gekostet**	regnen	**geregnet**
reden	**geredet**		

3. No **ge-** is added to
   a. verbs that end in **-ieren**

studieren	**studiert**	passieren	**passiert**
protestieren	**protestiert**	irritieren	**irritiert**

   b. verbs with inseparable prefixes (cf. Chap. 2, §8)

versuchen[1]	**versucht**	beleidigen	**beleidigt**
erledigen	**erledigt**	beneiden	**beneidet**

4. Verbs with separable prefixes insert **ge-** between prefix and stem.

auf•räumen[2]	**aufgeräumt**
aus•lachen[3]	**ausgelacht**
zu•hören	**zugehört**

PRACTICE 4   *State the past participles of the following verbs.*

1. lachen	10. antworten	19. versuchen	28. auf•räumen
2. aus•lachen	11. arbeiten	20. verdienen	29. irritieren
3. machen	12. mieten	21. kaufen	30. lächeln
4. auf•machen	13. heiraten	22. verkaufen	31. wandern
5. zu•machen	14. landen	23. schenken	32. bewundern
6. hören	15. studieren	24. schneien	33. beneiden
7. zu•hören	16. ignorieren	25. folgen	34. marschieren
8. holen	17. beleidigen	26. regnen	35. stören
9. ab•holen	18. bezahlen	27. kosten	36. warten

Word order in main clauses and questions

Haben occupies the position of the inflected verb; the past participle is in final position.

Main clause:	NORMAL WORD ORDER	Du glaubst das nicht.
		Du **hast** das nicht **geglaubt.**
	INVERTED WORD ORDER	Natürlich glaubst du das nicht.
		Natürlich **hast** du das nicht **geglaubt.**
Question:	WITHOUT A QUESTION WORD	Glaubst du das nicht?
		Hast du das nicht **geglaubt?**
	WITH A QUESTION WORD	Warum glaubst du das nicht?
		Warum **hast** du das nicht **geglaubt?**

1	**versuchen**	to try
2	**auf•räumen**	to tidy up, to straighten up
3	**aus•lachen**	to laugh at

PRACTICE 5   A. *Form sentences in normal and in inverted word order.*

> **Model:** a. Helga / diese Sache / erledigen
> **Helga hat diese Sache erledigt.**
> b. vielleicht / Helga / diese Sache / erledigen
> **Vielleicht hat Helga diese Sache erledigt.**

1. a. ich / Dietmar / beleidigen
   b. vielleicht / ich / Dietmar / beleidigen
2. a. du / mir / nicht / antworten
   b. leider / du / mir / nicht / antworten
3. a. es / mir / Spaß / machen[1]
   b. natürlich / es / mir / Spaß / machen
4. a. es / nicht / schneien
   b. hoffentlich / es / nicht / regnen
5. a. wir / eine Wohnung / mieten
   b. am Montag / wir / unser Haus / verkaufen
6. a. mein Freund / diese Frage / ignorieren
   b. vielleicht / diese Frage / meinen Freund / irritieren
7. a. Helga / auf einer Tankstelle / arbeiten
   b. leider / sie / sehr wenig Geld / verdienen
8. a. wir / dich / bewundern
   b. natürlich / wir / dich / auch / beneiden

B.   *Form questions in the present perfect tense.*

> **Model:** a. ihr / für die Prüfung / lernen?
> **Habt ihr für die Prüfung gelernt?**
> b. wann / ihr / für die Prüfung / lernen?
> **Wann habt ihr für die Prüfung gelernt?**

1. a. ihr / heiraten?
   b. wann / ihr / heiraten?
2. a. du / Margot / nicht / ab•holen?
   b. warum / du / Margot / nicht / ab•holen?
3. a. du / das Fenster / auf•machen?
   b. warum / Udo / das Fenster / zu•machen?
4. a. du / lachen?
   b. warum / du / mich / aus•lachen?
5. a. ihr / die Musik / hören?
   b. warum / ihr / nicht / zu•hören?
6. a. du / Rainer / eine Schallplatte[2] / schenken?
   b. wo / du / die Platte / kaufen?
7. a. das Motorrad / viel Geld / kosten?
   b. wieviel / Sie / für das Motorrad / bezahlen?

1 **Spaß machen**	to be fun
expression: **Es macht mir Spaß.**	It's fun to me. I enjoy it.
2 **die Schallplatte, -n**	record
short: **die Platte, -n**	

C. *Form questions and answers in the present perfect tense.*

Model: X: du / Andreas / manipulieren?
              Hast du Andreas manipuliert?
         Y: nein, / ich / ihn / nicht / manipulieren
              Nein, ich habe ihn nicht manipuliert.

1. X: du / die Post / ab.holen?
    Y: nein, / ich / sie / noch nicht / ab.holen
2. X: du / dein Zimmer / auf.räumen?
    Y: nein, / ich / es / noch nicht / auf.räumen
3. X: ich / Sie / stören?
    Y: natürlich / Sie / mich / stören
4. X: dein Freund / diese Sache / erledigen?
    Y: hoffentlich / er / sie / erledigen
5. X: was / Herr Schreiber / sagen?
    Y: er / viel Unsinn[1] / reden
6. X: ihr / zu.hören?
    Y: niemand / zu.hören
7. X: Sie / mich / aus.lachen?
    Y: ich / nur / lächeln
8. X: was / du / Barbara / zum Geburtstag / schenken?
    Y: ich / ihr / mein Herz / schenken / / das / nichts / kosten

Use of the auxiliary *sein* instead of *haben*

Sabine **ist** durch ganz Europa **gereist.**
Sabine has traveled through all of Europe.
or: *Sabine traveled through all of Europe.*

A few weak verbs use the auxiliary **sein** instead of **haben,** such as

folgen	*to follow*	**passieren**	*to happen*
landen	*to land*	**reisen**	*to travel*
marschieren	*to march*	**wandern**	*to wander, to hike*

These verbs are conjugated as the example **reisen**:

ich **bin** gereist   *I have traveled, I traveled*
du **bist** gereist

er ⎫
sie ⎬ **ist** gereist
es ⎭

wir **sind** gereist
ihr **seid** gereist
sie **sind** gereist
Sie **sind** gereist

1 **der Unsinn**   nonsense

PRACTICE 6   *Form sentences in the present perfect tense.*

Model: das / selten / passieren
Das ist selten passiert.

1. ich / durch ganz Europa / reisen
2. ein Polizeiwagen / uns / folgen
3. wir / nach Lichtenwalde / wandern
4. die Soldaten / zum Flugplatz / marschieren
5. wann / das Flugzeug / landen
6. wo / der Unfall[1] / passieren

Dependent word order

Compare the two sentences:

Sie **hat** die Wahrheit **gesagt.**
Ich nehme an, daß sie die Wahrheit **gesagt hat.**

As the inflected verb the auxiliary is in last position. It is preceded by the past
participle.

PRACTICE 7   *Restate the following sentences, using the indicated introductory*
clauses.

Model: Das ist am Montag oder Dienstag passiert.
**Ich weiß nicht genau, ob das am Montag oder Dienstag passiert
ist.**

1. Baumanns sind durch ganz Deutschland gereist.
   Ist es wahr, daß ...
2. Meine Frage hat den Chef irritiert.
   Ich bin überzeugt,[2] daß ...
3. Wieviel hat er für das Motorrad bezahlt?
   Ich habe keine Ahnung, wieviel ...
4. Er hat es nicht gemerkt.
   Es ist gut, daß ...
5. Was ist passiert?
   Wissen Sie, was ...
6. Wann hat Erika die neue Wohnung gemietet?
   Ich weiß nicht mehr,[3] wann ...

---

1 **der Unfall, ⁻e**	accident
2 **überzeugt sein**	to be convinced
3 **Ich weiß nicht mehr ...**	I don't remember ... (*lit.* I don't know anymore)
	Nicht mehr wissen is often used in the sense
	of not remembering something.

§3   PATTERNS FOR THE WORD ORDER IN THE PRESENT PERFECT TENSE

The patterns stated in Chapter 1, §6, may be applied to sentences in the present perfect tense:

		INFLECTED VERB		UNINFLECTED VERB
a. NORMAL WORD ORDER	Helga	**hat**	die Grammatik	**wiederholt.**
b. INVERTED WORD ORDER				
STATEMENT	Heute	**hat**	Helga die Grammatik	**wiederholt.**
DIRECT QUESTION				
WITH QUESTION WORD	Wann	**hat**	Helga die Grammatik	**wiederholt?**
WITHOUT QUESTION WORD		**Hat**	Helga die Grammatik	**wiederholt?**

The inflected verb is in second or first position; the uninflected verb (past participle) is in final position.

				UNINFLECTED VERB	INFLECTED VERB
c. DEPENDENT WORD ORDER					
STATEMENT	Es ist möglich,	daß	Helga die Grammatik	**wiederholt**	**hat.**
INDIRECT QUESTION	Ich weiß nicht,	wann	Helga die Grammatik	**wiederholt**	**hat.**
		ob	Helga die Grammatik	**wiederholt**	**hat.**

The inflected verb is in last position; it is preceded by the uninflected verb.

PRACTICE 8   *Translate into German, using the present perfect for the English past tense.*

Model: a. She doesn't notice it.   **Sie merkt es nicht.**
        b. She didn't notice it.   **Sie hat es nicht gemerkt.**
        c. It is possible that she didn't   **Es ist möglich, daß sie**
          notice it.   **es nicht gemerkt hat.**

1. a. I am trying it again.   **Ich versuche es noch einmal.**
   b. I tried it again.
   c. I am glad[1] that you tried it again. (fam. sing.)
2. a. Nobody is listening.   **Niemand hört zu.**
   b. Nobody was listening.

1 **froh**   glad

     c. Were they listening?

     d. Too bad that they weren't listening.

3. a. Are you waiting for him? **Wartest du auf ihn?**

     b. Were you waiting for him?

     c. Why were they waiting for him?

     d. I have no idea why they were waiting for him.

4. a. The boss is straightening up his desk. **Der Chef räumt seinen Schreibtisch auf.**

     b. He was straightening up his desk.

     c. When was he straightening up his desk?

     d. Do you know when he straightened up his desk? (formal)

5. a. Where is the plane going to land? **Wo landet das Flugzeug?**

     b. Where did the plane land?

     c. I don't know where the plane landed.

6. a. We travel a lot. **Wir reisen viel.**

     b. We have traveled a lot.

     c. I am glad that we have traveled a lot.

7. a. I don't make a lot of money. **Ich verdiene nicht viel Geld.**

     b. I didn't make a lot of money.

     c. Did you make a lot of money? (fam. sing.)

     d. Is it true that you made a lot of money? (fam. sing.)

8. a. Peter is laughing at me. **Peter lacht mich aus.**

     b. Perhaps he was laughing at me.

     c. Why was he laughing at me?

     d. I don't understand why he was laughing at me.

9. a. That happens often. **Das passiert oft.**

     b. That happened often.

     c. When did that happen?

     d. I don't remember when that happened.

10. a. Don't you notice it? **Merkst du es nicht?**

     b. Didn't you notice it?

     c. I noticed it.

     d. It is good that you noticed it. (formal)

The Simple Past and Present Perfect of Strong Verbs

§4 THE PRINCIPAL PARTS OF STRONG VERBS

As in English, all tenses can be derived from three basic verb forms called "principal parts," i.e. the infinitive, the simple past, and the past participle. Compare:

WEAK VERB	STRONG VERB
Barbara **lernt** Deutsch.	Der Tenor **singt** gut.
Barbara **lernte** Deutsch.	Der Tenor **sang** gut.
Barbara hat Deutsch **gelernt.**	Der Tenor hat gut **gesungen.**

<table>
<tr><td>

PRINCIPAL PARTS

lernen **lernte** **gelernt**
| |
-te ending -t ending

The verb stem remains unchanged.
</td><td>

PRINCIPAL PARTS

singen **sang** **gesungen**
| |
no ending -en ending

The stem vowel changes.
</td></tr>
</table>

The principal parts of strong verbs are not predictable. They have to be learned.

The strong verbs are divided into seven classes according to their vowel changes. It is helpful to learn the principal parts of strong verbs in association with other members of the same class. The following table lists some common examples of each class which will occur in the exercises. A more complete listing (in alphabetical order) appears in the Appendix, §2. **Ist** before a past participle indicates that the auxiliary **sein** is required.

CLASS	STEM VOWELS	INFINITIVE	SIMPLE PAST	PAST PARTICIPLE	MEANING
I	ei – ie – ie	bleiben	blieb	ist geblieben	to stay, remain
		schreiben	schrieb	geschrieben	to write
		steigen	stieg	ist gestiegen	to climb, go up
		ein•steigen	stieg ein	ist eingestiegen	to climb in, get on, board a vehicle
		aus•steigen	stieg aus	ist ausgestiegen	to get off
	ei – i – i	reiten	ritt	ist geritten	to ride, go on horseback
II	ie – o – o	fliegen	flog	ist geflogen	to fly
		verlieren	verlor	verloren	to lose
	e – o – o	heben	hob	gehoben	to raise, lift
III	i – a – u	finden	fand	gefunden	to find
		singen	sang	gesungen	to sing
		trinken	trank	getrunken	to drink
	i – a – o	beginnen	begann	begonnen	to begin
		gewinnen	gewann	gewonnen	to win
IV	e – a – o	brechen (bricht)	brach	gebrochen	to break
		unterbrechen (unterbricht)	unterbrach	unterbrochen	to interrupt
		helfen (hilft)	half	geholfen	to help
		nehmen (nimmt)	nahm	genommen	to take
		ab•nehmen (nimmt ab)	nahm ab	abgenommen	to decrease; lose weight
		zu•nehmen (nimmt zu)	nahm zu	zugenommen	to increase; gain weight
		übel•nehmen (nimmt übel)	nahm übel	übelgenommen	to take amiss, take offense, resent

CLASS	STEM VOWELS	INFINITIVE	SIMPLE PAST	PAST PARTICIPLE	MEANING
		sprechen (spricht)	sprach	gesprochen	to speak
		versprechen (verspricht)	versprach	versprochen	to promise
		sterben (stirbt)	starb	ist gestorben	to die
V	e – a – e	essen (ißt)	aß	gegessen	to eat
		vergessen (vergißt)	vergaß	vergessen	to forget
		geben (gibt)	gab	gegeben	to give
		auf•geben (gibt auf)	gab auf	aufgegeben	to give up
		nach•geben (gibt nach)	gab nach	nachgegeben	to give in
		lesen (liest)	las	gelesen	to read
		vor•lesen (liest vor)	las vor	vorgelesen	to read to (someone)
		sehen (sieht)	sah	gesehen	to see
	i – a – e	bitten	bat	gebeten	to ask for, request
		sitzen	saß	gesessen	to sit
	ie – a – e	liegen	lag	gelegen	to lie, be situated
VI	a – u – a	fahren (fährt)	fuhr	ist gefahren	to drive, go (by locomotion)
		mit•fahren (fährt mit)	fuhr mit	ist mitgefahren	to ride with (someone)
		laden (lädt)	lud	geladen	to load
		ein•laden (lädt ein)	lud ein	eingeladen	to invite
		tragen (trägt)	trug	getragen	to carry
VII	a –⌐ie⌐– a	fallen (fällt)	fiel	ist gefallen	to fall
		durch•fallen (fällt durch)	fiel durch	ist durchgefallen	to fall through, flunk (exam)
		gefallen (gefällt)	gefiel	gefallen	to please, like
		halten (hält)	hielt	gehalten	to hold, stop
		lassen (läßt)	ließ	gelassen	to let, leave
		schlafen (schläft)	schlief	geschlafen	to sleep
		ein•schlafen (schläft ein)	schlief ein	ist eingeschlafen	to fall asleep
	au– ie – au	laufen (läuft)	lief	ist gelaufen	to run, walk
	ei – ie – ei	heißen	hieß	geheißen	to be called
	u – ie – u	rufen	rief	gerufen	to call, shout
		an•rufen	rief an	angerufen	to phone
	o – ie – o	stoßen (stößt)	stieß	gestoßen	to push
	a – i – a	fangen (fängt)	fing	gefangen	to catch
		an•fangen (fängt an)	fing an	angefangen	to begin, start

All verbs in this class change the stem vowel to **ie** or **i** in the past.
The past participles retain the stem vowel.

Some common verbs that do not fit in the seven classes are:

tun	tat	getan	to do
stehen	stand	gestanden	to stand
auf•stehen	stand auf	ist aufgestanden	to rise, get up
bestehen	bestand	bestanden	to pass (exam)
verstehen	verstand	verstanden	to understand
gehen	ging	ist gegangen	to go
spazieren•gehen	ging spazieren	ist spazierengegangen	to go for a walk
kommen	kam	ist gekommen	to come
mit•kommen	kam mit	ist mitgekommen	to come along, join
bekommen	bekam	bekommen	to receive, get

§5   VERBS REQUIRING THE AUXILIARY *sein*

Verbs requiring the auxiliary **sein** are intransitive (they do not take an accusative object) and denote a change of location (**gehen, kommen, reisen, wandern**) or condition (**ein•schlafen**). There are exceptions to this, the most common of which are **bleiben** (*to stay, remain*) and **sein** (*to be* [cf. §9]) which take the auxiliary **sein** despite their meanings.

§6   THE SIMPLE PAST TENSE OF STRONG VERBS

The personal endings are added to the stem of the simple past (the second principal part).

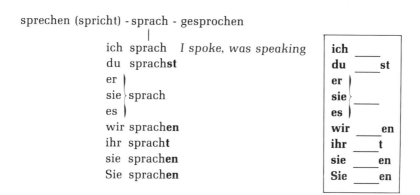

Note that the 1st and 3rd pers. sing. have no personal endings. When the stem ends in **d, t, s,** or **ß,** an **e** is inserted in the **du** and **ihr**-forms:

ich fand	ich hielt	ich ließ
du fand**est**	du hielt**est**	du ließ**est**
ihr fand**et**	ihr hielt**et**	ihr ließ**et**

§7   THE PRESENT PERFECT TENSE OF STRONG VERBS

The auxiliaries **haben** and **sein** are conjugated; the past participle does not change.

ich **habe** gesprochen		ich **bin** gefahren	
du **hast** gesprochen		du **bist** gefahren	
er ⎫		er ⎫	
sie ⎬ **hat** gesprochen		sie ⎬ **ist** gefahren	
es ⎭		es ⎭	
wir **haben** gesprochen		wir **sind** gefahren	
ihr **habt** gesprochen		ihr **seid** gefahren	
sie **haben** gesprochen		sie **sind** gefahren	
Sie **haben** gesprochen		Sie **sind** gefahren	

PRACTICE 9   A. *In this exercise the verbs of classes I, II, III, and IV will be practiced. Learn their principal parts before proceeding; then express the following sentences in the simple past and present perfect tenses.*

Model: Der Tenor singt sehr gut.
Der Tenor sang sehr gut.
Der Tenor hat sehr gut gesungen.

1. Der Redner spricht zu schnell.
2. Du versprichst zuviel.
3. Ein Student unterbricht den Redner.
4. Ihr trinkt zuviel.
5. Das Konzert beginnt um 8 Uhr.
6. Leider findet ihr den Film langweilig.[1]
7. Warum hebt Dieter die Hand?
8. Er schreibt uns nicht.
9. In diesem Fluß[2] sterben viele Fische.
10. Wir reiten durch den Park.
11. Schmidts fliegen nach Rom.
12. Sie bleiben drei Wochen in Italien.
13. Niemand hilft mir.
14. Mein Nachbar nimmt das übel.
15. Du nimmst ab, und ich nehme zu.
16. Wir gewinnen, und sie verlieren.
17. Wir steigen in Köln aus dem Bus aus, und ihr steigt dort ein.

B. *In this exercise the verbs of classes V, VI, VII, and the verbs that do not fit in the seven classes will be practiced. Learn their principal parts before proceeding, then express the following sentences in the simple past and present perfect tenses.*

1. Ich gehe zu Fuß.[3]

---

1 **langweilig**	boring
2 **der Fluß, ̈-sse**	river
3 **zu Fuß gehen**	to go on foot

2. Wir gehen spazieren.
3. Maria kommt nicht mit.
4. Monika bekommt ein Telegramm.
5. Niemand versteht mich.
6. Das tut mir leid.
7. Klaus steht am Fenster.
8. Meine Eltern stehen um 6 Uhr auf.
9. Nicht alle Studenten bestehen die Prüfung.
10. Ein paar[1] Studenten fallen durch.
11. Das gefällt meinen Eltern nicht.
12. Das Baby schläft schon.
13. Ich schlafe schnell ein.
14. Das Fußballspiel fängt um 2 Uhr an.
15. Klaus ruft seine Freundin an.
16. Wir lassen das Gepäck im Auto.
17. Margot läuft zum Briefkasten.[2]
18. Wie heißt das Hotel?
19. Der Bus hält an der Ecke.
20. Er ißt zuviel.
21. Helga vergißt nichts.
22. Sie bittet mich um Verzeihung.
23. Karin liest die Zeitung.
24. Leider gibt Peter nicht nach.
25. Martin sitzt in der ersten Reihe.
26. Deine Brille liegt auf dem Schreibtisch.
27. Andreas lädt alle seine Freunde ein.
28. Klaus trägt meinen Koffer.
29. Zimmermanns fahren nach Düsseldorf.
30. Hannelore fährt auch mit.

PRACTICE 10   *Express the dependent clauses in the present perfect tense.*

Model: Sie fürchtet, daß sie die Prüfung nicht besteht.
Sie fürchtet, daß sie die Prüfung nicht bestanden hat.

1. Sie fürchtet, daß sie in der Prüfung durchfällt.
2. Entschuldigen Sie bitte, daß ich zu spät komme.
3. Schade, daß ihr schon die Hoffnung aufgebt.
4. Ich möchte wissen, warum du mich stößt.
5. Ich verstehe nicht, warum Sie das tun.
6. Ich glaube nicht, daß er den Fehler sieht.
7. Es ist möglich, daß Frau Schmidt die Stelle[3] bekommt.
8. Ich bin überzeugt, daß Martin einen Job[4] findet.

1 **ein paar**	a few
2 **der Briefkasten, ⸚**	mailbox
3 **die Stelle, -n**	job, position
4 **der Job, -s**	job (*colloquially used by younger people*)

The Simple Past and Present Perfect of Irregular Verbs

§8   MIXED VERBS

A small group of verbs have the endings of weak verbs but the vowel change of strong verbs. They are therefore often referred to as *mixed verbs* or *hybrids*. Their principal parts are listed below.

brennen	brannte	gebrannt	*to burn, be on fire*
bringen	brachte	gebra**ch**t	*to bring*
denken	da**ch**te	geda**ch**t	*to think*
kennen	kannte	gekannt	*to know, be familiar with*
nennen	nannte	genannt	*to call, name*
rennen	rannte	ist gerannt	*to run*
senden	sandte	gesandt	*to send*
(rarely)	sendete	gesendet	
wenden	wandte	gewandt	*to turn*
(rarely)	wendete	gewendet	
wissen (weiß)	wußte	gewußt	*to know* (a fact)

Note that **bringen** and **denken** also change consonants in the simple past and past participle.

PRACTICE 11   *Express the following sentences in the simple past and present perfect.*

1. Ich denke an die Sommerferien.
2. Sie kennt mich nicht.
3. Sie wendet schnell den Kopf.
4. Unsere Nachbarn senden uns Grüße aus Heidelberg.
5. Alle nennen mich beim Vornamen.[1]
6. Ich bringe Renate nach Hause.[2]
7. Niemand weiß das.
8. Es brennt[3] in der Garage.
9. Wir rennen schnell zur Garage.

A note on the use of *kennen* and *wissen*

The English equivalent of both **kennen** and **wissen** is *to know*.

a. The verb **kennen** is used in the sense of *to be acquainted* or *familiar with* (persons, places, books, films, etc.). It must have a noun or pronoun as direct object.

1	**der Vorname, -n**	first name
2	**nach Hause bringen**	to take someone home
3	**es brennt**	*idiom.* there is a fire
		(*lit.* it burns)

Kennst du meine Freundin?
Kennen Sie Berlin?
Kennen Sie diesen Roman?[1]
Kennst du diese Komposition von Beethoven?

b. The verb **wissen** means *to know something as a fact,* or *to have information about something.* Its object is often **es, das** (referring to facts), or a clause.

Er weiß es vielleicht nicht.
Warum wissen Sie das nicht?
Du weißt doch, daß ich kein Geld habe.

PRACTICE 12 *Supply the German equivalent of* **to know**.

1. _____ Sie diesen Fußballspieler?
2. _____ du, daß wir morgen keine Schule haben?
3. _____ Sie Frankfurt?
4. _____ ihr diesen Schlager?[2]
5. _____ du, wie Peters neue Freundin heißt?
6. Niemand _____ mich hier.
7. Ich _____, was du jetzt denkst, denn ich _____ dich sehr gut.

§9   IRREGULAR FORMS OF *haben*, *sein*, AND *werden*

a. The principal parts of **haben** are | **haben - hatte - gehabt** |

Note the slight irregularity in the simple past tense:

PRESENT	SIMPLE PAST	PRESENT PERFECT
ich habe *I have*	ich hatte *I had*	ich habe gehabt *I have had, I had*
du hast	du hattest	du hast gehabt
er	er	er
sie} hat	sie} hatte	sie} hat gehabt
es	es	es
wir haben	wir hatten	wir haben gehabt
ihr habt	ihr hattet	ihr habt gehabt
sie haben	sie hatten	sie haben gehabt
Sie haben	Sie hatten	Sie haben gehabt

Remember: | er hat   *he has* |
           | er hatte   *he had* |

b. The principal parts of **sein** are | **sein - war - ist gewesen** |

Sein is a highly irregular verb.

---

1 **der Roman, -e**   novel
2 **der Schlager, -**   pop song

PRESENT	SIMPLE PAST	PRESENT PERFECT
ich bin *I am*	ich war *I was*	ich bin gewesen *I have been, I was*
du bist	du warst	du bist gewesen
er	er	er
sie ⟩ ist	sie ⟩ war	sie ⟩ ist gewesen
es	es	es
wir sind	wir waren	wir sind gewesen
ihr seid	ihr wart	ihr seid gewesen
sie sind	sie waren	sie sind gewesen
Sie sind	Sie waren	Sie sind gewesen

c. The principal parts of **werden** are | **werden (wird) - wurde - ist geworden** |

Note that **werden** has an **-e** ending in the 1st and 3rd person singular of the simple past.

PRESENT	SIMPLE PAST	PRESENT PERFECT
ich werde *I become*	ich wurd**e** *I became*	ich bin geworden *I have become,*
		I became
du wirst	du wurdest	du bist geworden
er	er	er
sie ⟩ wird	sie ⟩ wurd**e**	sie ⟩ ist geworden
es	es	es
wir werden	wir wurden	wir sind geworden
ihr werdet	ihr wurdet	ihr seid geworden
sie werden	sie wurden	sie sind geworden
Sie werden	Sie wurden	Sie sind geworden

PRACTICE 13   *Restate the following sentences, using the subjects indicated in parentheses.*

1. Ich war pleite.[1] (wir, er, du, ihr, Sie)
2. Ich bin schon oft bei Winklers gewesen. (du, ihr, Sie, wir)
3. Frank hatte recht. (wir, du, ihr, Sie, ich)
4. Haben Sie Lampenfieber[2] gehabt? (du, ihr)
5. Ich wurde böse. (er, du, Sie)
6. Warum sind Sie so böse geworden? (du, Martin)

The use of the simple past tense of *sein* and *haben*

Contrary to the general practice in conversational German of using the present perfect to refer to single past events, sentences with **sein** as the main verb frequently use the simple past. This occurs less often with **haben**.

Habt ihr gestern Karten **gespielt?**	Nein, wir **waren** im Kino.
Ist Rainer auch **mitgekommen?**	Nein, er **hatte** keine Zeit.

1 **pleite sein**   to be broke
2 **das Lampenfieber**   stage fright

PRACTICE 14   *The following exercise contains strong and irregular verbs. Translate the sentences into German, using the present perfect for the English past tense except where otherwise indicated.*

Model: a. Sabine isn't coming back.   **Sabine kommt nicht zurück.**
        b. She didn't come back.   **Sie ist nicht zurückgekommen.**
        c. Too bad that she didn't   **Schade, daß sie nicht**
           come back.   **zurückgekommen ist.**

1. a. We are late again.   **Wir kommen schon wieder zu spät.**
  b. We were late again.
  c. Why were you late again? (fam. sing.)
  d. I'd like to know why you were late again.
2. a. I hope you get the scholarship. (fam. sing.)   **Hoffentlich bekommst du das Stipendium.**
  b. I hope she got the scholarship.
  c. I'm glad that she got the scholarship.
3. a. I'm not going to do that.   **Ich tue das nicht.**
  b. I didn't do that.
  c. Who did that?
  d. Nobody knows who did that.
4. a. I am shocked.   **Ich bin schockiert.**
  b. I was shocked. (past)
  c. They were shocked. (past)
  d. Why were you so shocked? (fam. sing., past)
  e. I'd like to know why you were so shocked. (formal, past)
5. a. We are lucky.   **Wir haben Glück.**
  b. We were lucky. (past, pres. perf.)
  c. I hope they were lucky. (past, pres. perf.)
6. a. I hope I'll lose some weight.   **Hoffentlich nehme ich etwas ab.**
  b. I hope I lost some weight.
  c. Did you lose some weight? (formal)
  d. I am very glad that I lost some weight.
7. a. I hope I pass the exam.   **Hoffentlich bestehe ich die Prüfung.**
  b. I hope I passed the exam.
  c. Did you pass the exam? (fam. sing.)
  d. I assume that she passed the exam.
8. a. Perhaps I'll flunk the exam.   **Vielleicht falle ich in der Prüfung durch.**
  b. Perhaps I flunked the exam.
  c. Who flunked the exam?
  d. I don't know who flunked the exam.
9. a. Do you know him?   **Kennst du ihn?**
  b. Nobody knew him.
  c. I don't think that she knew him.
10. a. Don't you know that?   **Weißt du das nicht?**
  b. Didn't you know that?
  c. I assume that he didn't know that.

11. a. I resent that.   **Ich nehme das übel.**
    b. He resented that.
    c. Did you resent that? (formal)
    d. It is possible that she resented that.
12. a. I hope I won't lose the key.   **Hoffentlich verliere ich den Schlüssel nicht.**
    b. I hope I didn't lose the key.
    c. Where did you lose the key? (fam. sing.)
    d. I have no idea where I lost the key.
13. a. I hope you won't become angry. (formal)   **Hoffentlich werden Sie nicht böse.**
    b. He became very angry.
    c. I don't understand why he became so angry.
14. a. She is not inviting the Bergmanns.   **Sie lädt Bergmanns nicht ein.**
    b. They did not invite the Bergmanns.
    c. I'd like to know why they did not invite the Bergmanns.

The Past Perfect, Future, and Future Perfect of Weak, Strong, and Irregular Verbs

§10   THE PAST PERFECT TENSE

The past perfect expresses a past event that occurred previous to some other past event.

> Ein Polizist **gab** Klaus einen Strafzettel, weil er den Wagen auf der
> (past)
> falschen Straßenseite **geparkt hatte.**
> (past perfect)
> *A policeman **gave** Klaus a ticket because he **had parked** the car on the wrong side of the street.*

In this sentence two past events are expressed which did not occur simultaneously. First Klaus parked on the wrong side of the street, then the policeman gave him a ticket. The first event is in the past perfect tense, the other in the simple past tense.

The forms of the past perfect differ from the present perfect only in that the auxiliary verb **haben** or **sein** is in the simple past tense rather than in the present tense. Compare:

PRESENT PERFECT	PAST PERFECT
Sie **hat** mich nicht **angerufen.**	Sie **hatte** mich nicht **angerufen.**
	She had not called me.
Wir **sind** nach Hause **gefahren.**	Wir **waren** nach Hause **gefahren.**
	We had gone home.

PRACTICE 15   *Restate the following sentences in the past perfect tense.*

1. Ich habe Ihre Frage nicht verstanden.
2. Die Kinder sind zu Hause geblieben.
3. Er hat zuviel Geld ausgegeben.[1]
4. Wir haben Ellen gewarnt.[2]
5. Es ist kälter geworden.
6. Helga hat meinen Geburtstag vergessen.

Word order in dependent clauses:

> Wir gingen spazieren, nachdem wir gegessen **hatten**.
> *We went for a walk after we had eaten.*

The inflected verb is in last position.

PRACTICE 16   *Express the dependent clauses in the past perfect, using the indicated words.*

Model: Ich bat Erika um Verzeihung, weil / ich / eine dumme Bemerkung / machen
Ich bat Erika um Verzeihung, weil ich eine dumme Bemerkung gemacht hatte.

1. Sie hatte einen Nervenzusammenbruch,[3] weil / sie / zuviel / arbeiten
2. Wir räumten die Wohnung auf, nachdem / alle Gäste / nach Hause / gehen
3. Ich wurde sehr böse, weil / Klaus / sein Versprechen / nicht / halten[4]
4. Annerose bekam einen Strafzettel, weil / sie / zu schnell / fahren

§11   THE FUTURE TENSE

Formation

PRESENT   Barbara hilft mir bei den Hausaufgaben.
FUTURE   Barbara **wird** mir bei den Hausaufgaben **helfen**.
           Barbara will help me with the homework.

The future tense is formed with the present tense of the auxiliary **werden** and the infinitive of the main verb.

1 **Geld aus•geben**	to spend money
(gibt aus), gab aus, ausgegeben	
2 **warnen**	to warn
3 **der Nevenzusammenbruch, ¨-e**	nervous breakdown
4 **das Versprechen halten**	to keep the promise
(hält), hielt, gehalten	

Conjugation: ich **werde** helfen   *I will help*
du **wirst** helfen
er ⎫
sie ⎬**wird** helfen
es ⎭
wir **werden** helfen
ihr **werdet** helfen
sie **werden** helfen
Sie **werden** helfen

| **werden** + infinitive | | **will** + infinitive |

In main clauses and questions **werden** takes the position of the inflected verb; the infinitive is in last position. Compare these present and future tense sentences:

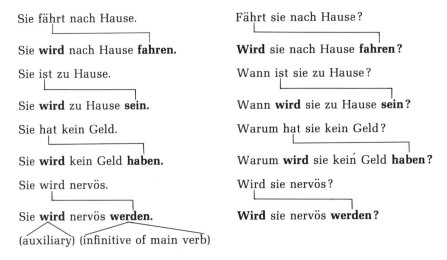

Sie fährt nach Hause.   Fährt sie nach Hause?

Sie **wird** nach Hause **fahren.**   **Wird** sie nach Hause **fahren?**

Sie ist zu Hause.   Wann ist sie zu Hause?

Sie **wird** zu Hause **sein.**   Wann **wird** sie zu Hause **sein?**

Sie hat kein Geld.   Warum hat sie kein Geld?

Sie **wird** kein Geld **haben.**   Warum **wird** sie kein Geld **haben?**

Sie wird nervös.   Wird sie nervös?

Sie **wird** nervös **werden.**   **Wird** sie nervös **werden?**
(auxiliary) (infinitive of main verb)

When the infinitive has a separable prefix, it is attached to the verb:

Sie ruft ihn an.   Ruft sie ihn an?

Sie wird ihn **anrufen.**   Wird sie ihn **anrufen?**

PRACTICE 17   *Express the following sentences in the future tense.*

Model: Ich komme nicht zurück.
Ich werde nicht zurückkommen.

1. Dietmar holt mich ab.
2. Wann holt er dich ab?
3. Wir verkaufen unseren Wagen.
4. Verkaufen Sie Ihren Wagen?
5. Du lachst mich aus.
6. Lachst du mich aus?
7. Er hält sein Versprechen.

8. Hält er sein Versprechen?
9. Helga hat keine Zeit für mich.
10. Hast du Zeit für mich?
11. Es wird noch kälter.
12. Wird es wirklich noch kälter?
13. Ist die Prüfung schwer?

Word order in dependent clauses

Er **wird** es mir nicht **sagen.**
Ich bin überzeugt, daß er es mir nicht **sagen wird.**
I am convinced that he won't tell me.

In dependent clauses the inflected auxiliary **werden** is in last position; it is preceded by the infinitive of the main verb.

PRACTICE 18   *Restate the following sentences beginning with* **Ich bin überzeugt, daß ...**

Model: Er wird es nicht übelnehmen.
       Ich bin überzeugt, daß er es nicht übelnehmen wird.

1. Du wirst nicht nachgeben.
2. Schmidts werden auch meine Freundin einladen.
3. Ihr werdet mich nicht verstehen.
4. Annette wird ihr Versprechen nicht halten.
5. Dieter wird sein Zimmer nicht aufräumen.
6. Du wirst das vergessen.
7. Diese Firma wird großen Erfolg[1] haben.

Use of the future tense

The present tense is often used to express future time if an adverb or the context indicates that the future is referred to (cf. Chap. 2, §7, 2).

Ich rufe dich morgen an.   *I'll call you tomorrow.*
Ich rufe dich bestimmt an.   *I'll certainly call you.*

The future tense has to be used if futurity is not otherwise indicated. Compare:

Sie **unterstützt** ihre Eltern.   She **supports** her parents.
Sie **wird** ihre Eltern **unterstützen.**   She **will support** her parents.

The future tense is occasionally used to express a supposition or probability referring to present or future time. Adverbs such as **wohl** (most commonly used), **wahrscheinlich, vielleicht** often enhance this notion. Compare:

Klaus ist wahrscheinlich krank.
Klaus **wird wohl** (wahrscheinlich) krank **sein.** } *Klaus is probably ill.*

Helga kommt wahrscheinlich nicht mit.
Helga **wird wohl** (wahrscheinlich) nicht **mitkommen.** } *Helga is probably not coming along.*

1 **der Erfolg, -e**   success

PRACTICE 19   *Restate the following sentences expressing the probability by using the future tense and* **wohl.**

Model: Fräulein Schmidt kennt mich wahrscheinlich nicht.
Fräulein Schmidt wird mich wohl nicht kennen.

1. Michael arbeitet wahrscheinlich in der Bibliothek.
2. Du vergißt mich wahrscheinlich sehr schnell.
3. Maria hat vielleicht Lampenfieber.
4. Das ist vielleicht nicht wahr.
5. Es wird vielleicht kälter.
6. Ich bleibe wahrscheinlich zu Hause.
7. Renate ruft mich wahrscheinlich nicht an.
8. Herr Kästner gibt vielleicht nicht nach.

§12   THE FUTURE PERFECT TENSE

FUTURE   Wir **werden** unser Haus im Sommer **verkaufen.**
FUTURE PERFECT   Wir **werden** es hoffentlich bis Ende des Sommers **verkauft haben.**
                  *We hope we **will have sold** it by the end of the summer.*

In the example above the future perfect tense expresses the anticipated conclusion of an action by a certain time in the future.

Compare the formation of the future and the future perfect:

FUTURE	FUTURE PERFECT	FUTURE	FUTURE PERFECT
er wird verkaufen	er wird **verkauft haben**	he will sell	he will *have sold*
er wird bezahlen	er wird **bezahlt haben**	he will pay	he will *have paid*
er wird gehen	er wird **gegangen sein**	he will go	he will *have gone*
er wird haben	er wird **gehabt haben**	he will have	he will *have had*
er wird sein	er wird **gewesen sein**	he will be	he will *have been*
er wird werden	er wird **geworden sein**	he will become	he will *have become*
werden + inf.	werden + perf. inf.	will + inf.	will + perf. inf.

In German the perfect infinitive consists of the past participle followed by the infinitive of the auxiliary **haben** or **sein,** depending on the past participle. In English the auxiliary *have* precedes the past participle.

PRACTICE 20   *Translate into English.*

1. Nächsten Freitag werden wir dieses Projekt beendet haben.
2. Bis dahin[1] werden wir unsere Schulden[2] bezahlt haben.
3. Ich werde diese Sache bis Mittwoch erledigt haben.
4. Ende dieses Jahres wird Frau Schramm drei Jahre bei dieser Firma gewesen sein.

1	**bis dahin**	by then
2	**die Schuld, -en**	debt

The future perfect tense expressing a supposition or probability

The future perfect tense is more commonly used to express a supposition or probability. Compare:

a. Sie **haben** wahrscheinlich Tennis **gespielt.**
b. Sie **werden** wohl Tennis **gespielt haben.** *They probably played tennis.*

The supposition refers to a past event. Sentence *a* uses the present perfect and sentence *b* the future perfect. Both sentences are rendered by the English past tense.

PRACTICE 21   *Translate the following sentences into English.*

Model: Ich werde wohl in der Prüfung durchgefallen sein.
I probably flunked the exam.

1. Der Lärm wird wohl meine Nachbarn gestört haben.
2. Anita wird wohl zum Arzt gegangen sein.
3. Du wirst wohl zu spät aufgestanden sein.
4. Es wird wohl in der Nacht geregnet haben.
5. Schuberts werden wohl nicht zu Hause gewesen sein.
6. Der Chef wird wohl nervös geworden sein.

§13   REFERENCE CHART: SYNOPSIS OF THE TENSES

Verbs selected as examples:
fragen   weak verb
mit•kommen   strong verb with separable prefix, using **sein**
haben
sein   functioning as main verbs
werden

MAIN CLAUSES	DEPENDENT CLAUSES
PRESENT	
Er **fragt** (nicht).	daß er (nicht) **fragt.**
Er **kommt** (nicht) **mit.**	daß er (nicht) **mitkommt.**
Er **hat** (kein) Geld.	daß er (kein) Geld **hat.**
Er **ist** (nicht) nervös.	daß er (nicht) nervös **ist.**
Er **wird** (nicht) nervös.	daß er (nicht) nervös **wird.**
PAST	
Er **fragte** (nicht).	daß er (nicht) **fragte.**
Er **kam** (nicht) **mit.**	daß er (nicht) **mitkam.**
Er **hatte** (kein) Geld.	daß er (kein) Geld **hatte.**
Er **war** (nicht) nervös.	daß er (nicht) nervös **war.**
Er **wurde** (nicht) nervös.	daß er (nicht) nervös **wurde.**

PRESENT PERFECT

Er **hat** (nicht) **gefragt**.	daß er (nicht) **gefragt hat**.
Er **ist** (nicht) **mitgekommen**.	daß er (nicht) **mitgekommen ist**.
Er **hat** (kein) Geld **gehabt**.	daß er (kein) Geld **gehabt hat**.
Er **ist** (nicht) nervös **gewesen**.	daß er (nicht) nervös **gewesen ist**.
Er **ist** (nicht) nervös **geworden**.	daß er (nicht) nervös **geworden ist**.

PAST PERFECT

Er **hatte** (nicht) **gefragt**.	daß er (nicht) **gefragt hatte**.
Er **war** (nicht) **mitgekommen**.	daß er (nicht) **mitgekommen war**.
Er **hatte** (kein) Geld **gehabt**.	daß er (kein) Geld **gehabt hatte**.
Er **war** (nicht) nervös **gewesen**.	daß er (nicht) nervös **gewesen war**.
Er **war** (nicht) nervös **geworden**.	daß er (nicht) nervös **geworden war**.

FUTURE

Er **wird** (nicht) **fragen**.	daß er (nicht) **fragen wird**.
Er **wird** (nicht) **mitkommen**.	daß er (nicht) **mitkommen wird**.
Er **wird** (kein) Geld **haben**.	daß er (kein) Geld **haben wird**.
Er **wird** (nicht) nervös **sein**.	daß er (nicht) nervös **sein wird**.
Er **wird** (nicht) nervös **werden**.	daß er (nicht) nervös **werden wird**.

FUTURE PERFECT

Er **wird** (nicht) **gefragt haben**.	daß er (nicht) **gefragt haben wird***.
Er **wird** (nicht) **mitgekommen sein**.	daß er (nicht) **mitgekommen sein wird**.
Er **wird** (kein) Geld **gehabt haben**.	daß er (kein) Geld **gehabt haben wird**.
Er **wird** (nicht) nervös **gewesen sein**.	daß er (nicht) nervös **gewesen sein wird**.
Er **wird** (nicht) nervös **geworden sein**.	daß er (nicht) nervös **geworden sein wird**.

The present and the simple past are formed without auxiliary; they are so-called *simple tenses*. The other four tenses are formed with the auxiliary **haben, sein,** or **werden;** they are *compound tenses*.

§14   THE POSITION OF SEPARABLE PREFIXES

The separable prefix is separated when the verb to which it belongs is in first or second position. This occurs in the following instances:

	MAIN CLAUSE	DIRECT QUESTION	IMPERATIVE
PRESENT	Sie kommt **mit**.	Kommt sie **mit**?	Komm **mit**!
PAST	Sie kam **mit**.	Wer kam **mit**?	

In all other instances the prefix is attached to the verb, i.e. in infinitives, past participles, and in dependent clauses (including indirect questions):

Sie wird nicht **mitkommen**.
Sie ist nicht **mitgekommen**.
Schade, daß sie nicht **mitkommt**.
Ich möchte wissen, warum sie nicht **mitkommt**.

* The future perfect hardly ever occurs in dependent clauses.

PRACTICE 22 Summarizing exercises.

A. *Express the following sentences in the past, present perfect, past perfect, and future.*

1. Das ist ein Skandal.
2. Irene ruft mich nicht an.
3. Sie wird böse.
4. Frank hat Lampenfieber.

B. *Express the following sentences in the tenses indicated in parentheses. (Do not change the boldface introductory clauses.)*

1. Rita hat recht. (past, past perf.)
2. Niemand hilft uns. (pres. perf., past perf., future)
3. Das ist nicht leicht. (past, future)
4. Udo weiß das nicht. (past, past perf.)
5. Die Sache wird problematisch. (past, pres. perf.)
6. Margot vergißt das bestimmt. (future, pres. perf.)
7. Wir haben Hunger und auch Durst. (past)
8. **Ich glaube nicht,** daß er Angst vor mir hat. (past)
9. Der Redner spricht zu leise und zu schnell. (past perf.)
10. Wir mieten eine kleine Wohnung. (future)
11. Kennen Sie Helgas Mann? (pres. perf.)
12. Ihr lacht mich vielleicht aus. (future)
13. Ich esse sehr wenig, und trotzdem[1] nehme ich nicht ab. (pres. perf.)
14. Frau Krause gibt dieses Mal nicht nach. (future)
15. **Ich glaube auch,** daß sie dieses Mal nicht nachgibt. (future)
16. Er wartet und wartet, aber sie kommt nicht. (past)
17. Kein Wunder, daß er böse wird. (past)
18. **Ist es wahr,** daß ihr im August in die Schweiz fliegt? (pres. perf.)
19. **Ich bin überzeugt,** daß er sein Versprechen hält. (future)
20. Meine Nachbarn stehen schon um 6 Uhr auf. (past perf.)
21. Sie essen, trinken und bezahlen nicht. Das ist nicht nett von ihnen. (past)
22. Diese Übung macht mir Spaß. (pres. perf.)
23. Das ist wohl nicht wahr. (future)

1 **trotzdem**   nevertheless

4

Modal Auxiliaries

KEY TO THE EXERCISES ON CASSETTE 2.
RUNNING TIME: APPROX. 40 MIN.

Introduction

Compare:

a.	Ich **helfe** Inge bei den Hausaufgaben.	*I am helping Inge with the homework.*
b.	Ich **kann** Inge bei den Hausaufgeben **helfen.**	*I can help Inge …*
	Ich **muß** Inge bei den Hausaufgaben **helfen.**	*I must help Inge …*
	Ich **soll** Inge bei den Hausaufgaben **helfen.**	*I am supposed to help Inge …*

Sentence *a* simply states the act of helping; it is modified in the three following sentences by the use of **können, müssen,** and **sollen.** These modal auxiliaries, commonly called *modals*, are inflected whereas the accompanying verb **helfen** is in the infinitive. In our further treatment, the accompanying verb will be referred to as the *dependent infinitive*.

In German there are six models:

dürfen	*may*	*expression of:*	permission
	to be allowed to		
	to be permitted to		
können	*can*		ability, possibility
	to be able to		
mögen	*to like to*		liking
	to care to		
müssen	*must*		necessity
	to have to		
sollen	*to be expected to*		obligation
	to be supposed to		
wollen	*to want to*		wish, desire, intention
	to intend to		

All German modals take the dependent infinitive without **zu.**

Wir dürfen hier parken.	*We may park here.*
	We are allowed to park here.
Wir können das nicht bezahlen.	*We cannot pay that.*
	We are not able to pay that.
Wir mögen jetzt nicht Tennis spielen.	*We don't care to play tennis now.*
Wir müssen auf Barbara warten.	*We must wait for Barbara.*
	We have to wait for Barbara.
Wir sollen den Fall der Polizei melden.	*We are expected to report the case to the police.*
	We are supposed to report the case to the police.
Wir wollen ein Haus kaufen.	*We want to buy a house.*
	We intend to buy a house.

The Modals in the Simple Tenses

§1   THE PRESENT TENSE

Formation

The modals are conjugated in the present tense as follows:

dürfen	**können**	**mögen**	**müssen**	**sollen**	**wollen**
ich darf	ich kann	ich mag	ich muß	ich soll	ich will
du darfst	du kannst	du magst	du mußt	du sollst	du willst
er	er	er	er	er	er
sie } darf	sie } kann	sie } mag	sie } muß	sie } soll	sie } will
es	es	es	es	es	es
wir dürfen	wir können	wir mögen	wir müssen	wir sollen	wir wollen
ihr dürft	ihr könnt	ihr mögt	ihr müßt	ihr sollt	ihr wollt
sie dürfen	sie können	sie mögen	sie müssen	sie sollen	sie wollen
Sie dürfen	Sie können	Sie mögen	Sie müssen	Sie sollen	Sie wollen
I may,	*I can,*	*I like to,*	*I must,*	*I am expected,*	*I want to,*
I am allowed to, etc.	*I am able to, etc.*	*I care to, etc.*	*I have to, etc.*	*I am supposed to, etc.*	*I intend to, etc.*

Note: a. The 1st and 3rd pers. sing. are identical.

b. The vowel change occurs throughout the singular but never in the plural; **sollen,** however, has no vowel change.

PRACTICE 1   A. *Supply the correct form of the modals in parentheses.*

1. Ich _____ nicht rauchen. (wollen, sollen, dürfen)
2. Du _____ Thomas helfen. (können, sollen, müssen)
3. Hannelore _____ das nicht essen. (mögen, wollen, dürfen)
4. Wir _____ jetzt nach Hause gehen. (müssen, wollen, sollen, können)
5. Ihr _____ hier parken. (können, dürfen)
6. Meine Eltern _____ das bezahlen. (sollen, müssen)

B. *Translate the following sentences into English.*

1. Niemand kann mir helfen.
2. Maria will mitkommen.
3. Ich mag ihn nicht fragen.
4. Du mußt das heute erledigen.
5. Hier dürft ihr nicht rauchen.
6. Darf ich Sie zu einer Tasse Kaffee einladen?
7. Was soll das bedeuten?

C. *Complete the following sentences in German, using the English cues in parentheses.*

1. Die Chefin _____ das Geld investieren. (*to want to, intend to*)
2. Ich _____ jetzt die Hausaufgaben machen. (*to have to*)
3. Wir _____ ihn um Erlaubnis bitten.[1] (*to be supposed to*)
4. Hier _____ du nicht überholen.[2] (*to be allowed to*)
5. Ihr _____ mich nicht überreden.[3] (*can*)
6. Ich _____ das nicht trinken. (*to like to*)

Introducing modals in main clauses and questions

When modals are introduced, the following changes occur in the structure of main clauses and questions:

Main clause

Ich glaube das nicht.

Ich **kann** das nicht **glauben**.

The inflected verb becomes the dependent infinitive and goes to the end of the sentence, while the modal becomes the inflected verb and thus occupies the second position.

Question   a. beginning with a question word—modal in second position:

Warum glaubst du das nicht?

Warum **kannst** du das nicht **glauben**?

1 **um Erlaubnis bitten**	to ask for permission
2 **überholen**	to overtake, pass
3 **überreden**	to persuade

b. without a question word—modal in first position:

Glaubst du das nicht?

Kannst du das nicht **glauben**?

PRACTICE 2   *Restate the following sentences, using the modals indicated in parentheses.*

Model: a. Wir fahren in die Stadt. (wollen)
Wir wollen in die Stadt fahren.
b. Wann fahrt ihr in die Stadt? (wollen)
Wann wollt ihr in die Stadt fahren?

1. a. Ich sage es dir nicht. (dürfen)
   b. Warum sagst du es mir nicht? (dürfen)
2. a. Meine Eltern verstehen das nicht. (können)
   b. Verstehen sie das wirklich nicht? (können)
3. a. Ich gehe jetzt nach Hause. (müssen)
   b. Gehst du wirklich schon nach Hause? (müssen)
4. a. Andreas bezahlt das. (sollen)
   b. Wer bezahlt das? (sollen)
5. a. Ich esse diesen Fisch nicht. (mögen)
   b. Warum essen Sie diesen Fisch nicht? (mögen)
6. a. Wir fliegen nach Alaska. (wollen)
   b. Fliegt ihr wirklich nach Alaska? (wollen)

Note the use of **haben, sein,** and **werden** as dependent infinitives:

Ich bin still.   Sie hat viel Geduld[1] mit mir.

Ich **soll** still **sein**.   Sie **muß** viel Geduld mit mir **haben**.

Er wird reich.

Er **will** reich **werden**.

Do not confuse **will** ... **werden** (*want to get* or *become*) with
wird ... **werden** (*will get* or *become* [future tense]).

PRACTICE 3   *Restate the following sentences using German modals.*

1. Meine Noten werden besser. (*must/have to*)
2. Neumanns haben keine Kinder. (*to want to*)
3. Wann ist die Arbeit fertig? (*to be supposed to*)
4. Heute hat niemand schlechte Laune. (*to be allowed to*)
5. Sabine wird nicht dick. (*to want to*)
6. Dietmar ist nicht treu.[2] (*can*)

---

1 **die Geduld**   patience
2 **treu**   faithful

Verbs with separable prefix as dependent infinitives:

Hans ruft mich heute nicht an.

Hans **kann** mich heute nicht **anrufen.**

Warum **kann** er dich heute nicht **anrufen?**

Kann er dich heute nicht **anrufen?**

The separable prefix is attached to the infinitive.

PRACTICE 4   *Restate the following sentences using the modals in parentheses.*

> **Model:** Lädst du Rainer ein? (wollen)
>   **Willst du Rainer einladen?**
>
> 1. Holst du Annerose ab? (wollen)
> 2. Wann fängt das Konzert an? (sollen)
> 3. Warum fahrt ihr nach Bonn zurück? (wollen)
> 4. Ich bringe die Bücher zur Bibliothek zurück. (müssen)
> 5. Bei diesem Wetter gehen wir nicht spazieren. (können)
> 6. Reicht Hannelore die Semesterarbeit[1] später ein?[2] (dürfen)
> 7. Wann stehst du morgen auf? (müssen)
> 8. Warum lädst du ihn nicht ein? (wollen)
> 9. Nehmen Sie die Einladung an?[3] (können)
> 10. Jörg räumt seinen Schreibtisch auf. (sollen)

Dependent word order

Barbara **kann** nicht mitkommen.

Ich weiß, daß Barbara nicht mitkommen **kann.**

In dependent clauses the inflected modal is in last position; the dependent infinitive precedes it.

PRACTICE 5   *Restate the following sentences, using the indicated introductory clauses.*

> **Model:** Wer kann dieses Problem lösen?
>   Ich möchte wissen, **wer dieses Problem lösen kann.**
>
> 1. Will Manfred seine Freundin mitbringen?
>   Ich weiß nicht, ob ...
> 2. Muß Astrid für eine Prüfung lernen?
>   Ich nehme an, daß ...
> 3. Dürfen wir hier über die Straße gehen?[4]
>   Ich glaube nicht, daß ...

---

1 **die Semesterarbeit, -en**	term paper
2 **ein•reichen**	to hand in
3 **die Einladung an•nehmen**	to accept the invitation
4 **über die Straße gehen**	to cross the street

4. Ihr sollt den Chef um Erlaubnis bitten.
   Wißt ihr nicht, daß ...
5. Ich muß am Wochenende die Nase ins Buch stecken.[1]
   Schade, daß ...
6. Du sollst nicht soviel klatschen.[2]
   Du weißt doch, daß ...

Use of modals without a dependent infinitive

Kannst du mir helfen? Nein, ich kann nicht. *No, I can't.*
   Nein, ich kann es nicht. *No, I can't do it.*
   Nein, ich kann das nicht. *No, I can't do that.*

Dependent infinitives need not be repeated in such sequences. They may be either omitted completely or replaced by **es** or **das.**

The verbs **fahren, gehen, machen,** and **tun** are often omitted because they are clearly understood from the context.

Ich muß in die Bibliothek. *I must go to the library.*
Wo willst du hin? *Where do you want to go?*
Was soll ich mit diesen Sachen? *What am I supposed to do with these things?*

PRACTICE 6   A. *Translate the following questions and answers into idiomatic English.*

1.   X: Müssen Sie schon nach Hause?
      Y: Leider ja. Unsere Kinder müssen jetzt ins Bett.
2.   X: Wo willst du hin?
      Y: Ich muß ins Studentenheim[3] zurück. Ich habe meine Brille[4] vergessen.
3.   X: Was macht ihr heute nachmittag?
      Y: Hans und Udo wollen zum Fußballspiel; Maria und ich wollen in den Zirkus.
4. a. X: Warum hast du mir diesen Katalog gegeben? Was soll ich damit?
      Y: Ein Geschenk bestellen. Jemand[5] hat bald Geburtstag.
   b. X: Ach so,[6] ein leiser Wink.[7] Und wer soll es bezahlen?
      Y: Du natürlich. Du kannst es doch.
   c. X: Wenn ich es aber nicht will?
      Y: Ich weiß, du kannst es, und du willst es auch.

1 **die Nase ins Buch stecken**	to hit the books
2 **klatschen**	to gossip
3 **das Studentenheim. -e**	dormitory
4 **die Brille, -n**	eyeglasses
5 **jemand**	somebody, someone
6 **ach so**	generally used in the sense of "oh, I see"
7 **ein leiser Wink**	a subtle hint

B. *Translate the responses into German, adding* **es** *to the modal.*

1. X: Willst du wirklich am Wochenende arbeiten?
   Y: (*I have to.*)
2. X: Warum essen Sie keine Schlagsahne?[1]
   Y: (*I'm not allowed to.*) Der Arzt hat es mir verboten.[2]
3. X: Du kannst doch mitfahren.
   Y: (*Yes, but I don't want to.*)
4. X: Wer soll diesen schweren Koffer tragen?
   Y: (*I'm supposed to, but I can't.*)
5. X: Niemand darf ihn jetzt bei der Arbeit stören.
   Y: (*I'm allowed to*), denn ich bin ein Jemand[3] und kein Niemand.*

PRACTICE 7   Summarizing exercises for the present tense.

A. *Form questions.*

Model: du / wollen / mit.kommen / wirklich nicht
   Willst du wirklich nicht mitkommen?

1. du / wollen / versuchen / es noch einmal?
2. Sie / können / lösen[4] / dieses Problem?
3. wir / sollen / warten / auf Marlene?
4. ihr / wollen / spazieren.gehen / heute nachmittag?
5. du / können / helfen / mir / bei den Hausaufgaben?
6. Sie / müssen / bitten / den Chef um Erlaubnis?
7. du / wollen / ab.holen / die Post?
8. wir / dürfen / parken / hier?
9. warum / du / können / mit.kommen / nicht?
10. warum / ihr / wollen / ein.laden / Bergmanns / nicht?
11. wann / Sie / können / reparieren / meinen Wagen?
12. was / du / wollen / schenken / deiner Freundin zum Geburtstag?
13. du / wollen / heiraten / mich?

B. *Form answers.*

Model: – X: Warum haben Sie diese Wohnung nicht gemietet?
      Y: weil / wir / wollen / kaufen / ein Haus
      Weil wir ein Haus kaufen wollen.

1. X: Warum fährst du zum Flughafen?
   Y: weil / ich / sollen / ab.holen / Volker
2. X: Warum überholst du den Wagen vor uns nicht?
   Y: weil / man / dürfen / über.holen / hier nicht
3. X: Warum gehst du nicht mit uns schwimmen?
   Y: weil / ich / müssen / stecken / die Nase ins Buch

1 **die Schlagsahne**	whipped cream
2 **der Arzt hat es mir verboten**	doctor's orders (*lit.: The doctor has forbidden it to me.*)
3 **ein Jemand**	a somebody
4 **lösen**	to solve

* **Jemand** and **niemand** are capitalized when preceded by a **der**-word or **ein**-word.

4. X: Warum erzählst du mir nicht, was du über Bergers gehört hast?
    Y: weil / ich / sollen / klatschen / nicht
5. X: Warum gehst du schon nach Hause?
    Y: weil / ich / müssen / sein / vor Mitternacht[1] zu Hause
6. X: Warum läufst du so schnell?
    Y: weil / ich / wollen / kommen / nicht zu spät
7. X: Warum heiratest du nicht?
    Y: weil / ich / können / sein / nicht treu

C. *Translate the following sentences into German.*

1. a. Frank is studying for an exam. **Frank lernt für eine Prüfung.**
    b. He has to study for an exam.
    c. He has to, but he doesn't want to.
2. a. Helga doesn't know (it). **Helga weiß es nicht.**
    b. She wants to know (it).
    c. I assume that she wants to know (it).
3. a. They are not telling me. **Sie sagen es[2] mir nicht.**
    b. They don't want to tell me.
    c. You don't want to tell me. (fam. sing.)
    d. I want to, but I am not allowed to.
4. a. When are you going to straighten up your room? **Wann räumst du dein Zimmer auf?**
    b. You have to straighten up your room.
    c. I'm supposed to, but I don't want to.
5. a. When are you handing in the term paper? **Wann reichst du die Semesterarbeit ein?**
    b. When do we have to hand in the term paper?
    c. I don't know when we have to hand in the term paper.
6. a. Who is taking care of that? **Wer erledigt das?**
    b. Who wants to take care of that?
    c. Who is supposed to take care of that?
    d. You have to take care of that. (fam. sing.)
    e. I can't take care of that.
7. a. I'm not losing weight. On the contrary, I'm gaining weight. **Ich nehme nicht ab. Im Gegenteil, ich nehme zu.**
    b. Do you want to gain weight? (formal)
    c. On the contrary, I want to lose weight.
    d. Ute wants to gain weight.
    e. I can't believe (it) that she wants to gain weight.
8. a. My grades are getting worse. **Meine Noten werden schlechter.**
    b. They have to get better.
    c. How can they get better?
    d. You have to hit the books. (fam. sing.)
    e. I have to hit the books so that[3] my grades get better.

1 **vor Mitternacht**	before midnight
2 **es sagen** (sagen + dir. obj.)	to tell
3 **damit**	so that

§2   THE SIMPLE PAST TENSE

Formation

The modals are conjugated in the simple past as follows:

dürfen	**können**	**mögen**	**müssen**	**sollen**	**wollen**
ich durfte	ich konnte	ich mochte	ich mußte	ich sollte	ich wollte
du durftest	du konntest	du mochtest	du mußtest	du solltest	du wolltest
er ⎫ sie ⎬ durfte es ⎭	er ⎫ sie ⎬ konnte es ⎭	er ⎫ sie ⎬ mochte es ⎭	er ⎫ sie ⎬ mußte es ⎭	er ⎫ sie ⎬ sollte es ⎭	er ⎫ sie ⎬ wollte es ⎭
wir durften	wir konnten	wir mochten	wir mußten	wir sollten	wir wollten
ihr durftet	ihr konntet	ihr mochtet	ihr mußtet	ihr solltet	ihr wolltet
sie durften	sie konnten	sie mochten	sie mußten	sie sollten	sie wollten
Sie durften	Sie konnten	Sie mochten	Sie mußten	Sie sollten	Sie wollten
I was allowed to, etc.	*I could, I was able to, etc.*	*I liked to, etc.*	*I had to, etc.*	*I was expected, I was supposed to, etc.*	*I wanted to, I intended to, etc.*

Note: a. Modals take the same endings in the simple past as weak verbs.

b. Modals have no umlaut in the past.

c. **Mochte** has a change of consonants.

The use of modals in the simple past tense

Modals generally use the simple past even to express single past events, while most other verbs are in the present perfect tense (cf. Chap. 3, §2).

> Warum **sind** Sie nur zwei Tage in München **geblieben**?
> *Why did you stay in Munich only two days?*

> Mein Freund **konnte** nicht länger bleiben.
> *My friend **could** not stay any longer.*

This parallels the English use of the simple past tense.

PRACTICE 8   A. *Supply the past tense forms of the infinitives in parentheses.*

1. Wir _____ das tun. (müssen, sollen, wollen, können, dürfen)
2. Hannelore _____ es mir sagen. (wollen, sollen, können, müssen)
3. _____ du das nicht? (können, wollen, dürfen, sollen, mögen)
4. _____ ihr mitfahren? (wollen, können, dürfen)

B. *Change the sentences to the past tense. (Do not change the boldface introductory clauses.)*

1. Kannst du Klaus nicht anrufen?
2. Warum wollen Sie nicht zum Arzt gehen?

3. Leider darf man da nicht parken.
4. Niemand mag den Pudding essen.
5. Wir sollen am Montag einen Vertrag[1] unterschreiben.[2]
6. Können Sie die Unterschrift[3] lesen?
7. Andreas will das Formular[4] nicht ausfüllen.[5]
8. **Es tut mir leid,** daß ich dich enttäuschen[6] muß.
9. **Ich glaube nicht,** daß Körners wirklich nach Afrika fliegen wollen.
10. **Niemand weiß,** ob der Chef es nicht kann oder nicht will.

The Modals in Compound Tenses

§3   THE PRESENT PERFECT TENSE

Formation

A distinction has to be made between the form of modals with and without a dependent infinitive.

without dependent infinitive	with dependent infinitive
Ich habe (es) nicht **gekonnt.**	Ich habe nicht **mitfahren können.**
gedurft.	**mitfahren dürfen.**
gemußt.	**mitfahren müssen.**
gewollt.	**mitfahren wollen.**
gemocht.	**mitfahren mögen.**
(past participle)	(double infinitive)

The past participle of the modal follows the pattern of weak verbs. It has no umlaut.
Mögen has a change of consonants: **gemocht.**

When a dependent infinitive is present, an alternative form of the past participle is used. It is identical to the infinitive of the modal and stands at the end of the clause. This produces the *double-infinitive construction.*

Modals use the auxiliary haben even if the dependent infinitive requires **sein** when occurring without a modal.

Er **ist** noch nie mitgefahren.
but: Er **hat** noch nie mitfahren **können.**

---

1 **der Vertrag, ¨-e**	contract
2 **unterschreiben,**	to sign
unterschrieb, unterschrieben	
3 **die Unterschrift, -en**	signature
4 **das Formular, -e**	form (*not* formula!)
5 **aus•füllen**	to fill out
6 **enttäuschen**	to disappoint

The use of modals in the present perfect tense

The present perfect tense of the modals tends to be used in contexts where English would also use the present perfect rather than the simple past. This occurs, for example, with the time expressions **noch nie, schon oft, schon immer.**

> **Frau Berger hat das noch nie zugeben wollen.**
> *Mrs. Berger has never wanted to admit that.*
>
> **Ich habe ihm schon oft bei den Hausaufgaben helfen müssen.**
> *I've often had to help him with the homework.*
>
> **Wir haben schon immer hier parken dürfen.**
> *We've always been allowed to park here.*

Note the position of these time expressions: they normally follow pronoun objects but precede all other elements.

PRACTICE 9   *Change the sentences to the present perfect tense, using the time expressions in parentheses.*

> **Model:** a. Ich kann meine Schulden nicht bezahlen. (schon oft)
> **Ich habe schon oft meine Schulden nicht bezahlen können.**
>
> b. Ich kann es nicht. (schon oft)
> **Ich habe es schon oft nicht gekonnt.**

1. a. Helga kann ihren Vater überreden. (schon oft)
   b. Sie kann es. (schon oft)
2. a. Wir müssen auf Dietmar warten. (schon oft)
   b. Wir müssen es. (schon oft)
3. a. Ich darf mit seinem Wagen fahren. (schon oft)
   b. Ich darf es. (schon oft)
4. a. Du kannst mich verstehen. (noch nie)
   b. Du kannst es. (noch nie)
5. a. Klaus will arbeiten. (noch nie)
   b. Klaus will es. (noch nie)
6. a. Ich muß nachgeben. (schon immer)
   b. Ich muß es. (schon immer)
7. a. Ich will deinen Freund kennenlernen.[1] (schon immer)
   b. Ich will es. (schon immer)
8. a. Martina mag keinen Käse essen. (schon immer)
   b. Sie mag keinen Käse. (schon immer)

§4   THE PAST PERFECT TENSE

The past perfect tense of modals is identical to the present perfect except that the past tense of **haben** is used as the auxiliary.

> **Ich hatte (es) nicht gekonnt.**   **Ich hatte nicht mitfahren können.**
> *I had not been able to.*   *I had not been able to come along.*

---

1 **kennen•lernen**   to get to know, meet (for the first time)

PRACTICE 10   *Express the following sentences in the past perfect tenses.*

1. Niemand kann Anita helfen.
2. Wir können es auch nicht.
3. Ich muß ihn leider enttäuschen.
4. Rainer will drei Tage bei uns bleiben.
5. Seine Freundin will es aber nicht.
6. Man darf ihm nicht widersprechen.[1]
7. Helga muß das zugeben.[2]

§5   THE FUTURE TENSE

Compare:

Er kann es nicht.   Er kann nicht mitkommen.

Er **wird** es nicht **können.**   Er **wird** nicht **mitkommen können.**
He will not be able to.   *He will not be able to come along.*

The future tense is formed with the auxiliary **werden**; the modal appears as an infinitive at the end of the clause. If there is a dependent infinitive, it precedes the modal (another instance of a *double-infinitive construction*).

If the future is to express supposition or probability, adverbs such as **wohl, wahrscheinlich,** or **vielleicht** are usually added (cf. Chap. 3, §11).

Sie werden mir wohl nicht helfen können.
You will probably not be able to help me.

PRACTICE 11   *Restate the following sentences in the future tense.*

Model: Frank will wahrscheinlich den Vertrag nicht unterschreiben.
Frank wird wahrscheinlich den Vertrag nicht unterschreiben wollen.

1. Frau Braun muß wahrscheinlich eine hohe Strafe[3] bezahlen.
2. Sie kann das wahrscheinlich nicht.
3. Andreas darf keinen Alkohol trinken.
4. Er will es auch nicht.
5. Diesen Kaffee mag wohl niemand.
6. Barbara kann wohl nicht treu sein.
7. Ich muß Sie leider enttäuschen.

---

1 **widersprechen (widerspricht),**   to contradict
    widersprach, widersprochen
2 **zu•geben (gibt zu), gab zu, zugegeben**   to admit
3 **die Strafe, -n**   fine

§6 THE FUTURE PERFECT TENSE

Modals with a dependent infinitive very rarely appear in the future perfect tense. Modals without a dependent infinitive are used occasionally in the future perfect expressing a past supposition or probability (cf. Chap. 3, §12).

> Er wird es wohl nicht **gekonnt haben.** *He probably could not do it.*
> (perfect infinitive)

§7 DEPENDENT WORD ORDER IN COMPOUND TENSES

<u>without dependent infinitive</u>

Ich weiß,

daß er es nicht **gekonnt hat.**
daß er es nicht **gekonnt hatte.**
daß er es nicht **können wird.**

<u>with dependent infinitive</u>

Ich weiß,

daß er nicht **hat mitkommen können.**
daß er nicht **hatte mitkommen können.**
daß er nicht **wird mitkommen können.**

The inflected auxiliary stands last in accordance with the general rule for dependent word order.

A double infinitive always has absolute right to final position in its clause.

PRACTICE 12 *Restate the following sentences, using the indicated introductory clauses.*

A. Without a dependent infinitive

Model: Er hat das nicht gekonnt.
Warum denken Sie, **daß er das nicht gekonnt hat?**

1. Sie hat es nicht gedurft.
   Warum denkst du, daß ...
2. Sie hatte es nicht gewollt.
   Es ist möglich, daß ...
3. Er wird das können.
   Ich nehme an, daß ...

B. With a dependent infinitive

Model: Ich habe ihm schon oft helfen können.
Ich bin froh, daß **ich ihm schon oft habe helfen können.**

1. Ich habe ihn noch nie verstehen können.
   Ich gebe zu, daß ...
2. Sie hatte schon um 5 Uhr morgens aufstehen müssen.
   Monika hatte schlechte Laune, weil ...
3. Man hatte das Problem nicht lösen können.
   Es war sehr schade, daß ...
4. Du wirst ihn überreden können.
   Ich bin überzeugt, daß ...
5. Ich werde Sie enttäuschen müssen.
   Es tut mir leid, daß ...

§8   REFERENCE CHART: SYNOPSIS OF THE TENSES OF MODALS AND THEIR BASIC MEANINGS

Keep in mind: With modals the use of the simple past and present perfect in German parallels the English use of these tenses (§2 and §3).

dürfen

PRESENT	ich darf es	ich darf anrufen	I may, I am allowed to
PAST	ich durfte es	ich durfte anrufen	I was allowed to
PRES. PERF.	ich habe es **gedurft**	ich habe **anrufen dürfen**	I have been allowed to
PAST PERF.	ich hatte es **gedurft**	ich hatte **anrufen dürfen**	I had been allowed to
FUTURE	ich werde es dürfen	ich werde anrufen dürfen	I will be allowed to

können

PRESENT	ich kann es	ich kann anrufen	I can, I am able to
PAST	ich konnte es	ich konnte anrufen	I could, I was able to
PRES. PERF.	ich habe es **gekonnt**	ich habe **anrufen können**	I have been able to
PAST PERF.	ich hatte es **gekonnt**	ich hatte **anrufen können**	I had been able to
FUTURE	ich werde es können	ich werde anrufen können	I will be able to

mögen

PRESENT	ich mag es nicht	ich mag nicht anrufen	I do not like to
PAST	ich mochte es nicht	ich mochte nicht anrufen	I did not like to
PRES. PERF.	ich habe es nicht **gemocht**	ich habe nicht **anrufen mögen**	I have not liked to
PAST PERF.	ich hatte es nicht **gemocht**	ich hatte nicht **anrufen mögen**	I had not liked to
FUTURE	ich werde es nicht mögen	ich werde nicht anrufen mögen	I will not like to

müssen

PRESENT	ich muß es	ich muß anrufen	I must, I have to
PAST	ich mußte es	ich mußte anrufen	I had to
PRES. PERF.	ich habe es **gemußt**	ich habe **anrufen müssen**	I have had to
PAST PERF.	ich hatte es **gemußt**	ich hatte **anrufen müssen**	I had had to
FUTURE	ich werde es müssen	ich werde anrufen müssen	I will have to

sollen

PRESENT	ich soll es	ich soll anrufen	I am expected to, I am supposed to
PAST	ich sollte es	ich sollte anrufen	I was expected to
PRES. PERF.	ich habe es **gesollt**	ich habe **anrufen sollen**	I have been expected to
PAST PERF.	ich hatte es **gesollt**	ich hatte **anrufen sollen**	I had been expected to
FUTURE	ich werde es sollen	ich werde anrufen sollen	I will be expected to

wollen

PRESENT	ich will es	ich will anrufen	I want to
PAST	ich wollte es	ich wollte anrufen	I wanted to
PRES. PERF.	ich habe es **gewollt**	ich habe **anrufen wollen**	I have wanted to
PAST PERF.	ich hatte es **gewollt**	ich hatte **anrufen wollen**	I had wanted to
FUTURE	ich werde es wollen	ich werde anrufen wollen	I will want to

§9   SUMMARY OF WORD ORDER IN DEPENDENT CLAUSES

Ich weiß,
daß er es nicht **kann.**
daß er es nicht **konnte.**
daß er es nicht gekonnt **hat.**
daß er es nicht gekonnt **hatte.**
daß er es nicht können **wird.**

Ich weiß,
daß er nicht anrufen **kann.**
daß er nicht anrufen **konnte.**
daß er nicht **hat** anrufen können.
daß er nicht **hatte** anrufen können.
daß er nicht **wird** anrufen können.

PRACTICE 13   Summarizing exercises

A. *Change the following sentences to the past, present perfect, past perfect, and future tenses. (Do not change the boldface introductory clauses.)*

1. Sie darf es mir nicht sagen.
2. Sie will es nicht.
3. **Ich glaube nicht,** daß er das Projekt aufgeben will.
4. **Ich nehme an,** daß er es nicht darf.

B. *Form sentences in the indicated tenses.*

Simple Past
Model: ich / müssen / bitten / die Chefin / um Erlaubnis
  Ich mußte die Chefin um Erlaubnis bitten.

1. der Chef / müssen / bezahlen / eine hohe Strafe
2. Frau Kästner / sollen / unterschreiben / einen Vertrag
3. ich / wollen / versuchen / es / noch einmal
4. wir / können / lösen / das Problem / nicht
5. die Kinder / dürfen / das nicht

Present Perfect
Model: ich / müssen / bezahlen / noch nie / eine Strafe
  Ich habe noch nie eine Strafe bezahlen müssen.

1. wir / müssen / aus•füllen / noch nie / so viele Formulare
2. man / wollen / überreden / mich / schon oft
3. ich / wollen / kennen•lernen / ihn / schon immer
4. du / können / verstehen / mich / noch nie
5. du / wollen / das / noch nie
6. wir / dürfen / das / noch nie
7. er / mögen / das / noch nie
8. ich / können / es / schon immer

Past Perfect
Model: Erika / wollen / unterschreiben / den Vertrag / nicht
  Erika hatte den Vertrag nicht unterschreiben wollen.

1. man / können / überreden / die Professorin / nicht
2. niemand / können / lesen / meine Unterschrift
3. er / dürfen / trinken / keinen Alkohol
4. ich / dürfen / das / auch nicht
5. wir / wollen / das / wirklich nicht

Future
Model: Sie / können / verstehen / mich / wohl
  Sie werden mich wohl verstehen können.

1. Sie / können / überreden / mich / wohl
2. du / müssen / zu•geben / das / wohl

3. ich / können / das / wohl / nicht
4. wir / dürfen / es / wahrscheinlich / nicht
5. ich / müssen / stecken / die Nase ins Buch

Mixed Tenses
  1. ich / können / helfen / dir / wohl / nicht (future)
  2. wir / müssen / auf•stehen / um 5 Uhr (simple past)
  3. ich / müssen / auf•stehen / noch nie / so früh (pres. perf.)
  4. Erika / wollen / sagen / es / mir / nicht (past perf.)
  5. ich / wollen / warnen / ihn (simple past)
  6. ich / müssen / warnen / ihn / wohl (future)
  7. Klaus / wollen / zu•geben / das / noch nie (pres. perf.)
  8. wir / dürfen / widersprechen / ihm / nicht (simple past)
  9. man / dürfen / widersprechen / ihm / noch nie (pres. perf.)
 10. niemand / wollen / stören / dich (past perf.)
 11. ich / müssen / enttäuschen / Sie / wohl (future)
 12. Elke / mögen / das / nicht (simple past)
 13. wir / dürfen / es / nicht (past perf.)

C. *Translate into German, using the same tenses as the English sentences.*

1. a. She doesn't understand that. **Sie versteht das nicht.**
   b. She can't understand that.
   c. Nobody was able to understand that.
   d. I've never been able to understand that.
2. a. I'm warning you. **Ich warne dich.**
   b. I must warn you.
   c. I didn't want to warn Dieter, but I had to.
   d. Nobody had wanted to warn Dieter.
   e. We'll have to warn Dieter.
3. a. When are you signing the contract? **Wann unterschreiben Sie den Vertrag?**
   b. You have to sign the contract. (formal)
   c. You'll have to sign the contract.
   d. She didn't want to sign the contract.
   e. Nobody knows why she didn't want to sign the contract.
4. a. I'm trying it again. **Ich versuche es noch einmal.**
   b. May I try it again?
   c. They wanted to try it again.
   d. They had wanted to try it again.
5. a. Who's going to solve this problem? **Wer löst dieses Problem?**
   b. Who can solve this problem?
   c. We weren't able to solve this problem.
   d. It's a pity that we weren't able to solve this problem.
   e. We will not be able to solve this problem.
   f. Will you be able to solve this problem? (fam. sing.)
6. a. He doesn't admit it. **Er gibt es nicht zu.**
   b. He has to admit it.

c. He'll have to admit it.

d. He doesn't want to admit it.

e. He didn't want to admit it.

f. He has never wanted to admit it.

Additional Meanings and Uses of Modal Auxiliaries

Modal auxiliaries may express various shades of meanings which largely depend on the context in which they occur. The preceding section focused on the basic meanings of modals. Here are some additional connotations.

§10   *können*

a. Just as English speakers often use *can* instead of *may*, Germans often use **können** instead of **dürfen**:

> Du kannst das Geld behalten

instead of

> Du darfst das Geld behalten.   *You may keep the money.*

b. Another meaning of **können** is *to know how to do something*:

Kannst du schwimmen?	*Do you know how to swim?*
Können Sie Deutsch?	*Do you know German? Do you speak German?*
Sie kann kein Englisch.	*She doesn't know English.* *She doesn't speak English.*

c. **Können** is used in the idiomatic expression: **Ich kann nicht anders.** *I can't help it.*

> **Ich konnte nicht anders, ich mußte lachen.**
> *I couldn't help it, I had to laugh.*
> *I couldn't help laughing.*

§11   *sollen*

a. **Sollen** may have the meaning of *shall*, principally in questions expressing a suggestion:

> **Soll** ich Ihnen einen Stuhl bringen?   ***Shall** I bring you a chair?*

b. **Sollen** is frequently used in the sense of *should*, expressing an obligation:

> Ich weiß nicht, ob ich es ihm sagen **soll**. *I don't know whether I **should** tell him.*

§12   *wollte gerade* or *wollte eben*

In conversational German **wollte gerade** or **wollte eben** is frequently used in the sense of *was on the point of* or *was (just) about to*.

Ich wollte Sie gerade anrufen.   *I was (just) about to call you.*
Wir wollten eben wegfahren.   *We were (just) about to leave.*

PRACTICE 14   *Translate into German.*

1. Shall I close the door?
2. I don't know whether I should call Dr. Krämer.
3. Dr. Krämer was just about to go home.
4. Does he know English?
5. Mary knows German.
6. Frank doesn't know German.
7. I couldn't help it, I had to protest.

§13   *mögen*

Mögen is used principally with **nicht** or some other negative to express dislike or reluctance.

Ich **mag** es ihm **nicht** sagen.   *I don't like to tell him.*

However, the subjunctive form **möchte** (*would like*) is frequently used in both positive and negative sentences.

Ich **möchte** es ihm (nicht) sagen.   *I would (not) like to tell him.*
Was **möchtest** du?   *What would you like?*
Ich **möchte** eine Tasse Kaffee.   *I would like a cup of coffee.*

Möchte is conjugated as follows:

ich möch**te**
du möch**test** | The same endings as the past tense **mochte.** |
er möch**te**

wir möch**ten**
ihr möch**tet**
sie möch**ten**

Sie möch**ten**

PRACTICE 15   *Translate into English, then reproduce the German from your translation.*

1. Ich möchte mehr Geld haben.
2. Meine Eltern möchten dich kennenlernen.
3. Möchtest du meine Frau[1] werden?
4. Möchtet ihr fernsehen?[2]
5. Wer möchte ein Plätzchen?[3]
6. Was möchten Sie?

1 **meine Frau**	my wife
(mein Mann)	(my husband)
2 **fern•sehen (sieht fern),**	to watch television
sah fern, ferngesehen	
3 **das Plätzchen, -**	cookie

§14   *nicht dürfen*

Sie müssen das tun.
- a. *You have to do that.*
- b. *You must do that.*

Both English sentences express the same thing as their German counterpart, i.e. the necessity of doing something. But notice the difference in meaning of the respective negative forms of the two English sentences:

a. *You don't have to do that.*   no obligation
b. *You mustn't do that.*   strong warning or prohibition

This distinction is expressed in German by **nicht müssen** or **nicht brauchen** (cf. §15 below) and **nicht dürfen**:

a. *You don't have to do that.*   Sie **müssen** das **nicht** tun.

or: Sie **brauchen** das **nicht** zu tun.

b. *You mustn't do that.*   Sie **dürfen** das **nicht** tun.

Remember: must not = **nicht dürfen**

PRACTICE 16   Translate into German.

1. We must not forget that.
2. I mustn't drink that.
3. You mustn't say that. (fam. sing.)
4. You mustn't disturb Mrs. Körner. (formal)
5. You mustn't be so stubborn.[1] (fam. pl.)
6. I must not gossip.

§15   THE USE OF *nicht brauchen* INSTEAD OF *nicht müssen*

Nicht brauchen is often used instead of **nicht müssen**. It takes the dependent infinitive with **zu** in contrast to the modal auxiliaries. Compare:

Sie müssen es mir nicht sagen.
Sie brauchen es mir nicht **zu** sagen. } *You don't have to tell me.*

Verbs with separable prefixes:

Sie brauchen die Platte nicht zurück**zu**geben. *You don't have to return the record.*

zu is inserted between the prefix and the verb

PRACTICE 17   *Substitute* **nicht brauchen** *for* **nicht müssen.**

Model: Er muß mir nicht in der Küche helfen.
Er braucht mir nicht in der Küche zu helfen.

1. Wir müssen heute nicht arbeiten.
2. Sie müssen ihn nicht um Erlaubnis bitten.

1 **stur**   stubborn

3. Du mußt nicht bar bezahlen.[1]
4. Diesen Stoff[2] muß man nicht bügeln.[3]
5. Sie müssen mein Angebot[4] nicht annehmen.
6. Ihr müßt Schreibers nicht einladen.

The use of **nicht brauchen** in the simple past and present perfect:

Wir **brauchten** das nicht **zu übersetzen.**
Wir **haben** das nicht **zu übersetzen brauchen.** } *We didn't have to translate that.*
inf.   inf.

Sie **brauchten** mein Angebot nicht **anzunehmen.**
Sie **haben** mein Angebot nicht **anzunehmen brauchen.** } *You didn't have to accept my offer.*
inf.   inf.

In compound tenses a double infinitive with **zu** is used.

PRACTICE 18 *Restate each sentence first in the simple past, then in the present perfect.*

Model: Sie brauchen das nicht noch einmal zu erklären.
Sie brauchten das nicht noch einmal zu erklären.
Sie haben das nicht noch einmal zu erklären brauchen.

1. Ich brauche die Rechnung nicht zu bezahlen.
2. Wir brauchen Helga nicht zu helfen.
3. Karin braucht das Formular nicht auszufüllen.
4. Wir brauchen nicht um Erlaubnis zu bitten.
5. Er braucht die Platte nicht zurückzugeben.

PRACTICE 19   Summarizing exercises for §10 to §15.

A. *The following sentences illustrate various uses of the modals. Render them into acceptable English.*

1. X: Herr Bauer, Sie wollten eben etwas sagen.
   Y: Ich weiß nicht mehr,[5] was ich eben sagen wollte.
2. X: Hier ist ein Stück Kuchen für dich.
   Y: Ich mache eine Schlankheitskur.[6] Du darfst mich nicht in Versuchung führen.[7]
3. X: Es ist sehr warm in diesem Zimmer.
   Y: Soll ich ein Fenster aufmachen?

1 **bar bezahlen**	to pay cash
2 **der Stoff, -e**	material, fabric
3 **bügeln**	to iron, press
4 **das Angebot, -e**	offer
das Angebot an•nehmen (nimmt an),	to accept the offer
nahm an, angenommen	
5 **ich weiß nicht mehr**	I don't remember (*lit.* I don't know anymore)
6 **eine Schlankheitskur machen**	to be *or* go on a diet
7 **in Versuchung führen**	to lead into temptation

4.   X: Warum brummst[1] du soviel?

 Y: Ich kann einfach[2] nicht anders, ich muß brummen.

5. a. X: Sie brauchen mir meinen alten Plattenspieler nicht zurückzugeben.

 Y: Kann ich ihn wirklich behalten?[3]

 b. X: Sie können und dürfen es.

6. a. X: Können Sie Italienisch?

 Y: Ich kann etwas Spanisch, aber kein Italienisch.

 b. X: Können Sie auch Deutsch?

 Y: Ein wenig. Wenn mich ein Deutscher sprechen hört, weiß er
nicht, ob er lachen oder weinen soll.

B. *Translate into German. (Use* **nicht brauchen** *for* ***not have to****.)*

1. a. I'm paying the bill.

 b. I have to pay the bill.

 c. You don't have to pay the bill. (fam. sing.)

 d. We didn't have to pay the bill. (past, pres. perf.)

2. a. Would you like a cookie? (formal)

 b. Would you like to meet my parents? (fam. sing.)

 c. I'd like to be in Hawaii.

3. a. I mustn't disappoint Monika.

 b. Ruth mustn't eat that because she's on a diet.

 c. We mustn't lead Ruth into temptation.

4. a. I was just about to call Martin.

 b. I was just about to protest.

 c. We were just about to go home.

 d. I don't remember what I was about to say.

5. a. She simply can't help it, she has to grumble.

 b. I simply can't help it, I have to gossip.

 c. They simply couldn't help it, they had to protest.

(The subjective use of modals is explained in Chapter 20, §10.)

---

1 **brummen**   to grumble
2 **einfach**   simple, simply
3 **behalten (behält),**   to keep
   behielt, behalten

5

The Nouns

KEY TO THE EXERCISES ON CASSETTE 3.
RUNNING TIME: APPROX. 20 MIN.

Gender and Plural

§1   GENDER

The definite article indicates the gender of the noun that follows it:

der (masculine)	der Vater
die (feminine)	die Mutter
das (neuter)	das Kind

In English, nouns referring to inanimate things and abstracts are neuter. In German, however, such nouns may be masculine, feminine, or neuter. It is imperative to learn German nouns with the corresponding definite article, since the gender of a noun is often the most important clue to the function of the noun in the sentence.

Here are a few useful guidelines for determining the gender of a noun.

Masculine
1. Nouns referring to male persons, their professions, nationalities:

> der Vater, der Bruder, der Junge, der Freund, der Lehrer, der Professor, der Arzt (*doctor*), der Chef (*boss*), der Polizist, der Komponist (*composer*), der Präsident, der Engländer, der Amerikaner, der Franzose, der Deutsche, der Ausländer (*foreigner*), der Verkäufer (*salesman*)

2. Names of all seasons, months, days of the week:

> der Frühling, der Sommer, der Herbst, der Winter;
> der Januar, der Februar, der März, etc.
> der Montag, der Dienstag, der Mittwoch, etc.

3. Most nouns ending in **-en**:

> der Wagen, der Regen, der Garten, der Osten, der Süden, der Westen, der Norden

Feminine

1. Nouns referring to female persons:

> die Mutter, die Frau, die Tante, etc.

Many feminine nouns are formed from masculine nouns by adding the suffix **-in**:

> die Freundin, die Lehrerin, die Professorin, die Assistentin, die Ärztin, die Sekretärin, die Amerikanerin, die Ausländerin

2. Most nouns ending in unstressed **-e**:

> die Liebe, die Frage, die Straße, die Karte, die Reise, die Schule

Common exceptions:

> der Name, der Käse, das Ende, das Auge

3. All nouns ending in **-ei, -ie, -ik, -ion, -heit, -keit, -schaft, -tät, -ung**:

> die Bäckerei (*bakery*), die Polizei (*police*), die Philosophie, die Musik, die Religion, die Freiheit (*freedom liberty*), die Möglichkeit (*possibility*), die Freundschaft (*friendship*), die Universität, die Meinung (*opinion*)

Neuter

1. Nouns referring to the young of animals and human beings:

> das Kalb (*calf*), das Fohlen (*foal, colt, filly*), das Lamm, das Kind, das Baby

2. Nouns with the diminutive suffix **-chen** or **-lein**:

> das Mädchen, das Fräulein

All nouns become neuter and usually add an umlaut when they take on the diminutive form:

> die Stadt (*town, city*)   das Städtchen (*small town*)
> der Hund (*dog*)   das Hündchen (*small dog, puppy*)
> die Katze (*cat*)   das Kätzchen (*kitten*)

The diminutive of names is sometimes used for children or simply for endearment:

> Hans—Hänschen.

The ending **-chen** is more common than **-lein.**

3. Most metals:

> das Gold, das Silber, das Eisen (*iron*), das Blei (*lead*), das Kupfer, das Metall

4. Infinitives used as nouns:

> das Rauchen (*smoking*), das Trinken (*drinking*), das Essen (*meal*).

5. Letters when used as nouns:

   das A, das B, das C

PRACTICE 1   *Add the definite article to the following nouns.*

1. _____ Frage	26. _____ Winter
2. _____ Platte	27. _____ Sonntag
3. _____ Lüge (*lie*)	28. _____ Schwester
4. _____ Rauchen	29. _____ Schwesterchen
5. _____ Essen	30. _____ Wagen
6. _____ A	31. _____ Garten
7. _____ F	32. _____ Osten
8. _____ Arzt	33. _____ Kind
9. _____ Ärztin	34. _____ Baby
10. _____ Verkäufer	35. _____ Universität
11. _____ Verkäuferin	36. _____ Spezialität
12. _____ Polizist	37. _____ Gold
13. _____ Polizistin	38. _____ Silber
14. _____ Polizei	39. _____ Freiheit
15. _____ Konditorei	40. _____ Krankheit
(*pastry shop*)	41. _____ Möglichkeit
16. _____ Religion	42. _____ Freundlichkeit
17. _____ Operation	(*friendliness*)
18. _____ Million	43. _____ Held (*hero*)
19. _____ Vorlesung	44. _____ Heldin
20. _____ Warnung	45. _____ C
21. _____ Erkältung (*cold*)	46. _____ Liebe
22. _____ Musik	47. _____ Information
23. _____ Grammatik	48. _____ Meinung (*opinion*)
24. _____ Fabrik (*factory*)	49. _____ Bruder
25. _____ Republik	50. _____ Brüderchen

Gender of Compound Nouns

    das Semester
                    → **die** Semesterarbeit (*term paper*)
    die Arbeit

Compound nouns have the gender of their last element.

§2   THE PLURAL

The plural definite article is the same for all genders: **die.**

    die Väter, die Mütter, die Kinder.

English ordinarily adds an **-s** to the singular of a noun to form the plural. There are a few exceptions, such as *child - children, foot - feet.*

In German, nouns form their plural in several different ways.
Some add an ending: **-e, -er, -en, -n,** or **-s.**

Examples:

Listed in the vocabulary
of this book:

der Tag	die Tage	der Tag, -e
das Lied	die Lied**er**	das Lied, -er
die Nation	die Nation**en**	die Nation, -en
die Frage	die Frage**n**	die Frage, -n
das Hotel	die Hotel**s**	das Hotel, -s

Some nouns add no ending to form the plural:

der Lehrer	die Lehrer	der Lehrer, -

Some umlaut the stem vowel in the plural:

der Gast	die Gäste	der Gast, ¨e

Because of the many ways German plurals are formed, it is very important to learn the plural (along with the gender) of each noun. You may find it helpful to study the following charts which provide an overview of the most common patterns of the plural formation. There are often exceptions to these patterns, however, and while these charts can help you to guess a plural, they are no substitute for the learning of individual plural forms.

Monosyllabics
(nouns of one syllable)

The majority of masculine and feminine nouns add **-e**; neuter nouns add **-er,** less frequently **-e.**

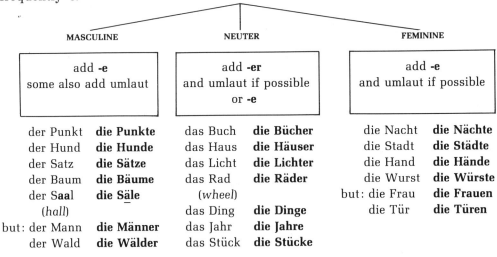

MASCULINE	NEUTER	FEMININE
add -e some also add umlaut	add -er and umlaut if possible or -e	add -e and umlaut if possible
der Punkt **die Punkte**	das Buch **die Bücher**	die Nacht **die Nächte**
der Hund **die Hunde**	das Haus **die Häuser**	die Stadt **die Städte**
der Satz **die Sätze**	das Licht **die Lichter**	die Hand **die Hände**
der Baum **die Bäume**	das Rad **die Räder**	die Wurst **die Würste**
der Saal **die Säle**	(wheel)	but: die Frau **die Frauen**
(hall)	das Ding **die Dinge**	die Tür **die Türen**
but: der Mann **die Männer**	das Jahr **die Jahre**	
der Wald **die Wälder**	das Stück **die Stücke**	

Keep in mind: **a, o, u,** and **au** umlaut to **ä, ö, ü,** and **äu; aa** umlauts to **ä.**

Polysyllabics
(nouns of more than one syllable)

MASCULINE AND NEUTER | FEMININE

1. add *no ending* to nouns that end in **-el, -en, -er, -chen, -lein;** some masculine nouns take umlaut

der Mantel	**die Mäntel**
der Wagen	**die Wagen**
der Lehrer	**die Lehrer**
das Mädchen	**die Mädchen**
das Fräulein	**die Fräulein**

2. ending **-e** added to most other nouns; some masculine nouns also add umlaut

der Anzug (suit)	**die Anzüge**
der Versuch	**die Versuche**
der Vertrag	**die Verträge**
das Paket	**die Pakete**
das Problem	**die Probleme**
das Gefängnis (prison)	**die Gefängnisse**
der Autobus	**die Autobusse**
short: der Bus	**die Busse**

Note: Nouns with the ending **-nis** and **-us** double the **s** when a declensional ending is added.

add **-n** to nouns ending in **-e, -el, -er;** add **-en** to all others

die Familie	**die Familien**
die Stunde	**die Stunden**
die Vokabel	**die Vokabeln**
die Schwester	**die Schwestern**
die Antwort	**die Antworten**
die Arbeit	**die Arbeiten**
die Nation	**die Nationen**
die Universität	**die Universitäten**
die Rechnung	**die Rechnungen**
die Studentin	**die Studentinnen**

Note: Feminine nouns with the ending **-in** have double **n** in the plural.

Mutter does not add a plural ending; it umlauts the stem vowel:

die Mutter	**die Mütter**

For masculine nouns adding **-(e)n,** see "Special Declensions," §5, 1.
For foreign nouns that add the plural ending **-s,** see §5, 3.

PRACTICE 2   *The following nouns form the plural in accordance with the above guidelines. (The neuter monosyllabics listed here add the ending* **-er.**) *State the plural forms of these nouns and add umlaut where indicated.*

Models:

der Freund	**die Freunde**
das Glas (umlaut)	**die Gläser**
der Koffer	**die Koffer**
das Programm	**die Programme**
die Straße	**die Straßen**

1. der Tag
2. der Schuh
3. der Kopf (umlaut)
4. der Film
5. der Saal (umlaut)
6. die Stadt (umlaut)
7. die Wand (*wall*) (umlaut)
8. das Haus (umlaut)
9. das Kleid
10. das Dorf (*village*) (umlaut)
11. der Mantel (umlaut)
12. der Löffel (*spoon*)
13. das Kapitel (*chapter*)
14. der Lehrer
15. der Reporter
16. der Ausländer
17. der Erfinder (*inventor*)
18. das Mädchen
19. das Märchen (*fairy tale*)
20. der Wagen
21. die Stunde
22. die Vase
23. die Chance
24. die Frage
25. die Freundin
26. die Reporterin
27. die Ausländerin
28. die Prüfung
29. die Sendung (*broadcast*)
30. die Erfindung
31. die Schwester
32. die Nummer
33. die Arbeit
34. die Religion
35. die Zigarette
36. die Serviette (*napkin*)
37. das Problem
38. das Experiment
39. das Paket
40. das Programm
41. das Kompliment
42. das Regal (*shelf*)
43. der Roman
44. der Anzug (umlaut)
45. das Rad (umlaut)
46. der Feind (*enemy*)
47. die Warnung
48. der Arbeiter (*worker*)
49. der Trainer (*coach*)
50. das Gefängnis
51. das Geheimnis (*secret*)
52. der Katalog
53. der Brief
54. der Faulenzer (*lazybones*)
55. die Faulenzerin

Compound Nouns in the Plural

The last element, which determines the gender of the compound noun, also determines its plural form. The other elements remain unchanged.

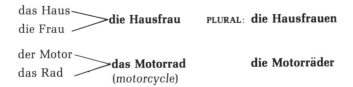

das Haus → **die Hausfrau**   PLURAL: **die Hausfrauen**
die Frau

der Motor → **das Motorrad**   **die Motorräder**
das Rad   (*motorcycle*)

PRACTICE 3   *Give the plurals of the following compound nouns.*

1. der Geburtstag
2. die Mathematikprüfung
3. die Telefonnummer
4. der Fußballtrainer
5. das Sommerkleid
6. der Handschuh (*glove*)
7. das Weinglas
8. das Bücherregal
9. das Krankenhaus
10. die Semesterarbeit
11. der Konzertsaal
12. der Wintermantel

The Cases

§3   GENERAL PATTERN FOR DECLINING GERMAN NOUNS

There are four cases in German: nominative, accusative, dative, and genitive. The following paradigm shows a typical masculine, neuter, and feminine noun in all its singular and plural forms.

		MASCULINE	NEUTER	FEMININE
SINGULAR	NOM.	**der** Freund	**das** Mädchen	**die** Stadt
	ACC.	**den** Freund	**das** Mädchen	**die** Stadt
	DAT.	**dem** Freund(e)	**dem** Mädchen	**der** Stadt
	GEN.	**des** Freund**es**	**des** Mädchen**s**	**der** Stadt
PLURAL	NOM.	**die** Freunde	**die** Mädchen	**die** Städte
	ACC.	**die** Freunde	**die** Mädchen	**die** Städte
	DAT.	**den** Freunde**n**	**den** Mädchen	**den** Städte**n**
	GEN.	**der** Freunde	**der** Mädchen	**der** Städte

Note: a. The nominative and the accusative are identical in form except for the masculine singular.

b. The dative masculine and neuter of monosyllabics may add **-e** in the singular. In present-day German, however, it is generally omitted.

In some fixed expressions the dative **-e** is still retained: **nach (zu) Hause, auf dem Lande** (in the country), **im Jahre** (in the year of). Even in these expressions, however, the **-e** may be omitted.

c. The dative plural adds **-n** to all nouns unless the plural ends in **-n** or **-s**.

d. The genitive masculine and neuter of monosyllabics may add **-es** or **-s**:

-es is usually added to monosyllabics (des Buch**es**, des Tisch**es**).
    It is mandatory with all nouns that end in
    -s, -ß, -z, -x (des Glas**es**, Gruß**es**, Gesetz**es**, Reflex**es**).
-s is added in all other instances.

e. Feminine nouns never take an ending in the singular.

PATTERN:	MASCULINE	NEUTER	FEMININE	PLURAL
NOM.	**der** —	**das** —	**die** —	**die** —
ACC.	**den** —	**das** —	**die** —	**die** —
DAT.	**dem** —(e)	**dem** —(e)	**der** —	**den** —n
GEN.	**des** —(e)s	**des** —(e)s	**der** —	**der** —

PRACTICE 4   *Change the following nominatives to the cases indicated.*

   Model: a. der Hund   b. die Katze   c. das Auto
          gen. sing.   **des Hundes**   **der Katze**   **des Autos**

	1. a. der Koffer	b. die Schule	c. das Wetter
acc. sing.	_____	_____	_____
	2. a. das Kind	b. die Frau	c. der Mann
dat. sing.	_____	_____	_____
	3. a. die Häuser	b. die Leute	c. die Wagen
dat. pl.	_____	_____	_____
	4. a. die Prüfung	b. das Mädchen	c. der Lehrer
gen. sing.	_____	_____	_____
	5. a. die Freunde	b. die Freundinnen	c. die Mädchen
gen. pl.	_____	_____	_____

§4   THE MAIN USES OF THE CASES

1. The nominative

a. The nominative is the case of the subject of the sentence.

Der Katalog liegt auf meinem Schreibtisch.
Die Studentin heißt Margot Bauer.
Das Mädchen kennt mich vielleicht nicht.
Die Leute glauben das nicht.

b. The nominative is the case of the predicate noun, also called *predicate nominative*. It is a noun that completes the meaning of the verbs **sein, werden, bleiben** (*to remain*), **heißen.**

Die Feier ist **der Höhepunkt** ihres Lebens. *The celebration is the high point of her life.*
Das wird **der Höhepunkt** seines Lebens.
Das bleibt **der Höhepunkt** meines Lebens.
Der Direktor heißt **Herr Bachmann.**

2. The accusative

The accusative is the case of the direct object of the verb. The direct object is the noun (or pronoun) that receives the direct action implied in the meaning of the verb.

Bitte fragen Sie **den Chef!**
Kennen Sie **den Musiklehrer?**

Do not confuse:

> Inge hat **den Katalog.** (direct object)
> Das ist **der Katalog.** (predicate nominative)

PRACTICE 5   *Insert the appropriate form of each noun in parentheses.*

1. Das ist _____ für Renate. (der Scheck, das Paket, die Zeitung)
2. Peter hat _____ für Renate. (der Scheck, das Paket, die Zeitung)

   3. Herr Wolf ist _____ des Reporters. (der Freund)
   4. Wissen Sie, wo _____ ist? (der Chef, die Chefin)
   5. Fragen Sie doch _____ ! (der Chef, die Chefin)
   6. Kennen Sie _____ ? (der Ausländer, die Ausländerin, die Ausländer, die Ausländerinnen)
   7. Wollen Sie _____ kaufen? (die Kamera, der Kalender, das Bild, die Bilder)
   8. Wann bringst du _____ in die Reinigung?[1] (das Kleid, die Kleider, der Anzug, die Anzüge)

3. The dative

a. The dative is the case of the indirect object: usually the person to whom something is given or said, or for whom something is done.

Bitte geben Sie **dem Chef die Post!** *Please give the boss the mail.*

INDIRECT   DIRECT
OBJ.   OBJ.

When both objects are nouns, the indirect object (person) usually precedes the direct object (thing).

PRACTICE 6   *Insert the appropriate forms in the direct and indirect objects.*

   1. Wer hat _____ _____ geschenkt?
      (die Reporterin) (die Kamera)
   2. Wer hat _____ _____ erzählt?
      (der Reporter) (der Klatsch[2])
   3. Wer hat _____ _____ erzählt?
      (die Kinder) (die Geschichte)
   4. Haben Sie _____ _____ gezeigt?
      (die Polizistin) (der Führerschein[3])
   5. Wer hat _____ _____ gegeben?
      (der Gepäckträger[4]) (das Trinkgeld[5])
   6. Wer hat _____ _____ gegeben?
      (die Polizei) (der Tip[6])
   7. Geben Sie doch _____ _____ !
      (der Mann) (die Chance)

1 **die Reinigung**	cleaning
in die Reinigung bringen	to take to the cleaners
2 **der Klatsch**	gossip
3 **der Führerschein, -e**	driver's licence
4 **der Gepäckträger, -**	porter
5 **das Trinkgeld, -er**	tip, gratuity
6 **der Tip, -s**	tip, hint, clue

8. Haben Sie _____ _____ zum Bahnhof gezeigt?
   (die Ausländerin) (der Weg)
9. Können Sie _____ _____ erklären?
   (die Ausländer) (die Grammatik)

b. Some verbs have only a dative object without an accusative object. These include:

antworten	*to answer*
danken	*to thank*
folgen	*to follow*
gefallen (gefällt),	*to please, like*
gefiel, gefallen	
gehören	*to belong to*
gratulieren	*to congratulate*
helfen (hilft),	*to help*
half, geholfen	
trauen	*to trust*
widersprechen (widerspricht),	*to contradict*
widersprach, widersprochen	

PRACTICE 7   *Insert the dative forms of the nouns in parentheses.*

1. Warum antworten Sie _____ nicht? (der Professor, die Dame)
2. Die Kamera gehört _____. (die Reporterin, der Reporter)
3. Matthias hat _____ nicht widersprochen. (der Dekan,[1] die Chefin)
4. Bitte folgen Sie _____! (der Reiseleiter,[2] die Reiseleiterin)
5. Haben Sie schon _____ zum Geburtstag gratuliert? (die Assistentin, der Hausmeister[3])
6. Warum hilfst du _____ nicht? (die Kinder, die Leute)
7. Wir möchten _____ danken. (der Schauspieler,[4] die Schauspielerin, die Schauspieler, die Schauspielerinnen)
8. Warum traust du _____ nicht? (der Mann, die Männer, die Frau, die Frauen)

Note the use of *gefallen*:

> **Der Protest gefällt dem Bürgermeister nicht.**
>
> lit: *The protest does not please the mayor.*
>
> idiom.: *The mayor does not like the protest.*

1 **der Dekan, -e**	dean
2 **der Reiseleiter, -**	male travel guide
die Reiseleiterin, -nen	female travel guide
3 **der Hausmeister, -**	janitor
4 **der Schauspieler, -**	actor
die Schauspielerin, -nen	actress

In German the person or thing liked or disliked is the subject of the sentence. The person who does the liking or disliking is the dative object of the verb.

PRACTICE 8   *Translate into English, then recall the German from your English translation.*

1. Das Regenwetter gefällt den Fußballspielern nicht.
2. Die Werbesendungen[1] haben den Leuten nicht gefallen.
3. Das Hotel Continental hat den Ausländern gefallen.
4. Die Arbeit (*job*) hat Fräulein Neumann nicht gefallen.
5. Das Theaterstück[2] hat Martin gefallen.

Frequently the dative is in first position:

> Dem Bürgermeister hat der Protest nicht gefallen.
> *The mayor did not like the protest.*

PRACTICE 9   *Translate into English, then recall the German from your English translation.*

1. Den Kindern gefällt Disneyland.
2. Den Arbeitern gefällt der Direktor nicht.
3. Der Dame hat das Motel nicht gefallen.
4. Dem Chef hat der Reporter gefallen.
5. Den Fußballspielern hat der Trainer nicht gefallen.

4. The genitive

The genitive case is used in German to show the possessive relationship or the relationship of belonging together. In English it is expressed by *of* or *'s*, as seen in the following examples:

Das ist der Vorname **des Vaters.**	*That's the first name **of the father.*** or: *That's **the father's** first name.*
Das ist der Vorname **des Kindes.**	*That's the first name **of the child**.* or: *That's **the child's** first name.*
Das ist die Verantwortung **der Mutter.**	*That's the responsibility **of the mother.*** or: *That's **the mother's** responsibility.*
Das ist die Pflicht **der Eltern.**	*That's the duty **of the parents.*** or: *That's **the parents'** duty.*

Except with proper names (see below), German normally uses the word order resembling the English *of*-construction.

PRACTICE 10   A. *Insert the genitive of the nouns in parentheses.*

Model: Das ist der Anfang _____ . (das Semester)
Das ist der Anfang des Semesters.

1. Das ist der Anfang _____ . (der Roman, die Geschichte)

---

1 **die Werbesendung, -en**   commercial (radio, television)
2 **das Theaterstück, -e**   stage play

2. Das ist das Ende _____ . (die Übung, die Übungen)
3. Das ist der Wagen _____ . (der Bürgermeister, die Journalistin)
4. Das ist der Name _____ . (die Musiklehrerin, der Hausmeister)
5. Das ist das Problem _____ . (der Lehrer, die Lehrer)
6. Das ist der Titel _____ . (das Buch, die Biographie)
7. Das ist die Telefonnummer _____ . (der Dekan)
8. Das ist der Mann _____ . (die Schauspielerin)
9. Das ist die Frau _____ . (der Schauspieler)
10. Das ist der Höhepunkt _____ . (das Konzert)

B. *Translate into German.*

1. That's the janitor's daughter.
2. That's the lady's son.
3. That's the mayor's brother.
4. That's the dean's car.
5. That's the reporter's (female) telephone number.
6. That's the reporter's (male) name.
7. That's the beginning of the semester.
8. That's the end of the story.
9. That's the title of the novel.

In spoken German, **von** + dative is often used instead of the genitive:

Das ist der Wagen **von der Sekretärin.**

The use of the genitive with proper names:

        Das ist **Barbaras** Hund.   *That's Barbara's dog.*
but: Das ist der Hund **des Hausmeisters.**   *That's the janitor's dog.*

The genitive **-s** is added to the name regardless of gender; it is not separated by an apostrophe. This form is commonly used with proper names, seldom with other nouns.
When the proper name ends in an **s**-sound (**-s, -ß, -z, -tz**), no **-s** is added to the name. The omission is indicated by an apostrophe:

Das ist **Thomas'** Wagen.

However, in these instances the construction with **von** is generally preferred:

Das ist der Wagen **von Thomas.**

PRACTICE 11   *Translate into German.*

1. a. That's Barbara's car.
   b. That's the janitor's car.
2. a. That's Dieter's telephone number.
   b. That's the dean's telephone number.
3. a. That's Renate's sister.
   b. That's the lady's sister.

4. a. That's Werner's friend.
   b. That's the mayor's friend.
5. a. That's Mathias' camera. (2 ways)
   b. That's the reporter's (female) camera.

§5   SPECIAL DECLENSIONS OF NOUNS

1. Some masculine nouns add **-(e)n** in all cases except in the nominative singular. They are usually referred to as *weak nouns*.

SINGULAR	NOM.	der Student	der Junge	der Herr
	ACC.	den Studenten	den Jungen	den Herrn
	DAT.	dem Studenten	dem Jungen	dem Herrn
	GEN.	des Studenten	des Jungen	des Herrn
PLURAL	NOM.	die Studenten	die Jungen	die Herren
	ACC.	die Studenten	die Jungen	die Herren
	DAT.	den Studenten	den Jungen	den Herren
	GEN.	der Studenten	der Jungen	der Herren

These nouns do not take the customary -s in the genitive singular.

Note that **Herr** adds **-n** in the singular and **-en** in the plural. When used with a name, **Herr** is declined in accordance with its function in the sentence:

Wo ist Herr Berger?
Haben Sie Herr**n** Berger gesehen?

In this group are:

a. nouns of foreign origin that are accented on the last syllable, such as **der Assistént, der Demokrát, der Komponíst, der Philosóph, der Polizíst, der Präsidént, der Studént, der Touríst;**
b. masculine nouns that end in an unstressed **-e**, such as **der Junge, der Kunde** (*customer*), **der Löwe;**
c. a few monosyllabic nouns, such as **der Mensch, der Christ, der Held, der Herr.**

2. A very few masculine nouns, such as **der Buchstabe** (*letter*), **der Friede** (*peace*), **der Gedanke** (*thought*), **der Glaube** (*faith*), **der Name, der Wille,** have the endings of the weak noun declension and an additional **-s** in the genitive.

One neuter noun, **das Herz,** adds the same endings except in the accusative singular.

SINGULAR	der Name	das Herz
	den Namen	das Herz
	dem Namen	dem Herzen
	des Namen**s**	des Herzen**s**
PLURAL	die Namen	die Herzen
	die Namen	die Herzen
	den Namen	den Herzen
	der Namen	der Herzen

3. Nouns of foreign origin that form the plural by adding **-s** have the ending **-s** in all cases of the plural.

		MASCULINE	NEUTER	FEMININE
SINGULAR	NOM.	der Scheck	das Auto	die Party
	ACC.	den Scheck	das Auto	die Party
	DAT.	dem Scheck	dem Auto	der Party
	GEN.	des Schecks	des Autos	der Party
PLURAL	NOM.	die Scheck**s**	die Auto**s**	die Party**s**
	ACC.	die Scheck**s**	die Auto**s**	die Party**s**
	DAT.	den Scheck**s**	den Auto**s**	den Party**s**
	GEN.	der Scheck**s**	der Auto**s**	der Party**s**

Other common nouns of this group are: **das Baby — die Babys, der Chef — die Chefs, das Hobby — die Hobbys, das Hotel — die Hotels, die Kamera — die Kameras, das Kino — die Kinos, das Restaurant — die Restaurants, der Tip — die Tips.**

Keep in mind:

> Only with these nouns may the declensional ending **-s** be a plural form; otherwise it signals the genitive singular case.

4. Some nouns of foreign origin have special plurals.

SING.	NOM.	das Thema[1]	das Drama	das Datum	das Museum	das Stipendium[2]
	ACC.	das Thema				
	DAT.	dem Thema				
	GEN.	des Themas				
PL.	NOM.	die Them**en**	die Dram**en**	die Dat**en**	die Muse**en**	die Stipendi**en**
	ACC.	die Them**en**				
	DAT.	den Them**en**				
	GEN.	der Them**en**				

PRACTICE 12   *Insert the German equivalents.*

1. In unserer Stadt haben wir _____, _____
   two museums' ten movie theaters
   und viele _____.
   restaurants'
2. Leider hat man _____ nicht erhöht.[3]
   (the scholarships)

---

1 **das Thema**   topic, theme
2 **das Stipendium**   stipend, scholarship
3 **erhöhen**   to raise

3. Diese _____ interessieren mich nicht.
   (topics)
4. Ich habe _____ von Schiller gelesen.
   (two dramas)
5. Diese Statue ist ein Symbol _____.
   (of peace)
6. Das ist eine Frage _____, nicht des Verstandes.[1]
   (of the heart)
7. Leider habe ich seinen _____ vergessen.
   (name)
8. Kennen Sie _____ da drüben?
   (the gentlemen)
9. Ich kenne nur _____.
   (Mr. Schreiber)
10. Zeigen Sie doch _____ Ihren Ausweis![2]
    (the policeman)
11. Mein Vater hat viele _____.
    (hobbies)
12. Ich muß in diesem Monat _____ geben.
    (two parties)
13. Das ist das Privileg _____.
    (of the president)
14. Haben Sie _____ gefragt?
    (the assistant)
15. Alle haben _____ gratuliert.
    (the hero)
16. Ich habe _____ bei den Hausaufgaben geholfen.
    (the boy)
17. Warum haben Sie _____ widersprochen?
    (the customer)
18. Wissen Sie _____?
    (the name of the customer)
19. Wer hat Ihnen diese _____ gegeben?
    (hints)
20. Ich vergesse Geburtstage und andere _____ sehr schnell.
    (dates)
21. Das kann man nicht beweisen,[3] denn das ist eine Sache _____.
    (of faith)

1 **der Verstand**   reason, mind
2 **der Ausweis, -e**   identification card
3 **beweisen, bewies, bewiesen** to prove

§6   FOR REFERENCE: THE DECLENSION OF NOUNS

1. Most masculine nouns and all neuter nouns add **-s** or **-es** to the genitive singular.
2. A small group of masculine nouns add **-n** or **-en** in all forms except in the nominative singular. This is the *weak declension.*
3. All nouns add **-n** to the dative plural unless the nominative plural ends in **-n** or **-s**.
4. Feminine nouns never take an ending in the singular.
5. The last word of a compound noun is declined.
6. Similar to the principal parts of verbs, from which all tenses can be derived, there are principal parts of nouns from which all cases can be derived. They are:
   a. the nominative singular (the case in which all nouns are listed in vocabularies and dictionaries)
   b. the genitive singular
   c. the nominative plural
   Good dictionaries list them in some form or other. Examples taken from one of them:

Film *m.* (-[e]s/-e)	which means:	
	nominative sing.	**der Film** (*m.* = masculine)
	genitive sing.	**Filmes** or **Films**
	nominative pl.	**Filme**
Student *m.* (-en/en)	which means:	
	nominative sing.	**der Student**
	genitive sing.	**Studenten**
	nominative pl.	**Studenten**
Studentin *f.* (-/-nen)	which means:	
	nominative sing.	**die Studentin** (*f.* = feminine)
	genitive sing.	**Studentin**
	nominative pl.	**Studentinnen**
Drama *n.* (-s/Dramen)	which means:	
	nominative sing.	**das Drama** (*n.* = neuter)
	genitive sing.	**Dramas**
	nominative pl.	**Dramen**

The principal parts of compound nouns that are not listed as such in a dictionary can be found by looking up the last element of the compound.

In this book, the nominative singular and plural of each noun are given, since the genitive singular for most nouns is predictable:
a. feminine nouns never add an ending,
b. masculine and neuter nouns add **-(e)s** with the exception of weak nouns, which add **-(e)n**. The latter are marked *weak* in this book.
The genitive is only stated in those rare instances when it has the weak ending plus **-s,** as in **der Name** (*weak;* gen. **-ns**), **-n.**

For the use of nouns with **der**-words and **ein**-words, see Chapter 6; with prepositions, see Chapter 7; in time expressions, see Chapter 11.

6

der-Words and *ein*-Words; Personal Pronouns

KEY TO THE EXERCISES ON CASSETTE 3.
RUNNING TIME: APPROX. 50 MIN.

der-Words

§1 FORMS

Compare the boldface words in the following sentences:

> **Der** Wagen gefällt mir nicht.
> **Dieser** Wagen gefällt mir nicht.
>
> Ich kaufe **den** Wagen.
> Ich kaufe **diesen** Wagen.

Dieser is one of several words that are called **"der-words"** because their declensional endings resemble those of the definite article. The most common **der**-words are listed below.

dieser	*this*
jener	*that*
jeder	*every*
mancher	*many a/pl. some, a few* (not: *many!*)
solcher	*such a/pl. such*
welcher	*which*
alle	*all*
beide	*both*

Declension of *der*-words

Compare the declension of the definite article and the **der**-word **dieser**:

	MASCULINE		NEUTER		FEMININE		PLURAL	
NOM.	der	dieser	das	dies**es**	die	dies**e**	die	dies**e**
ACC.	den	diesen	das	dies**es**	die	dies**e**	die	dies**e**
DAT.	dem	diesem	dem	diesem	der	dieser	den	diesen
GEN.	des	dieses	des	dieses	der	dieser	der	dieser

The boldface endings of the **der**-words are slightly different from the endings of the definite article.

PRACTICE 1   A. *Restate the following sentences, substituting the German equivalents of the words in parentheses for the boldface definite articles.*

1. **Der** Lehrer weiß das. (*this, every*)
2. Hoffentlich können Sie **die** Frage beantworten. (*every, this*)
3. **Das** Kompliment gefällt mir nicht. (*this*)
4. Er macht **der** Frau Komplimente. (*every*)
5. **Den** Unsinn[1] glaube ich nicht. (*this*)
6. Ich traue **dem** Hausmeister nicht. (*this*)
7. Rainer, **der** Faulenzer,[2] will nicht arbeiten. (*this*)
8. Fragen Sie doch **den** Polizisten! (*this*)
9. Ich glaube, meine Antwort hat **dem** Polizisten nicht gefallen. (*this*)
10. **Die** Studenten haben Probleme. (*some, such, all, both*)
11. Das sind die Probleme **der** Studenten. (*of these, of all*)
12. Das ist das Problem **der** Studentin. (*of this*)
13. Das ist das Problem **des** Studenten. (*of this*)
14. Das ist das Ende **der** Liebesgeschichte. (*of this*)

B. *Insert the appropriate* **der***-words.*

1. _____ Lehrer weiß das nicht? (*which*)
2. _____ Frage können Sie nicht beantworten? (*which*)
3. _____ Unsinn glauben Sie nicht? (*which*)
4. _____ Mann trauen Sie nicht? (*which*)
5. _____ Studenten haben Probleme? (*which*)
6. _____ Plattenspieler[3] gehört meiner Freundin. (*this*)
7. _____ Plattenspieler meinst du? (*which*)
8. Warum haben Sie _____ Warnung ignoriert? (*every*)
9. Er hat _____ Warnungen ignoriert. (*all*)
10. Das Picknick hat _____ Gästen gefallen. (*all*)
11. Ich habe _____ Reporterinnen nicht gekannt. (*both*)
12. Das ist der Höhepunkt _____ Romans. (*of this*)

---

1 **der Unsinn**   nonsense
2 **der Faulenzer, -**   lazybones
3 **der Plattenspieler, -** record player

13. Kennen Sie den Erfinder[1] _____ Maschinen? (*of these*)
14. Das war der Höhepunkt im Leben _____ Erfinderin.[2] (*of this*)
15. Das ist das Ende _____ Übungen. (*of these*)

§2   THE USE OF *dieser* AND *jener*

Zuerst müssen wir **dieses** und nicht **jenes** Problem besprechen.
First we have to discuss this problem, not that one.

The **der**-words **dieser** and **jener** are sometimes used together to express a contrast, as in the example above. **Jener** is rarely used otherwise. When no contrast is expressed, **dieser** is used as the equivalent of both *this* and *that*.

Nobody can answer this/that question.   Niemand kann **diese** Frage beantworten.
Nobody knows these/those people.   Niemand kennt **diese** Leute.

§3   THE DEFINITE ARTICLE MEANING *this/these* OR *that/those*

In conversational German the definite article, when spoken with heavy stress, is often the equivalent of English *this/these* or *that/those*. In print the letters are sometimes spaced to indicate this stress. Compare:

Dieser Wagen ist mein Traum.
D e r Wagen ist mein Traum.
  → *This/That car is my dream.*

Diesen Wagen möchte ich haben.
D e n Wagen möchte ich haben.
  → *I'd like to have this/that car.*

Dieses Mädchen möchte ich kennenlernen.
D a s Mädchen möchte ich kennenlernen.
  → *I'd like to meet this/that girl.*

Diese Mädchen sind sehr nett.
D i e Mädchen sind sehr nett.
  → *These/Those girls are very nice.*

PRACTICE 2   *Substitute the appropriate form of the definite article for* **dies-**.

Model: Diesem Mann traue ich nicht.
D e m Mann traue ich nicht.

1. **Diesen** Erfinder kenne ich.
2. **Dieser** Plattenspieler gehört Erika.
3. **Diesen** Witz[3] verstehe ich nicht.
4. **Diese** Frage ist zu persönlich.
5. **Dieses** Problem müssen wir lösen.
6. **Diese** Probleme kann niemand lösen.

---

1 **der Erfinder, -** male inventor
2 **die Erfinderin, -nen** female inventor
3 **der Witz, -e** joke

§4 **THE GERMAN EQUIVALENTS OF** *This/that is* **AND** *These/those are*

Compare:

a. **Diese** Schallplatte ist großartig.   *This record is great.*

b. **Dies**
   Das >**ist** die beste Schallplatte.

   This
   That > *is the best record.*

c. **Dies**
   Das >**sind** die besten Schallplatten.

   These
   Those > *are the best records.*

In sentence a. **diese** is a demonstrative adjective preceding the noun **Schall-platte.** It is declined and its ending agrees with **Schallplatte.**

In sentence b. **dies** does not take an ending since it does not precede the noun. It is a demonstrative pronoun pointing out **Schallplatte.** In conversational German it is more common to use **das** than **dies.**

In sentence c. the noun being pointed out, **Schallplatten,** is in the plural. In contrast to the English use of the plural forms *these* and *those,* the German **dies** and **das** do not change when pointing out a plural noun.

PRACTICE 3   *Insert German equivalents. (Use* **das** *as demonstrative pronoun.)*

1. Ich glaube _____ Unsinn nicht. (*this*)
2. _____ ist Unsinn. (*this*)
3. _____ Sendungen[1] sind interessant. (*these*)
4. _____ sind interessante Sendungen. (*these*)
5. _____ Sachen gehören Margot. (*these*)
6. _____ sind Margots Sachen. (*those*)
7. _____ ist Dieters Kugelschreiber.[2] (*this*)
8. _____ Kugelschreiber gehört Dieter. (*this*)
9. _____ ist der Katalog der Firma Schönemann. (*this*)
10. _____ Katalog ist neu. (*this*)

ein -Words

The **ein**-words take the endings of the indefinite article **ein**. Including the indefinite article, **ein**-words are **ein, kein,** and the possessives **mein, dein, sein, ihr, unser, euer, ihr, Ihr.**

§5 *Ein — kein*

Compare the declension of **der** and **(k)ein:**

1 **die Sendung, -en**   broadcast (radio, television)
2 **der Kugelschreiber, -**   ballpoint pen

	MASCULINE			NEUTER			FEMININE	
NOM.	der Mann	(k)ein Mann		das Kind	(k)ein Kind		die Frau	(k)eine Frau
ACC.	den Mann	(k)ein**en** Mann		das Kind	(k)ein Kind		die Frau	(k)ein**e** Frau
DAT.	dem Mann	(k)ein**em** Mann		dem Kind	(k)ein**em** Kind		der Frau	(k)ein**er** Frau
GEN.	des Mannes	(k)ein**es** Mannes		des Kindes	(k)ein**es** Kindes		der Frau	(k)ein**er** Frau

	PLURAL
NOM.	die / keine Männer, Frauen, Kinder
ACC.	die / keine Männer, Frauen, Kinder
DAT.	den / keinen Männern, Frauen, Kindern
GEN.	der / keiner Männer, Frauen, Kinder

Note: a. **Ein**, naturally, does not have a plural, but its negation **kein** does.

b. The **ein**-words have the same endings as the definite article with the exception of the three singular forms (boxed above) which take no ending:

nom. masc. **(k)ein Mann**   nom. neuter **(k)ein Kind**

acc. neuter **(k)ein Kind**

PRACTICE 4   *Insert German equivalents.*

1. a. Ist das _____ ? (*a novel*)
   b. Sie schreibt _____ . (*a novel*)
   c. Ist das der Titel _____ ? (*of a novel*)
2. a. Das ist _____ . (*a problem*)
   b. Haben Sie _____ ? (*a problem*)
   c. Ich habe _____ . (*no problems*)
3. a. Das ist _____ . (*a love story*)
   b. Liest du _____ ? (*a love story*)
   c. Das ist das Ende _____ . (*of a love story*)
4. a. Das ist _____ . (*a success*[1])
   b. Leider hatten wir _____ . (*no success*)
5. a. Bitte fragen Sie _____ . (*a policeman*)
   b. Wo ist _____ ? (*a policeman*)
6. a. Geben Sie doch dem Mann _____ ! (*a chance*)
   b. Man hat uns _____ gegeben. (*no chance*)
7. a. Haben Sie _____ der Firma Bauer? (*a catalogue*)
   b. Hier ist _____ dieser Firma. (*a catalogue*)
8. a. Das ist _____ . (*a secret*[2])
   b. Ich habe _____ . (*no secrets*)

---

1 **der Erfolg, -e**   success
2 **das Geheimnis, -se**   secret

The use of *kein*

When preceding a noun, **kein** may mean *no, not a, not any.*

Ich habe kein Auto. ─┬─*I have no car.*
                     └─*I don't have a car.*

Sie hat keine Geduld. ─┬─*She has no patience.*
                       └─*She doesn't have any patience.*

PRACTICE 5   *Translate into German.*

1. I don't have a catalogue.
2. I don't have any money.
3. She doesn't have a ballpoint pen.
4. He doesn't have a career.[1]
5. The Neumanns don't have any enemies.[2]
6. She doesn't make any mistakes.
7. I am not a lazybones.

Nicht ein is used instead of **kein** when **ein** is emphasized (often having the meaning of **one**).

Ordinary stress:

Ich habe kein Wort verstanden. *I did not understand a word.*

Ein emphasized:

Ich habe nicht **éin** Wort verstanden. *I did not understand óne word.*

PRACTICE 6   *Translate into German.*

1. Not one child was sick.
2. Not one broadcast was interesting.
3. Not one student protested. (pres. perf.)
4. She didn't make one mistake. (pres. perf.)
5. He didn't say one word. (pres. perf.)

Uses of *manch ein, solch ein,* and *welch ein*

a. **manch ein** (*many a*)
   The singular inflected forms of **mancher** mean *many a.* **Manch ein** is sometimes used instead. Note that **manch** remains uninflected and **ein** is inflected to agree with the noun that follows it.

   Mancher }
   Manch ein } Vater hat zu wenig Zeit für seine Kinder.
   Many a father has too little time for his children.

---

1 **die Karriere, -n**   career
2 **der Feind, -e**   enemy

Manche }
Manch eine } Mutter hat zuviel Verantwortung.

Many a mother has too much responsibility.

b. **solch ein** (*such a*)

More common than the inflected singular forms of **solcher** is the use of **solch ein.** Even more prevalent in conversational German is the expression of **so ein** as the equivalent of *such a.*

Solch ein }
So ein } Haus möchte ich haben.

I'd like to have such a house.

Solch eine }
So eine } Mutter verstehe ich nicht.

I don't understand such (that kind of) a mother.

Solch einen }
So einen } Film habe ich noch nie gesehen.

I have never seen such a film.

c. **welch ein** (*what a*)

Welch ein is used mainly in exclamations. It is often replaced by **was für ein,** particularly in conversational German.

Welch ein }
Was für ein } Dummkopf!   *What a blockhead! What a dummy!*

Welch eine }
Was für eine } Zeitverschwendung!   *What a waste of time!*

PRACTICE 7   A. *Insert the appropriate German equivalents. Give both possibilities for each.*

1. _____ Erfinder ist arm gestorben. (*many a*)
2. _____ Erfindung ist großartig. (*such a*)
3. _____ Überraschung![1] (*what a*)
4. _____ Tortur[2] ist grausam.[3] (*such a*)

B. *Translate expressing **such a** by **so ein** and **what a** by **was für ein.***

1. a. What a mother!
   b. What a lawyer!
   c. What a compliment!
   d. What a torture!
2. Such a car is a status symbol.[4]
3. I would like to have such a car.
4. I hate such a waste of time.

1 **die Überraschung, -en**   surprise
2 **die Tortur, -en**   torture
3 **grausam**   cruel
4 **das Statussymbol, -e**   status symbol

The use of *was für (ein)* in questions

Was für (ein) introducing a question has the meaning of *what kind of* (*a*).

Was für ein Hund ist das?	*What kind of a dog is that?*
Was für einen Hund haben Sie?	*What kind of a dog do you have?*
Was für Musik gefällt Ihnen?	*What kind of music do you like?*
Was für Filme gefallen Ihnen?	*What kind of films do you like?*

PRACTICE 8 *Insert German equivalents.*

1. _____ Wagen haben Sie? (*what kind of a*)
2. _____ Kamera hast du gekauft? (*what kind of a*)
3. _____ Haus wollt ihr bauen? (*what kind of a*)
4. _____ Freunde hast du? (*what kind of*)
5. _____ Experimente haben Sie gemacht? (*what kind of*)

§6 THE POSSESSIVES

The possessives are

mein	*my*
dein	*your* (fam. sing.)
sein	*his, its*
ihr	*her, its*
unser	*our*
euer	*your* (fam. pl.)
ihr	*their*
Ihr	*your* (formal)

When preceding a noun the possessive takes the ending of **ein/kein.** This ending is determined by the gender, number (singular or plural), and case of the noun that follows it.

Das ist **mein** Vater.
Das ist **meine** Mutter.
Das sind **meine** Eltern.

The nominative case

MASCULINE	NEUTER	FEMININE		PLURAL	
mein Freund	mein Auto	meine	Freundin	meine	Hobbys
dein Freund	dein Auto	deine	Freundin	deine	Hobbys
sein Freund	sein Auto	seine	Freundin	seine	Hobbys
ihr Freund	ihr Auto	ihre	Freundin	ihre	Hobbys
unser Freund	unser Auto	uns(e)re	Freundin	uns(e)re	Hobbys
euer Freund	euer Auto	eu(e)re	Freundin	eu(e)re	Hobbys
ihr Freund	ihr Auto	ihre	Freundin	ihre	Hobbys
Ihr Freund	Ihr Auto	Ihre	Freundin	Ihre	Hobbys

Note: a. **unser, euer: -er** is part of the stem, not a declensional ending.

b. **uns(e)re, eu(e)re:** The **e** before the **r** may be omitted when a declensional ending is added.

c. *your* ⟨ **dein** (sing. fam.) — referring to someone addressed as **du;**
euer (plur. fam.) — referring to two or more addressed as **ihr;**
Ihr (formal) — referring to one or more persons addressed as **Sie.**

PRACTICE 9   *Translate into German, repeating the nouns for each possessive in items 1 to 6.*

1. my father	2. my mother	3. my parents	4. my house
his	our	her	his
her	her	our	their
our	his	their	her
their	their	your (fam. sing., fam. pl., formal)	your (fam. sing., fam. pl., formal)

5. my brother and my sister   6. my son and my daughter

his	his	our	our
her	her	your	your (three forms)

7. his girlfriend   8. her boyfriend   9. our friends

10. your problem (three forms)   11. their house   12. her mistake

Declension of the possessives

As mentioned before, the possessives preceding nouns have the same case endings as **ein** and **kein.**

	MASCULINE	NEUTER	FEMININE	PLURAL
NOM.	mein	mein	mein**e**	mein**e**
ACC.	mein**en**	mein	mein**e**	mein**e**
DAT.	mein**em**	mein**em**	mein**er**	mein**en**
GEN.	mein**es**	mein**es**	mein**er**	mein**er**

Note the three forms without endings (boxed).

PRACTICE 10   *Insert the German possessives.*

1. Das ist _____ Wagen. (*my, his, her, your* [three forms])
2. Wollen Sie _____ Wagen kaufen? (*my, his, her, our, their*)
3. Haben Sie _____ Frage nicht verstanden? (*my, her, his*)
4. Dieses Fahrrad[1] gehört _____ Freund. (*my, her, your* [fam. sing., formal])

1 **das Fahrrad, ̈er,**   bicycle

5. Schäfers sind _____ Nachbarn. (*my, our, their*)
6. Sind das _____ Sachen? (*your* [three forms])
7. Das ist _____ Führerschein. (*my, his, her*)
8. Das ist der Führerschein _____ Bruders. (*of my, of your* [fam. sing., formal])
9. Das ist der Anfang _____ Karriere. (*of my, of his, of her*)
10. Ich werde _____ Versprechen halten.[1] (*my*)
11. Helga hat _____ Versprechen nicht gehalten. (*her*)
12. Haben Sie _____ Freund zum Geburtstag gratuliert? (*your*)
13. Hast du _____ Freundin einen Ring geschenkt? (*your*)
14. Fragen Sie doch _____ Rechtsanwalt! (*your*)
15. Was ist _____ Hauptfach?[2] (*your* [fam. sing.])
16. Soziologie ist _____ Nebenfach.[3] (*his, her*)
17. _____ Deutsch (*neut.*) ist besser geworden. (*your* [fam. sing., formal])
18. Dieses Haus ist _____ Traum.[4] (*my, our*)
19. Du bist die Frau _____ Träume. (*of my, of his*)

The German equivalent of English *its*

The German equivalent of *its* is **sein-** or **ihr-**:

    a. **der** Staat und **seine** Einwohner
       the state and its inhabitants

    b. **das** Dorf und **seine** Einwohner
       the village and its inhabitants

    c. **die** Stadt und **ihre** Einwohner
       the city and its inhabitants

In sentences *a* and *b* the possessors (**Staat/Dorf**) are masculine and neuter; the possessive **sein-** is used.
In sentence *c* the possessor (**Stadt**) is feminine; the possessive **ihr-** is used.

PRACTICE 11   *Insert the German equivalent of **its.***

1. die Universität und _____ Professoren
2. das Krankenhaus und _____ Ärzte
3. der Klub und _____ Mitglieder[5]
4. die Maschine und _____ Erfinder
5. das Bild und _____ Rahmen[6]
6. die Eskapade und _____ Folgen[7]

---

1 **das Versprechen halten (hält), hielt, gehalten**	to keep the promise
2 **das Hauptfach, ¨er**	major
3 **das Nebenfach, ¨er**	minor
4 **der Traum, ¨e**	dream
5 **das Mitglied, -er**	member
6 **der Rahmen, -**	frame
7 **die Folge, -n**	consequence

Uses of the Articles

§7   USES OF THE DEFINITE ARTICLE

1. Most names of countries are neuter. They are used without an article except when preceded by an adjective.

Deutschland	**in Deutschland**	but: **das** alte Deutschland
Schweden	**in Schweden**	**das** liberale Schweden
Italien	**in Italien**	**das** schöne Italien

The names of feminine, masculine, and plural countries require the definite article.

a. **Feminines**

die Schweiz
die Tschechoslowakei
die Türkei
die Bundesrepublik Deutschland (die BRD)
die Deutsche Demokratische Republik (die DDR)
die Union der Sozialistischen Sowjetrepubliken (die UdSSR)

b. **Masculines**

der Irak
der Iran
der Libanon

c. **Plurals**

die Niederlande (*The Netherlands*)
die Vereinigten Staaten von Amerika (die USA)

Note the use of the definite article with these countries:

Wir fahren **in die Schweiz.**
　　　　in die Türkei.
　　　　in die BRD.
　　　　in die UdSSR.
　　　　in die USA.
　　　　in den Libanon.

2. German normally uses the definite article rather than the possessive adjective with parts of the body and articles of clothing where reference to the subject of the sentence may be assumed.

Sie können den Nachtisch[1] mit **den** Fingern essen.
*You can eat the dessert with **your** fingers.*

Er hat immer **die** Hände in **den** Taschen.
*He always has **his** hands in **his** pockets.*

---

1 **der Nachtisch, -e**　　　dessert

Ich verliere **den** Verstand.
*I'm losing **my** mind.*

Sie hat **den** Kopf verloren.
*She has lost **her** head.*

3. In prepositional phrases with verbs of motion, the article is used in German but not in English:

in die Stadt gehen	*to go to town*
in die Schule gehen	*to go to school*
mit dem Auto fahren	*to go by car*
mit dem Wagen fahren	
mit dem Bus fahren	*to go by bus*
mit der Bahn fahren	*to go by train*
mit dem Zug fahren	
mit der U-Bahn[1] **fahren**	*to go by subway*

4. The article is used in English but not in German to express:
   a. playing an instrument

Klavier spielen	*to play **the** piano*
Violine/Geige spielen	*to play **the** violin*
Trompete spielen	*to play **the** trumpet*

but: **ein** Musikinstrument spielen *to play **a** musical instrument*

   b. the German equivalents of ***the Wagners, at the Winklers'***, etc.

Wagners haben Gäste.	***The Wagners*** *have guests.*
Wir waren **bei Winklers.**	*We were **at the Winklers'**.*

§8   USES OF THE INDEFINITE ARTICLE

Unlike English, German does not use the indefinite article after the verbs **sein, bleiben,** and **werden** when the following noun denotes a profession or social status.

Andreas ist Student.	*Andreas is **a** student.*
Karin ist Studentin.	*Karin is **a** student.*
Barbara wird Ärztin.	*Barbara is going to be **a** doctor.*
Herr Schmidt will nicht Rechtsanwalt bleiben.	*Mr. Schmidt does not want to remain **a** lawyer.*
Er ist Witwer.	*He is **a** widower.*
Sie ist Witwe.	*She is **a** widow.*

However, the article is used when the noun is modified by an adjective:

Ich bin **ein fauler Student.**
Du wirst bestimmt **ein guter Arzt** werden.

---

1 **die U-Bahn, -en** (*short for:* **die Untergrundbahn**)   subway

PRACTICE 12   *Translate into German.*

1. Are you a student? (formal, male, female)
2. Mrs. Bachmann is a widow.
3. Where do the Zimmermanns live?
4. Their children go to school.
5. Do you play the violin? (fam. sing.)
6. I play the piano.
7. Are you going by car or by train? (fam. pl.)
8. The Schmidts are going by subway.
9. Is Mr. Schreiber a lawyer?
10. He is going to be a teacher.
11. Is Helga at the Bergers'?
12. We are going to Turkey and Lebanon.
13. Germany and Switzerland are neighbors.
14. I am losing my mind.
15. Have you lost your mind? (fam. sing.)
16. He has lost his head.

PRACTICE 13   Summarizing exercises

A. *Insert German equivalents.*

1. a. X: Was ist _____ Hauptfach? (*your* [fam. sing.])
      Y: Psychologie ist _____ Hauptfach. (*my*)
   b. X: Hast du auch _____ Nebenfach? (*a*)
      Y: Nein, ich habe _____ Nebenfach. (*not a*)
2. a. X: Spielen Sie _____ Musikinstrument? (*a*)
      Y: Ich nicht, aber die Kinder _____ Nachbarin spielen
         _____ und _____ . (*of my, the piano, the trumpet*)
   b. X: Üben die Kinder viel?
      Y: Leider ja. Ich fürchte, ich verliere noch _____ . (*my mind*)
3.   X: Hier ist _____ Paket für Andreas. (*a*)
      Y: Schon wieder für Andreas? Warum bekomme ich _____
         Pakete? (*no*)
4.   X: Was hast du Inge erzählt?
      Y: Nichts. Ich habe _____ Wort mit ihr gesprochen. (*not one*)
5.   X: Kann man _____ Mann trauen? (*this*)
      Y: Das weiß ich nicht. Ich weiß nur, daß man _____ Frau nicht
         trauen kann. (*his*)
6.   X: Wem gehört _____ Kugelschreiber? (*this*)
      Y: Ich glaube, er gehört _____ Freundin. (*my*)
7.   X: Warum ist Karin so deprimiert?
      Y: _____ Noten sind nicht besser geworden. (*her*)
8.   X: Herr Winkler hat mir _____ Kompliment gemacht. (*a*)
      Y: _____ Mann macht _____ Frau Komplimente. (*this, every*)
9.   X: Ich habe heute _____ Zigarette (*fem.*) geraucht. (*not one*)
      Y: Du bist der Held _____ Tages. (*of the*)

10. X: Fahren Sie _____ zur Arbeit? (*by bus*)

     Y: Nein. Meistens fahre ich _____. (*by subway*)

11. X: Schenken Sie doch _____ Freundin _____ Diamantring! (*your, this*)

     Y: Ausgeschlossen![1] Ich bin doch _____ Millionär. (*no*)

12. X: Warum bist du so böse auf[2] Andreas?

     Y: Weil er _____ Versprechen nicht gehalten hat. (*his*)

13. X: Wo werden Sie die Flitterwochen verbringen?[3]

     Y: Das ist _____ Geheimmis. (*our*)

14. X: Ich glaube, ich bekomme _____ Glatze.[4] (*a*)

     Y: Ach, das macht nichts.[5] Du gefällst _____ Frau auch mit Glatze. (*your*)

B. *Express in German, using* **so ein** *for* **such a** *and* **was für ein** *for* **what a.**

1. a. That's a surprise.
   b. That's no surprise.
   c. What a surprise!
2. a. Is that a secret?
   b. That's no secret.
   c. I don't have any secrets.
   d. That's his secret.
3. a. This suggestion is very good.
   b. Which suggestion do you mean? (formal)
   c. Do you have a suggestion?
   d. That's only a suggestion.
   e. What a suggestion!
4. a. That's my record player.
   b. This record player belongs to my friend Dietmar.
   c. Helga, do you have a record player?
   d. What kind of a record player do you have?
   e. Andreas has such a record player.
5. a. Miss Winkler, do you have a driver's licence?
   b. That's my driver's licence.
   c. That's the driver's licence of my girlfriend.
6. a. Elke, is that your ring?
   b. Which ring do you mean?
   c. What kind of a ring did you buy? (pres. perf.)
7. a. Are you my friend or my enemy? (formal)
   b. I am not your enemy.
   c. You don't have any enemies.
   d. What kind of friends do you have?

---

1 **Ausgeschlossen!**   That's out of the question!
2 **böse sein auf** (*acc.*)   to be angry with
3 **die Flitterwochen verbringen, verbrachte, verbracht**   to spend the honeymoon
4 **die Glatze, -n**   bald head
   eine Glatze bekommen, bekam, bekommen   to go bald
5 **Das macht nichts.**   That doesn't matter.

8. a. Mr. Bayer is the inventor of this machine.
   b. Do you know this inventor? (fam. plural)
   c. This machine is his invention.
   d. What an invention!
9. a. Is that a warning?
   b. Why do you ignore the warning of a friend? (fam. sing.)
   c. Why do you ignore the warnings of your friends?
10. a. That's a torture.
    b. What a torture!
    c. Such a torture is cruel.
    d. That's the end of this torture.

C. *Using the cues, form sentences that fit the context.*

Model: Barbara war im Sommer in Deutschland. Der Deutschprofessor sagt zu ihr:

„Deutsch / besser / werden" (pres. perf.)

„Ihr Deutsch ist besser geworden."

1. Ich habe heute gute Laune. Warum?

   Noten / besser / werden (pres. perf.)

2. Ich brauche einen Koffer. Vielleicht bestelle ich ihn bei Schönemann. Ich frage Helga:

   „haben / Katalog / von Schönemann?"

3. Ich warte schon 20 Minuten auf den Bus und sage:

   „Zeitverschwendung!"

4. Das ist nicht meine Schreibmaschine.

   Freundin / gehören

5. Martin war in Europa. Er hatte versprochen, mir zu schreiben. Ich habe keine Post von ihm bekommen. Ich sage:

   „Versprechen / nicht halten" (pres. perf.)

6. Mein Bruder hat Schulden. Trotzdem (*in spite of this*) hat er heute ein neues Motorrad gekauft. Ich sage:

   „du / Verstand / verlieren?" (pres. perf.)

7. Dieter macht Hannelore ein Kompliment. Sie lacht und sagt:
   „du / jede Frau / Komplimente"

8. Herr Köhler ist Direktor der Firma Krause geworden. Er sagt zu seiner Frau:

   „Höhepunkt / Karriere"

9. Mein Haar wird dünn. Ich denke:
   hoffentlich / Glatze / bekommen

10. Gestern haben Andreas und Brigitte Schluß gemacht (*broke up*). Brigitte sagt:

    „Ende / Liebesgeschichte"

Personal Pronouns

§9   THE CASES OF PERSONAL PRONOUNS AND THEIR USES

The personal pronouns are declined as follows:

		1ST PERS.	2ND PERS. FAM.	3RD PERS. MASC.	3RD PERS. FEM.	3RD PERS. NEUT.
SINGULAR	NOM.	ich	du	er	sie	es
	ACC.	mich	dich	ihn	sie	es
	DAT.	mir	dir	ihm	ihr	ihm

FORMAL SING. + PL.

		1ST PERS.	2ND PERS. FAM.	3RD PERS.	FORMAL SING. + PL.
PLURAL	NOM.	wir	ihr	sie	Sie
	ACC.	uns	euch	sie	Sie
	DAT.	uns	euch	ihnen	Ihnen

Note: All cases of the formal address **Sie** are capitalized. The forms are the same as those of the 3rd pers. pl. **sie** except for the capitalization.

The genitive forms, which are rare and occur only in literary German, are:

SINGULAR	meiner	deiner	seiner ihrer seiner	
PLURAL	unser	euer	ihrer	Ihrer

Examples: Gedenke meiner!   *Think of me.*
                   (commonly: Denke an mich!)

                   Erbarme dich unser!   *Have mercy on us.*
                   (used in prayers)

PRACTICE 14   A. *Insert the correct German equivalents in the accusative.*

Frau Mensing haßt (*me, you* [fam. sing.], *him, her, it,
                          us, you* [fam. pl.], *them, you* [formal])

B. *Insert the correct German equivalents in the dative.*

Das gehört (*to me, to you* [fam. sing.], *to him, to her, to it,
                    to us, to you* [fam. pl.], *to them, to you* [formal])

C. *Insert the correct German equivalents in the accusative or dative.*

1. Verstehst du (*me, us, him, her, them*).
2. Er hilft (*me, him, us, them, her*).

3. Ich beneide (*you*, [fam. sing., fam. pl., formal]).
4. Ich danke (*you* [fam. sing., fam. pl., formal]).

D. *Substitute pronouns for the boldface noun subjects and objects.*

Model: Kennen Sie **Herrn Krause**?
Kennen Sie ihn?

1. Liebst du **Helga**?
2. **Helga** liebt **Klaus**.
3. Ich kenne **deine Eltern**.
4. **Elke** bringt **Bergers** zum Flughafen.
5. **Herr Berger** hat **seinen Rechtsanwalt** angerufen.
6. Hast du **den Kindern** bei den Hausaufgaben geholfen?
7. Haben Sie **der Chefin** zum Geburtstag gratuliert?
8. Ich weiß nicht, ob ich **dem Hausmeister** trauen kann.
9. Haben Sie **der Reporterin** die Wahrheit gesagt?
10. Hast du **dem Taxifahrer** ein Trinkgeld gegeben?

Personal pronouns referring to inanimate objects

Since inanimate objects are masculine, feminine, or neuter, they are referred to by masculine, feminine, or neuter personal pronouns.

Dieser Wagen ist nicht zu teuer.	Vielleicht kaufe ich **diesen Wagen.**	
Er ist nicht zu teuer.	Vielleicht kaufe ich **ihn.**	
It is not too expensive.	Maybe I'll buy *it.*	

PRACTICE 15   *Substitute pronouns for the boldface subjects and objects.*

1. Ich verstehe **diese Frage** nicht.
2. **Dieser Fernseher** ist kaputt.
3. Können Sie **den Fernseher** reparieren?
4. Bitte bringen Sie **diesen Anzug** in die Reinigung!
5. Sind **die Hausaufgaben** immer so leicht?
6. Hast du **die Dias**[1] gesehen?
7. Haben Sie **die Notiz**[2] gefunden?
8. Wann haben Sie **das Paket** bekommen?
9. Hast du **den Brief** gelesen?

PRACTICE 16   *Answer the following questions in the negative, substituting pronouns for the nouns.*

Model: Hast du die Post abgeholt? **Nein, ich habe sie noch nicht[3] abgeholt.**

1. Hast du den Scheck eingelöst?[4]

---

1 **das Dia, -s**	slide
short for: **das Diapositiv, -e**	
2 **die Notiz, -en**	note, memo
3 **noch nicht**	not yet
4 **den Scheck ein•lösen**	to cash the check

2. Haben Sie Ihre Eltern angerufen?
3. Haben Sie die Rechnung bezahlt?
4. Hast du den Koffer gepackt?
5. Hast du das Paket bekommen?
6. Hast du Hannelore gratuliert?
7. Haben Sie dem Hausmeister gedankt?
8. Hast du den Brief geschrieben?
9. Haben Sie die Hausaufgaben gemacht?
10. Hast du dein Zimmer aufgeräumt?
11. Hast du die Autoschlüssel gefunden?

A note on the use of personal pronouns referring to *das Mädchen* and *das Fräulein*

The nouns **Mädchen** and **Fräulein** are neuter. Normally personal pronouns must be in the same gender as the nouns to which they refer; however, for these two nouns the feminine **sie** is often used instead.

> Das Mädchen da drüben wohnt im Studentenheim. **Es/Sie** ist sehr nett.
> Kennst du das Fräulein da drüben? **Es/Sie** sieht wie Dieters Schwester aus.

When the name is mentioned, the feminine form has to be used:

> Das Mädchen
> Das Fräulein } heißt Maria Schreiber. **Sie** studiert in Köln.

The use of personal pronouns with *gefallen*

	Dieser Anzug	gefällt	**meinem Vater**	sehr gut.
	Er	gefällt	**ihm**	sehr gut.
lit.	*It*	*pleases*	*him*	*very much.*
idiom.	*He*	*likes*	*it*	*very much.*

As mentioned in Chapter 5, §4, the person or thing liked or disliked is the subject of the German sentence. The person who does the liking or disliking is the dative object of the verb.

PRACTICE 17   *Translate into German, following the models of sentences a.*

1. a. My brother likes this record player very much.
   Dieser Plattenspieler gefällt meinem Bruder sehr gut.
   b. He likes it very much.
   c. I like it very much.
   d. We like it very much.
   e. They like it very much.
2. a. My sister doesn't like this motorcycle.
   Dieses Motorrad gefällt meiner Schwester nicht.
   b. She doesn't like it.

      c. I don't like it.

      d. He doesn't like it.

      e. They don't like it.

      f. We don't like it.

  3. a. Marlene didn't like the reporter.

      Der Reporter hat Marlene nicht gefallen.

      b. She didn't like him.

      c. I didn't like him.

      d. You didn't like him. (fam. sing., formal)

      e. Why didn't you like him? (fam. sing., formal)

      f. Did you like him? (fam. plur.)

§10   POSITION OF PERSONAL PRONOUN OBJECTS

1. One personal pronoun object and one noun object

Compare the following three sentences:

a. Sie hat **meinem Bruder diesen Koffer** geschenkt. *She gave my brother this suitcase.*

         INDIRECT OBJECT   DIRECT OBJECT

          (dat./person)   (acc./thing)

b. Sie hat   **ihm**   **diesen Koffer** geschenkt. *She gave him this suitcase.*

c. Sie hat   **ihn**   **meinem Bruder** geschenkt. *She gave it **to** my brother.*

When there are two noun objects, the indirect object usually precedes the direct object, as in sentence *a* .

Personal pronoun objects precede noun objects regardless of which one is the direct or indirect object, as in sentences *b* and *c*.

In English the indirect object is preceded by *to* when it follows the direct object, as in sentence *c*.

PRACTICE 18   *Substitute personal pronouns for the boldface nouns and change the word order if necessary.*

  1. Frau Berger hat **ihrem Sohn** ein Paket geschickt.

  2. Hast du deinem Freund **die Dias** gezeigt?

  3. Ich habe dem Polizisten **meinen Ausweis**[1] gezeigt.

  4. Der Polizist hat **dem Fahrer** einen Strafzettel gegeben.

  5. Wer hat **deiner Freundin** diesen Witz erzählt?

  6. Wer hat **den Kindern** das Märchen[2] vorgelesen?[3]

  7. Ich habe **meinen Eltern** mein Ehrenwort gegeben.

  8. Sie hat ihrem Freund **ihr neues Kleid** gezeigt.

1 **der Ausweis, -e**	identity card
2 **das Märchen, -**	fairy tale
3 **vor•lesen (liest vor), las vor, vorgelesen**	to read to

9. Wer hat den Touristen **das Hotel** empfohlen?[1]
10. Bitte sagen Sie **der Reporterin** die Wahrheit!
11. Bitte gib der Sekretärin **diese Notiz!**
12. Bitte geben Sie **diesem Mann** eine Chance!

2. Two personal pronoun objects

When there are two personal pronoun objects, the accusative precedes the dative.

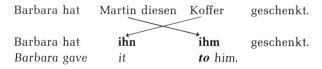

Barbara hat   Martin diesen   Koffer   geschenkt.

Barbara hat   **ihn**   **ihm**   geschenkt.
Barbara gave   *it*   ***to*** *him*.

PRACTICE 19   Substitute personal pronouns for the boldface nouns.

Model: Hast du **Margot das Geld** zurückgegeben?
Hast du es ihr zurückgegeben?

1. Kannst du **Barbara diese Sache** erklären?
2. Hast du **Udo die Hausaufgaben** erklärt?
3. Bitte geben Sie **dem Gepäckträger das Trinkgeld!**
4. Bitte geben Sie **den Kindern dieses Märchenbuch!**
5. Ich habe **meiner Frau diesen Witz** erzählt.
6. Ich habe **Herrn Baumann das Gerücht**[2] erzählt.
7. Ich habe **Dieter meine Dias** gezeigt.
8. Wir haben **den Touristen dieses Hotel** empfohlen.
9. Ich habe **meiner Freundin das Geld** noch nicht zurückgegeben.

3. A personal pronoun object and a noun subject

In sentences with inverted or dependent' word order, personal pronoun objects commonly precede noun subjects.

Compare: Hoffentlich hat der Film meinem Freund gefallen.

               Hoffentlich hat der Film   ihm   gefallen.
more common: Hoffentlich hat **ihm der Film** gefallen.

               Hat der Film deiner Freundin gefallen?

               Hat der Film   ihr   gefallen?
more common: Hat **ihr der Film** gefallen?

               Ich glaube nicht, daß der Film meinen Freunden gefallen hat.

               Ich glaube nicht, daß der Film   ihnen   gefallen hat.
more common: Ich glaube nicht, daß **ihnen der Film** gefallen hat.

1 **empfehlen (empfiehlt), empfahl, empfohlen**   to recommend
2 **das Gerücht, -e**   rumor

PRACTICE 20   *Replace the boldface noun objects with pronouns and change the word order accordingly.*

Model: Leider hat der Ring **meiner Freundin** nicht gefallen.
    Leider hat ihr der Ring nicht gefallen.

1. Leider hat der Koffer **meinem Freund** nicht gefallen.
2. Hoffentlich kann Udo **das Radio** reparieren.
3. Vielleicht hat Frau Krause **den Ausländer** nicht richtig verstanden.
4. Ich nehme an, daß Herr Zimmermann **die Rechnung** bezahlt hat.
5. Es ist möglich, daß meine Frau **den Anzug** in die Reinigung gebracht hat.
6. Hat Klaus **das Paket** schon aufgemacht?
7. Wie gefällt der Ring **deiner Freundin?**
8. Wann hat Monika **den Reisescheck** eingelöst?

PRACTICE 21   Summarizing exercises for §9 to §10

A. *Translate the answers into German, using the present perfect for the English past tenses.*

1.   X: Wer hat dir diese Schallplatte geschenkt?
     Y: Renate gave it to me.
2.   X: Wer hat Ihnen dieses Paket geschickt?
     Y: My parents sent it to me.
3.   X: Wer hat dir diesen Witz erzählt?
     Y: You told it to me.
4.   X: Hast du Frank dein neues Kleid gezeigt?
     Y: Yes, I showed it to him.
5.   X: Haben Sie der Polizistin Ihren Führerschein gezeigt?
     Y: Of course, I showed it to her.
6.   X: Haben Sie den Kindern dieses Märchen vorgelesen?
     Y: No, Annerose read it to them.
7.   X: Hast du die Notiz von Renate gelesen?
     Y: Yes, I read it.
8.   X: Haben Sie meine Frage verstanden?
     Y: No, I didn't understand it.
9.   X: Habt ihr das Problem schon gelöst?
     Y: No, we haven't solved it yet.
10.   X: Hast du den Reisescheck schon eingelöst?
     Y: No, I haven't cashed it yet.
11.   X: Hast du meinen Geburtstag vergessen?
     Y: Of course, I haven't forgotten it.
12.   X: Ist mein Deutsch (*neuter*) besser geworden?
     Y: Of course, it has improved (= become better).
13.   X: Wer hat Margot zum Flughafen gebracht?
     Y: Thomas and Elke took her to the airport.
14.   X: Wer hat deine Eltern am Flughafen abgeholt?
     Y: My brother picked them up.

15. X: Wirst du die Sache sofort erledigen?
    Y: Yes, I am giving you my word of honor.
16. X: Wer hat den Vertrag unterschrieben?
    Y: My wife signed it.
17. X: Wie gefällt Ihnen diese Sendung?
    Y: I don't like it.
18. X: Wie hat Ihnen die Reporterin gefallen?
    Y: I didn't like her.
19. X: Wie gefällt dir mein neuer Anzug?
    Y: I like it very much.
20. X: Und wie gefalle ich dir?
    Y: You are the man of my dreams.

B. *Form sentences that fit the context, using the present perfect except where otherwise indicated.*

Model: Ich habe viele Dias von meiner Europareise.
     ich / Freunde / zeigen
     Ich habe sie meinen Freunden gezeigt.

1. Ich bin zu schnell gefahren.
   Polizist / Strafzettel / geben
2. Ich frage Inge, warum sie so lacht. Sie antwortet:
   „Klaus / Witz / erzählen"
3. Herr Krause wollte nicht glauben, daß ich 20 Jahre alt bin.
   ich / Ausweis / zeigen
4. Ich habe Rainer 200 Mark geliehen (*lent*). Er gibt mir das Geld bestimmt zurück.
   er / Ehrenwort / geben
5. Gestern waren die Hausaufgaben in Mathematik sehr kompliziert. Ich bin zu Margot gegangen, denn sie ist in Mathematik besser als ich.
   sie / Hausaufgaben in Mathematik / erklären
6. Ich habe Müllers zum Flughafen gebracht.
   sie / nicht / danken
7. Ich habe heute Geburtstag.
   Freundin / noch nicht / gratulieren
8. Frank zeigt mir seine neue Kamera. Ich sage:
   „diese Kamera / gefallen" (present tense)
9. Frank war gestern im Konzert. Er sagt:
   „Konzert / nicht gefallen"
10. Ich habe Margots Freund kennengelernt. Sie fragt mich:
    „wie / mein Freund / gefallen?" (present tense)

7

Prepositions

KEY TO THE EXERCISES ON CASSETTE 4.
RUNNING TIME: APPROX. 25 MIN.

A preposition usually precedes a noun or pronoun, called its *object*. The preposition and its object constitute a phrase, called a *prepositional phrase*, e.g. **with a friend, for my friends, without them.** The use of prepositions is highly idiomatic. It is therefore imperative to pay close attention to these tricky words.

German prepositions are commonly divided into four groups:
    prepositions that govern the dative case,
    prepositions that govern the accusative case,
    prepositions that govern the dative or accusative case,
    prepositions that govern the genitive case.

In our treatment of these groups we shall consider only the most commonly used prepositions and their meanings. (For a fuller treatment of the use of prepositions in time expressions, see Chapter 11.)

§1   PREPOSITIONS THAT GOVERN THE DATIVE CASE

1. aus
a. *out of* (expressing motion)

> Sie kommt gerade **aus dem Haus.**
> *She's just coming out of the house.*

> Ich komme gerade **aus einer Vorlesung.**
> *I'm just coming from a lecture.*

b. *from* (being, coming from a place)

> Schreibers kommen **aus Deutschland.**
> *The Schreibers come from Germany.*

c. *made of* (a certain material)

> **Aus welchem Stoff** ist dieser Anzug?
> *What material is this suit made of?*
>
> Das Denkmal ist **aus Marmor.**
> *The monument is made of marble.*

d. expression: **aus diesem Grund** *for this/that reason*

> **Aus diesem Grund** haben wir die Einladung nicht angenommen.
> *For this/that reason we did not accept the invitation.*

2. außer *except for, besides*

> Außer meiner Schwester waren alle gekommen.
> *Except for my sister everybody had come.*
>
> **Außer diesem Paket** habe ich noch einen Scheck bekommen.
> *Besides this parcel I also received a check.*

3. bei

a. *at, near*

> Wir haben das Auto **beim Postamt** geparkt. (*at/near the post office*)
> Das ist eine Stadt **bei Nürnberg.** (*near Nuremberg*)

b. *at, with* (someone's home, business, or office)

> Er wohnt **bei seinen Eltern.** (*with his parents*)
> Ich war gestern **bei Schmidts.** (*at the Smiths'*)
> Sie arbeitet **bei der Firma Köhler.** (*at the Köhler company*)
> Andreas ist **beim Arzt.** (*at the doctor's*)
>   (bei dem)
> Inge hat die Handschuhe **bei Hertie** gekauft. (*at Hertie's*)

c. *in* (when used in connection with the weather)

> | **bei diesem Wetter** | *in this weather* |
> |---|---|
> | **bei diesem Regen** | *in this rain* |
> | **bei dieser Kälte** | *in this cold* |
> | **bei dieser Hitze** | *in this heat* |

4. gegenüber *opposite, across from*

> Das Postamt ist **dem Bahnhof gegenüber.**
> *or:* Das Postamt ist **gegenüber dem Bahnhof.**
> *The post office is across from the railway station.*

Gegenüber may precede or follow a noun, but it must follow a pronoun.

> Herr Schmidt saß **mir gegenüber.**
> *Mr. Schmidt was sitting across from me.*

5. mit

a. *with*

>Wir fliegen **mit Freunden** nach Europa.
>Haben Sie **mit ihm** gesprochen?

Mit corresponds very closely to English *with*.

b. *by* (with means of transportation)

Wir fahren **mit dem Wagen.**	*We are going by car.*
mit dem Bus.	*by bus.*
mit dem Zug / **mit der Bahn.**	*by train.*

Note the use of the definite article in German (cf. Chap. 6, §7, 3).

6. nach

a. *after* (in connection with time)

nach einer Stunde	*after an hour*
nach der Vorlesung	*after the lecture*
nach der Deutschstunde	*after German class*
nach dieser Stunde	*after this class*

b. *to* (with names of villages, towns, countries, islands, continents)

>Wir fahren **nach Wien.**
>Wir fliegen **nach England.**

>but: Wir fahren **in die Schweiz.** (*to Switzerland*)

Place names that are used with the definite article use the preposition **in** (cf. Chap. 6, §7, 1).
expression: **nach Hause gehen** *to go home*

c. *according to*

>Man kann nicht nur **nach dem Aussehen** urteilen.
>*One cannot judge by appearances only.*

expression: **meiner Meinung nach**	*in my opinion*
seiner	*his*
ihrer	*her*

Note that the preposition in this expression normally follows the noun.

7. seit *since, for a period of time*

Käte schwänzt **seit Montag.**	*Käte has skipped class since Monday.*
Klaus schwänzt **seit einer Woche.**	*Klaus has skipped class for a week.*

Note the use of the present tense in German and the present perfect in English to express a stretch of time that began in the past and continues into the present (cf. Chap. 2, §7, 3).

8. von

a. *from*

> Das ist ein Geschenk **von meiner Freundin.**
> *That is a gift from my girlfriend.*

b. *of,* frequently used in phrases that substitute for the genitive (cf. Chap. 5, §4, 4). Compare:

> Das ist die Adresse **eines Freundes.**
> Das ist die Adresse **von einem Freund.**
> *That is the address of a friend.*

c. *by* (author)

> Das ist ein Roman **von Thomas Mann.**
> Das ist eine Komposition **von Beethoven.**

9. zu *to*

a. direction, goal (cf. §6)

> Ich gehe **zum Arzt.** *I am going to the doctor.*
>   (zu dem)
> Sie geht **zum Briefkasten.** *She's going to the mail box.*
> Wir gehen **zur Bushaltestelle.** *We are going to the bus stop.*
>   (zu der)

b. attitude

> Er ist sehr nett **zu mir.** *He is very nice to me.*

c. idiomatic expressions:

> **(keine) Lust haben zu** (*not*) *to be in the mood to* ...
>   (*not*) *to feel like* ...
>
> Ich habe (keine) Lust **zur Arbeit.** *I am (not) in the mood to work.*
>   (zu der)   *I (don't) feel like working.*

zu Fuß gehen *to go on foot, walk*
zu Hause *at home*

Remember:

The following prepositions may be contracted with the definite article:

bei dem	= **beim**	Ich war **beim Arzt.**
von dem	= **vom**	Ich komme **vom Arzt.**
zu dem	= **zum**	Ich gehe **zum Arzt.**
zu der	= **zur**	Ich gehe **zur Bushaltestelle.**

PRACTICE 1   A. *Complete the following sentences with the German equivalents of the English words in parentheses.*

1. _____ Sonntag habe ich Zahnschmerzen. (since)
2. Frank hat schon _____ Woche Zahnschmerzen. (for a)
3. Er geht heute _____ Zahnarzt. (to the [contract])
4. Ich war gestern _____ Zahnarzt. (at the [contract])
5. Gehst du _____ U-Bahn?[1] (to the [contract])
6. Ich fahre _____ Freundin. (to my)
7. Haben Sie _____ Dekan gesprochen? (with the)
8. Wohnt Margot noch _____ Großeltern? (with her)
9. Hast du den Anzug _____ Neckermann gekauft? (at)
10. Meine Mutter arbeitet _____ Firma in Frankfurt. (at a)
11. Diese Uhr ist ein Geschenk _____ Eltern. (from my)
12. Das ist eine Oper _____ Verdi. (by)
13. _____ Freund Mathias haben alle getanzt. (except for my)
14. _____ Aktentasche[2] haben mir meine Eltern auch eine Brieftasche[3] geschenkt. (besides a)
15. Hast du Lust _____ Spaziergang?[4] (for a)
16. _____ Kälte gehe ich nicht gern spazieren. (in this)
17. Barbara ist nicht Amerikanerin. Sie kommt _____ Österreich. (from)
18. Diese Figur ist _____ Holz. (made of)
19. Wann fliegen Sie _____ München? (to)
20. _____ Deutschstunde gehe ich in die Sporthalle.[5] (after the)
21. Anita und Jörg kommen gerade _____ Sporthalle. (out of the)
22. Martins Eltern wohnen in einem Dorf _____ Heidelberg. (near)
23. _____ Augen, _____ Sinn.[6] (out of the; out of the)

B. *Complete the sentences, using German equivalents of the prepositional phrases in parentheses.*

1. Warum sprichst du nicht _____ ? (with me, with him, with her, with your girlfriend)
2. Dieses Paket ist _____ . (from my brother, from my sister, from my grandparents)
3. Schmidts sind sehr freundlich _____ . (to me, to their neighbors)
4. Das war sehr nett _____ . (of you [fam. sing., pl., formal])

1 **die U-Bahn, -en**	subway
short for: **die Untergrundbahn**	
2 **die Aktentasche, -n**	briefcase
3 **die Brieftasche, -n**	wallet
4 **der Spaziergang, ¨e**	walk
5 **die Sporthalle, -n**	gymnasium
6 **der Sinn**	sense, mind
	Here used in a German proverb which corresponds to English "Out of sight, out of mind."

5. Wir fliegen morgen _____ . (to England, to Switzerland)
6. Ich habe _____ gesessen. (across from him, across from her, across from them)
7. Das Postamt ist _____ . (across from the department store[1])
8. _____ gehen wir nicht einkaufen.[2] (in this rain)
9. Sind diese Schuhe _____ ? (made of leather[3])
10. _____ war niemand zu Hause. (except for the dog)
11. _____ haben alle die Prüfung bestanden. (except for him and her)
12. _____ sind wir in die Disko gegangen. (after the concert)
13. Wir sind _____ gefahren. (by train to Bremen)
14. _____ habe ich Sie nicht angerufen. (for this/that reason)
15. _____ haben Sie einen großen Fehler gemacht. (in my opinion)
16. Wir können _____ in die Stadt gehen. (on foot)
17. Haben Sie den Mantel _____ gekauft? (at Stern's)
18. _____ ist es gefährlich[4] zu fliegen. (in this weather)
19. Hannelore ist _____ krank. (since Wednesday)
20. Ich lerne schon _____ Deutsch. (for a year)
21. Was machst du _____ ? (after this class[5])

§2   PREPOSITIONS THAT GOVERN THE ACCUSATIVE CASE

1. bis

a. *till, until, by* (time)

Ich bin **bis Ende August** in Stuttgart.
I'll be in Stuttgart until the end of August.

Die Arbeit soll **bis nächste Woche** fertig sein.
The work is to be finished by next week.

b. *as far as, to, up to* (location)

Ich fahre nur **bis Köln.**
I'm only going to/as far as Cologne.

Ich habe den Roman **bis Seite 200** gelesen.
I read the novel up to page 200.

Bis is frequently used with a numeral or a place name and then the accusative case of the object is not evident. When **bis** occurs with another preposition, the latter one determines the case of the noun:

Wir haben **bis zur Kaffeepause** auf Sie gewartet.
We waited for you until coffee break.

Wir sind **bis zu einem** Dorf bei Stuttgart gefahren.
We went as far as a village near Stuttgart.

1 **das Warenhaus, ¨-er**	department store
2 **einkaufen gehen**	to go shopping
3 **das Leder**	leather
4 **gefährlich**	dangerous
5 **die Stunde, -n**	class (*instruction*)

2. **durch** *through*

Wir sind **durch die Stadt** gelaufen.
We walked through the town.

Ich habe den Job **durch einen Freund** bekommen.
I got the job through a friend.

3. **entlang** *along*

Wir fuhren **die Straße entlang.**
We were driving along the street.

Entlang generally follows its noun object. Occasionally it precedes; it then governs the dative case:

Entlang der Straße standen viele Zuschauer.
Many onlookers were standing along the street.

4. **für** *for*

Hier ist ein Brief **für dich.**
Here is a letter for you.

5. **gegen** *against*
a. denoting opposition, adversity

Die ganze Welt ist **gegen mich.**
The whole world is against me.

Haben Sie etwas **gegen mich?**
Do you have something against me?

b. denoting impact

Ich bin **gegen einen Baum gefahren.**
I ran/crashed into a tree.

6. **ohne** *without*

Ich kann nicht **ohne dich** leben.
I can't live without you.

7. **um** *around*

Wir sind **um den See (herum)** gefahren.
We drove around the lake.

The adverb **herum** is frequently added.

The following prepositions may be contracted with **das:**

durch das	= **durchs**	Der Dieb ist **durchs Feld** gelaufen.
für das	= **fürs**	Diese Milch ist **fürs Baby.**
um das	= **ums**	Der Hund ist **ums Haus** gerannt.

PRACTICE 2   A. *Complete the following sentences.*

1. Man macht viel Reklame[1] _____ Zigaretten. (*for these*)
2. Ich bin _____ Vorschlag. (*against this*)
3. Herr Helbig kann nicht _____ Briefmarken leben. (*without his*)
4. Wir sind _____ Marktplatz[2] gefahren. (*around the*)
5. Ich bin _____ Ende Juli in der Schweiz geblieben. (*until*)
6. Wir sind nur _____ München gefahren. (*as far as*)
7. Ich habe die Stelle _____ Dekan bekommen. (*through the*)

B. *Complete the sentences with the German equivalents of the prepositional phrases in parentheses.*

1. Warum sind alle _____ ? (*against me, against us, against him, against her*)
2. Sind Sie _____ ? (*for or against this suggestion*)
3. Das ist ein Geschenk _____ . (*for my girlfriend, for my boyfriend, for him, for her, for you* [*fam. sing., formal*])
4. Wir haben einen Bummel[3] _____ gemacht. (*through the village* [*contract*])
5. Ich kann nicht _____ leben. (*without my husband, without my wife*)
6. Möchten Sie eine Reise _____ machen? (*around the world*[4])
7. Wir sind _____ gelaufen. (*along the river*[5])
8. Sind Sie wirklich _____ gefahren? (*into a tree*)

§3   PREPOSITIONS THAT GOVERN BOTH THE DATIVE AND THE ACCUSATIVE

Some prepositions govern the dative or accusative, depending on meaning. The following rules will help you determine the appropriate case.

a. **Motion to a place:** The preposition governs **the accusative.**

Peter und Linda gehen **in den** Park.
(*into/to the*)

1 **die Reklame, -n**	advertising, advertisement
Reklame machen	to advertise
2 **der Marktplatz, ⸚e**	city square, marketplace
3 **der Bummel, -**	stroll
einen Bummel machen	to go for *or* take a stroll
4 **die Welt, -en**	world
5 **der Fluß, ⸚sse**	river

Answers the question: **Wohin** gehen Peter und Linda?
or: **Wo** gehen Peter und Linda **hin**?

Wohin or **wo … hin** are used in the sense of **where to** … asking for the direction of a motion.

b. **Being in a place:** The preposition governs **the dative.**

Peter und Linda sind **im** Park.
(in dem)

Answers the question: **Wo** sind Peter und Linda? (*where/in what place?*)

c. **Motion at or within a place:** The preposition governs **the dative.**

Peter und Linda laufen **im** Park herum.
Peter and Linda are walking around in the park.

Sie gehen **im** Park spazieren.
They are taking a walk in the park.

Answers the questions: **Wo** laufen Peter und Linda herum?
Wo gehen sie spazieren?

Remember:

> **Accusative:**
>
> motion to a place
> answering **wohin** (*where to*) questions
>
> **Dative:**
>
> being somewhere or motion within a place
> answering **wo** (*where/in what place*) questions

PRACTICE 3   *Complete the answers using the preposition* **in** *with the dative or accusative.*

1. X: Ist Werner in der Schule?
   Y: Nein, aber er geht jetzt _____. (*to school*)

2. X: Ist Inge in der Buchhandlung?
   Y: Nein, aber sie geht jetzt _____ . (*to the bookstore*)
3. X: Warum gehst du so oft in die Bibliothek?
   Y: Ich arbeite doch _____ . (*in the library*)
4. X: Gehst du jetzt in die Deutschstunde?
   Y: Nein, aber ich war heute morgen _____ . (*in the German class*)
5. X: Ist Professor Schiller jetzt in seinem Büro? (*neut.*)
   Y: Nein, aber ich glaube, er geht jetzt _____ . (*to his office*)
6. X: Sind Astrid und Dietmar in der Disko?
   Y: Nein, aber ich glaube, die zwei wollen _____ gehen. (*to the disco*)
7. X: Was habt ihr in diesem Warenhaus gekauft?
   Y: Nichts. Wir sind nur _____ herumgelaufen. (*in this department store*)

The following prepositions use the dative or the accusative case, depending on meaning. They are often called *two-way prepositions.*

Accusative	**Dative**
wohin? (*where to?*)	**wo?** (*where? in what place?*)

1. an

a. **an** *on* (vertical surface)

Ich hänge das Bild **an die** Wand.	Jetzt hängt das Bild **an der** Wand.
I am hanging the picture on the wall.	*Now the picture is hanging on the wall.*

b. **an** (*to go*) *to* or (*to be*) *at* (something)

Ich gehe **ans** Fenster.	Jetzt stehe ich **am** Fenster.
(an das)	(an dem)
I am going to the window.	*Now I am standing at the window.*
Der Kellner kommt **an den** Tisch.	Jetzt steht er **am** Tisch.
The waiter is coming to the table.	*Now he is standing at the table.*
Ich gehe **an die** Straßenecke.	Jetzt stehe ich **an der** Straßenecke.
I am going to the street corner.	*Now I am standing at the street corner.*
Wir fahren **an den** Rhein.	Jetzt sind wir **am** Rhein.
We are going to the Rhine.	*Now we are at the Rhine.*

2. auf

a. **auf** *on* (horizontal surface)

Ich stelle die Lampe **auf den** Tisch.	Die Lampe steht **auf dem** Tisch.
I am putting the lamp on the table.	*The lamp is standing on the table.*

b. **auf** *to*, *in*, and *at*

Ich gehe **auf den** Fußballplatz.	Jetzt bin ich **auf dem** Fußballplatz.
I am going to the soccer field.	*Now I am on the soccer field.*
auf den Marktplatz.	**auf dem** Marktplatz.
to the city square.	*on the city square.*

auf den Bahnhof.
to the railway station.

auf dem Bahnhof.
at/in the railway station.

aufs Postamt.
(auf das)
to the post office.

auf dem Postamt.
at/in the post office.

3. **hinter** behind

Ich habe den Mülleimer **hinter die** Garage gestellt.
I put the garbage can behind the garage.

Der Mülleimer steht **hinter der** Garage.

The garbage can is standing behind the garage.

4. **in** in, into, to

Wir gehen **ins** Auditorium.
        (in das)
We are going to the auditorium.

Jetzt sind wir **im** Auditorium.

Now we are in the auditorium.

5. **neben** next to, beside

Ich habe die Schlüssel **neben die** Brille gelegt.
I laid the keys next to the glasses.

Die Schlüssel liegen **neben der** Brille.

The keys are lying next to the glasses.

6. **über** above, over, across

Heute sind viele Flugzeuge **über die** Stadt geflogen.
Today many planes flew over the city.

Jetzt kreist ein Flugzeug **über der** Stadt.

Now a plane is circling over the city.

7. **unter** under

Bitte stellen Sie den Papierkorb **unter den** Schreibtisch!
Please put the waste basket under the desk.

Der Papierkorb steht **unter dem** Schreibtisch.
The waste basket is standing under the desk.

8. **vor** in front of, before

Ich habe das Fahrrad **vor die** Tür gestellt.
I put the bicycle in front of the door.

Das Fahrrad steht **vor der** Tür.

The bicycle is standing in front of the door.

9. **zwischen** between

Ich habe das Buchzeichen **zwischen die** Seiten 10 und 11 gelegt.
I put the bookmark between pages 10 and 11.

Das Buchzeichen liegt aber nicht mehr **zwischen den** Seiten 10 und 11.
But the bookmark isn't between pages 10 and 11 anymore.

Note that *parking, landing,* and *arriving* are done within an area. Thus two-way prepositions used with the verbs **parken, landen,** and **an•kommen** require the dative.

Ich habe den Wagen auf **dem** Marktplatz geparkt.
I parked the car on the town square.

Das Privatflugzeug kann nicht auf **diesem** Flugplatz landen.
The private plane cannot land on this *airfield.*

Wir sind um 10 Uhr in **der** Schweiz angekommen.
We arrived in Switzerland at 10 o'clock.

Contractions of two-way prepositions with the definite article:

DATIVE	ACCUSATIVE
an dem = **am**	an das = **ans**
in dem = **im**	auf das = **aufs**
	in das = **ins**

PRACTICE 4   A. *Insert the dative or accusative of the words in parentheses.*

1. Helga hat den Wagen hinter _____ geparkt. (das Studentenheim)
2. Wir sind um 3 Uhr in _____ angekommen. (das Hotel Excelsior)
3. Mein Mantel liegt auf _____. (das Bett)
4. Wer hat meinen Mantel auf _____ gelegt? (das Bett [contract])
5. Deine Brille liegt auf _____. (der Tisch)
6. Du hast deine Brille auf _____ gelegt. (der Tisch)
7. Frau Schubert hat mit uns an _____ gesessen. (der Tisch [contract])
8. Bitte stellen Sie den Sessel[1] in _____! (die Ecke)
9. Wer sitzt dort in _____? (die Ecke)
10. An _____ ist ein Zeitungsstand.[2] (die Ecke)
11. Mein Mantel hängt da drüben an _____. (der Haken[3] [contract])
12. Wollen Sie Ihre Jacke an _____ hängen? (der Haken)
13. Was liegt dort unter _____? (der Tisch)
14. Meine Serviette ist unter _____ gefallen. (der Tisch)
15. Das neue Restaurant ist zwischen _____. (eine Bäckerei und eine Fleischerei)
16. Wir können hier nicht über _____ gehen. (die Straße)
17. Wir haben eine kleine Wohnung über _____. (eine Buchhandlung)
18. Siehst du nicht, daß deine Handschuhe auf _____ liegen? (der Boden[4])

1 **der Sessel, -**   armchair
2 **der Zeitungsstand, ¨e** newsstand
3 **der Haken, -**   hook
4 **der Boden, ¨**   floor

19. Warum stehen so viele Studenten vor _____ ? (die Sporthalle)
20. Ich habe vor _____ gesessen. (er und seine Freundin)
21. Helga hat hinter _____ gestanden. (mein Freund und ich)
22. Warum gehst du nicht an _____ ? (das Telefon[1] [contract])
23. Marlene hängt die ganze Zeit an _____ . (das Telefon [contract])
24. Ein Spatz in _____ ist besser als eine Taube auf _____ *. (die Hand, das Dach)

B. *Insert German equivalents of the English prepositional phrases in parentheses.*

1. X: Warum hast du den Wagen nicht _____ gefahren? *(into the garage)*
    Y: _____ ist kein Platz mehr. *(in the garage)*
2. X: Was liegt da _____ ? *(under the table)*
    Y: Das ist eine Notiz. Sie ist _____ gefallen. *(under the table)*
3. X: Warum haben Sie den Sessel _____ gestellt? *(in this corner)*
    Y: Ich sitze gern _____ . *(in this corner)*
4. a. X: Wie heißt das Restaurant da _____ ? *(on the corner)*
    Y: Meinen Sie das Restaurant _____ ? *(next to the newsstand)*
   b. X: Nein. Ich meine das Restaurant _____ . *(between the bank and the hotel Excelsior)*
    Y: Es heißt „Goldner Schwan". _____ ißt man sehr gut.[2] *(in this restaurant)*
5. X: Wo sitzt Helga?
    Y: Dort _____ Rainer. *(next to)* Siehst du sie nicht? Renate sitzt _____ *(in front of her)*, und Barbara und Frank sitzen _____ . *(behind her)*
6. X: Ist Klaus _____ ? *(on the soccer field)*
    Y: Nein. Er sitzt mit Renate da _____ . *(at the table [contract])*
7. X: Bitte stellen Sie die Lampe _____ ! *(on the table)*
    Y: Sie steht doch schon _____ . *(on the table)*
8. X: Warum legst du die Mappen[3] _____ ? *(on the floor)*
    Y: Ich habe nicht genug Platz _____ . *(on my desk)*
9. X: Wo ist deine Semesterarbeit?
    Y: _____ . *(in this folder)*

---

1 **ans Telefon gehen**   to go to *or* answer the phone
2 **Dort ißt man gut.**   *idiomatic:* The food is good there.
3 **die Mappe, -n**   folder

* Proverb – *literal:* "A sparrow in the hand is better than a dove on the roof." *idiomatic:* "A bird in the hand is worth two in the bush."

10.   X: Geht ihr _____, oder wart ihr _____? (to the movies [contract]; at the movies [contract])
      Y: Wir waren _____ und gehen jetzt _____. (in the dormitory [contract]; to the auditorium [contract])
11.   X: Wie lange willst du noch _____ bleiben? (on the tennis court)
      Y: Nicht mehr lange. Um 3 Uhr gehe ich _____. (to the library)
12.   X: Hängt dein Mantel _____? (on the hook [contract])
      Y: Nein, ich habe ihn _____ gelegt. (on the bed [contract])
13.   X: Rainer hängt schon wieder _____. (on the phone [contract])
      Y: Du weißt doch, er hat die Telefonitis.

§4   PREPOSITIONS THAT GOVERN THE GENITIVE CASE

1. anstatt, statt instead of

Anstatt des Wagens hat er das Motorrad repariert.
or: **Statt des Wagens ...**
Instead of the car he repaired the motorcycle.

Nouns immediately following the preposition have no genitive ending:

Statt Fisch haben wir Sauerkrat mit Bratwurst gegessen.
Instead of fish we ate sauerkraut with bratwurst (fried sausage)

Statt Dieter habe ich Frank eingeladen.
Instead of Dieter I invited Frank.

2. trotz in spite of

Trotz des Gewitters sind wir in die Stadt gefahren.
In spite of the thunderstorm we went downtown.

3. während during

Während des Vortrags habe ich die Zeitung gelesen.
During the address I read the newspaper.

4. wegen because of

Wegen meiner Eltern haben wir die Reise verschoben.
Because of my parents we postponed the trip.

In elevated speech, **wegen** sometimes follows the noun:

Meiner Eltern wegen haben wir die Reise verschoben.

When used with pronouns, two forms are possible:

combination of genitive + **wegen**	**wegen** + dat.	
meinetwegen	wegen mir	*because of me, for my sake*
deinetwegen	wegen dir	*because of you, for your sake*
seinetwegen	wegen ihm	*because of him, for his sake*
ihretwegen	wegen ihr	*because of her, for her sake*
seinetwegen	wegen ihm	*because of it, for its sake*
unsretwegen or: unsertwegen	wegen uns	*because of us, for our sake*
euretwegen or: euertwegen	wegen euch	*because of you, for your sake*
ihretwegen	wegen ihnen	*because of them, for their sake*
Ihretwegen	wegen Ihnen	*because of you, for your sake*

Idiomatic expression:

meinetwegen *for all I care, as far as I am concerned*
Meinetwegen kannst du machen, was du willst.
For all I care, you can do what you want.

Colloquially, prepositions that normally govern the genitive are often used with the dative:

statt **dem** Wagen, während **dem** Vortrag, wegen **meinen** Eltern

PRACTICE 5   *Insert German equivalents.*

1. _____ sind wir zu Hause geblieben. (*because of the weather*)
2. Ich bin _____ nicht mitgefahren. (*because of him* [two forms])
3. Er hat das nur _____ getan. (*because of her* [two forms])
4. _____ kann er mitkommen. (*as far as I am concerned*)
5. _____ haben wir keinen Hund mehr. (*because of the neighbors*)
6. _____ mußten wir unseren Hund weggeben. (*because of them* [two forms])
7. Wo waren Sie _____ ? (*during the thunderstorm*)
8. Die Leute haben _____ viel geschrien.[1] (*during the soccer game*[2])
9. _____ haben wir einen kleinen Spaziergang gemacht. (*in spite of the rain*)
10. _____ habe ich ihm eine Brieftasche geschenkt. (*instead of a briefcase*)
11. _____ hat sie Italienisch gelernt. (*instead of Spanish*)
12. Der Kellner hat uns Tee _____ gebracht. (*instead of coffee*)

1 **schreien, schrie, geschrie(e)n**   to scream
2 **das Fußballspiel, -e**   soccer game

§5   SUMMARY OF COMMON PREPOSITIONS AND THEIR BASIC MEANINGS

Dative	*Accusative*	*Dative or Accusative*	*Genitive*
aus *out of, from*	**bis** *until,*	**an** *on (vertically), by,*	**anstatt** } *instead*
außer *except,*	*to, as*	*at the edge of*	**statt** }
besides	*far as*	**auf** *on (horizontally)*	**trotz** *in spite of*
bei *at, near,*	**durch** *through*	**hinter** *behind*	**während** *during*
at someone's	**entlang** *along*	**in** *in, into, to*	**wegen** *because of*
place	**für** *for*	**neben** *next to, beside*	
gegenüber *across from*	**gegen** *against*	**über** *above, over, across*	
mit *with, by*	**ohne** *without*	**unter** *under*	
nach *after, to,*	**um** *around*	**vor** *in front of, before*	
according to		**zwischen** *between*	
seit *since*			
von *from, of, by*			
zu *to, toward*			

Use the **accusative** when the verb denotes **motion toward a place** (answering the question "**where to?**").

Use the **dative** when the verb denotes either **position in a place or motion within a place** (answering the questions "**where?**" "**in what place?**").

Common contractions of the preposition with the definite article:

> preposition + **das** = **ans, aufs, durchs, fürs, ins, ums**
> preposition + **dem** = **am, beim, im, vom, zum**
> preposition + **der** = **zur**

Contractions are not used
a. when the article is stressed:

> Wir gehen ins Kino. but: In **das** Kino gehen wir nicht wieder.
> *We won't go to **that** movie again.*

b. when the noun is modified:

> Wir gehen in das kleine Kino da drüben. *We are going to the little moviehouse over there.*

§6   THE GERMAN COUNTERPARTS OF *to* WITH VERBS OF MOTION

Various German prepositions correspond to English *to* with verbs of motion.

1. *to* = **nach**
   This is the normal preposition used with names of towns, cities, regions, countries, or continents. It is not used when the name is accompanied by the article.

Wir fahren   **nach Bettendorf.**
              nach Frankfurt.
              nach England.
              nach Europa.
but: Wir fahren   **in die Schweiz.**
                   in die Vereinigten Staaten.

2. *to =* **zu**
This is the most generally acceptable word, and the only one possible if the object is a person.
a. Going to a person's home or business:

Ich gehe **zum Arzt.**
Er fährt **zu seiner Schwester.**
Wir gehen **zu Neumanns.**

b. Used with names of stores:

Wir gehen **zu Hertie.**

c. Going to places other than cities, regions, countries:

Sie geht **zum Briefkasten.**
Ich gehe **zur Bushaltestelle.**
Wir fahren **zum Flughafen.**

3. In many instances **in, auf,** or **an** with the accusative either may or must be used. This is especially true for public buildings and events in them.

a. *to =* **in** meaning *into a place, into a building:*

Wir gehen **in die Stadt.**	*We are going to town, downtown, uptown.*
in die Vorlesung.	*to the lecture.*
in die Deutschstunde.	*to the German class.*
ins Kino.	*to the movies.*
ins Konzert.	*to the concert.*
ins Theater.	*to the theater.*

b. *to =* **auf** meaning *onto a surface, base of operation:*

Wir gehen **auf den Fußballplatz.**	*We are going to the football field.*
auf den Tennisplatz.	*to the tennis court.*
auf den Marktplatz.	*to the town square.*

idiomatic:

Wir gehen **auf die Bank.**	*We are going to the bank.*
or: **zur Bank.**	
Wir gehen **aufs Postamt.**	*to the post office.*
or: **zum Postamt.**	
Wir gehen **auf den Bahnhof.**	*to the railway station.*
or: **zum Bahnhof.**	
Wir gehen **auf eine Party.**	*to a party.*
or: **zu einer Party.**	

c. *to* = **an** meaning *up to, to the edge of*:

Ich gehe **ans Fenster.**	*I am going to the window.*
an den Tisch.	*to the table.*
an die Tafel.	*to the (black)board.*
an die Wandtafel.	

PRACTICE 6   *Insert German equivalents.*

1. Gehst du heute _____ Vorlesung?
   (*to the*)

2. Sie fährt _____ Freundin.
   (*to her*)

3. Er ging _____ Fenster.
   (*to the*)

4. Wollen Sie ___ Bergmanns gehen?
   (*to*)

5. Bitte gehen Sie _____ Tafel!
   (*to the*)

6. Gehen Sie heute _____ Bank? (two ways)
   (*to the*)

7. Wann fahren Sie ___ Heidelberg?
   (*to*)

8. Der Kellner kam _____ Tisch.
   (*to our*)

9. Gehen Sie _____ Briefkasten?
   (*to the*)

10. Am Wochenende fahre ich _____ Freundin.
    (*to my*)

11. Wollen Sie _____ Postamt gehen? (two ways)
    (*to the*)

12. Käte fährt _____ Flughafen (*masc.*).
    (*to the*)

13. Gehst du _____ Party bei Schneiders? (two ways)
    (*to the*)

14. Vielleicht gehen wir heute abend _____ Theater.
    (*to the*)

15. Wir bringen dich _____ Bushaltestelle.
    (*to the*)

PRACTICE 7   Summarizing exercises

A. *Insert German equivalents.*

1. X: Ist Maria _____ gefahren? (*home*)
    Y: Ja. Sie ist wahrscheinlich schon _____. (*at home*)

2. X: Wohnst du _____ ? (*with your parents*)

    Y: Meine Eltern sind geschieden.[1] Ich wohne _____, und meine Schwester wohnt _____. (*with my father, with my mother*)

3. X: Warst du gestern _____ ? (*at the Bergers'*)

    Y: Ja. Ich gehe oft _____. (*to the Bergers*) Sie sind immer sehr nett _____. (*to me*)

4. X: Wer hat deinen Koffer _____ getragen? (*to the bus stop*)

    Y: Peter. Das war sehr nett _____. (*of him*)

5. X: Hast du diese Brieftasche _____ bekommen? (*from your girlfriend*)

    Y: Nein. Das ist ein Geschenk _____. (*from my parents*)

6. X: Hast du diesen Roman _____ gelesen? (*by Thomas Mann*)

    Y: Nein, aber ich möchte einen Roman _____ lesen. (*by him*)

7. X: Die ganze Stadt war _____. (*on the soccer field*)

    Y: Die ganze Stadt _____. (*except me*)

8. X: Bist du _____ mitgekommen? (*because of your girlfriend*)

    Y: Ja, nur _____. (*because of her* [two forms])

9. X: Hast du Karin _____ kennengelernt? (*through your brother*)

    Y: Nein, ich habe sie _____ kennengelernt. (*through a friend* [*masc., fem.*])

10. X: Wann gehst du _____ ? (*to the dentist*)

    Y: Ich war doch schon _____. (*at the dentist's*)

11. X: Wohnen Andreas und Frank auch _____ ? (*in this dormitory*)

    Y: Ja. Andreas wohnt _____, und Frank wohnt _____. (*above me, below me*)

12. X: Seid ihr _____ gefahren? (*to Düsseldorf*)

    Y: Nein. Wir sind nur _____ gefahren. (*as far as Bonn*)

13. X: Was hast du _____ ? (*against my friend* [*masc.*])

    Y: Ich habe nichts _____. (*against him*)

14. X: Was habt ihr _____ gekauft? (*in the town*)

    Y: Nichts. Wir haben nur einen Bummel _____ gemacht. (*through the town*)

15. X: Wollen Sie allein _____ fliegen? (*to Alaska*)

    Y: Natürlich nicht. Ich fliege _____. (*with my wife but perhaps without our son*)

16. X: Margot studiert schon _____ in Bonn. (*for a year*)

    Y: Ja. Leider schreibt sie mir nicht mehr. _____. ("*Out of sight, out of mind.*")

17. X: Ich verstehe nicht, warum Müllers den Vertrag so schnell unterschrieben haben.

---

1 **geschieden sein**   to be divorced

Y: Vielleicht haben sie gedacht:

_____.

("*A bird in the hand is worth two in the bush.*")˙

18.   X: _____ gehen wir nicht spazieren. (*in this weather*)

Y: Und wir sind _____ spazierengegangen. (*in spite of the weather*)

19.   X: _____ bin ich ein Dummkopf. (*in his opinion*)

Y: Und _____ bist du ein Schlaukopf.[1] (*in my opinion*)

20. a. X: Ihr Mann hat eine wunderbare Briefmarkensammlung.

Y: Das stimmt.[2] Er kann nicht _____ leben. (*without his stamp collection*)

b. X: Sagen wir,[3] er kann nicht _____ leben. (*without you and his stamp collection*)

Y: Hoffentlich in dieser Reihenfolge![4]

B. *Using the cues, form sentences that fit the context. Express them in the present tense except where otherwise indicated.*

Model: Karin fliegt heute nachmittag nach Berlin.

Martin / bringen / Flughafen

Martin bringt sie zum Flughafen.

1.   Werner Seifert wohnt nicht im Studentenheim.

er / wohnen / Eltern

2.   Ich sehe zuviel fern.

ich / können / leben / nicht / ohne Fernseher

3.   Ich habe lange meine Semesterarbeit gesucht. Endlich (*finally*) habe ich sie gefunden.

sie / sein / Mappe / Schreibtisch (*past*)

4.   Mein Bruder hat morgen Geburtstag.

heute nachmittag / ich / fahren / Stadt / / ich / wollen / kaufen / Geschenk / für / Bruder

5.   Ich bin müde und gähne die ganze Zeit.

gestern abend / ich / sein / Party (*past*) / / heute abend / ich / gehen / wieder / Party

6.   Unsere Nachbarn sind reich.

sie / machen / Reise / um Welt

7. a. Ich frage Klaus, wo Maria ist. Er antwortet:

„ vielleicht / sie / sein / Tennisplatz "

1	**der Schlaukopf, ̈e** (*male or female*)	whizz kid, smarty
2	**stimmen**	to be correct
3	**Sagen wir ...**	Let's say ...
4	**die Reihenfolge, -n**	order, sequence

    b. Dann sagt er:

       „Das stimmt nicht. sie / gehen / mit / Freund / Fußballplatz "
       (pres. perf.)

8. a. Ich frage Sabine, wo sie gestern abend war. Sie antwortet:

       „ich /sein / mit / Freund Andreas / Konzert " (past)

    b. Ich frage sie, wie ihr das Konzert gefallen hat. Sie antwortet:

       „Meinung nach / das Konzert / sein / nicht sehr gut " (past)

8

Verbs and Adjectives Used with Prepositions; *da*-Compounds; Interrogatives *wer* and *was*

KEY TO EXERCISES ON CASSETTE 4.
RUNNING TIME: APPROX. 20 MIN.

Verbs and Adjectives Used with Prepositions

§1 VERBS USED WITH PREPOSITIONS

Many verbs complete their meanings with prepositional phrases. Some common ones are listed below.

1. **Verbs with dative prepositions**

gratulieren **zu**	*to congratulate on*
handeln **von**	*to deal with, be about*
sprechen **mit**	*to talk with* or *to*
(spricht), sprach, gesprochen	
sprechen **von**	*to talk of* or *about*

2. **Verbs with accusative prepositions**

bitten **um,**	*to ask for, to request*
bat, gebeten	
danken **für**	*to thank for*

3. **Verbs with two-way prepositions**

antworten **auf** + *acc.*	*to answer something*
arbeiten **an** + *dat.*	*to work on*
denken **an** + *acc.*	*to think of* or *about*

lachen **über** + *acc.*   *to laugh at or about*
reagieren **auf** + *acc.*   *to react to*
warten **auf** + *acc.*   *to wait for*

Note that in these combinations the rules governing the use of the dative and the accusative with two-way prepositions do not apply, and the case for each must be learned individually. Most such constructions use the accusative.

PRACTICE 1   A. *Change the boldface prepositional phrases, using the dative or accusative of the words in parentheses.*

Model: Hast du ihm **zum Geburtstag** gratuliert? (sein Erfolg)
          Hast du ihm zu seinem Erfolg gratuliert?

1. Er hat noch nicht **auf meinen Brief** geantwortet. (meine Frage)
2. Arbeitest du noch **an deinem Referat?**[1] (der Aufsatz)
3. Haben Sie **mit der Chefin** gesprochen? (der Chef)
4. Eva hat nie **von ihrem Vater** gesprochen. (ihre Zukunftspläne[2])
5. Ich habe gerade **an meine Freundin** gedacht. (mein Freund)
6. Ich habe ihm noch nicht **für seinen Brief** gedankt. (sein Paket)
7. Der Film handelt **von der Französischen Revolution.** (ein Erfinder)
8. Ich habe den Chef **um Erlaubnis** gebeten. (eine Gehaltserhöhung[3])
9. Klaus hat nicht **über meinen Witz** gelacht. (sein Bruder)
10. Ich habe ihnen **zur Verlobung**[4] gratuliert. (die Hochzeit)
11. Wartest du **auf deine Freundin?** (der Bus)
12. Wie hat der Dekan **auf Ihren Brief** reagiert? (der Protest)

B. *Express the responses in German. (Use the pres. perf. for the English past tense.)*

Model: Denkst du oft an deinen Freund in Berlin?
      I think of him very often.
      Ich denke sehr oft an ihn.

1.   X: Arbeiten Sie noch an diesem Projekt?
      Y: No, I'm working on a seminar paper.
2.   X: Hast du schon mit Herrn Köhler gesprochen?
      Y: I talked with his wife but not with him.
3.   X: Haben Sie den Chef um Erlaubnis gebeten?
      Y: Of course I asked him for permission.
4.   X: Hast du Herrn Baumann für seine Hilfe gedankt?
      Y: Not yet, but I thanked Mrs. Baumann for her help.
5.   X: Wie hat Frau Klinger auf Ihren Vorschlag reagiert?
      Y: Unfortunately she has not yet reacted to my suggestion.
6.   X: Handelt dieser Roman vom Krieg?
      Y: No, it deals with a family in Alaska.

---

1 **das Referat, -e**   seminar paper (*oral presentation*)
2 **der Zukunftsplan, ̈e**   plan for the future
3 **die Gehaltserhöhung, -en** salary raise
4 **die Verlobung, -en**   engagement

7. X: Warum antwortest du nicht auf meine Frage?
    Y: Because you have not yet answered my question.
8. X: Hast du meiner Freundin zu ihrem Erfolg gratuliert?
    Y: Not yet, but I congratulated her brother on his success.
9. X: Wartest du auf Post von zu Hause?
    Y: I'm waiting for a letter with a check from home.
10. X: Du hörst nicht zu. Denkst du schon wieder an das Fußballspiel?
    Y: No, I'm thinking of my girlfriend.
11. a. X: Warum lachst du über mich?
       Y: I'm not laughing at you. I'm laughing at a joke.
    b. X: Und dieser Witz bin ich?
       Y: Of course not, my darling.[1]

§2   ADJECTIVES USED WITH PREPOSITIONS

The following frequently used adjectives complete their meanings with prepositional phrases:

begeistert sein **von** + dat.	to be enthusiastic about
böse sein **auf** + acc.	to be angry with
or: **mit** + dat.	
froh sein **über** + acc.	to be glad about
glücklich sein **über** + acc.	to be happy about
stolz sein **auf** + acc.	to be proud of
verliebt sein **in** + acc.	to be in love with
verlobt sein **mit** + dat.	to be engaged to
verheiratet sein **mit** + dat.	to be married to
verrückt sein **auf** + acc.	to be crazy about
verwandt sein **mit** + dat.	to be related to
zufrieden sein **mit** + dat.	to be satisfied, content with

Example:

Ich bin **von diesem Film** begeistert.
or: Ich bin begeistert **von diesem Film.**

> *I am enthusiastic about this film.*

Begeistert functions as a predicate adjective (following the verb **sein**; cf. Chap. 1, §7). Predicate adjectives may precede or follow prepositional phrases.

PRACTICE 2   *Translate the responses into German.*

1. X: Alle sind verrückt auf diesen Popstar.
   Y: I'm not crazy about him.
2. X: Sind Sie froh über diese Nachricht?[2]
   Y: Of course, I'm glad about this news.

---

1 **der Liebling, -e**   darling
  (the same form used for male and female)
2 **die Nachricht, -en**   news

3. X: Sind Sie mit dieser Dame verwandt?
   Y: Yes, I'm related to her. She's my mother.
4. X: Ich bin von Professor Klein begeistert.
   Y: Many students are enthusiastic about him.
5. X: Ist deine Schwester mit Dieter verlobt?
   Y: No, she's not engaged to him.
6. X: Bist du verliebt in Karin?
   Y: I don't know whether I'm in love with her.
7. X: Schuberts sind sehr stolz auf ihre Tochter.
   Y: And we are very proud of our son.
8. X: Meine Eltern sind sehr glücklich über meinen Erfolg.
   Y: We all are very happy about your success. (fam. sing.)
9. X: Ist Rainer mit Marias Schwester verheiratet?
   Y: No, he's not married to her.
10. X: Ich bin mit meinem Schicksal[1] zufrieden.
    Y: Not many people are satisfied with their destiny.
11. X: Ich bin sehr böse auf Manfred.
    Y: Why are you so angry with him? (formal)
12. X: Bist du böse mit Monika?
    Y: Why do you think that I am angry with her?

Using a dictionary

We have treated only a few common verbs and adjectives that complete their meanings with prepositional phrases. There are, of course, many more. A good dictionary will tell you what prepositions and cases are used with those verbs and adjectives.

da-Compounds

§3   *da-* AS PRONOUN SUBSTITUTE

Compare:

a. Haben Sie etwas **gegen Herrn Klein?**	*Do you have something against Mr. Klein?*
Haben Sie etwas **gegen ihn?**	*Do you have something against him?*
b. Haben Sie etwas **gegen den Vorschlag?**	*Do you have something against the suggestion?*
Haben Sie etwas **dagegen?**	*Do you have something against it?*

When referring to living beings, the appropriate dative or accusative pronoun is used as the object of the preposition. When referring to things or concepts, a *da*-compound replaces the preposition plus pronoun: **da-** (**dar-** before vowels) is attached as a prefix to the preposition.

---

1 **das Schicksal, -e**   destiny, fate

Commonly used **da**-compounds:

dabei	**daran**
dadurch	**darauf**
dafür	**daraus**
dagegen	**darin**
damit	**darüber**
danach	**darum**
davon	
davor	
dazu	

Since the **da**- does not change, this construction does not reflect the gender, number (sing. or pl.), or case of the noun it replaces.

Ich weiß nichts **von dieser Sache.**
         von diesen Dingen. } Ich weiß nichts **davon.**
         von seinen Plänen. *I know nothing about it/them.*

Ich habe keine Lust **zur Arbeit.**
         zum Lernen. } Ich habe keine Lust **dazu.**
         zum Kochen. *I'm not in the mood for it.*

Normally the accent is on the preposition: dazú, damít, davón, etc. When the **da**-compound is emphasized, the accent shifts to **da: dázu, dámit, dávon,** etc.

Dázu habe ich keine Lust.
Dávon weiß ich nichts.

The emphasized **da**-compound is generally in first position.

Frequently used expression:

Es kommt darauf an.	*It depends.*
Es kommt ganz darauf an.	*It all depends.*

PRACTICE 3   A. *Substitute* **da***-compounds for the boldface prepositional phrases.*

Model: Klaus hat viele Aufnahmen[1] **von dem Picknick** gemacht.
    Klaus hat viele Aufnahmen davon gemacht.

1. Ich habe viel Geld **für diese Brille** bezahlt.
2. Was machst du **mit diesen Sachen?**
3. Du kannst stolz **auf dein Zeugnis**[2] sein.
4. Ich bitte Sie **um einen Gefallen.**[3]

1 **die Aufnahme, -n**	picture, photograph
Aufnahmen machen	to take pictures
2 **das Zeugnis, -se**	report card
3 **der Gefallen, -**	favor
um einen Gefallen bitten	to ask for a favor

5. Er hat Schwierigkeiten[1] **mit seinem Führerschein.**
6. Ich habe keine Lust **zum Saubermachen.**[2]
7. Hast du Angst **vorm Fliegen?**
8. Die ganze Stadt spricht **von diesem Skandal.**
9. Arbeitest du noch **an dem Projekt?**
10. Barbara ist ganz verrückt **auf diese Schallplatte.**
11. Ich bin sehr froh **über diese Nachricht.**
12. Wer hat dir **bei diesen Hausaufgaben** geholfen?
13. Wie haben Sie **auf seinen Vorschlag** reagiert?
14. **Nach dem Konzert** sind wir in ein Café gegangen.
15. Herr Krause ist neutral: Er ist weder **für diesen Vorschlag** noch[3] **gegen diesen Vorschlag.**

B. *The boldface prepositional phrases refer to persons, things, or concepts. Complete the answers, using either the preposition and a personal pronoun or a* **da**-*compound.*

1. X: Sprecht ihr **von Frau Becker?**
   Y: Nein, wir sprechen nicht _____ .
2. X: Herr Schulze spricht immer nur **von seiner Arbeit.**
   Y: Warum spricht er denn[4] soviel _____ ?
3. X: Bist du **mit deinem Zeugnis** zufrieden?
   Y: Ja, aber meine Eltern sind nicht _____ zufrieden.
4. X: Sind Sie **mit Ihrer neuen Sekretärin** zufrieden?
   Y: Sie ist eine Perle.[5] Ich bin mehr als zufrieden _____ .
5. X: Ist Annerose verliebt in oder verlobt **mit Thomas?**
   Y: Beides,[6] und bald wird sie verheiratet _____ sein.
6. X: Haben Sie Angst **vor Prüfungen?**
   Y: Es kommt darauf an. Manchmal habe ich Angst _____ , und manchmal habe ich keine Angst _____ .
7. X: Hoffentlich hast du heute Lust **zum Saubermachen.**
   Y: _____ habe ich nie Lust.
8. X: Was haben Sie **auf seine Frage** geantwortet?
   Y: Ich weiß nicht mehr, was ich _____ geantwortet habe.
9. X: Frau Helbig ist böse **auf ihre Nachbarin.**
   Y: Weißt du, warum sie böse _____ ist?
10. X: Ich bin stolz **auf meine Note in Chemie.**
    Y: Sie können sehr stolz _____ sein.

1 **die Schwierigkeit, -en**	difficulty
Schwierigkeiten haben mit	to have trouble with
2 **das Saubermachen**	cleaning (generally housecleaning)
3 **weder ... noch**	neither ... nor
4 **denn**	here used as a flavoring particle implying a special interest on the part of the speaker (cf. Appendix, §4)
5 **die Perle, -n**	pearl; here used in the sense of *gem*
6 **beides**	both

11. X: Hat sie dich **um diesen Gefallen** gebeten?
    Y: Sie hat nicht _____ gebeten; sie hat ihn einfach befohlen.[1]
12. X: Niemand hat **über deinen Witz** gelacht.
    Y: Aber ich habe _____ gelacht, und das genügt.[2]

§4 PREPOSITIONS THAT DO NOT FORM *da*-COMPOUNDS

Da-compounds cannot be formed with the following prepositions:

ohne, seit, außer,

and all prepositions governing the genitive case (cf. Chap. 7, §4).

Pronouns or set expressions which convey the idea to be expressed are used instead.

ohne seine Hilfe	*without his help*
ohne sie	*without it*
seit seiner Krankheit	*since his illness*
seitdem	*since then*
außer seinem Geld	*except for or aside from his money*
außerdem	*aside from that, besides*
wegen seines Fleißes	*because of his diligence*
deswegen, deshalb	*because of that, therefore*
trotz meiner Faulheit	*in spite of my laziness*
trotzdem	*in spite of that*
statt eines Erfolgs	*instead of a success*
statt dessen	*instead of that*

PRACTICE 4   *Supply the German equivalents of the phrases in parentheses.*

1. X: Seit der Party bei Köhlers spricht Helga nicht mehr mit Andreas.
   Y: _____ spricht sie auch nicht mehr mit mir. (*since then*)
2. X: Wegen der großen Kälte sind wir am Wochenende nicht weggefahren.
   Y: _____ sind wir auch zu Hause geblieben. (*because of that*)
3. X: Meine Schwester liebt ihren Mann trotz seiner Trunksucht.[3]
   Y: Ich weiß selbst, daß man einen Mann _____ lieben kann. (*in spite of that*)
4. X: Winklers haben ein wunderbares Haus.
   Y: Und _____ haben sie noch ein Wochenendhaus[4] in den Bergen. (*aside from that*)

1 **befehlen (befiehlt), befahl, befohlen**	to order
2 **genügen**	to suffice, be enough
3 **die Trunksucht**	alcoholism
4 **das Wochenendhaus, ¨-er**	(weekend) cottage

5. X: Du wolltest doch ein Motorrad kaufen.

   Y: Ja, das wollte ich. _____ mußte ich armer Mann ein Fahrrad kaufen. (*instead of that*)

6. X: Ich habe deinen Großvater noch nie ohne Pfeife[1] gesehen.

   Y: _____ ist er nervös und unsicher.[2] (*without it*)

§5   ANTICIPATORY *da*-COMPOUNDS

Compare the following three sentences:

> Renate ist stolz **auf ihre Aussprache.**
> Renate ist stolz **darauf.**
> Renate ist stolz **darauf,** daß sie so eine gute Aussprache hat.
>
> *Renate is proud (of the fact) that she has such a good pronunciation.*
> or: *Renate is proud of having such a good pronunciation.*

In the third sentence the **da**-compound anticipates what is expressed in the following clause. It is an *anticipatory* **da**-compound. Depending on the context, the English translation of such a construction either disregards the **da**-compound or uses a prepositional phrase or gerund, as shown above.

PRACTICE 5   *Express the sentences in acceptable English.*

1. Ich habe nicht an deinen Geburtstag gedacht.
   Ich habe nicht daran gedacht.
   Ich habe nicht daran gedacht, daß du heute Geburtstag hast.
2. Wir danken Ihnen für Ihre Hilfe.
   Wir danken Ihnen dafür.
   Wir danken Ihnen dafür, daß Sie uns geholfen haben.
3. Helga spricht nie von ihren Zukunftsplänen.
   Helga spricht nie davon.
   Helga spricht nie davon, welche Zukunftspläne sie hat.
4. Ich bin sehr dankbar dafür, daß Sie mir diese Chance gegeben haben.
5. Es kommt darauf an, was man im Leben erreichen[3] will.
6. Hoffentlich können wir Andreas davon überzeugen, daß er nachgeben muß.
7. Ich bin sehr froh darüber, daß Helga meine dumme Bemerkung nicht übelgenommen hat.
8. Herr König ist dadurch berühmt[4] geworden, daß er diese Maschine erfunden hat.

§6   THE POSITION OF PREPOSITIONAL PHRASES AND *da*-COMPOUNDS

Prepositional phrases, including **da**-compounds, tend to stand toward the end of the sentence.

1	**die Pfeife, -n**	pipe
2	**unsicher**	insecure
3	**erreichen**	to achieve
4	**berühmt**	famous

PERSONAL PRONOUN	NOUN	PREP. + NOUN OR PRONOUN, DA-COMPOUND	

Margot	hat		Renate	**bei den Hausaufgaben**	geholfen.
Sie	hat	ihr		**dabei**	geholfen.
Ich	habe		die Uhr	**von meinen Eltern**	bekommen.
Ich	habe	sie		**von ihnen**	bekommen.

The Interrogative Pronouns *wer* and *was*

§7   THE INTERROGATIVE PRONOUN *wer*

The interrogative **wer** is used to refer to living beings of any gender in the singular and plural. Its forms are as follows:

NOM.	**wer**	*who*
ACC.	**wen**	*who(m)*
DAT.	**wem**	*to whom, who(m)*
GEN.	**wessen**	*whose*

Examples:

Herr Schmidt hat Peter angerufen.
NOM.
(subj.)

Wer hat Peter angerufen?
NOM.   *Who called Peter?*
(subj.)

Herr Schmidt hat **Peter** angerufen.
ACC.
(dir. obj.)

Wen hat Herr Schmidt angerufen?
ACC.   *Who(m) did Mr. Schmidt call?*
(dir. obj.)

Die Platte gehört **meinen Eltern.**
DAT.

Wem gehört diese Platte?
DAT.   *To whom does this record belong?*

Das sind **Barbaras** Kinder.
GEN.

Wessen Kinder sind das?
GEN.   *Whose children are these?*

The genitive **wessen** is quite rare, and some other construction is frequently used instead, such as:

Whose umbrella is that?   **Wem gehört dieser Regenschirm?**
(*Who does this umbrella belong to?*)

PRACTICE 6   *Translate the questions into German. (Use the present perfect for the English past tense.)*

Model: Klaus hat Ute angerufen.   **Wen hat Klaus angerufen?**
Whom did Klaus call?

1. Werner hat Ingrid eingeladen.

Whom has Werner invited?

2. Sabine haßt Ulrich.

_____
Who hates Ulrich?

3. Frau Kunze hat ihm geholfen.

_____
Whom did Mrs. Kunze help?

4. Astrid hat viele Aufnahmen gemacht.

_____
Who took a lot of pictures?

5. Dieser Koffer gehört meinem Freund.

_____
Who does this suitcase belong to?

6. Annerose hat ihm nicht geantwortet.

_____
Whom did Annerose not answer?

7. Rainer hat mich nicht erkannt.[1]

_____
Who didn't recognize you? (fam. sing.)

8. Ich habe meiner Freundin für das Geschenk gedankt.

_____
Whom did you thank for the gift? (formal)

Using _wer_ with prepositions

Das Geschenk ist für einen Freund.
     eine Freundin. ⎫ **Für wen** ist das Geschenk?
     Herrn und Frau Becker. ⎭

      For whom is the present?
     or: _Who is the present for?_

Das Geschenk ist von einem Freund.
     einer Freundin. ⎫ **Von wem** ist das Geschenk?
     Herrn und Frau Becker. ⎭

      From whom is the present?
     or: _Who is the present from?_

In German the preposition always precedes the interrogative and determines its case.

PRACTICE 7   _Translate the questions into German. (Use the present perfect for the English past tense.)_

Model: Karin arbeitet mit   **Mit wem arbeitet Karin im Labor?**
    Maria im Labor.   Who is Karin working with in the lab?

1. Die Leute haben über den Clown gelacht.

_____
Who did the people laugh at?

2. Ich habe Angst vor diesem Zahnarzt.

_____
Who are you afraid of? (fam. sing.)

---

1 **erkennen, erkannte, erkannt**   to recognize

3. Ich warte auf meine Freundin.

_____
Who are you waiting for? (formal)

4. Ich habe diese Blumen
von Mathias bekommen.

_____
Who did you get these flowers from?
(fam. sing.)

5. Volker ist in Margot
verliebt.

_____
Who is Volker in love with?

6. Meine Schwester ist mit
Rainer Stern verheiratet.

_____
Who is your sister married to?
(fam. sing.)

7. Wir sprechen von deinem
Freund Martin.

_____
Who are you talking of?
(fam. plural)

8. Ich gehe mit ein paar
Freunden kegeln.

_____
Who are you going bowling with?
(formal)

§8 THE INTERROGATIVE PRONOUN *was*

The interrogative **was** refers to things and concepts of any gender in the singular and plural. It has only one form, which is both nominative and accusative.

Was ist nicht richtig? *What is not correct?*
|
NOM.
(subj.)

Was verstehen Sie nicht? *What don't you understand?*
|
ACC.
(dir. obj.)

Using *was* with prepositions

Compare:

STATEMENT Ich habe Angst **vorm Fliegen.** *I am afraid of flying.*
Ich habe Angst **davor.** *I am afraid of it.*

QUESTION **Wovor** hast du Angst? *What are you afraid of?*
or: **Vor was** hast du Angst?

There are two ways of formulating the above question. In formal usage **wo-** is added as a prefix to the preposition: **wovor**. In colloquial usage the preposition is followed by **was: vor was.**

Compare the following **da-**compounds and **wo-**compounds:

da-compounds		**wo**-compounds	
(used in statements)		(used in questions)	
damit	*with it/them*	**womit?**	*with what?*
dafür	*for it/them*	**wofür?**	*for what?*
davon	*of it/them*	**wovon?**	*of what?*

r is inserted when the preposition begins with a vowel:

darin	*in it/them*	**worin?**	*in what?*
daran	*on or of it/them*	**woran?**	*on or of what?*
daraus	*from it/them*	**woraus?**	*from what?*
darauf	*on it/them*	**worauf?**	*on what?*

Examples:

Ich denke **daran.**   **Woran** denkst du?
             or: **An was** denkst du? ⟩*What are you thinking of?*

Ich warte **darauf.**   **Worauf** warten Sie?
             or: **Auf was** warten Sie? ⟩*What are you waiting for?*

The genitive prepositions and **außer, ohne, seit** form no **wo**-compounds, just as they form no **da**-compounds.

Ich kann nicht ohne Fernseher leben.
Ich kann nicht ohne   **ihn**   leben. ⟩**Ohne was** kannst du nicht leben?

PRACTICE 8   *Translate the questions into German, using* **wo**-*compounds. (Use the present perfect for the English past tense.)*

Model: Ich denke an die Ferien.   **Woran denkst du?** _____

What are you thinking of? (fam. sing.)

1. Ich warte auf eine Antwort von Udo.

   _____
   What are you waiting for? (fam. sing.)
2. Margot arbeitet an einem Referat.

   _____
   What is she working on?
3. Wir haben Angst vor der Prüfung.

   _____
   What are you afraid of? (fam. pl.)
4. Klaus ist ganz stolz auf sein Motorrad.

   _____
   What is he so proud of?
5. Ich bin mit dieser Gehaltserhöhung nicht zufrieden.

   _____
   What are you not satisfied with? (fam. sing.)
6. Der Film handelt von einer Liebesgeschichte.

   _____
   What does the film deal with? What is the film about?
7. Wir haben über unsere Dummheit gelacht.

   _____
   What were you laughing about? (fam. pl.)
8. Ich danke dir für das Geschenk.

   _____
   What are you thanking me for?

9. Ich denke an die Olympischen Spiele.

   _____
   What are you thinking of? (formal)
10. Uwe hat Schwierigkeiten mit seinem Führerschein.

    _____
    What is he having trouble with?
11. Wir sind begeistert von diesem Theaterstück.

    _____
    What are you so enthusiastic about? (fam. pl.)

PRACTICE 9   Summarizing exercises

A. _Translate into German._

1. a. She's having trouble with the boss.
   b. Are you having trouble with him? (fam. sing.)
   c. Who are you having trouble with?
2. a. I'm having trouble with my seminar paper.
   b. Are you having trouble with it? (formal)
   c. What are you having trouble with?
3. a. Are you working on this project? (formal)
   b. No, I'm not working on it.
   c. What are you working on?
4. a. I'm angry with Peter. (two forms)
   b. Why are you angry with him? (fam. sing., two forms)
   c. Who are you angry with? (two forms)
5. a. Martin is crazy about soccer.
   b. I know that he's crazy about it.
   c. What are you crazy about? (fam. sing.)
6. a. She's in love with Frank.
   b. Is she in love with him?
   c. Who are you in love with? (fam. sing.)
7. a. He's proud of his report card.
   b. He can be proud of it.
   c. What can you be proud of? (fam. sing.)
8. a. I'm thanking you for the gift. (formal)
   b. It's not necessary[1] that you thank me for it.
   c. What are you thanking me for?
9. a. Are you satisfied with your destiny? (fam. sing.)
   b. Yes and no. It depends.

B. _Form sentences that fit the context._
Model: Martins Vater hat den Nobelpreis bekommen.

   stolz sein / Vater
   Martin ist stolz auf seinen Vater.
   or: **Martin kann stolz auf seinen Vater sein.**

---

1 **nötig**   necessary

1. Mein Freund wollte mich gestern anrufen. Er hat es nicht getan.

    böse sein / Freund

2. Ich esse Kaviar sehr gern.

    verrückt sein / Kaviar

3. In diesem Brief steht, daß ich ein Stipendium (*scholarship*) bekomme.

    sehr froh sein / Nachricht

4. Ich weiß nicht, ob Peter und Andreas Freunde oder Verwandte (*relatives*) sind. Ich frage Peter:

    „verwandt sein / Andreas?"

5. Ich arbeite an einem Experiment.

    Schwierigkeiten / haben

6. Meine Freundin studiert in Hamburg.

    denken / oft

7. a. Heute abend gehe ich ins Kino.

    Film / handeln / eine Raumfahrt (*space trip*)

   b. Elke hat den Film gestern gesehen.

    begeistert sein / Film

8. Der Chef bezahlt nicht gut. Ich will mehr Geld verdienen.

    bitten / Gehaltserhöhung

9. Klaus ist mein Schwager (*brother-in-law*).

    er / verheiratet sein / Schwester

10. Meine Mutter hat mir am Telefon gesagt, daß sie mir einen Scheck schicken wird.

    warten / Scheck

11. Meine Freundin hat keine Angst vorm Fliegen.

    ich / Angst haben

12. Manchmal habe ich Lust zur Arbeit und manchmal habe ich keine.

    darauf an.kommen

9

Adjectives

KEY TO THE EXERCISES ON CASSETTE 5.
RUNNING TIME: APPROX. 30 MIN.

Introduction

Note the use of **vorsichtig** in the following sentences:

a. Herr Kästner ist **vorsichtig**.	*Mr. Kästner is careful.*
b. Herr Kästner fährt **vorsichtig**.	*Mr. Kästner drives carefully.*
c. Herr Kästner ist ein **vorsichtiger** Fahrer.	*Mr. Kästner is a careful driver.*

In sentence *a* **vorsichtig** is a predicate adjective with the verb **sein**; in sentence *b* it is an adverb modifying **fahren.** In both situations the base form **vorsichtig** is used with no ending. German does not distinguish between the base forms of adverbs and adjectives.

In sentence *c* **vorsichtig** is an attributive adjective directly preceding the noun **Fahrer,** which it modifies. Attributive adjectives have endings which are determined by the gender, number (singular or plural), and case of the nouns they modify.

In this chapter we shall consider only attributive adjectives, which we shall simply call "adjectives."

The Declension of Adjectives

There are three basic groups:
- adjectives that are not preceded by **der**-words or **ein**-words, referred to as *unpreceded adjectives,*
- adjectives preceded by **der**-words,
- adjectives preceded by **ein**-words.

§1   UNPRECEDED ADJECTIVES

	SINGULAR	PLURAL

Das ist ⟨ kalter Kaffee.
kaltes Wasser.   Das sind kalte Getränke.[1]
kalte Milch.

Unpreceded adjectives are declined almost exactly like **der**-words.
Review of the declension of the **der**-word **dieser**:

	MASCULINE	NEUTER	FEMININE	PLURAL
NOM.	dieser Kaffee	dieses Wasser	diese Milch	diese Getränke
ACC.	diesen Kaffee	dieses Wasser	diese Milch	diese Getränke
DAT.	diesem Kaffee	diesem Wasser	dieser Milch	diesen Getränken
GEN.	dieses Kaffees	dieses Wassers	dieser Milch	dieser Getränke

The endings attached to the **der**-words are known as *strong* endings. Compare them with the endings of the unpreceded adjectives below.

	MASCULINE	NEUTER	FEMININE	PLURAL
NOM.	kalter Kaffee	kaltes Wasser	kalte Milch	kalte Getränke
ACC.	kalten Kaffee	kaltes Wasser	kalte Milch	kalte Getränke
DAT.	kaltem Kaffee	kaltem Wasser	kalter Milch	kalten Getränken
GEN.	kalt [en] Kaffees	kalt [en] Wassers	kalter Milch	kalter Getränke

The difference between the two sets of endings occurs in the genitive singular masculine and neuter: the attributive adjective has the ending **-en** instead of **-es**.

PRACTICE 1   A. *Replace the boldface* **der**-*words with the appropriate forms of the adjectives in parentheses.*

Model: Trinken Sie **diesen** Tee gern? (englisch)
Trinken Sie englischen Tee gern?

1. Wo verkauft man **diesen** Käse? (holländisch)
2. **Dieser** Kaviar ist wirklich gut. (russisch)
3. Auf **solche** Fragen antworte ich nicht. (peinlich[2])
4. In dieser Bibliothek finden Sie **alle** Zeitungen. (ausländisch)
5. Ich habe **diese** Eier[3] bei Schneider gekauft. (frisch)
6. Wo ist **der** Zucker? (braun)
7. Bei **solchem** Wetter gehen wir nicht spazieren. (schlecht)
8. **Manche** Leute gehen mir auf die Nerven. (neugierig[4])
9. **Solches** Brot ist gut für die Gesundheit. (schwarz)
10. Ich liebe das Aroma **dieses** Kaffees. (frisch)

1 **das Getränk, -e**	beverage
2 **peinlich**	embarrassing
3 **das Ei, -er**	egg
4 **neugierig**	curious, nosy

B. *Insert adjective endings.*

1. X: Ist dieser Kaffee gut?
   Y: Ja, das ist gut____ Kaffee.
2. X: Ist dieser Kaffee zu stark für Sie?
   Y: Nein. Ich trinke stark____ Kaffee sehr gern.
3. X: Kommt dieser Wein aus Spanien?
   Y: Ja, das ist spanisch____ Wein.
4. X: Haben Sie diesen Tee in England gekauft?
   Y: Nein. Man kann englisch____ Tee auch hier kaufen.
5. X: Essen Sie diesen Käse gern?
   Y: Ja, denn das ist amerikanisch____ Käse. Wir essen meistens[1]
      amerikanisch____ Käse.
6. X: Hast du Hunger?
   Y: Ich habe sogar groß____ Hunger. (*masc.*)
7. X: War die Prüfung schwer?
   Y: Ja, aber ich habe groß____ Glück (*neut.*) gehabt.
8. X: Wie war das Wetter in Italien?
   Y: Wir hatten meistens schön____ Wetter.
9. X: Was für Laune hat der Chef?
   Y: Ich glaube, er hat schlecht____ Laune.
10. X: Sind diese Methoden noch modern, oder sind sie schon altmodisch?[2]
    Y: Meiner Meinung nach sind es altmodisch____ Methoden.
11. X: Ich finde dieses Theaterstück sehr interessant.
    Y: Ich auch. Dieser Autor schreibt meistens interessant____ Theaterstücke.
12. X: Sind Ihre Nachbarn nett?
    Y: Zum Glück[3] haben wir nett____ Nachbarn.
13. X: Gisela denkt, sie hat die Prüfung nicht bestanden.
    Y: Ach, das ist groß____ Unsinn. (*masc.*)
14. X: In Ihrer Wohnung riecht[4] es wunderbar. Haben Sie Brot gebakken?
    Y: Ja, das ist der Geruch[5] frisch____ Brotes.
15. X: Hannelores Kleid ist sehr schick.
    Y: Dieses Mädchen hat gut____ Geschmack.[6]
16. X: Deine Idee ist großartig.[7]
    Y: Ich habe immer großartig____ Ideen.

1 **meistens**	mostly, usually
2 **altmodisch**	old-fashioned
3 **zum Glück**	luckily
4 **riechen, roch, gerochen**	to smell
5 **der Geruch, ¨-e**	smell
6 **der Geschmack**	taste
7 **großartig**	great

§2   ADJECTIVES PRECEDED BY *der*-WORDS

Including the definite article, the **der**-words are **der, dieser, jeder, jener, mancher, solcher, welcher, alle,** and **beide** (cf. Chap. 6, §1). Adjectives preceded by **der**-words have *weak* endings. The following table shows the combinations of **der** and **dieser** + weak adjective + noun.

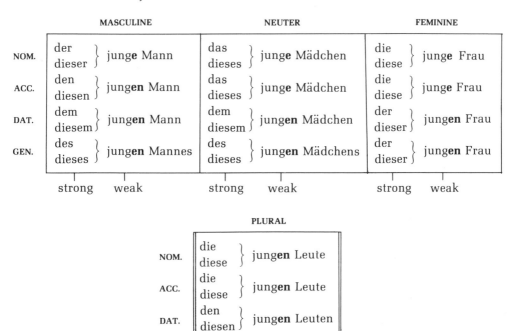

	MASCULINE	NEUTER	FEMININE
NOM.	der / dieser } jung**e** Mann	das / dieses } jung**e** Mädchen	die / diese } jung**e** Frau
ACC.	den / diesen } jung**en** Mann	das / dieses } jung**e** Mädchen	die / diese } jung**e** Frau
DAT.	dem / diesem } jung**en** Mann	dem / diesem } jung**en** Mädchen	der / dieser } jung**en** Frau
GEN.	des / dieses } jung**en** Mannes	des / dieses } jung**en** Mädchens	der / dieser } jung**en** Frau
	strong weak	strong weak	strong weak

PLURAL

NOM.	die / diese } jung**en** Leute
ACC.	die / diese } jung**en** Leute
DAT.	den / diesen } jung**en** Leuten
GEN.	der / dieser } jung**en** Leute
	strong weak

The weak adjective endings are either **-e** or **-en**:

> **-e** in the nominative masculine singular,
> > the nominative and accusative neuter singular,
> > the nominative and accusative feminine singular;
>
> **-en** in all other cases.

The following key shows the distribution of the endings **-e** and **-en** of adjectives preceded by **der**-words.

	MASC.	NEUT.	FEM.	PLURAL
NOM.	-e	-e	-e	-en
ACC.	-en	-e	-e	-en
DAT.	-en	-en	-en	-en
GEN.	-en	-en	-en	-en

The strong declension of **der**-words has a greater variety of endings which help to identify the gender, number, and case of the noun that follows. The weak declension with the two endings **-e** and **-en** is less distinctive. Remember that weak adjective endings do not occur unless preceded by a strong ending.

PRACTICE 2   *Insert the appropriate adjective endings.*

1. Wo ist der neu____ Chef?
2. Kennen Sie den neu____ Chef noch nicht?
3. Wieviel kostet dieses elegant____ Kleid?
4. Ich habe viel Geld für dieses elegant____ Kleid bezahlt.
5. Wo ist die deutsch____ Zeitung?
6. Haben Sie diese deutsch____ Zeitung schon gelesen?
7. Die deutsch____ Zeitungen liegen da drüben.
8. Diese braun____ Handschuhe gefallen mir.
9. Jeder ausländisch____ Student muß diese Prüfung machen.
10. Alle ausländisch____ Studenten wohnen in diesem Studentenheim.
11. Beide französisch____ Studenten sind meine Freunde.
12. Wer hat diese genial____[1] Idee gehabt?
13. Dieser neugierig____ Mensch geht mir auf die Nerven.
14. Wie heißt die neu____ Professorin?
15. Die neu____ Professoren haben noch keine Büros.
16. Auf dieser Liste stehen die Namen der neu____ Professoren und Professorinnen.
17. Haben Sie diesen interessant____ Roman gelesen?
18. Wie heißt der Autor dieses interessant____ Romans?
19. Mancher jung____ Arzt hat Schwierigkeiten mit seinen Patienten.
20. Bitte ignorieren Sie diese taktlos____[2] Bemerkung!
21. Ich versuche, alle taktlos____ Bemerkungen zu ignorieren.

Omission of the noun

Welche Handschuhe willst du kaufen?   Vielleicht kaufe ich **die braunen Handschuhe.**
or: Vielleicht kaufe ich **die braunen.**
Perhaps I'll buy the brown ones.

The fact that the noun **Handschuhe** is not repeated in the second sentence does not affect the adjective ending: **die braunen** is used in both sentences. In English *one*(s) is added when the noun is omitted.

PRACTICE 3   *Insert the appropriate adjective endings.*

1. X: Haben Sie den Chef gesehen?
   Y: Meinen Sie den jung____ oder den alt____?
2. X: Welches Kleid willst du anziehen?[3]
   Y: Ich weiß nicht, ob ich das grün____ oder das rot____ anziehen soll.

---

1 **genial**   ingenious
2 **taktlos**   tactless
3 **an•ziehen, zog an, angezogen**   to put on

3. X: Wie gefällt dir der Mantel?
   Y: Meinst du den schwarz____?
4. X: Welcher Fernseher ist kaputt?
   Y: Der kaputt____ steht im Nebenzimmer.[1]
5. X: Welches Restaurant haben Steins gekauft?
   Y: Ich glaube, sie haben das klein____ da an der Ecke gekauft.
6. X: Sind diese Formulare hier neu?
   Y: Ja, das sind die neu____.
7. X: Welche Formulare haben Sie schon ausgefüllt?
   Y: Ich habe alle neu____ ausgefüllt.

§3   ADJECTIVES PRECEDED BY *ein*-WORDS

The **ein**-words are **ein, kein,** and the possessives (cf. Chap. 6, §5 and §6).

The declension of **(k)ein** + adjective + noun is as follows:

	MASCULINE	NEUTER	FEMININE
NOM.	(k)ein jung**er** Mann	(k)ein jung**es** Mädchen	(k)eine jung**e** Frau
ACC.	(k)einen jung**en** Mann	(k)ein jung**es** Mädchen	(k)eine jung**e** Frau
DAT.	(k)einem jung**en** Mann	(k)einem jung**en** Mädchen	(k)einer jung**en** Frau
GEN.	(k)eines jung**en** Mannes	(k)eines jung**en** Mädchens	(k)einer jung**en** Frau

	PLURAL
NOM.	keine jung**en** Leute
ACC.	keine jung**en** Leute
DAT.	keinen jung**en** Leuten
GEN.	keiner jung**en** Leute

The **ein**-words have the same strong endings as the **der**-words except in three cases where they have no ending at all: see boxed forms above.

If an **ein**-word has an ending, the adjective has the same weak ending as after a **der**-word. But if the **ein**-word has no ending, the adjective has a strong ending: **-er** (masculine) or **-es** (neuter).

The following key shows the endings of adjectives preceded by an **ein**-word.

	MASC.	NEUT.	FEM.	PLURAL
NOM.	**-er**	**-es**	**-e**	**-en**
ACC.	**-en**	**-es**	**-e**	**-en**
DAT.	**-en**	**-en**	**-en**	**-en**
GEN.	**-en**	**-en**	**-en**	**-en**

1 **das Nebenzimmer, -**   adjoining room

Examples of possessive + adjective + noun combinations:

> Ist das dein neu**es** Auto?
>
> Ist das Ihr neu**er** Wagen?
>
> Das ist seine neu**e** Freundin.
>
> Das ist unser neu**es** Haus.
>
> Ist das euer neu**es** Hobby?

Keep in mind that -**er** of **unser** and **euer** is not a declensional ending (cf. Chap. 6, §6). The **e** before **r** may be omitted when the strong endings are added.

> Das ist **uns(e)re** neue Nachbarin.
>
> Wir haben **uns(e)rer** neuen Nachbarin geholfen.
>
> Ist das **eu(e)re** neue Nachbarin?
>
> Helft ihr **eu(e)rer** neuen Nachbarin?

PRACTICE 4   A. *Insert the appropriate adjective endings.*

> **Model:** a. Das ist ein gut**er** Film.
> > b. Ich habe gestern einen gut**en** Film gesehen.
> > c. In dieser Woche laufen hier keine gut**en** Filme.

1. a. Das ist ein nett____ Brief von Dietmar.
   b. Helga hat einen nett____ Brief von ihrem Freund bekommen.
   c. Warum bekomme ich keine nett____ Briefe von meinem Freund?
2. a. Das ist ein groß____ Problem.
   b. Das sind keine groß____ Probleme.
   c. Ich habe ein groß____ Problem.
   d. Das ist unser groß____ Problem.
3. a. Ist das ein neu____ Kleid?
   b. Hast du mein neu____ Kleid schon gesehen?
   c. Ich kann mir keine neu____ Kleider kaufen.
4. a. Hast du eine neu____ Freundin?
   b. Margot hat einen neu____ Freund.
   c. Rainer ist ihr neu____ Freund.
5. a. Wir haben eine modern____ Wohnung gemietet.
   b. Neumanns wohnen auch in einer modern____ Wohnung.
   c. In unserer Straße gibt es[1] keine modern____ Wohnungen.
6. a. Wir haben einen altmodisch____ Fernseher.
   b. Unser altmodisch____ Fernseher funktioniert noch sehr gut.
   c. Wir sind mit unserem altmodisch____ Fernseher sehr zufrieden.
7. a. Mein klein____ Bruder ist in der Prüfung durchgefallen.
   b. Warum hilfst du deinem klein____ Bruder nicht?
   c. Kennen Sie meinen klein____ Bruder?
   d. Ich kenne nur Ihre klein____ Schwester.

B. *Insert the appropriate adjective endings.*

1. X: Ich habe einen lang____ Brief von zu Hause bekommen.
   Y: Und ich habe ein groß____ Paket von zu Hause bekommen.

---

1 **es gibt (+** *acc.***)**   there is *or* are

2. X: Das war keine leicht＿＿ Mathematikprüfung.

 Y: In Mathematik gibt es keine leicht＿＿ Prüfungen.

3. X: Das ist ein interessant＿＿ Theaterstück.

 Y: Wir haben am Freitag ein langweilig＿＿ Theaterstück gesehen.

4. X: Dieser Fall[1] ist hoffnungslos.[2]

 Y: Ja, leider ist das ein hoffnungslos＿＿ Fall.

5. X: Haben Sie meine neu＿＿ Adresse?

 Y: Nein. Ich habe auch Ihre neu＿＿ Telefonnummer nicht.

6. X: Ist das dein neu＿＿ Auto?

 Y: Das ist unser neu＿＿ Auto, denn meine Frau fährt es natürlich auch.

7. X: Ist Andreas dein fest＿＿ Freund?[3]

 Y: Nein. Ich habe keinen fest＿＿ Freund.

8. X: Können Sie meine genial＿＿ Handschrift[4] lesen?

 Y: Natürlich nicht. Sie haben eine schrecklich＿＿ Handschrift.

9. X: Herr Neumann hat viel Unsinn geredet.

 Y: Dieser Mann hat keinen gesund＿＿ Menschenverstand.[5]

10. X: Ich bin heute deprimiert.[6] Kannst du mir einen gut＿＿ Witz erzählen?

 Y: Muß es ein gut＿＿ Witz sein? Ich weiß keine gut＿＿ Witze.

11. X: Du hast eine charmant＿＿[7] Freundin.

 Y: Stimmt.[8] Und ich bin ihr charmant＿＿ Freund.

§4   SLIGHTLY IRREGULAR FORMS OF ADJECTIVES

a. **hoch** (*high*)   Das Gebäude ist hoch.

                       das **hohe** Gebäude/ein **hohes** Gebäude

The **c** is omitted when an ending is added.

b. **dunkel** (*dark*)   Das Zimmer ist dunkel.

                       das **dunkle** Zimmer/ein **dunkles** Zimmer

 miserabel (*miserable*)   Das Wetter ist miserabel.

                       das **miserable** Wetter/ein **miserables** Wetter

Adjectives ending in **-el** omit **e** before **l** when an ending is added.

c. **teuer** (*expensive*)   Die Bücher sind teuer.

                       die **teuren** Bücher

 sauer (*sour*)   Die Milch ist sauer.

                       die **saure** Milch

Adjectives ending in **-er** after **eu** and **au** omit **e** before **r** when an ending is added.

1	**der Fall, ⁻e**	case
2	**hoffnungslos**	hopeless
3	**der feste Freund**	steady boyfriend
4	**die Handschrift, -en**	handwriting
5	**der gesunde Menschenverstand**	common sense
6	**deprimiert**	depressed
7	**charmant**	charming
8	**stimmt** (*short for:* **das stimmt**)	that's correct *or* right

§5 ADJECTIVES DERIVED FROM CITY NAMES

City names used as adjectives add **-er** regardless of the gender, number, or case of the following noun. These adjectives are capitalized.

> Das Flugzeug ist auf dem **Berliner** Flughafen gelandet.
> *The plane landed at the Berlin airport.*
> Das ist ein Bild vom **Kölner** Dom.
> *That's a picture of the cathedral of Cologne.*
> Wo haben Sie diese **Frankfurter** Würstchen gekauft?
> *Where did you buy these frankfurters?*

§6 SEVERAL ADJECTIVES MODIFYING THE SAME NOUN

> Das ist ein schön**er** Sommertag.
> Das ist ein schön**er**, warm**er** Sommertag.
> Das ist ein schön**er**, warm**er** und klar**er** Sommertag.

Since **schön, warm,** and **klar** all modify the same noun, they must have the same adjective ending.

§7 *alle* FOLLOWED BY A *der*-WORD OR *ein*-WORD

> all**e** dies**e** Sachen
> all**e** mein**e** Freunde

Alle may be followed by a **der**-word or **ein**-word; both have the same strong ending. Added adjectives have weak endings:

> alle meine gut**en** Freunde
> alle meine gut**en** alt**en** Freunde

PRACTICE 5   *Complete the responses.*

1.   X: Herr Schubert ist wirklich sehr nett.
      Y: Stimmt. Er ist ein _____ Mann. (*nice young*)
2.   X: Warum hast du schon wieder kein Geld?
      Y: Weil ich _____ Schulden bezahlt habe. (*all my old*)
3.   X: Mein Zimmer im Studentenheim ist etwas dunkel.
      Y: Leider habe ich auch ein _____ Zimmer. (*dark*)
4.   X: Ist diese Milch sauer?
      Y: Ja, das ist _____ Milch. (*sour*)
5.   X: Möchtest du etwas essen?
      Y: Hast du _____? (*frankfurters*)
6.   X: Das Wetter ist heute miserabel.
      Y: Dieses _____ Wetter geht mir auf die Nerven. (*miserable*)
7.   X: Dieser Mantel ist bestimmt sehr teuer.
      Y: Nein, das ist kein _____ Mantel. (*expensive*)
8.   X: Wo ist dein Gepäck?
      Y: Ich habe es auf dem _____ gelassen. (*Berlin airport*)

9. a. X: Haben Schmidts eine schöne Wohnung?

    Y: Ja. Sie haben eine _____ Wohnung. (*large and modern*)

  b. X: Sicher ist die Miete[1] sehr hoch.

    Y: Ich nehme an, daß sie eine _____ Miete bezahlen müssen. (*high*)

§8   SUMMARY OF THE MAIN FEATURES

1. Two sets of endings have to be kept in mind:

the strong endings of the **der**-words

	MASC.	NEUT.	FEM.	PLURAL
NOM.	-er	-es	-e	-e
ACC.	-en	-es	-e	-e
DAT.	-em	-em	-er	-en
GEN.	-es	-es	-er	-er

the weak endings of the adjectives

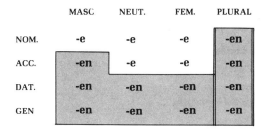

	MASC	NEUT.	FEM.	PLURAL
NOM.	-e	-e	-e	-en
ACC.	-en	-e	-e	-en
DAT.	-en	-en	-en	-en
GEN.	-en	-en	-en	-en

2. In the sequence (article)-adjective-noun, at least one strong ending must be present to signal gender, number, and case. Thus we find the following patterns:

a. Unpreceded adjectives have the strong **der**-word endings.

junger Mann	junges Mädchen	junge Frau	junge Leute
(NOM.)	(NOM./ACC.)	(NOM./ACC.)	(NOM./ACC.)

Exception: In the singular, the genitive masculine and neuter have the weak ending **-en** instead of the strong **-es.**

---

1 **die Miete, -n**   rent

b. Adjectives preceded by **der**-words have weak endings, i.e.

-**e** in the following five cases of the singular:

der jung**e** Mann	das jung**e** Mädchen	die jung**e** Frau
(NOM.)	(NOM./ACC.)	(NOM./ACC.)

-**en** in all other cases.

c. Adjectives preceded by **ein**-words

When the **ein**-word has a strong ending, the adjective has a *weak* ending. When the **ein**-word has no ending, the adjective has the strong ending -**er** or -**es**.

ein jung**er** Mann	ein jung**es** Mädchen	eine jung**e** Frau
(NOM.)	(NOM./ACC.)	(NOM./ACC.)

-**en** in all other cases.

3. Adjectives in a series

Adjectives modifying the same noun take the same endings.

    ein nett**er**, lang**er** Brief   ein hübsch**es**, aber altmodisch**es** Kleid

PRACTICE 6   Summarizing exercises
    A. *Insert the appropriate adjective endings.*

      Model: a. Das ist ein dumm**er** Fehler
             b. Ich habe einen dumm**en** Fehler gemacht.
             c. Das sind dumm**e** Fehler.
             d. Das sind keine dumm**en** Fehler.

      1. a. Das ist ein gut____ Witz.
         b. Wer hat Ihnen diesen gut____ Witz erzählt?
         c. Frau Zimmermann erzählt meistens gut____ Witze.
         d. Das sind keine gut____ Witze.
      2. a. Das ist ein groß____ Problem.
         b. Von welchem groß____ Problem sprechen Sie?
         c. Wir haben groß____ Probleme.
         d. Das sind doch keine groß____ Probleme.
      3. a. Kennst du dieses deutsch____ Lied?
         b. Das ist kein deutsch____ Lied.
         c. Singt ihr manchmal deutsch____ Lieder?
         d. Kennt ihr keine deutsch____ Lieder?

4. a. Das ist eine großartig____ Idee.
   b. Wer hat diese großartig____ Idee gehabt?
   c. Barbara hat oft großartig____ Ideen.
   d. Warum habe ich keine großartig____ Ideen?

5. a. Das war eine taktlos____ Bemerkung.
   b. Es tut mir leid, daß ich diese taktlos____ Bemerkung gemacht habe.
   c. Ich mache oft taktlos____ Bemerkungen.
   d. Bitte vergessen Sie meine taktlos____ Bemerkungen.

B. *Insert the appropriate adjective endings.*

1. X: Dieser Anzug ist altmodisch.
   Y: Aber dieser altmodisch____ Anzug hat Stil.

2. X: Soll ich den hell____ ¹ Anzug kaufen?
   Y: Der dunkl____ gefällt mir besser.

3. X: Diese Kritik ist nicht fair.
   Y: Ich finde auch, daß es eine unfair____ Kritik ist.

4. X: Können Sie mir einen gut____ Rechtsanwalt empfehlen?
   Y: Herr Krause ist ein ausgezeichnet____ ² Rechtsanwalt.

5. X: Ist das der neu____ Katalog?
   Y: Nein, das ist ein alt____ Katalog. Die neu____ Kataloge sind noch nicht herausgekommen.

6. X: Warum hast du dieses teur____ Kleid gekauft?
   Y: Weil es mir gefällt. Ich möchte wissen, warum mir nur teur____ Kleider gefallen.

7. X: Sie haben schon wieder Ihr Versprechen nicht gehalten.
   Y: Sie sehen, ich bin ein hoffnungslos____ Fall.

8. X: Bist du mit deinem Zeugnis zufrieden?
   Y: Ja. Ich habe gut____ Noten. Nur in Mathematik habe ich keine gut____ Note.

9. X: Deine Geschwister³ sind sehr nett.
   Y: Und ich? Bin ich kein nett____ Mensch? Ach ja, ich bin das schwarz____ Schaf in der Familie.

10. X: Die Preise in diesem Restaurant sind viel zu hoch für meinen Geldbeutel.⁴
    Y: Ich kann diese hoh____ Preise auch nicht bezahlen.

11. X: Wie kommt es,⁵ daß du immer so gut____ Ideen hast?
    Y: Ach, das ist nur gesund____ Menschenverstand.

12. X: Wie kommt es, daß du so beliebt⁶ bist?
    Y: Hm ... Das ist mein natürlich____ Charme (*masc.*).

13. X: Mein Fräulein, ich finde Sie sehr attraktiv.
    Y: Mein Herr, Sie haben gut____ Geschmack.

1	**hell**	light-colored
2	**ausgezeichnet**	excellent
3	**die Geschwister** (*pl.*)	brothers and sisters, siblings
4	**der Geldbeutel, -**	purse, pocketbook
5	**wie kommt es**	how come
6	**beliebt**	popular

14. a. X: Ich war mit Martin im Kino.

    Y: Mit Martin? Rainer ist doch dein fest____ Freund.

   b. X: Nicht mehr.[1] Das ist eine lang____ Geschichte.

15. a. X: Deine Handschrift ist miserabel.

    Y: Miserabl____ Handschriften sind genial.

   b. X: Und du bist doch so ein genial____ Mensch.

    Y: Stimmt. Ich bin ein neu____ Weltwunder (neut.).

16. a. X: Wo sind die ausländisch____ Zeitungen?

    Y: Alle ausländisch____ Zeitungen liegen da drüben.

   b. X: Verkaufen Sie auch portugiesisch____ Zeitungen?

    Y: Die portugiesisch____ Zeitungen liegen neben den französisch____ und spanisch____.

17. a. X: Ich glaube, Andreas hat einen neu____ Wagen.

    Y: Sein schick____ rot____ Sportwagen steht hinter der Bibliothek.

   b. X: Hast du auch ein schick____ Auto?

    Y: Natürlich. Dort steht mein alt____ Klapperkasten.[2]

C. *Form sentences using the following cues.*

Model: das / sein / ein / großartig / Idee

    Das ist eine großartige Idee.

1. das / sein / ein / taktlos / Bemerkung
2. das / sein / ein / langweilig / Theaterstück
3. das / sein / ein / interessant / Film?
4. das / sein / ein / unfair / Kritik? (past)
5. du / haben / ein / fest / Freund?
6. Frank / sein / mein / fest / Freund
7. Frau Krause / sein / ein / ausgezeichnet / Rechtsanwältin
8. ich / haben / ein / miserabel / Handschrift
9. ich / kaufen / ein / schick / Kleid (pres. perf.)
10. du / haben / gut / Geschmack
11. Anita / sein / schwarz / Schaf / in / Familie
12. mein Wagen / sein / ein / alt / Klapperkasten
13. ich / schenken / dir / mein / alt / Klapperkasten
14. dieser Fanatiker / haben / kein / gesund / Menschenverstand
15. er / sein / ein / hoffnungslos / Fall

Additional Uses of Adjectives

§9   ADJECTIVES PRECEDED BY UNINFLECTED ELEMENTS

Adjectives preceded by uninflected elements have strong endings to signal gender, number, and case of the noun that follows.

1 **nicht mehr**   not anymore
2 **der Klapperkasten, ∸**   boneshaker

a. **etwas** *some, a little*

    Wo kann ich etwas heiß**es** Wasser bekommen?

b. **ein wenig** *a little*

    Hier ist noch ein wenig schwarz**er** Kaffee.

    Etwas and **ein wenig** are interchangeable.

c. **ein paar** *a few, some* (generally more than two)

    Wir haben ein paar alt**e** Freunde besucht.

d. **genug** *enough*

    Haben wir genug kalt**e** Getränke für unser Picknick?

e. cardinal numbers **zwei, drei, vier,** etc.

    With the exception of **ein-,** cardinal numbers remain uninflected:

        drei neu**e** Experimente

When the cardinal number is preceded by a strong **der**-word or **ein**-word, the adjective has a weak ending:

die	drei	neu**en**	Experimente
seine	drei	neu**en**	Experimente
|	|	|	
strong	un-	weak	
	inflected		

f. **manch, solch, welch**

In literary German, **mancher, solcher,** and (in exclamations) **welcher** occur without endings.

manch gut**er** Freund	solch gut**er** Freund	Welch gut**er** Freund!
or: manch ein gut**er** Freund	solch ein gut**er** Freund	Welch ein gut**er** Freund!
many a good friend	*such a good friend*	*What a good friend!*

In informal German (everyday speech and informal writing) **so (ein)** is used in place of **solch (ein)** and **was für (ein)** is used instead of **welch (ein)**. (Cf. Chap. 6, §5).

So ein gut**er** Freund ist unbezahlbar.	*Such a good friend is prizeless.*
So gut**e** Freunde habe ich leider nicht.	*Unfortunately, I don't have such good friends.*
Was für ein gut**er** Freund!	*What a good friend!*
Was für gut**e** Freunde!	*What good friends!*

PRACTICE 7   *Insert the adjective endings, following the model of sentence 1.*

    1. Im Kühlschrank[1] ist noch ein wenig grün**er** Salat.
    2. Ist das genug heiß____ Wasser?
    3. Hast du noch etwas kalt____ Milch für mich?
    4. Wir haben ein paar nett____ Nachbarn eingeladen.

1 **der Kühlschrank, ¨e**   refrigerator

5. Köhlers haben zwei klein____ Kinder.
6. Haben Sie die zwei klein____ Kinder gesehen?
7. Welch schön____ Sonnenuntergang![1]
8. Was für ein herrlich____ Wetter!
9. So ein____ gut____ Lehrerin habe ich nicht wieder gehabt.
10. So leicht____ Hausaufgaben sind eine Beleidigung[2] für meine Intelligenz.

§10   ADJECTIVES PRECEDED BY *andere, einige, mehrere, viele, wenige*

The indefinite numerals **andere** (*other*), **einige** (*some, a few*), **mehrere** (*several*), **viele** (*many*), and **wenige** (*few, not many*), traditionally called *limiting adjectives*, are in fact normal attributive adjectives and may occur with either strong or weak endings, depending on whether or not they are preceded.

unpreceded:		preceded:	
viel**e** Studenten		die viel**en** Studenten	
ander**e** Projekte	strong endings	keine ander**en** Projekte	weak endings
wenig**e** Freunde		meine wenig**en** Freunde	

When another adjective is added, it has the same strong or weak ending:

unpreceded:	preceded:
viel**e** neu**e** Studenten	die viel**en** neu**en** Studenten
ander**e** groß**e** Projekte	keine ander**en** groß**en** Projekte
wenig**e** gut**e** Freunde	meine wenig**en** gut**en** Freunde

When used in the singular, unpreceded **viel** and **wenig** are usually not inflected; adjectives that follow them have strong endings:

viel/wenig Geld   viel/wenig ausländisch**es** Geld

For the use of **ander-** in the singular, see Chapter 20, §1.

PRACTICE 8   Insert the appropriate adjective endings.

1. Ich esse viel frisch____ Obst.[3]
2. Wir haben viel____ gut____ Freunde.
3. Einig____ ausländisch____ Studenten wohnen im Studentenheim.
4. Die ander____ ausländisch____ Studenten wohnen in der Stadt.
5. Mehrer____ neu____ Studenten suchen einen Job.
6. Es gibt zu viel____ Bewerber[4] für die wenig____ Jobs.
7. Ich habe viel____ dumm____ Fehler gemacht.
8. Meine viel____ dumm____ Fehler sind schockierend.

---

1 **der Sonnenuntergang, ¨e**   sunset
2 **die Beleidigung, -en**   insult
3 **das Obst**   fruit
4 **der Bewerber, -**   applicant

§11   FORMS AND USE OF *derselbe* (the same)

singular:	**derselbe** Mann	plural:
Das ist	**dasselbe** Mädchen	Das sind **dieselben** Leute.
	dieselbe Frau	

The English expression *the same* corresponds to German **der** + **selbe,** which is written as one word. **Der** has a strong ending, **selbe** a weak one.

d e r s e l b e
strong weak

The full declension is as follows:

	MASC.	NEUTER	FEM.	PLURAL
NOM.	derselbe	dasselbe	dieselbe	dieselben
ACC.	denselben	dasselbe	dieselbe	dieselben
DAT.	demselben	demselben	derselben	denselben
GEN.	desselben	desselben	derselben	derselben

Any additional adjective takes the same ending as **selbe.**

Das ist derselbe junge Mann.
         strong weak weak

PRACTICE 9   *Translate the sentences into German.*

1. That's the same mistake.
2. That's the same stupid mistake.
3. Is that the same young man?
4. That's not the same young lady.
5. I talked with the same janitor. (*pres. perf.*)
6. Barbara and Frank have the same teachers.
7. That's the same old story.
8. He's telling the same old stories.

§12   ADJECTIVAL NOUNS

Adjectives referring to persons, things, or abstractions may assume the function of nouns.

1. Referring to persons

Das ist ein Programm für Blind**e.**
  That's a program for the blind.

Ein Blind**er** und eine Blind**e** haben gestern im Konzert gesungen.
  A blind man and a blind woman sang in the concert yesterday.

Diese Blind**en** haben in unserem Chor gesungen.
  These blind people sang in our choir.

Adjectival nouns are capitalized. They follow the rules for the declension of adjectives and hence may have either strong or weak endings. They are frequently rendered into English by adding *man*, *woman*, or *people*.

SINGULAR		PLURAL	
male	**female**	**male and female**	
der Arm**e**	die Arm**e**	die Arm**en**	viele Arm**e**
ein Arm**er**	eine Arm**e**	keine Arm**en**	
		alle Arm**en**	
der Fremd**e**	die Fremd**e**	die Fremd**en**	einige Fremd**e**
the stranger			
ein Fremd**er**	eine Fremd**e**	keine Fremd**en**	
		alle Fremd**en**	
der Deutsch**e**	die Deutsch**e**	die Deutsch**en**	
ein Deutsch**er**	eine Deutsch**e**	keine Deutsch**en**	mehrere Deutsch**e**
		alle Deutsch**en**	

Unpreceded:
Sind Sie Deutsch**er?** (male)   Sind diese Touristen Deutsch**e?**
Sind Sie Deutsch**e** (female)

An attributive adjective has the same ending as the adjectival noun:

ein mysteriös**er** Fremd**er**   viele jung**e** Deutsch**e**
eine freundlich**e** Blind**e**

PRACTICE 10   Insert the appropriate endings.

1. a. In unserer Stadt gibt es viele Arm____.
   b. Ein Arm____ hat mich um Geld gebeten.
2. a. Kennen Sie den Blind____ da drüben?
   b. Mein Bruder it mit einer Blind____ verheiratet.
   c. Das ist eine Schule für Blind____.
3. a. Eine Fremd____ hat mich nach dem Weg zum Bahnhof gefragt.
   b. Als ich die Tür aufmachte, stand ein Fremd____ vor mir.
   c. Der Fremd____ war sehr höflich.
   d. Heute sind viele Fremd____ in unserer Stadt.
4. a. Unsere Nachbarn sind Deutsch____.
   b. Hier wohnen viele Deutsch____.
   c. Barbara ist mit einem Deutsch____ verlobt.
   d. Ich habe gestern mehrere jung____ Deutsch____ kennengelernt.

2. Referring to things or abstractions

The neuter forms of adjectives used as nouns are generally collectives or abstractions.

das Neue   *the new, the new stuff, that which is new*
das Alte   *the old*, etc.

das Gute   *the good*, etc.
das Böse   *the evil*, etc.

Das Gute an der Sache ist, daß wir keine Steuern bezahlen müssen.
The good thing (or part) about the matter is that we don't have to pay taxes.

These neuter forms are frequently preceded by **etwas, nichts, viel, wenig, alles.**

etwas Schön**es**	*something beautiful*	**alles** Schöne	*all that is beautiful*
un- strong		strong weak	
inflected			
wenig Neu**es**	*little that is new*	**alles** Neue	*all that is new*
	little news		*all news*
nichts Interessant**es**	*nothing interesting*	**alles** Interessante	*all that is interesting*
viel Gut**es**	*much that is good*	**alles** Gute	*all that is good*
	many good things	idiom: **Alles Gute!** *All the best!*	
			or: Good luck!

PRACTICE 11   *Insert the appropriate endings.*

1. Weißt du etwas Neu____?
2. Erika wird dir alles Neu____ erzählen.
3. Ich habe schon viel Gut____ über Sie gehört.
4. Wir wünschen Ihnen alles Gut____.
5. Ist etwas Interessant____ passiert?
6. Hier passiert nichts Interessant____.

§13   PARTICIPLES USED AS ADJECTIVES AND NOUNS

There are two types of participles: present participles and past participles.

1. Present participles

lachen**d**	*laughing*	bellen**d**	*barking*
weinen**d**	*crying*	folgen**d**	*following*

In English the present participle has the ending **-ing**; in German a **d** is added to the infinitive.

When the participle is used as an adjective preceding a noun, it follows the rules for the adjective declension.

der folgend**e** Satz	die folgend**en** Sätze	folgend**e** Sätze
das folgend**e** Beispiel[1]	die folgend**en** Beispiele	folgend**e** Beispiele
ein weinend**es** Kind	die weinend**en** Kinder	weinend**e** Kinder

Some present participles are commonly used as nouns. They follow the pattern of adjectival nouns explained in the preceding section.

der / die Reisend**e**	die Reisend**en**	Reisend**e**
the traveler (male/female)	*the travelers*	*travelers*

1 **das Beispiel, -e**   example

ein Reisend**er** (male)
eine Reisend**e** (female)

der / die Überlebend**e**	die Überlebend**en**	Überlebend**e**
the survivor (male/female)	*the survivors*	*survivors*

ein Überlebend**er** (male)
eine Überlebend**e** (female)

der / die Streikend**e**	die Streikend**en**	Streikend**e**
the striker (male/female)	*the strikers*	*strikers*

ein Streikend**er** (male)
eine Streikend**e** (female)

PRACTICE 12 *Insert the appropriate endings, following the model of sentence 1.*

1. Bei dem Flugzeugunglück hat es keine Überlebend**en** gegeben.
2. Es gibt nur einen Überlebend____.
3. Wissen Sie den Namen des Überlebend____?
4. Das folgend____ Beispiel spricht für sich selbst.
5. Folgend____ Beispiele sprechen für sich selbst.
6. Bitte übersetzen Sie den folgend____ Satz!
7. Die streikend____ Arbeiter marschieren vor der Fabrik auf und ab.
8. Werden die Streikend____ den neuen Vertrag unterschreiben?
9. Man hat dem Reisend____ eine falsche Auskunft[1] gegeben.
10. Ein Reisend____ hat laut protestiert.
11. Bellend____ Hunde beißen nicht.*

2. Past participles

When a past participle precedes a noun, it has normal adjective endings.

INFINITIVE	PAST PARTICIPLE
verdienen	**verdient**
(*to earn, deserve*)	das verdient**e** Geld (*the earned money*)
	eine verdient**e** Strafe (*a deserved punishment*)
gebrauchen	**gebraucht**
(*to use*)	die gebraucht**en** Bücher (*the used* or *second-hand books*)
stehlen	**gestohlen**
(*to steal*)	der gestohlen**e** Wagen (*the stolen car*)

Several past participles have come to be used as nouns. Like other adjectival nouns, they may have strong or weak adjective endings, depending on their usage. Here are some common examples:

1 **Auskunft geben**   to give information

---

* The literal translation is, "Barking dogs don't bite," which corresponds to the English saying, "His bark is worse than his bite."

der/die Angestellte (*the employee*)	der/die Gelehrte (*the scholar*)
ein Angestellter	ein Gelehrter
eine Angestellte	eine Gelehrte
der/die Erwachsene (*the adult*)	der/die Verlobte (*the fiancé[e]*)
ein Erwachsener	ein Verlobter
eine Erwachsene	eine Verlobte

When another adjective is added, it has the same ending as the participle:

der/die neue Angestellte   plural: die neuen Angestellten

ein neuer Angestellter   neue Angestellte

eine neue Angestellte   viele neue Angestellte

PRACTICE 13   *Insert the appropriate endings.*

1. Das ist eine verdient____ Medaille.
2. Das sind keine verdient____ Medaillen.
3. Warum kaufen Sie keine gebraucht____ Bücher?
4. Wo kann man gebraucht____ Bücher kaufen?
5. Er ist mit einem gestohlen____ Wagen nach Nürnberg gefahren.
6. Karin ist meine Verlobt____.
7. Klaus ist mein Verlobt____.
8. Dr. Herzog ist ein berühmt____ Gelehrt____.
9. Seine Frau ist auch eine berühmt____ Gelehrt____.
10. Die Angestellt____ der Firma Körner streiken.
11. Fragen Sie doch einen Angestellt____!
12. Ein freundlich____ Angestellt____ hat mir diese Auskunft gegeben.
13. Hier im Bus ist nur noch Platz für einen Erwachsen____ und ein Kind.
14. Dieser Film ist nur für Erwachsen____.

§14   SUMMARY OF ADDITIONAL USES OF ADJECTIVES

1. Adjectives have strong endings when preceded by uninflected elements, such as **etwas, ein wenig, ein paar, genug,** cardinal numbers (except **ein-**), and **manch, solch, welch.**

2. Adjectives following **andere, einige, mehrere, viele,** and **wenige** have the same strong or weak endings as these forms.

3. **Derselbe** combines the strong declension of **der** and the weak declension of **selbe** in one word. Additional adjectives take weak endings.

4. Participles preceding nouns follow the rules for the declension of adjectives.

5. Adjectives and participles used as nouns have the usual adjective endings.

PRACTICE 14   Summarizing exercises

A. *Insert the appropriate endings.*

1. X: Diese Gebäude sind schon sehr alt.
   Y: In dieser Stadt gibt es viel____ alt____ Gebäude.

2. X: Hat er denn diese Strafe wirklich verdient?
   Y: Meiner Meinung nach ist das eine verdient____ Strafe.
3. X: Sind diese Bücher neu oder gebraucht?
   Y: Das sind gebraucht____ Bücher.
4. X: Käte, ist das dein Verlobt____?
   Y: Kennst du denn meinen Verlobt____ noch nicht?
5. X: Hoffentlich wird das Wetter etwas besser.
   Y: Ja, wir haben genug schlecht____ Wetter gehabt.
6. X: Ich glaube, ein amerikanisch____ Gelehrt____ arbeitet an diesem Projekt.
   Y: Soviel ich weiß, arbeiten zwei amerikanisch____ Gelehrt____ daran.
7. X: Das war nicht fair von Ihrem Chef. Warum haben Sie nicht protestiert?
   Y: Ach, ich bin doch nur ein klein____ Angestellt____.
8. X: Hat ein Fremd____ Ihnen diese Auskunft gegeben?
   Y: Ich habe den Deutsch____ da drüben gefragt.
9. X: Wer hat das Glas zerbrochen? Ein Kind oder ein Erwachsen____?
   Y: Es war eine Erwachsen____. — Ich.
10. X: Was ist denn passiert?
    Y: Es ist etwas Schrecklich____ passiert.
11. X: Vergessen Sie doch alles Schlecht____ in Ihrem Leben und denken Sie nur an das Gut____!
    Y: Und es gibt viel Gut____ in meinem Leben.
12. X: Jetzt fahren wir in die Ferien.
    Y: Na, dann alles Gut____!
13. X: Warum denkst du, daß ich in Hannelore verliebt bin?
    Y: Ach, das sieht doch ein Blind____.
14. X: Was ist der Titel Ihrer Biographie?
    Y: „Ich und meine viel____ dumm____ Fehler."

B. *Translate into German. (Use the present perfect for the English past tense.)*

1. I made many stupid mistakes.
2. We visited a few (**ein paar**) good friends.
3. They told us something interesting.
4. We saw two interesting films.
5. These films are only for adults.
6. Here is some hot coffee.
7. Many Germans play soccer.
8. Her father is a famous scholar.
9. I asked an employee (fem.).
10. An employee (masc.) gave me this information.
11. That's the same old story.
12. I bought three second-hand books.
13. His bark is worse than his bite.
14. All the best!

10

Comparison of Adjectives and Adverbs

KEY TO THE EXERCISES ON CASSETTE 5.
RUNNING TIME: APPROX. 40 MIN.

Forms of Comparison

§1   BASIC PATTERN

There are three degrees of comparison:

the positive degree (base form)	**fast**	My car is fast.
the comparative degree	**faster**	Your car is faster.
the superlative degree	**fastest**	Her car is the fastest.

In English short adjectives form the comparative and superlative by adding the endings -*er* and -*est* to the base form, whereas longer adjectives use *more* and *most*: *more elegant, most elegant.*

The German forms are:

POSITIVE	schnell	elegant		
COMPARATIVE	schnell**er**	elegan**ter**	_____	**er**
SUPERLATIVE	schnell**st-**	elegan**test-**	_____	**(e)st-**

Regardless of length, German adjectives add **-er** to form the comparative and **-st** or **-est** to form the superlative. For the sake of pronunciation, **-est** is added to adjectives ending in **-d, -t, -s, -sch, -ß,** or **-z**:

mild	laut	hübsch (*pretty*)	heiß
milder	lauter	hübscher	heißer
mild**est-**	laut**est-**	hübsch**est-**	heiß**est-**

177

Polysyllabic adjectives ending in **-d, -t,** or **-sch** add **-st** in the superlative when the last syllable is unstressed:

interessánt	but: dríngend (*urgent*)	práktisch
interessánter	dríngender	práktischer
interessánt**est-**	dríngend**st-**	práktisch**st-**

§2   VARIATIONS AND IRREGULARITIES

a. Most monosyllabic adjectives with the stem vowels **a, o,** or **u** require an umlaut in the comparative and superlative:

alt	kalt	lang	warm	groß	jung	kurz (*short*)	dumm
älter	kälter	länger	wärmer	größer	jünger	kürzer	dümmer
ältest-	kältest-	längst-	wärmst-	größt-	jüngst-	kürzest-	dümmst-

Note the irregular form **größt-**: only **-t** is added to the stem in the superlative. §3 of the Appendix offers a list of adjectives that add an umlaut in the comparative and superlative.

b. Adjectives ending in **-e, -el,** and **-er** show a variation in the comparative:

leise (*soft*)	dunkel (*dark*)	teuer
leise**r**	dunk**l**er	teu**r**er
(only **r** added)	(**e** omitted)	
leisest-	dunkelst-	teuerst-

c. **Hoch** drops **c** in the comparative; **nahe** adds **c** in the superlative:

hoch	nahe (*close, near*)
höher	näher
höchst-	nächst-

d. The comparative and superlative of **gut** and **viel** are irregular, as are the forms of their English counterparts:

gut	(*good*)	**viel**	(*much, many*)
besser	(*better*)	**mehr**	(*more*)
best-	(*best*)	**meist-**	(*most*)

Note that in contrast to their English equivalents the comparative and superlative of **schlecht** and **wenig** are regular:

schlecht	(*bad*)	wenig	(*little*)
schlechter	(*worse*)	weniger	(*less*)
schlechtest-	(*worst*)	wenigst-	(*least*)

Using the Forms of Comparison

In German all three forms of adjectives — positive, comparative, and superlative — may function as a predicate adjective, an adverb, or an attributive adjective.

§3   COMPARISON OF PREDICATE ADJECTIVES AND ADVERBS

Heute ist es **kalt.**	Inge fährt **schnell.**	
kälter.	**schneller.**	_____ er
am kältesten.	**am schnellsten.**	am_____ (e)sten

The comparative has the ending **-er,** the superlative **-(e)sten.** The superlative is preceded by **am.** These forms do not change.

PRACTICE 1   A. _Complete the sentences with comparative forms._

> **Model:** Das ist _____. (interessant)
> **Das ist interessanter.**

1. Das ist _____. (dringend, praktisch, elegant, modern, hoch, nahe, gut, schlecht, viel, wenig)
2. Hannelore ist _____. (nett, freundlich, intelligent)
3. Ulrich ist _____. (jung, alt, unfreundlich, egoistisch)
4. Unsere Nachbarn sind _____. (neugierig, tolerant)
5. Diese Sache ist _____. (wichtig,[1] kompliziert, einfach[2])
6. Bitte fahren Sie _____. (langsam, vorsichtig[3])
7. Welches Kleid ist _____? (billig,[4] teuer)
8. Diese Farbe ist _____. (dunkel, hell)
9. Die Tage werden _____. (lang, kurz)
10. Bitte sprechen Sie _____! (laut, leise)

B. _Complete the sentences with superlative forms._

> **Model:** Das ist _____. (interessant)
> **Das ist am interessantesten.**

1. Das ist _____. (schwer, leicht, praktisch, gut, schlecht, langweilig,[5] einfach, wichtig, billig, teuer, hoch, nahe)
2. Klaus arbeitet _____. (schnell, langsam, viel, wenig)
3. Frau Büchner ist _____. (nett, tolerant, höflich,[6] neugierig)
4. Hier ist es _____. (warm, heiß, kalt)
5. Du gefällst mir _____. (gut)

Phrases of comparison expressing equality and inequality

In phrases of comparison, the positive degree is expressed with **so ... wie** and the comparative degree with **als**:

Marlene ist **so groß wie** ich.	
Marlene is as tall as I (am).	**so _____ wie** as _____ as

1 **wichtig**   important
2 **einfach**   simple
3 **vorsichtig**   careful(ly)
4 **billig**   cheap, inexpensive
5 **langweilig**   boring
6 **höflich**   polite

Klaus ist **größer als** ich.
Klaus is taller than I (am).

Helga ist **intelligenter als** ich.
Helga is more intelligent than I (am).

_____**er als**	_____er than
	more _____ than

Note that in comparisons

wie = *as*
als = *than*

PRACTICE 2   *Supply the German equivalents of the English phrases in parentheses.*

Model: X: Ich finde, daß Andreas sehr tolerant ist.
   Y: Er ist _____ seine Eltern. (*as tolerant as*)
   Er ist so tolerant wie seine Eltern.

1. X: Deine Schwester ist wirklich sehr hübsch.
   Y: Das stimmt. Sie ist _____ ich. (*as pretty as*)
2. X: Sind die neuen Schuhe bequem?[1]
   Y: Sie sind nicht _____ die alten. (*as comfortable as*)
3. X: Klaus ist immer sehr höflich.
   Y: Stimmt. Er ist _____ du. (*more polite than*)
4. X: Bist du dicker[2] geworden?
   Y: Nein. Ich bin _____ immer. (*as slim[3] as*)
5. X: Margot fährt _____ ich. (*more slowly than*)
   Y: Und sie fährt auch _____ du. (*more carefully than*)
6. X: Meine Noten sind nicht _____ deine. (*as good as*)
   Y: Aber meine Note in Biologie ist _____ deine. (*worse than*)
7. X: Du ißt _____ ich. (*more than*)
   Y: Das stimmt nicht. Ich esse _____ du. (*less than*)
8. X: Ist Margot _____ du? (*shorter[4] than*)
   Y: Nein. Sie ist _____ ich. (*as tall[5] as*)
9. X: Bist du ordentlich[6] oder liederlich?[7]
   Y: Sagen wir, ich bin _____ meine Schwester und
      _____ mein Bruder. (*neater than, sloppier than*)

1 **bequem**	comfortable
2 **dick**	fat, heavy
3 **schlank**	slim
4 **klein**	short ⎰
5 **groß**	tall ⎱ (a person's height)
6 **ordentlich**	orderly, neat
7 **liederlich**	sloppy

Strengthening the comparison

Certain words or prefixes may be added to strengthen a comparison.

a. **So** may be replaced by **ebenso** or **genauso**:

> Walter ist **ebenso/genauso groß wie** ich.
> *Walter is just as tall as I (am).*

b. The comparative form may be preceded by **noch, etwas,** or **viel**:

> Dieter ist **noch fauler als** ich.   *Dieter is even lazier than I (am).*
> Helga ist **etwas dicker als** du.   *Helga is somewhat (a little) heavier than you.*
> Ich bin **viel kleiner als** er.   *I am much shorter than he (is).*

c. In the superlative **aller-** may be added as a prefix:

> Das ist am **allerbesten.**   *That is best of all/the very best.*

PRACTICE 3   *Supply the German equivalents.*

> **Model:** Astrid spricht jetzt sehr gut Deutsch.
> Ja, ihr Deutsch ist _____ geworden. (*much better*)
> **Ja, ihr Deutsch ist viel besser geworden.**

1. X: War die Prüfung leicht oder schwer?
   Y: Sehr schwer. Sie war _____ sonst.[1] (*much harder than*)
2. X: Wer ist größer, du oder Thomas?
   Y: Thomas. Ich bin _____ er. (*a little shorter than*)
3. X: Merkst[2] du denn nicht, wie neugierig Rainer ist?
   Y: Ach, ich bin _____ er. (*even nosier than*)
4. X: Warum ist Monika Baumann immer so egoistisch?
   Y: Das liegt in der Familie.[3] Sie ist _____ alle Baumanns. (*just as egotistical as*)
5. X: Hoffentlich ist die neue Methode _____ die alte. (*just as simple as*)
   Y: Ich glaube, die neue ist _____ die alte. (*a little more complicated than*)
6. X: Ich weiß, meine Frage war sehr dumm.
   Y: Und meine Antwort war _____. (*even dumber*)
7. X: Astrid wiegt[4] _____ ich. (*much more than*)
   Y: Und ich wiege _____ Astrid. (*even more than*)
8. X: Wir alle fahren viel zu schnell.
   Y: Und du fährst _____. (*fastest of all*)
9. X: Ich glaube, dieser Punkt ist sehr wichtig.
   Y: Er ist _____. (*most important of all*)

1 **sonst**	usual(ly)
2 **merken**	to notice
3 **etwas liegt in der Familie**	something runs in the family
4 **wiegen, wog, gewogen**	to weigh

§4   COMPARISON OF ATTRIBUTIVE ADJECTIVES

Used attributively, comparative and superlative adjectives have the same strong or weak endings as any other adjective (cf. Chap. 9). The endings are added to the base forms as given in §1 and §2.

Der gro**ße** Koffer gehört mir.	Das ist ein gro**ßer** Koffer.
Der größe**re** Koffer gehört mir.	Das ist kein größe**rer** Koffer.
Der größ**te** Koffer gehört mir.	Das ist mein größ**ter** Koffer.

      | |
strong weak

          | |
          un- strong
          inflected

PRACTICE 4   A. *Replace the comparatives in the following sentences with appropriate comparative forms of the adjectives in parentheses.*

Model: Das ist der kürzere Weg. (lang)
        Das ist der längere Weg.

1. Das ist eine nettere Kollegin. (freundlich, jung, alt)
2. Das sind elegantere Schuhe. (bequem, billig, teuer)
3. Das ist ein kleinerer Wagen. (groß, alt, schick)
4. Frank Morgenstern ist ein jüngerer Fußballspieler. (gut, schlecht)
5. Das ist ein längerer Film. (kurz, interessant, langweilig)
6. Er hat ein schöneres Leben als wir. (leicht, schwer, gut)

B. *Change the attributive adjectives to the comparative.*

Model: Das ist ein kleiner Wagen.
        Das ist ein kleinerer Wagen.

1. Das ist ein freundlicher Briefträger.
2. Das ist ein bequemer Sessel.[1]
3. Das ist ein intelligentes Mädchen.
4. Herr Hofmann ist ein guter Pianist.
5. Haben Sie einen guten Vorschlag?
6. Das ist eine wichtige Sache.
7. Hoffentlich finden wir eine einfache Lösung.[2]
8. Ich muß eine praktische Tasche[3] kaufen.

C. *Insert superlative forms of the adjectives in parentheses.*

Model: Das ist das _____ Auto. (teuer)
        Das ist das teuerste Auto.

1. Das ist der _____ Wagen. (klein, groß, billig)
2. Das ist die _____ Übung. (leicht, schwer, einfach, kompliziert)
3. Renate hat den _____ Mann geheiratet. (reich, intelligent, nett, egoistisch)

---

1 **der Sessel, -**   armchair
2 **die Lösung, -en**   solution
3 **die Tasche, -n**   bag

4. Ich habe den _____ Aufsatz geschrieben. (lang, kurz, gut, schlecht)

Comparative and superlative forms of *viel* and *wenig*

viel	SINGULAR:	Sie hat **viel** Zeit.	(*much*)
		mehr Zeit.	(*more*)
		die meiste Zeit.	(*the most*)
	PLURAL:	**Viele** Leute sind dagegen.	(*many*)
		Mehr Leute	(*more*)
		Die meisten Leute	(*most*)
wenig	SINGULAR:	Sie hat **wenig** Zeit.	(*little*)
		weniger Zeit.	(*less*)
		die wenigste Zeit.	(*the least*)
	PLURAL:	**Wenige** Leute sind dagegen.	(*few*)
		Weniger Leute	(*fewer*)
		Die wenigsten Leute	(*the fewest*)

Note: a. **Viel** and **wenig** usually have endings in the plural but not in the singular.

b. The comparatives **mehr** and **weniger** never add an ending.

c. **Meist-** requires the definite article: **die** meisten Leute (*most people*).

PRACTICE 5   *Insert German equivalents.*

Model: Ich habe _____ du. (fewer hobbies than)
Ich habe weniger Hobbys als du.

1. Du hast _____ ich. (more stamps than)
2. Kaufmanns haben _____ wir. (more money than)
3. _____ arbeiten im Sommer. (most students)
4. Der neue Bürgermeister hat _____ der alte. (fewer problems than)
5. Ich habe _____ du. (less willpower[1] than)
6. Du hast _____. (the fewest worries[2])

PRACTICE 6   Summarizing exercises

A. *Translate into German.*

1. a. That's a simple solution.   **Das ist eine einfache Lösung.**
   b. That's a simpler solution.
   c. That's the simplest solution.
   d. That's simpler.
   e. That's the simplest.
2. a. That's a good suggestion.   **Das ist ein guter Vorschlag.**
   b. That's a better suggestion.

1 **die Willenskraft**   willpower
2 **die Sorge, -n**   worry

    c. Do you have a better suggestion? (formal)

    d. That's the best suggestion.

3. a. The brown shoes are very comfortable. **Die braunen Schuhe sind sehr bequem.**

    b. Are the black shoes as comfortable as the brown ones?

    c. The black shoes are even more comfortable.

    d. These are (**Das sind**) the most comfortable shoes.

4. a. This color isn't dark enough. **Diese Farbe ist nicht dunkel genug.**

    b. This color is a little darker.

    c. Do you have a darker color? (formal)

    d. That's the darkest color.

5. a. This composition isn't good. **Dieser Aufsatz ist nicht gut.**

    b. My composition is worse.

    c. That's the worst composition.

    d. Who wrote the worst composition? (pres. perf.)

6. a. This coffee tastes very good. **Dieser Kaffee schmeckt sehr gut.**

    b. Which coffee tastes better?

    c. Klaus makes[1] the best coffee.

    d. His coffee tastes best of all.

7. a. This bag isn't practical. **Diese Tasche ist nicht praktisch.**

    b. Do you have a more practical bag? (formal)

    c. I bought the most practical bag. (pres. perf.)

8. a. That's a big worry. **Das ist eine große Sorge.**

    b. That's my biggest worry.

    c. I've more worries than you. (fam. sing.)

    d. You have fewer worries than I.

9. a. Margrit is very neat. **Margrit ist sehr ordentlich.**

    b. She's much neater than you. (fam. sing.)

    c. I'm a little sloppier than my sister.

    d. You're just as sloppy as I. (fam. sing.)

B. *Supply the German equivalents.*

1.   X: Das ist ein wichtiger Punkt.

      Y: Meiner Meinung nach ist das der _____ Punkt. (*most important*)

2.   X: Hast du einen Job gefunden?

      Y: Noch nicht. Das ist jetzt mein _____ Problem. (*biggest*)

3.   X: Haben Sie jetzt _____ Zeit für Ihre Familie? (*more*)

      Y: Leider habe ich jetzt _____ Zeit für sie. (*even less*)

4.   X: Ich habe _____ du. (*fewer friends than*)

      Y: Aber du hast _____ ich. (*more girlfriends than*)

5.   X: Hoffentlich haben unsere Kinder ein _____ wir. (*better life than*)

      Y: Das hoffen _____. (*most parents*)

6.   X: Wer hat den _____ Aufsatz geschrieben? (*best*)

---

1 *idiom:* **Kaffee kochen**   to make coffee

Y: Das weiß ich nicht. Ich weiß nur, daß ich den _____
geschrieben habe. (*worst one*)

7. X: Ich finde, daß du jetzt _____ bist. (*slimmer*)
    Y: Leider stimmt das nicht. Ich bin _____ immer. (*as fat as*)

8. X: Ist dein neuer Freund _____ du? (*as tall as*)
    Y: Leider nicht. Er ist _____ ich. (*a little shorter than*)

9. X: Ich bin sehr liederlich. Bist du _____ ich? (*neater than*)
    Y: Nein. Ich bin _____ du. (*just as sloppy as*)

10. X: Sind die Hausaufgaben wieder so kompliziert?
    Y: Meiner Meinung nach sind sie _____.
    (*even more complicated*)

11. X: Sind deine Noten _____ geworden? (*a little better*)
    Y: Leider sind sie _____ geworden. (*even worse*)

12. X: Wer kocht den _____ Kaffee? (*best*)
    Y: Ich finde, mein Kaffee schmeckt _____. (*best*)

13. X: Meine Schwester ißt _____ ich. (*less than*)
    Y: Sie hat wahrscheinlich _____ du. (*more willpower than*)

14. a. X: Wieviel wiegst du?
       Y: _____ früher.[1] (*less than*)
    b. X: Und wieviel hast du früher gewogen?
       Y: _____ jetzt. (*more than*)
    c. X: Sehr logisch.
       Y: _____ immer.[2] (*as logical as*)

C. *Compare yourself with relatives and friends and form sentences expressing equality or inequality. Vary your sentences.*

Model: schlank sein

_____ (name) **ist so schlank wie ich.**

or: **genauso schlank wie ich.**

or: **nicht so schlank wie ich.**

or: **schlanker als ich.**

or: **viel (etwas) schlanker als ich.**

1. dick sein   6. vorsichtig fahren
2. liederlich sein   7. schnell lernen
3. neugierig sein   8. langsam arbeiten
4. egoistisch sein   9. viel essen
5. intelligent sein

D. *Answer the following questions:*

1. Wer in Ihrer Familie ißt am meisten?
2. Wer in Ihrer Familie spricht am wenigsten?

---

1 **früher**   earlier, before, in the past
2 **immer**   always

3. Wer von Ihren Freunden und Freudinnen hat die meiste Willenskraft?
4. Wen von Ihren Freunden und Freudinnen finden Sie am nettesten?
5. Welchen Schauspieler und welche Schauspielerin bewundern Sie am meisten?
6. Welche Fernsehsendung (*TV program*) gefällt Ihnen am besten oder hat Ihnen am besten gefallen?

Additional Features of Comparatives and Superlatives

§**5** TWO WAYS OF EXPRESSING THE SUPERLATIVE OF PREDICATE ADJECTIVES

> Meine Freunde sind sehr nett. Rainer ist **am nettesten.**
> > or: Rainer ist **der netteste** (Freund).
> > *My friends are very nice. Rainer is the nicest (one).*

When persons or things of a distinctive group are compared, the superlative predicate adjective frequently appears in the attributive form (in agreement with the noun to which it refers) rather than in the form that requires **am . . . (e)sten.**

Additional examples:

> Körners Töchter sind sehr intelligent.
> > Astrid is **am intelligentesten.**
> > or: Astrid ist **die intelligenteste** (Tochter).
> > *The Körners' daughters are very intelligent.*
> > *Astrid is the most intelligent (one).*

> Sie sehen hier sehr wertvolle Gemälde.
> > Dieses Gemälde ist **am wertvollsten.**
> > or: Dieses Gemälde ist **das wertvollste** (Gemälde).
> > *You are seeing here very valuable paintings.*
> > *This painting is the most valuable (one).*

PRACTICE 7   *Supply the German attributive forms.*

> **Model:** Wir haben sehr freundliche Nachbarn.
> > Kästners sind _____ (Nachbarn).
> > > *(the friendliest)*
> > **Kästners sind die freundlichsten.**

1. Die Mieter[1] in diesem Haus sind sehr tolerant.
   Köhlers sind _____ (Mieter).
   (the most tolerant)
2. Meine Schwester hat sehr strenge Lehrer.
   Ihr Mathematiklehrer ist _____ (Lehrer).
   (the strictest)

---

1 **der Mieter, -**   tenant

3. Die Kurzgeschichten in diesem Buch sind interessant.
   Diese hier ist _____ (Kurzgeschichte).
   (*the most interesting*)
4. In diesem Stadtteil[1] gibt es viele alte Häuser.
   Das hier ist _____ (Haus).
   (*the oldest*)
5. Ich habe viele dumme Fehler gemacht, und dieser hier ist
   _____ (Fehler).
   (*the most stupid*)
6. Alle Prüfungen waren schwer; die Biologieprüfung war
   _____ (Prüfung).
   (*the hardest*)

§6   THE COMPARATIVES AND SUPERLATIVES OF THE ADVERBS *bald*, *oft*, AND *gern*

a.	**bald**	soon	Besuchst du uns **bald**?
	eher	sooner	Kannst du nicht **eher** kommen?
	am ehesten	(*the*) *soonest*	Er hat **am ehesten** reagiert.
b.	**oft**	*often*	Er hat **oft** angerufen.
	öfter	*oftener/more often*	Sie hat **öfter** angerufen.
	(am öftesten)	*most often*	
	am häufigsten	*most frequently*	Du hast **am häufigsten** angerufen.

The superlative **am öftesten** is rare; **am häufigsten** is commonly used instead.

c.	**gern(e)**	etwas **gern** tun	*to like to do something*
	lieber	etwas **lieber** tun	*to prefer to do something*
	am liebsten	etwas **am liebsten** tun	*to like to do something most, best*

Gern(e), lieber, am liebsten are used together with a verb to express various degrees of liking. An **e** may be added to **gern**.

Note the use of **essen** and **trinken** when referring to food and drink:

Er **trinkt gern** Kaffee.	*He likes coffee.*
Ich **trinke lieber** Tee.	*I prefer tea.*
Sie **ißt am liebsten** Hummer.	*She likes lobster the best.*

PRACTICE 8   *Translate into English, then reproduce the German from your translation.*

1. Ich spiele gern Tennis, aber mein Freund spielt lieber Fußball.
2. Ich trinke gern Orangensaft,[2] aber Apfelsaft trinke ich lieber.
3. Was trinkst du am liebsten?
4. Meine Freundin ißt am liebsten Pizza.
5. Was tust du am liebsten?

1 **der Stadtteil, -e**	part of town
2 **der Orangensaft, ¨e**	orange juice

6. Ich tue am liebsten nichts.
7. Warum hast du mir das nicht eher gesagt?
8. Warum schreibst du mir nicht öfter?
9. Von allen meinen Freunden ruft Thomas am häufigsten an.

§7   THE USE OF *immer* + COMPARATIVE

The construction **immer** + comparative indicates a progressive change:

Es wird immer kälter.
It is getting colder and colder. It keeps getting colder.
(lit. *It is getting always/ever colder.*)

Du wirst immer egoistischer.
You are becoming more and more egotistical.

Immer mehr Arbeiter verlieren ihren Arbeitsplatz.
More and more workers are losing their jobs.

PRACTICE 9   *Insert German equivalents.*

> **Model:** _____ Leute sind politisch aktiv. *(fewer and fewer)*
> **Immer weniger Leute sind politisch aktiv.**

1. _____ Studenten suchen einen Job. *(more and more)*
2. _____ Studenten finden einen Job. *(fewer and fewer)*
3. Er ist _____ gefahren. *(faster and faster)*
4. Du wirst _____. *(prettier and prettier)*
5. Meine Noten werden _____. *(better and better)*
6. Das Wetter wird _____. *(worse and worse)*
7. Ich werde _____. *(fatter and fatter)*
8. Die Sache wird _____. *(more and more complicated)*
9. Das Benzin wird _____. *(more and more expensive)*
10. Ich verdiene _____ Geld. *(less and less)*

§8   THE USE OF *je ... desto* or *je ... um so*

Je schneller, desto besser.
or: **um so besser.** } *The faster the better.*

Je bequemer, desto besser.
or: **um so besser.** } *The more comfortable the better.*

Observe the word order:

Je mehr ich für dich **tue**, desto mehr **verlangst du** von mir.
└─DEPENDENT CLAUSE─┘ └──── MAIN CLAUSE────┘
   verb at the end   inverted word order
The more I do for you, the more you demand from me.

PRACTICE 10   *Translate into English, then reproduce the German from your translation.*

1. Je eher, desto besser.
2. Je praktischer, um so besser.
3. Je weniger Arbeit, um so besser.
4. Je mehr Geld ich verdiene, desto mehr Geld gebe ich aus.[1]
5. Es ist absurd: Je weniger ich esse, desto dicker werde ich.
6. Je mehr Sie ihn tadeln,[2] um so unsicherer wird er.

§9   ABSOLUTE COMPARATIVES AND SUPERLATIVES

Absolute comparatives

In certain expressions a comparative form is used where no comparison is actually implied:

ein **älterer** Herr	*an elderly gentleman*
ein **größerer** Geldbetrag	*a rather large amount of money*
eine **längere** Reise	*a rather long trip*
Neuere Sprachen	*modern languages*

Absolute superlatives

Superlative forms may be used merely to indicate a very high degree of some quality. As adjectives such superlatives are often unpreceded:

liebste Barbara	*dearest Barbara*
liebster Peter	*dearest Peter*
beste Grüße	*best greetings or regards*

As adverbs these superlatives modify an adjective or another adverb; they lack **am** and the ending **-en:**

Das war **höchst** interessant.	*That was most interesting.*
Das ist **äußerst** unangenehm.	*That is extremely unpleasant.*

Special adverbial superlatives with the ending *-ens*

höchstens	*at the most*	Sie ist **höchstens** 20 Jahre alt.
mindestens	*at least*	Er arbeitet **mindestens** 8 Stunden am Tag.
frühestens	*at the earliest*	Ich komme **frühestens** am Freitag zurück.
spätestens	*at the latest*	Wir rufen Sie **spätestens** am Sonnabend an.
meistens ⎫	*mostly, most of*	Ich komme **meistens/meist** zu spät.
meist ⎭	*the time, usually*	*I'm usually late. I'm late most of the time.*

1 **aus•geben (gibt aus),**   to spend
   gab aus, ausgegeben
2 **tadeln**   to reprimand

PRACTICE 11   *Insert German equivalents.*

1. Ich muß _____ die Dreckarbeit[1] machen. (*most of the time*)
2. Wenn wir Pizza essen wollen, gehen wir _____ in dieses Restaurant. (*usually*)
3. Klaus wiegt _____ 200 Pfund. (*at least*)
4. Wir haben _____ zehn Minuten gewartet. (*at the most*)
5. Ich kann dich _____ um 7 Uhr abholen. (*at the earliest*)
6. Ich gebe dir das Geld _____ am Freitag zurück. (*at the latest*)
7. Das war eine _____ peinliche Frage. (*most*)
8. Das ist ein _____ kompliziertes Problem. (*extremely*)
9. Frau Krause ist eine _____ Dame. (*elderly*)
10. Renate studiert _____ in Hamburg. (*modern languages*)
11. Alle unsere Nachbarn haben _____ Familien. (*rather large*)
12. Wir senden Dir,* _____ , _____ aus München. (*dearest Karin, best regards*)

§10   COMPARATIVES AND SUPERLATIVES USED AS NOUNS

Like other adjectives, comparatives and superlatives may be used as nouns. They retain their usual adjective endings (cf. Chap. 9, §12).

Comparatives

der/die/das Stärker**e**	*the stronger one*
die Stärker**en**	*the stronger ones*
nichts Leichter**es**	*nothing easier*
nichts Schöner**es**	*nothing more beautiful*
nichts Besser**es**	*nothing better*
etwas Besser**es**	*something better*
etwas Billiger**es**	*something cheaper, something less expensive*
etwas Interessanter**es**	*something more interesting*
etwas Praktischer**es**	*something more practical*
etwas Wichtiger**es**	*something more important*

Superlatives

Thomas ist **der Beste** in Chemie.	*Thomas is the best (one) in chemistry.*
Er ist **der Allerbeste.**	*He is the best (one) of all.*
Du bist **die Schönste.**	*You are the most beautiful one.*
Du bist **die Allerschönste.**	*You are the most beautiful one of all.*
Der Nächste bitte!	*The next (one) please.*
Das ist **das Schwerste.**	*That is the hardest thing.*
Das ist **das Wichtigste.**	*That is the most important thing.*

---

1 **die Dreckarbeit**	dirty work
der Dreck	dirt

* The familiar address is capitalized in letters, cards, and notes (cf. Appendix, §7).

Heben Sie **das Neu(e)ste** gehört?   *Have you heard the latest?*
Ich habe **mein Bestes** getan.   *I did my best.*

PRACTICE 12   *Insert the German equivalents.*

1. Ich konnte nichts _____ finden. (*better*)
2. Du mußt immer das _____ haben. (*best*)
3. Ich werde mein _____ tun. (*best*)
4. Frau Stern, Sie sind die _____. (*next one*)
5. Nicht immer gewinnt der _____. (*stronger one*)
6. Es gibt für ihn nichts _____ als Fußball. (*more interesting*)
7. Haben Sie nicht etwas _____? (*more practical*)
8. Werner besucht uns nie. Immer hat er etwas _____ vor. (*more important*)
9. Was ist für dich das _____? (*most important thing*)
10. Ich finde, Selbstbeherrschung[1] ist das _____. (*hardest thing*)
11. Haben Sie Frau Bergmann schon das _____ erzählt? (*latest*)
12. Helga ist die _____. (*best of all*)

PRACTICE 13   Summarizing exercises for §5 to §10.

A. *Translate into German.*

1. a. That's important.   **Das ist wichtig.**
   b. That's extremely important.
   c. There's[2] nothing more important than that.
   d. That's the most important thing.
2. a. This music is very romantic.   **Diese Musik ist sehr romantisch.**
   b. It's getting more and more romantic.
   c. The more romantic the better.
   d. There's nothing more romantic than that.
3. a. I have to buy something cheap.   **Ich muß etwas Billiges kaufen.**
   b. The cheaper the better.
   c. Do you have something cheaper? (*formal*)
   d. Do you have something more practical?
   e. Do you have something more interesting?
4. a. Life is hard.   **Das Leben ist schwer.**
   b. Life is becoming harder and harder.
   c. What's the hardest thing for you? (*fam. sing.*)
   d. What's the easiest thing for you?
   e. There's nothing easier than that.
   f. There's nothing better than that.

B. *Insert the German equivalents.*

1. a. X: Meine Klavierlehrerin ist sehr streng.
      Y: Meine auch. Ich finde, sie wird _____. (*stricter and stricter*)

1 **die Selbstbeherrschung**   self-control
2 **es gibt** (+ *acc.*)   there is *or* are

   b. X: Strenge Lehrer sind gut für mich.

       Y: Für mich auch. _____ . (*The stricter the better.*)

2. a. X: Die deutsche Grammatik ist sehr schwer.

       Y: Nur am Anfang. Später wird sie _____ . (*easier and easier*)

   b. X: Ich finde, sie wird _____ . (*more and more complicated*)

3.   X: Werden deine Noten _____ ? (*better*)

     Y: Leider werden sie _____ . (*worse and worse*)

4.   X: Wollt ihr wirklich schon im Mai heiraten?

     Y: Ja. _____ . (*The sooner the better.*)

5.   X: Ich finde diesen Tanz verrückt.

     Y: Mir gefällt er. _____ . (*The crazier the better.*)

6.   X: Soll ich Ihnen Kaffee oder Tee bringen?

     Y: Für mich Tee. Meine Freundin _____ . (*prefers coffee*)

7.   X: Ist deine Freundin immer so nett?

     Y: Nicht immer, aber _____ . (*most of the time*)

8.   X: Was machst du sonnabends?

     Y: Da gehe ich _____ einkaufen. (*usually*)

9.   X: Wie lange willst du in Wien studieren?

     Y: _____ zwei Semester. (*at least*)

10.   X: Hast du die Prüfung bestanden?

     Y: Hoffentlich. Ich habe _____ getan. (*my best*)

11.   X: Ich verstehe nicht, wie du in der Prüfung durchfallen konntest.

     Y: Es gibt _____ als das. (*nothing easier*)

12.   X: Ich werde _____ . (*dumber and dumber*)

     Y: Keine Angst![1] Das merkt hier niemand.

13.   X: Es ist schrecklich, wie oft Barbara in den Spiegel[2] sieht.

     Y: Und jedesmal[3] fragt sie:

       „Spieglein, Spieglein an der Wand,

       wer ist die _____ im ganzen Land?"* (*most beautiful*)

---

1 **keine Angst!**   don't worry (*lit.*: no fear)
2 **der Spiegel, -**   mirror
3 **jedesmal**   every *or* each time

* In English, "Mirror, mirror on the wall, who is the fairest of them all?"

11

Numerals; Time Expressions

KEY TO THE EXERCISES ON CASSETTE 6.
RUNNING TIME: APPROX. 40 MIN.

Cardinal and Ordinal Numbers

§1 CARDINAL NUMBERS AND THEIR USES

0	null	30	**dreißig**
1	eins	31	einunddreißig
2	zwei	40	vierzig
3	drei	41	einundvierzig
4	vier	50	fünfzig
5	fünf	60	**sechzig**
6	sechs	70	**siebzig**
7	sieben	80	achtzig
8	acht	90	neunzig
9	neun	100	(ein)hundert
10	zehn	101	hunderteins
11	elf	102	hundertzwei
12	zwölf	150	hundertfünfzig
13	dreizehn	151	hunderteinundfünfzig
14	vierzehn	199	hunderteinundfünfzig
15	fünfzehn	200	zweihundert
16	**sechzehn**	201	zweihunderteins
17	**siebzehn**	300	dreihundert
18	achtzehn	400	vierhundert
19	neunzehn	500	fünfhundert
20	zwanzig	600	sechshundert
21	**einundzwanzig**	700	siebenhundert
22	zweiundzwanzig	800	achthundert
23	dreiundzwanzig	900	neunhundert

999 neunhundertneunundneunzig	1 000 000 eine Million
1 000 (ein)tausend	10 000 000 zehn Millionen
2 000 zweitausend	100 000 000 hundert Millionen
10 000 zehntausend	200 500 000 zweihundert Millionen
100 000 (ein)hunderttausend	fünfhunderttausend
250 320 zweihundertfünfzigtausend-	1 000 000 000 eine Milliarde (*one billion*)
dreihundertzwanzig	1 000 000 000 000 eine Billion (*one trillion*)

Note: a. **Eins** is used in counting. It is the only cardinal number that changes when modifying a noun. It then uses the endings of the **ein**-words (cf. Chap. 6, §5).

> Ich habe nur **einen** Freund.
> Ich habe zwei Freunde.

b. **Eins** is written 1.

Sieben is usually written 7 to distinguish it from **eins**.

c. The boldface numbers are irregular:

> eins but **einundzwanzig (s** omitted)
> sechs but **sechzehn, sechzig (s** omitted)
> sieben but **siebzehn, siebzig (en** omitted)
> **dreißig** (ending **-ßig** instead of **-zig**)

d. To separate thousands, German leaves a space or inserts a period. It does not insert a comma, as English does.

> 10 570 or 10.570   zehntausendfünfhundertsiebzig

e. All numbers of less than a million are written with small letters. Numbers of a million or more are feminine nouns; their plural forms end in **-en**:

> **zwei Millionen, Milliarden, Billionen.**

Remember:

> **eine Milliarde** = *one billion*
> **eine Billion**   = *one trillion (one thousand billions)*

PRACTICE 1   *Read aloud the following figures.*

1. 26	5. 126	9. 1 317	13. 431 690
2. 67	6. 247	10. 4 255	14. 919 900
3. 88	7. 739	11. 19 387	15. 1 500 000
4. 94	8. 966	12. 51 674	16. 10 800 750

Approximate figures

etwa		**etwa hundert**
rund	} *about, approximately, roughly*	**rund zwanzig**
ungefähr		**ungefähr zehn**
über	*over, more than*	**über fünfzig**

Decimals

The German equivalent of a decimal point is a comma:

0,5   (read: null Komma fünf)
2,75   (read: zwei Komma sieben fünf)

Amounts in *Deutsche Mark* (DM) and *Pfennig*

Diese Schallplatte kostet DM 30,50. (read: dreißig Mark fünfzig [Pfennig])

Note: a. **Mark** and **Pfennig** are in the singular.
b. **Pfennig** is generally omitted except, of course, when it is the only currency:

Ich habe nur noch 50 Pfennig.

Simple Arithmetic

$12 + 4 = 16$ zwölf und vier ist sechzehn
                or: zwölf plus vier ...
$12 - 4 = 8$ zwölf weniger vier ist acht
                or: zwölf minus vier ...
$$\left. \begin{array}{l} 12 \times 4 \\ \text{or: } 12 \cdot 4 \end{array} \right\} = 48$$ zwölf mal vier ist achtundvierzig
$12 : 4 = 3$ zwölf geteilt durch 4 ist drei
                (short: zwölf durch vier ist drei)

German uses a colon to express division.

PRACTICE 2   *Read aloud the following sentences and equations.*

1. Diese Uhr kostet DM 124,95.
2. Bergmanns haben über 100 000 Mark gewonnen.
3. Etwa 20 000 Ausländer haben diese Ausstellung[1] besucht.
4. Unsere Stadt hat rund 600 000 Einwohner.
5. Haben Sie 4,5 oder 5,4 gesagt?
6. $56 + 21 = 77$
7. $75 - 45 = 30$
8. $7 \times 9 = 63$
9. $150 : 10 = 15$

§2   ORDINAL NUMBERS AND THEIR USES

der, das, die 1.   der, das, die **erste**   *the first*
              2.   zweite   *the second*
              3.   **dritte**   *the third*
              4.   vierte

1 **die Ausstellung, -en**   exhibition

5.	fünfte
6.	sechste
7.	siebente
	or: **siebte**
8.	**achte**
9.	neunte
10.	zehnte
11.	elfte
12.	zwölfte
13.	dreizehnte
19.	neunzehnte
20.	zwanzigste
21.	einundzwanzigste
22.	zweiundzwanzigste
23.	dreiundzwanzigste
30.	dreißigste
31.	einunddreißigste
40.	vierzigste
50.	fünfzigste
60.	sechzigste
70.	siebzigste
80.	achtzigste
90.	neunzigste
100.	hundertste
200.	zweihundertste
1 000.	tausendste
1 000 000.	millionste

Note: a. The ordinal numbers **erste, dritte, siebte,** and **achte** are irregular. The others from 2nd to 19th are formed by adding **-te** to the cardinal number. Higher numbers add **-ste.**

b. Ordinal numbers take normal adjective endings (cf. Chap. 9, §8).

der erst**e** Sonntag   die erst**e** Frage
am erst**en** Sonntag   nach der erst**en** Frage

c. When numerals are used, ordinal numbers are indicated by placing a period after the number.

Mein Büro ist im 19. Stock.   *My office is on the 19th floor.*

The use of the adverbs *erstens, zweitens, drittens,* etc.

1. **erstens**   *first(ly), in the first place*
2. **zweitens**   *second(ly), in the second place*
3. **drittens**   *third(ly), in the third place*
4. **viertens**   *fourth(ly), in the fourth place*

Warum willst du nicht mit uns ins Kino gehen?
Erstens bin ich müde, **zweitens** habe ich keine Zeit, und **drittens** bin ich pleite.

The use of *-mal* and *Mal* with cardinal and ordinal numbers

cardinal number + **-mal**:		ordinal number used as adjective:	
einmal	*once*	**das erste Mal**	*the first time*
noch einmal	*once more*	**zum ersten Mal**	*for the first time*
zweimal	*twice, two times*	**das zweite Mal**	
dreimal	*three times*	**das dritte Mal**	
zehnmal	*ten times*	**das vierte Mal**	
hundertmal	*a hundred times*		
tausendmal	*a thousand times*		

Fractions

$\frac{1}{2}$	**ein halb-**	Das ist **ein halber Kuchen.**	*This is half a cake.*
	die Hälfte	**Die Hälfte** gehört mir.	*Half of it is mine.*
$\frac{1}{3}$	**ein Drittel**		
$\frac{1}{4}$	**ein Viertel**		
$\frac{2}{5}$	**zwei Fünftel**		
$\frac{3}{10}$	**drei Zehntel**		
$\frac{1}{100}$	**ein Hundertstel**		

With the exception of **ein halb-** and **die Hälfte**, fractions are neuter nouns. They are formed by adding **-l** to the ordinal number. **Ein halb-** takes the normal adjective endings. However, in compounds like **eineinhalb** and **anderthalb** ($1\frac{1}{2}$) no adjective ending is used.

$1\frac{1}{2}$	**eineinhalb**	Wir haben **eineinhalb (anderthalb) Jahre** in
	or: **anderthalb**	Zürich gewohnt.
$2\frac{1}{2}$	**zweieinhalb**	Martin hat **zweieinhalb Jahre** Deutsch gelernt.
$3\frac{1}{2}$	**dreieinhalb**	Helgas Eltern sind **dreieinhalb Wochen** in
		Florida geblieben.

PRACTICE 3   A. *Replace the boldface words with German equivalents of the English words and phrases in parentheses.*

1. Wir haben in der **ersten** Reihe gesessen. (*third, fifth, tenth*)
2. Ich habe die **zweite** Frage nicht verstanden. (*fourth, sixth, eighth*)
3. Wir haben das **dritte** Kapitel noch nicht behandelt. (*seventh, seventeenth*)
4. Alle diese Gedichte sind aus dem **sechzehnten** Jahrhundert.[1] (*nineteenth, twentieth*)
5. Du hast nun schon **dreimal** gewonnen. (*five times, nine times*)
6. Sie hat **zum ersten Mal** nachgegeben. (*for the second time*)
7. Ich kann nur **die Hälfte** von meinen Schulden bezahlen. (*one fourth*)
8. Müllers waren **anderthalb** Monate in Europa. (*three and a half*)

B. *Insert German equivalents of the English words and phrases in parentheses.*

1.   X: Wollen Sie es _____ versuchen? (*once more*)
     Y: Ich habe es schon _____ versucht. (*twice*)

---

1 **das Jahrhundert, -e**   century

2. X: _____ hat Helga gewonnen und _____ Thomas.
    (*the first time, the second time*)

    Y: Und _____ werde ich gewinnen. (*the third time*)

3. X: Warum hast du mich nicht angerufen?

    Y: _____ wollte ich dich nicht bei der Arbeit stören, und _____ dachte ich, du würdest vielleicht später anrufen. (*in the first place, in the second place*)

4. a. X: Kennst du Herrn Morgensterns _____ Frau? (*first*)

    Y: Ich kenne nur seine jetzige[1] Frau. Ist das seine _____ Frau? (*second*)

  b. X: Nein, seine _____. (*third*) *Vielleicht* lernen wir noch eine _____ kennen. (*fourth*)

    Y: Hoffentlich nicht.

5. X: Du hast nun schon _____ gesagt, daß du Monika nicht leiden kannst.[2] (*ten times*) Wann hörst du endlich damit auf?

    Y: Wenn ich es _____ gesagt habe. (*a hundred times*)

6. X: Möchten Sie eine Tasse Kaffee?

    Y: Bitte nur _____. (*half a cup*)

7. X: Michael, du vernachlässigst[3] mich. Liebst du mich nicht mehr?

    Y: Unsinn! Du weißt doch, daß du meine _____ bist. (*better half*)

The use of ordinal numbers with dynastic names

Papst Paul **der Erste**	written: Papst Paul I.
Kaiser Wilhelm **der Zweite**	Kaiser Wilhelm II.
König Ludwig **der Vierzehnte**	König Ludwig XIV.

Here the ordinal numbers are capitalized, since they are regarded as part of a proper name. They have the usual adjective endings.

NOM.	Kaiser Friedrich **der Dritte**	Kaiser Friedrich III. war sein Freund.
ACC.	Kaiser Friedrich **den Dritten**	Er haßte Kaiser Friedrich III.
DAT.	Kaiser Friedrich **dem Dritten**	Sie halfen Kaiser Friedrich III.
GEN.	Kaiser Friedrich**s des Dritten**	Sie war die Tochter Kaiser Friedrichs III.

Note that the genitive **-s** is attached to the name only, not to the title.

PRACTICE 4   *Read the following sentences aloud:*

1. Das war ein großes Problem für Kaiser Friedrich III.
2. Das waren die Kinder Kaiser Karls VI.
3. Sie mußten mit König Ludwig XIV. verhandeln.[4]
4. Papst Gregor VII. bannte[5] König Heinrich IV.

1	**jetzig**	present, current
2	**nicht leiden können**	to dislike, not like
3	**vernachlässigen**	to neglect
4	**verhandeln**	to negotiate
5	**bannen**	to excommunicate

Time Expressions

Introduction

In using time expressions, one must pay particular attention to the gender of the nouns. Here is a list of frequently occurring nouns grouped according to gender.

MASCULINE	NEUTER	FEMININE
der Monat, -e	das Jahr, -e	die Sekunde, -n
der Tag, -e	das Wochenende, -n	die Minute, -n
		die Stunde, -n
days of the week		die Nacht, ̈e
der Sonntag, -e		die Mitternacht, ̈e
Montag, -e		die Zeit, -en
Dienstag, -e		die Jahreszeit, -en (*season*)
Mittwoch, -e		die Woche, -n
Donnerstag, -e		die Uhr, -en (*clock, watch*)
Freitag, -e		
Sonnabend, -e		
or: Samstag, -e		

Remember:

> **die Stunde** = *hour*
> **die Uhr**   = *clock, watch*

parts of the day
der Morgen, -
    Vormittag, -e
    Mittag, -e
    Nachmittag, -e
    Abend, -e
(but: die Nacht)

months
der Januar
    Februar
    März
    April
    Mai
    Juni
    Juli
    August
    September
    Oktober
    November
    Dezember

seasons
der Frühling, -e
    Sommer, -
    Herbst, -e
    Winter, -

§3   TIME EXPRESSIONS REFERRING TO SEASONS, MONTHS, DAYS OF THE WEEK, AND PARTS OF THE DAY

Most time expressions that include a preposition are in the dative case.

1. Seasons and Months

im Frühling	*in the* spring	**im** Januar	*in* January
im Sommer	*in the* summer	**im** Februar	
im Herbst	*in the* fall	**im** März	
im Winter	*in the* winter		

In contrast to English usage, German names of the months require the definite article.

Wir heiraten **im Januar**. (contraction of **in** + **dem**)
Der Juli war dieses Jahr sehr heiß.

2. Days of the week

(am) Sonntag *on Sunday*	(Am) Sonntag bin ich in Berlin.
(am) Montag	
(am) Dienstag	

Note that **am** (**an** + **dem**) may be omitted.

3. Parts of the day

am Morgen	*in the (early) morning*	Am Morgen war ich zu Hause.
am Vormittag	*in the (late) morning* or *forenoon* (from 10 to noon)	
am Mittag ⟍ ⟋ *at noon* **zu** Mittag		
am Nachmittag	*in the afternoon*	
am Abend ⟨ *in the evening* / *at night (before bedtime)*		
in der Nacht	*at night (after bedtime)*	

Note that *at night* (*before bedtime*) is expressed by **am Abend**.

4. The days of the week combined with parts of the day

(am) Sonntag morgen   (Am) Sonntag morgen ist unser Hund davongelaufen.
(am) Montag vormittag
(am) Dienstag mittag
(am) Mittwoch abend (*Wednesday evening/night*)
in der Nacht vom Donnerstag zum Freitag

With the exception of **Nacht**, the parts of the day are used as adverbs in these combinations and are therefore not capitalized.

PRACTICE 5   *Insert German equivalents of the English phrases in parentheses.*

1. Vielleicht mieten wir _____ eine größere Wohnung. (*in the spring; in the fall*)
2. Dieses Jahr fahren wir schon _____ nach Italien. (*in June; in May*)
3. _____ habe ich an meinem Referat[1] gearbeitet. (*on Tuesday, on Thursday*)
4. Ich besuche dich vielleicht _____. (*on Wednesday, on Saturday*)
5. Wir sind _____ einkaufen gegangen. (*Saturday morning, Friday afternoon, Thursday evening*)
6. Hast du _____ etwas vor? (*Friday night, Sunday afternoon*)
7. Ich war _____ im Supermarkt. (*Monday morning, Tuesday noon*)
8. _____ hatten wir ein schweres Gewitter.[2] (*the night from Wednesday to Thursday*)

5. Adverbial forms ending in -s

a. Herr Zimmermann arbeitet **am Montag** nicht.
b. Herr Zimmermann arbeitet **montags** nicht.

Sentence *a* may mean that Mr. Zimmermann will not work this coming Monday or that he usually does not work on Mondays. The use of **montags** in sentence *b* clearly indicates that he does not work on Mondays.

Forms ending in **-s** normally denote repeated occurrences. Because they function as adverbs, they are not capitalized.

sonntags, montags, dienstags, mittwochs, donnerstags, freitags, sonnabends/ samstags

on Sundays, Mondays ...

Parts of the day functioning as adverbs:

morgens, vormittags, mittags, nachmittags, abends, nachts
in the morning(s) ...

Meistens lerne ich **abends**. *I usually study at night.*

These forms may also refer to one event:

Ich war gestern zu Hause. Nur **am Nachmittag**⎱
　　　or: Nur **nachmittags**　⎰ war ich bei Kleins.

I was at home yesterday. Only in the afternoon I was at the Kleins'.

---

1 **das Referat, -e**　　seminar paper
2 **das Gewitter, -**　　thunderstorm

The days of the week combined with parts of the day have two forms:

Frau Berger ist **donnerstags nachmittags** immer in ihrem Büro.

(two adverbs)

or: **Donnerstag nachmittags**

(noun + adverb)

PRACTICE 6   *Insert German equivalents of the English phrases in parentheses, using adverbial* **s**-*forms.*

1. _____ ist Frau Morgenstern meistens zu Hause. (*on Mondays, on Tuesdays*)
2. Meistens gehe ich _____ einkaufen. (*on Fridays, on Thursdays*)
3. Diese Bank ist _____ geschlossen. (*on Saturdays and on Wednesday afternoons*)
4. _____ mache ich die Wohnung sauber. (*on Thursday evenings*)
5. Ich weiß meistens nicht, was ich _____ machen soll. (*on Sunday afternoons*)
6. _____ mache ich immer die Hausaufgaben für Montag. (*on Sunday nights*)

§4   ADDITIONAL TIME EXPRESSIONS

1. Adverbs

vorgestern	gestern	heute	morgen	übermorgen
the day before yesterday	*yesterday*	*today*	*tomorrow*	*the day after tomorrow*

The parts of the day used with **heute, gestern,** and **morgen:**

heute morgen } **heute früh**	*this morning*	**gestern morgen** **gestern früh**	**morgen früh** *tomorrow morning* (only this form)
heute vormittag	*this morning* *this forenoon*	**gestern vormittag** etc.	**morgen vormittag** etc.
heute mittag	*this noon*		
heute nachmittag	*this afternoon*		
heute abend	{ *this evening* *tonight*		
heute nacht	*tonight*		

The adverb **morgen** may have two meanings: *morning* or *tomorrow*. When it follows another time expression, it has the meaning of *morning*:

Heute morgen habe ich den Wecker nicht gehört.
This morning I didn't hear the alarm clock.

When it precedes another time expression or stands alone, it has the meaning of *tomorrow*:

> Ich fahre **morgen nachmittag** nach Münster.
>> *I'm going to Münster **tomorrow afternoon.***
> Dieter fährt **morgen** auch nach Münster.
>> *Dieter is also going to Münster **tomorrow**.*

Keep in mind that until bedtime (about 11 P.M.) **abend** corresponds to English *night*:

tonight	**heute abend**
tomorrow night	**morgen abend**
last night	**gestern abend**

Last night after bedtime is expressed by **letzte Nacht.** Compare:

> Ich habe **gestern abend** in der Bibliothek gearbeitet.
> *I worked in the library last night.*

> Ich habe **letzte Nacht** nicht gut geschlafen.
> *I didn't sleep well last night.*

PRACTICE 7   *Insert the German equivalents of the English phrases in parentheses.*

1. Arnold hat _____ an seinem Referat gearbeitet. (*last night*)
2. Vielleicht räume ich _____ mein Zimmer auf. (*tonight, tomorrow night*)
3. Ich habe _____ von dir geträumt. (*last night*)
4. _____ habe ich meinen Wagen gewaschen. (*this noon, yesterday noon*)
5. Wahrscheinlich geht Ursula _____ zum Arzt. (*this afternoon, tomorrow afternoon*)
6. _____ arbeite ich im Labor. (*this morning, tomorrow morning*)
7. _____ habe ich die Deutschstunde geschwänzt. (*this morning, yesterday morning* [use **vormittag**])
8. Ellen ist _____ weggefahren, und _____ kommt sie zurück. (*the day before yesterday, the day after tomorrow*)

2. Time expressions in the accusative case

Most time expressions that do not include a preposition are in the accusative case.

dies**e** Woche	nächst**e** Woche	jed**e** Woche
this week	*next week*	*every week*
dies**es** Wochenende	nächst**es** Wochenende	jed**es** Wochenende
dies**en** Monat	nächst**en** Monat	jed**en** Monat
dies**es** Jahr	nächst**es** Jahr	jed**es** Jahr
	nächst**en** Freitag	jed**en** Freitag
	but: <u>am</u> nächst**en** Tag	
	the next day	

vorige }
letzte } Woche   den ganzen Tag

last week   *all day*
voriges }   *the whole/entire day*
letztes } Wochenende   den ganzen Abend
vorigen }   die ganze Nacht
letzten } Monat   den ganzen Monat
voriges }   das ganze Jahr
letztes } Jahr   die ganze Zeit

3. Time expressions with prepositions + dative case

in ein paar Minuten	vor ein paar Minuten	nach einer Weile
in a few minutes	*a few minutes ago*	*after a while*
in einer Stunde	vor einer Stunde	nach der Deutschstunde
in einer Woche	vor drei Wochen	nach ein paar Tagen
in einem Monat	vor fünf Monaten	nach einer Woche
in einem Jahr	vor zwei Jahren	nach einem Jahr

heute in einer Woche   heute vor einer Woche
  a week from today   *a week ago today*
heute in einem Monat   heute vor einem Monat
  a month from today   *a month ago today*
heute in einem Jahr   heute vor einem Jahr
  a year from today   *a year ago today*

einmal, zweimal, dreimal **am Tag**   *once, twice, three times a day*
                         in der Woche   *a week*
                     or: **die Woche**
                         (accusative)
                         im Monat   *a month*
                         im Jahr   *a year*

Note that **ein paar** is not inflected (cf. Chap. 9, §9).
(For the use of **seit** + dative, cf. Chap. 2, §7,3 and Chap. 7, §1,7.)

4. Set expressions in the genitive case denoting indefinite time

Eines Tages ist Frank davongelaufen.   *One day Frank ran away.*

Eines Morgens }   *One morning* }
Eines Abends } ist er zurückgekommen.   *One evening* } *he came back.*
Eines Nachts }   *One night*   }

Although **Nacht** is of feminine gender, the masculine form **eines Nachts** is used by analogy with **eines Morgens** and **eines Abends**.

PRACTICE 8   *Insert German equivalents of the English phrases in parentheses.*

1. Meine Frau und ich waren _____ in Österreich. (*a week ago, a month ago, a year ago*)
2. _____ waren wir in Wien. (*a week ago today, a month ago today, a year ago today*)
3. Wo werden wir _____ sein? (*a week from today, a month from today, a year from today*)
4. _____ muß diese Arbeit fertig sein. (*in a week, in a month, in a year*)
5. _____ muß ich sehr sparsam[1] sein. (*this week, this month, this year*)
6. Vielleicht sehen wir uns _____ wieder. (*next week, next month, next year*)
7. Erst[2] hat er ja gesagt, aber _____ hat er nein gesagt. (*the next day*)
8. Erst waren wir begeistert von unserem Haus, aber _____ hat es uns nicht mehr gefallen. (*after a few years*)
9. Die ganze Familie Berger war _____ bei uns. (*last Sunday, last weekend, last week*)
10. Käte fährt _____ nach Hause. (*every day, every weekend, every month*)
11. Maria hat mich _____ angerufen. (*a few minutes ago, an hour ago*)
12. Er ruft mindestens _____ an. (*once a day, twice a week, four times a month*)
13. Wir haben _____ Ferien. (*three times a year*)
14. Mein Freund hat _____ vor dem Fernseher gesessen. (*all evening, all the time*)
15. _____ war mein Fahrrad verschwunden.[3] (*one day, one night*)
16. _____ brachte die Polizei mein Fahrrad zurück. (*one morning*)

5. Expressing dates

a. Heute ist **der elfte Mai.**   written: Heute ist **der 11. Mai.**
b. Heute haben wir **den elften Mai.**   Heute haben wir **den 11. Mai.**
c. Ich habe **am elften Mai** Geburtstag.   Ich habe **am 11. Mai** Geburtstag.

In sentence a. **der elfte Mai** is a predicate nominative (after **sein**). In sentence b. **den elften Mai** is in the accusative (direct object). In sentence c. **am elften Mai** is in the dative (prepositional phrase).

1 **sparsam**	thrifty, economical
2 **erst**	at first
3 **verschwinden,**	to disappear
verschwand, ist verschwunden	

Asking about today's date:

> **Welches Datum haben wir heute?** ⎫
> or: **Den wievielten haben wir heute?** ⎬ *What is today's date?*

Dates in letterheads and documents:

> **Berlin, den 11. Mai 1972**
> (spoken: den elften Mai neunzehnhundertzweiundsiebzig)
> **Bonn, den 31. Oktober 1985**
> (spoken: den einunddreißigsten Oktober neunzehnhundertfünfundachtzig)

The day always precedes the month, even when the month is indicated by an ordinal number:

> 31.10.1985 = 31. Oktober 1985

The English phrase *in 1950* is in German **im Jahr(e) 1950** or simply **1950** (never ~~in 1950~~).

> Der Komponist starb **im Jahr(e) 1929.** ⎫
> or: Der Komponist starb **1929.**   ⎬ *The composer died in 1929.*

PRACTICE 9   A. *Insert German equivalents of the English phrases in parentheses.*

Model: Dieses Jahr beginnen die Sommerferien _____. (on May 31)
   Dieses Jahr beginnen die Sommerferien am 31. Mai.

1. Schuberts geben _____ (on December 2) eine große Party.
2. Karin hat _____ Geburtstag. (on July 21)
3. Ich habe _____ Geburtstag. [insert your birthday]
4. Heute ist _____ (April 1)
5. Haben wir heute _____? (June 5)
6. _____ hatten wir eine Explosion in unserem Studentenheim. (in 1979 [two ways])

B. Write the following dates in German, then read them aloud.

1. Hamburg, August 3, 1982
2. Berlin, December 31, 1946
3. Vienna, January 1, 1985

PRACTICE 10   Summarizing exercises for §3 and §4.

A. *Complete the sentences in German.*

1. X: Welches Datum haben wir heute?
   Y: Ich glaube, heute haben wir _____ [insert today's date]
2. X: In welchem Jahr waren die Olympischen Spiele in München?
   Y: Weißt du das nicht mehr? Das war doch _____ (in 1972 [two ways])

3. X: Fährst du am Wochenende mit Gisela nach Hause?

   Y: _____ sind wir zu ihren Eltern gefahren, und _____ fahren wir zu meinen Eltern. (*last weekend, this weekend*)

4. X: Wann ist dieses Museum geöffnet?

   Y: Das weiß ich nicht genau. Ich weiß nur, daß es _____ geschlossen ist. (*Wednesday afternoons*)

5. X: Weißt du, ob Elke jetzt zu Hause ist?

   Y: _____ ist sie nie zu Hause. (*Friday nights*)

6. X: Wann kann man Sie zu Hause erreichen?[1]

   Y: _____ bin ich meistens zu Hause. (*Sunday noons*)

7. X: Warum gehst du nicht zum Zahnarzt?

   Y: Ich war doch _____ dort. (*yesterday noon*)

8. X: Hat es in der Nacht geregnet?

   Y: Es hat _____ geregnet. (*all night*)

9. X: Wann beginnen die Semesterprüfungen?

   Y: Leider schon _____. (*tomorrow morning*)

10. X: Wie oft mußt du diese Tabletten einnehmen?[2]

   Y: _____. (*three times a day*)

11. X: Wie oft geht ihr schwimmen?

   Y: _____. (*twice a week*)

12. X: Wann haben die Schulferien angefangen?

   Y: _____. (*three days ago*)

13. X: Wann werden Sie mit dem Studium fertig?[3]

   Y: Hoffentlich _____. (*in the spring*)

14. X: Was hast du heute gemacht?

   Y: Ich habe _____ die Wohnung saubergemacht. (*all day*)

15. X: Wann hast du Peter das letzte Mal gesehen?

   Y: Er war _____ hier. (*the day before yesterday*)

16. X: Wann hast du Post von Margot bekommen?

   Y: _____. (*a few days ago*)

17. X: Wann haben Frank und Barbara geheiratet?

   Y: _____. (*a week ago today*)

18. X: Ich möchte wissen, ob dein Bruder jemals[4] gute Laune hat.

   Y: Ich glaube, das passiert nur _____. (*once or twice a year*)

19. X: Du ißt _____. (*all the time*)

   Y: Nicht _____. (*all the time*) Ich esse doch nur _____. (*ten times a day*)

B. *Form sentences using the time expressions in the left column. You may combine them with expressions from the column on the right or create your own.*

---

1 **erreichen**   to reach, contact

2 **eine Tablette ein•nehmen**   to take a tablet, pill
   (nimmt ein), nahm ein, eingenommen

3 **mit dem Studium fertig werden**   to graduate

4 **jemals**   ever

Model: heute nachmittag
> **Heute nachmittag habe ich meine Freundin zum Flughafen gebracht.**

1. gestern abend	mit Professor Zimmermann sprechen
2. heute morgen	Peter Geburtstag haben
3. morgen früh	mein Zimmer sauber.machen
4. mittwochs nachmittags	einen Job suchen
5. nächsten Sonnabend	für eine Prüfung lernen
6. vorgestern	nichts vor.haben
7. übermorgen	Bank geschlossen
8. am ersten August	mit meiner Freundin aus.gehen
9. vorigen Sonntag	zu spät auf.stehen
10. im Sommer	nur Unsinn reden
11. voriges Wochenende	einkaufen gehen
12. jeden Donnerstag	die Semesterferien beginnen
13. einmal in der Woche	nach Hause fahren
14. heute abend	zu Hause bleiben
15. die ganze Zeit	schwimmen gehen

Clock Time

In official statements of time (such as timetables, office hours, performance time) the 24-hour system is used (explained in §6). Otherwise time is expressed according to the 12-hour system.

§**5**   USING THE 12-HOUR SYSTEM

Wie spät ist es?
Wieviel Uhr ist es? } *What time is it?*

Time is most commonly expressed as follows:

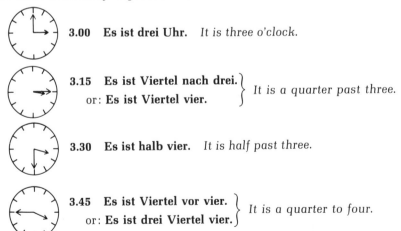

3.00   Es ist drei Uhr.   *It is three o'clock.*

3.15   Es ist Viertel nach drei.
or: **Es ist Viertel vier.** } *It is a quarter past three.*

3.30   Es ist halb vier.   *It is half past three.*

3.45   Es ist Viertel vor vier.
or: **Es ist drei Viertel vier.** } *It is a quarter to four.*

In German, hours are separated from minutes by a period rather than a colon. Alternatively, the minutes may be raised:

    3.15 or 3^{15}

Note the use of **ein** when it precedes **Uhr,** and **eins** when it stands alone:

    1.00   Es ist **ein Uhr.**
    1.15   Es ist Viertel nach **eins.**
  12.30   Es ist halb **eins.**
  12.45   Es ist Viertel vor **eins.**

PRACTICE 11   *Give the time in German. Use also the options.*

    Model: 8.15 Es ist Viertel nach acht.
                   Es ist Viertel neun.

1. 10.15	5. 6.15	9. 11.45	13. 1.00
2. 10.30	6. 7.15	10. 12.45	14. 2.15
3. 10.45	7. 8.30	11. 1.45	15. 3.45
4. 11.00	8. 9.30	12. 7.00	16. 12.30

Five-minute intervals

The most usual forms of five-minute intervals are shown below.

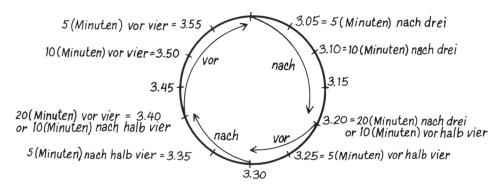

PRACTICE 12   *Give the time in German following the above pattern.*

    Model: 6.20 Es ist 20 (Minuten) nach sechs.
       or: Es ist 10 (Minuten) vor halb sieben.

1. 5.20	5. 11.05	9. 8.10	13. 12.05	17. 2.20
2. 5.40	6. 11.25	10. 8.25	14. 12.35	18. 9.40
3. 5.50	7. 11.35	11. 8.40	15. 1.10	19. 7.50
4. 5.10	8. 11.55	12. 8.50	16. 1.25	20. 10.35

Other intervals may be expressed the same way.

    3.02   Es ist zwei (Minuten) nach drei.
    3.12   Es ist zwölf (Minuten) nach drei.
    3.22   Es ist acht (Minuten) vor halb vier.

3.32 Es ist zwei (Minuten) nach halb vier.
3.38 Es ist acht (Minuten) nach halb vier.
3.48 Es ist zwölf (Minuten) vor vier.
3.58 Es ist zwei (Minuten) vor vier.

Minute cannot be omitted after **eine.**

3.01 Es ist **eine Minute** nach drei.
3.59 Es ist **eine Minute** vor vier.

PRACTICE 13   *Give the time in German.*

Model: 10.04   Es ist 4 (Minuten) nach zehn.

1. 10.13	5. 6.09	9. 12.07	13. 2.01
2. 10.29	6. 6.17	10. 12.39	14. 3.29
3. 10.36	7. 6.27	11. 1.06	15. 11.59
4. 10.57	8. 6.54	12. 1.33	

Advice to students: If you don't remember the above ways of expressing the time, you may resort to a simpler way:

5.10 Es ist fünf Uhr zehn.
7.20 Es ist sieben Uhr zwanzig.
1.55 Es ist ein Uhr fünfundfünfzig.
12.33 Es ist 12 Uhr dreiunddreißig.

People will understand you. However, when German-speaking people express the time as explained in this section, you should be able to understand them.

To make clear whether A.M. or P.M. is meant, **morgens, vormittags, mittags, nachmittags, abends** or **nachts** is frequently added.

7:00 A.M. = 7 Uhr morgens   10:00 A.M. = zehn Uhr vormittags
7:00 P.M. = 7 Uhr abends   10:00 P.M. = zehn Uhr abends

1:00 A.M. = ein Uhr nachts
1:00 P.M. = ein Uhr mittags

§6   USING THE 24-HOUR SYSTEM

Official statements of time are based on the 24-hour system.

Der Zug fährt 13.40 (dreizehn Uhr vierzig) ab.
The train leaves at 1:40 P.M.

Das Konzert beginnt 19.30 (neunzehn Uhr dreißig).
The concert begins at 7:30 P.M.

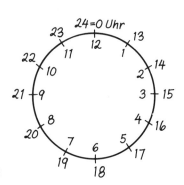

English A.M. = German	1–12 Uhr
P.M. =	13–24 Uhr

1:15 A.M. = 1.15   **ein Uhr fünfzehn**
1:15 P.M. = 13.15   **dreizehn Uhr fünfzehn**
                        (= English p.m. time + 12)

8:45 A.M. = 8.45	**acht Uhr fünfundvierzig**
8:45 P.M. = 20.45	**zwanzig Uhr fünfundvierzig**
11:56 A.M. = 11.56	**elf Uhr sechsundfünfzig**
11:56 P.M. = 23.56	**dreiundzwanzig Uhr sechsundfünfzig**
12:15 A.M. = 0.15	**null Uhr fünfzehn**
12:15 P.M. = 12.15	**zwölf Uhr fünfzehn**

Note: **Viertel, halb, drei Viertel, vor,** and **nach** are not used in the 24-hour system.

PRACTICE 14   A. *Give the time according to the 24-hour system.*

Model: 4:13 A.M. **vier Uhr dreizehn**
4:13 P.M. **sechzehn Uhr dreizehn**

1. 7:20 A.M.	3. 10:45 A.M.	5. 3:15 A.M.
7:20 P.M.	10:45 P.M.	3:15 P.M.
2. 9:30 A.M.	4. 6:10 A.M.	6. 12:30 A.M.
9:30 P.M.	6:10 P.M.	12:30 P.M.

B. *Convert to English* P.M. *time.*

Model: 14.30 = **2:30 P.M.**

1. 19.00	3. 20.45	5. 23.45
2. 17.15	4. 13.30	

§7   COMMON EXPRESSIONS USED WHEN TELLING TIME

um 1 Uhr *at* 1 *o'clock*
Um 1 Uhr esse ich zu Mittag und **um** 7 Uhr zu Abend.
At 1 o'clock I have lunch/dinner (noon meal) and **at** *7 o'clock supper/dinner (evening meal).*

When telling time, **um** is the German equivalent of English *at.*

Punkt 3 Uhr *3 o'clock sharp*

gegen 3 Uhr ⎫
so gegen 3 Uhr ⎭ *around 3 o'clock*

von ... bis ... *from ... to ...*	Das Postamt ist **von 9 bis 5 Uhr** offen.
vor.gehen (Uhr) *to be fast*	Meine Uhr **geht etwas vor.** *My watch is a little fast.* Diese Uhr **geht 5 Minuten vor.**
nach.gehen (Uhr) *to be slow*	Meine Uhr **geht etwas nach.** *My watch is a little slow.* Diese Uhr **geht 10 Minuten nach.**
richtig gehen (Uhr) *to be correct*	**Geht** diese Uhr **richtig?** *Is that clock correct? Is that the right time?*

nicht gehen *not work, not run*	Meine Uhr **geht nicht.**
	My watch doesn't work.
stehen.bleiben *to stop*	Meine Uhr **ist** schon wieder
	stehengeblieben.
	My watch has stopped again.
die Uhr stellen *to set the clock*	Ich habe vergessen,
	den Wecker zu stellen.
	I forgot to set the alarm clock.
nach meiner Uhr	**Nach meiner Uhr** ist es 3 Uhr.
according to my watch	*According to my watch it is 3 o'clock.*

PRACTICE 15.   A. *Insert German equivalents.*

1. X: Warum kommen Sie schon wieder zu spät?
   Y: _____. (*Because my watch has stopped.*)
2. X: Wissen Sie, wann Dr. Lippert heute Sprechstunde[1] hat?
   Y: Soviel ich weiß, hat er heute _____ Sprechstunde.
   (*from 9 to 12 o'clock*)
3. X: Es kann doch nicht schon zwölf Uhr sein.
   Y: _____. (*This clock is a little fast.*)
4. X: Geht Ihre Uhr richtig?
   Y: _____. (*It is two or three minutes slow.*)
5. X: Wann mußt du morgen früh aufstehen?
   Y: _____. (*At 5 o'clock. I have to set the alarm clock.*)
6. X: Heute morgen habe ich verschlafen.[2]
   Y: _____. (*Did you forget to set the alarm clock?* [fam.;
   pres. perf.])
7. X: Können Sie mir sagen, wie spät es ist?
   Y: _____. (*According to my watch it is 7:30.*)
8. X: Wann beginnt das Konzert?
   Y: Soviel ich weiß, beginnt es _____. (*at 8 o'clock*)
9. X: Wo ist deine Uhr?
   Y: Ich habe sie zu Hause gelassen. _____. (*It doesn't
   work.*)
10. X: Wann bist du gestern abend ins Bett gegangen?
    Y: Ich glaube, es war _____. (*around 11 o'clock*)
11. X: Wann ist der Zug abgefahren?
    Y: _____. (*9 o'clock sharp*)

B. *Form sentences using the following cues.*

Model: meine Uhr / ein paar Minuten / vor.gehen
   Meine Uhr geht ein paar Minuten vor.

1. diese Uhr / fünf Minuten / nach.gehen
2. leider / meine Uhr / stehen.bleiben (pres. perf.)

---

1 **Sprechstunde haben**   to have office hours, consultation
2 **verschlafen (verschläft),**   to oversleep
   verschlief, verschlafen

3. um 4 Uhr / ich / beim Zahnarzt / müssen / sein
4. von 5 bis 9 Uhr / ich / auf der Tankstelle / arbeiten
5. gegen 2 Uhr / ich / Margot /ab.holen

C. Ein Tag im Leben einer Studentin.
   State the indicated time and form sentences using the cues.

Model: _____ Margot / auf.stehen
Um Viertel vor sieben steht Margot auf.

1. _____ sie / zur Universität / fahren

2. _____ sie / im Hörsaal / sitzen

3. _____ sie / zu Mittag / essen

4. _____ sie / in die Bibliothek / gehen

5. _____ sie / nach Hause / fahren

6. _____ sie / zu Abend / essen

7. _____ sie / Dieter / an.rufen

8. _____ sie / an einem Referat / arbeiten

9. _____ sie / ins Bett / gehen

12

Conjunctions; Infinitive Phrases

KEY TO THE EXERCISES ON CASSETTE 6.
RUNNING TIME: APPROX. 35 MIN.

Conjunctions

There are two basic types of conjunctions: coordinating and subordinating.

§1   COORDINATING CONJUNCTIONS

Coordinating conjunctions connect words, phrases, and clauses of equal importance, *coordinating* them, not subordinating one to the other. Common coordinating conjunctions are:

aber	*but (however, nevertheless)*
denn	*for, because*
oder	*or*
sondern	*but (rather)*
und	*and*

Coordinating conjunctions have no effect on the word order. Sentences joined by them retain their normal or inverted word order, as the following sentences illustrate.

1. a. Monika spielt gern Tennis. **Ihr Freund spielt** lieber Fußball.
   b. Monika spielt gern Tennis, aber **ihr Freund spielt** lieber Fußball.
      Monika likes to play tennis, but her friend prefers to play soccer.

2. a. Ich rufe Martin um 7 Uhr an. Dann **ist er** bestimmt zu Hause.
   b. Ich rufe Martin um 7 Uhr an, denn dann **ist er** bestimmt zu Hause.
      I'll call Martin at 7 o'clock, because he definitely will be home then.

In sentences 2. *a* and *b* the inversion is caused by the adverb **dann**.

Do not confuse:

> **denn** = *for, because* (coordinating conjunction)
> **dann** = *then* (adverb)

The German equivalents of *but*

but = **sondern** when used in the sense of *but on the contrary* or *but rather* (only after a negative).

> Klaus ist **nicht** dumm, **sondern** sehr intelligent.
> *Klaus is not stupid but (on the contrary) very intelligent.*

> Wir sprechen **nicht** von dir, **sondern** von Klaus.
> *We are not talking of you but (rather) of Klaus.*

Observe the use of **sondern** in the phrase **nicht nur ... sondern auch**:

> Diese Transaktion ist **nicht nur** kompliziert, **sondern auch** riskant.
> *This transaction is **not only** complicated **but also** risky.*

but = **aber** in all other instances. **Aber** is also used in the sense of *however* or *nevertheless*. The preceding clause may or may not be negated.

> Ulrich ist nicht dumm, **aber** er hat immer schlechte Noten.
> *Ulrich is not stupid, but (however, nevertheless) he has always bad grades.*

> Sabine ist intelligent, **aber** ihre Noten sind nicht gut.
> *Sabine is intelligent, but (however, nevertheless) her grades are not good.*

PRACTICE 1   A. *Insert* **sondern** *or* **aber** *and state the reason for your choice.*

1. Wir wohnen in einem kleinen alten Haus, _____ es gefällt uns sehr.
2. Müllers fahren nicht nach Spanien, _____ nach Italien.
3. Dieses Dokument ist nicht das Original, _____ eine Kopie.
4. Ich habe nicht viel Geld, _____ einmal im Monat kaufe ich mir etwas Besonderes.
5. Nicht Lore, _____ Klaus hat das Geschirr gespült.[1]
6. Ich verstehe nicht immer alles, was mein mexikanischer Freund sagt, _____ meistens weiß ich, was er sagen will.

B. *Translate the responses into German, using the expression* **nicht nur ... sondern auch**.

Model: X: Hast du Hunger?
  Y: I am not only hungry but also thirsty.
    Ich habe nicht nur Hunger, sondern auch Durst.

1. X: Heute ist es wirklich sehr heiß.
   Y: It is not only hot but also humid.[2]

---

1 **das Geschirr spülen**   to do the dishes (*lit.*: rinse the dishes)
2 **feucht**   humid

2. X: Heinz hat ja[1] eine sehr dumme Bemerkung gemacht.
   Y: His observation was not only stupid but also dangerous.[2]
3. X: Findest du auch, daß die Prüfung zu lang war?
   Y: It was not only too long but also too hard.
4. X: Deine neue Freundin ist wirklich sehr nett.
   Y: She is not only very nice but also very interesting.

PRACTICE 2   *Combine the following sentences using German coordinating conjunctions.*

1. Sie hat mich nicht erkannt.[3] (*or*) Sie wollte mich nicht erkennen.
2. Ich bin sehr böse auf Klaus. (*for*) Er hat sein Versprechen nicht gehalten.
3. Das ist ein langweiliger Film. (*but*) Meine Freundin will ihn unbedingt[4] sehen.
4. Mein Bruder hat den Motor repariert. (*and*) Jetzt läuft er ausgezeichnet.
5. Wir gehen immer morgens schwimmen. (*for*) Dann ist das Hallenbad[5] nicht so voll.

§2   SUBORDINATING CONJUNCTIONS

Subordinating conjunctions introduce dependent clauses. Compare these sentences:

a. **Ich bin** jetzt oft in der Bibliothek,   denn **ich schreibe** eine Semesterarbeit.
   MAIN CLAUSE   MAIN CLAUSE

b. **Ich bin** jetzt oft in der Bibliothek,   weil **ich** eine Semesterarbeit **schreibe.**
   MAIN CLAUSE   DEPENDENT CLAUSE

c. Weil **ich** eine Semesterarbeit **schreibe,** **bin ich** jetzt oft in der Bibliothek.
   DEPENDENT CLAUSE   MAIN CLAUSE

In sentence *b* the clause introduced by the subordinating conjunction **weil** has dependent word worder: the inflected verb is in last position. When the dependent clause precedes the main clause, as in sentence *c*, the latter has inverted word order (cf. Chap. 1, §3).

Common subordinating conjunctions are:

als	*when*
bevor }	
ehe }	*before*
bis	*until*

1 **ja**	here used as a flavoring particle (cf. Appendix, §4)
2 **gefährlich**	dangerous
3 **erkennen, erkannte, erkannt**	to recognize
4 **unbedingt**	absolutely, by all means
5 **das Hallenbad, ⁻er**	indoor swimming pool

da	*since* (stating reason), *because*
damit	*so that, in order that*
daß	*that*
indem	*by* (doing something)
nachdem	*after*
ob	*whether, if*
obwohl } obgleich }	*although*
seit } seitdem }	*since* (referring to time)
sobald	*as soon as*
solange	*as long as*
während	*while*
weil	*because*
wenn	*when, whenever, if*

Observe the use of the following subordinating conjunctions.

Three German equivalents of *when*

1. *when* = **wann** in direct and indirect questions.

Direct question:

Wann kommt Sonja nach Hause?

Indirect question (preceded by an introductory clause; cf. Chap. 1, §5):

Weißt du, **wann** Sonja nach Hause **kommt**?
Ich weiß nicht, **wann** Sonja nach Hause **kommt.**

In indirect questions, the question word **wann** functions as a subordinating conjunction.

2. *when* = **als** in clauses that refer to a single past occurrence or state:

Leider hat es gestern geregnet, **als** wir ein Picknick machen wollten.
Unfortunately it rained yesterday when we were planning to have a picnic.

Sie war sehr vorsichtig, **als** sie am Montag mit dem Chef sprach.
She was very careful when she talked with the boss on Monday.

Ich habe mich erkältet, **als** ich gestern in der Stadt war.
I caught a cold when I was in town yesterday.

The occurrence or state may cover a period of time:

Sabine hat Peter kennengelernt, **als** sie in München studierte.
Sabine met Peter when she was studying in Munich.

Er hatte viele Freunde, **als** er jung und unternehmungslustig war.
He had many friends when he was young and enterprising.

Exception: **Als** is also used in present-tense summaries of stories, plays, and films:

> **Als** der Held seinen Gegner kommen sieht, stellt er sich tot.
> *When the hero sees his opponent coming, he pretends to be dead.*

3. *when* = **wenn** in all other instances:

a. when referring to repeated occurrences in the past. (In such cases, English often uses *whenever*.)

> Leider hat es immer geregnet, **wenn** wir ein Picknick machen wollten.
> *Unfortunately, it always rained when (whenever) we wanted to have a picnic.*

> Sie war immer sehr vorsichtig, **wenn** sie mit dem Chef gesprochen hat.
> *She was always very careful when (whenever) she talked with the boss.*

b. in all clauses referring to the present and future (single or repeated occurrences).

> Hoffentlich regnet es nicht, **wenn** ihr morgen ein Picknick macht.
> Sie ist immer sehr vorsichtig, **wenn** sie mit dem Chef spricht.

Remember:

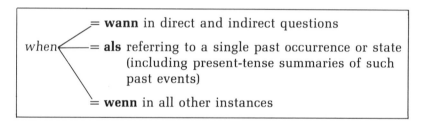

when
= **wann** in direct and indirect questions
= **als** referring to a single past occurrence or state (including present-tense summaries of such past events)
= **wenn** in all other instances

PRACTICE 3   *Supply the German equivalent of **when**.*

1. Ich habe mich sehr gefreut,[1] _____ ich am Montag die gute Nachricht bekam.
2. Ich habe mich immer gefreut, _____ du mich angerufen hast.
3. _____ rufst du Renate an? Ich weiß noch nicht, _____ ich sie anrufen kann.
4. Natürlich werde ich dir alles erzählen, _____ du morgen zu mir kommst.
5. _____ er mich gestern sah, wurde er verlegen.[2]
6. _____ er mich sieht, wird er immer verlegen.
7. Weißt du noch, _____ du den Brief abgeschickt hast?
8. _____ Sonja in Frankfurt studierte, hatte sie einen französischen Freund.
9. a. Wir haben Goethes „Faust" gesehen, _____ wir vorige Woche im Theater waren.
   b. Faust sieht Margarete zum ersten Mal, _____ sie gerade aus der Kirche kommt.

1 **sich freuen**   to be happy, glad
2 **verlegen**   embarrassed

The German equivalents of *if*

if = **wenn** in conditional statements.

> **Wenn** das wahr ist, (dann) gibt es bestimmt einen Skandal.
> *If that is true, (then) there will certainly be a scandal.*

if = **ob** in indirect questions. (English also uses *whether* in this context; cf. Chap. 1, §5.)

> Ist das wahr? Ich weiß nicht, **ob** das wahr ist.
> *Is that true? I don't know if (whether) that is true.*

Remember:

> *if* = **wenn** unless it is replaceable by *whether*, in which case it is **ob**.

PRACTICE 4   *Supply the German equivalents of **if**.*

1. Ich weiß nicht, _____ er die Wahrheit gesagt hat.
2. Sie wird bestimmt sehr böse, _____ er ihr nicht die Wahrheit sagt.
3. Ich möchte wissen, _____ Kästners jetzt zu Hause sind.
4. _____ ich mein Stipendium verliere, muß ich mit dem Studium aufhören.
5. Wissen Sie, _____ der Zug aus München Verspätung hat?[1]
6. _____ der Zug pünktlich abfährt, kommen wir um 12 Uhr in Bonn an.

The German equivalents of *since*

since = **seitdem** or **seit** when it refers to time.

> **Seitdem** (**seit**) Maria in Bonn studiert, schreibt sie mir nicht mehr.
> *Since Maria has been studying at Bonn, she does not write to me anymore.*

Seitdem and **seit** are used with the present tense if the action is not yet completed, while English **since** is used with the present perfect (often in the progressive form). (See Chap. 2, §7,3.)

since = **da** when it is replaceable by *because*.

> **Da** wir nicht wissen, wo er jetzt ist, können wir ihn nicht anrufen.
> *Since (Because) we don't know where he is now, we can't call him.*

PRACTICE 5   *Supply the German equivalents of **since**.*

1. _____ es nicht aufhörte zu regnen, sind wir den ganzen Sonntag zu Hause geblieben.
2. Wir haben nicht wieder von Winklers gehört, _____ sie in Basel wohnen.

---

1 **Verspätung haben**   to be late (*train, bus, plane*)

3. Leider kann ich Martin nicht schreiben, _____ ich seine Adresse nicht weiß.

4. _____ Maria für eine Prüfung lernen mußte, bin ich mit Sonja ins Kino gegangen.

5. _____ Wagners vom Urlaub[1] zurückgekommen sind, haben sie uns noch nicht wieder besucht.

The use of *indem*

> Wir haben das Problem gelöst, **indem** wir einen Kompromiß geschlossen haben.
> *We solved the problem by making a compromise.*

The German dependent clause introduced by **indem** states a means by which something is, was, or will be done. The English equivalent is usually expressed with **by** plus a gerund.

The use of tenses in clauses introduced by *nachdem*

a. Er duscht meistens, **nachdem** er den Rasen **gemäht hat.**
    PRESENT   PRES. PERF.

He usually takes a shower, after he has mowed the lawn.
                    or: after he mows the lawn.
                    or: after mowing the lawn.

b. Er duschte gestern, **nachdem** er den Rasen **gemäht hatte.**
    PAST   PAST PERF.

He took a shower yesterday, after he had mowed the lawn.
                    or: after he mowed the lawn.
                    or: after mowing the lawn.

The clause introduced by **nachdem** expresses an action which precedes that of the main clause. If the verb in the main clause is in the present or future tense, the **nachdem** clause is in the present perfect tense. If the main clause is in the past, present perfect, or past perfect tense, the **nachdem** clause is in the past perfect tense. German lacks the choice of tenses that English has.

Subordinating conjunctions that are frequently confused with other words

The best way to recognize subordinating conjunctions is the position of the inflected verb at the end of the clause.

    _since, as (subordinating conjunction)
da —there (adverb of place)
    `then (adverb of time)

Da Martin nicht weit von mir **wohnt**, sehe ich ihn oft. (verb last; dependent clause)

Since Martin doesn't live far from me, I often see him.

---

1 **der Urlaub, -e**   vacation

Da wohnt Martin. (verb second; main clause with inverted word order)
*Martin lives **there**.*

Da war es schon zu spät.
***Then** it was already too late.*

während⟨ *while* (subordinating conjunction)
                during (preposition)

Während wir uns **unterhielten**, rauchte Dietmar.
While we were talking, Dietmar was smoking.

Während unserer Unterhaltung rauchte Dietmar.
During our conversation Dietmar was smoking.

PRACTICE 6   A. *Combine the sentences, using the appropriate subordinating conjunction.*

Model: Ich rufe dich an. (*as soon as*) Ich bin mit der Arbeit fertig.
Ich rufe dich an, sobald ich mit der Arbeit fertig bin.

1. Ich bin sehr böse auf Dieter. (*because*) Er hat sein Versprechen nicht gehalten.
2. Mein Wagen läuft ausgezeichnet. (*since* [*time*]) Ich habe ihn repariert.
3. Wir haben nicht gewartet. (*until*) Das Flugzeug ist abgeflogen.
4. Ich habe nachgegeben. (*in order that*) Es gibt keinen Streit.[1]
5. Ich weiß nicht. (*whether, if*) Ich kann mitfahren.
6. Natürlich können Sie mitfahren. (*if*) Sie haben nichts anderes vor.[2]
7. Leider kann ich nicht mitfahren. (*since, because*) Ich habe etwas anderes vor.[3]
8. Ein Reifen[4] ist geplatzt.[5] (*when*) Der Fahrer wollte einen anderen Wagen überholen.[6]
9. Ein Reifen platzte. (*after*) Der Fahrer hatte einen anderen Wagen überholt.
10. Frau Krause hat einen Streit vermieden.[7] (*by*) Sie hat geschwiegen.[8]

B. *Introduce the first sentence in each pair with the appropriate subordinating conjunction.*

Model: (*as long as*) Ich habe keinen Job. Ich kann dir das Geld nicht zurückgeben.
Solange ich keinen Job habe, kann ich dir das Geld nicht zurückgeben.

1 **der Streit**	quarrel, fight
2 **nichts anderes vor•haben**	to have nothing else planned
3 **etwas anderes vor•haben**	to have something else planned
4 **der Reifen, -**	tire
5 **platzen (ist)**	to blow out, burst
6 **überholen**	to overtake, pass
7 **vermeiden, vermied, vermieden**	to avoid
8 **schweigen, schwieg, geschwiegen**	to remain silent

1. (*since, because*) Wir konnten keinen Parkplatz finden. Wir sind einfach weitergefahren.
2. (*before*) Sabine fährt nach Hause. Sie ruft mich hoffentlich an.
3. (*if*) Der Kurs wird zu schwer. Ich muß damit aufhören.[1]
4. (*while*) Du spülst das Geschirr. Ich räume die Wohnung auf.
5. (*although*) Ich habe wenig Geld. Ich werde einen Kassettenrecorder kaufen.
6. (*as long as*) Man widerspricht ihm nicht. Man kommt gut mit ihm aus.[2]
7. (*as soon as*) Man widerspricht ihm. Es gibt Streit.

PRACTICE 7   Summarizing exercises

A. *Combine the following sentences using the appropriate coordinating and subordinating conjunctions.*

1. Ich konnte nicht mit Frau Krause sprechen. (*because*) Die Leitung war immer besetzt.[3]
2. Ich habe fünfmal angerufen. (*but*) Es war immer besetzt.
3. Ich mache Überstunden.[4] (*for*) Ich muß unbedingt mehr Geld verdienen.
4. Frank macht auch Überstunden. (*in order that*) Er verdient mehr Geld.
5. (*after*) Ich habe meine Schulden bezahlt. Ich schlafe bestimmt besser.
6. Rita war pleite. (*after*) Sie hatte ihre Schulden bezahlt.
7. Wir können das Problem lösen. (*if*) Wir schließen einen Kompromiß.[5]
8. Ich weiß nicht. (*whether, if*) Annette will einen Kompromiß schließen.
9. Wir haben das Problem gelöst. (*by*) Wir haben einen Kompromiß geschlossen.
10. Helga treibt viel Sport.[6] (*in order that*) Sie bleibt fit.
11. (*if*) Du willst fit bleiben. Du mußt viel Sport treiben.
12. (*since, because*) Wir wollten einen Streit vermeiden. Wir haben geschwiegen.
13. Wir haben einen Streit vermieden. (*by*) Wir haben geschwiegen.
14. Ich gehe nicht gern zum Supermarkt. (*when*) Ich habe großen Hunger. (*for*) Dann kaufe ich zuviel.
15. Peter ist eingeschlafen. (*when*) Ich war gestern mit ihm im Kino.

1 **mit einem Kurs auf•hören**	to drop a course
2 **aus•kommen, kam aus, ist ausgekommen mit** (*dat.*)	to get along with
3 **Die Leitung ist besetzt.** or *simply*: **Es ist besetzt.**	The line is busy.
4 **Überstunden machen**	to work overtime
5 **einen Kompromiß schließen, schloß, geschlossen**	to make a compromise
6 **viel Sport treiben, trieb, getrieben**	to do a lot of sport

16. Ich habe Peter sehr gern.[1] (*although*) Er schläft oft ein. (*when*) Ich bin mit ihm im Kino.

B. *Translate into German. (Use the present for the English future and the present perfect for the English simple past except where otherwise indicated.)*

1. a. I hear from Ellen. I call you.
    Ich höre von Ellen. Ich rufe dich an.
   b. When I hear from Ellen, I'll call you.
   c. I'll call you, as soon as I hear from Ellen.
   d. I'll call you, after I have heard from Ellen.
   e. I called Mathias, after I had heard from Ellen.

2. a. I help him. He never thanks me.
    Ich helfe ihm. Er dankt mir nie.
   b. He never thanks me when I help him.
   c. I help him, although he never thanks me.
   d. He always thanked me when I helped him.
   e. He thanked me when I helped him yesterday.

3. a. I am waiting. She is coming back.
    Ich warte. Sie kommt zurück.
   b. I'll wait until she comes back.
   c. I waited but she didn't come back.
   d. Nobody knows when she is coming back.

4. a. I am not coming along. I have other plans.
    Ich komme nicht mit. Ich habe etwas anderes vor.
   b. Are you coming along or do you have other plans? (fam. sing.)
   c. I can't come along, because I have other plans.
   d. I couldn't come along, since I had other plans. (past)
   e. Since Elke had other plans, she couldn't come along. (past)

5. a. She is doing the dishes. I am straightening up the room.
    Sie spült das Geschirr. Ich räume das Zimmer auf.
   b. I am straightening up the room while she is doing the dishes.
   c. If you do the dishes, I'll straighten up the room. (fam. sing.)
   d. After I have done the dishes, I'll straighten up the room.
   e. After I had done the dishes, I straightened up the room.

6. a. We'll solve the problem. We'll make a compromise.
    Wir lösen das Problem. Wir schließen einen Kompromiß.
   b. We can solve the problem, if we make a compromise.
   c. We can solve the problem by making a compromise.
   d. If we want to solve the problem, we must make a compromise.
   e. I don't know whether we can solve the problem.

7. a. I am remaining silent. I want to avoid a fight.
    Ich schweige. Ich will einen Streit vermeiden.
   b. I am remaining silent because I want to avoid a fight.
   c. Perhaps I can avoid a fight if I remain silent.
   d. Perhaps we can avoid a fight by remaining silent.

1 **sehr gern haben**   to be very fond of

Infinitive Phrases

§3   BASIC STRUCTURE

Ich hatte nicht den Mut **zu fragen**.
*I didn't have the courage **to ask**.*

Ich hatte nicht den Mut, ihn **zu fragen**.
*I didn't have the courage **to ask** him.*

Ich hatte nicht den Mut, ihn gestern **zu fragen**.
*I didn't have the courage **to ask** him yesterday.*

Note: a. The German infinitive stands at the end. All modifiers and objects precede it, though in English they would follow.

     b. Infinitive phrases are usually set off by commas. However, the bare infinitive with no modifiers or objects is not set off (as in the first example).

Zu, when accompanying a verb with a separable prefix, stands between the prefix and verb:

Ich habe vor, dieses Mal nach**zu**geben.
I am planning to give in this time.

PRACTICE 8   A. *Complete the responses in German.*

Model: X: Hast du die Dias mitgebracht?
            Y: Leider habe ich vergessen, _____.
                 (to bring them along)
            Leider habe ich vergessen, sie mitzubringen.

   1. X: Hast du Marlene angerufen?
       Y: Ich habe versucht, _____ (*to call her*), aber es war immer besetzt.
   2. X: Hat Peter die Post abgeholt?
       Y: Ich glaube, er hat vergessen, _____. (*to pick up the mail*)
   3. X: Hast du dein Zimmer aufgeräumt?
       Y: Ich habe noch keine Zeit gehabt, _____. (*to straighten it up*)
   4. X: Warum ist Dagmar nicht mitgekommen?
       Y: Ich nehme an, daß sie keine Lust hatte[1] _____. (*to come along*)
   5. X: Ich weiß nicht, was ich zu dieser Sache sagen soll.
       Y: Ich glaube, es ist besser, _____. (*to say nothing*)
   6. X: Warum suchst du dir keinen besseren Job?
       Y: Ach, du weißt doch, wie schwer es ist, _____. (*to find a better job*)
   7. X: Hoffentlich hältst du dein Versprechen (neut.).
       Y: Ich werde versuchen, _____. (*to keep it*)

---

1 **ich habe keine Lust**   I don't feel like, I am not in the mood

8. X: Ich weiß nicht, ob ich den Chef um einen Gefallen bitten kann.
   Y: Es hat keinen Zweck,[1] _____ . (*to ask him for a favor*). Er sagt doch immer nein.

9. X: Wollt ihr zu Morgensterns gehen?
   Y: Nein. Wir haben vor, _____ . (*to go to the Seiferts'*)

10. X: Wie kommst du mit Rainer aus?
    Y: Nicht besonders gut. Es ist nicht leicht, _____ . (*to get along with him*)

11. X: Ich habe noch nie gehört, daß jemand dem Chef widersprochen hat.
    Y: Niemand wagt,[2] _____ . (*to contradict him*)

12. X: Hast du auch Frau Dr. Schubert zu deiner Party eingeladen?
    Y: Nein. Ich habe nicht gewagt, _____ . (*to invite her*)

13. X: Will Dietmar den Magister machen?[3]
    Y: Ich glaube, er hat nicht vor, _____ . (*to get his* [*the*] *Master's*)

B. *Translate the following sentences into German.*

1. I don't feel like playing tennis.
2. It's not easy to remain silent.
3. It's hard to avoid a quarrel.
4. It's no use to warn him.
5. I am trying to get along with her.
6. She is planning to get her (the) Master's.
7. She doesn't dare to ask Mrs. Bauer.
8. He doesn't have the courage to contradict the boss.

§4   INFINITIVE PHRASES INTRODUCED WITH *um, ohne, anstatt* OR *statt*

Um introduces infinitive phrases that express a purpose or intention:

Ich habe das getan, **um** Geld zu sparen.
        I did this (in order) to save money.

                um nicht in Schulden zu geraten.
                in order not to run up debts.

When the infinitive phrase is introduced with **ohne, anstatt** or **statt,** the English equivalents include gerunds:

Monika legte den Hörer auf, **ohne** ein Wort **zu sagen.**

Monika put down the receiver⎫
                                ⎬ ***without saying*** a word.
or: *Monika hung up*   ⎭

---

1 **es hat keinen Zweck**   it's no use, there is no point
2 **wagen**   to dare
3 **den Magister machen**   to get one's Master's degree
  (*with the definite article*)

Ich bin auf eine Party gegangen, **anstatt/statt** für die
  Prüfung **zu lernen**.

*I went to a party **instead of studying** for the exam.*

PRACTICE 9   A. *Complete the sentences with infinitive phrases.*

Model: Barbara hat mit meiner Kamera Aufnahmen gemacht,[1]
  ohne / bitten / mich / um Erlaubnis
  ohne mich um Erlaubnis zu bitten.

1. Hannelore ist einkaufen gegangen, ohne / warten / auf mich
2. Ich mache Überstunden, um / verdienen / mehr Geld
3. Manfred hat uns ausgelacht, anstatt / helfen / uns
4. Die ganze Familie treibt Sport, um / bleiben / fit
5. Renate hat geschwiegen, um / vermeiden / einen Streit
6. Wir können das Problem nicht lösen, ohne / schließen / einen
   Kompromiß
7. Ich habe den ganzen Abend ferngesehen, anstatt / machen / die Hausaufgaben

B. *Translate the English sentences into German. (Use the present perfect
for the English past tense.)*

Model: Ich habe geschwiegen. Ich wollte Helga nicht ärgern.
  Ich habe geschwiegen, um Helga nicht zu ärgern.
  I remained silent in order not to annoy Helga.

1. Wir haben alles getan. Wir wollten einen Streit vermeiden.

   _____

   We did everything (in order) to avoid a quarrel/fight.
2. Er treibt viel Sport. Er will fit bleiben.

   _____

   He does a lot of sport (in order) to stay fit.
3. Ich habe ja gesagt. Ich habe nicht an die Folgen[2] gedacht.

   _____

   I said yes without thinking of the consequences.
4. Meine Schwester hat meine Kamera mitgenommen. Sie hat mich nicht
   um Erlaubnis gebeten.

   _____

   My sister took my camera along without asking me for permission.
5. Thomas hat über meinen Vorschlag gelacht. Er hat ihn nicht ernst
   genommen.[3]

   _____

   Thomas laughed at my suggestion instead of taking it seriously.

---

1 **Aufnahmen machen**   to take pictures
2 **die Folge, -n**   consequence
3 **ernst nehmen (nimmt),**   to take seriously
  nahm, genommen

C. *Cover up the German sentences of exercise B and state the German equivalents of the English sentences.*

Model: I remained silent in order not to annoy Helga.

   Ich habe geschwiegen, um Helga nicht zu ärgern.

§5   THE INFINITIVE PHRASE PRECEDING THE MAIN CLAUSE

The main clause has inverted word order when it is preceded by an infinitive phrase. Compare:

Ich habe geschwiegen, um Anita nicht zu ärgern.

Um Anita nicht zu ärgern, **habe ich** geschwiegen.

PRACTICE 10   A. *Translate the English sentences into German. (Use the present perfect for the English past tense.)*

Model: Wir haben die Hausaufgaben nicht gemacht.

   Wir haben Schach gespielt.

   Anstatt die Hausaufgaben zu machen, haben wir Schach gespielt.

   Instead of doing the homework, we played chess.

1. Sie hat mir nicht geholfen. Sie ist davongelaufen.

   _____

   Instead of helping me, she ran away.
2. Ich habe mein Zimmer nicht aufgeräumt. Ich habe die ganze Zeit vorm Fernseher gesessen.

   _____

   Instead of straightening up my room, I sat in front of the TV the whole time.
3. Ich habe kein Wort gesagt. Ich habe den Hörer aufgelegt.

   _____

   Without saying a word, I put down the receiver. (I hung up.)
4. Ich will nicht dick werden. Ich gehe jeden Tag schwimmen.

   _____

   In order not to get fat, I go swimming every day.
5. Wir wollten Geld sparen. Wir haben in einem miesen[1] Motel übernachtet.[2]

   _____

   In order to save money, we stayed overnight in a crummy motel.

B. *Cover up the German sentences of exercise A and state the German equivalents of the English sentences.*

Model: Instead of doing the homework, we played chess.

   Anstatt die Hausaufgaben zu machen, haben wir Schach gespielt.

---

1 **mies**   crummy
2 **übernachten**   to stay overnight

§6   ENGLISH INFINITIVE CONSTRUCTIONS EXPRESSED IN GERMAN BY DEPENDENT CLAUSES

1. English infinitives with subjects in the objective case

As the following example illustrates, an English infinitive may have a subject in the objective case.

> My parents want **me** to continue with my studies.

In this sentence, **me** is not a direct object, since it does not mean "My parents want me," but rather "My parents want that I should continue with my studies." **Me** is the implied subject of the infinitive **to continue**. This English construction occurs frequently after verbs of wishing, expecting, and believing.

Sentences of this type are expressed in German by means of a **daß** clause. The German equivalent of the above English example is:

> Meine Eltern wollen, **daß ich weiterstudiere**.

Additional examples:

Sie erwartet, **daß ich sie heute abend anrufe**.	*She expects me to call her tonight.*
Ich glaube, **daß er ehrlich ist**.	*I believe him to be honest.*
Meine Eltern wollen, **daß wir heiraten**.	*My parents want us to get married.*

PRACTICE 11   A. *Translate into German.*

1. a. I want you to tell me the truth. **Ich will, daß du mir die Wahrheit sagst.**
   b. He wants me to tell him the truth.
   c. Do you want me to tell you the truth? (formal)
   d. We all want you to tell us the truth. (formal)
2. a. I don't expect him to pay the bill. **Ich erwarte nicht, daß er die Rechnung bezahlt.**
   b. They expect me to pay the bill.
   c. Do you expect me to pay the bill? (fam. sing.)
   d. Nobody expects you to pay the bill. (fam. sing.)
3. a. I don't believe him to be reliable. **Ich glaube nicht, daß er zuverlässig ist.**
   b. I don't believe her to be reliable.
   c. Nobody believes them to be reliable.
   d. Do you believe them to be reliable? (formal)

B. *Translate the responses into German.*

1. X: Wer holt Käte ab?
   Y: She wants me to pick her up.
2. X: Denkst du, daß sie dir die Wahrheit sagen wird?
   Y: I don't expect her to tell me the truth.
3. X: Soll ich es noch einmal versuchen?
   Y: We all want you to try it again. (formal)

4. X: Ich nehme diese Sache nicht ernst.
   Y: But I want you to take this matter seriously. (fam. sing.)
5. X: Ist Monika deinem Bruder wirklich treu?
   Y: He believes her to be faithful to him.
6. X: Der Chef gibt uns vielleicht eine Gehaltserhöhung.
   Y: I don't expect him to give us a raise.

2. English infinitives introduced with a question word

In English but not in German infinitives may be introduced with a question word. Compare:

I don't know   Ich weiß nicht,
   a. *what I am supposed to do.*⎫
                             ⎬ **was ich machen soll.**
   b. ***what to do.***⎭

She told me   Sie hat mir gesagt,
   a. *where I should buy the record.*⎫
                             ⎬ **wo ich die Platte kaufen soll.**
   b. ***where to buy the record.***⎭

He will tell you   Er wird dir sagen,
   a. *how you can solve this problem.*⎫
                             ⎬ **wie du dieses Problem lösen kannst.**
   b. ***how to solve this problem.***⎭

Since German does not permit an infinitive phrase after a question word, the English option *b* in each case has no German counterpart.

PRACTICE 12   A. *Complete the German responses using the modals occurring in the questions.*

Model: X: Weißt du, was du machen sollst?
       Y: Natürlich weiß ich, _____. (*what to do*)
      Natürlich weiß ich, was ich machen soll.

1. X: Weißt du, was du ihm sagen sollst?
   Y: Natürlich weiß ich, _____. (*what to tell him*)
2. X: Können Sie mir sagen, wo ich meinen Wagen parken kann?
   Y: Nein, aber der Polizist da drüben kann Ihnen sicher sagen,
   _____. (*where to park it*)
3. X: Wißt ihr, wo ihr übernachten könnt?
   Y: Leider wissen wir noch nicht, _____. (*where to stay overnight*)
4. X: Weißt du, wie du mehr Geld verdienen kannst?
   Y: Nein, aber du kannst mir vielleicht sagen, _____. (*how to make more money*)
5. X: Wir wissen nicht, wie wir dieses Theaterstück interpretieren sollen.
   Y: Ich weiß auch nicht, _____. (*how to interpret it*)
6. X: Du ißt zuviel. Du weißt nie, wann du aufhören mußt.
   Y: Ach, ich weiß genau, _____ : eine Sekunde, bevor ich platze. (*when to stop*)

B. *Translate the following sentences into German, using the modals in parentheses.*

Model: I don't know who(m) to invite. (sollen)
      Ich weiß nicht, wen ich einladen soll.

1. I don't know who(m) to ask. (sollen)
2. I don't know what to say. (sollen)
3. I can't tell you what to do. (müssen [formal])
4. Peter can tell you how to do that. (müssen [fam. sing.])
5. We know how to handle[1] him. (müssen)
6. I don't know how to convince[2] her. (können)
7. I don't know how to solve this problem. (sollen)

PRACTICE 13   Summarizing exercises containing various types of infinitive constructions.

A. *Translate the following sentences into German.*

1. a. I am doing him a favor.   **Ich tue ihm einen Gefallen.**
   b. It is not easy to do him a favor.
   c. He wants me to do him a favor.
   d. I don't know how to do him a favor.
2. a. I am giving (it) up.   **Ich gebe es auf.**
   b. I am planning to give (it) up.
   c. My friends don't want me to give (it) up.
3. a. I am not trying (it) again.   **Ich versuche es nicht noch einmal.**
   b. It's no use trying (it) again.
   c. They expect me to try (it) again.
   d. She is giving (it) up instead of trying (it) again.
4. a. You must ask the boss for permission.   **Sie müssen den Chef um Erlaubnis bitten.**
   b. You cannot do that without asking him for permission.
   c. He expects you to ask him for permission.
   d. I don't know what to say.
5. a. I am taking a few days vacation.   **Ich mache ein paar Tage Urlaub.**
   b. He is trying to take a few days vacation.
   c. Why are you working instead of taking a few days vacation? (formal)
   d. My boss doesn't want me to take a few days vacation.
   e. I don't know what to do.

B. *Using the cues, form sentences that fit the context.*

Model: Ich habe zwei Einladungen für Freitag abend.
        nicht wissen—was / sollen / machen
      Ich weiß nicht, was ich machen soll.

---

1 **behandeln**   to handle, treat
2 **überzeugen**   to convince

1. Dieter schwindelt (*is telling a fib*). Ich sage zu ihm:
   „ich / wollen—mir / sagen / Wahrheit "
2. Ich möchte fit bleiben, und deshalb treibe ich viel Sport.
   ich / Sport / treiben—fit / bleiben
3. Ich habe die Hausaufgaben nicht gemacht.
   ich / fern•sehen (pres. perf.)—anstatt / machen / Hausaufgaben
4. Ich möchte mit meiner Freundin ins Kino gehen und frage sie:
   „du / Lust / haben—gehen / ins Kino? "
5. Wenn man Barbara um einen Gefallen bittet, sagt sie immer nein.
   keinen Zweck / haben—sie / bitten / um einen Gefallen
6. a. Margot ist etwas schwierig. Karin sagt:
   „nicht leicht / sein—aus•kommen / mit ihr "
   b. Meine Freundin und ich kommen gut mit Margot aus.
   wir / wissen—wie / müssen / behandeln / Margot

13

The Subjunctive
Part I

KEY TO THE EXERCISES ON CASSETTE 7.
RUNNING TIME: APPROX. 50 MIN.

Introduction

Both English and German possess two sets of verb forms which indicate how real or how likely the speaker believes a statement to be. The more usual forms, called *indicative*, indicate that an utterance is either factual or relatively likely:

She is Miss America.	Sie ist „Miss Amerika".
I am not Mr. Körner.	Ich bin nicht Herr Körner.
Perhaps he'll come tomorrow.	Vielleicht kommt er morgen.

The other set of forms, called *subjunctive*, indicates that a statement is relatively unlikely, implausible, conjectural, or simply contrary to fact:

*If he **were** to come tomorrow, ...*	Wenn er morgen **käme,** ...
*If I **were** Miss America, ...*	Wenn ich „Miss Amerika" **wäre,** ...
*If I **were** Mr. Körner, ...*	Wenn ich Herr Körner **wäre,** ...

Were, wäre, and **käme** in the sentences above are subjunctive forms. English has few distinct subjunctive forms, whereas German has many recognizable subjunctives.

German distinguishes between a *general subjunctive* (also called *subjunctive II*) and a *special subjunctive* (also called *subjunctive I*). This chapter deals only with the general subjunctive. For convenience's sake, we shall refer to it simply as the *subjunctive*. It is used mainly to signal unreal conditions. They are divided into two time categories: those that deal with the present or future and those that deal with the past.

Unreal conditions referring to the present or future

§1   UNREAL CONDITIONS IN ENGLISH

Compare these two sentences:

> When I lived in Vienna, I often went to the opera.
> If I lived in Vienna, I would go to the opera often.

In the first sentence **lived** is the past tense indicative: the speaker once lived in Vienna. In the second sentence **lived** refers to the present and is called *present tense subjunctive.* "If I lived in Vienna " is a hypothesis, an **unreal condition.**

Note the difference between an indicative conditional sentence and a subjunctive (unreal) conditional sentence:

> a. If **I have** the money, **I'll go** to Europe.
> b. If **I had** the money, **I would go** to Europe.

In sentence *a* the speaker considers it possible that he/she will have the money. Since the condition may be fulfilled, it is real and hence in the indicative. In sentence *b* the condition is purely hypothetical. The speaker does not have the money (but if he/she had it ...); hence the verb **had** is subjunctive (identical in form, but not in meaning, to the past indicative).

Hypothetical (unreal) conditions are generally accompanied by equally hypothetical conclusions. Observe the verb forms used in the following sentences:

CONDITION	CONCLUSION
If I **had** the money,	I **would go** to Europe.
If she **had** the time,	she **would join** us.
If I **could** pay my debts,	I **would be** very relieved.
If he **became** angry,	I **would become** angry, too.
subjunctive	**conditional**
(usually identical in form to the past indicative)	*would* + verb

The subjunctive and the conditional may refer to either the present or future.

> If I had more money, I would not be living in such a small apartment.
> PRESENT   PRESENT
> If I had the money, I would buy a house next spring.
> PRESENT   FUTURE
> If I lost my scholarship, I would have to quit school.
> FUTURE   FUTURE

PRACTICE 1   *The following sentences contain real conditions. Change them to unreal conditions.*

> **Model:** If it is raining, we won't walk to school.
> **If it were raining, we would not walk to school.**

1. If she invites me, I will not accept.
2. If I can, I'll help you.
3. If you have a fever, you'll have to see a doctor.
4. If that is true, I'll never speak to her again.
5. If we have a choice, we won't sign the contract.
6. If I don't call them, they'll be very angry with me.
7. If she loves me, she'll forgive me.
8. If she does that, she'll make me very happy.

§2   UNREAL CONDITIONS IN GERMAN

	CONDITION	CONCLUSION
Real condition:	Wenn Sie es ihr **sagen,**	**ist** sie bestimmt schockiert.
	If you tell her,	*she will certainly be shocked.*
Unreal condition:	Wenn Sie es ihr **sagten,**	**wäre** sie bestimmt schockiert.
	If you told her,	*she would certainly be shocked.*

The real condition and conclusion are expressed in the indicative, their unreal counterparts in the subjunctive.

A note on the word order

The conditional clause, or **wenn**-clause, is a dependent clause; hence the verb stands at the end. The conclusion is the main clause. It has inverted word order because it is preceded by a dependent clause (cf. Chap. 12, §2).

§3   FORMS OF THE PRESENT SUBJUNCTIVE

Weak verbs

The forms of the present subjunctive and of the past indicative are identical (cf. Chap. 3, §1).

PAST INDICATIVE = PRESENT SUBJUNCTIVE

ich sagte	ich arbeitete
du sagtest	du arbeitetest
er, sie, es sagte	er, sie, es arbeitete
wir sagten	wir arbeiteten
ihr sagtet	ihr arbeitetet
sie sagten	sie arbeiteten
Sie sagten	Sie arbeiteten

(An **e** is added when the stem ends in **-d, -t,** or consonant clusters.)

PRACTICE 2   *Supply the appropriate subjunctive forms of the verbs in parentheses. (Keep in mind that in dependent clauses the separable prefix is attached to the verb.)*

Model: Wenn er nicht _____, ... (bezahlen, studieren, auf•passen)
    Wenn er nicht bezahlte, ...
    Wenn er nicht studierte, ...
    Wenn er nicht aufpaßte, ...

1. Wenn er _____, ... (fragen, schwänzen, warten, zu•hören)
2. Wenn es _____, ... (stören, regnen, passieren)
3. Wenn wir es _____, ... (glauben, ab•holen, parken, zu•machen)
4. Wenn sie (she) ihn _____, ... (lieben, heiraten, manipulieren)
5. Wenn du mich _____, ... (fragen, aus•lachen, ignorieren)
6. Wenn die Arbeiter _____, ... (streiken, protestieren)
7. Wenn ihr es noch einmal _____, ... (versuchen)
8. Wenn das Motorrad nicht soviel Geld _____, ... (kosten)
9. Wenn die Leute ihr Geld _____, ... (investieren)

Strong verbs

(cf. Chap. 3, §4, §6, and Appendix, §2)
The personal endings of the subjunctive are identical to the past-tense endings of weak verbs minus **t**:

ich	_____	**e**
du	_____	**est**
er, sie, es	_____	**e**
wir	_____	**en**
ihr	_____	**et**
sie	_____	**en**
Sie	_____	**en**

These endings are attached to the past-tense stem of strong verbs, i.e. the second principal part:

gehen   ging   ist gegangen

PAST INDICATIVE   PRESENT SUBJUNCTIVE

ich	ging		ich	ging**e**
du	gingst		du	ging**est**
er, sie, es	ging	er, sie, es	ging**e**
wir	gingen	(identical)	wir	ging**en**
ihr	gingt		ihr	ging**et**
sie	gingen	(identical)	sie	ging**en**
Sie	gingen	(identical)	Sie	ging**en**

Further examples in the **ich** form:

	PAST INDICATIVE	PRESENT SUBJUNCTIVE
bleiben	ich blieb	**ich bliebe**
lassen (läßt)	ich ließ	**ich ließe**
schreiben	ich schrieb	**ich schriebe**

Strong verbs with the vowels **a, o,** and **u** in the past indicative require an umlaut in the present subjunctive:

essen (ißt)	ich aß	**ich äße**
tun	ich tat	**ich täte**
fliegen	ich flog	**ich flöge**
fahren (fährt)	ich fuhr	**ich führe**

A few strong verbs have irregular subjunctives, such as

gewinnen	ich gewann	**ich gewönne** (also: ich gewänne)
helfen (hilft)	ich half	**ich hülfe** (also: ich hälfe)
schwimmen	ich schwamm	**ich schwömme** (also: ich schwämme)
stehen	ich stand	**ich stünde** (also: ich stände)
sterben (stirbt)	sie starb	**sie stürbe**

Because these irregular subjunctives rarely occur, they will not be practiced. (The use of substitute forms is explained in §6.)

PRACTICE 3   A. *Restate the following* **wenn-***clauses, using the subjects in parentheses.*

1. Wenn ich jetzt nach Hause ginge, ... (wir, er, Sie, du, ihr)
2. Wenn ich zu Hause bliebe, ... (du, ihr, Sie)
3. Wenn ich nicht schriebe, ... (Ruth, meine Eltern)
4. Wenn ich das äße, ... (wir, Ralf, die Kinder)

B. *First state the second principal part of the verb in parentheses, then supply the appropriate subjunctive form.*

Model: Wenn wir unseren Hund _____, ... (mit•nehmen / _____)
   Wenn wir unseren Hund mitnähmen, ... (nahm mit)

1. Wenn Sie _____, ... (mit•kommen / _____)
2. Wenn ich ein Stipendium[1] _____, ... (bekommen / _____)
3. Wenn er mir den Gefallen _____, ... (tun / _____)
4. Wenn Sie etwas langsamer _____, ... (sprechen / _____)
5. Wenn ich Ursula das Geld _____, ... (geben / _____)
6. Wenn er heute abend _____, ... (an•rufen / _____)
7. Wenn ich keine Stelle _____, ... (finden / _____)
8. Wenn das Geschenk meiner Freundin nicht _____, ... (gefallen / _____)

_____

1 **das Stipendium,** *pl.* **die Stipendien**   scholarship

9. Wenn wir sofort _____, ... (an•fangen / _____)
10. Wenn ihr zu spät _____, ... (kommen / _____)
11. Wenn er mich _____, ... (sehen / _____)

Irregular verbs

1. Mixed verbs (cf. Chap. 3, §8)

	PAST INDICATIVE	PRESENT SUBJUNCTIVE
denken	ich dachte	**ich dächte**
bringen	ich brachte	**ich brächte**
wissen	ich wußte	**ich wüßte**

These verbs form the subjunctive by adding an umlaut to the past indicative form. The following mixed verbs that require an **e** in their subjunctive forms occur only in literary German. (The use of substitute forms is explained in §6.)

brennen	es brannte	es brennte
kennen	ich kannte	ich kennte
nennen	ich nannte	ich nennte
rennen	ich rannte	ich rennte

2. haben, sein, werden (cf. Chap. 3, §9)

haben	ich hatte	**ich hätte**
sein	ich war	**ich wäre**
werden	ich wurde	**ich würde**

Haben and **werden** form the subjunctive by adding an umlaut to the past indicative forms. The subjunctive forms of **sein** follow the pattern of strong verbs.

Haben, sein, and **werden** are frequently used in the subjunctive. Their conjugations are listed below.

haben	**sein**	**werden**
ich hätte	ich wäre	ich würde
du hättest	du wär(e)st	du würdest
er, sie, es hätte	er, sie, es wäre	er, sie, es würde
wir hätten	wir wären	wir würden
ihr hättet	ihr wär(e)t	ihr würdet
sie hätten	sie wären	sie würden
Sie hätten	Sie wären	Sie würden

(The **e** of the fam. sing. and pl. may be omitted.)

PRACTICE 4   *Restate the following* **wenn**-*clauses, substituting the subjects indicated.*

1. Wenn ich mehr Zeit hätte, ... (er, Sie, du, ihr)
2. Wenn ich nicht so egoistisch wäre, ... (du, ihr, wir)

3. Wenn ich krank würde, ... (Rita, die Kinder, ihr, du, Sie)
4. Wenn ich daran dächte, ... (Sie, Marlene, wir, du)
5. Wenn ich Schmidts nach Hause brächte, ... (wir, du, ihr, Sie)
6. Wenn ich es wüßte, ... (Sie, er, du, ihr)

Modal auxiliaries

(cf. Chap. 4, §2)

INFINITIVE	PAST INDICATIVE	PRESENT SUBJUNCTIVE	
können	ich konnte	**ich könnte**	
dürfen	ich durfte	**ich dürfte**	(with umlaut)
müssen	ich mußte	**ich müßte**	
mögen	ich mochte	**ich möchte**	
wollen	ich wollte	**ich wollte**	(without umlaut)
sollen	ich sollte	**ich sollte**	

The present subjunctive of modals is like the past indicative except that those that have umlaut in the infinitive add umlaut in the subjunctive.

Remember: | **wollen** and **sollen** never have umlaut.

PRACTICE 5   *Supply the appropriate subjunctive forms of the modals in parentheses.*

1. Wenn wir das _____, ... (müssen, wollen, können, dürfen, sollen)
2. Wenn Monika zu Hause bleiben _____, ... (müssen, mögen, wollen, sollen)
3. Wenn du mitkommen _____, ... (dürfen, mögen, können, wollen)
4. Wenn Sie das bezahlen _____, ... (sollen, können, müssen)
5. Wenn ihr das nicht _____, ... (wollen, mögen, dürfen, können)

§4   USE OF THE PRESENT SUBJUNCTIVE IN UNREAL CONDITIONS AND CONCLUSIONS

Real condition and conclusion:

Wenn er wirklich in Gefahr **ist, müssen** wir ihn warnen.
If he is really in danger, we have to warn him.

Unreal condition and conclusion:

Wenn er wirklich in Gefahr **wäre, müßten** wir ihn warnen.
If he were really in danger, we would have to warn him.

The conclusion may be introduced by **dann** or **so** (the latter has a literary flavor):

Wenn er wirklich in Gefahr wäre, **dann (so)** müßten wir ihn warnen.

PRACTICE 6   *Convert the following sentences with real conditions to unreal conditions. Render the unreal version into English.*

Model: Wenn der Kurs in Physik noch schwerer wird, muß ich damit aufhören.

Wenn der Kurs in Physik noch schwerer würde, müßte ich damit aufhören.

If the course in physics got any harder, I would have to drop it.

1. Wenn dieses Projekt zu teuer wird, müssen wir es aufgeben.
2. Wenn Margot in die Stadt fahren will, dann kann sie meinen Wagen nehmen.
3. Wenn Egon nach 8 Uhr anruft, ist Renate nicht zu Hause.
4. Wenn er die Stelle beim Konsulat bekommt, hat er großes Glück.[1]
5. Wenn Sie Lisas Adresse wissen, dann können wir ihr eine Karte aus Berlin schicken.
6. Wenn du willst, kannst du es noch einmal versuchen.

§5   USE OF *würde* + INFINITIVE IN THE CONCLUSION

Conclusions with the verbs **haben, sein, wissen,** and the modals are normally expressed in the present subjunctive. With other verbs, however, a form of **würde** (subjunctive of **werden**) + infinitive of the main verb is usually preferred. This corresponds to the English use of **would** + verb.

> Wenn wir hier parken könnten, **sparten** wir Zeit und Geld.
> more common: Wenn wir hier parken könnten, **würden** wir Zeit und Geld **sparen.**
> *If we could park here, we would save time and money.*

Würde plus infinitive of the main verb is structurally the future subjunctive (cf. Chap. 14, §6, 3); however, it frequently serves as a substitute for the present subjunctive.

PRACTICE 7   A. *Replace the present subjunctive in the conclusion with* **würde** + *infinitive forms. (Keep in mind that the separable prefix is attached to the infinitive.)*

Model: Wenn es nicht schneite, holten wir heute unseren neuen Wagen ab.

Wenn es nicht schneite, würden wir heute unseren neuen Wagen abholen.

1. Wenn ich es könnte, gäbe ich dir das Geld sofort zurück.
2. Wenn wir noch Platz im Wagen hätten, dann nähmen wir Sie natürlich mit.
3. Wenn sie es dürften, dann versuchten sie es noch einmal.
4. Wenn ich immer soviel arbeiten müßte, bekäme ich bestimmt einen Nervenzusammenbruch.[2]

---

1 **großes Glück haben**   to be very lucky

2 **der Nervenzusammenbruch, ¨e**   nervous breakdown

5. Wenn ich an deiner Stelle wäre,[1] bliebe ich nicht zu Hause.
6. Wenn du an meiner Stelle wärest,[2] sagtest du wahrscheinlich nein.

B. *Convert the following real conditions to unreal conditions, using* **würde** + *infinitive forms in the conclusions.*

Model: Wenn ich es kann, tue ich dir diesen Gefallen.
      Wenn ich es könnte, würde ich dir diesen Gefallen tun.

1. Wenn meine Noten nicht gut genug sind, bekomme ich kein Stipendium.
2. Wenn sie mich fragt, dann sage ich ihr die Wahrheit.
3. Wenn der Chef uns nicht gut bezahlt, streiken wir.
4. Wenn er kein sicherer Fahrer ist, dann fahre ich nicht mit.
5. Wenn du ein Fenster aufmachst, dann macht er es wieder zu.
6. Wenn sie mich auslacht, dann lache ich sie auch aus.

C. *Convert to unreal conditions. In the conclusions, use the present subjunctive with* **haben, sein, wissen,** *and the modals but* **würde** + *infinitive forms with other verbs.*

1. Wenn er mich ignoriert, dann ignoriere ich ihn auch.
2. Wenn Frau Schneider das hört, ist sie bestimmt schockiert.
3. Wenn Sie eine Gehaltserhöhung[3] bekommen, dann haben Sie großes Glück.
4. Wenn der Chef gute Laune hat, bitte ich ihn um eine Gehaltserhöhung.
5. Wenn es nicht regnet, gehen wir zu Fuß ins Theater.
6. Wenn meine Noten gut genug sind, studiere ich Medizin.
7. Wenn er ein gutes Gedächtnis[4] hat, dann weiß er den Namen des Hotels noch.
8. Wenn man mich manipulieren will, dann protestiere ich sofort.
9. Wenn er mir einen Heiratsantrag macht,[5] dann sage ich nein.
10. Wenn du es wirklich willst, dann kannst du es auch.
11. Wenn ich Martina diesen Gefallen tue, dann muß sie mir auch einen Gefallen tun.

§6   USE OF *würde* + INFINITIVE IN THE *wenn*-CLAUSE

In formal German (literary works, lectures, papers, official statements), **wenn**-clauses usually avoid the **würde** + infinitive forms. However, an exception is

1 **Wenn ich an deiner Stelle wäre**	If I were in your place
	If I were you
2 **Wenn du an meiner Stelle wärest**	If you were in my place
	If you were me
3 **die Gehaltserhöhung, -en**	raise (*salary*)
4 **das Gedächtnis**	memory
5 **einen Heiratsantrag machen**	to propose marriage

often made in the case of a strong verb with the subjunctive stem vowel **ö** or **ü** and a mixed verb with the stem vowel **e** .

Possible but somewhat stiff:	Alternative:
Wenn er uns **hülfe,** ...	Wenn er uns **helfen würde,** ...
Wenn er **stürbe,** ...	Wenn er **sterben würde,** ...
Wenn wir den Krieg **verlören,** ...	Wenn wir den Krieg **verlieren würden,** ...
Wenn man sie beim Vornamen **nennte,** ...	Wenn man sie beim Vornamen **nennen würde,** ...

It is, however, considered poor practice in formal style to have **würde** + infinitive forms in both the **wenn**-clause and the conclusion.

poor style: Wenn die Regierung helfen würde, würde diese Firma nicht bankrott machen.
If the government would help, this company would not go bankrupt.

rephrased: Wenn die Regierung helfen könnte, würde diese Firma nicht bankrott machen.

or: Wenn die Regierung helfen würde, machte diese Firma nicht bankrott.

Colloquial German frequently uses **würde** + infinitive forms with verbs other than those above.

Wenn du mich anriefest, ...	Wenn du mich anrufen würdest, ...
Wenn ihr nicht soviel schwänztet, ...	Wenn ihr nicht soviel schwänzen würdet, ...

It is also rather common in colloquial German to use **würde** + infinitive forms both in the **wenn**-clause and in the conclusion.

§7   OMISSION OF *wenn*

Compare the following sentences:

Wenn ich eine Schreibmaschine hätte, (dann/so) würde ich dir öfter schreiben.
Hätte ich eine Schreibmaschine, **dann/so** würde ich dir öfter schreiben.

Note: The inflected verb is at the beginning of the clause. The otherwise optional particle **dann** or **so** is required. Literal translations of such sentences frequently sound stiff:

Had I a typewriter, then I would write to you more often.
idiomatic: *If I had a typewriter, I would write to you more often.*

§8   REVERSAL OF THE *wenn*-CLAUSE AND CONCLUSION

Compare the following two sentences:

Wenn ich an seiner Stelle wäre, **würde ich** die Rechnung nicht bezahlen.
Ich würde die Rechnung nicht bezahlen, wenn ich an seiner Stelle wäre.
I would not pay the bill if I were in his place.

Note the change to normal word order when the conclusion (main clause) precedes the **wenn**-clause.

PRACTICE 8   A. *Omit* **wenn**, *change the word order, and insert* **dann**. *Follow the model of sentence 1.*

     1. Wenn ich nicht für eine Prüfung lernen müßte, würde ich ins Theater gehen.
     Müßte ich nicht für eine Prüfung lernen, dann würde ich ins Theater gehen.
     2. Wenn wir eine größere Wohnung hätten, würden wir mehr Leute einladen.
     3. Wenn mein Wagen nicht kaputt wäre, würde ich Erika vom Flughafen abholen.
     4. Wenn es nach mir ginge[1], würden wir aufs Land ziehen.[2]
     5. Wenn Hans nicht so egoistisch wäre, hätte er bestimmt mehr Freunde.

B. *Begin each sentence with the conclusion, following the model of sentence 1.*

     1. Wenn du es wirklich wolltest, könntest du uns helfen.
     Du könntest uns helfen, wenn du es wirklich wolltest.
     2. Wenn meine Noten besser wären, würde ich Medizin studieren.
     3. Wenn Sie mir diesen Gefallen tun könnten, wäre ich Ihnen sehr dankbar.
     4. Wenn ich nicht pleite wäre, würde ich heute abend ins Theater gehen.

§9   UNREAL CONDITIONS WITH QUESTIONS

Unreal conditions may follow questions.

     Was würdest du sagen, wenn ich nicht zurückkäme?
     What would you say if I didn't come back?

     Was würden Sie tun, wenn Sie an ihrer Stelle wären?
     What would you do if you were in her place?

PRACTICE 9   *Complete the questions, following the model of sentence 1.*

     1. Was würdest du sagen, **wenn ich zu Hause bleiben wollte?**
                   if I wanted to stay at home?
     2. Was würden Sie sagen, _____
                   if I could not pay this bill?
     3. Was würdest du tun, _____
                   if you were in my place?

---

1 idiom: **es geht nach mir, dir, ihm,** *etc.*   it is up to me, you, him, *etc.*
2 **aufs Land ziehen, zog, ist gezogen**   to move to the country

4. Was würden Sie tun, _____

if you were in his place?

5. Würden Sie es übelnehmen, _____

if I said no?

6. Könntest du es verstehen, _____

if I wanted to move to the country?

§10   CONCLUSIONS STANDING ALONE

Although an unreal condition is not always expressed, one is often implied. In such instances the main clause (conclusion) stands alone.

Ich würde den Vertrag nicht unterschreiben. (wenn ich an deiner Stelle wäre)
I would not sign the contract. (if I were you)

Ich würde ihm gern helfen. (wenn ich es könnte)
I would gladly help him. (if I could)

Das wäre schade. (wenn das passierte)
That would be a pity. (if that happened)

Das wäre großartig. (wenn wir das tun könnten)
That would be great. (if we could do that)

PRACTICE 10   *Translate the responses into German following the model of sentence 1.*

1. X: Ich habe etwas Angst vor ihm.
   Y: **Ich hätte keine Angst vor ihm.**
   I would not be afraid of him.
2. X: Vielleicht sage ich es ihr nicht.
   Y: _____
   I would tell her.
3. X: Ich weiß nicht, ob ich den Chef um eine Gehaltserhöhung bitten soll.
   Y: _____
   I would ask him for a raise.
4. X: Klaus nimmt es vielleicht übel, wenn wir seine Freundin nicht einladen.
   Y: _____
   He would resent it.
5. X: Vielleicht laden wir auch Helga und Dieter ein.
   Y: _____
   That would be great.
6. X: Vielleicht kann ich nicht mitfahren.
   Y: _____
   That would be a pity.

§11 *wenn*-CLAUSES STANDING ALONE

Wenn ich nur mehr Zeit **hätte!**
less common: **Hätte** ich nur mehr Zeit! } *If only I had more time.*

Wenn Sie mich nur verstehen **könnten!** } *If only you could*
less common: **Könnten** Sie mich nur verstehen! } *understand me.*

Wenn ich nur ihren Namen **wüßte!**
less common: **Wüßte** ich nur ihren Namen! } *If only I knew her name.*

These are wishes one does not expect to be fulfilled. In German they end with an exclamation point. Just as English uses the particle *only*, German uses **nur**. In most instances **nur** follows the subject and pronoun objects but precedes all other elements.

PRACTICE 11 *Translate into German following the model of sentence 1.*

1. Klaus hat viele Vorurteile.[1]
   Wenn er nur nicht so viele Vorurteile hätte!
   If only he didn't have so many prejudices.
2. Leider habe ich nicht viel Willenskraft.[2]
   _____
   If only I had more will power.
3. Meine Freundin ist sehr stur. _____
   If only she weren't so stubborn.
4. Leider weiß ich es nicht. _____
   If only I knew it.
5. Ich suche eine bessere Stelle. _____
   If only I could find a better job.
6. Ich beneide Annerose. _____
   If only I were in her place.
7. Schade, daß Herr Krause verheiratet ist. _____
   If only he were single.[3]

Unreal Conditions Referring to the Past

§12 IN ENGLISH

	CONDITION	CONCLUSION
PRESENT	**If I knew,**	**I would tell you.**
	PRES. SUBJ.	PRESENT CONDITIONAL
PAST	**If I had known,**	**I would have told you.**
	PAST SUBJ.	PAST CONDITIONAL

1 **das Vorurteil, -e**   prejudice
2 **die Willenskraft**   willpower
3 **ledig**   single

Note: a. The past subjunctive form (**I had known**) in the conditional clause is identical to the past perfect indicative.

b. The conclusion is expressed in the past conditional (**would have told**).

PRACTICE 12   *Change the unreal conditions from the present to the past, following the model of sentence 1.*

1. If I told you, you would not believe it.
   If I had told you, you would not have believed it.
2. If they invited me, I would not accept.
3. If they printed that, they would ruin our reputation.
4. If I did not call her, she would become very angry.
5. If they were in trouble, we would help them.
6. If I had the money, I would study abroad for a year.

§13   IN GERMAN

	WENN-CLAUSE	CONCLUSION
PRESENT	Wenn ich es wüßte,	(dann/so) würde ich es dir sagen.
PAST	Wenn ich es **gewußt hätte**,	(dann/so) **hätte** ich es dir **gesagt**.
	PAST SUBJ.	PAST SUBJ.

Both the **wenn**-clause and the conclusion are expressed in the past subjunctive. The **würde**-substitute is not used when referring to the past.

The forms of the past subjunctive will be practiced first in main clauses (conclusions), then in **wenn**-clauses, and finally in sentences consisting of a **wenn**-clause plus a conclusion.

§14   MAIN CLAUSES IN THE PAST SUBJUNCTIVE

Using weak, strong, and irregular verbs

The forms of the past subjunctive are derived from the past perfect indicative (cf. Chap. 3, §10).

PAST PERFECT INDICATIVE	PAST SUBJUNCTIVE	ENGLISH EQUIVALENT
verbs with auxiliary **haben**		
ich hatte gewußt	**ich hätte gewußt**	*I would have known*
ich hatte gefragt	**ich hätte gefragt**	*I would have asked*
ich hatte eingeladen	**ich hätte eingeladen**	*I would have invited*
ich hatte gehabt	**ich hätte gehabt**	*I would have had*
verbs with auxiliary **sein**		
Ich war gegangen	**ich wäre gegangen**	*I would have gone*
ich war geblieben	**ich wäre geblieben**	*I would have stayed*
ich war gewesen	**ich wäre gewesen**	*I would have been*
ich war geworden	**ich wäre geworden**	*I would have become*

Note: The auxiliaries **haben** and **sein** are in the subjunctive; the past participle remains unchanged.

PRACTICE 13   *Supply the past subjunctive forms of the sentences given in the present subjunctive. Follow the model of sentence 1.*

A. Verbs requiring **haben**

1. Ich würde ihn um eine Gehaltserhöhung bitten.
    Ich hätte ihn um eine Gehaltserhöhung gebeten.
    I would have asked him for a raise.
2. Ich würde es Klaus nicht sagen.

    _____
    I wouldn't have told Klaus.
3. Wir würden Bergmanns nicht einladen.

    _____
    We wouldn't have invited the Bergmanns.
4. Annerose würde mir die Wahrheit sagen.

    _____
    Annerose would have told me the truth.
5. Er hätte keine Probleme damit.

    _____
    He wouldn't have had any problems with that.
6. Ich hätte keine Angst davor.

    _____
    I wouldn't have been afraid of that.

B. Verbs requiring **sein**

1. Margot würde sehr böse werden.
    Margot wäre sehr böse geworden.
    Margot would have become very angry.
2. Die Sache würde zu kompliziert werden.

    _____
    The matter would have become too complicated.
3. Ich würde etwas länger in Wien bleiben.

    _____
    I would have stayed in Vienna a little longer.
4. Ich würde vor Angst sterben.

    _____
    I would have died of fear.
5. Das würde nicht passieren.

    _____
    That wouldn't have happened.
6. Das wäre schade.

    _____
    That would have been a pity.

7. Deine Freunde wären schockiert.

_____

Your friends would have been shocked.

C. *Cover up the German sentences of exercises A and B and translate the English sentences.*
Model: I would have asked him for a raise.
   Ich hätte ihn um eine Gehaltserhöhung gebeten.

Using modals

Modals always use the auxiliary **haben** (cf. Chap. 4, §3 and §4).

a. Modals with a dependent infinitive

Ich **hätte** ihm **helfen können.**	*I could have helped him.*
	or: *I would have been able to help him.*
Ich **hätte** ihm **helfen sollen.**	*I should have helped him.*
Er **hätte** dort nicht **parken dürfen.**	*He would not have been allowed to park there.*
Sie **hätte** lange **warten müssen.**	*She would have had to wait for a long time.*
Niemand **hätte** das **essen wollen.**	*Nobody would have wanted to eat that.*
Niemand **hätte** das **essen mögen.**	*Nobody would have liked to eat that.*

> hätte + _____
>   DOUBLE INFINITIVE

b. Modals without a dependent infinitive

Ich hätte es **gekonnt, gesollt, gedurft, gemußt, gewollt, gemocht.**

> hätte + _____
>   PAST PARTICIPLE

Note the difference between the German and English constructions:

Ich hätte ihm helfen können.	**Ich hätte es gekonnt.**
*I **could have** helped him.*	*I **could have** (done it).*
Ich hätte ihm helfen sollen.	**Ich hätte es gesollt.**
*I **should have** helped him.*	*I **should have** (done it).*

PRACTICE 14   A. *Supply the past subjunctive forms of the sentences given in the present subjunctive. Follow the model of sentences 1a and b.*

1. a. Ich könnte es nicht bezahlen.
   Ich hätte es nicht bezahlen können.
   I couldn't have paid it.

b. Ich könnte es nicht.

Ich hätte es nicht gekonnt.

I couldn't have (done it).

2. a. Niemand könnte das voraussehen.

_____

Nobody could have foreseen that.

b. Niemand könnte das.

_____

Nobody could have (done that).

3. a. Ich sollte mehr für die Prüfung lernen.

_____

I should have studied more for the exam.

b. Wir alle sollten das.

_____

We all should have done that.

4. a. Sie wollte ihn nicht heiraten.

_____

She wouldn't have wanted to marry him.

b. Sie wollte das nicht.

_____

She wouldn't have wanted to (do that).

5. a. Niemand dürfte ihm widersprechen.

_____

Nobody would have been allowed to contradict him.

b. Niemand dürfte das.

_____

Nobody would have been allowed to (do that).

6. a. Eigentlich müßte die Versicherungsgesellschaft alle Rechnungen bezahlen.

_____

Actually, the insurance company would have had to pay all the bills.

b. Eigentlich müßte die Versicherungsgesellschaft das.

_____

Actually, the insurance company would have had to (do that).

B. _Cover up the German sentences of exercise A and translate the English sentences._

Model: I couldn't have paid it.

Ich hätte es nicht bezahlen können.

§15   _wenn_-CLAUSES IN THE PAST SUBJUNCTIVE

The following wishes refer to the past:

Wenn er mich nur **angerufen hätte**!	If only he had called me.
Wenn ich nur mehr Zeit **gehabt hätte**!	If only I had had more time.

> Wenn ich nur zu Hause **gewesen wäre**!   If only I had been at home.
> Wenn ich nur nicht nervös **geworden wäre**!   If only I had not become nervous.

The **wenn**-clause has dependent word order: the inflected form is in final position.

Exception: The inflected form must precede a double infinitive (cf. Chap. 4, §7).

> Wenn ich dir nur **hätte** helfen können!   If only I could have helped you.
> but: Wenn ich es nur gekonnt **hätte**!   If only I could have (done it).

PRACTICE 15   A. *Supply the past subjunctive forms of the sentences given in the present subjunctive. Follow the model of sentence 1.*

1. Wenn das nur möglich wäre!
   Wenn das nur möglich gewesen wäre!
   If only that had been possible.
2. Wenn das Wetter nur besser wäre!

   If only the weather had been better.
3. Wenn ich nur mehr Geduld hätte!

   If only I had had more patience.
4. Wenn ich nur nicht soviel Angst hätte!

   If only I had not been so afraid.
5. Wenn er mich nur verstehen könnte!

   If only he could have understood me.
6. Wenn ich nur rauchen dürfte!

   If only I had been allowed to smoke.
7. Wenn ich das nur dürfte!

   If only I had been allowed to (do that).

B. *Cover up the German sentences of exercise A and translate the English sentences.*
Model: If only that had been possible.
   Wenn das nur möglich gewesen wäre.

§16   *wenn*-CLAUSE + CONCLUSION IN THE PAST SUBJUNCTIVE

The **wenn**-clause precedes the conclusion:

> **Wenn ich es gewußt hätte, (dann/so) hätte ich es dir gesagt.**
> *If I had known it, I would have told you.*

The conclusion precedes the **wenn**-clause:

> **Ich hätte es dir gesagt, wenn ich es gewußt hätte.**

PRACTICE 16   *Change the following present subjunctive sentences to past subjunctive.*

A. The **wenn**-clause preceding the conclusion:

Model: Wenn meine Noten besser wären, würde ich nicht mit dem Studium aufhören.

Wenn meine Noten besser gewesen wären, hätte ich nicht mit dem Studium aufgehört.

If my grades had been better, I would not have dropped out of school.

1. Wenn es möglich wäre, würde ich dir helfen.

_____

If it had been possible, I would have helped you.

2. Wenn ich an deiner Stelle wäre, würde ich es noch einmal versuchen.

_____

If I had been in your place, I would have tried it again.

3. Wenn wir Zeit hätten, würden wir Sie am Sonntag besuchen.

_____

If we had had time, we would have visited you on Sunday.

4. Wenn sie es wollte, würde ich mit ihr in die Oper gehen.

_____

If she had wanted it, I would have gone to the opera with her.

5. Wenn ich es dürfte, würde ich etwas länger bleiben.

_____

If I had been allowed to, I would have stayed a little longer.

6. Wenn ich rauchen dürfte, wäre ich nicht so nervös.

_____

If I had been allowed to smoke, I would not have been so nervous.

B. The conclusion preceding the **wenn**-clause:

Model: Ich würde nicht mit dem Studium aufhören, wenn meine Noten besser wären.

Ich hätte nicht mit dem Studium aufgehört, wenn meine Noten besser gewesen wären.

I would not have dropped out of school, if my grades had been better.

1. Ich würde den Fernseher kaufen, wenn er nicht so teuer wäre.

_____

I would have bought the TV set, if it hadn't been so expensive.

2. Sie wäre schockiert, wenn sie das hörte.

_____

She would have been shocked, if she had heard that.

3. Wir würden etwas länger in Wien bleiben, wenn es nur nach mir ginge.

_____

We would have stayed in Vienna a little longer, if it had been only up to me.

4. Er würde vor Neugierde[1] sterben, wenn wir es ihm nicht sagten.

_____

He would have died of curiosity, if we hadn't told him.

5. Sie könnten es noch einmal versuchen, wenn Sie es wollten.

_____

You could have tried it again, if you had wanted to.

C. *Cover up the German sentences of exercises A and B, and translate the English sentences.*

Model: If my grades had been better, I would not have dropped out of school.

Wenn meine Noten besser gewesen wären, hätte ich nicht mit dem Studium aufgehört.

Omission of *wenn*

Wenn ich es gewußt hätte, (dann/so) hätte ich es dir gesagt.
Hätte ich es gewußt, **dann/so** hätte ich es dir gesagt.

When the sentence begins with the inflected verb signaling an omitted **wenn**, the otherwise optional **dann** or **so** is required.

PRACTICE 17   *Omit* **wenn,** *change the word order, and add* **dann.**

1. Wenn ich an seiner Stelle gewesen wäre, hätte ich den Chef um eine Gehaltserhöhung gebeten.
2. Wenn es nur nach mir gegangen wäre, wären wir etwas länger in Wien geblieben.
3. Wenn wir nicht so schnell gefahren wären, wäre der Unfall vielleicht nicht passiert.
4. Wenn ich es gekonnt hätte, hätte ich Ihnen den Gefallen getan.

§17   *wenn*-CLAUSE AND CONCLUSION IN DIFFERENT TENSES

Observe the use of the tenses in the **wenn**-clause and conclusion:

a. Wenn Ute nicht krank wäre, könnten wir jetzt ins Konzert gehen.
     PRESENT   PRESENT
   If Ute weren't sick, we could go to the concert now.

b. Wenn Ute nicht krank gewesen wäre, wären wir gestern ins Konzert gegangen.
     PAST   PAST
   If Ute hadn't been sick, we would have gone to the concert yesterday.

c. Wenn Ute nicht krank wäre, wären wir gestern ins Konzert gegangen.
     PRESENT   PAST
   If Ute weren't sick, we would have gone to the concert yesterday.

In sentence *c* the **wenn**-clause is in the present, since Ute is still sick. The conclusion is in the past tense, since the concert was yesterday.

1 **die Neugierde**   curiosity

PRACTICE 18   *Translate the English sentences into German.*

> **Model:** Der Roman ist sehr lang. Deshalb habe ich ihn nicht gelesen.
> **Wenn der Roman kürzer wäre, hätte ich ihn gelesen.**
> If the novel were shorter, I would have read it.

1. Das Benzin ist sehr teuer. Wir haben einen kleinen Wagen gekauft.

   _____

   If gasoline weren't so expensive, we would have bought a bigger car.
2. Ich bin sehr kleinlich.[1] Ich habe die Rechnung nicht bezahlt.

   _____

   If I weren't so petty, I would have paid the bill.
3. Ich habe nicht viel Ausdauer.[2] Ich habe mit dem Studium aufgehört.

   _____

   If I had more perseverance, I would not have dropped out of school.
4. Mein Vater hat keine bessere Stelle gefunden. Wir können diese moderne Wohnung nicht mieten.

   _____

   If my father had found a better job, we could rent this modern apartment.
5. Wir haben nicht in der Lotterie gewonnen. Wir machen keine Reise um die Welt.

   _____

   If we had won in the lottery, we would take a trip around the world.

§18   SUMMARY OF THE MAIN FEATURES

Unreal Conditions

   1. **General pattern:**

	WENN-CLAUSE	CONCLUSION
PRES./ FUT.	Wenn ich es **wüßte,** PRES. SUBJ.	(dann/so) **würde** ich es dir **sagen.** **würde** + infinitive or: PRES. SUBJ. (especially with **haben, sein, wissen,** and the modals)
PAST	Wenn ich es **gewußt hätte,** PAST SUBJ.	(dann/so) **hätte** ich es dir **gesagt.** PAST SUBJ.

1 **kleinlich**   petty
2 **die Ausdauer**   staying power, perseverance

2. Omission of **wenn**:

> **Wüßte** ich es, dann **würde** ich es dir sagen.
> **Hätte** ich es **gewußt**, dann **hätte** ich es dir **gesagt**.

3. The conclusion precedes the **wenn**-clause:

> Ich **würde** es dir **sagen**, wenn ich es **wüßte**.
> Ich **hätte** es dir **gesagt**, wenn ich es **gewußt hätte**.

4. The **wenn**-clause and the conclusion in different tenses:

> Wenn ich es **wüßte**, dann **hätte** ich es dir **gesagt**.

5. The **wenn**-clause standing alone:

> Wenn ich es nur **wüßte**!
> Wenn ich es nur **gewußt hätte**!

6. The main clause (conclusion) standing alone:

> Ich **würde** es dir **sagen**.
> Ich **hätte** es dir **gesagt**.

§19 REFERENCE TABLE

Selected verbs:

fragen	weak verb (using **haben**)
gehen	strong verb (using **sein**)
haben **sein** **werden**	functioning as main verbs
können	modal without dependent infinitive
gehen können	modal with dependent infinitive

WENN-CLAUSES

PRESENT	PAST
Wenn ich ... **fragte**	Wenn ich ... **gefragt hätte**
If I asked	*If I had asked*
Wenn ich ... **ginge**	Wenn ich ... **gegangen wäre**
If I went	*If I had gone*
Wenn ich ... **hätte**	Wenn ich ... **gehabt hätte**
If I had	*If I had had*
Wenn ich ... **wäre**	Wenn ich ... **gewesen wäre**
If I were	*If I had been*
Wenn ich ... **würde**	Wenn ich ... **geworden wäre**
If I became	*If I had become*
Wenn ich ... **könnte**	Wenn ich ... **gekonnt hätte**
If I could	*If I could have*
Wenn ich ... **gehen könnte**	Wenn ich ... **hätte gehen können**
If I could go	*If I could have gone*

MAIN CLAUSES

PRESENT				PAST	

Ich **würde** ... **fragen**   *I would ask*   Ich **hätte** ...   **gefragt**
                                                                         I would have asked

Ich **würde** ... **gehen**   *I would go*   Ich **wäre** ...   **gegangen**
                                                                         I would have gone

Ich **hätte**   *I would have*   Ich **hätte** ...   **gehabt**
                                                                         I would have had

Ich **wäre**   *I would be*   Ich **wäre** ...   **gewesen**
                                                                         I would have been

Ich **würde** ... **werden**   *I would become*   Ich **wäre** ...   **geworden**
                                                                         I would have become

Ich **könnte** (es)   *I could (do it)*   Ich **hätte** (es)   **gekonnt**
                                                                         I could have (done it)

Ich **könnte** ... **gehen**   *I could go*   Ich **hätte** ...   **gehen können**
                                                                         I could have gone

PRACTICE 19   Summarizing exercises

A. *Translate into German.*

1. a. I can't tell you because I don't know it.   **Ich kann es dir nicht sagen, weil ich es nicht weiß.**
    b. If only I knew it.
    c. If I knew it, I would tell you.
    d. If I had known it, I would have told you.
2. a. She is dying of curiosity.   **Sie stirbt vor Neugierde.**
    b. She would die of curiosity.
    c. She would have died of curiosity.
3. a. He is in a bad mood.   **Er hat schlechte Laune.**
    b. If only he were in a good mood.
    c. If only he had been in a good mood.
4. a. I am asking my boss for a raise.   **Ich bitte meinen Chef um eine Gehaltserhöhung.**
    b. I should ask my boss for a raise.
    c. I should have asked my boss for a raise.
    d. If my boss were in a good mood, I would ask him for a raise.
    e. If my boss had been in a good mood, I would have asked him for a raise.
5. a. Life is hard.   **Das Leben ist schwer.**
    b. If only life were easier.
    c. Life would be easier, if I had more money.
6. a. Karin has found a better job.   **Karin hat eine bessere Stelle gefunden.**
    b. If only I could find a better job.
    c. If only I had found a better job.
    d. Life would be easier, if I had found a better job.
7. a. I can't go with you to the theater because I am broke.   **Ich kann nicht mit euch ins Theater gehen, weil ich pleite bin.**

    b. If only I could go with you to the theater.
    c. If only I had not been broke.
    d. If I had not been broke, I would have gone with you to the theater.
 8. a. Is she single? **Ist sie ledig?**
    b. If only she were single.
    c. If she were single, I would invite her.
    d. If she were single, I would have invited her.
 9. a. Please do me this favor. **Bitte tun Sie mir diesen Gefallen!**
    b. If only you could do me this favor.
    c. I would be very grateful, if you could do me this favor.
10. a. I'd like to be in her place. **Ich möchte an ihrer Stelle sein.**
    b. If only I were in her place.
    c. If I were in her place, I would marry Frank.
    d. What would you do, if you were in my place? (fam. sing.)
11. a. Why am I so afraid? **Warum habe ich soviel Angst?**
    b. If only I weren't so afraid.
    c. If only I had not been so afraid.
    d. I should not be so afraid.
    e. I should not have been so afraid.
    f. I would tell you the truth if I weren't so afraid. (formal)
    g. I would have told you the truth if I had not been so afraid.

B. *Complete the responses in German.*

 1. X: Warum werden deine Noten immer schlechter?
    Y: Weil ich faul bin. _____
                          If only I weren't so lazy.
 2. X: Liebst du Renate?
    Y: Ja, sehr. _____
                  I could not live without her.
 3. X: Hast du die Semesterarbeit getippt? Du hast doch eine Schreib-
       maschine.
    Y: _____
       I would have typed it if I had a typewriter.
 4. X: Du warst ja gestern sehr stur.
    Y: Ja, leider. _____
                   If only I had not been so stubborn.
 5. X: Bist du immer so kleinlich?
    Y: Nicht immer, aber meistens. _____
                                   I shouldn't be so petty.
 6. X: Ist es nicht großartig, daß Sie in der Lotterie gewonnen haben?
    Y: _____
       It would be great if it were true.
 7. X: Warum hast du nicht länger gewartet?
    Y: Es war schon spät. _____
                          I could not have waited any longer.

8. X: Fahren wir oder gehen wir zu Fuß?
   Y: Es ist sehr windig.

   _____

   If it weren't so windy, we could walk. (go on foot)
9. X: Wie ist denn der Unfall passiert? Ist Frank kein sicherer Fahrer?
   Y: _____

   If Frank were a safe driver, the accident would not have happened.
10. X: Haben Sie die Krise nicht vorausgesehen?
    Y: _____

    Nobody could have foreseen it.
11. X: Es ist schade, daß Hans so viele Vorurteile hat.
    Y: Ja, sehr schade. _____

                    Everything (**alles**) would be easier, if he did not

    _____
    have so many prejudices.
12. X: Wie ich höre, studiert deine Schwester Medizin.
    Y: Ich beneide sie sehr.

    _____

    If my grades were better, I would also study medicine.
13. X: Mußt du das ganze Wochenende lernen?
    Y: Zum Glück nicht.

    _____

    It would be very boring if I had to study all weekend.
14. X: Wollen Sie wirklich Neumanns Haus kaufen?
    Y: Meine Frau will, daß wir es kaufen.

    _____

    If it were only up to me, we would not buy it.
15. X: Warum wollen Sie nicht mit Herrn Körner ausgehen?
    Y: Weil das Goldstück¹ verheiratet ist.

    _____

    Of course, I would go out with him if he were single.

C. _Using the cues, make sentences that fit the context._

Model: Hannelore klatscht zuviel. Eine Freundin sollte es ihr sagen. Ich
    bin nicht ihre Freundin und kann es deshalb nicht.

        Wenn / Freundin—ihr / sagen

    Wenn ich ihre Freundin wäre, würde ich es ihr sagen.

1. Mein Freund Thomas will ein Jahr in Frankfurt studieren. Leider kann
   ich das nicht, denn ich habe nicht genug Geld.

        Wenn / mehr Geld—auch in Frankfurt / studieren

---

1 **das Goldstück, -e**   gem (_lit.:_ gold piece)

2. Ich habe eine sehr kleine Wohnung und kann nicht viele Leute einladen.

   Wenn / größere Wohnung—mehr Leute / ein.laden

3. Marlene hat mehr Ausdauer als ich.

   Wenn / nur / mehr Ausdauer!

4. Renate will mit dem Studium aufhören. Ich finde, daß sie das nicht tun
   sollte.

   Wenn / ich / an ihrer Stelle—nicht / mit dem Studium / auf.hören

5. Mein Bruder ist sehr egoistisch. Wahrscheinlich hat er deshalb nicht
   viele Freunde.

   Er / mehr Freunde—wenn / nicht so egoistisch

6. Ich soll Karin vom Flughafen abholen, kann es aber nicht, denn mein
   Wagen ist kaputt.

   Ich / ab.holen—wenn / Wagen / nicht kaputt

7. Meiner Meinung nach ist dieser Film etwas langweilig, weil er zu lang
   ist.

   Film / interessanter—wenn / kürzer

8. Andreas hat einen Sportwagen und fährt wie der Teufel. Ich fahre nie
   mit ihm.

   Ich / sterben / vor Angst

D. Sagen Sie in fünf Sätzen, was Sie tun würden, wenn Sie eine Million
Dollar in der Lotterie gewonnen hätten.

14

The Subjunctive
Part II

KEY TO THE EXERCISES ON CASSETTE 7.
RUNNING TIME: APPROX. 40 MIN.

Various Uses of the Subjunctive

§1   WISHES INTRODUCED BY *Ich wollte* OR *Ich wünschte*

**referring to the present
or future**

Ich wollte, Ich wünschte, }	ich **hätte** mehr Freizeit.	*I wish I had more leisure time.*
	ich **wäre** nicht so schüchtern.	*I weren't so shy.*
	ich **wüßte** es.	*I knew it.*
	ich **könnte** Sie überzeugen.	*I could convince you.*
	er **würde** nicht so schnell fahren.	*he would not drive so fast.*

Note: a. The introductory statement **Ich wollte** or **Ich wünschte** is a form of the present subjunctive. The English counterpart *I wish* is, of course, present indicative.

   b. The wish itself is expressed in the present subjunctive with **haben, sein, wissen,** and the modals; with other verbs the **würde** + infinitive forms are commonly used.

referring to the past

Ich wollte, Ich wünschte, }	ich **wäre** vorsichtiger **gewesen.**	*I wish I had been more careful.*
	ich **hätte** das im voraus **gewußt.**	*I had known that beforehand.*

| ich **hätte** das **voraussehen können.** | *I could have foreseen that.* |
| er **wäre** nicht so schnell **gefahren.** | *he had not been driving so fast.* |

Wishes referring to the past are expressed in the past subjunctive.

PRACTICE 1   *Complete the responses in German.*

A. **present or future wishes**

Model: X: Können Sie Klavier spielen?
      Y: **Leider nein, aber ich wollte, ich könnte es.**

        I wish I could (do it).

1. X: Sind Ihre Nachbarn immer so laut?
   Y: Nicht immer, aber meistens. _____

        I wish they weren't so loud.

2. X: Du hast ja nicht viel Ausdauer.
   Y: Das stimmt. _____

        I wish I had more perseverance.

3. X: Kommst du mit?
   Y: Leider kann ich nicht. _____

        I wish I could come along.

4. X: Wann kommt Karin zurück?
   Y: Ich habe keine Ahnung. _____

        I wish I knew (it).

5. X: Hat dich Werner angerufen?
   Y: Bis jetzt noch nicht.[1] _____

        I wish he would call soon.[2]

6. X: Bringt dich Gisela zum Bahnhof?
   Y: Leider nein. _____

        I wish she would take me to the railway station.

B. **past wishes**

Model: X: Hast du es ihm gesagt?
      Y: **Ja, aber ich wünschte, ich hätte es ihm nicht gesagt.**

      I wish I hadn't told him.

1.   X: Hast du Leonores Wagen gekauft?
      Y: Ja, aber _____

      I wish I hadn't bought it.

---

1 **bis jetzt noch nicht**   not yet so far
2 **bald**   soon

2. X: Du warst schon wieder in der Stadt. Sicher hast du wieder viel
       Geld ausgegeben.

    Y: Leider ja. _____

       I wish I hadn't spent so much money.

3. X: Ulrich hat heute Geburtstag. Hast du daran gedacht?

    Y: Leider nein. _____

       I wish I had thought of it.

4. a. X: Wie war die Party bei Köhlers?

    Y: Sehr langweilig. _____

       I wish I had stayed at home.

   b. X: Wenn man sich langweilt,[1] ißt man meistens zuviel.

    Y: Stimmt. _____

       I wish I had not eaten so much.

5. X: Jemand hat gesagt: „Die Herrschaft über den Augenblick ist die
       Herrschaft über das ganze Leben."*

    Y: Großartig! _____

       I wish I had said that.

§2   CLAUSES INTRODUCED BY *als ob, als wenn,* OR *als*

Er sieht (sah) so aus⟨ **als ob (als wenn)** er krank **wäre.**
                     ⟨ **als wäre** er krank.

He looks (looked) as if he were sick.

Note: a. Clauses introduced by **als ob, als wenn** (used less frequently), or their
shortened form **als** express conjectures.

  b. **Als ob/als wenn** clauses have dependent word order. When **ob** or **wenn**
is omitted, the inflected verb follows immediately after **als**.

Additional examples:

Sie hat ihr Geld verschwendet,⟨ **als ob (als wenn) sie Millionärin wäre.**
                              ⟨ **als wäre sie Millionärin.**

She was wasting her money as if she were a millionaire.

Er tut so,⟨ **als ob (als wenn) er viele Freunde hätte.**
          ⟨ **als hätte er viele Freunde.**

He acts as if he had many friends. He pretends to have many friends.

Idioms: **Tun Sie so,**⟨ **als ob (als wenn) Sie zu Hause wären.**
                       ⟨ **als wären Sie zu Hause.**

Make yourself at home.

Sie tut nur so.

She is only pretending.

---

1 **sich langweilen**   to be bored

* "Control over the moment is control over one's entire life."

PRACTICE 2   *Complete the German responses using both* **als ob** *and* **als**.

Model: X: Ist Herr Körner wirklich so intelligent, wie er tut?

Y: Ach, das ist nur Angabe.[1]

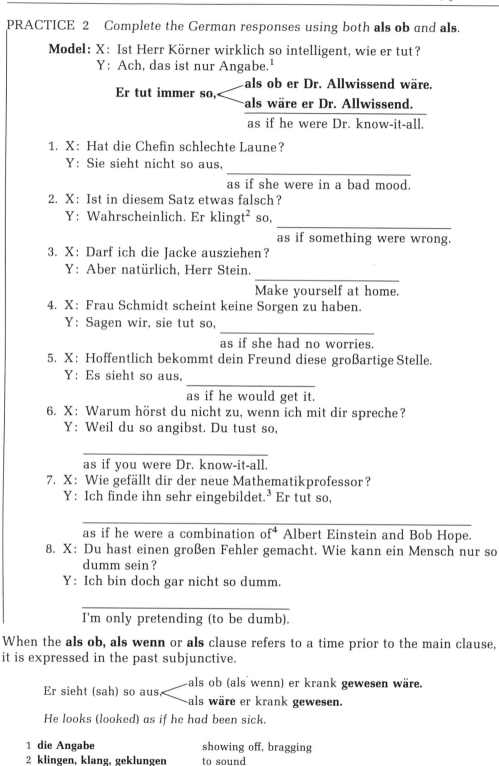

Er tut immer so,   **als ob er Dr. Allwissend wäre.**

                   als wäre er Dr. Allwissend.

                       as if he were Dr. know-it-all.

1. X: Hat die Chefin schlechte Laune?

    Y: Sie sieht nicht so aus, _____

                  as if she were in a bad mood.

2. X: Ist in diesem Satz etwas falsch?

    Y: Wahrscheinlich. Er klingt[2] so, _____

                    as if something were wrong.

3. X: Darf ich die Jacke ausziehen?

    Y: Aber natürlich, Herr Stein. _____

                 Make yourself at home.

4. X: Frau Schmidt scheint keine Sorgen zu haben.

    Y: Sagen wir, sie tut so, _____

                  as if she had no worries.

5. X: Hoffentlich bekommt dein Freund diese großartige Stelle.

    Y: Es sieht so aus, _____

              as if he would get it.

6. X: Warum hörst du nicht zu, wenn ich mit dir spreche?

    Y: Weil du so angibst. Du tust so,

    _____

    as if you were Dr. know-it-all.

7. X: Wie gefällt dir der neue Mathematikprofessor?

    Y: Ich finde ihn sehr eingebildet.[3] Er tut so,

    _____

    as if he were a combination of[4] Albert Einstein and Bob Hope.

8. X: Du hast einen großen Fehler gemacht. Wie kann ein Mensch nur so dumm sein?

    Y: Ich bin doch gar nicht so dumm.

    _____

    I'm only pretending (to be dumb).

When the **als ob, als wenn** or **als** clause refers to a time prior to the main clause, it is expressed in the past subjunctive.

                                als ob (als wenn) er krank **gewesen wäre.**

    Er sieht (sah) so aus,

                                  als **wäre** er krank **gewesen.**

    He looks (looked) as if he had been sick.

1	**die Angabe**	showing off, bragging
2	**klingen, klang, geklungen**	to sound
3	**eingebildet**	conceited
4	**eine Kombination von**	a combination of

PRACTICE 3   *Complete the German responses using both* **als ob** *and* **als**.

Model: X: War Barbara beim Friseur?

Y: **Sie sieht so aus,** ⟨ **als ob sie beim Friseur gewesen wäre.**
                                    als wäre sie beim Friseur gewesen.

as if she had been at the hairdresser's.

1. X: Hat es geregnet?
   Y: Es sieht so aus, _____

   as if it had rained.

2. X: Hast du zugenommen?
   Y: Sehe ich so aus, _____

   as if I had gained weight?

3. X: Warum denkst du, daß Marlene den ersten Preis gewonnen hat?
   Y: Sie strahlt[1] so, _____

   as if she had won the first prize.

4. X: Wie hast du auf Renates taktlose Bemerkung reagiert?
   Y: Ich habe so getan, _____

   as if I hadn't heard it.

5. X: Hast du diesen Film schon gesehen?
   Y: Es kommt mir so vor,[2] _____

   that (als ob) I have seen it already.

A note on the use of the special subjunctive in *als ob* and *als* clauses

In literary German these clauses are also expressed in the special subjunctive (cf. §7).

Er sah so aus, ⟨ als ob er krank **sei.**
                      als **sei** er krank.

Er sah so aus, ⟨ als ob er krank **gewesen sei.**
                      als **sei** er krank **gewesen.**

§3   *beinah(e)* OR *fast* INDICATING THAT SOMETHING ALMOST OCCURRED

Ich hätte es beinah(e) (fast) vergessen.   *I almost forgot it.*
Ich wäre beinah(e) (fast) gestorben.   *I almost died.*

Note: a. To indicate that something almost happened, German often uses the past subjunctive while English uses the past indicative.
   b. The **-e** of **beinahe** may be omitted. **Beinah(e)** and **fast** mean *almost* and are used interchangeably.

---

1 **strahlen**   to beam
2 *idiom:* **es kommt mir so vor**   it seems to me

Beinah(e) and **fast** normally follow subjects and personal pronoun objects but precede all other elements.

PRACTICE 4   *Translate the responses into German.*

> **Model:** X: Habt ihr den Zug verpaßt?
>
> Y: **Nein, aber wir hätten ihn beinahe verpaßt.**
>
> No, but we almost missed it.

1. X: Hoffentlich hast du den Vertrag nicht unterschrieben.

   Y: _____

   I almost signed it.

2. X: Hoffentlich hast du nicht schon wieder den Schlüssel vergessen.

   Y: _____

   I almost forgot it.

3. X: Warum seid ihr so aufgeregt?[1] Habt ihr einen Autounfall gehabt?

   Y: _____

   No, but we almost had a car accident.

4. X: Hast du verschlafen?

   Y: _____

   I almost overslept.

5. X: Bist du in der Vorlesung eingeschlafen?

   Y: _____

   I almost fell asleep.

6. X: Haben Sie Frau Berger sofort erkannt?

   Y: _____

   No. I almost didn't recognize her.

7. X: War Klaus wirklich so schwer krank,[2] wie seine Freundin sagt?

   Y: _____

   Yes. He almost died.

§4   TENTATIVE AND POLITE STATEMENTS AND QUESTIONS

In German the subjunctive is frequently used to make statements and questions more tentative, modest, or polite. Compare:

> a. INDICATIVE   Ich rate Ihnen, diese dumme Bemerkung zu ignorieren.
>
> *I advise you to ignore this stupid remark.*
>
> b. SUBJUNCTIVE   Ich **würde** Ihnen **raten**, diese dumme Bemerkung zu ignorieren.
>
> *I **would advise** you to ignore this stupid remark.*

The use of the subjunctive **würde** + **raten** in sentence *b* makes the statement more tentative. It expresses the advice with modesty and caution in contrast to

1 **aufgeregt**   excited, upset
2 **schwer krank sein**   to be seriously ill

the somewhat blunt tone of sentence *a*. This distinction is clear in the two English sentences above. However, subjunctive constructions occur more frequently in German than in English. They often have to be rendered into English with indicative forms, as the following examples illustrate:

Wir **hätten** also wieder einmal Glück **gehabt**.
So we have been lucky again.

Damit **hätte** ich endlich mein Ziel **erreicht**.
With that I have finally achieved my goal.

Questions are frequently made more polite by using the subjunctive. Compare:

INDICATIVE	SUBJUNCTIVE
Haben Sie einen Zettel für mich?	**Hätten** Sie einen Zettel für mich?
Do you have a piece of paper for me?	*Would you have a piece of paper for me?*
Ist Ihnen das recht?	**Wäre** Ihnen das recht?
Is that OK with you?	*Would that be OK with you?*
Können Sie einen Augenblick warten?	**Könnten** Sie einen Augenblick warten?
Can you wait a moment (minute)?	*Could you wait a moment (minute)?*
Tun Sie mir diesen Gefallen?	**Würden** Sie mir diesen Gefallen **tun**?
Are you going to do me this favor?	*Would you do me this favor?*

Note that the **würde** + infinitive forms are used with most verbs other than **haben, sein,** and the modals.

PRACTICE 5   *Express the following questions in a more polite way.*

> **Model:** Passen Sie ein paar Minuten auf meine Sachen auf?
> **Würden Sie ein paar Minuten auf meine Sachen aufpassen?**
>
> 1. Hilfst du mir?
> 2. Hast du etwas Zeit für mich?
> 3. Darf ich Sie um einen Gefallen bitten?
> 4. Ist das möglich?
> 5. Haben Sie Lust mitzufahren?
> 6. Ist dir das recht?
> 7. Paßt du auf meinen Koffer auf?
> 8. Bringt ihr mich zum Flughafen?
> 9. Kannst du mir 100 Mark leihen?[1]

PRACTICE 6   Summarizing exercises

> A. *Translate into German.*
>
> 1. a. He should speak a little more slowly. **Er sollte etwas langsamer sprechen.**
>   b. I wish he would speak a little more slowly.
>   c. I wish he had spoken a little more slowly.
>   d. Would you speak a little more slowly? (formal)
>   e. Could you speak a little more slowly?

1 **leihen, lieh, geliehen**   to lend

2. a. Who is taking care of that? **Wer erledigt das?**
   b. I wish she would take care of that.
   c. I wish she had taken care of that.
   d. Would you take care of that? (formal)
   e. Could you take care of that? (fam. sing.)
3. a. I don't have a typewriter. **Ich habe keine Schreibmaschine.**
   b. I wish I had a typewriter.
   c. I wish I had bought a typewriter.
   d. I almost bought a typewriter.
4. a. Don't give up hope. **Geben Sie die Hoffnung nicht auf!**
   b. It looks as if they would give up hope. (two ways: **als ob/als**)
   c. It looks as if they had given up hope. (two ways)
   d. We almost gave up hope.
5. a. He is a second Albert Einstein. **Er ist ein zweiter Albert Einstein.**
   b. He acts as if he were a second Albert Einstein. (two ways)
   c. He acts as if he had been Albert Einstein's right hand. (two ways)
6. a. She is shy. **Sie ist schüchtern.**
   b. She pretends to be shy. (two ways)
   c. She is only pretending.

B. *Using the cues, form sentences that fit the context.*

1. Hannelore war ein Jahr in Europa. Gestern ist sie zurückgekommen. Sie sieht anders aus als vor einem Jahr.

   ich / beinahe / nicht erkennen

2. Der neue Professor gefällt mir nicht.

   so tun, / Dr. Allwissend sein

3. Herberts Eltern feiern die Silberne Hochzeit. Herbert soll eine kleine Rede halten. Hat er Lampenfieber? (*stage fright*)

   so aus•sehen, / haben / Lampenfieber

4. Frau Klinger hat Gäste. Sie möchte, daß sie sich wie zu Hause fühlen, und sagt:

   „so tun, / zu Hause sein" (formal)

5. Gestern war die Vorlesung sehr langweilig.

   beinahe / ein•schlafen

6. Ich bin auf dem Bahnhof und habe einen schweren Koffer. Ich sehe einen Zeitungsstand. Neben mir steht eine ältere Dame. Sie sieht vertrauenswürdig (*trustworthy*) aus. Ich sage zu ihr:

   „Zeitung / kaufen. // auf Koffer auf•passen?"

7. Der Deutschprofessor hat mich etwas gefragt, aber ich habe seine Frage nicht verstanden. Ich sage höflich:

   „Frage / wiederholen?"

8. Ich habe keine Ahnung, wie lange meine Freundin in der Schweiz bleiben will.

   wollte, / ich / es / wissen

9. Ich habe Jürgen einen Lügner (*liar*) genannt. Jetzt tut es mir leid, daß ich das gesagt habe.

   wünschte, / das / nicht / sagen

10. Was gefällt Ihnen an Ihren Freunden und Freundinnen nicht? (drei Sätze)

    Ich wollte, er/sie ...

Using the Indicative and Subjunctive in Indirect Discourse

Introduction

Compare:

> **He says, "I like my brother's car."** (DIRECT DISCOURSE)
> **He says he likes his brother's car.** (INDIRECT DISCOURSE)

In indirect discourse one person reports what another has said without quoting him directly. Note that in the example, *I* and *my* are replaced by *he* and *his*.

In German, indirect discourse may be expressed in the indicative and in the subjunctive. Native speakers of German choose indicative or subjunctive forms according to what they want to imply and what they feel would sound right in a given context. The more refined their "Sprachgefühl" (feeling for the language) is, the more discriminating they are in the use of these forms. On the other end of the scale are those who use them rather haphazardly.

This can be quite puzzling to those who study German as a foreign language. Not yet being able to resort to a German "Sprachgefühl," they need rules and guidelines which give them a solid basis to work with. The following detailed explanations are designed to provide it.

Indirect discourse is treated somewhat differently in informal German (everyday speech, informal writing) and in formal German (literary works, lectures, papers, official statements).

§5   INFORMAL GERMAN USING THE INDICATIVE

When speakers use the indicative to report what someone has said, they indicate that they do not doubt the correctness of what they are reporting.

DIRECT QUOTE

Frau Köhler sagt: „**Mein Mann arbeitet** im Garten."

INDIRECT QUOTE

Frau Köhler sagt, daß **ihr Mann** im Garten **arbeitet**.
          or: **ihr Mann arbeitet** im Garten.

Note: a. When the subordinating conjunction **daß** is omitted, the indirect quote has the word order of a main clause.

b. The direct quote is preceded by a colon. The opening quotation mark is set on the line.

Additional examples:

Herr Köhler hat gesagt: „**Meine Frau und ich haben** im Garten **gearbeitet.**"
Herr Köhler hat gesagt, daß **seine Frau und er** im Garten **gearbeitet haben.**
or: **seine Frau und er haben** im Garten **gearbeitet.**

Köhlers haben gesagt: „**Unsere Kinder arbeiten** nicht gern im Garten."
Köhlers haben gesagt,   daß **ihre Kinder** nicht gern im Garten **arbeiten.**
or: **ihre Kinder arbeiten** nicht gern im Garten.

PRACTICE 7   *Change the following direct quotations to indirect discourse, using* **daß.** *(Keep in mind that in dependent clauses the separable prefix is attached to the verb.)*

Model: Sigrid hat gesagt: „Ich rufe dich Freitag abend an."
Sigrid hat gesagt, daß sie mich Freitag abend anruft.

1. Klaus hat gesagt: „Ich hole Inge um 7 Uhr ab."
2. Helga sagt: „Ich habe Dieters Telefonnummer vergessen."
3. Frau Körner hat gesagt: „Ich bin nur drei Tage in Berlin geblieben."
4. Zimmermanns haben gesagt: „Wir wollen aufs Land ziehen."
5. Inge sagt: „Ich habe heute keine Lust zur Arbeit."
6. Rainer hat gesagt: „Das Konzert fängt schon um 4 Uhr an."
7. Fräulein Klinger hat gesagt: „Der Zug ist pünktlich abgefahren."

Questions are quoted indirectly as follows:

DIRECT QUOTE

Herr Schreiber hat Herrn Köhler gefragt:
a. „Wann arbeiten Sie in Ihrem Garten?"
b. „Arbeiten Sie oft in Ihrem Garten?"

INDIRECT QUOTE

Herr Schreiber hat Herrn Köhler gefragt,
a. **wann** er in seinem Garten **arbeitet.**
b. **ob** er oft in seinem Garten **arbeitet.**

Note: Indirect questions always have dependent word order. They are introduced either by a question word, as in sentence *a*, or by **ob,** as in sentence *b* (cf. Chap. 1, §5).

Another example:

Ich habe Andreas gefragt:
a. „Warum hast du Renate eingeladen?"
b. „Hast du Renate eingeladen?"

Ich habe Andreas gefragt,
a. **warum** er Renate eingeladen **hat.**
b. **ob** er Renate eingeladen **hat.**

PRACTICE 8   *Change the following direct quotations to indirect discourse, using the introductory clauses indicated.*

Model: „Kommt Inge auch mit?"
Hans hat mich gefragt, <u>ob Inge auch mitkommt.</u>
„Warum kommst du nicht mit?"
Ich habe Klaus gefragt, <u>warum er nicht mitkommt.</u>

1. „Holst du Annerose ab?"
   Ich habe Hartmut gefragt, _____

2. „Rufst du mich heute abend an?"
   Ich habe Ruth gefragt, _____

3. „Wo hast du Renate kennengelernt?"
   Ich habe Martin gefragt, _____

4. „Wann kommt der Zug in München an?"
   Margot hat einen Beamten[1] gefragt, _____

5. „Wieviel kostet der Kassettenrecorder?"
   Ich habe die Verkäuferin gefragt, _____

6. „Haben Sie das Theaterstück gelesen?"
   Professor Krause hat mich gefragt, _____

§6   INFORMAL GERMAN USING THE SUBJUNCTIVE

The subjunctive is used in cautious reporting, usually when the speaker has reservations about the truth or accuracy of what was said.

1. The direct quote is in the present tense

Frank hat gesagt: Frank hat gesagt,
„Professor Bauer ist nicht fair."   Professor Bauer **wäre** nicht fair.
                                          (PRESENT SUBJUNCTIVE)

The speaker doubts the veracity of Frank's statement. By using the subjunctive he/she makes clear that he/she is merely reporting what Frank said.

Indirect quotations expressed in the subjunctive are usually not introduced by **daß**.

Additional examples:

Sie sagte: Sie sagte,
„Ich habe Angst."   sie **hätte** Angst.
„Ich kann das nicht essen."   sie **könnte** das nicht essen.
„Ich werde verrückt."   sie **würde** verrückt.
„Ich weiß seinen Namen nicht mehr."   sie **wüßte** seinen Namen nicht
                                          mehr.

---

1 **der Beamte** (*adj. noun* [Chap. 9, §12])   official

PRACTICE 9   *Change to indirect quotations.*

> **Model:** Frau Kästner hat gesagt: „ Ich kann sehr stur sein."
> **Frau Kästner hat gesagt, sie könnte sehr stur sein.**
>
> 1. Helga hat gesagt: „ Ich muß immer nachgeben."
> 2. Professor Wagner hat gesagt: „ Die Prüfung ist nicht schwer."
> 3. Margot hat gesagt: „ Ich habe nicht genug Willenskraft."
> 4. Michael hat gesagt: „ Ich weiß nichts davon."
> 5. Fräulein Bauer hat gesagt: „ Frau Stern will nicht zu ihrem Mann zurückgehen."
> 6. Herr Berger hat gesagt: „ Ich habe nie schlechte Laune."
> 7. Frau Berger hat gesagt: „ Das ist eine Lüge."

2. **The direct quote is in the past, present perfect, or past perfect**

Maria hat gesagt:	Maria hat gesagt,
„Ich **wußte** nichts davon."	
„Ich **habe** nichts davon **gewußt**."	sie **hätte** nichts davon **gewußt**.
„**Ich hatte** nichts davon **gewußt**."	(PAST SUBJUNCTIVE)
	Maria said she had known nothing about it.

The past subjunctive is used in indirect discourse to replace all three indicative tenses in the original statement.

Additional examples:

Er hat gesagt:	Er hat gesagt,
„ Ich hatte keine Angst.	er **hätte** keine Angst **gehabt**.
„ Das war eine Lüge."	das **wäre** eine Lüge **gewesen**.
„ Der Film hat niemand gefallen."	der Film **hätte** niemand **gefallen**.
„ Viele Leute sind im Kino eingeschlafen	viele Leute **wären** im Kino **eingeschlafen**.
„ Ich mußte immer nachgeben."	er **hätte** immer **nachgeben müssen**.
„ Ich wollte es nicht."	er **hätte** es nicht **gewollt**.

PRACTICE 10   *Change the following direct quotations to indirect discourse using the subjunctive.*

> **Model:** Peter hat gesagt: " Ich konnte meine Eltern nicht überzeugen."
> **Peter hat gesagt, er hätte seine Eltern nicht überzeugen können.**
>
> 1. Margot hat gesagt: „ Ich konnte die Rechnung nicht bezahlen."
> 2. Klaus hat gesagt: „ Ich konnte es auch nicht."
> 3. Herr Körner hat gesagt: „ Ich wollte den Vertrag nicht unterschreiben."
> 4. Frau Körner hat gesagt: „ Ich wollte es auch nicht."
> 5. Renate hat gesagt: „ Mein Freund hat gelogen."[1]

---

1 **lügen, log, gelogen**   to lie, tell a lie

6. Ihr Freund sagte: „Ich habe das nur zum Spaß gesagt."[1]
7. Meine Nachbarin hat gesagt: „Herr Schubert ist gestorben."
8. Frau Müller hat gesagt: „Das war nicht fair von meinem Chef."
9. Bauers sagten: „Wir hatten Schwierigkeiten an der Schweizer Grenze."
10. Sabine hat gesagt: „Thomas hat mir einen Heiratsantrag gemacht."
11. Thomas hat gesagt: „Sabine hat mich mißverstanden."

3. The direct quote is in the future tense

So far we have used **würde** + infinitive of the main verb as a substitute for the present subjunctive; however, as mentioned in Chap. 13, §5, these forms are actually the future subjunctive. They are used as such in indirect discourse.

Frau Morgenstern hat gesagt:
  „Ich werde das bei der Polizei melden."

Frau Morgenstern hat gesagt,
  sie **würde** das bei der Polizei **melden**.

  Mrs. Morgenstern *said she would report that to the police.*

The future subjunctive is frequently used when the direct present-tense quote has a future connotation:

Frau Morgenstern hat gesagt:
  „Ich melde das morgen bei der Polizei."

Frau Morgenstern hat gesagt,
  sie **würde** das morgen bei der Polizei **melden**.

The use of the future subjunctive is extremely common in indirect discourse and does not necessarily imply reservations as to what was said. It is virtually required if the event has already happened when reported:

Rainer und Monika haben im Juni geheiratet. Sie haben mir schon im Februar gesagt, sie **würden** im Juni **heiraten**.

PRACTICE 11   *Change the following direct quotations to indirect discourse using the future subjunctive.*

1. Petra sagte: „Ich werde meine Reise verschieben."[2]
2. Die Studenten haben gesagt: „Wir werden protestieren."
3. Anita hat gesagt: „Ich werde meine Eltern nicht enttäuschen."[3]
4. Der Bankdirektor hat gesagt: „Die Firma Schütze wird bankrott machen."[4]
5. Unsere Fußballmannschaft hat gewonnen. Vor Beginn des Spieles sagte der Trainer[5] siegesbewußt[6] zur Presse: „Wir werden gewinnen."

1 **zum Spaß sagen**	to say as a joke
2 **verschieben, verschob, verschoben**	to postpone
3 **enttäuschen**	to disappoint
4 **bankrott machen**	to go bankrupt
5 **der Trainer, -**	coach
6 **siegesbewußt**	confident of victory

Indirect reporting of commands

Commands are reported in indirect discourse with the modal **sollen**. Either the indicative or the subjunctive may be used, the latter option not implying reservations.

> „Bitte rufen Sie mich an!"
> Er hat mir gesagt, ich **soll** ihn anrufen. (indicative)
> > or: ich **sollte** ihn anrufen. (subjunctive)
> > *He told me I should call him.*
> or: *He told me **to call him**.*

In English indirect commands are frequently expressed with the infinitive, as in the example above. German does not have this option.

PRACTICE 12   *Express the following indirect commands in German using indicative and subjunctive forms.*

> **Model:** „Habt keine Angst!"
> > **Wir haben den Kindern gesagt,**
> > **sie sollen/sollten keine Angst haben.**
> >
> > not to be afraid (they shouldn't be afraid).

1. „Bitte seid still!"
   Wir haben den Kindern gesagt, _____
   > to be quiet (they should be quiet).
2. „Versuchen Sie es noch einmal!"
   Er hat uns gesagt, _____
   > to try again (we should try again).
3. „Rauchen Sie nicht soviel!"
   Der Arzt hat ihm gesagt,

   _____
   not to smoke so much (he shouldn't smoke so much).
4. „Gib die Hoffnung nicht auf!"
   Wir haben Frau Fischer gesagt,

   _____
   not to give up hope (she shouldn't give up hope).
5. „Glauben Sie diese Gerüchte nicht!"
   Ich habe meinem Freund gesagt,

   _____
   not to believe these rumors (he shouldn't believe these rumors).

§7   INDIRECT DISCOURSE IN FORMAL GERMAN

Indirect discourse in formal German is normally a matter of noncommittal reporting requiring the subjunctive. Here the subjunctive forms merely denote indirectness of speech and not reservations as to what is reported.

So far we have used only the forms of the general subjunctive. Formal German uses the forms of the special subjunctive in indirect discourse, but only where they are not identical to indicative forms. If they are identical, the general subjunctive is used.

1. Present subjunctive

The forms of the special subjunctive are based on the stem of the infinitive.

Example: sprechen (spricht), sprach, gesprochen

SPECIAL SUBJUNCTIVE	GENERAL SUBJUNCTIVE
subjunctive endings added to infinitive stem **sprech-**	subjunctive endings added to past tense stem **sprach** + umlaut
ich spreche	ich spräche
du sprechest	du sprächest
er, sie, es spreche	er, sie, es spräche
wir sprechen	wir sprächen
ihr sprechet	ihr sprächet
sie sprechen	sie sprächen
Sie sprechen	Sie sprächen

Some forms of the special subjunctive are identical to present indicative forms and hence cannot be readily recognized as subjunctive. These forms are replaced by forms of the general subjunctive, as indicated by the arrows in the following table.

INDICATIVE		SPECIAL SUBJ.		GENERAL SUBJ.
ich spreche	identical	(ich spreche)	⟶	ich spräche
du sprichst		du sprechest		du sprächest
er spricht		er spreche		er spräche
wir sprechen	identical	(wir sprechen)	⟶	wir sprächen
ihr sprecht		ihr sprechet		ihr sprächet
sie sprechen	identical	(sie sprechen)	⟶	sie sprächen
Sie sprechen	identical	(Sie sprechen)	⟶	Sie sprächen

Example:

Der Konsul sagte: „Meine Frau spricht zwei Fremdsprachen, meine Kinder sprechen sogar drei Fremdsprachen."
Der Konsul sagte, seine Frau **spreche** zwei Fremdsprachen, seine Kinder **sprächen** sogar drei Fremdsprachen.

More than 90 percent of the subjunctives used in formal indirect discourse are either third person singular or third person plural. The special subjunctive is used in the third singular, while the general subjunctive replaces it in the third plural.

Examples:

	SPECIAL SUBJUNCTIVE	GENERAL SUBJUNCTIVE
machen	er, sie, es **mache**	sie **machten**
geben	**gebe**	**gäben**

gehen	er, sie, es **gehe**	sie **gingen**
haben	**habe**	**hätten**
werden	**werde**	**würden**
wissen	**wisse**	**wüßten**
können	**könne**	**könnten**
müssen	**müsse**	**müßten**

(stem of inf. + **e**)

Exception: All forms of the special subjunctive of **sein** differ from the indicative forms and are not replaced by the general subjunctive **wäre**.

PRESENT INDICATIVE	PRESENT SPECIAL SUBJUNCTIVE
ich bin	ich **sei**
du bist	du **sei(e)st**
er, sie, es ist	er, sie, es **sei**
wir sind	wir **seien**
ihr seid	ihr **seiet**
sie sind	sie **seien**
Sie sind	Sie **seien**

Note: a. ich **sei** ⎫
       er, sie, es **sei** ⎬ no -**e** added to the stem of the infinitive.

b. The **e** in **seiest** is generally omitted.

Example for the use of the special subjunctive of **sein**:

Der Direktor sagte: „Das ist ein großes Problem, aber meine Mitarbeiter[1] sind sehr optimistisch, daß sie es lösen können."

Der Direktor sagte, das **sei** ein großes Problem, aber seine Mitarbeiter **seien** sehr optimistisch, daß sie es lösen könnten.

PRACTICE 13   *Change the following direct quotations to indirect discourse. Begin each sentence with* **Sie sagte,** ...

Model: „Man kann die Unzufriedenheit der Arbeiter verstehen."
          Sie sagte, man könne die Unzufriedenheit der Arbeiter verstehen.

1. „Man muß dieses Problem lösen."
2. „Der Chef und die Arbeiter müssen zusammenarbeiten."
3. „Es gibt keine andere Lösung."
4. „Der Chef weiß das, und die Arbeiter wissen das auch."
5. „Diese Firma hat finanzielle Schwierigkeiten, aber andere Firmen haben noch größere Schwierigkeiten."
6. „Die Spannung[2] zwischen dem Chef und seinen Mitarbeitern wird immer größer, und die Debatten werden immer länger."
7. „Der Chef ist nicht diplomatisch, und seine Mitarbeiter sind es auch nicht."

---

1 **der Mitarbeiter, -**   collaborator
2 **die Spannung, -en**   tension

2. Past subjunctive

The auxiliary **haben** uses the special subjunctive in the 3rd pers. sing. and the general subjunctive in the 3rd pers. pl. The auxiliary **sein** uses the special subjunctive in both forms.

	3RD PERS. SING.	3RD PERS. PL.
	special subjunctive	general subjunctive
verbs requiring **haben**	er, sie, es habe vergessen	sie hätten vergessen
	habe gehabt	hätten gehabt
	habe fahren können	hätten fahren können
	habe gekonnt	hätten gekonnt
		special subjunctive
verbs requiring **sein**	er, sie, es sei gefahren	sie seien gefahren
	sei gewesen	seien gewesen
	sei geworden	seien geworden

Examples:

Direct quote in any past tense	Indirect quote in the past subjunctive
Sie sagten:	Sie sagten,
„Wir waren in großer Gefahr.	sie **seien** in großer Gefahr **gewesen**.
„Niemand konnte uns helfen."	niemand **habe** ihnen **helfen können**.
„Zwei Polizisten haben es versucht."	zwei Polizisten **hätten** es **versucht**.
„Sie hatten kein Glück."	sie **hätten** kein Glück **gehabt**.

PRACTICE 14   *Change the following direct quotations to indirect discourse.*

Model: „Man konnte nicht alles verstehen, was der Redner sagte."
Sie hat behauptet[1], man habe nicht alles verstehen können, was der Redner gesagt habe.

1. „Ich mußte diesen Plan aufgeben."
   Sie sagte, _____
2. „Ich wußte nichts davon."
   Er hat behauptet, _____
3. „Die Leser haben mich mißverstanden."
   Die Journalistin sagte, _____
4. „Ich hatte meine Frage nicht gut formuliert."[2]
   Der Reporter sagte, _____
5. „Die zwei Zeugen[3] haben sich widersprochen."[4]
   Der Richter[5] erklärte, _____
6. „Ich bin die ganze Zeit in meinem Wagen geblieben."
   Ein Zeuge sagte, _____

1 **behaupten**	to claim, assert
2 **formulieren**	to phrase
3 **der Zeuge** (*weak*), **-n**	witness
4 **sich widersprechen**	to contradict oneself
5 **der Richter, -**	judge

7. „ Ich bin schnell über die Straße gelaufen."
Dann sagte er, _____

8. „ Der Mann hat eine Sonnenbrille getragen."
Der andere Zeuge sagte, _____

9. „ Ich habe den Mann nur von hinten gesehen."
Später sagte er, _____

10. „ Ich habe den Prozeß verloren,[1] weil die Zeugen ihre Aussagen[2] geändert[3] haben."
Die Rechtsanwältin betonte,[4] _____

3. Future subjunctive

The auxiliary **werden** uses the special subjunctive in the 3rd pers. sing. and the general subjunctive in the 3rd pers. pl.

SPECIAL SUBJUNCTIVE	GENERAL SUBJUNCTIVE
er, sie, es **werde** fahren	sie **würden** fahren

Examples:

Der Chef sagte:	Der Chef sagte,
„Ich werde den Fall klären."	er **werde** den Fall klären.
„Meine Mitarbeiter werden den Fall klären."	seine Mitarbeiter **würden** den Fall klären.

PRACTICE 15   *Change the following direct quotations to indirect discourse.*

1. „ Ich werde den Vertrag ändern."
Die Rechtsanwältin sagte, _____

2. „ Die Arbeiter werden bestimmt streiken."
Die Journalistin prophezeite,[5] _____

3. „ Der Bürgermeister wird wohl zurücktreten."[6]
Ein Stadtrat[7] sagte, _____

4. „ Viele Stadträte werden das begrüßen."[8]
Ein anderer sagte, _____

Indirect reporting of questions

The rules for the use of the subjunctive in formal indirect discourse apply to questions as well as to statements. Note that dependent word order is required:

1 **den Prozeß verlieren**	to lose the case
2 **die Aussage, -n**	testimony
3 **ändern**	to change
4 **betonen**	to emphasize, stress
5 **prophezeien**	to prophesy, predict
6 **zurück•treten (tritt zurück), trat zurück, ist zurückgetreten**	to resign
7 **der Stadtrat, ¨e**	town councilor, councilman
8 **begrüßen**	to welcome

Der Reporter fragte:

„Wann ist der Unfall passiert?"

„Hat man die Polizei informiert?"

„Ist der Fahrer an dem Unfall schuld?"[1]

Der Reporter fragte,

wann der Unfall passiert **sei**.

ob man die Polizei informiert **habe**.

ob der Fahrer an dem Unfall schuld **sei**.

PRACTICE 16   *Change to indirect discourse, beginning each sentence with* **Die Chefin fragte ihn,** ...

Model: „Haben Sie konkrete Vorschläge?"

Die Chefin fragte ihn, ob er konkrete Vorschläge habe.

1. „Haben Sie Schwierigkeiten mit Ihren Kollegen?"
2. „Sind Sie gegen den neuen Arbeitsplan?"
3. „Wann haben Sie Überstunden[2] gemacht?"
4. „Warum sind Sie zu Hause geblieben?"
5. „Werden Sie den neuen Vertrag unterschreiben?"

Indirect reporting of commands

The special subjunctive of **sollen** is used in the singular and the general subjunctive in the plural.

„Bitte stören Sie mich nicht!"

Sie sagte ihm, **er solle** sie nicht stören.

> She told him ⟨ he should not disturb her.
> not to disturb her.

Sie sagte ihnen, **sie sollten** sie nicht stören.

> She told them ⟨ they should not disturb her.
> not to disturb her.

PRACTICE 17   *Express the following indirect commands in German.*

1. „Bitte sprechen Sie lauter!"
   Der Richter sagte Frau Stein, _____
                                              to speak louder.
2. „Sagen Sie die Wahrheit!"
   Die Rechtsanwältin sagte den zwei Zeugen, _____
                                              to tell the truth.
3. „Unterbrechen Sie mich nicht!"
   Der Stadtrat sagte dem Reporter, _____
                                              not to interrupt him.
4. „Manipulieren Sie mich nicht!"
   Die Stadträtin sagte der Reporterin, _____
                                              not to manipulate her.

---

1 **schuld sein an (***dat.***)**   to be to blame for
2 **Überstunden machen**   to work overtime

5. „Enttäuschen Sie mich nicht!"
   Der Trainer sagte den Fußballspielern, _____

   not to disappoint him.

Lengthy indirect quotations

In German, lengthy statements may be quoted indirectly by using the subjunctive. In English, remarks such as "he continued," "he also mentioned," "he stated further" have to be added as reminders to the listener or reader that the indirect quotation continues. This is not necessary in German, because the subjunctive itself signals the continuation of the indirect quote.

Example:

A direct quotation by councilman Schmidt:

„Die Sitzung[1] war sehr stürmisch. Der Bürgermeister und die Stadträte führten lange Debatten. Man konnte sich nicht einigen,[2] und der Bürgermeister drohte mit seinem Rücktritt."[3]

The newspaper quotes:

Stadtrat Schmidt sagte, die Sitzung **sei** sehr stürmisch **gewesen**. Der Bürgermeister und die Stadträte **hätten** lange Debatten **geführt**. Man **habe** sich nicht einigen **können**, und der Bürgermeister **habe** mit seinem Rücktritt **gedroht**.

PRACTICE 18   *Change to indirect discourse using the introductory clauses provided.*

1. „Stadtrat Schubert hatte eine geniale Idee. Sein Vorschlag war ein Kompromiß. Der Bürgermeister und die Stadträte fanden diesen Kompromiß akzeptabel."
   Die Reporterin sagte, ...
2. „Die Debatte mit meinen Mitarbeitern hat mich sehr enttäuscht. Zwei Mitarbeiter sind nicht objektiv geblieben. Ich mußte die Diskussion abbrechen."[4]
   Der Chef sagte, ...
3. „Der Vortrag[5] über China war interessant. Der Redner sprach über die politischen und wirtschaftlichen[6] Probleme Chinas. Am Schluß stellten einige Zuhörer Fragen. Leider konnte der Redner nur kurz darauf antworten."
   Die Journalistin schrieb, ...

1 **die Sitzung, -en**	session
2 **sich einigen**	to come to an agreement
3 **der Rücktritt, -e**	resignation
4 **ab•brechen (bricht ab), brach ab, abgebrochen**	to break off
5 **der Vortrag, ¨-e**	lecture
6 **wirtschaftlich**	economical

§8   FINAL REMARKS ON THE USE OF THE INDICATIVE AND SUBJUNCTIVE IN INDIRECT DISCOURSE

As discussed, informal indirect discourse is expressed in the indicative when the one providing the account has no doubt about the validity of what is reported. The general subjunctive is used in cautious reporting, usually when the speaker has reservations as to what was said.

In formal German, the subjunctive is normally required for indirect discourse. The special subjunctive is used unless it is identical to the indicative, in which case the general subjunctive is substituted.

However, there is a growing tendency to use the indicative in certain formal indirect statements.

a. When the introductory verb is in the present tense:

> Der Rechtsanwalt sagt: „Dieser Text kann zu Mißverständnissen führen."
> Der Rechtsanwalt sagt, daß dieser Text zu Mißverständnissen führen **kann.**

In order to distinguish the indirect quote from the direct quote, a **daß** clause is normally used.

b. When quoting oneself, since one is usually willing to vouch for one's own claims:

> Ich sagte vor Gericht[1]: „Der Polizist hat mich mißverstanden."
> Ich sagte vor Gericht, daß der Polizist mich mißverstanden **hat.**

c. When reporting something that is undeniably true:

> Galilei hat als erster gesagt, daß sich die Erde um die Sonne **bewegt.**

Subjunctives in original statements are retained in both formal and informal indirect discourse.

> Frau Morgenstern sagte: „Ich **möchte** Architektin werden."
> Frau Morgenstern sagte,   sie **möchte** Architektin werden.
> Herr Morgenstern sagte: „Wenn meine Frau Architektin **wäre, würden** wir in einem Palast wohnen."
> Herr Morgenstern sagte,   wenn seine Frau Architektin **wäre, würden** sie in einem Palast wohnen.

---

1 **vor Gericht**   in court

15

der-Words and *ein*-Words Used as Pronouns; Uses of *man, jemand, niemand, irgend,* and *es*

KEY TO THE EXERCISES ON CASSETTE 8.
RUNNING TIME: APPROX. 20 MIN.

der-Words and *ein*-Words Used as Pronouns

§1   *der*-WORDS USED AS PRONOUNS

The definite article denotes gender, number, and case of nouns; it is a *determiner*. The **der**-words **dieser, jeder, jener, mancher, solcher, welcher, alle,** and **beide** function much like the definite article and are also referred to as *determiners* when they precede nouns. When they stand alone, they function as pronouns. In either case they have the same endings.

DETERMINER	PRONOUN
Welchen Wagen wollen Sie kaufen?	**Welchen** wollen Sie kaufen?
Which car do you want to buy?	*Which one do you want to buy?*
Jeder Student ist dagegen.	**Jeder** ist dagegen.
Every student is against it.	*Everyone is against it.*

§2   *der, das, die* USED AS DEMONSTRATIVE PROUNOUNS

When used as demonstrative pronouns, **der, das, die** are declined as follows:

	MASCULINE	NEUTER	FEMININE	PLURAL
NOM.	der	das	die	die
ACC.	den	das	die	die
DAT.	dem	dem	der	**denen**
GEN.	**dessen**	**dessen**	**deren**	**deren**

The forms in boldface differ from the forms of the definite article: The genitive singular and plural and the dative plural have the *long forms* **dessen, deren,** and **denen.**

The demonstrative pronouns **der, das, die** occur frequently in informal German:

1. Pointing out persons and things

Welches Bild gefällt dir besser? **Das hier** oder **das da?**
This one or that one?
Mit welchem Mechaniker hast du gesprochen? **Mit dem hier** oder **mit dem da?**
With this one or with that one?
In welchen Katalogen sind die Preise reduziert? **In denen hier** oder in **denen da?**
In these or in those?

In informal German, **this one** and **that one** (pl.: **these** and **those**) are generally expressed by **der, das, die + hier** (close to the speaker) or **da** (more distant from the speaker). The pronouns are always stressed.

PRACTICE 1   *Add the appropriate forms of* **der, das, die + hier** *or* **da.**

Model: X: In welchem Haus wohnt Frau Rose?
Y: **Das weiß ich nicht genau; vielleicht in
dem hier oder in dem da.**
　　　　this one 　　 *that one*

1. X: Welches Kleid willst du kaufen?
   Y: Ich glaube, ich nehme _____ . _____ ist zu teuer.
   　　　　　　　　this one 　 *That one*
2. X: Wieviel kosten diese Strümpfe?[1]
   Y: ____ kosten 10 Mark das Paar, ____ kosten 12 Mark das Paar.
   These 　　　　　　　　　 *those*
3. X: Welches Formular soll ich ausfüllen?
   Y: _____ und _____ .
   This one 　 *that one*
4. X: Von welchen Formularen sprecht ihr?
   Y: Von ____ und ____ .
   　　 these 　 *those*

1 der **Strumpf,** ⸚e 　 stocking

5. X: Welche Rechnung willst du bezahlen?

   Y: Keine, aber ich muß heute _____ bezahlen. _____

                                     this one   *That one*

   bezahle ich nächsten Monat.

6. X: In welchem Gebäude ist Professor Sterns Büro?

   Y: In _____ .

          that one

2. Third-person pronouns

Conversational German frequently uses **der, das, die** as third-person pronouns. They may be stressed or unstressed and are translated into English with the normal third-person pronouns. In the following examples stress is indicated by spacing the letters:

Herr Müller   kann uns nicht helfen.

      Er   kann uns nicht helfen.

      Der

or: D e r   kann uns nicht helfen.

    He   *cannot help us.*

   Ich spreche nicht mehr mit diesen Leuten.

   Ich spreche nicht mehr mit   ihnen.

   Ich spreche nicht mehr mit   denen.

or: Mit d e n e n spreche ich nicht mehr.

     *I don't talk with **them** any more.*

The stressed pronouns are frequently placed at the beginning of main clauses.

PRACTICE 2   A. *Add sentences c. and d., following the model of sentence 1.*

1. a. Ich helfe meinen Nachbarn gern.
   b. Ich helfe ihnen gern.
   c. **Ich helfe denen gern.**
   d. **Denen helfe ich gern.**
2. a. Ich habe seine Telefonnummer nicht.
   b. Ich habe sie nicht.
   c.
   d.
3. a. Wir können diese komplizierten Probleme nicht lösen.
   b. Wir können sie nicht lösen.
   c.
   d.
4. a. Helga hat diesen Film nicht gesehen.
   b. Helga hat ihn nicht gesehen.
   c.
   d.
5. a. Ich werde es meinen Freunden nicht sagen.
   b. Ich werde es ihnen nicht sagen.
   c.
   d.

B. *Insert the appropriate form of the pronoun* **der, das, die,** *following the model of sentence 1.a.*

1. a. X: Kann man diesem Mann glauben?
      Y: **Nein, dem kann man nicht glauben.**
   b. X: Aber seiner Frau kann man doch glauben?
      Y: _____ glaube ich auch nicht.
2.   X: Willst du Dagmar anrufen?
      Y: Nein, _____ rufe ich nie wieder an.
3.   X: Wie kommst du mit Ruth aus?[1]
      Y: Mit _____ komme ich sehr gut aus.
4.   X: Hoffentlich laden Müllers auch meinen Freund Peter ein.
      Y: _____ laden Müllers bestimmt ein.
5.   X: Alle Nachbarn haben Schulzes beim Umzug[2] geholfen.
      Y: Schulzes sind nette Leute. _____ hilft jeder gern.
6.   X: Hast du Post von Monika?
      Y: Von _____ bekomme ich keine Post mehr.
7.   X: Gehst du heute abend mit Udo aus?
      Y: Mit _____ gehe ich nie wieder aus.
8.   X: Ich bin ganz begeistert von diesen Fußballspielern.
      Y: Von _____ sind alle begeistert.

3. Alternatives to *da*-compounds

Normally pronoun objects of prepositions which refer to inanimate objects are replaced by **da**-compounds (cf. Chap. 8, §3).

> Er ist **stolz auf seinen Sportwagen.**
> Er ist stolz **darauf.**

However, when speakers wish to emphasize the pronoun, they have two choices. They may stress the **da**-element:

> **Dárauf** ist er stolz

or use a form of **der, das, die** as the object of the preposition:

> **Auf dén** ist er stolz.

The second option is more emphatic than the stressed **da**-compound.

PRACTICE 3   *Begin the following sentences with the preposition + the appropriate form of the pronouns* **der, das, die.**

> **Model:** Für diese Briefmarken hat Herr Berger kein Interesse.
> **Für die hat Herr Berger kein Interesse.**

1. Für diesen Ring hat Klaus viel Geld bezahlt.
2. Mit diesem Bleistift kann ich nicht schreiben.
3. Auf diesen Scheck mußte ich lange warten.

---

1 **aus•kommen mit** (*dat.*)   to get along with
  kam aus, ist ausgekommen
2 **der Umzug, ¨e**   move (*change of residence*)

4. Von diesem Haus ist meine Mutter begeistert.
5. Auf diese Platte ist Udos Freundin ganz verrückt.
6. Aus dieser Tasse hat Einstein getrunken.

4. Special use of the genitive forms *dessen* and *deren*

> Hans, sein Freund Peter und **dessen** Schwester Barbara haben uns besucht.
> *Hans, his friend Peter, and the latter's sister Barbara visited us.*

Seine Schwester would leave the question open whether Barbara is the sister of Hans or Peter. **Dessen** (*the latter's*) makes it clear that she is Peter's sister. The gender and number of **dessen** is determined by the possessor, i.e. Peter; thus the masculine singular is used.

Additional examples:

> Helga, Margot und **deren** Schwester / **deren** Bruder
> *Helga, Margot, and the latter's sister / the latter's brother*

Margot is the possessor, thus the feminine singular is used.

> Schmidts, Müllers und **deren** Sohn / **deren** Tochter
> *The Smiths, the Müllers, and the latter's son / the latter's daughter*

The Müllers are the possessors, thus the plural form is used.

The case of the noun that follows has no influence on **dessen** or **deren**:

> Wir sind mit <u>**einer Freundin, einer Nachbarin**</u> und **deren Brüdern**
>   DATIVE   DATIVE   GEN.   DATIVE
> nach Wien gefahren.

PRACTICE 4   *Translate into German.*

1. Helmut, Martin, and the latter's girlfriend went to the movies. (pres. perf.)
2. Barbara, Hannelore, and the latter's dog were in the car.
3. Mrs. Zimmermann, the Körners, and the latter's children are in the park.
4. Mr. Schubert, his brother, and the latter's wife visited us. (pres. perf.)
5. This is a present from Monika, Renate, and the latter's parents.

§3   *ein*-WORDS USED AS PRONOUNS

The **ein**-words (**ein, kein,** and the possessives) are also determiners when preceding nouns, but pronouns when standing alone.

1. *ein* and *kein*

DETERMINER   PRONOUN
Ist das **ein** Fehler?   Ja, das ist **einer**. *Yes, that is one.*
                          Nein, das ist **keiner**. *No, that isn't one.*
                                            No, that's none.

Ist das **ein** Problem?	Ja, das ist **ein(e)s.**
	Nein, das ist **kein(e)s.**
Ist das **eine** Warnung?	Ja, das ist **eine.**
	Nein, das ist **keine.**

Used as determiners, the **ein**-words have three forms without endings: the nominative masculine singular and the nominative and accusative neuter singular. All other forms have the same endings as the **der**-words (cf. Chap. 6, §5).

Used as pronouns, the **ein**-words have the same endings as the **der**-words in all forms, including the nominative masculine singular (**-er**) and the nominative and accusative neuter singular (**-es,** usually shortened to **-s**).

The following table combines the declension of the determiner and the pronoun:

	MASCULINE		NEUTER		FEMININE	PLURAL
NOM.	ein	einer	ein	ein(e)s	eine	keine
ACC.	einen		ein	ein(e)s	eine	keine
DAT.	einem		einem		einer	keinen
GEN.	eines		eines		einer	keiner

Remember: | The forms of the determiner and pronoun differ only in three cases in the singular.

PRACTICE 5   A. *Answer the questions, following the model of sentence 1.*

1. Wo ist ein Supermarkt? **Da drüben ist einer.**
2. Wo ist ein Parkplatz? (masc.)
3. Wo ist ein Restaurant? (neuter)
4. Wo ist eine Bank?

B. *Answer the questions positively and negatively, following the model of sentence 1.*

1. Hast du einen Regenschirm? **Ja, ich habe einen. Nein, ich habe keinen.**
2. Hast du eine Kamera?
3. Hast du ein Auto?
4. Hast du einen Fernseher?

2. The possessives

The possessives take the same endings as **ein** and **kein,** as the following nominative masculine and neuter forms illustrate.

DETERMINERS		PRONOUNS	
Das ist mein Wagen.	(*my car*)	Das ist mein**er.**	(*mine*)
mein Auto.		mein**(e)s.**	
Das ist dein Wagen.	(*your car*)	Das ist dein**er.**	(*yours*)
dein Auto.		dein**(e)s.**	

Das ist sein Wagen.	(his car)	Das ist seiner.	(his)
sein Auto.		sein**(e)s**.	
Das ist ihr Wagen.	(her car)	Das ist ihrer.	(hers)
ihr Auto.		ihr**(e)s**.	
Das ist unser Wagen.	(our car)	Das ist uns(e)rer.	(ours)
unser Auto.		uns(e)r**es**.	
Das ist euer Wagen.	(your car)	Das ist eu(e)rer	(yours)
euer Auto.		eu(e)r**es**.	
Das ist ihr Wagen.	(their car)	Das ist ihrer.	(theirs)
ihr Auto.		ihr**(e)s**	
Das ist Ihr Wagen.	(your car)	Das ist Ihrer	(yours)
Ihr Auto.		Ihr**(e)s**	

Note: a. German equivalents of *your* and *yours*:

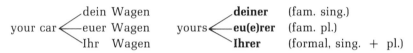

your car	dein Wagen	yours	**deiner**	(fam. sing.)
	euer Wagen		**eu(e)rer**	(fam. pl.)
	Ihr Wagen		**Ihrer**	(formal, sing. + pl.)

b. The **e** of **unser** and **euer** may be omitted when the ending **-e** or an ending beginning with **-e** is added (cf. Chap. 6, §6).

PRACTICE 6   A. *Insert the German equivalents of the pronouns in parentheses.*

1. Hier ist Peters Plattenspieler, (masc.)
   und da drüben ist auch _____ . (*mine, yours* [three forms])
2. Hier ist Karins Radio, (neut.)
   und da drüben ist auch _____ . (*mine, yours* [three forms])
3. Hier ist Herrn Bergers Kamera,
   und da drüben ist auch _____ (*mine, yours* [three forms])
4. Hier sind Helgas Sachen,
   und da drüben sind _____ . (*mine, ours, theirs*)
5. Wir sind nicht mit meinem Wagen gefahren;
   wir sind mit _____ gefahren. (*his, hers*)

B. *Insert the appropriate forms of* **ein, kein,** *and the possessives.*

1. X: Ist das hier mein Glas? (neut.)
   Y: Ja, das ist _____ . (*yours* [fam. sing., formal])
2. X: Wir haben sehr nette Nachbarn.
   Y: Wir nicht. _____ sind sehr unfreundlich. (*ours*)
3. X: Da drüben ist ein Briefkasten. (masc.)
   Y: Hier ist auch _____ . (*one*)
4. X: Wo ist hier eine Tankstelle?
   Y: Da an der Ecke ist _____ . (*one*)
5. X: Hast du ein Motorrad? (neut.)
   Y: Leider habe ich _____ . (*not one* = **kein**)

6. X: Hat Dieter einen Job gefunden?
   Y: Soviel ich weiß,[1] hat er noch _____ gefunden. (*not one* = **kein**)
7. X: Ich muß in die Stadt, habe aber keinen Wagen. _____ ist kaputt. (*mine*)
   Y: Du kannst _____ nehmen. (*mine*)
8. X: Ist das Ihr Hund, der draußen bellt?
   Y: Nein, das ist nicht _____. (*ours*)
9. X: Haben Sie mit Ihren Freunden über Ihre Pläne gesprochen?
   Y: Ich habe nur mit _____ darüber gesprochen. (*one*)
10. X: Leider habe ich deinen Geburtstag vergessen.
    Y: Ach, das macht nichts.[2] Ich habe ja bald wieder _____. (*one*)

3. The German equivalents of the genitive phrases *of mine, of yours,* etc.

German uses the preposition **von** with the dative case of the personal pronoun to express the English genitive phrases *of mine, of yours,* etc.

He is a friend of mine.	Er ist ein Freund **von mir.**
	(lit.: *He is a friend of me.*)
He is a friend of his.	Er ist ein Freund **von ihm.**
of hers.	**von ihr.**
of ours.	**von uns.**
of theirs.	**von ihnen.**
of yours.	⎧ **von dir.**
(three forms)	⎨ **von euch.**
	⎩ **von Ihnen.**

PRACTICE 7   *Insert German equivalents.*

1. X: Ist Thomas ein Freund von Barbara?
   Y: Ich weiß nicht, ob er ein Freund _____ ist. (*of hers*)
2. X: Sind Schmidts Verwandte[3] _____? (*of yours* [fam. pl., formal])
   Y: Ja, sie sind Verwandte _____. (*of ours*)
3. X: Ist sie eine Kollegin _____? (*of his*)
   Y: Nein, sie ist eine Kollegin _____. (*of mine*)
4. X: Sind das Freunde von Brauns?
   Y: Das sind sehr gute Freunde _____. (*of theirs*)

---

1 **soviel ich weiß**   as far as I know
2 **das macht nichts**   that doesn't matter
3 **der Verwandte**   relative
   (*adj. noun* [cf. Chap. 9, §12])

Uses of *man, jemand, niemand, irgend,* and *es*

§4   THE INDEFINITE PRONOUNS *man, jemand,* and *niemand*

1. *man*

The English equivalents of **man** may be *one, you, they,* or *people,* depending on the context.

Man weiß das nicht im voraus.	***One*** *doesn't know that beforehand.*
	You *don't know that beforehand.*
Man hat mich gewarnt.	***They*** *warned me.*
	People *warned me.*

The form **man** exists only in the nominative case. For the accusative and dative **einen** and **einem** are used.

> Diese Unsicherheit macht **einen** nervös.
> *This insecurity makes one (you, people) nervous.*
>
> Fräulein Braun dankt **einem** nie.
> *Miss Braun never thanks you (anyone).*

Sein is used as the possessive of **man**.

> Man sollte immer **seine** Meinung sagen.
> *One should always speak one's mind.*

In English, a second occurrence of **man** is sometimes replaced by **he**. This cannot be done in German.

> *If one wants to help, one/he will find a way.*
> Wenn **man** helfen will, findet **man** einen Weg.

Expression: **Man kann nie wissen.** *One never knows.*
You never know.

PRACTICE 8   *Restate the following sentences substituting* **man, einen,** *or* **einem** *for the boldface pronouns.*

> **Model: Wir** können auch unsere Kinder mitbringen.
> **Man kann auch seine Kinder mitbringen.**

1. **Wir** können unsere Sachen in der Bibliothek lassen.
2. Hier müssen **Sie** Ihren Hund an der Leine führen.[1]
3. Wie übersetzen **Sie** das?
4. Wie sagen **Sie** das auf deutsch?
5. Er hilft **mir** nie.
6. Das ärgert[2] **mich** natürlich.

---

1 **an der Leine führen**   to keep on a leash
2 **ärgern**   to annoy

7. Wenn **ich** mit Barbara spreche, muß **ich** besonders vorsichtig sein.
8. Wenn **du** zu schnell fährst, bekommst **du** einen Strafzettel.
9. Er tut **mir** leid, wenn **ich** ihn vor Schmerzen schreien[1] höre.

2. *jemand* AND *niemand*

Jemand (*somebody, someone, anybody, anyone*) and **niemand** (*nobody, no one*) may remain uninflected or take the ending **-en** in the accusative and **-em** in the dative.

Jemand
Niemand >hat mich gefragt.

Somebody
Nobody >*asked me.*

Ich habe< **jemand(en)**
niemand(en) gefragt.

I asked < *somebody.*
nobody.

Ich habe mit< **jemand(em)**
niemand(em) gesprochen.

I talked with < *someone.*
no one.

Expression: **Das geht niemand(en) etwas an.**
  That is nobody's business.

Note the use of **jemand** and **niemand** with **anders**:

jemand anders (als)   *somebody/someone else (but)*
niemand anders (als)   *nobody/no one else (but)*

Nicht Frank, sondern **jemand anders** hat mir das erzählt.
Not Frank but someone else told me that.

Ich habe mit **niemand anders als** mit Helga darüber gesprochen.
I talked with no one else but with Helga about it.

PRACTICE 9   *Complete the sentences using the German equivalents of **somebody, nobody** (uninflected forms) and **one**.*

1. X: Kennen Sie _____ in Berlin? (*somebody*)
   Y: Leider kenne ich dort _____ . (*nobody*)
2. X: Hast du den Ring von Werner bekommen?
   Y: Nein. Ich habe ihn von _____ bekommen. (*somebody else*)
3. X: Da ist ein Paket für dich.
   Y: Das kann von _____ von meinen Eltern sein. (*nobody else but*)
4. X: Alle möchten gern wissen, warum du Ulrich nicht heiraten willst.
   Y: _____ . (*That is nobody's business.*)
5. X: Er redet und redet, aber in Wirklichkeit[2] sagt er nichts. Warum ist er nicht still?
   Y: Das verstehe ich auch nicht. Wenn _____ nichts zu sagen hat, sollte _____ still sein. (*one, one*)

---

1 **vor Schmerzen schreien, schrie, geschrie(e)n**   to cry out in pain
2 **in Wirklichkeit**   in reality, in actual fact, actually

6. X: Frau Winkler hat mich schon wieder unterbrochen.[1]
   Y: Sie unterbricht _____ oft. (one)
7. X: Ingrid wird mich bestimmt nicht betrügen.[2]
   Y: _____. (One never knows.)

§5   USES OF *irgend*

Irgend expresses indefiniteness. It is often used to intensify an indefinite pronoun. Compare:

   a. Jemand hat das der Polizei gemeldet.
      Someone reported that to the police.
   b. **Irgend jemand** hat das der Polizei gemeldet.
      Someone or other reported that to the police.
   a. Ich möchte Monika etwas geben.
      I'd like to give Monika something.
   b. Ich möchte Monika **irgend etwas** geben.
      I'd like to give Monika something or other.

In sentences *b* **irgend** enhances the indefiniteness of **jemand** and **etwas**.

Irgend may be prefixed to another word:

irgendein *a, some, any* (singular)
irgendwelche *some, any* (plural)

   Haben Sie **irgendeinen** Vorschlag?
   Do you have any suggestion (at all)?
   Haben Sie **irgendwelche** Vorschläge?
   Do you have any suggestions (at all)?

irgendwann *some time or other, sometime, anytime*

   Irgendwann ist sie zur Vernunft gekommen.
   At some time or other she came to her senses.
   Hoffentlich sehe ich Sie **irgendwann** mal wieder.
   I hope to see you again sometime.

irgendwie *somehow (or other)*

   Wir müssen das Problem **irgendwie** lösen.
   We have to solve this problem somehow (or other).

irgendwo *somewhere (or other), anywhere* (denoting the place at which)
irgendwohin *somewhere (or other), anywhere* (denoting motion to a place)

   Ich habe Hannelore **irgendwo** in der Stadt gesehen.
   I saw Hannelore somewhere in town.
   Martin fährt morgen **irgendwohin.**
   Martin is going somewhere tomorrow.

   1 **unterbrechen (unterbricht),**   to interrupt
     unterbrach, unterbrochen
   2 **betrügen,**   to cheat
     betrog, betrogen

The negation of **irgendwo** is **nirgendwo** or **nirgends** *nowhere, not anywhere (place at which)*; the negation of **irgendwohin** is **nirgend(s)wohin** *nowhere, not anywhere (motion to a place)*.

> Wir haben unseren Hund gesucht, konnten ihn aber **nirgends** finden.
> *We were looking for our dog but couldn't find him anywhere.*
> Ich fahre dieses Wochenende **nirgendwohin.**
> *I'm not going anywhere this weekend.*

PRACTICE 10   *Insert German equivalents using combinations with **irgend**.*

1. X: Ich weiß nicht, wie ich aus diesem Dilemma herauskommen soll.
   Y: Kann ich dir _____ helfen? (*somehow*)
2. X: Wo sollen wir zu Mittag essen?
   Y: Es ist mir ganz gleich.[1] _____. (*Anywhere*)
3. X: Ist dein Bruder heute abend zu Hause?
   Y: Ich glaube, er geht heute abend _____. (*somewhere*)
4. X: Bist du heute abend zu Hause?
   Y: Ja. Heute abend gehe ich _____ (*not anywhere, nowhere*)
5. X: Warum bist du so nervös?
   Y: Ich kann meine Brille _____ finden. (*not anywhere, nowhere*)
6. X: Ich glaube, Renate gefällt mein Geschenk nicht.
   Y: Hat sie _____ Bemerkung gemacht? (*any*)
7. X: Ich glaube, die Chefin ist nicht zufrieden mit meiner Arbeit.
   Y: Warum denkst du das? Hat sie _____ Bemerkungen gemacht? (*any*)
8. X: Wann hat Margot Geburtstag?
   Y: _____ im August. (*sometime*)
9. X: Warum ist Rainer so deprimiert?
   Y: _____ ist schiefgegangen.[2] (*Something*)

§6   USES OF *es*

1. Impersonal use of verbs

Verbs used impersonally have **es** as their subject. The inflected verb is always in the third person singular. Compare:

USED PERSONALLY	USED IMPERSONALLY
Die Kinder klopfen an die Tür.	**Es** klopft.
The children are knocking at the door.	*There is a knock at the door.*
Der Briefträger klingelt (läutet).	**Es** klingelt (läutet).
The mailman is ringing.	*Someone is ringing the bell.*
	The bell is ringing.
Die Kerzen brennen.	**Es** brennt.
The candles are burning.	*There is a fire.*

1 **es ist mir ganz gleich**   it's all the same to me
2 **schief•gehen, ging schief, ist schiefgegangen**   to go wrong

Note the use of the impersonal expression **es gibt** (+ acc.):

> **Es gibt** nur **einen ausländischen Studenten** in unserem Studentenheim.
> SUBJ.   DIRECT OBJECT
> *There is* only one foreign student in our dormitory.

> **Es gibt** nur **zwei ausländische Studenten** in unserem Studentenheim.
> *There are* only two foreign students in our dormitory.

Es gibt is used with both singular and plural accusative nouns. The English equivalent is *there is* or *there are*.

Some idiomatic uses of **es gibt**:

> **Es gibt heute noch Regen (Schnee, ein Gewitter).**
> *We are going to have rain (snow, a thunderstorm) today.*
> **Was gibt's (gibt es) heute zu Mittag (zum Abendessen/Abendbrot)?**
> *What is there (are we having) for lunch (dinner/supper) today?*
> **Gibt's (gibt es) noch Kaffee (Kuchen, etc.)?**
> *Is there any coffee (cake, etc.) left?*
> **Es gibt keinen Kaffee (Kuchen, etc.) mehr.**
> *There is no coffee (cake, etc.) left.*

2. Introductory *es* in main clauses

For reasons of style or emphasis (cf. Chap. 19, §5, 4), an introductory **es** may be used in main clauses. Compare:

> **Niemand** ist zu Hause geblieben.
> SUBJECT
> **Es ist niemand** zu Hause geblieben. } *Nobody stayed at home.*
> SUBJECT

The subject follows the inflected verb.

Note that the verb agrees with the subject, not with **es**:

> Drei Studenten fehlen. } *Three students are absent.*
> Es **fehlen drei Studenten.** }

When another element is placed in first position, **es** may not be used:

> Es fehlen drei Studenten.
> **Heute fehlen** drei Studenten.

The introductory **es** cannot be used in questions and dependent clauses.

3. *es* anticipating a dependent clause or infinitive phrase

> Ich kann **es** verstehen, daß er böse auf mich ist.
> *I can understand that he is angry with me.*

> Ich hasse **es**, morgens um 6 Uhr aufzustehen.
> *I hate getting up at 6 o'clock in the morning.*

German often uses **es** to anticipate a clause or infinitive phrase where English would use nothing.

PRACTICE 11   *The following sentences illustrate various uses of* **es**. *Express them in English.*

    1. X: Hat jemand protestiert?
       Y: Es haben alle protestiert.
    2. X: Es schwänzen immer ein paar Studenten.
       Y: Heute hat aber niemand geschwänzt.
    3. X: Ich kann es nicht glauben, daß so viele Studenten durchgefallen sind.
       Y: So viele? Es sind nur zwei Studenten durchgefallen.
    4. X: Arbeitet Fräulein Kluge auch an dem neuen Projekt?
       Y: Leider hat sie es abgelehnt,[1] an dem neuen Projekt zu arbeiten.
    5. X: Brennt es irgendwo?
       Y: Es brennt im Nachbarhaus.
    6. X: Hat es geklopft?
       Y: Es hat schon zweimal geklopft. Da klopft es wieder.
    7. X: Vielleicht gibt's heute Fisch zu Mittag.
       Y: Ach nein. Gestern hat es doch schon Fisch gegeben.
    8. X: Könnte ich ein Stück Kuchen haben?
       Y: Leider gibt's keinen Kuchen mehr, aber es gibt noch ein paar Plätzchen.[2]
    9. X: Warum hast du keine Bananen gekauft?
       Y: Im Supermarkt gab es keine mehr.
   10. X: Heute gibt es bestimmt Regen.
       Y: Hoffentlich gibt es kein Gewitter.
   11. X: Ist die Deutschstunde schon zu Ende?
       Y: Nein, es hat noch nicht geklingelt.

PRACTICE 12   Summarizing exercises.

    Express the responses in German.

    1.   X: Gibt es eine Konzerthalle in dieser Stadt?
          Y: There are two concert halls in this city.
    2.   X: Warum gehst du zur Tür?
          Y: There was a knock at the door. (pres. perf.)
    3.   X: Hoffentlich ist die Deutschstunde bald zu Ende.
          Y: The bell is ringing in two minutes.
    4.   X: Ich glaube, wir kommen zu spät ins Labor.
          Y: Yes. The bell rang already. (pres. perf.)
    5.   X: Was möchtest du? Kaffee und Plätzchen?
          Y: Is there any cake left?

---

1 **ab·lehnen**   to decline
2 **das Plätzchen, -**   cookie

6.   X: Welche Kamera gefällt dir am besten?
     Y: This one.

7.   X: In welchem Gebäude ist Ihr Büro?
     Y: In that one.

8.   X: Hier ist dein Koffer.
     Y: That's not mine.

9.   X: Ist das Renates Kassettenrecorder?
     Y: Yes, that's hers.

10. X: Haben viele Studenten gestern geschwänzt?
     Y: No, only one cut class. (pres. perf.)

11. X: Ist diese Dame eine Verwandte oder Freundin von Herrn
        Krause?
     Y: She's a relative of his.

12. X: Warum sagst du uns nicht, warum du mit Walter Schluß
        gemacht hast?
     Y: That's nobody's business.

13. X: Mit wem sind Sie in die Ferien gefahren?
     Y: With Thomas, Peter, and the latter's brother.

14. X: Ist dieser Brief von deiner Freundin?
     Y: No, it's from someone else.

15. X: Warum stehen so viele Leute vor dem Auditorium?
     Y: There's a fire in the auditorium.

16. a. X: Es riecht nach[1] Bratwurst. (fem.)
        Y: Today we are having Bratwurst for lunch.

    b. X: Ich esse Bratwurst nicht gern.
        Y: May I eat yours? (fam. sing.)

17. X: Wo möchten Sie sitzen?
     Y: It's all the same to me. Anywhere.

18. X: Wann kommen Andreas und Ulrich aus Mexiko zurück?
     Y: Sometime in July.

19. X: Ich glaube nicht, daß wir dieses Problem lösen können.
     Y: We have to solve it somehow or other.

20. X: Weißt du, warum der Chef so schlechte Laune hat?
     Y: I assume that something or other went wrong. (pres. perf.)

---

1 **riechen nach** (*dat.*), **roch, gerochen**   to smell of

16

Relative Pronouns and Relative Clauses

KEY TO THE EXERCISES ON CASSETTE 8.
RUNNING TIME: APPROX. 25 MIN.

§1 RELATIVE PRONOUNS AND RELATIVE CLAUSES IN ENGLISH

The gentleman **who** just came in is the mayor of this city.

    ANTECEDENT   RELATIVE CLAUSE

"The Turn of the Screw," **which** I have read many times, is very interesting.

        ANTECEDENT   RELATIVE CLAUSE

The story **that** you told me is unbelievable.

ANTECEDENT   RELATIVE CLAUSE

Note: a. The relative pronouns **who** (referring to persons), **which** (referring to things), and **that** (referring to persons or things) introduce dependent clauses, which are called *relative clauses*.

b. Relative clauses commonly modify nouns, less frequently pronouns, by giving further information. The nouns or pronouns modified are called *antecedents*.

Relative pronouns can have various functions within the relative clause:

The student **who** is talking with Mr. Clark is my sister.

           |
           SUBJ. of the relative clause

The student **whom you** see in this picture is my sister.

           | |
          DIR. OBJ. SUBJ. of the relative clause

People **that** I owe **money** keep bothering me.

        | | |
     INDIR. OBJ.   SUBJ.   DIR. OBJ. of the relative clause

In English the relative pronoun is rarely used as a true indirect object. Instead, it is used as the object of the preposition **to**:

This is the city councilor   **to whom the policeman** gave **a ticket**.
                              OBJ. OF   SUBJ.   DIR. OBJ.
                              PREP. **to**

The preposition often stands at the end of the relative clause:

This is an important point   **that**   the speaker did not go **into**.
                             OBJ. OF
                             PREP. **into**

When the relative pronoun expresses possession, it is in the possessive (genitive) case:

The student **whose** name is mentioned in the newspaper is my brother.

Anyone learning German must be able to recognize the function of a given relative pronoun. As a first step, the following exercise will deal with English relative pronouns.

PRACTICE 1   *State the function of the boldface relative pronouns.*

> **Model:** This is a remark **that** I resent.
> **The relative pronoun *that* functions as direct object.**

1. This is a matter **that** you will never understand.
2. I know the artist **who** painted this picture.
3. The figures **that** she quoted are appalling.
4. The lady **whose** picture is on the front page is our neighbor.
5. Professor Johnson, **who** received the Nobel Prize, is the dean of the college.
6. People **who** do such things must be mentally disturbed.
7. The patient to **whom** the nurse gave the wrong medication is recovering.
8. This is a problem for **which** there is no solution.
9. This is only one of the inconveniences **that** they will have to contend with.

The English relative pronoun is often omitted:

This is a matter you will never understand.
The figures she quoted are appalling.
This is only one of the inconveniences they will have to contend with.

§2   RELATIVE PRONOUNS AND RELATIVE CLAUSES IN GERMAN

Most forms of the relative pronoun are the same as those of the definite article.

1. a. Der junge Mann, **der** mich angerufen hat, ist Lindas Bruder.
         who
      SUBJ.

    b. Der junge Mann, **den** ich angerufen habe, ist Lindas Bruder.
           whom
           DIR. OBJ.

2. a. Der Wagen, **der** da vor der Garage steht, gehört meiner Schwester.
         which/that
         SUBJ.

    b. Der Wagen, **den** Sie da vor der Garage sehen, gehört meiner Schwester.
         which/that
         DIR. OBJ.

Note: a. The antecedents in the above examples are masculine nouns: **der junge Mann** and **der Wagen**. The relative pronouns refer to both persons and things.

    b. In sentences 1. *a* and 2. *a* the relative pronoun is the subject of the relative clause and therefore in the nominative case: **der**.
       In sentences 1. *b* and 2. *b* the relative pronoun is the direct object of the relative clause and therefore in the accusative case: **den**.

       RULE: The relative pronoun agrees in gender and number (singular or plural) with the antecedent. Its case, however, is determined by its function in the relative clause.

    c. The relative clause is a dependent clause; hence, the inflected verb stands at the end.

    d. Normally, the relative clause follows the antecedent immediately. It is always set off by commas.

    e. In German the relative pronoun cannot be omitted.

     The young man I called is Linda's brother.
     Der junge Mann, **den** ich angerufen habe, ist Lindas Bruder.

§3   DECLENSION OF THE RELATIVE PRONOUN

	MASC.	NEUT.	FEM.	PLURAL
NOM.	der	das	die	die
ACC.	den	das	die	die
DAT.	dem	dem	der	**denen**
GEN.	**dessen**	**dessen**	**deren**	**deren**

Depending on context, English equivalents may be:

who, which, that
whom, which, that, (who)
(to) whom, which, that, (who)
whose, of which

Only the boldface "long" forms differ from the definite article. (The forms of the relative pronoun are the same as those of **der, das, die** functioning as demonstrative pronouns [cf. Chap. 15, §2].)

Examples for all cases:

1. The relative pronoun as the subject of the relative clause (nominative):

    Der Student, **der** da drüben steht, ist mein Bruder.
    Das Mädchen, **das** da drüben steht, ist meine Schwester.
    Die Studentin, **die** da drüben steht, ist meine Freundin.
    Die Leute, **die** da drüben stehen, sind meine Freunde.

2. The relative pronoun as the direct object of the relative clause (accusative):

Der Student, **den** Sie dort sehen, ist mein Bruder.
Das Mädchen, **das** Sie dort sehen, ist meine Schwester.
Die Studentin, **die** Sie dort sehen, ist meine Freundin.

Die Leute, **die** Sie dort sehen, sind meine Freunde.

3. The relative pronoun as the indirect object of the relative clause (dative):

Der Student, **dem** ich das Geld gegeben habe, ist mein Bruder.
Das Mädchen, **dem** ich das Geld gegeben habe, ist meine Schwester.
Die Studentin, **der** ich das Geld gegeben habe, ist meine Freundin.

Die Leute, **denen** ich das Geld gegeben habe, sind meine Freunde.

4. The relative pronoun showing possession (genitive):

Der Student, **dessen** Name in der Zeitung steht, ist mein Bruder.
Das Mädchen, **dessen** Name in der Zeitung steht, ist meine Schwester.
Die Studentin, **deren** Name in der Zeitung steht, ist meine Freundin.

Die Leute, **deren** Namen in der Zeitung stehen, sind meine Freunde.

Remember:

> relative pronoun: a. gender and number determined by
> the antecedent;
> b. case determined by its function
> in the relative clause.

PRACTICE 2   *State the function and give the case and gender (if singular) or*
number (if plural) of each relative pronoun in the following sentences.

Model: Ist das die Dame, **die** uns das Museum zeigen soll?
subject, nominative, feminine
Sind das die Leute, **die** das Museum sehen wollen?
subject, nominative, plural

1. Ist das der Herr, **der** uns das Museum zeigen soll?
2. Ist das der Tourist, **dem** wir die Stadt zeigen sollen?
3. Sind das die Touristen, **denen** wir unsere Stadt zeigen sollen?
4. Sind das die Touristen, **die** unsere Stadt sehen wollen?
5. Wie heißen die Leute, **deren** Haus Sie kaufen wollen?
6. Wo ist das Paket, **das** Ihre Eltern geschickt haben?
7. Das große Paket, **das** vor der Tür steht, ist für Hannelore.
8. Wo wohnt Ihre Tochter, **der** Sie dieses Paket schicken wollen?
9. Ist das Mädchen, **das** dich immer anruft, deine feste Freundin?[1]
10. Ist das Mädchen, **das** du immer anrufst, deine feste Freundin?

---

1 **die feste Freundin**   steady girlfriend
  der feste Freund   steady boyfriend

Note that a relative pronoun referring to **Mädchen** or **Fräulein** must be neuter, though the personal pronoun would often be feminine rather than neuter (cf. Chap. 6, §9).

Keep in mind that some verbs have dative objects, such as **helfen, antworten, danken, folgen, gratulieren, trauen** (cf. Chap. 5, §4, 3b).

> Das ist ein Mann, **dem** man nicht trauen kann.
> Das sind Leute, **denen** man nicht trauen kann.

Some of these verbs occur in the next exercise.

PRACTICE 3   *Replace the boldface antecedents with the words given in parentheses. Change the relative pronouns (and if necessary the verbs) to match the new antecedents.*

> **Model: Der Student,** der im Zimmer neben mir wohnt, ist krank. (die zwei Studenten)
> **Die zwei Studenten, die im Zimmer neben mir wohnen, sind krank.**

1. **Das Buch,** das ich für den Kurs in Chemie brauche, ist sehr teuer. (die Bücher)
2. **Die Bemerkung,** die Rita gemacht hat, werde ich ignorieren. (die Bemerkungen)
3. Das ist **ein Apparat,** der noch nie funktioniert hat. (eine Maschine)
4. Das ist nicht **die Suppe,** die ich bestellt habe. (der Nachtisch)[1]
5. Hast du **das Radio** gesehen, das ich Monika schenken will? (der Ring)
6. Das ist **ein Punkt,** den wir noch klären[2] müssen. (eine Sache)
7. **Das Theaterstück,** das ich gestern gesehen habe, ist sehr langweilig. (der Film)
8. Das ist **eine Haltung,**[3] die ich nicht verstehe. (ein Problem)
9. Da drüben steht **der Polizist,** dem ich meinen Führerschein zeigen mußte. (die Polizistin)
10. **Die Studentin,** der ich bei den Hausaufgaben geholfen habe, hat die Prüfung bestanden. (der Student)
11. Das ist **der Wagen,** dem wir folgen müssen. (die Limousine)
12. Dort sind **Herr und Frau Schreiber,** denen wir für die schöne Party danken müssen. (Frau Krause)
13. **Der Herr,** dem Frau Berger gratuliert, hat eine Gehaltserhöhung bekommen. (die zwei Damen)
14. **Herr Berger,** dessen Vater gestorben ist, hat viel Geld geerbt.[4] (Frau Schiller)
15. Das ist **die Kamera,** die ich geerbt habe. (der Schreibtisch)

---

1 **der Nachtisch, -e**   dessert
2 **klären**   to clarify
3 **die Haltung, -en**   attitude
4 **erben**   to inherit

PRACTICE 4   A. *In the following English sentences, two statements are combined by using a relative clause. Translate them into German. (Keep in mind that the relative pronoun may be omitted in English but not in German.)*

Model: Das ist eine Chance. Man bekommt sie nicht jeden Tag.
      Das ist eine Chance, die man nicht jeden Tag bekommt.
      That's a chance one doesn't get every day.

  1. Das ist ein Problem. Ich kann es nicht lösen.

      _____

      That's a problem I can't solve.
  2. Das ist eine grammatische Konstruktion. Ich verstehe sie nicht.

      _____

      That's a grammatical construction I don't understand.
  3. Wie gefällt Ihnen der antike Wagen? Ich habe ihn geerbt.

      _____

      How do you like the antique car I inherited?
  4. Das sind peinliche Fragen. Man muß sie ignorieren.

      _____

      These are embarrassing questions that one has to ignore.
  5. Da drüben ist der neue Student. Ich möchte ihn kennenlernen.

      _____

      Over there is the new student who(m) I'd like to meet.
  6. Das ist eine Leistung. Ich bewundere sie.

      _____

      That's an achievement I admire.
  7. Das ist ein modernes Gedicht. Sie sollten es lesen.

      _____

      That's a modern poem you should read.
  8. Das ist ein Fehler. Professor Naumann hat ihn übersehen.

      _____

      That's a mistake Professor Naumann has overlooked.
  9. Rainer gibt heute abend eine Party. Seine Freundin hat den ersten Preis gewonnen.

      _____

      Rainer, whose girlfriend has won the first prize, is giving a party tonight.
 10. Zimmermanns ziehen nach Köln. Wir haben ihr Haus gekauft.

      _____

      The Zimmermanns, whose house we bought, are moving to Cologne.

B. *Cover up the German sentences of exercise A and state the German equivalents of the English sentences.*

Model: That's a chance one doesn't get every day.
      Das ist eine Chance, die man nicht jeden Tag bekommt.

§4   RELATIVE PRONOUNS AS OBJECTS OF PREPOSITIONS

(For cases governed by prepositions, see Chap. 7, §5, and Chap. 8, §1 and §2.)

> Das ist ein Lehrer, **von dem** ich begeistert bin.
> > *about whom I am enthusiastic.*
> > or: *whom I am enthusiastic about.*
> Das ist eine Lehrerin, **von der** ich begeistert bin.
> Das sind zwei Lehrer, **von denen** ich begeistert bin.

Note: a. In German the preposition always precedes the relative pronoun.

   b. As usual, gender and number of the relative pronoun are in agreement with the antecedent. The case of the relative pronoun is determined by the preceding preposition: **von** governs the dative; thus the relative pronouns are in the dative case in the examples above.

   c. The genitive case—**dessen, deren**—is not affected by any preceding preposition because the object of the preposition is not the relative pronoun but the noun following it:

> Das ist Herr Schmidt, mit **dessen** Frau wir verwandt sind.
> > (*whose wife we are related to*)

The masculine form of the genitive is used because its antecedent is **Herr Schmidt,** regardless of the fact that it precedes the feminine noun **Frau.** For the same reason, the feminine form **deren** is used in the following example:

> Das ist Frau Schmidt, mit **deren** Mann wir verwandt sind.
> > (*whose husband we are related to*)

PRACTICE 5   *Replace the boldface antecedents with the words given in parentheses. Change the relative pronouns (and if necessary the verb) to match the new antecedents.*

Model: Das ist **eine Sache,** von der ich nicht gern spreche. (Sachen)
Das sind Sachen, von denen ich nicht gern spreche.

1. Wie heißt **die Studentin,** mit der Sie in einem Zimmer wohnen?[1] (der Student)
2. Das ist **ein Problem,** für das es keine Lösung gibt. (Probleme)
3. Das ist **ein Punkt,** auf den ich später eingehen[2] werde. (zwei Punkte)
4. Das ist **ein Nachbar,** mit dem wir gut auskommen.[3] (Nachbarn)
5. Das ist **der Brief,** auf den ich lange gewartet habe. (das Paket)
6. Kennen Sie **das Ehepaar,**[4] bei dem unsere Tochter in Heidelberg wohnt? (die Familie)

1 **in einem Zimmer wohnen mit** (*dat.*)	to room with
2 **ein•gehen auf** (*acc.*),	to go into
ging ein, ist eingegangen	
3 **aus•kommen mit** (*dat.*),	to get along with
kam aus, ist ausgekommen	
4 **das Ehepaar, -e**	(married) couple

7. **Der Kurs,** mit dem ich aufhören[1] will, ist zu schwer für mich. (die Kurse)

8. Das ist **eine Chance,** an die niemand gedacht hat. (ein Problem)

9. Wo wohnt **die Familie,** zu der Sie am Wochenende fahren? (die Freunde)

10. **Bergmanns,** mit deren Sohn ich befreundet bin,[2] haben mir eine Geburtstagskarte geschickt. (Herr Bergmann, Frau Bergmann)

PRACTICE 6   A. *Translate the following sentences into German.* (*Again, keep in mind that the relative pronoun may be omitted in English but not in German.*)

Model: Das ist ein Erfolg. Sie können auf diesen Erfolg stolz sein.

Das ist ein Erfolg, auf den Sie stolz sein können.

That's a success you can be proud of.

1. Das ist eine Leistung. Du kannst stolz auf diese Leistung sein.

_____

That's an achievement you can be proud of.

2. Das ist ein modernes Theaterstück. Ich bin begeistert von dem Theaterstück.

_____

That's a modern stage play I am enthusiastic about.

3. Das ist der Scheck von zu Hause. Ich habe auf den Scheck gewartet.

_____

That's the check from home I have been waiting for.

4. Kennst du die Studentin? Ich wohne mit ihr in einem Zimmer.

_____

Do you know the student (female) I room with?

5. Wie heißt der junge Mann? Hannelore ist verliebt in den jungen Mann.

_____

What's the name of the young man Hannelore is in love with?

6. Das sind Einzelheiten.[3] Wir können nicht auf diese Einzelheiten eingehen.

_____

These are details we cannot go into.

7. Das ist ein Student. Jeder kommt mit ihm aus.

_____

That's a student everybody gets along with.

8. Das ist ein Problem. Es gibt keine Lösung für das Problem.

_____

That's a problem for which there is no solution.

---

1 **mit dem Kurs auf•hören**	to drop the course
2 **befreundet sein mit** (*dat.*)	to be friends with
3 **die Einzelheit, -en**	detail

9. Erika Stein wird uns im Juli besuchen. Wir sind mit ihrem Bruder durch ganz Europa gereist.

Erika Stein, with whose brother we traveled through all of Europe, will visit us in July.

B. *Cover up the German sentences of exercise A and state the German equivalents of the English sentences.*
Model: That's a success you can be proud of.
   Das ist ein Erfolg, auf den Sie stolz sein können.

Other Forms of Relative Pronouns

§5   *welcher, welches, welche* AS RELATIVE PRONOUNS

Welcher, welches, welche may function as relative pronouns in the nominative, accusative, and dative cases. These forms have a bookish ring and occur mainly in formal German.

Der Botschafter, **welcher** die Verhandlungen geführt hat, muß den Vertrag unterschreiben.
   The ambassador who conducted the negotiations must sign the treaty.
Das war eine Niederlage für die Arbeiter, **welche** keinen Kompromiß schließen wollten.
   That was a defeat for the workers who did not want to compromise.

§6   *was* AS A RELATIVE PRONOUN

Was is used as a relative pronoun in the following instances:

1. When the antecedent is a neuter indefinite pronoun, such as **etwas** (*something*), **nichts** (*nothing*), **alles** (*all, everything*), **wenig** (*little*), **viel** (*much*), **vieles** (*many things*).

Das ist **etwas, was** ich nicht verstehen kann.
   That is something (that) I cannot understand.
Nicht **alles, was** er sagt, ist wahr.
   Not everything he says is true.
Es gibt nicht **viel, was** ihm wirklich gefällt.
   There is not much he really likes.
Vieles, was sie sagt, ist übertrieben.
   Many things she says are exaggerated.

English uses the relative pronouns *that* and *which* or omits them completely.

Note the distinction between **viel** and **vieles**:

viel = *much* (refers to something as a whole)	vieles = *many things* (refers to a number of individual, separate things, not taken together as one quantity)
Er weiß viel. *He knows much, a lot.* (referring to his knowledge as a whole) **Er sagt nicht viel.** *He doesn't say much.*	**Er weiß vieles nicht.** *There are many things he doesn't know.* **Er sagt mir vieles nicht.** *There are many things he doesn't tell me.*

2. When the antecedent is a neuter adjective in the superlative used as a noun, such as **das Beste** (*the best* [*thing*]), **das Klügste** (*the smartest* [*thing*]), **das Interessanteste** (*the most interesting* [*thing*]). (Cf. Chap. 10, §13).

> Das ist **das Beste, was** wir für Sie tun konnten.
> *That's the best we could do for you.*
> Das ist **das Klügste, was** man in so einer Situation tun kann.
> *That's the smartest thing one can do in such a situation.*

3. When the antecedent is a neuter ordinal (such as **das erste** [*the first thing*], **das zweite** [*the second thing*], etc.) or **das letzte** (*the last thing*), **das einzige** (*the only thing*).

Although these words seem to be used as nouns, they are not capitalized.

> Das war **das erste, was** er sagte.
> *That was the first thing he said.*
> Das ist **das letzte, was** ich tun würde.
> *That's the last thing I would do.*
> **Das einzige, was** mir Sorgen macht, ist meine notorische Faulheit.
> *The only thing that worries me is my notorious laziness.*

4. When the antecedent is an entire clause rather than a single element.

> Er will seinen Wagen vor dem Eingang parken, **was** verboten ist.
> *He wants to park his car in front of the entrance, **which** is forbidden.*

§7   *wo*-COMPOUND INSTEAD OF PREPOSITION + *was*

> Das ist etwas, ~~über was~~ er sich immer beschwert.
>   **worüber**
> *That is something about which he is always complaining.*
> or: *That is something he is always complaining about.*

When preceded by a preposition, **was** functioning as relative pronoun must be replaced by **wo** as part of a **wo**-compound.

PRACTICE 7   A. *Translate the following sentences into acceptable English and then reproduce the German from your translation.*

1. Herr Baumann sitzt jeden Abend vorm Fernseher, was seine Frau schrecklich ärgert.
2. Bernhard war pünktlich, was nicht sehr oft passiert.
3. Das war das erste, was Margot wissen wollte.
4. Das ist das Billigste, was ich finden konnte.
5. Das war das letzte, was wir für ihn tun konnten.
6. Das ist nicht das einzige, was mich stört.
7. Es gibt wenig, worauf ich wirklich stolz sein kann.
8. Das ist etwas, wovor ich wirklich Angst habe.

B. *Complete the responses in German, following the model of sentence 1.*

1. X: Ich möchte wissen, warum Klaus und Ruth Schluß gemacht haben.[1]

   Y: Das ist etwas, **was ich auch wissen möchte.**
   I also would like to know.

2. X: Warum sagst du es mir nicht?

   Y: Das ist etwas, _____
   I can't tell you.

3. X: Das verstehe ich wirklich nicht.

   Y: Liebling,[2] es gibt vieles, _____
   you don't understand.

4. X: Ich danke dir für deine Hilfe.

   Y: Ach, du brauchst mir nicht zu danken. Es war ja nicht viel,

   _____
   I could do for you.

5. X: Können Sie uns etwas mehr von dem neuen Projekt erzählen?

   Y: Leider nicht. Das ist alles, _____
   I know.

6. X: Ich möchte Dagmar etwas schenken, kann aber nur fünf Dollar dafür ausgeben.

   Y: Da hast du keine große Auswahl.[3] Es gibt wenig,

   _____
   that costs only five dollars.

7. X: Warum sagst du nichts?

   Y: Alles, ____, scheint falsch zu sein.
   I say

8. X: Macht Sie dieser Lärm nicht verrückt?

   Y: Es gibt nichts, _____
   that can drive me crazy.

---

1 **Schluß machen**   to break up
2 **der Liebling, -e** (*male and female*)   darling
3 **die Auswahl**   selection, choice

9. X: Seid ihr stolz auf das Resultat eurer Experimente?

   Y: Natürlich. Das ist etwas, _____

   we can be proud of.

10. X: Der Redner ist nicht auf diesen Punkt eingegangen.

    Y: Es gibt vieles, _____

    he didn't go into.

§8   THE RELATIVE PRONOUNS *wer* AND *was* WITH NO ANTECEDENT

The relative pronouns **wer** and **was** are used without an antecedent in the sense of

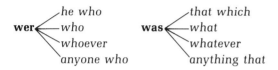

Compare:

wer / was

used as interrogative pronouns (inflected verb in second position)	used as relative pronouns without antecedents (inflected verb in last position)
Wer hat einen Wagen? *Who has a car?*	**Wer** einen Wagen **hat,** (der) geht selten zu Fuß. *He who has a car seldom walks.* or: *Anyone who has a car seldom walks.*
Was sagst du? *What are you saying?*	**Was** du **sagst,** (das) ist Unsinn. *What you are saying is nonsense.*

Note: a. **Wer** and **was** functioning as relative pronouns introduce dependent clauses; thus the inflected verb is in final position.

   b. In the above examples the demonstratives **der** and **das** are in parentheses because they are generally omitted in sentences with the following combinations:

Wer ...,	(der)
(nom.)	(nom.)
Was ...,	(das)
(nom. or acc.)	(nom. or acc.)

   In all other instances they must be added.

   Wer nicht arbeiten will, **den** sollte man nicht unterstützen.
   He who (Whoever) does not want to work should not be supported.
   (lit. *one should not support*)
   Wem das nicht gefällt, **der** kann ja protestieren.
   He who (Whoever) does not like it can protest.

The notion of generalization or indefiniteness may be enhanced by adding **immer, auch,** or **auch immer**:

> **Wer immer** uns besucht,
> or: **Wer** uns **auch** besucht,
> or: **Wer** uns **auch immer** besucht, } (der) ist willkommen.
> *Whoever visits us is welcome.*

> **Was immer** sie unternimmt,
> or: **Was** sie **auch** unternimmt,
> or: **Was** sie **auch immer** unternimmt, } (das) ist gut überlegt.
> *Whatever she undertakes is well thought out.*

The relative pronouns **wer** and **was** frequently occur in advertisements, proverbs, and sayings:

> **Wer gesund bleiben will, trinkt Obstsaft.**
> *Whoever wants to stay healthy drinks fruit juice.*
> or: *People who want to ...*

> **Wer Qualität liebt, kauft bei Merkur.**
> *Whoever loves quality buys at Merkur.*
> or: *People who love quality ...*

> PROVERB: **Wer im Glashaus sitzt, soll nicht mit Steinen werfen.**
> *People who live in glass houses shouldn't throw stones.*

PRACTICE 8   Translate into acceptable English.

1. Wer zuletzt lacht, lacht am besten. (proverb)
2. Was ich nicht weiß, macht mich nicht heiß.[1] (proverb)
3. Wer einmal lügt, dem glaubt man nicht, und wenn er auch[2] die Wahrheit spricht. (proverb)
4. Wer die Wahl[3] hat, hat die Qual.[4] (proverb)
5. Was man auch immer zu ihm sagt, geht zum einen Ohr hinein, zum anderen wieder hinaus.
6. Wen diese Musik stört, der soll es sagen.
7. Wem es Spaß macht,[5] der kann mitsingen.
8. Wem dieser Witz nicht gefällt, der braucht nicht darüber zu lachen.
9. Wer zuviel ißt, begeht Selbstmord[6] mit Messer und Gabel.

§9   SUMMARY OF THE MAIN FEATURES

1. Relative clauses are dependent clauses that ordinarily modify antecedents. They are set off by commas.

1 **heiß**	hot; *here:* angry
2 **wenn auch**	even though, even when
3 **die Wahl, -en**	choice
4 **die Qual, -en**	pain; *here:* pain of having to make a decision
5 *idiom:* **es macht mir Spaß**	it's fun for me, I enjoy it
6 **Selbstmord begehen, beging, begangen**	to commit suicide

2. They are introduced by a relative pronoun that cannot be omitted. This pronoun agrees in gender and number with its antecedent, but its case is determined by its function in the relative clause.

3. Relative pronouns usually resemble the definite article.

4. The alternative forms of the relative pronoun **welcher** occur mainly in formal German.

5. The relative pronoun **was** is used after the following antecedents:
   a. indefinite pronouns, such as **etwas, nichts, alles, wenig, viel, vieles**;
   b. neuter adjectives in the superlative used as nouns, such as **das Beste, das Dümmste**;
   c. neuter ordinals and **das letzte, das einzige**;
   d. entire clauses.

6. **wo**-Compounds must be used in place of a preposition + **was**.

7. **Wer** and **was** are used as relative pronouns when there is no antecedent.

PRACTICE 9   Summarizing exercises

A. *Express in German.*[1]

1. a. We must clarify this point.   **Wir müssen diesen Punkt klären.**
   b. That's a point we must clarify.
   c. That's something we must clarify.
2. a. I cannot understand this attitude.   **Ich kann diese Haltung nicht verstehen.**
   b. That's an attitude I cannot understand.
   c. That's something I cannot understand.
   d. That's not the only thing I cannot understand.
3. a. She did that for me.   **Sie hat das für mich getan.**
   b. That's the first thing she did for me.
   c. That's the only thing she did for me.
4. a. I would not do that.   **Ich würde das nicht tun.**
   b. That's something I would not do.
   c. That's the last thing I would do.
5. a. That worries me.   **Das macht mir Sorgen.**
   b. That's a problem that worries me.
   c. That's something that worries me.
   d. That's not the only thing that worries me.
6. a. I dropped a course.   **Ich habe mit einem Kurs aufgehört.**
   b. The course I dropped was too hard for me.

1 Render	the first thing	by	**das erste**
	the last thing	by	**das letzte**
	the only thing	by	**das einzige**
	many things	by	**vieles**
	there is/are	by	**es gibt**

c. The courses I dropped were too hard for me.
d. There is nothing that is too hard for you. (formal)

7. a. I cannot go into details.   **Ich kann nicht auf Einzelheiten eingehen.**
   b. These are (Das sind) details I cannot go into.
   c. That is something I cannot go into.
   d. There are many things I cannot go into.

8. a. She can be proud of this achievement.   **Sie kann auf diese Leistung stolz sein.**
   b. That is an achievement she can be proud of.
   c. That is something she can be proud of.
   d. That is not the only thing she can be proud of.
   e. There is not much I can be proud of.
   f. There are many things you can be proud of. (fam. sing.)

B. *Insert the appropriate relative pronouns.*

1.   X: Ich weiß etwas, _____ du nicht weißt.
     Y: Was könnte das sein? Wahrscheinlich ein Gerücht,[1] _____
        du auf der Party bei Neumanns gehört hast.

2.   X: Bist du wirklich schon mit dieser Arbeit fertig?
     Y: Ja. _____ mir Spaß macht, tue ich sehr schnell … Hm, mei-
        stens.

3.   X: Diese Radiosendung wird nicht allen Leuten gefallen.
     Y: _____ sie nicht gefällt, der kann sie ja abschalten.[2]

4.   X: Ich habe zwei Stellenangebote.[3] Jetzt weiß ich wirklich nicht,
        welches Angebot ich annehmen soll.
     Y: _____ die Wahl hat, hat die Qual. Das ist übrigens[4] eine
        Qual, _____ ich auch haben möchte.

5.   X: Dieter findet, daß du arrogant bist. Er hat gesagt …
     Y: Ach, das will ich gar nicht wissen. _____ ich nicht weiß,
        macht mich nicht heiß.

6. a. X: Wie hast du auf seine ironische Bemerkung reagiert?
      Y: Ich bin still geblieben, _____ wirklich nicht leicht für mich
         ist.
   b. X: Das ist das Klügste, _____ du tun konntest.

C. *Form sentences that fit the context.*

Model: Dieter hat eine neue Studentin gesehen. Er möchte sie
         kennenlernen. Ich frage ihn:

         „ Wo ist die Studentin—du / kennen•lernen? "

         „ Wo ist die Studentin, die du kennenlernen möchtest? "

---

1 **das Gerücht, -e**   rumor
2 **ab•schalten**   to turn off
3 **das Stellenangebot, -e**   job offer
4 **übrigens**   by the way

1. Andreas sagt, daß er ein nettes Mädchen kennengelernt hat. Ich frage ihn:

   „Wie heißt das Mädchen—du / kennen.lernen" (pres. perf.)

2. Helga liest einen Brief. Ich frage sie:

   „Ist das der Brief—du / so lange / warten" (pres. perf.)

3. In Margots Zimmer steht eine Kuckucksuhr. Ich frage sie:

   „Ist das die Kuckucksuhr—du / erben" (pres. perf.)

4. Ich habe eine großartige Stelle gefunden und sage:

   „Das ist eine Chance—nicht wieder / bekommen"

5. Ich frage Michael, ob es wahr ist, daß er mit dem Kurs in Trigonometrie aufgehört hat. Er antwortet:

   „Das ist nicht der Kurs—auf.hören" (pres. perf.)

6. Ich frage Rainer, wie ihm der neue Chemieprofessor gefällt. Er antwortet:

   „Das ist ein Professor—alle Studenten / begeistert"

7. Ich frage Barbara, mit wem sie in einem Zimmer wohnt. Sie antwortet:

   „Dort am Fenster steht die Studentin—Zimmer / wohnen"

8. Ich habe den ersten Preis im Hochsprung (high jump) gewonnen.

   Das ist etwas—ich / stolz

9. Fischers haben ihr schönes Haus verkauft. Jetzt finden sie, daß das ein großer Fehler war. Herr Fischer sagt:

   „Das war das Dümmste—wir / machen / können" (past)

10. Ich habe zwei Einladungen für Freitag abend. Welche soll ich annehmen?

    Wahl—Qual

11. Der Bürgermeister kritisiert zuviel. Ich finde, er sollte vorsichtiger mit seiner Kritik sein.

    Glashaus sitzen—nicht werfen

12. Ihr Freund ißt zuviel. Sie warnen ihn:

    „zuviel essen—begehen Selbstmord / Messer und Gabel"

17

Reflexive Pronouns and Reflexive Verbs; Reciprocal Pronouns; Uses of *selbst* (*selber*)

KEY TO THE EXERCISES ON CASSETTE 9.
RUNNING TIME:APPROX. 25 MIN.

Reflexive Pronouns and Reflexive Verbs

Introduction

Compare the following three sentences:

> a. **John** is defending **his friend.**
> b. **John** is defending **him.**
> c. **John** is defending **himself.**

In sentences *a* and *b* the subject and the object are two different persons. In sentence *c* the subject and object are identical, and the object is expressed with a reflexive pronoun.

In most instances the reflexive pronoun is the direct object, as in the above example, but it may also function as indirect object:

> He has to give **himself**   more time.
> | |
>   **INDIRECT**   **DIRECT**
>   **OBJ.**   **OBJ.**

310

The reflexive pronoun also occurs as the object of a preposition:

> He was **beside himself.**
> He was talking **to himself.**
> He was laughing **at himself.**

There is no difference in form, regardless of whether the reflexive pronoun functions as direct object, indirect object, or object of a preposition.

German reflexive pronouns have the same three functions, but they show some changes in form.

§1   THE REFLEXIVE PRONOUN IN THE ACCUSATIVE CASE

The reflexive pronoun is in the accusative when it functions as a direct object.

> Compare: a. **Hans** verteidigt **seinen Freund.**
> *Hans is defending his friend.*
>
> b. **Hans** verteidigt **ihn.** (personal pronoun)
> c. **Hans** verteidigt **sich.** (reflexive pronoun)

Here is a complete set of the reflexive pronoun in the accusative case:

Ich verteidige **mich.** *I am defending myself.*
Du verteidigst **dich.** *You are defending yourself.*

Er verteidigt | **sich.** | *He is defending himself.*
Sie verteidigt | **sich.** | *She is defending herself.*
Es verteidigt | **sich.** | etc.

Wir verteidigen **uns.**
Ihr verteidigt **euch.**
Sie verteidigen | **sich.** |
Sie verteidigen | **sich.** | (formal)

The reflexive pronouns are identical to the accusative personal pronouns except for the form **sich**
    in the 3rd person sing. and plural, and in the formal address.

Note that the formal reflexive **sich** is the only formal pronoun not capitalized.

All transitive verbs can be used reflexively, for example:

sich fragen *to ask oneself*
sich kennen *to know oneself*
sich loben *to praise oneself*
sich täuschen *to deceive oneself*

PRACTICE 1 *Restate the following sentences, using the subjects in parentheses. Change the reflexive pronoun to match the new subject.*

> **Model:** Ich frage mich, ob das wahr ist. (Astrid, wir, meine Eltern)
> **Astrid fragt sich, ob das wahr ist.**
> **Wir fragen uns, ob das wahr ist.**
> **Meine Eltern fragen sich, ob das wahr ist.**

1. Er lobt sich zuviel. (ich, du, ihr)
2. Helga täuscht sich vielleicht. (Herr Berger, wir, Sie)
3. Mein Bruder hat sich nicht verteidigt. (die Kinder, ich)
4. Er fragt sich das oft. (ich, wir)
5. Ich kenne mich doch. (du)

Some common verbs that are used reflexively in German but not in English:

sich entschuldigen	*to apologize*
sich erinnern an (acc.)	*to remember*
sich erkälten	*to catch a cold*
sich freuen auf (acc.)	*to look forward to*
sich freuen über (acc.)	*to be happy about*
sich gewöhnen an (acc.)	*to get used or accustomed to*
sich interessieren für (acc.)	*to be interested in*
sich irren	*to be mistaken*
sich konzentrieren auf (acc.)	*to concentrate on*
sich langweilen	*to be bored, get bored*
sich rasieren	*to shave*
sich setzen	*to sit down*
sich verfahren (verfährt), verfuhr, verfahren	*to lose one's way (driving)*
sich verlaufen (verläuft), verlief, verlaufen	*to lose one's way (walking)*
sich waschen (wäscht), wusch, gewaschen	*to wash (oneself)*

Because they are transitive, verbs used reflexively form the present perfect and the past perfect with the auxiliary **haben**, even if they are derivatives of verbs that employ **sein**, such as **sich verfahren** and **sich verlaufen**. Compare:

Wir **sind** in die Stadt gefahren/gelaufen.	*We drove/walked to town.*
Wir **haben** uns verfahren/verlaufen.	*We lost our way (driving/walking).*

The position of the reflexive pronouns

The position of the reflexive pronoun is governed by the same rules as the personal pronoun object (cf. Chap. 6, §10).

a. In sentences with **normal word order**, the reflexive pronoun follows the inflected verb:

> Er hat **sich** gestern auf dem Fußballplatz erkältet.

b. In sentences with **inverted** or **dependent word order**, the reflexive pronoun follows the personal pronoun subject:

> Vielleicht hat er **sich** gestern auf dem Fußballplatz erkältet.
> Es ist möglich, daß er **sich** gestern auf dem Fußballplatz erkältet hat.

It precedes all other elements, usually also noun subjects:

> Vielleicht hat **sich** Herr Zimmermann gestern auf dem Fußballplatz erkältet.
> Es ist möglich, daß **sich** Herr Zimmermann gestern auf dem Fußballplatz erkältet hat.

PRACTICE 2   A. *Translate into German.*

1. a. I'm bored.   **Ich langweile mich.**
   b. We are bored.
   c. They are bored.
   d. Are you bored? (fam. sing., pl., formal)
2. a. I'm mistaken.   **Ich irre mich.**
   b. Perhaps I'm mistaken.
   c. Perhaps you are mistaken. (fam. sing., formal)
   d. We are not mistaken.
3. a. I apologize.   **Ich entschuldige mich.**
   b. I have to apologize.
   c. I'd like to apologize.
   d. I'm not apologizing.
4. a. Martin is shaving.   **Martin rasiert sich.**
   b. I'm shaving.
   c. You have to shave. (fam. sing.)
   d. Where can I shave?
5. a. Why aren't we sitting down?   **Warum setzen wir uns nicht?**
   b. Why aren't you sitting down? (fam. sing., pl., formal)
   c. Would you like to sit down? (formal)
6. a. I hope I won't catch a cold.   **Hoffentlich erkälte ich mich nicht.**
   b. I hope we won't catch a cold.
   c. I hope you won't catch a cold. (fam. sing., pl., formal)
7. a. I hope we won't lose our way.   **Hoffentlich verfahren/verlaufen wir uns nicht.**
   b. I hope I won't lose my way.
   c. I hope you won't lose your way. (formal, fam. sing., pl.)
8. a. I'm defending myself.   **Ich verteidige mich.**
   b. I must defend myself.
   c. You must defend yourself. (fam. sing., formal)
   d. She doesn't defend herself.
   e. He can't defend himself.

B. *Translate the responses into German, using the present perfect for the English past tense.*

1. X: Sie haben sich geirrt.
   Y: No, I wasn't mistaken.

2. X: Habt ihr euch sehr gelangweilt?
   Y: Yes, we were very bored.

3. X: Alle haben sich am Sonntag erkältet.
   Y: I didn't catch a cold.

4. X: Haben sich die Kinder heute morgen gewaschen?
   Y: Of course, they washed.

5. X: Hat sich Ihre Nachbarin entschuldigt?
   Y: No, she didn't apologize.

6. X: Hast du dich rasiert?
   Y: Of course, I shaved.

7. X: Warum hat er sich nicht verteidigt?
   Y: I don't know why he didn't defend himself.

8. X: Maria ist noch nicht zurückgekommen. Hat sie sich verfahren oder verlaufen?
   Y: It is possible that she lost her way.

Particular attention must be paid to verbs associated with a preposition, such as **sich erinnern an** (*acc.*).

Sie erinnert sich noch an meinen Bruder.
She (still) remembers my brother.
Sie erinnert sich noch an ihn.
She (still) remembers him.
(**noch** is commonly added)

Sie erinnert sich nicht mehr an das Picknick.
She doesn't remember the picnic (anymore).
Sie erinnert sich nicht mehr daran.
She doesn't remember it (anymore).
(**mehr** is commonly added to **nicht**)

Note the use of the **da**-compound **daran** (cf. Chap. 8, §3).

PRACTICE 3   A. *Translate into German.*

1. a. I (still) remember this soccer player. **Ich erinnere mich noch an diesen Fußballspieler.**
   b. I (still) remember him.
   c. My sister (still) remembers him.
   d. Many people (still) remember him.
   e. Do you (still) remember him? (formal, fam. sing., pl.)

2. a. I don't remember this soccer game. **Ich erinnere mich nicht mehr an dieses Fußballspiel.**
   b. I don't remember it.
   c. Andreas doesn't remember it.
   d. My friends don't remember it.

3. a. I'm happy about this message. **Ich freue mich über diese Nachricht.**
   b. I'm happy about it.
   c. We are happy about it.
   d. Are you happy about it? (fam. sing., formal)

4. a. I'm looking forward to this trip.   **Ich freue mich auf diese Reise.**
   b. We are looking forward to this trip.
   c. I'm not looking forward to it.
   d. Are you looking forward to it? (fam. sing., pl., formal)
5. a. Margot is interested in karate.   **Margot interessiert sich für Karate.**
   b. Many people are interested in karate.
   c. I'm not interested in it.
   d. Are you interested in it? (fam. sing., formal)
6. a. I have to concentrate more on my work.   **Ich muß mich mehr auf meine Arbeit konzentrieren.**
   b. I have to concentrate more on it.
   c. I can't concentrate on it.
7. a. They are getting used to this noise.   **Sie gewöhnen sich an diesen Lärm.**
   b. They are getting used to it.
   c. I'm getting used to it.
   d. I must get used to it.
   e. I can't get used to it.
   f. You have to get used to it. (fam. sing., pl., formal)

B. *Translate the responses into German, using the present perfect for the English past tense.*

1. X: Habt ihr euch an das Leben im Studentenheim gewöhnt?
   Y: Yes, we got used to it.
2. X: Hat sich Herr Lange noch an mich erinnert?
   Y: Yes, he (still) remembered you. (fam. sing.)
3. X: Hat sich Renate über Michaels Geschenk gefreut?
   Y: Of course, she was happy about it.
4. X: Die ganze Familie Wetzel hat sich auf das Wochenende in den Bergen gefreut.
   Y: Mrs. Wetzel wasn't looking forward to it.
5. X: Hat sich Herr Rothe für deine Briefmarkensammlung interessiert?
   Y: No, he wasn't interested in it.
6. X: Hast du gehört, was Annerose gesagt hat?
   Y: No. I was concentrating on my work.

§2   THE REFLEXIVE PRONOUN IN THE DATIVE CASE

The reflexive pronoun will be in the dative case if there is a direct object in the sentence.

Example:

sich etwas überlegen   *to think about something*
Ich überlege   **mir**   **die Sache**.   *I am thinking about the matter.*
            | |
       INDIRECT   DIRECT
         OBJ.   OBJ.

Except for the first and second person singular, the dative reflexive pronouns are identical to their accusative counterparts:

Ich überlege $\boxed{\textbf{mir}}$ die Sache.
Du überlegst $\boxed{\textbf{dir}}$ die Sache.
Er $\Big\}$
Sie $\Big\}$überlegt **sich** die Sache.
Es $\Big\}$

Wir überlegen **uns** die Sache.
Ihr überlegt **euch** die Sache.

Sie überlegen **sich** die Sache.

Sie überlegen **sich** die Sache. (formal)

Some common verbs with dative reflexive pronouns:

sich etwas an•sehen
sich etwas an•schauen $\longrightarrow$ *to (take a) look at*

sich etwas leisten   *to treat oneself to something*
sich etwas leisten können   *to be able to afford something*

sich etwas überlegen   *to think about something, think it over*

sich etwas vor•stellen   *to imagine something*

When referring to parts of the body, the dative reflexive pronoun is used in combination with the definite article where English uses the possessive:

Ich wasche **mir die** Hände/**die** Haare.   *I'm washing **my** hands/**my** hair.*
Ich putze **mir die** Zähne.   *I'm brushing **my** teeth.*
Ich habe **mir den** Arm gebrochen.   *I broke **my** arm.*

Verbs requiring a dative object (cf. Chap. 5, §4, 3.b) naturally have a dative rather than an accusative reflexive pronoun:

Ich gefalle **mir** nicht in diesem Kleid.   *I don't like myself in this dress.*
Ich widerspreche **mir.**   *I'm contradicting myself.*

With some verbs, such as **kaufen, bestellen** (*to order*), and **holen** (*to [go and] get, fetch*), the use of the dative reflexive pronoun is optional:

Frau Schmidt hat (sich) einen Wagen gekauft.
  Mrs. Schmidt bought (herself) a car.

Was hast du (dir) bestellt?
  What did you order (for yourself)?

Ich habe (mir) eine Coca-Cola aus dem Kühlschrank geholt.
  I got (myself) a Coca-Cola from the refrigerator.

PRACTICE 4   *Restate the following sentences, using the subjects in parentheses.*

1. Maria hat sich keinen Nachtisch bestellt. (ich, wir)
2. Martin hat sich widersprochen. (du, ihr)

3. Haben Sie sich die Hand gebrochen? (du)
4. Herr Krause gefällt sich in der Rolle eines Hausmanns.[1] (ich)
5. Sie können sich die Hände im Bad waschen. (du)
6. Käte hat sich eine Morgenzeitung geholt. (ich)
7. Wollen Sie sich die Zähne putzen? (du, ihr)

A note on word order

Compare the following three sentences:

a. Ich kann **mir** diesen Fernseher nicht leisten.   *I can't afford this TV set.*

b. Ich kann **ihn mir** nicht leisten.   *I can't afford it.*
c. Ich kann **mir das** nicht leisten.   *I can't afford that.*

By analogy with the position of personal pronoun objects (cf. Chap. 6, §10) the dative reflexive follows the accusative personal pronoun, as in sentence *b*. However, it precedes other accusative pronouns, for instance, the demonstrative pronoun **das,** as in sentence *c*.

Additional examples:

Ich kann **es mir** vorstellen.   *I can imagine it.*
Ich kann **mir das** vorstellen.   *I can imagine that.*

Ich werde **es mir** überlegen.   *I'll think about it.*
Ich werde **mir das** überlegen.   *I'll think about that.*

PRACTICE 5   A. *Replace the direct object noun with the appropriate form of the personal pronoun; then substitute* **das** *for the personal pronoun.*

Model: Hast du dir die Dias angesehen?
  Hast du sie dir angesehen?
  Hast du dir das angesehen?

1. Hast du dir diese Fernsehsendung angeschaut?
2. Ich kann mir das Fiasko gut vorstellen.
3. Er hat sich meine Briefmarkensammlung nicht angesehen.
4. Ich habe mir die Sache überlegt.
5. Wir können uns dieses Haus nicht leisten.

B. *Translate into German.*

1. a. I can't imagine it.   **Ich kann es mir nicht vorstellen.**
   b. I can't imagine that.
   c. You can't imagine that. (fam. sing., pl.)
   d. Can you imagine that? (fam. sing., formal)
2. a. My parents can't afford it.   **Meine Eltern können es sich nicht leisten.**
   b. I can't afford it.

---

1 **der Hausmann, ¨er**   house husband

c. I can't afford that.

d. Can you afford that? (fam. sing., formal)

3. a. I'm thinking about it.   **Ich überlege es mir.**

b. I must think about it.

c. I must think about that.

d. I thought about that. (pres. perf.)

4. a. They are watching the soccer match on TV.   **Sie schauen sich das Fußballspiel im Fernsehen an.**

b. Are you watching the soccer match on TV? (formal, fam. sing., pl.)

c. I was watching the soccer match on TV. (pres. perf.)

5. a. We are only window-shopping. **Wir sehen uns nur die Schaufenster[1] an.**

b. I'm only window-shopping.

c. I was only window-shopping. (pres. perf.)

d. They were only window-shopping. (pres. perf.)

§3   THE IMPERATIVE OF REFLEXIVE VERBS

Reflexive verbs must include the appropriate reflexive pronoun in the imperative. (For the formation of the imperative, see Chap. 2, §12 to §14.)

REFLEXIVE IN THE ACCUSATIVE CASE	REFLEXIVE IN THE DATIVE CASE
fam. sing.	
Wasch(e) **dich** !	Wasch(e) **dir** die Hände!
fam. pl.	
Wascht **euch!**	Wascht **euch** die Hände!
formal	
Waschen Sie **sich!**	Waschen Sie **sich** die Hände!
wir form = Let's ...	
Waschen wir **uns!**	Waschen wir **uns** die Hände!

Only the familiar singular imperative distinguishes dative and accusative reflexive pronouns.

PRACTICE 6   A. *Add the familiar singular, plural, and* **wir** *imperatives.*

Model: Sehen Sie sich diese Fotos an!
  Sieh dir diese Fotos an!
  Seht euch diese Fotos an!
  Sehen wir uns diese Fotos an!

---

1 **das Schaufenster, -**   shop window
  sich die Schaufenster an•sehen   to window-shop
  (sieht an), sah an, angesehen

1. Bestellen Sie sich doch etwas!
2. Stellen Sie sich das mal vor!
3. Setzen Sie sich doch!
4. Täuschen Sie sich nicht!

B. *Add the familiar singular and plural imperatives.*

1. Erkälten Sie sich nicht!
2. Bitte bedienen Sie sich![1]
3. Schauen Sie sich mal diese Sendung an!
4. Überlegen Sie sich das doch!

§4   THE REFLEXIVE PRONOUN AS THE OBJECT OF A PREPOSITION

Compare the following three sentences:

a.	**Ich** habe über **ihn** gelacht.	*I laughed at **him**.*
b.	**Ich** habe über **mich** gelacht.	*I laughed at **myself**.*
c.	**Er** hat über **sich** gelacht.	*He laughed at **himself**.*

When the reflexive pronoun is the object of a preposition, as in b and c, its case is determined by the preceding preposition. (For cases governed by prepositions, see Chap. 7, §5 and Chap. 8, §1 and §2.)

Additional examples:

Du kannst stolz auf **dich** sein.	*You can be proud of **yourself**.*
Bist **du** nun zufrieden mit **dir**?	*Are you now content with **yourself**?*
Ich bin außer **mir**.	*I'm beside **myself**.*

Note that German uses the reflexive pronoun in the expression **bei sich haben** (*to have on you, to carry with you*):

Ich habe kein Geld **bei mir**. *I have no money **on me**.*
Haben Sie Ihren Ausweis **bei sich**? *Do you have your ID card **on you**?*

PRACTICE 7   A. *Substitute the indicated subjects and use the appropriate reflexive pronouns.*

Model: Ich bin nicht zufrieden mit mir. (Helga, wir)
Helga ist nicht zufrieden mit sich.
Wir sind nicht zufrieden mit uns.

1. Er kann stolz auf sich sein. (Sie, du, wir)
2. Lachst du über dich? (Sie, ihr)
3. Ich spreche zuviel von mir. (du, viele Leute)
4. Ich bin außer mir. (wir, Bergers)
5. Ich habe kein Geld bei mir. (Herr Berger, die Kinder)

---

1 **sich bedienen**   to help or serve oneself (*lit.*: to wait on oneself)
  Bitte bedienen Sie sich!   Please help yourself.

6. Haben Sie Ihren Ausweis bei sich? (du ... deinen)
7. Leonore hat ihren Führerschein[1] nicht bei sich. (ich ... meinen)

B. *Translate into German.*

1. I'm not talking of myself.
2. They can be proud of themselves.
3. She was beside herself.
4. He's laughing at himself.
5. I don't have my ID card on me.
6. Do you have your driver's licence on you? (fam. sing.)

Reciprocal Pronouns and Uses of *selbst* (*selber*)

§5   RECIPROCAL PRONOUNS

1. The reciprocal pronoun **einander** (*each other* or *one another*) is never inflected.

   Sie helfen **einander**. *They help each other/one another.*

   When following a preposition, **einander** is written together with it.

   Wir hören oft **voneinander**.   *We often hear from each other.*
   Wir sitzen **nebeneinander**.   *We are sitting next to each other.*

2. The reflexive pronouns are often used to express reciprocity.

   Sie hassen **sich**. Possible meanings: *They hate themselves.*
                                          They hate each other.

   The context must clarify the appropriate meaning.

Normally, **einander** and the reciprocal reflexive pronouns are interchangeable; however, after prepositions only **einander** can be used.

PRACTICE 8   *Translate the following sentences, then reproduce the German from your translation.*

1. Es ist klar, daß die zwei sich lieben.
2. Wir schreiben uns nicht, aber wir rufen uns manchmal an.
3. Sie küssen sich nicht, sie umarmen[2] sich nur.
4. Markus und Volker grüßen[3] sich nicht. Sie gehen stumm[4] aneinander vorbei.[5]

---

1 **der Führerschein, -e**	driver's licence
2 **umarmen**	to embrace, hug
3 **grüßen**	to greet, say hello
4 **stumm**	silent(ly)
5 **vorbei•gehen an** (*dat.*), **ging vorbei, ist vorbeigegangen**	to pass by

5. Heidrun und Petra kommen sehr gut miteinander aus.[1]
6. Wir sind nicht miteinander ausgekommen.
7. Wir helfen einander bei den Hausaufgaben.

§6   USES OF *selbst (selber)*

Selbst is an intensifier rather than a reflexive pronoun. The form **selber** is preferred in colloquial German.

    a. Er glaubt das nicht.   *He doesn't believe that.*
    b. Er glaubt das **selbst (selber)** nicht.   *He doesn't believe that **himself**.*

In sentence *b* **selbst (selber)** is used for emphasis. This intensifier has no case endings. English uses the reflexive pronoun as intensifier.

Additional examples:

Waschen Sie Ihren Wagen **selber**?	*Do you wash your car yourself?*
Herr Schreiber macht alle Reparaturen **selbst**.	*Mr. Schreiber does all repair work himself.*
Hast du den Bericht **selber** getippt?	*Did you type the report yourself?*
Kochen Sie **selbst**?	*Do you do your own cooking?* (translation!)
Meine Mutter ist die Güte **selbst**.	*My mother is kindness itself.*

Selbst (selber) may also reinforce reflexives:

Er hat nicht mich, sondern **sich selbst** getäuscht.
He did not deceive me but himself.

When **selbst** (never **selber**) precedes the element it qualifies, it means *even*:

Selbst sie hat kein Geld.   ***Even she** has no money.*

PRACTICE 9   *Translate the following sentences, then reproduce the German from your translation.*

1. Herr Körner hat das selbst zugegeben.
2. Selbst Herr Körner hat das zugegeben.
3. Haben Sie den Kuchen selbst gebacken?
4. Ich gehe nicht oft essen.[2] Meistens koche ich selber.
5. Haben Sie mich gefragt, oder haben Sie mit sich selbst gesprochen?
6. Ich lache nicht über dich, ich lache über mich selber.
7. Selbst der Professor hat es nicht gewußt.
8. Du bist die Bescheidenheit[3] selbst.

---

1 **aus•kommen mit** (*dat.*)**, kam aus, ist ausgekommen**	to get along with
2 **essen gehen**	to eat out
3 **die Bescheidenheit**	modesty

§7   SUMMARY OF THE MAIN FEATURES

Reflexive pronouns

1. The reflexive pronouns are identical in form to the personal pronouns except for the form *sich* in the third person singular and plural, and in the formal address.

2. The reflexive pronoun occurs more frequently in the accusative than in the dative. The forms of the accusative and dative differ only in the first and second person singular.

	ACC.	DAT.
ich	**mich**	**mir**
du	**dich**	**dir**
er		
sie	**sich**	
es		
wir	**uns**	
ihr	**euch**	
sie	**sich**	
Sie		

3. The forms of the imperative:

   Wasch(e) **dich!**   Wasch(e) **dir** dis Hände!
   Wascht **euch!**   Wascht **euch** die Hände!
   Waschen Sie **sich!**   Waschen Sie **sich** die Hände!

   Only the familiar singular imperative distinguishes dative and accusative reflexive pronouns.

4. The reflexive pronoun usually follows the inflected verb form or a personal pronoun (subject or direct object), but precedes all other elements.

Reciprocal pronouns

Each other/one another may be expressed by **einander** or by the appropriate reflexive pronoun (except after prepositions).

Uses of *selbst* (*selber*)

Selbst (selber) is used as intensifier and to strengthen reflexive pronouns.
Selbst preceding a noun or pronoun corresponds to English **even.**

PRACTICE 10   Summarizing exercise
      Using the cues, form statements and questions that fit the context.
      Model: Es ist sehr kalt, und ich trage nur eine dünne Jacke. Ich denke:

               „ sich erkälten "

            „ Vielleicht erkälte ich mich."
         or: „ Hoffentlich erkälte ich mich nicht."

1.   Margot sitzt vorm Fernseher.

sich an.schauen / Film

2.   Ich habe Martin beleidigt. Ich denke:

„ müssen / sich entschuldigen "

3.   Der Chef ist nicht fair zu Andreas. Warum protestiert Andreas nicht? Ich sage zu ihm:

„ müssen / sich verteidigen "

4.   Ich habe Gäste und sage zu ihnen:

„ bitte / sich bedienen! " (fam. pl.)

5.   Man hat Dieters Brieftasche (wallet) gestohlen. Dieter sagt:

„ außer sich sein "

6.   Annerose fragt mich, was ich am Wochenende gemacht habe. Ich antworte:

„ sich langweilen " (pres. perf.)

7.   Mein Freund sagt, daß das Benzin bestimmt billiger wird. Ich sage:

„ können / das / sich vor.stellen / nicht "

8.   Ich will einen Scheck einlösen. Leider kann ich es nicht.

Ausweis / nicht / bei sich haben

9.   Ich habe viele alte Münzen (coins) und möchte sie meiner Freundin zeigen. Ich frage sie:

„ sich interessieren / Münzen? "

10.   Ich niese (sneeze) sehr viel. Ich denke:

vielleicht / sich erkälten / am Sonntag (pres. perf.)

11.   Margot und Renate kommen aus der Stadt. Ich frage sie, was sie gekauft haben. Renate sagt:

„ Nichts. wir / sich an.sehen / nur die Schaufenster " (pres. perf.)

12.   Marlene will ihren Wagen verkaufen. Sie fragt mich, ob ich ihn kaufen will. Ich sage:

„ müssen / sich überlegen "

13.   Barbara und Karin haben ein Doppelzimmer im Studentenheim. Im nächsten Semester will Barbara ausziehen (move out). Warum? Sie sagt:

„ wir / nicht aus.kommen "

14.   Klaus wohnt nicht mehr mit Rainer in einem Zimmer. Helga sagt:

„ sie / nicht aus.kommen " (pres. perf.)

15. a. Ich bin bei Barbara. Wir trinken Kaffee und essen Kuchen. Ich frage sie:

„ Kuchen / selbst backen? " (pres. perf.)

    b. Sie antwortet:

„ nur Kaffee / selbst kochen " (pres. perf.)

16. a. Frank fährt im Sommer nach Kalifornien. Ich frage ihn:

„ sich freuen / Reise? "

    b. Frank fragt mich, ob ich mitfahren will. Ich habe kein Geld und sage:

„ können / sich leisten / nicht "

17. Andreas Neumann ist ein Freund von mir. Er hat mir eine Karte aus Berlin geschickt. Ich sage zu Käte:

„ du / sich erinnern an? / / diese Karte / bekommen (pres. perf.) / / sich sehr freuen / darüber "

18

The Passive Voice

KEY TO THE EXERCISES ON CASSETTE 9.
RUNNING TIME: APPROX. 40 MIN.

Basic Differences Between the Active and the Passive Voices

§1   IN ENGLISH

Compare:

> a. The policeman caught the thief.   (ACTIVE VOICE)
> b. The thief was caught by the policeman.   (PASSIVE VOICE)

In sentence *a* the subject, the policeman, does something; it is active. The sentence is expressed in the active voice.

In sentence *b* the subject, the thief, is acted upon by someone, i.e. the policeman. Sentences in which the subject is not active but acted upon are expressed in the passive voice. The grammatical term for the element that acts upon the subject of a passive sentence—in the above example, the policeman—is the *agent*.

When converting a sentence from the active to the passive voice, the following changes occur:

> ACTIVE: a. **The policeman** caught **the thief.**
>   SUBJECT————————DIRECT OBJECT
>
> PASSIVE: b. **The thief** was caught by **the policeman.**
>   SUBJECT   AGENT

The direct object of the active voice becomes the subject of the passive, and the subject of the active voice becomes the agent of the passive.

When you compare sentences *a* and *b*, you will notice a shift of emphasis: In sentence *a* the attention focuses on the fact that the policeman caught the thief. In sentence *b* the focus of attention is the thief and what happened to him.

In many passive sentences the agent is not stated:

> The thief was caught.
> The houses were torn down.
> The Bauers will not be invited.

The formation of the tenses in the active and passive voices

It is very important to keep in mind that the active and the passive voices use different infinitives.

INFINITIVE OF THE ACTIVE VOICE	INFINITIVE OF THE PASSIVE VOICE
to catch	to be caught
to invite	to be invited
to ask	to be asked
to watch	to be watched

The tenses are based on these infinitives, as seen in the following synopsis.

	ACTIVE VOICE	PASSIVE VOICE
	infinitive: **to watch**	infinitive: **to be watched**
PRESENT	he watches/is watching	he is (being) watched
PAST	he watched/was watching	he was (being) watched
PRES. PERF.	he has watched	he has been watched
PAST PERF.	he had watched	he had been watched
FUTURE	he will watch	he will be watched
FUT. PERF.	he will have watched	he will have been watched

PRACTICE 1   A. *Express the following sentences in the tenses indicated in parentheses.*

1. This project is financed by the government. (past, pres. perf., past perf., future)
2. His name was not mentioned. (future, pres., pres. perf., past perf.)

B. *Express the following sentences in the corresponding tenses of the passive voice.*

1. Many adolescents are reading his latest book.
2. The speaker did not mention this point.
3. A real estate agent has just sold this house.
4. The police had informed the mayor.
5. The interviewer will ask you to give all your qualifications.

§2   IN GERMAN

Compare:

Ein Mechaniker   repariert   **meinen Wagen.**
    subject   direct object
 NOMINATIVE   ACCUSATIVE

Mein Wagen   wird   von **einem Mechaniker** repariert.
    subject   agent
 NOMINATIVE   DATIVE
My car is being repaired by a mechanic.

Note: a. As in English, the direct object of the active voice becomes the subject of the passive voice, which means a switch from the accusative **meinen Wagen** to the nominative **mein Wagen.**

b. The subject of the active voice, **ein Mechaniker,** becomes the agent of the passive, **einem Mechaniker** (the dative object of **von**).

c. English uses the auxiliary *to be* + past participle to express the passive; German uses the auxiliary **werden** + past participle. The past participle is in final position in German main clauses.

d. In the German passive infinitive, **werden** follows the past participle:

repariert werden *to be repaired*

(For the formation of past participles, see Chap. 3, §2 and §4.)

Compare the following infinitives of the active and passive which will occur in the exercises:

ACTIVE		PASSIVE	
absagen	*to call off, cancel*	**abgesagt werden**	*to be called off, be canceled*
ändern	*to change*	**geändert werden**	*to be changed*
aus.nutzen	*to exploit*	**ausgenutzt werden**	*to be exploited*
bedienen	*to serve, wait on*	**bedient werden**	*to be served, be waited on*
behandeln	*to treat, deal with*	**behandelt werden**	*to be treated, be dealt with*
erledigen	*to take care of*	**erledigt werden**	*to be taken care of*
erwähnen	*to mention*	**erwähnt werden**	*to be mentioned*
loben	*to praise*	**gelobt werden**	*to be praised*
manipulieren	*to manipulate*	**manipuliert werden**	*to be manipulated*
unterbrechen	*to interrupt*	**unterbrochen werden**	*to be interrupted*
verwöhnen	*to spoil (someone)*	**verwöhnt werden**	*to be spoiled*

The Tenses in the Passive Voice

§3   THE PRESENT TENSE

Compare the following conjugations:

ACTIVE	PASSIVE
infinitive: **fragen**	infinitive: **gefragt werden**
ich frage *I ask, am asking*	ich **werde** gefragt *I am (being) asked*
du fragst	du **wirst** gefragt
er, sie, es fragt	er, sie, es **wird** gefragt
wir fragen	wir **werden** gefragt
ihr fragt	ihr **werdet** gefragt
sie fragen	sie **werden** gefragt
Sie fragen	Sie **werden** gefragt

werden + past participle

The auxiliary **werden** is conjugated;
the past participle remains the same.

Remember:

> In passive sentences, **werden** has to be rendered by a form of *to be*.

PRACTICE 2   *Translate into English.*

1. Das wird oft vergessen.
2. Diese Instrumente werden aus Schweden importiert.
3. Du wirst von deinen Großeltern verwöhnt.
4. Wir werden sehr unfair behandelt.
5. Ihr werdet wahrscheinlich ausgenutzt.
6. Dieser Punkt wird im ersten Kapitel erwähnt.
7. Werden Sie schon bedient?
8. Wird dieser Plan geändert?
9. Wie wird das Projekt finanziert?
10. Wie wird das gemacht?

Sometimes the best English equivalent of a German passive construction is in the active voice.

Fräulein Schmidt wird oft angerufen.
lit.: *Miss Schmidt is called often.*
idiom.: *Miss Schmidt gets lots of calls.*

Diese Spielzeuge werden gern gekauft.
lit.: *These toys are gladly bought.*
idiom.: *People like to buy these toys.*

When stating the English equivalent of a German passive construction, it is advisable to translate it first literally and then make the necessary adjustments to English usage. This sometimes means employing the generalizing *they* or *people* as a subject.

PRACTICE 3   *Translate into acceptable English.*

1. Ich werde oft von meinen Geschwistern[1] ausgelacht.
2. Barbara wird von uns allen beneidet.
3. Von wem wird diese Sache erledigt?
4. Diese Zeitung wird von jungen Leuten sehr gern gelesen.
5. Hier wird viel Obst[2] angebaut[3] und natürlich auch gegessen.

PRACTICE 4   *Convert the following sentences from the active to the passive voice.*

Model: Diese Verkäuferin bedient uns.
     Wir werden von dieser Verkäuferin bedient.

1. Der Autor erwähnt diesen Punkt.
2. Mein Mann verwöhnt mich.
3. Deine Frau manipuliert dich.
4. Die Regierung finanziert dieses Projekt.
5. Sein Chef lobt ihn oft.
6. Meine Freundin erledigt diese Sache.
7. Helga lacht dich aus.
8. Dieser Chef nutzt die Arbeiter aus.

§4   THE PAST, PRESENT PERFECT, PAST PERFECT, FUTURE, AND FUTURE PERFECT

You are familiar with the tenses of **werden** used as the main verb, meaning *to become.*

PRES.	Sie **wird** nervös.	*She is becoming nervous.*
PAST	Sie **wurde** nervös.	*She became nervous.*
PRES. PERF.	Sie **ist** nervös **geworden.**	*She has become nervous.*
		or: *She became nervous.*
PAST PERF.	Sie **war** nervös **geworden.**	*She had become nervous.*
FUT.	Sie **wird** nervös **werden.**	*She will become nervous.*
FUT. PERF.	Sie **wird** nervös **geworden sein.**	*She will have become nervous.*

When **werden** functions as the main verb, its principal parts are

werden (wird), wurde, ist geworden.

In the passive the auxiliary **werden** governs the tense of the sentence, and the form of its past participle is modified from **geworden** to **worden:**

1 **die Geschwister** (*pl.*)	brothers and sisters
2 **das Obst**	fruit
3 **an•bauen**	to grow, cultivate, plant

ACTIVE	PASSIVE

infinitive: **fragen**   infinitive: **gefragt werden**

PRESENT

Sie fragt nicht.   Sie wird nicht gefragt.

She does not ask.   *She is not (being) asked.*

PAST

Sie fragte nicht.   Sie wurde nicht gefragt.

She did not ask.   *She was not (being) asked.*

PRESENT PERFECT

Sie hat nicht gefragt.   Sie ist nicht | gefragt worden. |

She has not asked.   *She has not been asked.*

or: *She did not ask.*   or: *She was not (being) asked.*

PAST PERFECT

Sie hatte nicht gefragt.   Sie war nicht | gefragt worden. |

She had not asked.   *She had not been asked.*

FUTURE

Sie wird nicht fragen.   Sie wird nicht gefragt werden.

She will not ask.   *She will not be asked.*

FUTURE PERFECT

Sie wird nicht gefragt haben.   Sie wird nicht | gefragt worden | sein.

She will not have asked.   *She will not have been asked.*

Note: a. The past participle of the main verb, i.e. **gefragt,** does not change.

   b. **Werden** requires **sein;** thus the perfect tenses of the passive voice are formed with **sein.**

   c. As in the active voice, the future is formed with **werden** + infinitive of the main verb:

   Sie **wird** nicht **fragen.**   Sie **wird** nicht **gefragt werden.**

   active infinitive   passive infinitive

   d. The future perfect is hardly ever used in the passive. It will therefore not be practiced.

Pattern:

PRES.	sie **wird**	(past part.)		she is (being)	(past part.)
PAST	sie **wurde**	(past part.)		she was (being)	(past part.)
PRES. PERF.	sie **ist**	(past part.)	**worden**	she has been or: she was (being)	(past part.)
PAST PERF.	sie **war**	(past part.)	**worden**	she had been	(past part.)
FUT.	sie **wird**	(past part.)	**werden**	she will be	(past part.)

PRACTICE 5   *Express the following sentences in the tenses indicated and translate them into English.*

1. Herr Köhler wird ins Krankenhaus gebracht.   *Mr. Köhler is being taken to the hospital.*

    past
    pres. perf.
    past perf.
    future

2. Wird dieser Fall vom FBI untersucht?   *Is this case being investigated by the FBI?*

    past
    pres. perf.
    past perf.
    future

Conjugation of the tenses in the passive

PRESENT	ich werde gefragt	*I am (being) asked*
	du wirst	
er, sie, es	wird	
	wir werden	
	ihr werdet	
	sie werden	
	Sie werden	

PAST	ich wurde gefragt	*I was (being) asked*
	du wurdest	
er, sie, es	wurde	
	wir wurden	
	ihr wurdet	
	sie wurden	
	Sie wurden	

PRESENT PERFECT	ich bin gefragt worden	*I have been asked*
	du bist	*I was (being) asked*
er, sie, es	ist	
	wir sind	
	ihr seid	
	sie sind	
	Sie sind	

PAST PERFECT	ich war gefragt worden	*I had been asked*
	du warst	
er, sie, es	war	
	wir waren	
	ihr wart	
	sie waren	
	Sie waren	

FUTURE   ich werde gefragt werden   *I will be asked*
                               du wirst
                   er, sie, es wird
                              wir werden
                              ihr werdet
                              sie werden
                              Sie werden

PRACTICE 6   *Restate the following sentences in the tenses indicated.*

1. Du wirst von dieser Firma ausgenutzt. (pres. perf., past perf., fut.)
2. Ihr werdet nicht verwöhnt. (fut., pres. perf.)
3. Wir werden wie Stiefkinder[1] behandelt. (past, pres. perf.)
4. Die Fernsehsendung wird unterbrochen. (past, past perf., future)
5. Wie wird das neue Projekt finanziert? (fut., past)
6. Wird das Programm geändert? (fut.)
7. Warum wird Ulrike nicht gewarnt? (past, pres. perf.)
8. Wo wird Dieters Geburtstag gefeiert? (pres. perf.)
9. Warum wird das Konzert abgesagt? (past perf.)
10. Hoffentlich wird der Junge nicht verhaftet.[2] (pres. perf.)
11. Unser Haus wird am Montag versteigert.[3] (past)
12. Du wirst vielleicht befördert.[4] (fut.)
13. Das Picknick wird verschoben.[5] (past)
14. Hoffentlich werdet ihr nicht betrogen.[6] (pres. perf.)

§5   DEPENDENT WORD ORDER

The inflected verb form is in final position.

Ich glaube nicht, daß er von seinem Bruder betrogen **wird**.
                                        betrogen **wurde**.
                                        betrogen worden **ist**.
                                        betrogen worden **war**.
                                        betrogen werden **wird**.

PRACTICE 7   *Restate the following sentences, using dependent word order after the indicated introductory clauses.*

Model: Das Programm wurde geändert.
        Wissen Sie, warum ...
        Wissen Sie, warum das Programm geändert wurde?

1. Frank ist befördert worden.
   Weißt du, ob ...

1 **das Stiefkind, -er**	stepchild
2 **verhaften**	to arrest
3 **versteigern**	to auction off
4 **befördern**	to promote (*to a new position*)
5 **verschieben, verschob, verschoben**	to postpone
6 **betrügen, betrog, betrogen**	to cheat

2. Wann wird das nächste Kapitel behandelt?
   Können Sie mir sagen, wann ...
3. Die Prüfung ist verschoben worden.
   Wir sind überglücklich,[1] daß ...
4. Wie wird dieses Fenster aufgemacht?
   Wissen Sie, wie ...
5. Ist das Haus schon versteigert worden?
   Peter weiß vielleicht, ob ...
6. Von wem wurde das Projekt finanziert?
   Ich habe keine Ahnung, von wem ...
7. Ich werde wie ein Stiefkind behandelt.
   Ich möchte wissen, warum ...

PRACTICE 8 Summarizing exercise.

Translate into German.

1. a. The broadcast is being interrupted. **Die Sendung wird unterbrochen.**
   b. The broadcast has been interrupted.
   c. Why has the broadcast been interrupted?
   d. I have no idea why the broadcast has been interrupted.
2. a. They are being arrested. **Sie werden verhaftet.**
   b. They were arrested.
   c. Why were they arrested?
   d. Nobody knows why they were arrested.
3. a. This house is being auctioned off. **Dieses Haus wird versteigert.**
   b. It will be auctioned off.
   c. Will it be auctioned off?
   d. It has already been auctioned off.
   e. Too bad that it has already been auctioned off.
4. a. Why is the picnic being postponed? **Warum wird das Picknick verschoben?**
   b. Why has it been postponed?
   c. Will it be postponed?
   d. It will probably[2] be postponed.
5. a. The strike is being called off. **Der Streik wird abgesagt.**
   b. Has the strike been called off?
   c. Why has it been called off?
   d. It will probably be called off.
6. a. She is being promoted. **Sie wird befördert.**
   b. She was not promoted.
   c. Who has been promoted?
   d. Perhaps Klaus knows who has been promoted.
7. a. You are being exploited by this company. **Sie werden von dieser Firma ausgenutzt.**

1 **überglücklich**   overjoyed
2 **wohl**   probably

b. You will be exploited by this company.
c. Mr. Neumann had been exploited by this company.
d. I have never been exploited.
e. I cannot believe (it) that you have never been exploited. (fam. sing.)

Meanings of *werden*

In order to recognize the meaning of **werden** in a given context, you have to first determine whether it is accompanied by an adjective, a noun, or a verb.

1. **werden** + predicate adjective or predicate noun

   Es **wird** kälter.   *It **is getting** colder.*
   Er **wurde** Präsident.   *He **became** president.*

   Werden is the main verb. The English equivalent is ***to become, get.***

2. **werden** + verb

   When **werden** is an auxiliary, the main verb may be an infinitive or a past participle.
   a. If the verb is an infinitive, **werden** is the future auxiliary in the active voice.

      Sie **wird** den Fall **untersuchen**. *She **will investigate** the case.*

   b. If the verb is a past participle, **werden** is the passive auxiliary.

      Der Fall **wird untersucht**. *The case **is being investigated**.*

English equivalents of **werden**
- *to become, get* when used with adjective or noun
- *shall/will* when used with an infinitive (expressing the future tense)
- a form of *to be* when used with a past participle (expressing the passive)

PRACTICE 9   *Analyze the use of* **werden** *in the following sentences and translate them into English.*

Model: Ich fürchte, Sie werden mich auslachen.
       Werden + infinitive *auslachen* express the future tense.
       I am afraid you will laugh at me.

1. Niemand wird das glauben.
2. Dein Deutsch wird jeden Tag besser.

3. Das wird anders[1] gemacht.
4. Hoffentlich wirst du das verstehen.
5. Wie werden Sie Ihr Geld investieren?
6. Das Projekt wird von einem Millionär finanziert.
7. Hoffentlich wird es nicht kälter.
8. Ich fürchte, ich werde von Ihnen manipuliert.
9. Das wird nie passieren.
10. Dieses Projekt wird eine Katastrophe.

Miscellaneous Features of Passive Sentences

§6   THE AGENT PRECEDED BY *von, durch,* OR *mit*

In most passive sentences the agent is preceded by the preposition **von** (+ dat.).
Occasionally **durch** (+ acc.) is used to indicate the intermediary or the inanimate
means by which an action is brought about.

> Wir wurden **durch einen Boten** benachrichtigt.
> *We were notified through a messenger.*
> Die Kirche wurde **durch Bomben** zerstört.
> *The church was destroyed by bombs.*

The preposition **mit** (+ dat.) is used when the reference is to an instrument or a
tool. This parallels the English use of *with*.

> Die Tür wurde **mit einem Hauptschlüssel** geöffnet.
> *The door was opened with a master key.*

§7   INTRODUCTORY *es* IN PASSIVE SENTENCES

(Its use with active verbs is explained in Chap. 15, §5, 2.)
Es is often placed at the beginning of passive main clauses. It cannot be used in
questions or dependent clauses. Compare:

> **Viele Fabriken** werden geschlossen.
> SUBJECT
> **Es** werden **viele Fabriken** geschlossen.
> SUBJECT

Many factories are being closed.

Naturally, the verb agrees with the subject **viele Fabriken** rather than with **es**.

Es is omitted if another element is placed at the beginning of the sentence.
Compare:

> Einige Fragen wurden nicht beantwortet.
> **Es** wurden einige Fragen nicht beantwortet.

Some questions were not answered.

> **Leider** wurden einige Fragen nicht beantwortet.
> *Unfortunately, some questions were not answered.*

---

1 **anders**   different(ly)

§8   DATIVE OBJECTS IN PASSIVE SENTENCES

1. English permits either the direct or indirect object of an active sentence to become the subject of a passive sentence:

> ACTIVE   They awarded **this inventor the Nobel Prize.**
>   INDIR. OBJ.   DIRECT OBJ.

> PASSIVE   a. **The Nobel Prize** was awarded to this inventor.
>   SUBJECT

>   b. **This inventor** was awarded the Nobel Prize.
>   SUBJECT

In German, only the accusative (direct) object of the active sentence may become the subject of the passive voice:

> ACTIVE   Sie verliehen diesem Erfinder den Nobelpreis.

> PASSIVE   a. **Der Nobelpreis** wurde diesem Erfinder verliehen.
>   SUBJECT

>   b. **Diesem Erfinder** wurde **der Nobelpreis** verliehen.
>   INDIRECT OBJ.   SUBJECT

>   or: Es wurde **diesem Erfinder der Nobelpreis** verliehen.

In contrast to the English passive sentence *b*, the subject in the German passive sentence *b* is **der Nobelpreis,** the direct object of the active sentence. The indirect object **diesem Erfinder** is retained. It is frequently placed in first position, or it follows the inflected verb when an introductory **es** is used.

Additional examples:

> **Ihm** wurde auch eine französische Medaille verliehen.
> or: Es wurde **ihm** auch eine französische Medaille verliehen
> *He was also awarded a French medal.*

> **Mir** wurde eine zweite Chance gegeben.
> or: Es wurde **mir** eine zweite Chance gegeben.
> *I was given a second chance.*

> **Uns** wurden nur die Vorteile gezeigt, nicht die Nachteile.
> or: Es wurden **uns** nur die Vorteile gezeigt, nicht die Nachteile.
> *We were shown only the advantages, not the disadvantages.*

2. Dative verbs that lack accusative objects (cf. Chap. 5, §7), such as **danken, drohen** (*to threaten*), **gratulieren, helfen, widersprechen** (*to contradict*), can form only subjectless passives, since there is no accusative object in the active sentence to become the subject in the passive. The verb is in the third person singular. An introductory **es** is frequently added. Compare:

ACTIVE   Man hat mir nie geholfen.

PASSIVE   **Mir** ist nie geholfen worden.
    or: **Es** ist **mir** nie geholfen worden.
        I have never been helped.

ACTIVE   Man gratuliert ihm.

PASSIVE   **Ihm** wird gratuliert.
    or: **Es** wird **ihm** gratuliert.
        He is being congratulated.

3. The implied subject of a passive verb may be a dependent clause or an infinitive phrase:

Mir wurde gesagt,
    or: **Es** wurde **mir** gesagt, } daß sie Margot Bauer heißt.

I was told that her name is Margot Bauer.

Ihm wurde geraten,
    or: **Es** wurde **ihm** geraten, } weniger aggressiv zu sein.

He was advised to be less aggressive.

PRACTICE 10   A. *Restate the following sentences in the present, past, and present perfect of the passive. Begin the sentence with the boldface dative pronouns.*

Model: Man hilft **mir** nicht.
        Mir wird nicht geholfen.
        Mir wurde nicht geholfen.
        Mir ist nicht geholfen worden.

1. Man dankt **mir** nicht.
2. Man widerspricht **ihr** selten.
3. Man gibt **ihm** eine zweite Chance.
4. Man zeigt **mir** das Geschenk für Marlene nicht.

B. *Translate into English.*

1. Mir wurde gesagt, daß ich mehr arbeiten sollte.
2. Es wurde ihr geraten, eine Bewerbung[1] einzureichen.
3. Es wurde mir nicht die Gelegenheit[2] gegeben, mich zu verteidigen.[3]
4. Uns wurde die Erlaubnis erteilt,[4] hier zu zelten.[5]
5. Es wurde den streikenden Arbeitern mit Entlassung gedroht.[6]

1 **die Bewerbung, -en**	application
2 **die Gelegenheit, -en**	opportunity, chance
3 **sich verteidigen**	to defend oneself
4 **die Erlaubnis erteilen**	to give permission
5 **zelten**	to camp (*in a tent*)
6 **mit Entlassung drohen**	to threaten with dismissal

§9   PASSIVES WHICH LACK BOTH SUBJECT AND OBJECT

The following sentences illustrate a peculiar passive construction.

Es wurde nicht applaudiert.	*There was no applause (applauding).*
Leider wurde nicht applaudiert.	*Unfortunately, there was no applause (applauding).*

There is neither a subject nor an object; the verb is in the third person singular. The introductory **es** is not used when another element is in first position.

Passives which lack both subject and object are often difficult to translate into English.

Es wird hier viel gestohlen.
or: **Hier wird viel gestohlen.**
> *There is a lot of stealing going on around here.*

Es wurde viel gegessen und getrunken.
or: **Da wurde viel gegessen und getrunken.**
> *There was a lot of eating and drinking going on.*
> *They ate and drank a lot.*

Heute wird gefaulenzt.[1]
> *Today we are loafing.*
> *Today I am loafing.*

The subject has to be supplied according to the context.

Occasionally, this construction has the force of a command:

Hier wird nicht geraucht!
> *No smoking here.*

PRACTICE 11   *Translate into English.*

1. Ihr faulenzt schon wieder. Heute wird gearbeitet!
2. Kinder, warum paßt ihr nicht auf? Hier wird aufgepaßt!
3. Es wird zuviel geschwänzt.
4. Warum ist es so laut im Nachbarhaus?—Ach, da wird heute gefeiert.
5. Wie feiert ihr das Semesterende?—Meistens wird getanzt.
6. Wie wollt ihr gegen die neue Anordnung[2] protestieren?—Es wird einfach gestreikt.

§10   MODAL AUXILIARIES IN PASSIVE SENTENCES

In passive sentences modal auxiliaries usually occur in two tenses: the present and the simple past.

---

1 **faulenzen**	to loaf
2 **die Anordnung, -en**	regulation, rule

The present tense

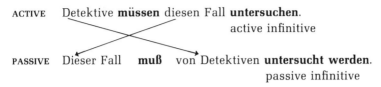

ACTIVE   Detektive **müssen** diesen Fall **untersuchen.**

active infinitive

PASSIVE   Dieser Fall   **muß**   von Detektiven **untersucht werden.**

passive infinitive

This case has to be investigated by detectives.

Note: a. The direct object of the active sentence, **diesen Fall,** becomes the subject of the passive setence, **dieser Fall.**

b. The modal must agree with the subject, thus **müssen** becomes **muß.**

c. The infinitive **untersuchen** becomes **untersucht werden,** which is the passive infinitive.

Keep in mind:

> The modal is not in the passive, but it is complemented by a passive infinitive.

Here are some active and passive infinitives which occur in the exercises:

ACTIVE		PASSIVE	
benachrichtigen	*to notify*	**benachrichtigt werden**	*to be notified*
ein•reichen	*to hand in*	**eingereicht werden**	*to be handed in*
klären	*to clarify*	**geklärt werden**	*to be clarified*
lösen	*to solve*	**gelöst werden**	*to be solved*
stören	*to disturb*	**gestört werden**	*to be disturbed*
übersehen	*to overlook*	**übersehen werden**	*to be overlooked*
vergessen	*to forget*	**vergessen werden**	*to be forgotten*
vermeiden	*to avoid*	**vermieden werden**	*to be avoided*
voraus•sehen	*to foresee*	**vorausgesehen werden**	*to be foreseen*

PRACTICE 12   A. *Add the German passive infinitives.*

Model: Dieser Punkt muß sofort _____ . *(be clarified)*
Dieser Punkt muß sofort geklärt werden.

1. Solche Fehler können leicht _____ . *(be overlooked)*
2. Die Semesterarbeit soll am Freitag _____ . *(be handed in)*
3. Das kann nicht _____ . *(be avoided)*
4. Das darf nicht[1] _____ . *(be forgotten)*
5. Fischers müssen sofort _____ . *(be notified)*
6. Der Chef will nicht _____ . *(be disturbed)*
7. Solche Dinge können nicht _____ . *(be foreseen)*
8. Die Arbeiter wollen nicht _____ . *(be exploited)*

---

1 **nicht dürfen**   must not (cf. Chap. 4, §14)

B. *Express the following sentences in the passive omitting the agent.*

Model: Wir müssen ihn sofort benachrichtigen.
      Er muß sofort benachrichtigt werden.

1. Wir müssen ihn warnen.
2. Wir müssen dieses Problem lösen.
3. Ich muß diesen Fehler vermeiden.
4. Ich kann diesen Fall sofort klären.
5. Du darfst den Redner nicht unterbrechen.
6. Wir können die Chefin nicht manipulieren.

The simple past

The modal as the inflected verb is in the past tense (cf. Chap. 4, §2); the passive infinitive remains unchanged. Compare:

ACTIVE	PASSIVE
Ich **mußte** ihn **benachrichtigen.**	Er **mußte benachrichtigt werden**.
	He had to be notified.
Ich **konnte** ihn **benachrichtigen**	Er **konnte benachrichtigt werden**
	He could be notified.
Ich **wollte** ihn **benachrichtigen**	Er **wollte benachrichtigt werden**
	He wanted to be notified.
Ich **sollte** ihn **benachrichtigen**	Er **sollte benachrichtigt werden**
	He was supposed to be notified.

Dependent word order

The inflected modal is in final position.

Ich nehme an, daß er benachrichtigt werden **muß.**
Schade, daß er nicht benachrichtigt werden **konnte.**

PRACTICE 13   *Translate into German.*

1. a. They are exploiting us.   **Sie nutzen uns aus.**
   b. We don't want to be exploited.
   c. We didn't want to be exploited.
2. a. We have to avoid that.   **Wir müssen das vermeiden.**
   b. That has to be avoided.
   c. That had to be avoided.
3. a. They want to manipulate me.   **Sie wollen mich manipulieren.**
   b. I don't want to be manipulated.
   c. Nobody wants to be manipulated.
   d. We didn't want to be manipulated.
4. a. We must notify his family.   **Wir müssen seine Familie benachrichtigen.**
   b. His family must be notified.
   c. I assume that his family must be notified.

5. a. We are supposed to hand in the term paper on Monday. **Wir sollen die Semesterarbeit am Montag einreichen.**
   b. The term paper is supposed to be handed in on Monday.
   c. It was supposed to be handed in on Monday.
   d. Is it true that it was supposed to be handed in on Monday?
6. a. We have to solve this problem. **Wir müssen dieses Problem lösen.**
   b. This problem has to be solved.
   c. It had to be solved.
   d. It cannot be solved.
   e. Unfortunately, it could not be solved.
   f. Too bad that it could not be solved.

The present perfect, past perfect, and future

The tenses of passive sentences with modal auxiliaries parallel their active counterparts. The passive sentences are distinguished merely by the presence of a passive infinitive in place of the active infinitive of the main verb. Compare:

active infinitive: **fragen**   passive infinitive: **gefragt werden**

to ask   *to be asked*

PRESENT PERFECT

Ich habe ihn nie **fragen müssen.**   Er hat nie **gefragt werden müssen.**

(double infinitive)   (double infinitive)

*I have never had **to ask** him.*   *He has never had **to be asked**.*

PAST PERFECT

Ich hatte ihn **fragen müssen.**   Er hatte **gefragt werden müssen.**

(double infinitive)   (double infinitive)

*I had had **to ask** him.*   *He had had **to be asked**.*

FUTURE

Ich werde ihn **fragen müssen.**   Er wird **gefragt werden müssen.**

(double infinitive)   (double infinitive)

*I will have **to ask** him.*   *He will have **to be asked**.*

These awkward passive constructions are rarely used and will therefore not be practiced.

§11   THE STATAL PASSIVE

Ordinarily, passive sentences describe a process: something is, was, or will be done to the subject. For many passive sentences, there is also a *statal* counterpart, as the following examples illustrate.

1. a. Die Tür **wird geschlossen.**   *The door is being closed.*
   b. Die Tür **ist geschlossen.**   *The door is closed (= not open).*
2. a. Mein Wagen **wird repariert.**   *My car is being repaired.*
   b. Mein Wagen **ist repariert.**   *My car is repaired*
                                         (= back in working order).

Sentences 1. a and 2. a indicate the process of closing and repairing; sentences 1. b and 2. b denote the result of that process, i.e. a state or condition. The latter, called *statal passives*, employ **sein**; the past participles **geschlossen** and **repariert** function as predicate adjectives.

PRACTICE 14   A. *Translate into English.* (**Doch** is used for emphasis; cf. Appendix, §4.)

    1. Der Krieg wird nicht verloren, er ist doch schon verloren.
    2. Hoffentlich wird die Prüfung verschoben.—Sie ist doch schon verschoben.
    3. Werde ich zu eurer Hochzeit eingeladen?—Du bist doch schon eingeladen.
    4. Hoffentlich wird der Streit[1] bald vergessen.—Er ist doch schon vergessen.

    B. *Translate the responses into German using* **doch.**

    1. Wann wird diese Sache erledigt?

       _____

       It is already taken care of.
    2. Hoffentlich wird dieses Problem bald gelöst.

       _____

       It is already solved.
    3. Wann werden diese Rechnungen endlich bezahlt?

       _____

       They are already paid.
    4. Wird dieses herrliche Schloß[2] wirklich verkauft?

       _____

       It is already sold.

A note on the use of *geboren werden* and *geboren sein*

    a. Wann **wurde** Lincoln **geboren?**   When *was* Lincoln **born?**
    b. Wann **sind** Sie **geboren?**   When *were* you **born?**
       (lit.: *When are you born?*)
    c. Ich **bin** 1960 **geboren.**   *I was born* in 1960.

The three English sentences are in the simple past of the passive voice. German uses the simple past of the passive voice for the dead, as in *a*, and the present statal forms for the living, as in *b* and *c*. However, a living person frequently uses the simple past of the passive voice when listing biographical data in a personal report, such as a curriculum vitae:

    Ich **wurde** am 5. Mai 1960 in Düsseldorf **geboren.**

---

    1 **der Streit, -e**   quarrel, fight
    2 **das Schloß, ¨-sser**   castle

Alternatives to the Passive Voice

The passive voice is used less in German than in English. Here are some German alternative constructions.

§12   THE USE OF *man*

The most common alternative to the passive is the use of **man** as the subject of a sentence in the active voice.

PASSIVE   **Der Autor** wird nicht erwähnt.   *The author is not mentioned.*
ACTIVE   **Man** erwähnt **den Autor** nicht.   *They don't mention the author.*
          (lit.: *One doesn't mention the author.*)

The subject of the passive sentence becomes the direct object of the active sentence with **man** as the subject.

PRACTICE 15   *Express the following sentences in the active voice, using* **man** *as the subject. Follow the models of sentences 1.*

A. PRESENT

1. Ich werde nie gelobt.
   Man lobt mich nie.
2. Ich werde nicht gefragt.
3. Er wird ausgelacht.
4. Wir werden nicht verwöhnt.

B. PAST

1. Sein Vorschlag wurde ignoriert.
   Man ignorierte seinen Vorschlag.
2. Das Geld wurde investiert.
3. Der Fall wurde untersucht.
4. Die Arbeit wurde nicht gut bezahlt.

C. PRESENT PERFECT

1. Der Fehler ist übersehen worden.
   Man hat den Fehler übersehen.
2. Der Plan ist geändert worden.
3. Ich bin ausgenutzt worden.
4. Du bist betrogen worden.

D. PAST PERFECT

1. Alle Studenten waren benachrichtigt worden.
   Man hatte alle Studenten benachrichtigt.
2. Die Kritik war falsch interpretiert worden.
3. Der Scheck war noch nicht eingelöst worden.
4. Er war nicht fair behandelt worden.

E. FUTURE

1. Er wird wohl nicht befördert werden.
   Man wird ihn wohl nicht befördern.
2. Du wirst wohl nicht verwöhnt werden.
3. Ich werde vielleicht ausgenutzt werden.
4. Diese Arbeit wird gut bezahlt werden.

F. VARIOUS TENSES

1. Der Fall wird untersucht.
2. Der Fall wird untersucht werden.
3. Ich bin manipuliert worden.
4. Der Dieb ist verhaftet worden.
5. Mein Vorschlag war zweimal ignoriert worden.
6. Ich werde nicht verwöhnt.
7. Helga wird wie ein Stiefkind behandelt.
8. Wir wurden nicht gefragt.
9. Ich werde wohl nicht gefragt werden.
10. Der Autor ist nicht erwähnt worden.

The following alternatives to the passive are far less common than the **man**-construction.

§13 THE USE OF *sein* + *zu* + INFINITIVE

> Hunde **sind** an der Leine **zu führen.**
> *Dogs **are to be kept** on a leash.*
> or: *Dogs **must be kept** on a leash.*

> **Ist** Fräulein Berger telefonisch **zu erreichen**?
> *Can Miss Berger **be reached** by phone?*

Such constructions indicate that something is to be done, must be done, or can be done. They also occur in the past tense:

> Die Katastrophe **war** nicht **vorauszusehen.**
> *The catastrophe **could** not **be foreseen.**

Note that verbs with separable prefixes have **zu** inserted between prefix and verb, as in the example above.

PRACTICE 16 *Restate the following sentences using **sein** + **zu** + infinitive as alternative to the passive.*

> **Model:** Diese Rechnungen müssen sofort bezahlt werden.
> **Diese Rechnungen sind sofort zu bezahlen.**

1. Diese zwei Punkte müssen noch geklärt werden.
2. Peters Eltern müssen sofort benachrichtigt werden.
3. Dieser Fehler muß unbedingt vermieden werden.

4. Dieses hohe Ziel[1] kann bestimmt nicht erreicht werden.
5. Diese Entwicklung[2] konnte nicht vorausgesehen werden.
6. Seine Schuld[3] kann nicht bewiesen[4] werden.
7. Frau Neumanns Schuld konnte auch nicht bewiesen werden.
8. Der Rechtsanwalt konnte telefonisch nicht erreicht werden.

§14   THE USE OF REFLEXIVE VERBS

1. **lassen** + **sich** + infinitive is frequently used as a substitute for **können** + passive infinitive.

Das kann nicht vorausgesehen werden.⎫
Das läßt sich nicht voraussehen. ⎬ *That cannot be foreseen.*

Das konnte nicht vorausgesehen werden.⎫
Das ließ sich nicht voraussehen. ⎬ *That could not be foreseen.*

Idiom: | **Das/Es läßt sich nicht ändern.** *That/It cannot be helped.*
Das/Es ließ sich nicht ändern. *That/It could not be helped.*

2. Some other verbs permit the reflexive to substitute for the passive.

Dieses Wort wird anders geschrieben.⎫
Dieses Wort schreibt sich anders. ⎬ *This word is spelled differently.*

Wie wird Ihr Name ausgesprochen?⎫
Wie spricht sich Ihr Name aus? ⎬ *How is your name pronounced?*

Expression:

Das versteht sich.   ⎫ *That is understood. That goes without*
or: **Das versteht sich von selbst.**⎬ *saying.*

PRACTICE 17 A. *Restate the following sentences using* **lassen** + **sich** + *infinitive as alternative to the passive.*

Model: Das kann nicht vermieden werden.
         Das läßt sich nicht vermeiden.

1. Das kann nicht bewiesen werden.
2. Das konnte nicht bewiesen werden.
3. Dein Wunsch kann leicht erfüllt werden.
4. Dieser Wunsch konnte nicht erfüllt werden.
5. Meine Enttäuschung[5] kann nicht in Worten ausgedrückt[6] werden.

---

1 **das Ziel, -e**   goal
2 **die Entwicklung, -en**   development
3 **die Schuld**   guilt
4 **beweisen, bewies, bewiesen** to prove
5 **die Enttäuschung, -en**   disappointment
6 **aus•drücken**   to express

B. *Restate the following sentences, using the reflexive verb as alternative to the passive.*

Model: Hoffentlich wird bald eine Lösung gefunden.
Hoffentlich findet sich bald eine Lösung.

1. Hoffentlich wird bald ein Ausweg[1] aus diesem Dilemma gefunden.
2. Dieses Wort wird anders ausgesprochen.
3. Wie wird Ihr Name geschrieben?
4. Diese Tür wird automatisch geschlossen.
5. Solche Gerüchte werden schnell verbreitet.[2]

PRACTICE 18   A. *The following sentences illustrate various features of the passive voice and its alternatives. Translate them into acceptable English.*

1.   X: Habe ich Ihren Namen richtig ausgesprochen?
     Y: Nein. Er spricht sich anders aus.
2.   X: Die Situation ist hoffnungslos.
     Y: Vielleicht findet sich noch ein Ausweg.
3.   X: Willst du wirklich Tierarzt werden?
     Y: Ja. Hoffentlich läßt sich dieser Wunsch erfüllen.
4.   X: Von hier aus haben wir einen schönen Blick auf die Stadt.
     Y: Und in der Ferne[3] sind sogar die Alpen zu sehen.
5.   X: Bei dem Bankrott[4] der Firma Neubert haben wir viel Geld verloren.
     Y: Wir auch. Dieser Bankrott war nicht vorauszusehen.
6.   X: Wie ich höre, haben Sie in der Lotterie gewonnen.
     Y: Ich bin überglücklich. Meine Freude läßt sich nicht in Worten ausdrücken.
7.   X: Werden Sie schon bedient?
     Y: Hoffentlich werde ich noch von der Verkäuferin da drüben bedient.
8.   X: Passen Sie gut auf Ihre Sachen auf!
     Y: Warum? Wird hier viel gestohlen?
9.   X: Hoffentlich schickst du mir eine Ansichtskarte[5] von Berlin.
     Y: Natürlich. Das versteht sich von selbst.
10. X: Hast du schon das Neuste gehört? Ich habe einen Job gefunden.
     Y: Großartig. Das muß unbedingt gefeiert werden.
11. X: Ich glaube nicht, daß Gisela gestern wirklich krank war. Sie ist in der Stadt gesehen worden.
     Y: Hat man sie da wirklich gesehen?

1 **der Ausweg, -e**	way out
2 **verbreiten**	to spread
3 **in der Ferne**	in the distance
4 **der Bankrott**	bankruptcy
5 **die Ansichtskarte, -n**	picture postcard *or simply* postcard

12.   X: Kann dieser Stoff[1] gewaschen werden?

        Y: Natürlich läßt er sich waschen.

13.   X: Es ist schade, daß du kein Stipendium bekommen hast.

        Y: Ja, das ist schade, aber es läßt sich nicht ändern.

14.   X: Spricht man in diesem Laden[2] Deutsch?

        Y: Da ist ein Schild[3] „Hier wird Deutsch gesprochen."

15.   X: Wie wird diese Flasche aufgemacht?

        Y: Frag doch Dieter! Er weiß, wie alle Flaschen aufgemacht werden.

16.   X: Wissen Sie, wann Schuberts umziehen?

        Y: Mir wurde gesagt, daß sie nächste Woche umziehen.

17. a. X: Wann sind Sie geboren?

        Y: Ich bin am 14. August 1950 geboren.

    b. X: Und in welchem Jahr ist Ihr Mann geboren?

        Y: Mein Mann lebt nicht mehr. Er wurde 1940 geboren.

18. a. X: Warum warst du auf der Party bei Zimmermanns so still?

        Y: Mir wurde von einem guten Freund geraten, nicht soviel zu reden.

    b. X: Wir alle reden zuviel und handeln[4] zu wenig.

        Y: Ja, das ist ein altes Problem: Es wird zuviel geredet und nicht genug gehandelt.

B. *Form sentences that fit the context.*

1. Sie sind froh, daß das Semester bald zu Ende ist. Sie sagen zu ihren Freunden:

    „das Semesterende / müssen / gefeiert"

2. Annerose sagt, daß sie älter ist als Sie. Sie können das nicht glauben und fragen sie:

    „in welchem Jahr / geboren?"

3. Sie sind in einer Buchhandlung und blättern (leaf) durch ein paar Bücher. Ein Verkäufer kommt und fragt Sie:

    „schon / bedient?"

4. Sie besuchen einen Freund und stellen Ihr Fahrrad hinters Haus. Dann fragen Sie Ihren Freund:

    „hier / gestohlen?"

5. Sie haben einen Kanister Farbe (paint) gekauft, können ihn aber nicht aufmachen. Sie fragen Ihre Schwester:

    „wie / aufgemacht?"

---

1 **der Stoff, -e**   material
2 **der Laden, ⸚**   store
3 **das Schild, -er**   sign
4 **handeln**   to act

6. Ihr Freund fragt sie, warum sie nicht gern zu politischen Versamm-
lungen (meetings) gehen. Sie antworten:

   „ zuviel geredet / nicht genug gehandelt "

7. Sie mußten das ganze Wochenende die Nase ins Buch stecken und für
eine Prüfung lernen. Sie sagen:

   „ das / schrecklich / sein,—aber es / sich nicht ändern lassen " (past)

8. Ihr Freund fragt Sie, ob Sie ihn verteidigen würden, wenn jemand
etwas Schlechtes über ihn sagte. Sie antworten:

   „ das / von selbst / sich verstehen "

19

The Position of Objects, Adverbial Modifiers, and Complements; Variations in the Sequence of Elements

KEY TO THE EXERCISES ON CASSETTE 10.
RUNNING TIME: APPROX. 20 MIN.

This chapter supplements what has been said about German word order in previous chapters (Chap. 1; 5, §4, 3; 6, §10; 8, §6; 12, §1 to §3; 17, §1 and §2 [Note]).

The Position of Objects

§1   THE SEQUENCE OF DIRECT AND INDIRECT OBJECTS

The indirect object (usually a person) precedes the direct object (usually a thing), unless the latter is a personal pronoun.

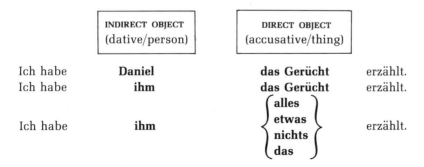

	INDIRECT OBJECT (dative/person)	DIRECT OBJECT (accusative/thing)	
Ich habe	**Daniel**	**das Gerücht**	erzählt.
Ich habe	**ihm**	**das Gerücht**	erzählt.
Ich habe	**ihm**	**alles etwas nichts das**	erzählt.

349

When the direct object is a personal pronoun, however, the sequence is reversed. (For the cases of pers. pronouns, see Chap. 6, §9)

DIRECT OBJECT	INDIRECT OBJECT	
Ich habe	**es**	**Daniel**	erzählt.
Ich habe	**es**	**ihm**	erzählt.

Note:
> Ich habe **es ihm** erzählt.
> but: Ich habe **ihm das** erzählt.

Since **das** is a demonstrative pronoun rather than a personal pronoun, it follows the personal pronoun indirect object.

PRACTICE 1   *Insert the objects in parentheses in the proper sequence.*

1. X: Wer hat _____ gesagt? (das / dir)
   Y: Elke hat _____ gesagt. (es / mir)

2. X: Hat die Polizistin _____ gegeben? (einen Strafzettel / dem Fahrer)
   Y: Ich glaube nicht, daß sie _____ gegeben hat. (einen Strafzettel / ihm)

3. X: Hast du _____ erklärt? (deinem Freund / die Hausaufgaben)
   Y: Ich habe versucht, _____ zu erklären. (ihm / sie)

4. X: Bitte erklären Sie _____! (diese grammatische Konstruktion / mir)
   Y: Fragen Sie doch den Assistenten! Er wird _____ erklären. (sie / Ihnen)

5. a. X: Hast du _____ nachgeschickt?[1] (die Post / Dieter)
      Y: Helga hat _____ nachgeschickt. (sie / ihm)
   b. X: Hat sie _____ nachgeschickt? (ihm / auch die Zeitungen)
      Y: Sie hat _____ nachgeschickt. (alles / ihm)

6. X: Ich möchte _____ zum Geburtstag schenken. (Helga / etwas)
   Y: Ich kann _____ schenken, denn ich bin wieder einmal pleite. (nichts / ihr)

7. X: Hat die Chefin _____ gegeben? (eine Gehaltserhöhung / der Sekretärin)
   Y: Soviel ich weiß, hat sie _____ gegeben. (ihr / keine Gehaltserhöhung)

8. X: Wollen Sie _____ zeigen? (die Dias / den Studenten)
   Y: Ich habe _____ schon gezeigt. (ihnen / sie)

---

1 **die Post nach•schicken**   to forward the mail

9. X: Wer hat _____ gegeben? (Ihnen / das)
    Y: Meine Nachbarin hat _____ gegeben. (mir / es)

§2   THE POSITION OF PREPOSITIONAL OBJECTS AND da-COMPOUNDS

Prepositional objects and **da**-compounds usually follow pronoun objects and noun objects.

personal or reflexive pronouns	other pronouns or nouns	prepositions + pronouns or nouns, **da**-compounds

Ich habe		ein Paket	von meinen Eltern	bekommen.
Ich habe	es		von ihnen	bekommen.
Ich habe		das / alles / etwas / nichts	von ihnen	bekommen.
Ich habe	ihnen		dafür	gedankt.
Er hat	sich		über die Einladung	gefreut.

PRACTICE 2   *Insert the elements in parentheses in the proper sequence.*

1. X: Haben Sie _____ besprochen?[1] (mit Ihrer Frau / diesen Plan)
    Y: Natürlich habe ich _____ besprochen. (mit ihr / ihn)
2. X: Hast du _____ gewarnt? (Herrn Berger / vor dieser Gefahr)
    Y: Ich habe versucht, _____ zu warnen. (davor / ihn)
3. X: Hat Barbara den Führerschein bekommen?
    Y: Ja. Du kannst _____ gratulieren. (dazu / ihr)
4. X: Haben Sie _____ entschuldigt? (sich / bei[2] Andreas)
    Y: Ich habe vergessen, _____ zu entschuldigen. (bei ihm / mich)
5. X: Leider habe ich vergessen, _____ mitzubringen. (für Helga / das Geburtstagsgeschenk)
    Y: Und ich habe vergessen, _____ mitzubringen. (für sie / die Geburtstagskarte)
6. X: Michael hat _____ erzählt. (von dieser Sache / nichts / mir)
    Y: Und du? Hast du _____ erzählt? (etwas / davon / ihm)
7. X: Hoffentlich gewöhnen Sie _____. (sich / an dieses Klima)
    Y: Ich glaube, es ist nicht sehr schwer, _____ zu gewöhnen. (daran / sich)

---

1 **besprechen (bespricht), besprach, besprochen**   to discuss, talk about
2 **sich entschuldigen bei** (*dat.*)   to apologize to

The Position of Adverbial Modifiers and Complements

§3   THE POSITION OF ADVERBIAL MODIFIERS

Adverbial modifiers include simple adverbs, such as **heute, dort, gut,** or phrases, such as **diesen Freitag, in diesem Monat, in der Stadt, mit dem Bus.** For simplicity's sake both will be called *adverbs* here.

An adverb often stands at the beginning of a main clause.

> **Gestern** war ich nicht in der Vorlesung.
> **Dort** steht mein Wagen.

Otherwise adverbs normally have the following positions:

1. **Adverbs of time** (answering the question *when?*), such as **oft, manchmal, immer, vorher** (*before*), **nachher** (*afterwards*), **heute, nach der Deutschstunde, vor ein paar Minuten** (*a few minutes **ago***), occur early in the sentence, following personal pronouns and usually preceding all other elements.

   > Ich rufe dich **nach der Deutschstunde** an.
   > *I am going to call you after German class.*
   >
   > Haben Sie **manchmal** Schwierigkeiten mit Ihren Nachbarn?
   > *Do you sometimes have trouble with your neighbors?*
   >
   > Ich habe vor, Sie **morgen** zu besuchen.
   > *I am planning to visit you tomorrow.*

2. **Adverbs of place** (answering the question *where/at what place?*), such as **dort, da drüben** (*over there*), **vorn** (*in front*), **hinten** (*behind, in the back*), **oben** (*at the top, upstairs*), **unten** (*at the bottom, below, downstairs*), **bei Müllers** (*at the Müllers'*), **auf einer Party** (*at a party*), come toward the end of the sentence and follow adverbs of time. This is unlike English, in which adverbs of place precede adverbs of time.

   > Wir sind nur ein paar Tage **in Hamburg** geblieben.
   > *We stayed in Hamburg only a few days.*
   >
   > Ich war gestern abend **bei Köhlers.**
   > *I was at the Köhlers' last night.*

Do not confuse the following adverbs and prepositions:

> ADVERBS
> **vorn—hinten**
> Frank sitzt **vorn,** and Käte sitzt **hinten.**
> *Frank sits in front and Käte sits in the back.*
>
> **oben—unten**
> Helga wohnt **oben,** und Ute wohnt **unten.**
> *Helga lives upstairs, and Ute lives downstairs.*

PREPOSITIONS (preceding nouns or pronouns)

vor—hinter

Frank sitzt **vor mir,** und Käte sitzt **hinter mir.**
Frank sits in front of me and Käte sits behind me.

über—unter

Helga wohnt **über mir,** und Ute wohnt **unter mir.**
Helga lives above me, and Ute lives below me.

The prepositional phrases **vor mir, hinter mir, über mir,** and **unter mir** function as adverbs of place.

3. **Other adverbs** generally follow pronouns and nouns. When they occur with adverbs of time and place, they normally follow expressions of time but precede expressions of place. In our examples we shall concentrate on **adverbs of manner** (answering the questions *how? in what way?*). Many such adverbs are identical to adjectives, for instance, **schnell, langsam, gut, schlecht, freundlich, höflich** (*polite*). They also include prepositional phrases, such as **mit dem Bus (Wagen, Zug), zu Fuß** (*on foot*), **mit lauter (leiser) Stimme** (*in a loud [low] voice*).

Sie hat mich **gestern   höflich**   gegrüßt.
                     TIME   MANNER
She greeted me politely yesterday.

Wir sind **langsam   durch den Park**   gelaufen.
              MANNER   PLACE
We walked slowly through the park.

Wir sind **heute nachmittag   langsam   durch den Park**   gelaufen.
                 TIME   MANNER   PLACE
We walked slowly through the park this afternoon.

PRACTICE 3   *Insert the adverbs in parentheses in the proper sequence.*

1. Wir haben vor, _____ zu bleiben. (im Schwarzwald / eine Woche)
2. Ich habe ihn _____ kennengelernt. (auf einer Party / vor einem Jahr)
3. Meine Freundin hat _____ gestanden. (am Fenster / still)
4. Unser Hund ist _____ gerannt. (bellend / um das ganze Haus)
5. Zwei Studenten haben _____ protestiert. (mit lauter Stimme / gestern)
6. Peter hat _____ gesessen. (vor mir / oft)
7. Sitzt du _____? (vorn / immer)
8. Ich sitze _____ (manchmal / hinten)
9. Ich glaube, Karin hat _____ gesessen. (hinter mir / gestern)
10. Wir wohnen _____. (oben / seit Montag)

11. Schuberts wohnen _____ . (jetzt / unten)

12. Wir sind _____ gefahren. (mit dem Wagen / um den See)

13. Renate und ich sind _____ gelaufen. (den Fluß entlang / am Sonntag / zu Fuß)

14. Kästners haben uns gebeten, sie _____ zu besuchen. (nächsten Sonnabend / in ihrem Wochenendhaus)

15. Weißt du nicht, daß der Bericht[1] _____ gestanden hat? (in der Zeitung / vorige Woche)

16. Ich habe Lisa _____ gesehen. (beim Friseur / vor ein paar Minuten)

17. Lehmanns wollen _____ fahren. (mit dem Dampfer[2] / auf dem Rhein / morgen)

§4   THE POSITION OF VERB COMPLEMENTS

In this book the term "verb complements" is used for certain sentence elements which have a particularly close relationship to the verb and may be said to *complete its meaning*. They stand at the end of a clause, immediately before the final verb elements (if any). The main complement types are listed below.

1. Predicate adjectives and predicate nouns

(Cf. Chap. 1, §7)

    a. Rainer ist **krank**.

    b. Rainer ist schon eine Woche **krank**.   *Rainer has been ill for a week.*

    a. Sie ist **Journalistin**.

    b. Sie ist seit einem Jahr **Journalistin**.   *She has been a journalist for a year.*

    a. Er ist **Lehrer** geworden.

    b. Er ist vor zwei Jahren **Lehrer** geworden.   *He became a teacher two years ago.*

Note that most other sentence elements must precede the predicate adjective or noun. However, prepositional phrases may often stand either before or after a predicate adjective (cf. Chap. 8, §2).

    Sie ist **zu mir** sehr nett.
    or: Sie ist sehr nett **zu mir**. } She is very nice to me.

2. Necessary adjuncts of verb phrases

    a. Many common noun objects, adjectives, adverbs, and prepositional phrases are construed to be verb complements and therefore stand at the end of the clause, followed only by closing verb forms.

    Examples:

    Tennis (Fußball, Karten, Schach, Klavier) spielen
        Wir haben gestern hinter dem Studentenheim **Fußball** gespielt.
        We played soccer behind the dormitory yesterday.

1 **der Bericht, -e**   report
2 **der Dampfer, -**   steamship

zu Mittag (zu Abend) essen   *to have lunch (dinner)*
Wir haben in einem kleinen Restaurant **zu Mittag** gegessen.
We had lunch in a little restaurant.

die Wahrheit sagen   *to tell the truth*
Haben Sie auf der Polizeiwache **die Wahrheit** gesagt?
Did you tell the truth at the police station?

auswendig lernen   *to learn by heart, memorize*
Ich nehme an, daß wir das Gedicht **auswendig** lernen müssen.
I assume that we have to memorize the poem.

ernst nehmen   *to take seriously*
Man kann nicht alles, was er sagt, **ernst** nehmen.
One can't take everything he says seriously.

einen Kompromiß schließen   *to compromise, make a compromise*
Ich werde versuchen, mit meinem Vater **einen Kompromiß** zu schließen.
I'll try to make a compromise with my father.

eine Rede halten   *To make a speech*
Dr. König hat im Auditorium **eine Rede** gehalten.
Dr. König made a speech in the auditorium.

einen Heiratsantrag machen   *to propose (marriage)*
Er hat ihr in Wien **einen Heiratsantrag** gemacht.
He proposed to her in Vienna.

b. **Directionals**

Adverbs of place that merely locate (as in the examples above) are not verb complements. However, when adverbs of place denote motion to or from a place, they are called *directionals*. As necessary adjuncts of the verbs of motion, they are verb complements and stand at the end of the clause followed only by final verb forms.

in die Stadt (nach Hause, nach Bremen) fahren   *to go to town (home, to Bremen)*
Möchten Sie mit uns **in die Stadt** fahren?
Would you like to go to town with us?

auf eine Party gehen   *to go to a party*
Inge ist vor ein paar Minuten mit Erika **auf eine Party** gegangen.
Inge went to a party with Erika a few minutes ago.

nach oben (nach unten, nach vorn, nach hinten) gehen
to go upstairs (downstairs, to the front, to the back)
Herr und Frau Berger sind soeben mit ihren Gästen **nach unten** gegangen.
Mr. and Mrs. Berger have just gone downstairs with their guests.

Bitte kommen Sie mit Ihrem Freund **nach vorn**!
Please come to the front with your friend.

A note on the position of *nicht*

Nicht precedes verb complements in sentences with normally accented negation (cf. Chap. 1, §7):

Ich habe meinem Freund **nicht** die Wahrheit gesagt.
Wir haben **nicht** Fußball gespielt.

PRACTICE 4   *Form sentences arranging the elements in the proper sequence.*

> **Model:** ich / gehen / in den Zirkus / mit ein paar Freunden / gestern abend (pres. perf.)
>
> **Ich bin gestern abend mit ein paar Freunden in den Zirkus gegangen.**

1. Ich / fahren / in die Stadt / mit einer Freundin / gestern nachmittag (pres. perf.)
2. ich / gehen / ins Theater / mit Inge / am Sonnabend (pres. perf.)
3. Helga / gehen / auf eine Party / mit Rainer / gestern abend (pres. perf.)
4. wir / spielen / Tennis / nicht (pres. perf.)
5. wir / spielen / Fußball / im neuen Stadion / am Freitag nachmittag (pres. perf.)
6. Renate / spielen / Schach / jeden Mittwoch abend / mit Dietmar
7. ich / spielen / Karten / mit meinen Freunden / manchmal
8. Klaus / gehen / nach unten / mit dem Hund (pres. perf.)
9. ich / laufen / nach oben / schnell (pres. perf.)
10. Inge / gehen / zum Friseur[1] / vor ein paar Minuten / mit Margot (pres. perf.)
11. a. wir / schließen / einen Kompromiß / mit Dieter
    b. Wir werden versuchen, / zu schließen / einen Kompromiß / mit ihm
12. a. der Bürgermeister / halten / eine Rede / heute abend / auf dem Marktplatz
    b. Der Bürgermeister hat nicht vor, / zu halten / eine Rede / heute abend / auf dem Marktplatz
13. a. vielleicht / er / machen / einen Heiratsantrag / in Hollywood / dir
    b. Ich glaube nicht, daß er vorhat, / zu machen / einen Heiratsantrag / in Hollywood / mir
14. a. wir / essen / zu Mittag / in der Stadt / gestern (pres. perf.)
    b. Es ist möglich, daß / wir / essen / zu Abend / im Hotel / morgen
15. a. Klaus / nehmen / zu ernst / das Leben
    b. Ich glaube nicht, daß / Andreas / nehmen / ernst / unsere Warnung
    c. Wir bitten dich, / zu nehmen / ernst / unsere Warnung
16. a. du / sagen / die Wahrheit / nicht (pres. perf.)
    b. Frau Schubert / sagen / die Wahrheit / dem Rechtsanwalt / nicht (pres. perf.)
    c. hoffentlich / Frau Schubert / sagen / die Wahrheit / vor Gericht[2] (pres. perf.)
    d. Ich bitte dich, / zu sagen / die Wahrheit / vor Gericht
17. a. ich / lernen / auswendig / dieses Gedicht (pres. perf.)
    b. Meine Freundin denkt, daß es keinen Zweck hat,[3] / zu lernen / auswendig / ein Gedicht

---

1 **der Friseur, -e**   hairdresser
2 **vor Gericht**   in court
3 **keinen Zweck haben**   be of no use or purpose

18. a. Dr. Steinbach / sein / Tierarzt / schon seit 20 Jahren

    b. seine Tochter / werden / Tierärztin / auf eigenen Wunsch[1]

PRACTICE 5 *Translate into German, using the present perfect for the English past tense.*

1. a. I am going to the theater. **Ich gehe ins Theater.**
   b. I am going to the theater tomorrow night.
   c. I am going to the theater with Maria tomorrow night.
   d. I am planning to go to the theater with her tomorrow night.
   e. It is possible that I'll go to the theater with her tomorrow night. (pres.)
2. a. We are going to the hairdresser. **Wir gehen zum Friseur.**
   b. We went to the hairdresser yesterday.
   c. Yesterday I went to the hairdresser with Hannelore.
   d. I am glad that I went to the hairdresser with her yesterday.
   e. I don't have time to go to the hairdresser today.
3. a. He proposed to her. **Er hat ihr einen Heiratsantrag gemacht.**
   b. Did he propose to her in Bonn?
   c. She proposed to him in Heidelberg.
   d. Is it true that she proposed to him in Heidelberg?
4. a. We have to make a compromise. **Wir müssen einen Kompromiß schließen.**
   b. I have to make a compromise with my father.
   c. I am trying to make a compromise with him.
5. a. Are they playing chess? **Spielen sie Schach?**
   b. They are not playing chess.
   c. They played chess on Monday.
   d. I played chess with Margot on Friday.
   e. I am planning to play chess with her tomorrow.
6. a. I am memorizing a speech. **Ich lerne eine Rede auswendig.**
   b. I am trying to memorize a speech.
   c. I have to make a speech tomorrow.
   d. Tomorrow I have to make a speech in the auditorium.
   e. I am nervous because I have to make a speech in the auditorium tomorrow.

Variations in the Sequence of Elements

§5   SHIFTING ELEMENTS FURTHER TO THE END OF A SENTENCE

Important elements are placed close to the end of a German sentence. You have already seen that the complement, which is vital, is placed immediately before the final verb forms. Any other element to which in a given context special importance is attached may also be placed unusually close to the end of the sentence, particularly if it represents new information.

---

1 **auf eigenen Wunsch**   at one's own request

1. Changes in the order of adverbial modifiers

Compare the following two statements:

> X: Monika ist fünf Tage in Hamburg geblieben.
>   TIME   PLACE
> *Monika stayed in Hamburg for five days.*

> Y: Soviel ich weiß, ist sie in Hamburg **nur drei Tage** geblieben.
>   PLACE   TIME
> *As far as I know, she stayed in Hamburg only for three days.*

The statement of X is a sentence with normal intonation, i.e. every element carries its natural stress. No element is given more emphasis than usual, and thus the adverb of time precedes the adverb of place.

In Y's response, the place expression **in Hamburg** is the known element; the time expression **nur drei Tage** is more important, for it provides new information. It is more heavily stressed than usual and moves closer to the end of the sentence. The normal order time before place is reversed.

The same change may occur in questions, dependent clauses, and infinitive phrases.

> Ist sie in Hamburg wirklich **nur drei Tage** geblieben?
> Ich habe gehört, daß sie in Hamburg **nur drei Tage** geblieben ist.
> Sie hatte vor, in Hamburg **nur drei Tage** zu bleiben.

2. Alternative order of objects

Compare the following two sentences:

> Ich habe meinem Freund einen Kalender gegeben.
>   INDIR. OBJ.   DIR. OBJ.
> *I gave my friend a calendar.*

> Er hat den Kalender **einer Freundin** gegeben.
>   DIR. OBJ.   INDIR. OBJ.
> *He gave the calendar **to** a girl friend.*

The first sentence shows the normal order of noun objects: indirect object before direct object. In the second sentence the direct object represents old information, while the indirect object is new information and is therefore placed toward the end of the sentence. A similar ordering of the objects occurs in English, with the difference that the English indirect object is used with a preposition (*to*, sometimes *for*) when placed after the direct object.

Note the shift from **einen Kalender** in the first sentence to **den Kalender** in the second. Objects preceded by the definite article usually refer to something that is known and have less news value than those preceded by the indefinite article.

3. Alternative order of prepositional phrases

> X: Klaus hat tausend Mark von seinem Vater bekommen.
> Y: Ich glaube, er hat von ihm **nur fünfhundert Mark** bekommen.

Prepositional phrases normally follow direct and indirect objects. But when an object represents new information, it may be placed after a prepositional phrase that communicates old information (as in Y's response) or is less important.

4. Alternative position of subjects

    a. Es ist soeben auf dem Marktplatz **ein schwerer Autounfall** passiert.
    b. Soeben ist auf dem Marktplatz **ein schwerer Autounfall** passiert.
    A serious car accident just now happened on the marketplace.

The subject, **ein schwerer Autounfall,** has been moved to the end for greater emphasis. Sentence *a* begins with an introductory **es,** which is omitted in sentence *b* because another element is in first position (cf. Chap. 15, §5, 2).

The standard beginning of a fairytale contains such a " delayed " subject:

    Es war einmal **eine schöne Prinzessin** (ein armes Mädchen, ein weiser König).
    Once upon a time there was a beautiful princess (a poor girl, a wise king).

PRACTICE 6   *Form sentences placing the boldface elements toward the end.*

    Model: X: Ich habe gestern einen Brief an Renate geschrieben.
            Y: du / ab.schicken/ **auch gestern** / den Brief an Renate ? (pres. perf.)
            Hast du den Brief an Renate auch gestern abgeschickt?

    1. X: Ich habe vorige Woche jeden Tag in der Bibliothek gearbeitet.
       Y: du / arbeiten / **auch am Sonntag** / da? (pres. perf.)
    2. X: Wir sind um 9 Uhr in Frankfurt angekommen.
       Y: ihr / an.kommen/ **wirklich schon um 9 Uhr** / in Frankfurt? (pres. perf.)
    3. X: Ich glaube, Helga hat vier Semester in Wien studiert.
       Y: sie / studieren / **nur zwei Semester** / in Wien (pres. perf.)
    4. X: Wer hat Margot das Gerücht erzählt?
       Y: Das war Rainer. er / erzählen / **allen Leuten** / das Gerücht. (pres. perf.)
    5. X: Wer hat der Polizei den Tip gegeben?
       Y: Unsere Nachbarin. sie / geben / **auch einem Rechtsanwalt** / den Tip. (pres. perf.)
    6. X: Hast du das Paket von deinen Eltern bekommen?
       Y: Ja, und ich / bekommen / **auch einen Scheck** / von ihnen. (pres. perf.)
    7. X: Hat der Polizist Renate einen Strafzettel gegeben?
       Y: er / geben / **Renates Freundin** / den Strafzettel. (pres. perf.)
    8. X: Bitte geben Sie der Dame die Speisekarte!
       Y: warum / Sie / geben / **dem Herrn und nicht der Dame** / die Speisekarte?
    9. X: Bitte sagen Sie dem Polizisten, was gestern abend passiert ist.
       Y: Es war gegen 10 Uhr. Ich ging von der Garage zur Haustür. plötzlich[1] / **ein Mann** / stehen / vor mir. (past)

    1 **plötzlich**   suddenly, all of a sudden

10. X: Das ist ein Bild von mir, als ich zehn Jahre jünger war.
    Y: Wie im Märchen: es / **ein schöner Prinz** / sein / einmal (past)

§6 PLACING ELEMENTS AFTER THE FINAL VERB FORMS

1. *Als* and *wie* phrases in comparisons

In comparisons **als** and **wie** phrases (cf. Chap. 10, §3) are normally placed after all other sentence elements, including separable prefixes and final verb forms. Compare:

a. Ich rufe nicht oft zu Hause **an.**
b. Ich rufe nicht so oft zu Hause an **wie mein Bruder.**
c. Er ruft mehr an **als ich.**

In sentence *a* the separable prefix occupies its normal position at the end of the sentence. In sentences *b* and *c* it is followed by the **als** and **wie** phrases.

Additional examples:

a. Du kannst sehr schnell laufen.
b. Du kannst schneller laufen **als ich.**
c. Du weißt doch, daß du schneller laufen kannst **als ich.**

a. Ich bin dicker geworden.
b. Ich bin nicht so dick geworden **wie Renate.**
c. Ich bin froh, daß ich nicht so dick geworden bin **wie Renate.**

PRACTICE 7 *Translate into German, using the present perfect for the English past tense.*

1. a. I type faster than you. **Ich tippe schneller als du.**
   b. I can type faster than you.
   c. I don't think that I can type faster than you.
2. a. He's making more money than I. **Er verdient mehr Geld als ich.**
   b. He made more money than I.
   c. I assume that he made more money than I.
3. a. She cuts class just as often as he. **Sie schwänzt genauso oft wie er.**
   b. She cut class just as often as he.
   c. It's not true that she cut class just as often as he.
4. a. Their vacation starts sooner than ours. **Ihre Ferien fangen früher an als unsere.**
   b. Their vacation started sooner than ours.
   c. It is possible that their vacation started sooner than ours.

2. Other elements

a. Wir sind trotz des schlechten Wetters an den Strand gegangen.
b. Wir sind an den Strand gegangen **trotz des schlechten Wetters.**
   We went to the beach in spite of the bad weather.

In sentence *a* the past participle is in its usual final position. In sentence *b* the prepositional phrase **trotz des schlechten Wetters** has been placed after the past participle. Such an *extraposition* is sometimes done for special emphasis, but often the extraposed element (usually a prepositional phrase) is a mere afterthought.

Additional examples:

a. Ich bin aus finanziellen Gründen nicht nach Florida geflogen.
b. Ich bin nicht nach Florida geflogen **aus finanziellen Gründen**.
   I didn't fly to Florida for financial reasons.

a. Mein Vater ist nach vielen Jahren harter Arbeit in den Ruhestand getreten.
b. Mein Vater ist in den Ruhestand getreten **nach vielen Jahren harter Arbeit**.
   My father retired after many years of hard work.

20

Special Problems

KEY TO THE EXERCISES ON CASSETTE 10.
RUNNING TIME: APPROX. 40 MIN.

This chapter focuses on several grammatical features that can be treated better separately than in the context of preceding chapters. The discussion of each feature is self-contained to allow instructors to select only those sections that are of particular value for given classes.

The German Equivalents of *another*

§1   The German equivalent of *another* may be **ein ander-** or **noch ein**:

     a. Dieser Kaffee ist kalt.   Bitte geben Sie mir **eine andere Tasse Kaffee.**
                               *Please give me **another cup of coffee.***
     b. Dieser Kaffee ist gut.   Bitte geben Sie mir **noch eine Tasse Kaffee.**
                                 *Please give me **another cup of coffee.***

In sentence *a* ***another cup of coffee*** means "a different cup of coffee." The German equivalent is **eine andere Tasse Kaffee.** In sentence *b* ***another cup of coffee*** means "one more cup" or "an additional cup of coffee." The German equivalent is **noch eine Tasse Kaffee.**

Remember:
> another ⟨ **ein ander-**   meaning: a different (one)
>   **noch ein**   meaning: one more, an additional (one)

In both expressions **ein** has its usual **ein**-word endings; **ander-** has normal adjective endings (cf. Chap. 9, §8).

362

PRACTICE 1   A. *Explain the choice of* **ein ander-** *or* **noch ein** *in the following sentences.*

1. Diese Handschuhe gefallen mir. Vielleicht kaufe ich noch ein Paar.
2. Diese Bluse ist schmutzig. Ich muß eine andere anziehen.[1]
3. Der Kuchen schmeckt ausgezeichnet. Könnte ich noch ein Stück haben?
4. Leider habe ich die Stelle nicht bekommen. Sie haben sie einem anderen Studenten gegeben.
5. Dieser Verkäufer hat mich nicht bedient. Es war ein anderer.

B. *Insert German equivalents.*

1. Ich wollte Herrn Klein meinen Wagen verkaufen. Leider hat er _____ gekauft. (*another car*)
2. Schmidts haben schon zwei Wagen. Wissen Sie, warum sie _____ kaufen wollen? (*another one*)
3. Ich habe schon zwei Semesterarbeiten getippt. Leider muß ich _____ tippen. (*another one*)
4. Diese Fernsehsendung ist ja schrecklich langweilig. Können wir uns nicht _____ anschauen? (*another one*)
5. Wir haben nur einen Sohn und möchten gern _____ haben. (*another child*)

Another with the plural:

another three weeks⎫
                        ⎬ **noch drei Wochen**
= *three more weeks*⎭

PRACTICE 2   *Insert German equivalents.*

1. X: Wie lange wollt ihr noch in Wien bleiben?
   Y: Ich glaube, wir bleiben _____. (*another five days*)
2. X: Hast du den Bericht schon getippt?
   Y: Ich habe drei Seiten getippt und muß _____ tippen. (*another two*)
3. X: Hast du nun alle Rechnungen bezahlt?
   Y: Nein. Ich muß _____ bezahlen. (*another four*)
4. X: Wieviel Pfund hast du abgenommen?
   Y: 20 Pfund,[2] und ich will _____ abnehmen. (*another 10 pounds*)

---

1 **an•ziehen, zog an, angezogen**   to put on
2 **20 Pfund**   20 pound**s**
   (**Pfund** *is in the singular* [cf. Appendix, §5])

German Equivalents of *to like*

§2   TO LIKE DOING SOMETHING

1. The most frequent expression uses the adverb **gern** with a verb.

Ich singe **gern.**	*I like to sing.*
Ich singe **sehr gern.**	*I like to sing very much.*
Er tanzt **nicht gern.**	*He doesn't like to dance.*

When English adds (*very*) *much*, German uses **sehr.**

2. The modal **mögen** + infinitive is not common.

> Ich **mag** sie nicht um Geld bitten.   *I don't like to ask her for money.*

Only the subjunctive **möchte** (*would like*) is frequently used (cf. Chap. 4, §13).

> Ich **möchte** ihr helfen.   *I'd like to help her.*

§3   TO LIKE SOMETHING OR SOMEONE

1. The verb **gefallen** expresses pleasure or displeasure in a non-emotional fashion.

> Dieses Bild **gefällt mir.**   *I like this picture.*
>
> Dieses Bild **gefällt mir sehr.**
> or: Dieses Bild **gefällt mir gut.**   } *I like this picture very much.*
> or: Dieses Bild **gefällt mir sehr gut.**
>
> Dieses Bild **gefällt mir nicht.**   *I don't like this picture.*

For emphasis, **sehr, gut,** or **sehr gut** can be added; all correspond to *very much.*

Remember:

> The verb **gefallen** is used like English *to please.* Its subject is the thing or person that is liked or disliked. Its dative object is the person who has these feelings (cf. Chap. 6, §9).
>
> **Das gefällt mir.**   *I like that. (That pleases me.)*

2. **Mögen** is more emotionally colored than **gefallen.**

> Ich **mag** dieses Bild nicht.   *I don't like this picture.*
> Wir **mögen** unsere neuen Nachbarn nicht.   *We don't like our new neighbors.*

Used with food or drink:

Mögen Sie Käse?	*Do you like cheese?*
Mögen Sie Tomatensaft?	*Do you like tomato juice?*

It is very common to use **gern** with the verbs **essen** or **trinken** instead:

> **Essen** Sie **gern** Käse?
> **Trinken** Sie **gern** Tomatensaft?

3. **Gern haben** is used in the sense of *to be fond of.*

> Ich **habe** Barbara **sehr gern,** aber ich liebe sie nicht.
> *I am very fond of Barbara, but I don't love her.*

4. People one finds pleasant and likeable are often said to be **sympathisch.**

> **Sie ist mir sympathisch.**   *I like her* (in the sense of *I find her pleasant/likeable*).

> **Sie ist mir nicht sympathisch.** }
> or: **Sie ist mir unsympathisch.** } *I don't like her.*

Occasionally **sympathisch** is used with things:

> **Dieser Vorschlag ist mir nicht sympathisch.**
> *I don't like this suggestion.*
> *This suggestion doesn't appeal to me.*

§4   THE POSITION OF *gern*

Gern is an adverb of manner; it usually follows adverbs of time and precedes adverbs of place (cf. Chap. 19, §3, 3).

> Ich habe vorigen Sommer **gern** im Garten gearbeitet.

It follows pronoun objects:

> Ich helfe Ihnen **gern.**

It follows or precedes noun objects:

> Essen Sie **gern** Fisch?
> Essen Sie Fisch **gern?**

It usually precedes prepositional phrases and verb complements:

> Ich spreche **gern** mit ihm.
> Sie spielt **gern** Tennis.

Exception: With **haben, gern** is a verb complement and stands at the end of the clause followed only by the closing verb forms (cf. Chap. 19, §4):

> Ich habe als Kind diesen Teddybären[1] sehr **gern** gehabt.
> *As a child I was very fond of this teddy bear.*

PRACTICE 3   A. *Translate into German.*

> 1. a. I am fond of my brother.   **Ich habe meinen Bruder gern.**
>   b. I am fond of my brother and his girlfriend.

1 **der Bär** (*weak*), **-en**   bear

   c. Are you fond of your sister? (formal)

   d. Are you fond of me? (fam. sing.)

   e. You know that I am very fond of you. (fam. sing.)

2. a. I like this play very much.   **Dieses Theaterstück gefällt mir sehr.**

   b. She likes it very much.

   c. Does she like it?

   d. Do you like it? (fam. sing., formal)

   e. I don't like it.

3. a. I don't like this music.   **Ich mag diese Musik nicht.**

   b. My parents don't like this music.

   c. Why don't they like this music?

4. a. I like pineapple punch.   **Ich trinke gern Ananasbowle.**

   b. My friend likes pineapple punch.

   c. I know that he likes pineapple punch.

   d. Do you like pineapple punch? (fam. sing., formal)

5. a. I like shrimp.[1]   **Ich esse gern Krabben.**

   b. Many people like shrimp.

   c. Do you like shrimp? (formal, fam. sing., fam. pl.)

   d. Do you know whether Hannelore likes shrimp? (fam. sing.)

6. a. I like to play tennis.   **Ich spiele gern Tennis.**

   b. Do you like to play tennis? (fam. sing.)

   c. My girlfriend doesn't like to play tennis.

   d. Too bad that she doesn't like to play tennis.

7. a. I like her.   **Sie ist mir sympathisch.**

   b. I like him.

   c. I like his friends.

   d. I like them.

   e. I don't like this man.

   f. I don't like these people.

8. a. My parents don't like my boyfriend.   **Mein Freund ist meinen Eltern unsympathisch.**

   b. They don't like him.

   c. Too bad that they don't like him.

B. *Respond using the cues.*

Model: Wie gefällt dir mein Motorrad?

        <u>**Es gefällt mir sehr gut.**</u>

        (sehr gut gefallen)

  1. Wie gefällt dir mein Freund?   _____

                                             (sehr gut gefallen)

  2. Wie gefällt Ihnen mein neues Kleid?   _____

                                             (sehr gefallen)

  3. Wie hat dir der Film gefallen?   _____

                                             (gut gefallen)

---

1 **die Krabbe, -n**   shrimp
   (*here used in the plural*)

4. Wie hat Ihnen das Konzert gefallen? _____
   (nicht gefallen)

5. Wie gefällt Ihnen die neue
   Assistentin? _____
   (unsympathisch)
6. Haben Sie nette Nachbarn?
   _____
   (sehr sympathisch)

7. Warum lädst du Lore nicht ein? _____
   (nicht mögen)

8. Weißt du, daß du schon fünf Stück
   Kuchen gegessen hast? _____
   (sehr gern essen)
9. Du hast nicht eine einzige[1] Tasse
   Kaffee getrunken. _____
   (nicht gern trinken)
10. Spielt dein Freund Fußball? _____
   (sehr gern spielen)

11. Willst du Andreas heiraten? _____
   (sehr gern haben / nicht lieben)

C. *Ask yourself the following questions and answer them.*

Model: Was mache ich gern?
   Ich faulenze gern. Ich esse gern ...

1. Was mache ich gern?
2. Was mache ich nicht gern?
3. Wer ist mir sympathisch?
4. Wer ist mir unsympathisch?
5. Wen habe ich gern?
6. Wen habe ich sehr gern?

Uses of *hängen, legen, stellen, setzen,* and *liegen, stehen, sitzen*

§5   *hängen* USED TRANSITIVELY AND INTRANSITIVELY

A transitive verb is capable of taking a direct object in the accusative case.

   Ich schreibe **einen Brief.**
   Sie trinkt **keinen Kaffee.**

An intransitive verb cannot take a direct object but is often complemented by a prepositional phrase.

   Wir **reisen durch Deutschland.**
   Ich **bleibe in Frankfurt.**

Some verbs are used either transitively or intransitively. One of them is **hängen.**

   1 **einzig**   single

Used transitively: expressing an activity	Used intransitively: expressing a condition

PRESENT	
Sie hängt **das Bild an die Wand.***	Das Bild hängt **an der Wand.**†
(dir. obj.) (prep. phrase)	(prep. phrase)
PAST	
Sie hängte das Bild an die Wand.	Das Bild hing an der Wand.
PRESENT PERFECT	
Sie hat das Bild an die Wand gehängt.	Das Bild hat an der Wand gehangen.

———— PRINCIPAL PARTS ————

hängen—hängte—gehängt	**hängen—hing—gehangen**
Used transitively, **hängen** is a <u>weak</u> verb.	Used intransitively, **hängen** is a <u>strong</u> verb.

A good rule of thumb: When **hängen** is used in the sense of *to put*, it is weak; otherwise it is strong.

PRACTICE 4   *State whether the following sentences express an activity or a condition; then restate them in the simple past and present perfect.*

1. Frau Braun hängt die Wäsche auf die Leine.[1]
2. Frau Zimmermanns Wäsche hängt auf der Leine.
3. Klaus hängt seinen Mantel an den Haken.[2]
4. Mein Mantel hängt am Haken neben der Tür.
5. Ingrids Mantel hängt auf einem Bügel.[3]
6. Dieter hängt den Anzug auf den Bügel.
7. Wo hängt die Fahne?[4]

1 **die Leine, Wäscheleine, -n**	(clothes)line
2 **der Haken, -**	hook
3 **der Bügel, Kleiderbügel, -**	(clothes)hanger
4 **die Fahne, -n**	flag

* The two-way preposition **an** requires the accusative because the sentence expresses motion toward a place: the picture is being put someplace it wasn't before.

† The sentence expresses location; thus the dative case is used: **an der Wand.** (For two-way prepositions, see Chap. 7, §3 and §5.)

Forms of *hängen* with a prefix

TRANSITIVE (weak)	INTRANSITIVE (strong)
erhängen *to hang someone* Sie haben ihn **erhängt.** *They hanged him.* **sich erhängen** *to hang oneself* Er hat **sich erhängt.** *He hung himself.*	**ab•hängen von** (*dat.*) *to be dependent on* Bergers wollen nicht von ihren Kindern **abhängen.** *The Bergers don't want to be dependent on their children.* Sie haben nie von ihren Kindern **abgehangen.** *They have never been dependent on their children.*

EXPRESSION:

Das hängt von dir ab. ⎰ *That depends on you.*
⎱ *That's up to you.*

Das hing von dir ab.
Das hat von dir abgehangen.

PRACTICE 5 *Insert the appropriate past participles of* **hängen, erhängen,** *or* **ab•hängen.**

1. Früher hat man Verbrecher[1] hier _____ .
2. Niemand weiß, warum sich unser Nachbar _____ hat.
3. Herr Schubert hat zu lange finanziell von seinen Eltern _____ .
4. Die Entscheidung[2] hat nicht von mir _____ .
5. Ich habe das Schild[3] „Bitte nicht stören!" an die Tür _____ .
6. Das Schild „Bitte nicht stören!" hat an der Tür _____ .

§6   THE USE OF THE TRANSITIVE VERBS *legen*, *stellen*, AND *setzen*

English *put* has no good German counterpart. Instead, one uses specialized verbs of placing, such as **hängen,** or the following:

legen *to put* (in a lying position), *lay, make lie*
Bitte **legen Sie** das Buch auf den Schreibtisch!
Please put (lay) the book on the desk.

stellen *to put* (in an upright position), *make stand*
Bitte **stellen Sie** das Buch ins Regal!
Please put the book on the shelf.

setzen *to put, set, make sit*
Bitte **setzen Sie** das Kind auf die Couch!
Please put (set) the child on the couch.

---

1 **der Verbrecher, -** criminal
2 **die Entscheidung, -en** decision
3 **das Schild, -er** sign

Since these verbs imply motion toward a goal, two-way prepositions used with them require accusative objects.

The three transitive verbs are weak:

legen   — legte   — gelegt
stellen — stellte — gestellt
setzen — setzte — gesetzt

PRACTICE 6   *Translate the responses into German, using the present perfect.*
(Remember: **schon** usually follows personal pronouns and precedes all other elements.)

Model: X: Bitte stellen Sie die Gläser auf den Tisch!
Y: **Ich habe sie schon auf den Tisch gestellt.**
I already put them on the table.

1. X: Bitte legen Sie Ihre Sachen aufs Bett!
   Y: _____
   We already put them on the bed.
2. X: Bitte stellen Sie den nassen Regenschirm ins Bad!
   Y: _____
   I already put it in the bathroom.
3. X: Bitte legen Sie die Mappe[1] auf den Schreibtisch!
   Y: _____
   I already put it on the desk.
4. X: Warum setzen Sie kein Inserat[2] in die Zeitung?
   Y: _____
   I already put two ads in the newspaper.
5. X: Wir sollten die Milch in den Kühlschrank stellen.
   Y: _____
   Margot has just[3] put it into the refrigerator.
6. X: Vielleicht können Sie die Teller auf den Tisch stellen.
   Y: _____
   Günter has just put them on the table.

Note the expression **die Teller auf den Tisch stellen** or **setzen** (*to put the plates on the table*) although it means placing the plates in a horizontal position.

§7   THE USE OF THE INTRANSITIVE VERBS *liegen*, *stehen*, AND *sitzen*

Just as German uses specialized verbs of putting, it often prefers to use specialized verbs of location. Compare:

1 **die Mappe, -n**	folder
2 **das Inserat, -e**	ad, advertisement
ein Inserat in die Zeitung setzen	to put an ad in the newspaper
3 **gerade**	just (now)

transitive verbs (weak): expressing an activity	intransitive counterparts (strong): expressing a condition
legen — legte — gelegt stellen — stellte — gestellt setzen — setzte — gesetzt	liegen — lag — gelegen stehen — stand — gestanden sitzen — saß — gesessen

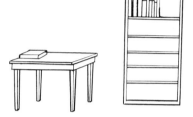

Examples:

a. Sie legt das Buch auf den Tisch.
   legte
   hat ... gelegt.
 	
She lays (laid) the book on the table.
(principal parts: to lay—laid—laid)
 	
or: *She puts (put) the book on the table.*
	Das Buch **liegt** auf dem Tisch.
	   lag
	   hat ... gelegen
	
	The book lies (lay) on the table.
	(principal parts: to lie—lay—lain)
	
	or: *The book is (was) on the table.*

b. Sie stellt die Bücher ins Regal.
   stellte
   hat ... gestellt.
 	
She puts (put) the books on the shelf.
	Die Bücher **stehen** im Regal.
	   standen
	   haben ... gestanden.
	
	The books are (were) on the shelf.

c. Sie setzt das Kind aufs Sofa.
   setzte
   hat ... gesetzt.
 	
She puts (put) the child on the sofa.
	Das Kind **sitzt** auf dem Sofa.
	   saß
	   hat ... gesessen.
	
	The child sits (sat) on the sofa.

Note: ┌─────two-way prepositions─────┐
      │ require the accusative   require the dative │

PRACTICE 7   A. *Form sentences expressing a condition in the present, simple past, and present perfect.*

Model: die Milch / im Kühlschrank / stehen
   Die Milch steht im Kühlschrank.
   Die Milch stand im Kühlschrank.
   Die Milch hat im Kühlschrank gestanden.

1. das Buch / im Regal / stehen
2. die Brille / neben der Zeitung / liegen
3. Rainer / neben seiner Freundin / sitzen
4. das Foto[1] / auf dem Schreibtisch / stehen
5. deine Handschuhe / auf dem Fußboden[2] / liegen

B. *State whether the following sentences express an activity or a condition, then express them in the simple past and present perfect.*

1. In seinem Zimmer liegen alle Sachen auf dem Boden.
2. Rainer legt alle Sachen auf den Boden.
3. Der Teddybär sitzt auf Helgas Schreibtisch.
4. Helga setzt den Teddybären neben die Schreibtischlampe.
5. Monika stellt den neuen Sessel neben die Couch.
6. Der alte Sessel steht in der Ecke.

PRACTICE 8   *Form sentences that fit the context.*

Model: Hannelore gibt Ihnen ein Glas Milch. Sie ist lauwarm (lukewarm).

Sie denken: Milch / nicht / Kühlschrank (pres. perf.)

Die Milch hat nicht im Kühlschrank gestanden.

1. Ingrid sucht wieder einmal ihre Brille. Sie sehen die Brille und sagen:

   „neben / Zeitung"

2. Warum ist Ihr Mantel so zerknittert (creased)? Sie sagen:

   „nicht / auf Bügel" (pres. perf.)

3. a. Meine Eltern erwarten Gäste. Ich frage, ob ich irgendwie helfen kann. Meine Mutter sagt:

   „du / können / Teller und Gläser / auf Tisch"

   b. Die Gäste wollen nach Hause gehen. Meine Mutter sagt:

   „mein Mann / alle Mäntel / auf Bett" (pres. perf.)

4. In Rainers Zimmer liegen die meisten Bücher auf dem Boden. Sie fragen ihn:

   „warum / du / Bücher / nicht / Regal?"

5. Meine neue Freundin hat mir ein Foto geschenkt.

   ich / auf Schreibtisch (pres. perf.)

6. Frank sagt, daß er gestern im Konzert war. Sie haben ihn nicht gesehen. Sie fragen:

   „wo / du / sitzen?" (pres. perf.)

---

1 **das Foto, -s**   photo(graph)
  short form of **die Fotografie, -n**
  (*note the change of gender*)
2 **der Fußboden, ⸚**   floor
  short: **der Boden, ⸚**

7. Sie wollten gestern Sabine etwas fragen, sind aber nicht in ihr Zimmer gegangen. Warum nicht?

    Schild „Bitte nicht stören!" / Tür (pres. perf.)

8. Wenn man mich fragt, ob ich den Magister machen will, antworte ich:

    „das / von Noten / ab.hängen"

9. Ich frage Barbara, wie oder wo sie ihren neuen Freund kennengelernt hat. Sie antwortet:

    „ich / Inserat / Zeitung / setzen" (pres. perf.)

The Use of *sein* and *haben* With Some Verbs of Motion

§8   Compare the following two uses of **fahren**:

fahren ⟨ used intransitively: **Wir sind** nach München **gefahren**.
                                    We drove to Munich.
           used transitively: **Haben** Sie **den Wagen** gefahren?
                                                        DIR. OBJ.
                                    Did you drive the car?

Some verbs that are normally intransitive and take the auxiliary **sein** occasionally have a direct object. Then, of course, they must use the auxiliary **haben**. Some of the most common verbs that belong to this class are **fahren, fliegen, landen,** and **reiten.**

Examples:

a. Bergers **sind** mit ihrem Privatflugzeug nach Düsseldorf **geflogen**.
    The Bergers flew to Düsseldorf in their private plane.

b. Frau Berger **hat das Flugzeug** zum ersten Mal **geflogen**.
    Mrs. Berger flew the plane for the first time.

a. Wann **seid** ihr in Berlin **gelandet?**
    When did you land in Berlin?

b. Wo **hat** der Pilot **das Flugzeug gelandet?**
    Where did the pilot land the plane?

a. Wir **sind** heute morgen durch die Felder **geritten.**
    We rode on horseback through the fields this morning.

b. Welcher Jockei **hat dieses Pferd geritten?**
    Which jockey rode this horse?

PRACTICE 9   *Restate the following sentences in the present perfect.*

1. Barbara reitet viel zu schnell.
2. Warum reitet sie immer das schwarze Rennpferd?[1]

---

1 **das Rennpferd, -e**   racehorse

3. Fahren Sie mit dem Bus?
4. Wer fährt den Bus?
5. Wann fliegen Sie in die Schweiz?
6. Welcher Pilot fliegt diese Maschine?[1]
7. Hoffentlich landet er nicht im Gefängnis.[2]
8. In meinen schönsten Träumen lande ich ein Raumschiff[3] auf dem Mond.

Double Infinitive Constructions with *sehen, lassen, hören,* and *helfen*

§9   When accompanied by another verb, **sehen, lassen, hören,** and **helfen** occur with double infinitive constructions in compound tenses. They follow the example of the modal auxiliaries (cf. Chap. 4, §3 to §5).

1. **sehen**

without a dependent infinitive	with a dependent infinitive
Wir sehen ihn.	Wir sehen ihn kommen.
We see him.	*We see him coming.*
Wir sahen ihn.	Wir sahen ihn kommen.
Wir haben ihn **gesehen.**	Wir haben ihn **kommen sehen.**
Wir hatten ihn **gesehen.**	Wir hatten ihn **kommen sehen.**
Wir werden ihn **sehen.**	Wir werden ihn **kommen sehen.**
	The accompanying verb precedes **sehen.**

2. **lassen**

Wir haben den Koffer im Wagen **gelassen.**	Wir haben Klaus nicht allein **fahren lassen.**
We left the suitcase in the car.	*We didn't let Klaus drive alone.*

3. **hören** and **helfen**

Ich habe ihn nicht **gehört.**	Ich habe ihn nie **lachen hören.**
I didn't hear him.	or: Ich habe ihn nie lachen **gehört.**
	I have never heard him laugh.
Ich habe ihr **geholfen.**	Ich habe ihr **packen helfen.**
I helped her.	or: Ich habe ihr packen **geholfen.**
	I helped her pack.
	Careful usage prefers the double infinitive, but the use of the past participle **gehört** or **geholfen** is also considered to be correct.

---

1 **die Maschine, -n**   plane
  (frequently used instead
  of **das Flugzeug)**
2 **im Gefängnis landen**   to wind up in prison
3 **das Raumschiff, -e**   spaceship

PRACTICE 10   A. *Restate the following sentences in the present perfect tense.*

1. Ich sehe Karin oft im Garten arbeiten.
2. Sehen Sie auch manchmal Peter im Garten?
3. Klaus hilft Andreas umziehen.[1]
4. Wir alle helfen ihm.
5. Hören Sie den Hund bellen?
6. Die ganze Nachbarschaft hört ihn.
7. Man läßt mich nicht rauchen.
8. Unser Baby läßt uns nicht schlafen.
9. Ich lasse meine Sachen im Schließfach.[2]
10. Man läßt mich nicht in Ruhe.[3]
11. Warum lassen Sie mich nicht ausreden?[4]
12. Wir lassen unsere Kinder nicht gern allein zu Hause.
13. Sehen Sie die zwei Polizisten winken?[5]
14. Ich sehe nur einen Polizisten.

B. *Translate into German, using the present perfect for the English past tense.*

1. a. I hear the baby crying. **Ich höre das Baby weinen.**
   b. Do you hear the baby crying? (formal)
   c. Did you hear the baby crying?
   d. I didn't hear it.
2. a. I see her waving. **Ich sehe sie winken.**
   b. Do you see her waving? (fam. sing.)
   c. Did you see her waving? (fam. plural)
   d. I didn't see that.
3. a. Let him finish (talking). (fam. sing.) **Laß ihn ausreden!**
   b. Please let me finish (talking). (fam. sing., formal)
   c. They didn't let me finish (talking).
4. a. Leave her alone. (fam. sing.) **Laß sie in Ruhe!**
   b. Please leave me alone. (fam. sing., formal)
   c. We left him alone.

The causative meaning of *lassen*

> **Ich lasse ihn den Wagen waschen.**
> *I let him wash the car.* (expressing permission)
> or: *I'm having him wash the car.* (expressing causation)

In German **lassen** is used to express both permission and causation; the meaning must be determined from context. The sentences in the preceding

1 **um•ziehen, zog um, ist umgezogen**	to move
2 **das Schließfach, ̈er**	locker
3 **in Ruhe lassen (läßt), ließ, gelassen**	to leave alone
4 **aus•reden lassen**	to let finish (*talking*)
5 **winken**	to wave

section use **lassen** in the sense of *to leave* and *to let*. In this section we shall deal with the causative use of **lassen.**

In German, as in English, the person who actually carries out the action need not be mentioned. When this person is omitted, German continues to use a complementary infinitive, whereas English uses a past participle.

PRESENT	Ich lasse meinen Wagen **waschen.**	*I am having my car* ***washed.***	
	Ich lasse ihn **waschen.**	*I am having it* ***washed.***	
PRES. PERF.	Ich habe meinen Wagen **waschen lassen.**	*I had my car* ***washed.***	
	Ich habe ihn **waschen lassen.**	*I had it* ***washed.***	

PRACTICE 11   A. *Express the responses in German using the present tense.*

Model: X: Kannst du den Fernseher selbst reparieren?

Y: <u>**Nein. Ich lasse ihn reparieren.**</u>

No. I'll have it repaired.

1. X: Kannst du die Bewerbung selbst tippen?
   Y: _____
   No. I'll have it typed.
2. X: Wollen Sie den Rasen selbst mähen?[1]
   Y: _____
   No. I'll have it mowed.
3. X: Wollen Sie das Paket selbst abholen?
   Y: _____
   No. I'll have it picked up.
4. X: Putzen[2] Sie die Fenster selbst?
   Y: _____
   No. I have them washed.
5. X: Entwickeln[3] Sie Ihre Filme selbst?
   Y: _____
   No. I have them developed.
6. X: Wollen Sie Ihr Haus selbst streichen?[4]
   Y: _____
   No. We'll have it painted.

B. *Express the responses in German using the present perfect tense.*

Model: X: Wann läßt du den Fernseher reparieren?

Y: <u>**Ich habe ihn schon reparieren lassen.**</u>

I already had it repaired.

1 **den Rasen mähen**	to mow the lawn
2 **die Fenster putzen**	to clean *or* wash the windows
3 **entwickeln**	to develop
4 **streichen, strich, gestrichen**	to paint

1. X: Wann läßt du den Film entwickeln?
   Y: _____
      I already had it developed.
2. X: Wann lassen Sie Ihr Haus streichen?
   Y: _____
      We already had it painted.
3. X: Läßt du deine Semesterarbeit tippen?
   Y: _____
      I already had it typed.
4. X: Wann lassen Sie den Rasen mähen?
   Y: _____
      We already had it mowed.
5. X: Wann läßt du deinen Mantel reinigen?[1]
   Y: _____
      I already had it cleaned.

Lassen is also used reflexively: **sich etwas machen lassen** means *to have some-thing done to* or *for oneself.*

sich die Haare schneiden lassen   *to have one's hair cut, get a haircut*

PRESENT   Ich lasse **mir** die Haare schneiden.⟨ *I'm having my hair cut.*
⟨ *I'm getting a haircut.*

PRES. PERF. Ich habe **mir** die Haare schneiden lassen.⟨ *I had my hair cut.*
⟨ *I got a haircut.*

sich eine Dauerwelle machen lassen   *to get a permanent*

Sie läßt **sich** eine Dauerwelle machen.   *She is getting a permanent.*
Sie hat **sich** eine Dauerwelle machen lassen.   *She got a permanent.*

Note that the reflexive pronoun is in the dative case because the sentences contain a direct object: **die Haare, eine Dauerwelle** (cf. Chap. 17, §2).

PRACTICE 12   *Translate into German, using the present perfect for the English past tense.*

1. a. I am getting a haircut.   **Ich lasse mir die Haare schneiden.**
   b. She is getting a haircut.
   c. He got a haircut.
   d. Did he get a haircut?
   e. Did you get a haircut? (fam. sing., formal)
2. a. I am getting a permanent.   **Ich lasse mir eine Dauerwelle machen.**
   b. He is getting a permanent.
   c. She got a permanent.
   d. Did you get a permanent? (fam. sing., formal)

---

1 **reinigen lassen**   to have dry-cleaned

PRACTICE 13   *Form sentences that fit the context.*

> **Model:** Frank hat gestern wunderbar Flöte (flute) gespielt. Ich frage Margot:
>
> > du / hören / spielen?" (pres. perf.)
> >
> > **„Hast du ihn Flöte spielen hören?"**

1. Neumanns haben seit gestern einen Hund. Er hat die ganze Nacht gebellt. Ulrich fragt mich:

   > „du / hören / bellen?" (pres. perf.)

2. Ich gehe mit Susanne spazieren. Ihre Schwester fährt an uns vorbei. Susanne fragt mich:

   > „du / sehen / winken?" (pres. perf.)

3. Hartmut hat schlechte Laune. Ich will ihn aufheitern (cheer up). Er sagt sehr unfreundlich:

   > „lassen / in Ruhe!"

4. Martin unterbricht mich immer. Ich sage:

   > „bitte / lassen / aus.reden!"

5. Brigitte hatte mich mißverstanden. Ich wollte die Sache klären, konnte es aber nicht.

   > Brigitte / mich / nicht / lassen / aus.reden. (pres. perf.)

6. Mein Wagen läuft jetzt ausgezeichnet. Warum?

   > ich / lassen / reparieren (pres. perf.)

7. Wir haben unser Wochenendhaus nicht selbst gestrichen.

   > „wir / lassen / streichen (pres. perf.)

8. Sie fragen Uwe, ob er die Bewerbung selbst getippt hat. Er antwortet:

   > „Nein, / ich / lassen / tippen." (pres. perf.)

9. Ich frage Anita, ob ihr Mantel neu ist. Sie antwortet:

   > „Nein, das ist der alte. ich / lassen / reinigen." (pres. perf.)

10. Irene hat eine neue Frisur. (hairdo)

    > sie / sich / lassen / machen / Dauerwelle. (pres. perf.)

11. Meine Freundin findet, daß ich heute viel jünger aussehe. Ich sage:

    > „ich / sich / lassen / schneiden / die Haare" (pres. perf.)

The Subjective Use of Modal Auxiliaries

§10   Compare the use of **müssen** in the following sentences:

> a. Thomas sucht eine bessere Stelle. Er **muß** mehr Geld verdienen.
> *Thomas is looking for a better job. He must make more money.*

b. Unser Nachbar hat ein großes neues Haus gekauft. Er **muß** viel Geld verdienen.
Our neighbor bought a big new house. He must make a lot of money.

In *a* the modal **müssen** expresses the necessity of making more money. In *b* the speaker concludes that his neighbor is making a lot of money from the fact that he has bought a big new house. That is his judgment, a subjective sizing up of the situation. **Müssen** is used subjectively rather than objectively, as in *a*.

Structurally, the objective and subjective uses look identical. The meaning of the modal must be derived from the context. However, when the subjective modal refers to a past act or state, it differs structurally from the objective modal. Compare:

Thomas **mußte** mehr Geld verdienen.   *Thomas had to make more money.*

The objective modal is in the simple past.

Herr Berger hat einige Jahre in Alaska gearbeitet. Als er zurückkam, hat er ein
Hotel gekauft.
Er **muß** viel Geld **verdient haben,** als er in Alaska war.

perfect infinitive
*Mr. Berger worked in Alaska for a few years. When he came back, he bought a
hotel.*
He ***must have made*** *a lot of money when he was in Alaska.*

perfect infinitive

This is a present inference about a past situation. Thus in both languages the modal is in the present tense and the accompanying verb in the perfect infinitive (cf. Chap. 3, §12).

Additional examples of the subjective use of **müssen**:

PRESENT   Das **muß** ein Mißverständnis **sein.**
That ***must be*** *a misunderstanding.*

PAST   Das **muß** ein Mißverständnis **gewesen sein.**
That ***must have been*** *a misunderstanding.*

PRESENT   Er **muß** Schwierigkeiten in Chemie **haben.**
He ***must have*** *problems in chemistry.*

PAST   Er **muß** Schwierigkeiten in Chemie **gehabt haben.**
He ***must have had*** *problems in chemistry.*

Keep in mind:
> The modal is in the present tense; the dependent infinitive is either a *simple infinitive* (referring to a present action or state) or a *perfect infinitive* (referring to a past action or state).

Examples for the objective and subjective uses of *können,* *mögen,* *sollen,* **and** *wollen*

können

objective: a. expressing ability

> Ich kann (konnte) das verstehen.
> *I can (could) understand that.*

b. expressing objective possibility

> Wir können (konnten) mit dem Bus vom Flughafen in die Stadt fahren.
> *We can (could) go by bus from the airport to town.*

subjective: expressing a subjectively perceived possibility

> PRESENT   Das **kann** wahr **sein.**
> *That may be true.*

> PAST   Das **kann** wahr **gewesen sein.**
> *That may have been true.*

mögen

objective: expressing liking

> Ich mag (mochte) ihn nicht fragen.
> *I don't (didn't) like to ask him.*

subjective: expressing a subjectively perceived possibility similar to the use of **können. (Mögen** has a more literary connotation.)

> PRESENT   Das **mag sein.**
> *That may be so.*

> PAST   Das **mag** eine gute Idee **gewesen sein.**
> *That may have been a good idea.*

sollen

objective: expressing obligation

> Der Bürgermeister soll (sollte) eine Rede halten.
> *The mayor is (was) expected to make a speech.*
> or: *The mayor is (was) supposed to make a speech.*

subjective: expressing rumors, hearsay

> PRESENT   Sie **soll** sehr reich **sein.**
> *She is said to be very rich.*
> or: *She is supposed to be very rich.*

> PAST   Sie **soll** sehr reich **gewesen sein.**
> *They say she was very rich.*
> or: *She is supposed to have been very rich.*

Note that English **to be supposed to** has a similar dual function: it has both objective meaning (*to be expected to*) and subjective meaning (*to be said to*).

wollen

objective: expressing a wish or an intention

> Hannelore will (wollte) das erledigen.
> *Hannelore wants (wanted) to take care of that.*
> or: *Hannelore intends (intended) to take care of that.*

subjective: expressing the speaker's or writer's reservation about someone's claim

PRESENT	Er **will** ein großer Musiker **sein.**
	He claims to be a great musician.
	(But I have my doubts.)
PAST	Er **will** ein großer Musiker **gewesen sein.**
	He claims to have been a great musician.
	(But I have my doubts.)
	or: *He claims that he was a great musician.*

PRACTICE 14   *Translate the following sentences into English and then reproduce the German from your translation.*

1. Das kann eine Lüge sein.
2. Das kann ein Irrtum[1] gewesen sein.
3. Das mag ein Fehler sein.
4. Das mag eine Ausrede[2] gewesen sein.
5. Sabine Richter soll eine gute Schauspielerin sein.
6. Herr Bachmann soll in seiner Jugend ein guter Fußballspieler gewesen sein.
7. Schreibers wollen ein Haus an der Riviera haben, aber das glaubt niemand.
8. Rainer will zwei Jahre in Rom studiert haben, aber ich kann das nicht glauben.
9. Renate schreibt mir nicht mehr. Sie muß mich vergessen haben.
10. Der junge Tenor aus Hamburg hat nicht gut gesungen.
    Er muß Lampenfieber[3] gehabt haben.
11. Petra und Martin wollen eine fliegende Untertasse[4] gesehen haben.

The modal in the subjunctive

To make a statement seem more tentative and cautious, the subjective modal may be expressed in the subjunctive mood. This is particularly true with **können.**

PRESENT	Das **könnte** wahr **sein.**
	That might (could) be true.
PAST	Das **könnte** wahr **gewesen sein.**
	That might (could) have been true.

1 **der Irrtum, ̈-er**	error
2 **die Ausrede, -n**	excuse, pretended reason, pretext
3 **das Lampenfieber**	stage fright
4 **die fliegende Untertasse, -n**	flying saucer

PRACTICE 15   *Express the responses in German.*

1. X: Warum spricht der Redner so leise und so schnell?
   Y: He might be nervous.
2. X: Marlene hat gestottert,[1] als sie sich entschuldigte.
   Y: She might have been nervous.
3. X: Warum sagt Jürgen seinen Eltern nicht die Wahrheit?
   Y: He might be afraid.
4. X: Warum hat mir meine Freundin nicht die Wahrheit gesagt?
   Y: She might have been afraid.
5. X: Ich möchte wissen, warum mich Ruth nicht angerufen hat.
   Y: She might have forgotten it.

PRACTICE 16   *Translate into German.*

1. a. That's an error.   **Das ist ein Irrtum.**
   b. That must be an error.
   c. That must have been an error.
2. a. That's a coincidence.   **Das ist ein Zufall.**
   b. That may be a coincidence. (Use **können**)
   c. That may have been a coincidence.
   d. That might be a coincidence.
   e. That might have been a coincidence.
3. a. She is a child prodigy.   **Sie ist ein Wunderkind.**
   b. She is supposed (said) to be a child prodigy.
   c. She is supposed (said) to have been a child prodigy.
4. a. He's very popular.   **Er ist sehr beliebt.**
   b. He must be very popular.
   c. He must have been very popular.
   d. He claims to be very popular.
   e. He claims to have been very popular.
5. a. They know many famous artists in Europe.   **Sie kennen viele berühmte Künstler in Europa.**
   b. They claim to know many famous artists in Europe.
   c. They are supposed (said) to know many famous artists in Europe.
   d. They must know Janna Hendrik.
   e. They must have known Picasso.
   f. They might have known your famous grandfather. (fam. sing.)

Appositives

§11   An appositive is an explanatory noun phrase which follows immediately the noun or pronoun it modifies.

---

1 **stottern**   to stutter

Peter Stein, **der berühmte Pianist,** hat den Beethoven-Preis gewonnen.

SUBJ.,   NOM

NOM.

Peter Stein, the famous pianist, won the Beethoven Prize.

The appositive is normally in the same case as the element it modifies. In the above example, the appositive, **der berühmte Pianist,** is in the nominative because it modifies the subject of the sentence, **Peter Stein.**

Examples in other cases:

Wir haben ihm, **dem berühmten Pianisten,** zu seinem Erfolg gratuliert.

        DAT.   DAT.

We congratulated him, the famous pianist, on his success.

Wir haben ihn, **den berühmten Pianisten,** um ein Autogramm gebeten.

        ACC.   ACC.

We asked him, the famous pianist, for an autograph.

Sie ist die Tochter Peter Steins, **des berühmten Pianisten.**

             GEN.   GEN.

She is the daughter of Peter Stein, the famous pianist.

Sie kommt aus Rossau, **einem kleinen Dorf** in Sachsen.

          DAT.   DAT.

She comes (is) from Rossau, a little village in Saxony.

Diese Blumen sind für meine Großmutter, **die Mutter** meines Vaters.

                 ACC.   ACC.

These flowers are for my grandmother, the mother of my father (my father's mother).

PRACTICE 17   *The elements in parentheses are stated in the nominative. Insert them as appositives in the appropriate cases.*

Model: Wir haben Herrn Bauer, _____, in der Stadt getroffen. (ein guter Freund meiner Eltern)

Wir haben Herrn Bauer, einen guten Freund meiner Eltern, in der Stadt getroffen.

1. Frau Zimmermann, _____, hat mich gestern angerufen. (eine gute Freundin meiner Mutter)
2. Das ist ein Geschenk für meinen Onkel Werner, _____. (der Bruder meines Vaters)
3. Kennen Sie Ulf Schreiber, _____? (der erste Preisträger[1])
4. Das ist Andreas Krause, _____. (der zweite Preisträger)
5. Ich habe mit Thomas Köhler, _____ gesprochen. (der dritte Preisträger)
6. Erika hat mir viel von Berlin, _____, erzählt. (ihre Heimatstadt)

1 **der Preisträger, -**   prize winner

7. Wir wollen mit Körners, _____, in die Stadt fahren. (unsere Nachbarn)
8. Maria kommt aus Villingen, _____. (eine kleine Stadt im Schwarzwald)
9. Wir sprechen von Hannelore, _____. (die jüngste Tochter von Schmidts)
10. Mit Herrn Winkler, _____, möchte ich nicht verheiratet sein. (dieser Schürzenjäger[1])

Extended Adjective Constructions

§12   Adjectives preceding nouns may be *extended* by additional modifiers.

> Herr Krause hat die **schon lange überfällige** Entschädigung noch nicht erhalten.
> *Mr. Krause has not yet received the **long overdue** compensation.*

In this sentence, the adjective **überfällig** is modified by a time expression, **schon lange.** Because this expression is relatively short, both English and German permit the modified adjective to precede the noun. But if the modification of the adjective is more extensive, only German permits the construction to precede the noun. English requires that the adjective construction be placed after the noun, often as part of a relative clause.

> Herr Krause hat die **schon seit mehr als drei Monaten fällige** Entschädigung noch nicht erhalten.
>
> *Mr. Krause has not yet received the compensation **due for more than three months.***
>
> or: *Mr. Krause has not yet received the compensation **which has been due for more than three months.***

These *extended adjective constructions* occur frequently in written German (literary and scientific texts, newspapers and periodicals). In most instances the adjective is a present or past participle (cf. Chap. 9, §13).

Present participle:

> Der schon seit Monaten **steigende** Preis für Benzin hat zu wirtschaftlichen Schwierigkeiten geführt.
>
> *The price of gas, which has been rising for months, has led to economic difficulties.*

When preceded by **zu,** the present participle has passive meaning and implies obligation or possibility. There are several English equivalents: *to be, can be, may be, must be, should be* + past participle, depending on the context.

> die heute **zu** bezahlenden Rechnungen
>
> *the bills to be paid today*
> or: *the bills that must be paid today*
> or: *the bills that should be paid today*

---

1 **der Schürzenjäger, -**   womanizer (*lit.*: apron hunter)

Note the position of **zu** if the participle has a separable prefix:

die nicht voraus**zu**sehenden Schwierigkeiten

the difficulties that cannot be foreseen
or: *the difficulties that may not be foreseen*

Past participle:

Der im vorigen Jahr so hoch **gestiegene** Preis für Benzin hat zu wirtschaftlichen Schwierigkeiten geführt.

The price of gas, which has climbed so high in the past year, has led to economic difficulties.

Alle noch nicht **bezahlten** Rechnungen sind in dieser Mappe.
All bills that have not yet been paid are in this folder.

Rendering extended adjective constructions into idiomatic English often poses considerable problems. Here are a few hints as to how to proceed.

Auf Seite 10 finden wir die bei jungen Leuten sehr beliebten Fernsehsendungen.

First bring together the beginning and the end of the extended adjective construction, i.e. the article **die** (1) and the noun **Fernsehsendungen** (2). Then proceed backwards: Take first the adjective that immediately precedes the noun, i.e. **beliebten** (*popular*). It is modified by the adverb **sehr.** Thus **sehr beliebten** is the third unit. It is preceded by the fourth unit, **bei jungen Leuten.** The result is:

On page 10 we find the TV programs that are very popular with young people.

PRACTICE 18   *Translate into acceptable English.*

1. Das ist eine erst neuerdings[1] aufgetauchte[2] Frage.
2. Die Regierung muß dieses von vielen nicht erkannte Problem lösen.
3. Er ist ein auf der ganzen Welt bekannter Gelehrter.
4. Der Höhepunkt des Konzerts war ein vom Komponisten selbst dirigiertes[3] Werk.
5. Die von vielen Gegnern[4] angegriffene[5] Journalistin ist ihren Grundsätzen[6] treu geblieben.
6. In diesem 100 km von München entfernt liegenden Dorf gibt es ein reizendes[7] Gasthaus mit einem ausgezeichneten Koch.

1 **erst neuerdings**	only recently
2 **auf•tauchen**	to emerge, come up
3 **dirigieren**	to conduct (*music*)
4 **der Gegner, -**	opponent
5 **an•greifen,**	to attack
griff an, angegriffen	
6 **der Grundsatz, ̈-e**	principle
7 **reizend**	charming

7. Die Lohnerhöhungen[1] bleiben hinter den von Monat zu Monat steigenden Lebenshaltungskosten[2] zurück.
8. Der in eine Seitenstraße einbiegende[3] Bus stieß mit einem Lastwagen[4] zusammen.[5]
9. Man hat die bei diesem Unfall verletzten Fahrgäste[6] in das Albert-Schweitzer-Krankenhaus gebracht.
10. Die Bürgermeisterin gab einen Überblick[7] über die in diesem Jahr zu lösenden Probleme.
11. Die Diskussionen über die noch zu klärenden Fragen beginnen am Montag.
12. Die am Anfang des zwanzigsten Jahrhunderts viel gelesenen Romane dieses Autors sind jetzt völlig[8] in Vergessenheit geraten.[9] Das ist eine nicht zu leugnende[10] Tatsache.[11]

1 **die Lohnerhöhung, -en**	wage increase
2 **die Lebenshaltungskosten** (pl.)	cost of living
3 **ein•biegen,**	to turn into (a street)
bog ein, ist eingebogen	
4 **der Lastwagen, -**	truck
5 **zusammen•stoßen (stößt zusammen),**	to collide
stieß zusammen, ist zusammengestoßen	
6 **der Fahrgast, ˗e**	passenger
7 **der Überblick, -e**	overview
8 **völlig**	completely
9 **in Vergessenheit geraten**	to fall into oblivion, be forgotten
10 **leugnen**	to deny
11 **die Tatsache, -n**	fact

Appendix

§1   ss or ß?

ss is used between two vowels if the preceding vowel is short:

> Wasser   Flüsse   wissen   lassen   messen   essen   hassen   müssen

ss must also be used in compounds if the two s's belong to different parts of the compound:

> aussprechen (aus + sprechen) diesseits (dies + Seite)

ß is used in all other cases, for example,

a. between vowels if the preceding vowel is long or is a diphthong:

> grüßen   heißen   schließen   Preußen   außer

b. at the end of a word:

> Gruß   Fluß   Fuß   weiß   Kongreß   Maß   bloß

c. before a consonant:

> ihr wißt   sie ißt   er läßt   wir mußten

d. in compounds if both s's belong to the first element:

> Mißernte (*crop failure*) (miß- + Ernte)
> Meßinstrument (*measuring instrument*) (messen + Instrument)
> Großstadt (groß + Stadt)

These rules are not always observed. Although ß cannot be used where ss is required, it is not regarded as wrong to use ss instead of ß.

§2   PRINCIPAL PARTS OF STRONG AND IRREGULAR VERBS

The third person singular forms of verbs with a vowel change in the present tense are shown in parentheses after the infinitive. The third person singular general subjunctive present is also shown. For verbs with separable or inseparable prefixes not listed, see the main verb.

A-1

infinitive (3rd. pers. sing.)	simple past	past participle	subjunctive present	meaning
backen (bäckt)	backte	gebacken	backte	to bake
befehlen (befiehlt)	befahl	befohlen	beföhle or: befähle	to command
beginnen	begann	begonnen	begänne or: begönne	to begin
beißen	biß	gebissen	bisse	to bite
betrügen	betrog	betrogen	betröge	to deceive
beweisen	bewies	bewiesen	bewiese	to prove
biegen	bog	gebogen	böge	to bend
bieten	bot	geboten	böte	to offer
binden	band	gebunden	bände	to bind, tie
bitten	bat	gebeten	bäte	to ask (for), request
blasen (bläst)	blies	geblasen	bliese	to blow
bleiben	blieb	ist geblieben	bliebe	to stay, remain
braten (brät)	briet	gebraten	briete	to roast, fry
brechen (bricht)	brach	gebrochen	bräche	to break
brennen	brannte	gebrannt	brennte	to burn
bringen	brachte	gebracht	brächte	to bring
denken	dachte	gedacht	dächte	to think
empfangen (empfängt)	empfing	empfangen	empfinge	to receive
empfehlen (empfiehlt)	empfahl	empfohlen	empföhle or: empfähle	to recommend
empfinden	empfand	empfunden	empfände	to feel
erlöschen (erlischt)	erlosch	ist erloschen	erlösche	to go out (light, fire)
erschrecken (erschrickt)	erschrak	ist erschrocken	erschräke	to be startled
essen (ißt)	aß	gegessen	äße	to eat
fahren (fährt)	fuhr	ist gefahren	führe	to drive, travel
fallen (fällt)	fiel	ist gefallen	fiele	to fall
fangen (fängt)	fing	gefangen	finge	to catch
finden	fand	gefunden	fände	to find
fliegen	flog	ist geflogen	flöge	to fly
fliehen	floh	ist geflohen	flöhe	to flee
fließen	floß	ist geflossen	flösse	to flow
fressen (frißt)	fraß	gefressen	fräße	to eat (animals)
frieren	fror	gefroren	fröre	to freeze, be cold
geben (gibt)	gab	gegeben	gäbe	to give
gehen	ging	ist gegangen	ginge	to go
gelingen	gelang	ist gelungen	gelänge	to succeed
gelten (gilt)	galt	gegolten	gölte or: gälte	to be valid, carry weight
genesen	genas	ist genesen	genäse	to recover (from illness)
genießen	genoß	genossen	genösse	to enjoy
geschehen (geschieht)	geschah	ist geschehen	geschähe	to happen
gewinnen	gewann	gewonnen	gewönne or: gewänne	to win
gießen	goß	gegossen	gösse	to pour
gleichen	glich	geglichen	gliche	to equal, resemble
gleiten	glitt	ist geglitten	glitte	to glide, slide
graben (gräbt)	grub	gegraben	grübe	to dig
greifen	griff	gegriffen	griffe	to grip, seize
haben (hat)	hatte	gehabt	hätte	to have
halten (hält)	hielt	gehalten	hielte	to hold, stop
hängen	hing	gehangen	hinge	to hang (intransitive)
heben	hob	gehoben	höbe	to lift

infinitive (3rd. pers. sing.)	simple past	past participle	general subjunctive present	meaning
heißen	hieß	geheißen	hieße	to be called
helfen (hilft)	half	geholfen	hülfe or: hälfe	to help
kennen	kannte	gekannt	kennte	to know, be acquainted with
klingen	klang	geklungen	klänge	to sound
kneifen	kniff	gekniffen	kniffe	to pinch
kommen	kam	ist gekommen	käme	to come
kriechen	kroch	ist gekrochen	kröche	to crawl
laden (lädt)	lud	geladen	lüde	to load
lassen (läßt)	ließ	gelassen	ließe	to leave, let, cause to
laufen (läuft)	lief	ist gelaufen	liefe	to run, walk
leiden	litt	gelitten	litte	to suffer
leihen	lieh	geliehen	liehe	to lend
lesen (liest)	las	gelesen	läse	to read
liegen	lag	gelegen	läge	to lie, be situated
lügen	log	gelogen	löge	to (tell a) lie
meiden (vermeiden)	mied	gemieden	miede	to avoid
messen (mißt)	maß	gemessen	mäße	to measure
nehmen (nimmt)	nahm	genommen	nähme	to take
nennen	nannte	genannt	nennte	to name, call
pfeifen	pfiff	gepfiffen	pfiffe	to whistle
preisen	pries	gepriesen	priese	to praise
raten (rät)	riet	geraten	riete	to advise; guess
reiben	rieb	gerieben	riebe	to rub
reißen	riß	ist gerissen	risse	to tear
reiten	ritt	ist geritten	ritte	to ride (on an animal)
rennen	rannte	ist gerannt	rennte	to run
riechen	roch	gerochen	röche	to smell
rufen	rief	gerufen	riefe	to call
saufen (säuft)	soff	gesoffen	söffe	to drink (animal)
scheiden	schied	geschieden	schiede	to separate
scheinen	schien	geschienen	schiene	to shine; seem
schelten (schilt)	schalt	gescholten	schölte	to scold
schieben	schob	geschoben	schöbe	to shove, push
schießen	schoß	geschossen	schösse	to shoot
schlafen (schläft)	schlief	geschlafen	schliefe	to sleep
schlagen (schlägt)	schlug	geschlagen	schlüge	to hit, beat
schleichen	schlich	ist geschlichen	schliche	to creep
schließen	schloß	geschlossen	schlösse	to close
schmelzen (schmilzt)	schmolz	geschmolzen	schmölze	to melt
schneiden	schnitt	geschnitten	schnitte	to cut
schreiben	schrieb	geschrieben	schriebe	to write
schreien	schrie	geschrie(e)n	schriee	to shout, scream
schreiten	schritt	ist geschritten	schritte	to stride
schweigen	schwieg	geschwiegen	schwiege	to be silent
schwimmen	schwamm	ist geschwommen	schwömme or: schwämme	to swim
schwingen	schwang	geschwungen	schwänge	to swing
schwören	schwor	geschworen	schwöre	to swear, vow
sehen (sieht)	sah	gesehen	sähe	to see
sein (ist)	war	ist gewesen	wäre	to be
senden	sandte	gesandt	sendete	to send
singen	sang	gesungen	sänge	to sing

infinitive (3rd. pers. sing.)	simple past	past participle	general subjunctive present	meaning
sinken	sank	ist gesunken	sänke	to sink
sitzen	saß	gesessen	säße	to sit
spinnen	spann	gesponnen	spönne	to spin
sprechen (spricht)	sprach	gesprochen	spräche	to speak
springen	sprang	gesprungen	spränge	to jump
stechen (sticht)	stach	gestochen	stäche	to prick, sting
stehen	stand	gestanden	stünde or: stände	to stand
stehlen (stiehlt)	stahl	gestohlen	stähle or: stöhle	to steal
steigen	stieg	ist gestiegen	stiege	to climb, rise
sterben (stirbt)	starb	ist gestorben	stürbe	to die
stinken	stank	gestunken	stänke	to stink
stoßen (stößt)	stieß	gestoßen	stieße	to push
streichen	strich	gestrichen	striche	to paint
streiten	stritt	gestritten	stritte	to quarrel
tragen (trägt)	trug	getragen	trüge	to carry; wear
treffen (trifft)	traf	getroffen	träfe	to meet
treiben	trieb	getrieben	triebe	to drive (cattle); pursue (an activity)
treten (tritt)	trat	ist getreten	träte	to step, tread
trinken	trank	getrunken	tränke	to drink
tun	tat	getan	täte	to do
verderben (verdirbt)	verdarb	verdorben	verdürbe	to spoil
vergessen (vergißt)	vergaß	vergessen	vergäße	to forget
verlieren	verlor	verloren	verlöre	to lose
verschwinden	verschwand	ist verschwunden	verschwände	to disappear
verzeihen	verzieh	verziehen	verziehe	to pardon
wachsen (wächst)	wuchs	ist gewachsen	wüchse	to grow
waschen (wäscht)	wusch	gewaschen	wüsche	to wash
weichen	wich	ist gewichen	wiche	to yield, give way
wenden	wandte	gewandt	wendete	to turn
werben (wirbt)	warb	geworben	würbe	to recruit; woo
werden (wird)	wurde	ist geworden	würde	to become
werfen (wirft)	warf	geworfen	würfe	to throw
wiegen	wog	gewogen	wöge	to weigh
winden	wand	gewunden	wände	to wind, twist
wissen (weiß)	wußte	gewußt	wüßte	to know
ziehen	zog	gezogen	zöge	to pull
zwingen	zwang	gezwungen	zwänge	to force

§3 ADJECTIVES THAT ADD UMLAUT IN THE COMPARATIVE AND SUPERLATIVE (cf. Chap. 10, §2)

The following monosyllabic adjectives add an umlaut in the comparative and superlative:

alt	älter	ältest-
arg (bad)	ärger	ärgst-

arm	ärmer	ärmst-
dumm	dümmer	dümmst-
grob (coarse, rude)	gröber	gröbst-
groß	größer	größt-
hart	härter	härtest-
hoch	höher	höchst-
jung	jünger	jüngst-
kalt	kälter	kältest-
klug	klüger	klügst-
krank	kränker	kränkst-
kurz	kürzer	kürzest-
lang	länger	längst-
nah	näher	nächst-
oft	öfter	(öftest-) häufigst-
scharf (sharp)	schärfer	schärfst-
schwach (weak)	schwächer	schwächst-
schwarz	schwärzer	schwärzest-
stark	stärker	stärkst-
warm	wärmer	wärmst-

The following adjectives have comparative and superlative forms with and without umlaut. The boldface forms are more common.

blaß (pale)	**blasser**	**blassest-**
	blässer	blässest-
fromm (religious, devout)	frommer	frommst-
	frömmer	frömmst-
		(either form)
gesund (healthy)	gesunder	gesundest-
	gesünder	**gesündest-**
glatt (smooth, slippery)	**glatter**	**glattest-**
	glätter	glättest-
naß (whet)	**nasser**	**nassest-**
	nässer	nässest-
rot (red)	roter	rotest-
	röter	**rötest-**
schmal (narrow)	**schmaler**	**schmalst-**
	schmäler	schmälst-

§4   FLAVORING PARTICLES

Certain adverbs and conjunctions, such as **doch, schon, aber, denn,** are often used as flavoring particles. They express the speaker's attitude toward what is said and are difficult to translate into English in any consistent way. Nevertheless, it is possible to state when, and often why, they are used. Here are some frequently occurring flavoring particles and their most common uses.

aber

Aber merely strengthens the thought expressed.

> **Das hast du aber fein gemacht.**
> *You really did a fine job.*
> *You did a fine job, I must say.*

auch

1. **Auch** may confirm that a possibility or supposition is reality.

> **Köhlers hatten vor, ein Haus zu kaufen.—Sie haben auch eins gekauft.**
> *The Köhlers were planning to buy a house—They did buy one.*

> **Frau Schreiber soll sehr nett sein.—Sie ist auch sehr nett.**
> *Mrs. Schreiber is supposed to be very nice.—She indeed is very nice.*

2. **Auch** used in questions may express a certain doubt.

> **Hast du mich auch verstanden?**
> *Did you really understand me? (I wonder.)*

> **Kann man sich auch auf dich verlassen?**
> *Can one really rely on you?*

3. **Auch** used in commands reinforces them.

> **Vergiß das auch nicht!**
> *Be sure not to forget that.*

> **Komm auch nicht zu spät!**
> *Be sure not to be late.*

denn

1. **Denn** used in questions may imply special interest, impatience, or surprise on the part of the speaker.

> **Wann ist denn der Unfall passiert?**
> *When did the accident happen? (I'd like to know.)*

> **Warum kommt denn der Bus nicht?**
> *Why isn't the bus coming? (We've been waiting at least 15 minutes.)*

> **Kommst du denn nicht mit?**
> *Aren't you coming along? (I thought you would.)*

2. **Denn** may make questions less abrupt.

> **Wieso denn?**   *How so?*
> **Wo denn?**   *Where?*
> **Wann denn?**   *When?*

doch

1. **Doch** is frequently used for emphasis.

> **Das ist doch die Höhe!**
> *That is the limit. (stress on is)*

Das ist doch kaum zu glauben.
That certainly (indeed) is hard to believe.

2. **Doch** may express opposition: what is said is opposite to what one would have expected.

Wir haben Müllers doch noch eingeladen.
We invited the Müllers after all (contrary to what we said or planned to do before).

Such a statement is often strengthened by adding **noch**.

einmal, (mal)

1. **Nun einmal (nun mal)** indicates acceptance of something that cannot be helped.

Ich bin nun einmal (nun mal) sehr unbeliebt.
I am very unpopular (and there is nothing to be done about it).

Das ist nun einmal (nun mal) so.
That's how it is. That's how it goes.

2. **Mal** (seldom **einmal**) usually makes a sentence sound more casual, less abrupt or blunt.

Komm mal her!
Come here, will you?

Ich muß mir das mal überlegen.
I have to think about that.

ja

1. **Ja** is frequently used when stating facts that are known or when making assertions with confidence. **Ja** either remains untranslated or remarks such as " you know," " as is known," are added.

Das ist ja kein Geheimnis.
That's no secret, you know.

Das weiß ja jeder.
Everybody knows that.

2. **Ja** conveys admonition in imperatives.

Vergiß das (nur) ja nicht!
Be sure not to forget that.

Machen Sie das (nur) ja nicht wieder!
Don't ever do that again.

Ja is stressed in these cases; **nur** is frequently added for reinforcement (see below).

nur, bloß

Colloquially, **bloß** is frequently used instead of **nur.**

1. **Nur (bloß)** may express intense interest in learning the answer to some puzzling question.

> **Warum hat er nur (bloß) gelogen?**
> *Why did he lie? (I'd really like to know.)*
>
> **Wie konntest du nur (bloß) soviel Geld verschwenden?**
> *How on earth could you waste so much money?*

2. In imperative sentences **nur** may express encouragement and reassurance.

> **Kommen Sie nur herein!**
> *Do come in.*
> **Haben Sie nur keine Angst!**
> *Don't be afraid.*

It may also express admonition, frequently reinforcing **ja.**

> **Beleidige ihn nur nicht!** ⎫
> **Beleidige ihn nur ja nicht!** ⎬ *Don't insult him. (by all means)*
> ⎭

schon

1. **Schon** may express reassurance that something will be so, although it may seem to be doubtful.

> **Du wirst es schon schaffen.**
> *Don't worry, you'll make it.*
>
> **Wir werden schon eine Lösung finden.**
> *Don't worry, we'll find a solution.*

2. **Schon** may express a concession.

> **Das ist schon richtig, aber das ist nicht die ganze Wahrheit.**
> *That's correct, I admit (I grant you), but that's not the whole truth.*
>
> In den Ferien hast du doch genug Zeit zum Schreiben.—**Das schon, aber ich habe keine Lust dazu.**
>
> *During vacation you do have enough time to write.—That's true, I admit, but I don't have the urge to.*

As the above sentences illustrate, this concessive use can easily be recognized by the conjunction **aber** introducing a qualifying remark, frequently a counterargument.

3. **Schon** is used in rhetorical questions in the sense of *after all, but then.*

> Ich habe nichts gesagt. **Was kann man schon in so einem Fall sagen?**
> *I said nothing. After all, what can one say in such a case?*
>
> Natürlich ist das eine herrliche Jacht. **Aber wer kann sich schon so einen Luxus leisten?**
> *Of course, that is a magnificent yacht. But then, who can afford such a luxury?*

§5   COMMON GERMAN MEASUREMENTS AND THEIR ENGLISH EQUIVALENTS*

Most measures (except those ending in **-e**) add no ending in the plural when they follow a numeral.

das Pfund, -e	zwei Pfund	*two pounds*
der Grad, -e	zwei Grad	*two degrees*
die Meile, -n	zwei Meilen	*two miles*
die Gallone, -n	zwei Gallonen	*two gallons*

German	English equivalents	English	German equivalents
1 Zentimeter (1 cm)	0.4 inch	1 inch	2,5 Zentimeter
1 Meter (1 m)	3.3 feet	1 foot	0,3 Meter
	or: 1.1 yard	1 yard	0,9 Meter
1 Kilometer (1 km)	0.62 mile	1 mile	1,6 Kilometer

Illustration of how many miles correspond to 1–500 km:

Mile	0.6 1.8 3.1	4.9 6.2	9.3	12.4	15.5	18.6	21.7	24.8	27.9	31.0	62.1	93.1	124.2	155.2	186.4	217.4	248.5	279.5	310.6
Kilometer	1 3 5 8 10	15	20	25	30	35	40	45	50	100	150	200	250	300	350	400	450	500

1 Quadratmeter (1 qm) = 10.8 square feet	1 square foot = 0,092 Quadratmeter (qm)
1 Quadratkilometer (1 qkm) = 0.39 square mile	1 square mile = 2,6 Quadratkilometer (qkm)
1 Liter (1 l) = 2.1 U.S. pints 1.05 U.S. quarts	1 U.S. pint = 0,47 Liter (l) 1 U.S. quart = 0,94 Liter (l) 1 U.S. gallon = 3,76 Liter (l)
1 Gramm (1 g) = 0.04 ounce 1 Pfund (1 Pfd) = 1.1 pounds 1 Kilogramm (1 kg) = 2.2 pounds or: Kilo	1 ounce = 28 Gramm (g) 1 pound = 454 Gramm (g)

Some practical hints:

A **Meter** is a little more than a yard.
A **Pfund** is a little more than a pound.
A **Liter** is a little more than a quart. **3 3/4 Liter** = 1 gallon.
A **Kilometer** is 5/8 of a mile. **5 Kilometer** = approx. 3 miles.

When you weigh yourself on a German scale, your weight is 10 percent less than on an American scale; for example, Barbara weighs 120 pounds in America, but **108 Pfund** in Germany.

* Data and illustrations from "These Strange German Ways," courtesy Atlantik-Brücke e. V., Hamburg.

Fahrenheit and Centigrades (Celsius)

Wieviel Grad haben wir heute?

Heute haben wir zehn Grad Celsius. (written: 10° C)

If you have the centigrade reading and want to find out the temperature in Fahrenheit, multiply the centigrades by 9, divide by 5, and add 32.

$$\text{Formula: } F = \frac{9C}{5} + 32$$

If you have the Fahrenheit reading and want to find out the temperature in centigrade, deduct 32 from the Fahrenheit reading, multiply by 5, and divide by 9.

$$\text{Formula: } C = \frac{5(F - 32)}{9}$$

The dual scales on the thermometer shown below give you some equivalents.

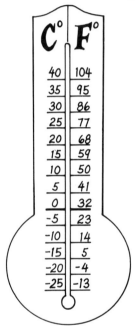

Conversion Tables

SKIRTS, DRESSES, COATS		SHIRTS		SHOES	
U.S.	EUROPE	U.S.	EUROPE	U.S.	EUROPE
10	38	14	36	6	37
12	40	14 1/2	37	7	38
14	42	15	38	8	39
16	44	15 1/2	39	9	40
18	46	16	41	10	41
20	48	16 1/2	42	11	42
		17	43	12	43
				13	44

SUITS		BLOUSES		HATS	
U.S.	EUROPE	U.S.	EUROPE	U.S.	EUROPE
36	46	30	38	7	57
38	48	32	40	7 1/8	58
40	50	34	42	7 1/4	59
42	52	36	44	7 3/8	60
44	54	38	46	7 1/2	61
46	56	40	48		
48	58				

KITCHEN HINTS

U.S.	EUROPE
1 cup sugar	200 g
1 cup flour	150 g
1 tsp.	5 g
1 tbsp.	12 g

§6   PUNCTUATION

The following punctuation rules differ from English usage.

The comma

1. In enumerations the last item is not set off by a comma if preceded by **und** or **oder.**

> Klaus, Margot und Renate haben einen Preis gewonnen.
> *Klaus, Margot, and Renate won a prize.*

> Klaus, Margot oder Renate haben den ersten Preis gewonnen.
> *Klaus, Margot, or Renate won first prize.*

2. Main clauses joined by **und** or **oder** are more often separated by commas than in English.

> Helga las die Zeitung, und ihre Schwester schrieb Briefe.
> *Helga read the newspaper and her sister wrote letters.*

> Das Eis auf dem See taut schon, oder es wird bald tauen.
> *The ice on the lake is thawing already or it is going to thaw soon.*

But if the clauses share one or more elements, no comma is used.

> Das Eis auf dem See taut schon oder wird bald tauen.
> *The ice on the lake is thawing already or is going to thaw soon.*

Das Eis is the subject of both **taut** and **wird ... tauen.**

3. The conjunctions **aber** and **sondern** are preceded by a comma if the following element is a phrase or clause.

Sie ist sehr intelligent, aber leider etwas faul.
She is very intelligent but unfortunately a little lazy.

Er wohnt nicht in Bonn, sondern in Köln.
He doesn't live in Bonn but in Cologne.

4. All dependent clauses are set off by commas.

Ich weiß, daß er jetzt zu Hause ist.
I know that he is at home now.

Ich weiß, er ist jetzt zu Hause.
I know he is at home now.

Das ist ein Film, der mir gefällt.
That's a film I like.

Die Schallplatte, die ich gestern gekauft habe, ist verschwunden.
The record I bought yesterday has disappeared.

5. Infinitive phrases are set off by commas unless they consist only of **zu** + infinitive.

Ich versuche zu arbeiten.
I'm trying to work.

Ich versuche, mich zu konzentrieren.
I'm trying to concentrate.

Ich versuche, mich auf meine Arbeit zu konzentrieren.
I'm trying to concentrate on my work.

6. Adverbs and prepositional phrases are normally not set off by commas.

Natürlich weiß er das.
Of course, he knows that.

Zum Glück war Margot zu Hause.
Luckily, Margot was at home.

Nach vielen Jahren schwerer Arbeit ist mein Vater endlich in den Ruhestand getreten.
After many years of hard work, my father finally retired.

7. The comma is used as a decimal point (cf. Chap. 11, §1).

3,50 (read: drei Komma fünf null) = *3.50 (three point five O)*

Keep in mind:

> German leaves a space or uses a period to separate thousands and millions (cf. Chap. 11, §1).
> 10 000   or   10.000 = English 10,000
> 1 000 000   or   1.000.000 = English 1,000,000

Punctuation of direct quotations

Er sagte: „ Ich habe keine Zeit."
He said, "I don't have time."

Direct quotations are preceded by a colon. Except in typing, the opening quotation mark is set on the line.

The end quote precedes a comma:

> „ Ich habe keine Zeit ", sagte er.

The exclamation point

> Bitte kommen Sie!
> or: Bitte kommen Sie. — *Please come.*

Imperative sentences end with an exclamation point or, if there is no special emphasis, with a period.

The hyphen in compounds

German often omits an element belonging to two different compound nouns. The hyphen is then used to show where it has been omitted.

> Er ist Mathematik- und Physikprofessor.
>   (for: Mathematikprofessor und Physikprofessor)
> Ich habe einen Sonnenaufgang und -untergang fotografiert.
>   (for: Sonnenaufgang und Sonnenuntergang)

§7   WRITING LETTERS AND ADDRESSES

For writing the date, see Chapter 11, §4, 5.

Formal letter

```
Sehr geehrter Herr Krause,

ich danke Ihnen für Ihren Brief vom 23. August. Ich verstehe
natürlich, daß....

Mit freundlichen Grüßen
```

Maria Schoelber

The salutation **Sehr geehrter Herr Krause** (lit. *Very esteemed Mr. Krause*) corresponds to English *Dear Mr. Krause*. When the letter is directed to a company, it may begin with **Sehr geehrte Herren** or no salutation.

Some people hesitate to begin a letter with **ich** because it might be considered impolite. They begin with another element and use inversion:

```
Sehr geehrter Herr Krause,
für Ihren Brief vom 23. August danke ich Ihnen...
```

Note that there are no indentations.

Informal letters

Note that the personal pronouns of the familiar address and the corresponding possessives are capitalized:

```
Liebe Monika,

lange habe ich nichts von Dir und Deiner Familie gehört.
Hast Du meinen Brief vom 1. September nicht erhalten?...

              Mit herzlichen Grüßen
                    Deine
                   Sabine

Liebe Barbara und lieber Dietmar,

lange habe ich nichts von Euch gehört. Habt Ihr meinen Brief
vom 30. Juli nicht erhalten?...

              Beste Grüße
              von Eurem
                   Klaus
```

Addresses

Familie	Frau
Martin Schramm	Dr. Käte Wolf
Beethovenstraße 21	Jenaer Str. 2
D–6000 Frankfurt/Main	DDR–5300 Weimar
Fräulein	Herrn
Maria Renner	Professor Dr. H. Spörli
Schubertring 2	Mainaustr. 12
A–1011 Wien	CH–8008 Zürich

Note: a. The house number follows the street.
      b. The ZIP code precedes the city name.
      c. Letters sent to another country have a country symbol prefixed to the ZIP code. Some of the common ones are:

D	Federal Republic of Germany (West Germany)
DDR	German Democratic Republic (East Germany)
A	Austria
CH	Switzerland

§8   THE GERMAN ALPHABET

Modern German books and newspapers use the same type fonts as are used in English, and German handwriting is similar to ours. Until the second quarter of the twentieth century Gothic type (Fraktur) was commonly used in Germany. Since you may encounter this type in older books, the following table provides Roman and Gothic styles, together with handwritten Gothic forms.

ROMAN TYPE		GOTHIC TYPE AND GERMAN SCRIPT		PRONUNCIATION OF LETTER NAME
A	a	𝔄	a	ah
B	b	𝔅	b	beh
C	c	ℭ	c	tseh
D	d	𝔇	d	deh
E	e	𝔈	e	eh
F	f	𝔉	f	eff
G	g	𝔊	g	geh
H	h	ℌ	h	hah
I	i	ℑ	i	ee
J	j	𝔍	j	yot
K	k	𝔎	k	kah
L	l	𝔏	l	ell
M	m	𝔐	m	em
N	n	𝔑	n	en
O	o	𝔒	o	oh

ROMAN TYPE		GOTHIC TYPE AND GERMAN SCRIPT		PRONUNCIATION OF LETTER NAME
P	p	𝔓	p	peh
Q	q	𝔔	q	coo
R	r	ℜ	r	err
S	s	𝔖	ſ ß	ess
T	t	𝔗	t	teh
U	u	𝔘	u	oo
V	v	𝔙	v	fow (as in fowl)
W	w	𝔚	w	veh
X	x	𝔛	x	iks
Y	y	𝔜	y	üpsilon
Z	z	ℨ	z	tset

UMLAUTE

Ä	ä			ah umlaut
Ö	ö			oh umlaut
Ü	ü			oo umlaut

DIPTHONGS

Au	au	Au	au	= ow (as in owl)
Äu	äu	Äu	äu	= ow umlaut
Eu	eu	Eu	eu	= oy (as in boy)
Ai	ai	Ai	ai	} = eye
Ei	ei	Ei	ei	

GERMAN SCRIPT

Herbstlied

Bunt sind schon die Wälder,
Gelb die Stoppelfelder,
Und der Herbst beginnt.
Und die Blätter fallen,
Und die Nebel wallen,
Kühler weht der Wind.

EXAMPLE IN ROMAN TYPE

Herbstlied

Bunt[1] sind schon die Wälder,
Gelb die Stoppelfelder,[2]
Und der Herbst beginnt.
Und die Blätter fallen,
Und die Nebel[3] wallen,[4]
Kühler weht[5] der Wind.

—Salis-Seewis

GOTHIC TYPE

Herbstlied

Bunt sind schon die Wälder,
Gelb die Stoppelfelder,
Und der Herbst beginnt.
Und die Blätter fallen,
Und die Nebel wallen,
Kühler weht der Wind.

—Salis-Seewis.

1 bunt — many-colored
2 das Stoppelfeld, -er — stubble field
3 der Nebel, - — fog
4 wallen — to surge
5 wehen — to blow

German-English Vocabulary

With the exception of numerals and personal pronouns, all vocabulary items that appear in the exercises are included. The number in parentheses indicates the chapter in which each vocabulary item is introduced. A second number indicates that the word in question is reintroduced in a subsequent chapter with additional information about its use.

The nouns are given in the nominative singular and plural:

$$\text{die Stadt, ¨e} = \text{nom. sing. } \textbf{die Stadt}$$
$$\text{nom. pl. } \textbf{die Städte}$$

$$\textbf{der Lehrer, } - = \text{nom. sing. } \textbf{der Lehrer}$$
$$\text{nom. pl. } \textbf{die Lehrer}$$

Irregular plurals are written out:

das Drama, die Dramen

Weak nouns (cf. Chap. 5, §5) are listed as follows:

der Student (*weak*), **-en**

The genitive singular is added when it is irregular:

der Name (*weak; gen.* **-ns**), **-n**

Adjectival nouns (cf. Chap. 9, §12–§13) are listed as follows:

der Fremde (*adj. noun*)

Only the infinitive is provided for weak verbs; (**ist**) after the infinitive indicates that the present perfect and past perfect tenses require the auxiliary **sein**:

reisen (ist)

The principal parts are given for all strong and irregular verbs:

geben (gibt), gab, gegeben
gehen, ging, ist gegangen

ab•brechen (bricht ab), brach ab, abgebrochen (14) to break off
der Abend, -e (11) evening, night (*before bedtime*)
    zu Abend essen (19) to have dinner (*evening meal*)
    aber (1, 12) but, however, nevertheless

ab•hängen (hängt ab), hing ab, abgehangen von (*dat.*) (20) to depend on
ab•holen (2) to pick up
ab•lehnen (15) to decline
ab•nehmen (nimmt ab), nahm ab, abgenommen (2, 3) to decrease, lose weight
ab•sagen (18) to call off

ab•schalten (16) to turn off
ach so (4) oh, I see
die **Ahnung: keine Ahnung haben** (2) to have no idea
die **Aktentasche, -n** (7) briefcase
der **Alkohol, -e** (4) alcohol
alle (*pl.*) (6) all
allein (20) alone
Allwissend: Dr. Allwissend (14) Dr. know-it-all
als (10) than
als (*sub. conj.*) (12) when
alt (10) old
altmodisch (9) old-fashioned
amerikanisch (9) American
an (*acc./dat.*) (7) on (*vertically*), by, at the edge of
die **Ananasbowle, -n** (20) pineapple punch
an•bauen (18) to grow, cultivate, plant
ändern (14) to change; **das läßt sich nicht ändern** (18) that cannot be helped
anders (18) different(ly)
der **Anfang, ⁻e** (5) beginning
an•fangen (fängt an), fing an, angefangen (2, 3) to begin, start
die **Angabe** (14) showing off, bragging
an•geben (gibt an), gab an, angegeben (2, 3) to show off, brag, put on airs
das **Angebot, -e** (4) offer; **das Angebot an•nehmen (nimmt an), nahm an, angenommen** to accept the offer
der **Angestellte** (*adj. noun*) (9) employee
an•greifen, griff an, angegriffen (20) to attack
die **Angst, ⁻e** (2) fear; **Angst haben vor** (*dat.*) (2, 8) to be afraid of; **keine Angst!** (10) don't be afraid, don't worry
an•kommen, kam an, ist angekommen (7) to arrive; **an•kommen auf** (*acc.*) (8) to depend on; **es kommt (ganz) darauf an** it (all) depends
an•nehmen (nimmt an), nahm an, angenommen (2, 3) to accept; to assume
die **Anordnung, -en** (18) regulation, rule
an•rufen, rief an, angerufen (1, 3) to call (*by phone*)
sich (*dat.*) **etwas an•schauen** (17) to (take a) look at
sich (*dat.*) **etwas an•sehen (sieht an), sah an, angesehen** (17) to (take a) look at
die **Ansichtskarte, -n** (18) picture postcard

anstatt (*gen.*) (7) instead
antik (16) antique
antworten (*dat.*) (5) to answer someone; **antworten auf** (*acc.*) (8) to answer something
an•ziehen, zog an, angezogen (9) to put on
der **Anzug, ⁻e** (5) suit
applaudieren (2) to applaud
der **April** (11) April
die **Arbeit, -en** (2) work
arbeiten an (*dat.*) (1, 8) to work on
der **Arbeiter, —** (5) worker
ärgern (15) to annoy
der **Arme** (*adj. noun*) (9) the poor man
das **Aroma, die Aromen** (9) aroma
der **Arzt, ⁻e** (2) male doctor; **der Arzt hat es mir verboten** (4) doctor's orders
die **Ärztin, -nen** (5) female doctor
die **Aspirintablette, -n** (1) aspirin (tablet)
der **Assistent** (*weak*), **-en** (5) male assistant
die **Assistentin, -nen** (5) female assistant
atmen (2) to breathe
attraktiv (9) attractive
auch (2) also, too
auf (*acc./dat.*) (7) on (*horizontally*)
auf•geben (gibt auf), gab auf, aufgegeben (2, 3) to give up
aufgeregt (14) excited, upset
auf•hören (2) to stop, end, cease; **mit einem Kurs auf•hören** (12) to drop a course
auf•machen (2) to open
die **Aufnahme, -n** (8) picture, photograph; **eine Aufnahme machen** to take a picture
auf•passen (2) to pay attention, watch, keep an eye on
auf•räumen (3) to tidy up, to straighten up
auf•stehen, stand auf, ist aufgestanden (3) to rise, get up
auf•tauchen (20) to emerge, come up
der **Augenblick, -e** (2) moment
der **August** (11) August
aus (*dat.*) (7) out of, from
die **Ausdauer** (13) staying power, perseverance
aus•drücken (18) to express
aus•füllen (4) to fill out
aus•geben: Geld aus•geben (gibt aus), gab aus, ausgegeben (3) to spend money

aus•gehen, ging aus, ist ausgegangen (2, 3) to go out

ausgeschlossen (6) out of the question

ausgezeichnet (9) excellent

aus•kommen, kam aus, ist ausgekommen mit (*dat.*) (12) to get along with

die Auskunft, ⁻e (9) information; Auskunft geben (gibt), gab, gegeben to give information

aus•lachen (3) to laugh at

der Ausländer, — (5) male foreigner

die Ausländerin, -nen (5) female foreigner

ausländisch (9) foreign

aus•nutzen (18) to exploit

die Aussage, -n (14) testimony

aus•sehen (sieht aus), sah aus, ausgesehen (2, 3) to appear, look

außer (*dat.*) (7) except, besides

außer sich (*dat.*) sein (17) to be beside oneself

außerdem (8) besides, aside from that

die Ausrede, -n (20) excuse, pretext

aus•reden lassen (20) to let finish (*talking*)

aus•steigen, stieg aus, ist ausgestiegen (3) to get off (*a vehicle*)

die Auswahl (16) selection, choice

der Ausweg, -e (18) way out

auswendig lernen (19) to learn by heart

der Ausweis, -e (5) identification card

das Auto, -s (1) car

automatisch (18) automatic

der Autoschlüssel, — (1) car key

der Autounfall, ⁻e (14) car accident

das Baby, -s (5) baby

die Bäckerei, -en (7) bakery

das Bad (das Badezimmer, —) (20) bathroom

baden (2) to bathe

der Bahnhof, ⁻e (1) railway station

bald (10) soon

der Ball, ⁻e (2) Ball

die Bank, -en (7) bank

der Bankrott, -e (18) bankruptcy

bankrott machen (14) to go bankrupt

bannen (11) to excommunicate

bar bezahlen (4) to pay cash

der Beamte (*adj. noun*) (14) official

bedeuten (1) to mean

bedienen (18) to wait on

sich (*acc.*) bedienen (17) to help *or* serve oneself

beenden (3) to finish

befehlen (befiehlt), befahl, befohlen (8) to order, give orders

befördern (18) to promote

befreundet sein mit (*dat.*) (16) to be friends with

begeistert sein von (*dat.*) (8) to be enthusiastic about

beginnen, begann, begonnen (1, 3) to begin

begraben (begräbt), begrub, begraben (2) to bury; die Sache begraben to bury the matter

begrüßen (14) to welcome

behalten (behält), behielt, behalten (4) to keep

behandeln (12) to treat, deal with

behaupten (14) to claim, assert

bei (*dat.*) (7) at, near, at someone's place; bei sich (*dat.*) haben: ich habe kein Geld bei mir (17) I have no money on me

beide (6) both

das Beispiel, -e (9) example

beißen, biß, gebissen (9) to bite

bekommen, bekam, bekommen (2, 3) to get, receive

beleidigen (2) to insult

die Beleidigung, -en (9) insult

beliebt (9) popular

bellen (9) to bark; bellend barking

die Bemerkung, -en (2) remark, observation

benachrichtigen (18) to notify

beneiden (2) to envy

bequem (10) comfortable

der Bericht, -e (19) report

berühmt (8) famous

die Bescheidenheit (17) modesty

besetzt: die Leitung ist besetzt (12) the line is busy

besprechen (bespricht), besprach, besprochen (19) to discuss

bestehen: die Prüfung bestehen, bestand, bestanden (3) to pass the exam

sich (*dat.*) bestellen (17) to order for oneself

bestimmt (3) certain(ly), definite(ly)

besuchen (1) to visit

betonen (14) to emphasize

betrügen, betrog, betrogen (15) to cheat

das **Bett, -en** (7) bed
bevor (*sub. conj.*) (12) before
beweisen, bewies, bewiesen (5) to prove
der **Bewerber, —** (9) applicant
die **Bewerbung, -en** (18) application
bewundern (2) to admire
bezahlen (1) to pay
die **Bibliothek, -en** (1) library
das **Bild, -er** (6) picture
billig (10) cheap, inexpensive
die **Billion, -en** (11) trillion
die **Biographie, -en** (9) biography
bis (*acc.*) (7) until *or* as far as, to, up to
(*location*)
bis jetzt (2) until now, so far;
bißchen: ein bißchen (9) a little (bit)
bitten, bat, gebeten um (*acc.*) (2, 3, 8) to
ask for, request
bleiben, blieb, ist geblieben (3) to stay,
remain
der **Blinde** (*adj. noun*) (9) the blind man
der **Boden, ⸚** (7) floor
böse sein auf (*acc.*) *or* **mit** (*dat.*) (1, 6, 8) to
be angry with
brauchen (4) to need; **etwas nicht zu**
machen brauchen (4) not to have to do
something
braun (9) brown
brechen (bricht), brach, gebrochen (17) to
break; **sich** (*dat.*) **den Arm brechen** to
break one's arm
die **Bremse, -n** (2) brake
brennen, brannte, gebrannt (3) to burn;
es brennt there is a fire
der **Brief, -e** (1) letter
der **Briefkasten, ⸚** (7) mailbox
die **Briefmarke, -n** (2) stamp
die **Briefmarkensammlung, -en** (7) stamp collection
die **Brieftasche, -n** (7) wallet
die **Brille, -n** (4) (eye) glasses
bringen, brachte, gebracht (3) to bring;
nach Hause bringen to bring *or* take
home
der **Bruder, ⸚** (5) brother
das **Brüderchen** (*diminutive*) (5) little brother
brummen (4) to grumble
die **Buchhandlung, -en** (7) bookstore
das **Bücherregal, -e** (5) book shelf
der **Bügel, der Kleiderbügel, —** (20)
(clothes)hanger
bügeln (4) to iron, press

der **Bummel, —** (7) stroll; **einen Bummel**
machen to go for *or* take a stroll
der **Bürgermeister, —** (5) mayor
das **Büro, -s** (1) office
der **Bus, -se** (2) bus
die **Bushaltestelle, -n** (7) bus stop

die **Chance, -n** (5) chance
charmant (9) charming
der **Charme** (9) charm
der **Chef, -s** (1) male boss
die **Chefin, -nen** (5) female boss

da (12) then *or* there; **da drüben** (19) over
there; **da** (*sub. conj.*) (12) since (*stating*
reason), because
das **Dach, ⸚er** (2) roof
damit (*sub. conj.*) (12) so that, in order
that
der **Dampfer, —** (19) steamship
danken (*dat.*) **für** (*acc.*) (5, 8) to thank for
dann (12) then
das (1) that
daß (*sub. conj.*) (1) that
das **Datum, die Daten** (5) date
die **Dauerwelle, -n** (20) permanent; **sich** (*dat.*)
eine Dauerwelle machen lassen to get a
permanent
die **Debatte, -n** (14) debate
der **Dekan, -e** (5) dean
denken, dachte, gedacht an (*acc.*) (3, 8) to
think of
denn (12) for, because
deprimiert (6) depressed
deshalb (8) because of that, therefore
deswegen (8) because of that, therefore
der **Deutsche** (*adj. noun*) (9) the German
die **Deutschstunde, -n** (7) German class
der **Dezember** (11) December
das **Dia, -s** (*short for* das **Diapositiv, -e**) (6)
slide
der **Diamantring, -e** (6) diamond ring
dick (2) fat
der **Dieb, -e** (18) thief
der **Dienstag, -e** (3) Tuesday
dieser, dieses, diese (1) this
diplomatisch (14) diplomatic
dirigieren (20) to conduct (*music*)
die **Disko, -s** (*short for* die **Diskothek, -en**) (7)
disco
der **Donnerstag, -e** (11) Thursday
das **Dorf, ⸚er** (5) village
dort (2) there

das **Drama, die Dramen** (5) drama

der **Dreck** (10) dirt; **die Dreckarbeit** dirty work

dringend (10) urgent

drohen (*dat.*) (18) to threaten; **mit Entlassung drohen** to threaten with dismissal

dumm (3) stupid, silly, dumb

die **Dummheit, -en** (8) stupidity

der **Dummkopf, ⁻e** (*male and female*) (7) dumbbell

dunkel (9) dark

dünn (2) thin

durch (*acc.*) (3) through

durch•fahren (fährt durch), fuhr durch, ist durchgefahren (2) to go nonstop

durchfahren (durchfährt), durchfuhr, hat durchfahren (2) to run through (*figuratively*); **ein großer Schreck durchfährt die Menge** a feeling of great horror runs through the crowd

durch•fallen (fällt durch), fiel durch, ist durchgefallen (3) to flunk (exam)

dürfen (darf), durfte, gedurft (4) may, to be allowed to

Durst haben (3) to be thirsty

die **Ecke, -n** (7) corner

egoistisch (10) egotistical

ehe (*sub. conj.*) (12) before

das **Ehepaar, -e** (16) (married) couple

das **Ehrenwort** (6) word of honor

das **Ei, -er** (9) egg

eilig: es eilig haben (2) to be in a hurry

einander (17) each other, one another

ein•biegen, bog ein, ist eingebogen (20) to turn into (*a street*)

einfach (4) simple, simply

eingebildet (14) conceited

ein•gehen, ging ein, ist eingegangen auf (*acc.*) (16) to go into (*question, point*)

sich (*acc.*) **einigen** (14) to come to an agreement

einkaufen gehen (7) to go shopping

ein•laden (lädt ein), lud ein, eingeladen (2, 3) to invite

die **Einladung, -en** (2) invitation; **die Einladung an•nehmen (nimmt an), nahm an, angenommen** to accept the invitation

ein•lösen: den Scheck ein•lösen (6) to cash the check

ein•reichen (4) to hand in

ein•schlafen (schläft ein), schlief ein, ist eingeschlafen (3) to fall asleep

ein•steigen, stieg ein, ist eingestiegen (3) to climb in, get on, board a vehicle

die **Einzelheit, -en** (16) detail

einzig (20) single; **nicht eine einzige Tasse Kaffee** not a single cup of coffee

das **einzige** (16) the only thing

das **Eis** (2) ice, ice cream

elegant (9) elegant

die **Eltern** (1) parents

empfehlen (empfiehlt), empfahl, empfohlen (2, 6) to recommend

englisch (9) English

entlang (*acc.*) (7) along

entlassen (entläßt), entließ, entlassen (2) to dismiss, fire

die **Entlassung, -en** (18) dismissal; **mit Entlassung drohen** to threaten with dismissal

die **Entscheidung, -en** (20) decision

entschuldigen (2) to excuse

sich (*acc.*) **entschuldigen bei** (*dat.*) (17, 19) to apologize to

enttäuschen (4) to disappoint

die **Enttäuschung, -en** (18) disappointment

entwickeln (20) to develop

die **Entwicklung, -en** (18) development

erben (16) to inherit

der **Erfinder, —** (5) male inventor

die **Erfinderin, -nen** (5) female inventor

die **Erfindung, -en** (5) invention

der **Erfolg, -e** (3) success

erhöhen (5) to raise

sich (*acc.*) **erinnern an** (*acc.*) (17) to remember

sich (*acc.*) **erkälten** (17) to catch a cold

die **Erkältung, -en** (5) cold

erkennen, erkannte, erkannt (12) to recognize

erklären (2) to explain

die **Erlaubnis: die Erlaubnis erteilen** (18) to give permission; **um Erlaubnis bitten** (4) to ask for permission

erledigen (2) to take care of, settle

ernst nehmen (nimmt), nahm, genommen (12) to take seriously

erreichen (8, 11) to achieve; to reach, contact

der **Erwachsene** (*adj. noun*) (9) adult

erwähnen (18) to mention

erzählen (4) to tell, relate

das **Essen, —** (5) meal
 essen (ißt), aß, gegessen (2, 3) to eat
 etwas (2, 16) a little; something
das **Experiment, -e** (2) experiment

die **Fabrik, -en** (5) factory
die **Fahne, -n** (2) flag
 fahren (fährt), fuhr, ist gefahren (1, 3) to
  drive, ride, go
der **Fahrer, —** (6) driver
der **Fahrgast, ⁓e** (20) passenger
das **Fahrrad, ⁓er** (6) bicycle
der **Fall, ⁓e** (9) case
 fallen (fällt), fiel, ist gefallen (3) to fall
 falsch (16) false, wrong
die **Familie, -n** (8) family
 faulenzen (18) to loaf
der **Faulenzer, —** (5) male lazybones
die **Faulenzerin, -nen** (5) female lazybones
der **Februar** (11) February
der **Fehler, —** (1) mistake
 feiern (18) to celebrate
der **Feind, -e** (5) enemy
das **Fenster, —** (3) window
die **Ferne** (18) distance; **in der Ferne** in the
  distance
 fern•sehen (sieht fern), sah fern, fern-
  gesehen (4) to watch television
der **Fernseher, —** (6) TV set
 feucht (12) humid
das **Fieber (1)** fever
die **Figur, -en** (7) figure
der **Film, -e** (5) film
 finanzieren (18) to finance
 finden, fand, gefunden (2, 3) to find
die **Firma, die Firmen** (7) company, firm
der **Fisch, -e** (3) fish
 fit bleiben, blieb, ist geblieben (12) to stay
  fit
die **Fleischerei, -en** (17) butcher's shop
 fliegen, flog, ist geflogen (1) to fly
die **Flitterwochen** (pl.) (6) honeymoon; **die**
  Flitterwochen verbringen, verbrachte,
  verbracht (6) to spend the honeymoon
die **Flöte, -n** (20) flute
der **Flughafen, ⁓** (4) airport
der **Flugplatz, ⁓e** (3) airport
das **Flugzeug, -e** (15) airplane
der **Fluß, ⁓sse** (7) river
die **Folge, -n** (6) consequence
 folgen (ist) (dat.) (3) to follow
 folgend (9) following

das **Formular, -e** (4) form
 formulieren (14) to formulate, phrase
das **Foto, -s** (20) photo(graph)
die **Frage, -n** (5) question; **eine Frage stellen**
  (14) to ask a question
 fragen (1) to ask; **sich** (acc.) **fragen** (17) to
  ask oneself
 französisch (9) French
die **Frau, -en** (2, 4) woman; wife; **Frau ...**
  Mrs. ...
 frech (2) fresh, impudent
die **Freiheit, -en** (5) freedom, liberty
der **Freitag, -e** (2) Friday
der **Fremde** (adj. noun) (9) stranger
 sich (acc.) **freuen auf** (acc.) (17) to look
  forward to
 sich (acc.) **freuen über** (acc.) (17) to be
  happy about
der **Freund, -e** (1) male friend; **der feste**
  Freund (9) steady boyfriend
die **Freundin, -nen** (1) female friend
 freundlich (1) friendly
die **Freundlichkeit, -en** (5) friendliness
der **Friede** (weak; gen. -ns) (5) peace
der **Friseur, -e** (19) hairdresser
die **Frisur, -en** (20) hairdo
 froh sein über (acc.) (3, 8) to be glad
  about
 früher (10) earlier, before, in the past
 frühestens (10) at the earliest
der **Frühling, -e** (11) spring
der **Führerschein, -e** (5) driver's licence
 funktionieren (1) to function, work
 für (acc.) (1, 7) for
 fürchten (3) to fear, be afraid of
 Fuß: zu Fuß gehen (3) to go on foot, to
  walk
die **Fußballmannschaft, -en** (1) soccer team
das **Fußballspiel, -e** (7) soccer game
der **Fußballspieler, —** (3) soccer player
der **Fußballtrainer, —** (5) soccer coach
der **Fußboden, ⁓** (20) floor

 gähnen (3) to yawn
 ganz (2) whole
 gar nicht (14) not at all
die **Garage, -n** (3) garage
der **Garten, ⁓** (5) garden
das **Gebäude, —** (9) building
 geben (gibt), gab, gegeben (2, 3) to give;
  es gibt (acc.) (9, 15) there is, there are

gebrauchen (9) to use; **ein gebrauchter Wagen** a used car; **gebrauchte Bücher** second-hand books

der **Geburtstag, -e** (3) birthday; **ich habe Geburtstag** (11) it is my birthday

das **Gedächtnis** (12) memory

das **Gedicht, -e** (16) poem

die **Geduld** (4) patience

die **Gefahr, -en** (14) danger

gefährlich (7) dangerous

der **Gefallen, —** (8) favor; **um einen Gefallen bitten** to ask for a favor

gefallen (gefällt), gefiel, gefallen (dat.) (1, 3, 5) to like

sich (dat.) **gefallen** (17) to like oneself

das **Gefängnis, -se** (5) prison

gegen (acc.) (7) against

gegenüber (dat.) (7) across from

der **Gegner, —** (20) opponent

die **Gehaltserhöhung, -en** (8) salary raise

gehen, ging, ist gegangen (1, 3) to go; idiom: **es geht nach mir, dir, ihm,** etc. (13) it is up to me, you, him, etc.

das **Geheimnis, -se** (5) secret

gehören (dat.) (5) to belong to

das **Geld** (1) money

der **Geldbeutel, —** (9) purse, pocketbook

die **Gelegenheit, -en** (18) opportunity, chance

der **Gelehrte** (adj. noun) (9) scholar

genau (2) exact(ly), precise(ly)

genial (9) ingenious

genug (1) enough

genügen (8) to suffice, be enough

das **Gepäck** (2) luggage

der **Gepäckträger, —** (5) porter

gerade (4) just (now)

das **Gericht, -e** (19) court; **vor Gericht** in court

gern (2) gladly; **etwas gern tun** (2, 20) to like doing something; **gern haben** (12, 20) to be fond of

der **Geruch, ̈-e** (9) smell

das **Gerücht, -e** (6) rumor

das **Geschenk, -e** (7) gift, present

die **Geschichte, -n** (5) story

geschieden sein (7) to be divorced

das **Geschirr** (12) dishes; **das Geschirr spülen** to do the dishes

der **Geschmack, ̈-e** (9) taste

die **Geschwister** (9) brothers and sisters

das **Gesetz, -e** (2) law

die **Geste, -n** (2) gesture

gestern (1) yesterday

die **Gesundheit** (9) health

gewinnen, gewann, gewonnen (2, 3) to win

das **Gewitter, —** (15) thunderstorm

sich (acc.) **gewöhnen an** (acc.) (17) to get used or accustomed to

die **Glatze, -n** (6) bald head; **eine Glatze bekommen** to go bald

der **Glaube** (weak; gen. **-ns**) (5) faith

glauben (1) to believe

gleich: es ist mir (ganz) gleich (15) it is (all) the same to me

das **Glück** (12) luck; **großes Glück haben** to be very lucky; **zum Glück** (9) luckily

glücklich sein über (acc.) (8) to be happy about

das **Gold** (5) gold

die **Grammatik, -en** (1) grammar

gratulieren (dat.) **zu** (dat.) (5, 8) to congratulate on

grausam (16) cruel

die **Grippe, -n** (1) flu

groß (3, 10) big, large, tall (referring to a person's height)

großartig (6) great

die **Großeltern** (7) grandparents

grün (9) green

der **Grund, ̈-e** (7) reason; **aus diesem Grund** for this reason

der **Grundsatz, ̈-e** (20) principle

der **Gruß, ̈-e** (10) greeting

grüßen (17) to greet, say hello

gut (10) good

das **Haar, -e** (20) hair; **sich** (dat.) **die Haare schneiden lassen** to get a haircut

haben, hatte, gehabt (1, 3) to have

der **Haken, —** (7) hook

die **Hälfte, -n** (11) half

das **Hallenbad, ̈-er** (12) indoor swimming pool

halten (hält), hielt, gehalten (2, 3) to hold; stop

die **Haltung, -en** (16) attitude

die **Hand, ̈-e** (3) hand

handeln von (dat.) (8) to deal with, be about

die **Handschrift, -en** (9) handwriting

der **Handschuh, -e** (5) glove

hängen (20) to hang (activity)

hängen, hing, gehangen (20) to hang (condition)

hassen (2) to hate

das **Hauptfach, ¨er** (6) major
das **Haus, ¨er** (2) house; **zu Hause sein** (1) to be at home; **zu Hause bleiben** (13) to stay at home; **nach Hause gehen** (7) to go home
die **Hausaufgaben** (*pl.*) (1) homework
der **Hausmann, ¨er** (17) house husband
der **Hausmeister, —** (5) janitor
die **Hautcreme** (2) skin cream
heben, hob, gehoben (3) to raise, lift
heiraten (1) to marry, get married
der **Heiratsantrag, ¨e** (12) marriage proposal; **einen Heiratsantrag machen** to propose marriage
heiß (10) hot
heißen, hieß, geheißen (1) to be called, be named
der **Held** (*weak*), **-en** (5) hero
die **Heldin, -nen** (5) heroine
helfen (hilft), half, geholfen (*dat.*) (2, 3) to help
hell (9) light, light-colored
der **Herbst, -e** (11) fall
der **Herr** (*weak; -n*), **-en** (5) gentleman; **Herr** ... Mr. ...
herrlich (18) magnificent
das **Herz** (*weak; gen. -ns*), **-en** (3, 5) heart
heute (1) today; **heute abend** (11) tonight (*before bedtime*); **heute nacht** tonight (*after bedtime*)
hier (2) here
die **Hilfe, -n** (8) help
hinten (19) behind, in the back; **nach hinten gehen** to go to the back
hinter (*acc./dat.*) (7) behind
das **Hobby, -s** (5) hobby
hoch (10) high
höchstens (10) at the most
hoffen (2) to hope
hoffentlich (1) hopefully, I hope
die **Hoffnung, -en** (2) hope
hoffnungslos (9) hopeless
höflich (9) polite
der **Höhepunkt, -e** (5) high point
holen (2) to (go and) get, fetch; **sich** (*dat.*) **etwas holen** (17) to get something for oneself
das **Holz, ¨er** (7) wood
hören (4) to hear
der **Hörsaal, die Hörsäle** (11) lecture hall
das **Hotel, -s** (6) hotel
hübsch (10) pretty

der **Hund, -e** (9) dog
der **Hunger** (3) hunger; **Hunger haben** to be hungry

die **Idee, -n** (9) idea
immer (2) always
importieren (18) to import
in (*acc./dat.*) (7) in, into, to
indem (*sub. conj.*) (12) by (*doing something*)
die **Information, -en** (5) information
das **Inserat, -e** (20) ad, advertisement; **ein Inserat in die Zeitung setzen** to put an ad in the newspaper
intelligent (10) intelligent
die **Intelligenz** (9) intelligence
interessant (2) interesting
sich (*acc.*) **interessieren für** (*acc.*) (17) to be interested in
investieren (4) to invest
sich (*acc.*) **irren** (17) to be mistaken
irritieren (2) to irritate
der **Irrtum, ¨er** (20) error
das **Italien** (3) Italy
italienisch (1) Italian

die **Jacke, -n** (14) jacket
das **Jahr, -e** (2) year
die **Jahreszeit, -en** (11) season
das **Jahrhundert, -e** (11) century
der **Januar** (11) January
jeder, jedes, jede (6) every, each
jemals (11) ever
jemand (4) somebody, someone
jener, jenes, jene (6) that
jetzig (11) present
jetzt (1) now
der **Job, -s** (3) job
der **Journalist** (*weak*), **-en** male journalist
die **Journalistin, -nen** (5) female journalist
der **Juli** (11) July
jung (10) young
der **Junge** (*weak*), **-n** (5) boy
der **Juni** (1) June

der **Kaffee** (4) coffee; **Kaffee kochen** (10) to make coffee
der **Kalender, —** (5) calendar
kalt (1) cold
die **Kälte: bei dieser Kälte** (7) in this cold
die **Kamera, -s** (5) camera

das Kapitel, — (5) chapter
kaputt sein (6) to be broken (*not working*)
die Karriere, -n (6) career
der Käse (9) cheese
der Katalog, -e (5) catalogue
die Karte, -n (1) card; **Karten spielen** (3) to play cards
der Kassettenrecorder, — (1) cassette recorder
die Katastrophe, -n (18) catastrophe
kaufen (1) to buy; **sich** (*dat.*) **etwas kaufen** (17) to buy something for oneself
der Kaviar, -e (9) caviar
kein (1) no, not a, not any
kennen, kannte, gekannt (1, 3) to know, be acquainted with
kennenlernen (4) to get to know, meet (*for the first time*)
das Kind, -er (2) child
das Kino, -s (1) movie theater
der Klapperkasten, ⁻ (9) boneshaker
klären (16) to clarify
der Klatsch (5) gossip
klatschen (4) to gossip
das Klavier, -e (6) piano; **Klavier spielen** to play the piano
das Kleid, -er (5) dress
klein (10) small, little, short (*referring to a person's height*)
kleinlich (13) petty
klingeln (15) to ring the bell; **es klingelt** the bell is ringing
klingen, klang, geklungen (14) to sound
klopfen (15) to knock; **es klopft** there is a knock at the door
klug (16) smart
das Klügste (16) the smartest thing
kochen (4) to cook; **Kaffee kochen** to make coffee; **selbst (selber) kochen** (17) to do one's own cooking
der Koffer, — (3) suitcase
die Kombination, -en (14) combination
kommen, kam, ist gekommen (1, 3) to come; **wie kommt es?** (9) how come?
das Kompliment, -e (2) compliment
kompliziert (2) complicated
der Kompromiß, -sse (12) compromise; **einen Kompromiß schließen, schloß, geschlossen** to make a compromise, to compromise
die Konditorei, -en (5) pastry shop
können (kann), konnte, gekonnt (4) can,

to be able to; **ich kann nicht anders** I can't help it
die Konstruktion, -en (16) construction; **die grammatische Konstruktion** the grammatical construction
sich (*acc.*) **konzentrieren auf** (*acc.*) (17) to concentrate on
das Konzert, -e (1) concert
der Konzertsaal, die Konzertsäle (5) concert hall
der Kopf, ⁻e (5) head
der Kopfschmerz, -en (1) headache
korrigieren (2) to correct
kosten (1) to cost
die Krabbe, -n (20) shrimp
krank (2) ill, sick; **schwer krank sein** (14) to be seriously ill
das Krankenhaus, ⁻er (2) hospital
die Krankheit, -en (5) illness, sickness, disease
der Krieg, -e (8) war
kritisieren (2) to criticize
der Kuchen, — (4) cake
der Kugelschreiber, — (6) ballpoint pen
der Kühlschrank, ⁻e (9) refrigerator
der Kunde (*weak*), -n (5) customer
der Künstler, — (20) artist
der Kurs, -e (12) course; **mit einem Kurs auf•hören** to drop a course
kurz (10) short
der Kuß, ⁻sse (2) kiss

lächeln (2) to smile
lachen über (*acc.*) (1, 8) to laugh at *or* about
der Laden, ⁻ (18) shop, store
laden (lädt), lud, geladen (2) to load
die Lampe, -n (7) lamp
das Lampenfieber (3) stage fright
das Land, ⁻er (13) country; **aufs Land ziehen, zog, ist gezogen** to move to the country
landen (ist) (3) to land
lang (10) long
lange (2) a long time
langsam (10) slow
sich (*acc.*) **langweilen** (17) to be bored, get bored
langweilig (3) boring
der Lärm (3) noise
lassen (läßt), ließ, gelassen (3) to let, leave
der Lastwagen, — (20) truck

laufen (läuft), lief, ist gelaufen (2, 3) to run

die **Laune** (1) mood; **gute/schlechte Laune haben** to be in a good/bad mood

laut (10) loud

das **Leben** (13) life

die **Lebenshaltungskosten** (*pl.*) (20) cost of living

das **Leder** (7) leather

ledig (13) single

legen (20) to put (*in a lying position*), lay, make lie

der **Lehrer,** — (5) male teacher

die **Lehrerin, -nen** (5) female teacher

leicht (3) easy

leider (1) unfortunately

leihen, lieh, geliehen (14) to lend

die **Leine, -n** (15) line, rope; **an der Leine führen** to keep on a leash

leise (3) soft, low (*tone, voice*)

sich (*dat.*) **etwas leisten** (17) to treat oneself to something; **sich etwas leisten können** to be able to afford something

die **Leistung, -en** (16) achievement

die **Leiter, -n** (2) ladder

lernen (2) to learn

lesen (liest), las, gelesen (2) to read

leugnen (20) to deny

die **Leute** (*pl.*) (1) people

die **Liebe** (5) love

lieben (1) to love

die **Liebesgeschichte, -n** (6) love story

der **Liebling, -e** (*male or female*) (8) darling

das **Lied, -er** (9) song

liederlich (10) sloppy

liegen, lag, gelegen (3) to lie, be situated

loben (18) to praise

der **Löffel,** — (5) spoon

logisch (10) logical

die **Lohnerhöhung, -en** (20) wage increase

lösen (4) to solve

die **Lösung, -en** (10) solution

die **Lotterie, -n** (13) lottery

die **Lüge, -n** (4) lie

lügen, log, gelogen (14) to lie, tell a lie

(keine) Lust haben zu (*dat.*) (7) (not) to be in the mood to, (not) to feel like

machen (2) to make; **das macht nichts** (6) that doesn't matter

das **Mädchen,** — (5) girl

der **Magister** (12) the Master's; **den Magister machen** to get one's Master's degree

der **Mai** (11) May

Mal: dieses Mal (3) this time

mancher, manches, manche (6) many a; *pl.* some, a few

manchmal (1) sometimes

manipulieren (2) to manipulate

der **Mantel, ⁻** (5) coat

die **Mappe, -n** (7) folder

das **Märchen,** — (5) fairy tale

der **Marktplatz, ⁻e** (7) marketplace

marschieren (ist) (3) to march

der **März** (11) March

die **Maschine, -n** (20) machine, plane

die **Medaille, -n** (9) medal

mehr (1) more

meinen (2) to mean

meinetwegen (7) as far as I am concerned, for all I care

die **Meinung, -en** (5) opinion; **meiner Meinung nach** (7) in my opinion

meistens (9) mostly, usually

der **Mensch** (*weak*), **-en** (9) man, human being

der **Menschenverstand** (9) human understanding; **gesunder Menschenverstand** common sense

merken (3) to notice

die **Methode, -n** (9) method

mies (12) crummy

der **Miesepeter,** — (*male or female*) (2) grouch

die **Miete, -n** (9) rent

mieten (3) to rent

der **Mieter,** — (10) tenant

die **Milch** (9) milk

die **Milliarde, -n** (11) billion

die **Million, -en** (5) million

der **Millionär, -e** (6) millionaire

mindestens (10) at least

die **Minute, -n** (11) minute

miserabel (9) miserable

mißachten (2) to disregard

mißverstehen, mißverstand, mißverstanden (2, 3) to misunderstand

mit (*dat.*) with

der **Mitarbeiter,** — (14) collaborator

mit•bringen, brachte mit, mitgebracht (2, 3) to bring along

mit•fahren (fährt mit), fuhr mit, ist mitgefahren (3) to ride with (*someone*)

das **Mitglied, -er** (6) member

mit.kommen, kam mit, ist mitgekommen (2) to come along

mit.nehmen (nimmt mit), nahm mit, mitgenommen (2, 3) to take along

der Mittag, -e (11) noon; zu Mittag essen (19) to have lunch

die Mitternacht (11) midnight

der Mittwoch, -e (11) Wednesday

mögen (mag), mochte, gemocht (4) to like; ich möchte I would like

möglich (1) possible

die Möglichkeit, -en (5) possibility

der Monat, -e (2) month

der Mond, -e (20) moon

der Montag, -e (1) Monday

der Morgen, — (11) morning

morgen (1, 11) tomorrow

das Motel, -s (5) motel

das Motorrad, ¨er (3) motorcycle

müde (2) tired

das Museum, die Museen (5) museum

die Musik (5) music

das Musikinstrument, -e (6) musical instrument

müssen (muß), mußte, gemußt (4) must, to have to

mysteriös (9) mysterious

nach (dat.) (7) after, to, according to

der Nachbar, -n (2) male neighbor

die Nachbarin, -nen (2) female neighbor

die Nachbarschaft, -en (20) neighborhood

nachdem (sub. conj.) (3, 12) after

nach.geben (gibt nach), gab nach, nachgegeben (2, 3) to give in, yield

nach.gehen, ging nach, ist nachgegangen (11) to be slow (clock)

nachher (19) afterwards

der Nachmittag, -e (11) afternoon

die Nachricht, -en (8) news

die Nacht, ¨e (11) night (after bedtime)

der Nachtisch, -e (16) dessert

nächst- (1) nearest, next

nahe (10) near

der Name (weak; gen. -ns), -n (1, 5) name

die Nase, -n (4) nose; die Nase ins Buch stecken to hit the books

naß (20) whet

natürlich (1) naturally, of course

neben (acc./dat.) (7) next to, beside

das Nebenfach, ¨er (6) minor

das Nebenzimmer, — (9) adjoining room

nehmen (nimmt), nahm, genommen (2, 3) to take

nennen, nannte, genannt (3) to call, name

der Nerv, -en (1) nerve; diese Leute gehen mir auf die Nerven (9) these people are getting on my nerves

der Nervenzusammenbruch, ¨e (3) nervous breakdown

nervös (2) nervous

nett (1) nice

neu (1) new

neuerdings (20) recently; erst neuerdings only recently

die Neugierde (13) curiosity; vor Neugierde sterben to die of curiosity

neugierig (9) curious, nosy

nicht (1) not; nicht mehr (9) not anymore

nichts (2) nothing

nie (2) never

niemand (2) nobody

noch nicht (2) not yet

die Note, -n (1) grade

die Notiz, -en (6) note

der November (11) November

die Nummer, -n (5) number

nur (13) only

ob (sub. conj.) (1, 12) whether, if

oben (19) at the top, upstairs; nach oben gehen to go upstairs

obgleich (sub. conj.) (12) although

das Obst (9) fruit

obwohl (sub. conj.) (12) although

oder (12) or

öffnen (2) to open

oft (2) often

ohne (acc.) (7) without

der Oktober (11) October

die Olympischen Spiele (11) Olympic Games

die Oper, -n (7) opera

die Operation, -en (5) operation

optimistisch (14) optimistic

der Orangensaft, ¨e (10) orange juice

ordentlich (10) orderly, neat

organisieren (2) to organize

der Osten (5) east

paar: ein paar (2) a few, some

das Paket, -e (5) parcel

der Park, -s (3) park

parken (4) to park

der **Parkplatz, ¨e** (12) parking space, parking lot

die **Party, -s** (5) party

passieren (ist) (3) to happen

der **Patient** (*weak*), **-en** (2) patient

die **Pause, -n** (2) recess, break; **eine Pause machen** to take a break

peinlich (9) embarrassing

die **Perle, -n** (8) pearl; **sie ist eine Perle** she is a gem

die **Pfeife, -n** (8) pipe

das **Picknick, -e** *or* **-s** (8) picnic

der **Plan, ¨e** (14) plan

der **Plattenspieler, —** (4) record player

das **Plätzchen, —** (4) cookie

platzen (ist) (12) to blow out, burst

pleite sein (3) to be broke

plötzlich (19) suddenly, all of a sudden

die **Polizei** (5) police

der **Polizeiwagen** (3) police car

der **Polizist** (*weak*), **-en** (5) policeman

die **Polizistin, -nen** (5) policewoman

portugiesisch (9) Portuguese

die **Post** (2) mail; **die Post nachschicken** (19) to forward the mail

das **Postamt, ¨er** (2) post office

praktisch (10) practical

der **Präsident** (*weak*), **-en** (5) president

der **Preis, -e** (2) prize; (9) price

der **Preisträger, —** (20) prize winner

das **Problem, -e** (5) problem

problematisch (3) problematic

der **Professor** (*weak*), **-en** (5) male professor

die **Professorin, -nen** (6) female professor

das **Programm, -e** (5) program

das **Projekt, -e** (3) project

prophezeien (14) to prophesy, predict

der **Protest, -e** (5) protest

der **Prozeß, -sse** (14) trial; **den Prozeß verlieren, verlor, verloren** to lose the case

die **Prüfung, -en** (2) exam, test

der **Punkt, -e** (16) point

pünktlich (1) punctual, on time

putzen (17, 20) to clean; **das Fenster putzen** to wash the window; **sich** (*dat.*) **die Zähne putzen** to brush one's teeth

dia **Qual, -en** (16) pain

das **Rad, ¨er** (5) wheel

das **Radio, -s** (6) radio

der **Rahmen, —** (6) frame

der **Rasen, -n** (20) lawn; **den Rasen mähen** to mow the lawn

sich (*acc.*) **rasieren** (17) to shave

raten (rät), riet, geraten (2, 3) to advise

rauchen (1) to smoke

das **Raumschiff, -e** (20) spaceship

reagieren auf (*acc.*) (8) to react to

die **Rechnung, -en** (1) bill

recht haben (2) to be right

der **Rechtsanwalt, ¨e** (6) male lawyer

die **Rechtsanwältin, -nen** (14) female lawyer

die **Rede, -n** (19) speech; **eine Rede halten (hält), hielt, gehalten** to make a speech

reden (2) to speak, talk

der **Redner, —** (3) speaker

das **Referat, -e** (8) seminar paper (*oral presentation*)

das **Regal, -e** (5) shelf

der **Regenschirm, -e** (20) umbrella

das **Regenwetter** (5) rainy weather

regnen (2) to rain

der **Reifen, —** (12) tire

die **Reihe, -n** (2) row; **in der ersten Reihe** in the first row

die **Reihenfolge, -n** (7) sequence, order

reinigen lassen (20) to have dry-cleaned

die **Reinigung** (5) cleaning; **in die Reinigung bringen** to take to the cleaners

die **Reise, -n** (13) trip; **eine Reise um die Welt machen** to take a trip around the world

der **Reiseleiter, —** (5) male travel guide

die **Reiseleiterin, -nen** female travel guide

reisen (ist) (2, 3) to travel

der **Reisende** (*adj. noun*) (9) traveler

reiten, ritt, ist geritten (3) to ride, go on horseback

reizend (20) charming

die **Reklame, -n** (7) advertisement; **Reklame machen** to advertise

die **Reklamesendung, -en** (5) commercial (*radio, television*)

die **Religion, -en** (5) religion

rennen, rannte, ist gerannt (3) to run

das **Rennpferd, -e** (20) racehorse

reparieren (4) to repair

der **Reporter, —** (5) male reporter

die **Reporterin, -nen** (5) female reporter

die **Republik, -en** (5) republic

das **Restaurant, -s** (5) restaurant

das **Resultat, -e** (16) result

der **Richter, —** (14) judge

richtig (6) right, correct

riechen, roch, gerochen nach (*dat.*) (9, 15) to smell of

der **Ring, -e** (1) ring

der **Roman, -e** (3) novel

der **Rücktritt, -e** (14) resignation

die **Ruhe** (20) quiet, peace; **in Ruhe lassen (läßt), ließ, gelassen** to leave alone

russisch (9) Russian

der **Saal, die Säle** (5) hall

die **Sache, -n** (2) matter, thing

sagen (1) to say; **sagen wir ...** (7) let's say ...

der **Salat, -e** (9) salad

sammeln (2) to collect

der **Samstag, -e** (11) Saturday

der **Satz, ̈-e** (2) sentence

das **Saubermachen** (8) cleaning (*generally house cleaning*)

sauer (9) sour

der **Schach** (19) chess; **Schach spielen** to play chess

schade sein (1) to be a pity

schade (2) too bad

das **Schaf, -e** (9) sheep; **das schwarze Schaf sein** to be the black sheep

die **Schallplatte, -n** (3) record; *short:* **die Platte, -n**

das **Schaufenster, —** (17) shop window; **sich** (*dat.*) **die Schaufenster an•sehen (sieht an), sah an, angesehen** to window-shop

der **Schauspieler, —** (5) male actor

die **Schauspielerin, -nen** (5) actress

der **Scheck, -s** (5) check

schenken (3) to give (*as a gift*)

schick (2) chic

schicken (16) to send

das **Schicksal, -e** (8) destiny, fate

schief•gehen, ging schief, ist schiefgegangen (15) to go wrong

das **Schild, -er** (18) sign

schlafen (schläft), schlief, geschlafen (2, 3) to sleep

der **Schlager, —** (3) pop song

die **Schlagsahne** (4) whipped cream

schlank (10) slim

die **Schlankheitskur, -en** (4) slimming diet; **eine Schlankheitskur machen** to be or go on a diet

der **Schlaukopf, ̈-e** (7) male or female whiz kid, smarty

schlecht (10) bad

schließen, schloß, geschlossen (2) to close

das **Schließfach, ̈-er** (20) locker

das **Schloß, ̈-sser** (18) castle

schneien (3) to snow

schnell (1) fast

schockierend (9) shocking

schockiert sein (1) to be shocked

schon (2) already

schreiben, schrieb, geschrieben (1, 3) to write

die **Schreibmaschine, -n** (13) typewriter

der **Schreibtisch, -e** (7) desk

schreien, schrie, geschrie(e)n (7, 15) to scream, cry out; **vor Schmerzen schreien** to cry out in pain

schüchtern (14) shy

der **Schuh, -e** (5) shoe

die **Schuld, -en** (3) debt; **die Schuld** (18) guilt; **schuld sein an** (*dat.*) (14) to be to blame for

der **Schürzenjäger, —** (20) womanizer

schwänzen (2) to cut or skip class

schwarz (9) black

schweigen, schwieg, geschwiegen (12) to remain silent

schwer (4, 9) heavy; difficult, hard

die **Schwester, -n** (5) sister

die **Schwierigkeit, -en** (8) difficulty; **Schwierigkeiten haben mit** (*dat.*) to have trouble with

das **Schwimmbad, ̈-er** (2) swimming pool

der **See, -n** (19) lake

sehen (sieht), sah, gesehen (2, 3) to see

sehr (1) very

sein, war, ist gewesen (2, 3) to be

seit (*dat.*) (2, 7) since; **seitdem** (8) since then

seit, seitdem (*sub. conj.*) (12) since (*referring to time*)

die **Sekunde, -n** (11) second

selbst (17) oneself; even

der **Selbstmord, -e** (16) suicide; **Selbstmord begehen, beging, begangen** to commit suicide

das **Semester, —** (4) semester, term

die **Semesterarbeit, -en** (4) term paper

senden, sandte, gesandt (3) to send

die **Sendung, -en** (5) broadcast

der **September** (11) September

die **Serviette, -n** (5) napkin

der **Sessel, —** (7) armchair

setzen (20) to put, set, make sit

sich (*acc.*) **setzen** (17) to sit down
siegesbewußt (14) confident of victory
das **Silber** (5) silver
singen, sang, gesungen (3) to sing
der **Sinn, -e** (7) sense, mind
sitzen, saß, gesessen (2, 3) to sit
die **Sitzung, -en** (14) session
der **Skandal, -e** (3) scandal
so ... wie (10) as ... as
sobald (*sub. conj.*) (12) as soon as
sofort (2) immediately, at once
sogar (9) even
solange (*sub. conj.*) (12) as long as
solcher, solches, solche (6) such a; *pl.* such
sollen, sollte, gesollt (4) to be supposed to, expected to, should
der **Sommer, —** (11) summer
die **Sommeferien** (*pl.*) summer vacation
das **Sommerkleid, -er** (5) summer dress
sondern (12) but, rather
der **Sonnabend, -e** (11) Saturday
der **Sonnenuntergang, ⁻e** (6) sunset
der **Sonntag, -e** (1) Sunday
die **Sorge, -n** (10) worry
soviel (2) so much; **soviel ich weiß** (15) as far as I know
das **Spanien** (9) Spain
spanisch (9) Spanish
die **Spannung, -en** (14) tension
sparsam (11) thrifty, economical
der **Spaß** (3) fun; **es macht mir Spaß** it's fun to me, I enjoy it; **zum Spaß sagen** (14) to say as a joke
spät (2) late; **zu spät kommen** (3) to be late
spätestens (10) at the latest
der **Spaziergang, ⁻e** (7) walk
spazieren.gehen, ging spazieren, ist spazierengegangen (3) to go for a walk
die **Spezialität, -en** (5) specialty
spielen (1) to play
der **Sport** (12) sport; **viel Sport treiben, trieb, getrieben** to do a lot of sport
die **Sporthalle, -n** (7) gymnasium
sprechen (spricht), sprach, gesprochen mit (*dat.*) (1, 3, 8) to speak with *or* to; **sprechen von** (*dat.*) (8) to talk of *or* about; **von sich** (*dat.*) **sprechen** to talk of oneself
die **Sprechstunde, -n** (11) consultation (hour); **Sprechstunde haben** to have office hours

die **Stadt, ⁻e** (1) city, town
der **Stadtrat, ⁻e** (14) male town councilor
die **Stadträtin, -nen** (14) female town councilor
der **Stadtteil, -e** (10) part of town
stark (9) strong
statt (*gen.*) (7) instead; **statt dessen** (8) instead of that
das **Statussymbol, -e** (6) status symbol
stehen, stand, gestanden (3) to stand
stehen.bleiben, blieb stehen, ist stehengeblieben (11) to stop (clock)
stehlen (stiehlt), stahl, gestohlen (9) to steal; **der gestohlene Wagen** the stolen car
steigen, stieg, ist gestiegen (3) to climb, go up
die **Stelle, -n** (3) position, job
stellen (20) to put (*in an upright position*)
das **Stellenangebot, -e** (16) job offer
sterben (stirbt), starb, ist gestorben (3) to die; **vor Angst sterben** (13) to die of fear
die **Steuer, -n** (2) tax
das **Stiefkind, -er** (18) stepchild
die **Stimme, -n** (19) voice; **mit lauter (leiser) Stimme** in a loud (low) voice
stimmen (9) to be correct; **das stimmt** *or* **stimmt** that's correct *or* correct
das **Stipendium, die Stipendien** (2) scholarship
der **Stoff, -e** (4) material, fabric
stolz sein auf (*acc.*) (8) to be proud of
stören (2) to disturb
stoßen (stößt), stieß, gestoßen (2, 3) to push
stottern (20) to stutter
die **Strafe, -n** (4) fine
der **Strafzettel, —** (3) traffic ticket
strahlen (14) to beam
streichen, strich, gestrichen (20) to paint (*house*)
streiken (9) to strike, be on strike
der **Streikende** (*adj. noun*) (9) striker
der **Streit** (12) quarrel, fight
streng (10) strict
der **Strumpf, ⁻e** (15) stocking
das **Stück, -e** (4) piece
der **Student** (*weak*), **-en** (5) male student
die **Studentin, -nen** (5) female student
das **Studentenheim, -e** (4) dormitory
studieren (2) to study

das **Studium, die Studien** (11) study; **mit dem Studium auf•hören** (13) to drop out of school (*higher education*); **mit dem Studium fertig werden** to graduate
stumm (17) silent(ly)

die **Stunde, -n** (5, 7) hour; class (*instruction*); **die Deutschstunde** German class
stur (4) stubborn
suchen (9) to seek, to look for

der **Supermarkt** (12) supermarket

das **Symbol, -e** (5) symbol
sympathisch sein (20) to be likeable, pleasant

die **Tablette, -n** (11) tablet, pill; **eine Tablette ein•nehmen (nimmt ein), nahm ein, eingenommen** to take a tablet, pill
tadeln (10) to reprimand

der **Tag, -e** (5) day
taktlos (9) tactless

die **Tankstelle, -n** (1) gas station
tanzen (2) to dance

die **Tasche, -n** (10) bag

die **Tasse, -n** (15) cup

die **Tatsache, -n** (20) fact
sich (*acc.*) **täuschen** (17) to deceive oneself

das **Taxi, -s** (6) taxi

der **Taxifahrer, —** (6) taxi driver

der **Tee, -s** (9) tea

das **Telefon, -e** (7) telephone; **ans Telefon gehen** to go to or answer the phone

das **Telegramm, -e** (3) telegram

der **Tennisplatz, -̈e** (7) tennis court

das **Theater, —** (7) theater

das **Theaterstück, -e** (5) stage play
teuer (9) expensive
tief (2) deep
tippen (13) to type

der **Tisch, -e** (7) table

die **Telefonnummer, -n** (5) telephone number

das **Thema, die Themen** (5) topic, theme

der **Tip, -s** (5) tip, hint, clue

der **Titel, —** (5) title

die **Tortur, -en** (6) torture
tragen (trägt), trug, getragen (3) to carry

der **Trainer, —** (5) coach
trauen (*dat.*) (5) to trust

der **Traum, -̈e** (6) dream

die **Toilette, -n** (1) toilet, lavatory
tolerant (1) tolerant
treten (tritt), trat, getreten (2) to step

treu (4) faithful
trinken, trank, getrunken (3) to drink

das **Trinkgeld, -er** (5) tip, gratuity

die **Trompete, -n** (6) trumpet; **die Trompete spielen** to play the trumpet
trotz (*gen.*) (7) in spite of
trotzdem (3) nevertheless, in spite of that

die **Trunksucht** (8) alcoholism
tun, tat, getan (2, 3) to do; **so tun, als ob ...** (14) to act as if ..., pretend

die **Tür, -en** (2) door

die **U-Bahn, -en** (*short for* **Untergrundbahn**) (7) subway
übel•nehmen (nimmt übel), nahm übel, übelgenommen (2, 3) to take amiss, resent, take offense
üben (6) to practice
über (*acc./dat.*) (7) above, over, across

der **Überblick, -e** (20) overview
überglücklich (18) overjoyed
überholen (4) to overtake, pass

der **Überlebende** (*adj. noun*) survivor
sich (*dat.*) **etwas überlegen** (17) to think about something
übermorgen (11) the day after tomorrow
übernachten (12) to stay overnight

die **Überraschung, -en** (6) surprise
überreden (4) to persuade
übersehen (übersieht), übersah, übersehen (16) to overlook
übersetzen (2) to translate
über•setzen (2) to ferry across
Überstunden machen (12) to work overtime
überzeugen (3) to convince; **überzeugt sein** to be convinced
übrigens (16) by the way

die **Übung, -en** (5) exercise

die **Uhr, -en** (7) clock, watch; **die Uhr stellen** (11) to set the clock
um (*acc.*) (7) around
umarmen (17) to embrace, hug
umgehen, umging, umgangen (2) to circumvent, dodge, evade, bypass
um•gehen, ging um, ist umgegangen (2) to go around, circulate
um•ziehen, zog um, (ist) umgezogen (20) to move (*change residence*)

der **Umzug, -̈e** (15) move (*change of residence*)
unbedingt (12) absolutely, by all means
und (12) and

der **Unfall, ¨e** (3) accident
unfreundlich (2) unfriendly
unhöflich (2) impolite
die **Universität, -en** (5) university
unsicher (8) insecure
der **Unsinn** (3) nonsense
unten (19) at the bottom, below, downstairs; **nach unten gehen** to go downstairs
unter (*acc./dat.*) (7) under
unterbrechen (unterbricht), unterbrach, unterbrochen (18) to interrupt
unterschreiben, unterschrieb, unterschrieben (4) to sign
die **Unterschrift, -en** (4) signature
untersuchen (18) to investigate
die **Untertasse, -n** (20) saucer; **die fliegende Untertasse** flying saucer
die **Unzufriedenheit** (12) dissatisfaction
der **Urlaub, -e** (12) vacation (*from a job*)

die **Vase, -n** (5) vase
der **Verbrecher, —** (20) criminal
verbreiten (18) to spread
verdienen (3, 9) to earn; deserve
sich (*acc.*) **verfahren (verfährt), verfuhr, verfahren** (17) to lose one's way (*driving*)
vergessen (vergißt), vergaß, vergessen (2, 3) to forget
Vergessenheit: in Vergessenheit geraten (20) to fall into oblivion, be forgotten
verhaften (18) to arrest
verhandeln (11) to negotiate
verheiratet sein mit (*dat.*) (8) to be married to
verkaufen (2) to sell
der **Verkäufer, —** (5) salesman
die **Verkäuferin, -nen** (3) saleslady
sich (*acc.*) **verlaufen (verläuft), verlief, verlaufen** (17) to lose one's way (*walking*)
verlegen sein (12) to be embarrassed
verliebt sein in (*acc.*) (8) to be in love with
verlieren, verlor, verloren (3) to lose
verlobt sein mit (*dat.*) (8) to be engaged to
der **Verlobte** (*adj. noun*) (9) fiancé
die **Verlobung, -en** (8) engagement
vermeiden, vermied, vermieden (12) to avoid
vernachlässigen (11) to neglect
vernünftig (2) sensible, reasonable

verrückt sein auf (*acc.*) (8) to be crazy about
verschieben, verschob, verschoben (14) to postpone
verschlafen (verschläft), verschlief, verschlafen (11) to oversleep
verschwinden, verschwand, ist verschwunden (11) to disappear
die **Versicherungsgesellschaft, -en** (13) insurance company
Verspätung haben (12) to be late (*train, bus, plane*)
versprechen (verspricht), versprach, versprochen (3) to promise
das **Versprechen halten (hält), hielt, gehalten** (3) to keep the promise
der **Verstand** (5) reason, mind; **den Verstand verlieren** (6) to lose one's mind
verstehen, verstand, verstanden (1, 3) to understand; **das versteht sich (von selbst)** (18) that is understood, that goes without saying
versteigern (18) to auction off
versuchen (3) to try
die **Versuchung, -en** (4) temptation; **in Versuchung führen** to lead into temptation
sich (*acc.*) **verteidigen** (17) to defend oneself
der **Vertrag, ¨e** (4) contract
verwandt sein mit (*dat.*) (8) to be related to
der **Verwandte** (*adj. noun*) (15) relative
verwöhnen (18) to spoil (*someone*)
Verzeihung: um Verzeihung bitten, bat, gebeten (2, 3) to apologize
viel (2) much, a lot
vieles (16) many things
vielleicht (1) perhaps
völlig (20) completely
von (*dat.*) (7) from, of, by
vor (*acc./dat.*) (7) in front of, before
voraus•sehen (sieht voraus), sah voraus, vorausgesehen (13) to foresee
vorbei•gehen, ging vorbei, ist vorbeigegangen an (*dat.*) (17) to pass by
vor•gehen, ging vor, ist vorgegangen (11) to be fast (*clock*)
vorgestern (11) the day before yesterday
vor•haben, hatte vor, vorgehabt (2) to plan, have plans; **etwas anderes vor•haben** (12) to have something else planned

vorher (19) before

vor•kommen: es kommt mir so vor (14) it seems to me

vor•lesen (liest vor), las vor, vorgelesen (3) to read to (*someone*)

die **Vorlesung, -en** (1) lecture

der **Vormittag, -e** (11) late morning, forenoon

vorn (19) in front; **nach vorn gehen** to go to the front

der **Vorname, -n** (3) first name

der **Vorschlag, ⸚e** suggestion

vorsichtig (2) careful

sich (*dat.*) **etwas vor•stellen** (17) to imagine something

der **Vortrag, ⸚e** (14) lecture

das **Vorurteil, -e** (13) prejudice

wagen (12) to dare

wahr (2) true

während (*gen.*) (7) during

während (*sub. conj.*) (12) while

die **Wahrheit, -en** (1) truth

wahrscheinlich (3) probably

die **Wand, ⸚e** (5) wall

wandern (ist) (3) to wander, hike

die **Wandtafel, -n** or die **Tafel, -n** (7) (black)board

wann (1) when

das **Warenhaus, ⸚er** (7) department store

warm (10) warm

warnen (3) to warn

die **Warnung, -en** (2) warning

warten auf (*acc.*) (2, 8) to wait for

warum (1) why

was (1) what; **was für (ein)** (6) what kind of (a)

sich (*acc.*) **waschen (wäscht), wusch, gewaschen** (17) to wash (*oneself*)

sich (*dat.*) **die Hände waschen** (17) to wash one's hands

das **Wasser** (9) water

weder ... noch (8) neither ... nor

wegen (*gen.*) (7) because of

weil (*sub. conj.*) (12) because

der **Wein, -e** (9) wine

das **Weinglas, ⸚er** (5) wine glass

weiter•lesen (liest weiter), las weiter, weitergelesen (2, 3) to continue reading, go on reading

weiter•machen (2) to continue (*doing something*)

weiter•sprechen (spricht weiter), sprach weiter, weitergesprochen (2, 3) to continue talking, go on talking

welcher, welches, welche (6) which

die **Welt, -en** (7) world

das **Weltwunder, —** (9) wonder of the world

wenden, wandte, gewandt (3) to turn

wenig (2) little; **ein wenig** (4) a little

wenn (*sub. conj.*) (12) when, if; **wenn auch** (16) even though

werden (wird), wurde, ist geworden (1, 3) to get, become

wichtig (10) important

widersprechen (widerspricht), widersprach, widersprochen (*dat.*) (4) to contradict

sich (*dat.*) **widersprechen** (14, 17) to contradict oneself

wie (2) how; **wie lange** how long; **wie oft** how often

wieder (1) again; **schon wieder** (2) again (*emphatic*)

wiederholen (2) to repeat; **die Grammatik wiederholen** to review grammar

wieder•holen (2) to (go and) get something back

wiegen, wog, gewogen (10) to weigh

wieviel (1) how much

die **Willenskraft** (10) willpower

der **Wink, -e** (4) hint; **ein leiser Wink** a subtle hint

winken (20) to wave

der **Winter, —** (5, 11) winter

der **Wintermantel, ⸚** (5) winter coat

wirklich (1) real(ly)

die **Wirklichkeit** (15) reality; **in Wirklichkeit** in reality, in actual fact, actually

wirtschaftlich (14) economical

wissen (weiß) wußte, gewußt (1, 3) to know; **ich weiß es nicht mehr** (3) I don't remember

der **Witz, -e** (6) joke

wo (1) where, at what place

die **Woche, -n** (3) week

das **Wochenende, -n** (8) weekend

das **Wochenendhaus, ⸚er** (8) (weekend) cottage

wohnen (1) to live

die **Wohnung, -en** (3) apartment

wollen (will), wollte, gewollt (4) to want to, intend to; **ich wollte gerade** I was on the point of, I was (just) about to das **Wunder,** — (2) wonder, miracle; **kein Wunder** no wonder

der **Wunsch, ∸e** (18) wish; **einen Wunsch erfüllen** to make a wish come true; **auf eigenen Wunsch** (19) at one's own request

der **Zahnarzt, ∸e** (7) dentist

der **Zahnschmerz, -en** (7) toothache

zeichnen (2) to draw

zeigen (5) to show

die **Zeit, -en** (1) time

die **Zeitung, -en** (2) newspaper

der **Zeitungsstand, ∸e** (7) newsstand

die **Zeitverschwendung, -en** (6) waste of time

zelten (18) to camp (*in a tent*)

zerreißen, zerriß, zerrissen (2) to tear up

der **Zeuge** (*weak*), **-n** (14) witness

das **Zeugnis, -se** (8) report card

das **Ziel, -e** (18) goal; **das Ziel erreichen** to reach the goal

die **Zigarette, -n** (5) cigarette

das **Zimmer,** — (2) room; **in einem Zimmer wohnen mit** (*dat.*) (16) to room with

zu (1) too

zu (*dat.*) (7) to, toward

der **Zucker** (9) sugar

zuerst (2) at first

der **Zufall, ∸e** (20) coincidence

zufrieden sein mit (*dat.*) (8) to be satisfied, content with

der **Zug, ∸e** (14) train; **den Zug verpassen** to miss the train

zu•geben (gibt zu), gab zu, zugegeben (4) to admit

zu•hören (2) to listen

der **Zukunftsplan, ∸e** (8) plan for the future

zu•machen (2) to close

zu•nehmen (nimmt zu), nahm zu, zugenommen (2, 3) to gain weight

zurück•bringen, brachte zurück, zurückgebracht (2, 3) to bring back, take back

zurück•fahren (fährt zurück) fuhr zurück, ist zurückgefahren (2, 3) to drive back, return

zurück•geben (gibt zurück), gab zurück, zurückgegeben (2, 3) to give back, return

zurück•gehen, ging zurück, ist zurückgegangen (2, 3) to go back, return

zurück•treten (tritt zurück, trat zurück, ist zurückgetreten (14) to resign

zusammen•arbeiten (14) to work together, collaborate

zusammen•stoßen (stößt zusammen), stieß zusammen, ist zusammengestoßen (20) to collide

zuviel (2) too much

der **Zweck, -e** (12) purpose; **es hat keinen Zweck** it's no use, there is no point

zwischen (*acc./dat.*) (7) between

English-German Vocabulary

The explanations at the beginning of the German-English vocabulary apply also to the English-German vocabulary. The following listing contains the vocabulary items of the exercises that require translation from English into German.

to be able to (4) können (kann), konnte, gekonnt

above, over (7) über (*acc./dat.*)

achievement (16) die Leistung, -en

across from (7) gegenüber (*dat.*)

ad, advertisement (20) das Inserat, -e

admire (16) bewundern

to admit (4) zu•geben (gibt zu), gab zu, zugegeben

adult (9) der Erwachsene (*adj. noun*)

afford: to be able to afford something (17) sich (*dat.*) etwas leisten können

after (*prep.*) (7) nach (*dat.*)

after (*sub. conj.*) (12) nachdem

afternoon (11) der Nachmittag, -e

to be afraid (2) Angst haben

against (7) gegen (*acc.*)

airport (6) der Flughafen, ˙-; **to take to the airport** zum Flughafen bringen, brachte, gebracht

alarm clock (11) der Wecker, —; **to set the alarm clock** den Wecker stellen

all (6) alle

to be allowed to (4) dürfen (darf), durfte, gedurft

almost (14) beinah(e), fast

along (7) entlang (*acc.*)

although (12) obgleich, obwohl (*sub. conj.*)

always (2) immer

to be angry with (8) böse sein auf (*acc.*) or mit (*dat.*)

to become angry (3) böse werden (wird), wurde, ist geworden

to answer something (7) antworten auf (*acc.*)

antique (16) antik

to apologize (2) um Verzeihung bitten, bat, gebeten; (17) sich (*acc.*) entschuldigen

around (7) um (*acc.*)

artist (20) der Künstler, —

to arrest (18) verhaften

aside from that, besides (8) außerdem

to ask for, request (8) bitten, bat, gebeten um (*acc.*)

assistant (5) der Assistent (*weak*), -en

to assume (2) an•nehmen (nimmt an), nahm an, angenommen

at, at someone's place (6) bei (*dat.*)

attitude (16) die Haltung, -en

to auction off (18) versteigern

auditorium (7) das Auditorium, die Auditorien

to avoid (18) vermeiden, vermied, vermieden

bad: too bad (2) schade

bag (10) die Tasche, -n

ballpoint pen (6) der Kugelschreiber, —

bank (7) die Bank, -en

to bark (9) bellen

beginning (5) der Anfang, ˙-e

because (12) weil (*sub. conj.*)

because of (7) wegen (gen.); **because of me** wegen mir or meinetwegen; **because of that, therefore** (8) deswegen, deshalb

bed (7) das Bett, -en

before (*prep.*) (7) vor (acc./*dat.*)

before (*sub. conj.*) (12) bevor, ehe

behind (7) hinter (*acc./dat.*)

to begin (2, 3) an•fangen (fängt an), fing an, angefangen

to believe (1) glauben
bell: the bell is ringing (15) es klingelt
beside (7) neben (acc./dat.); to be beside
  oneself (17) außer sich (dat.) sein
besides (7) außer (dat.)
best: all the best (9) alles Gute!
better: to get better (4) besser werden (wird),
  wurde, ist geworden
between (7) zwischen (acc./dat.)
bill (4) die Rechnung, -en
black (10) schwarz
bookstore (7) die Buchhandlung, -en
to be or get bored (17) sich (acc.) langweilen
boss (5) der Chef, -s; die Chefin, -nen
both (6) beide
to bowl (8) kegeln; to go bowling kegeln
  gehen, ging, ist gegangen
break: to take a break (2) eine Pause machen
briefcase (7) die Aktentasche, -n
to bring along (12) mit•bringen, brachte mit,
  mitgebracht
broadcast (6) die Sendung, -en
to be broke (13) pleite sein
brother (5) der Bruder, ¨
brown (10) braun
to bury (2) begraben (begräbt), begrub, begraben
business: that's nobody's business (15) das
  geht niemand etwas an
but (however, nevertheless) (12) aber
but (rather) (12) sondern
to buy (2) kaufen

cake (15) der Kuchen, —
to call (phone) (4) an•rufen, rief an, angerufen
to call off (18) ab•sagen
can (4) können (kann), konnte, gekonnt;
  I can't help it ich kann nicht anders
camera (5) Kamera, -s
car (1) der Wagen, —; das Auto, -s; to go by
  car (6) mit dem Wagen (Auto) fahren
car accident (14) der Autounfall, ¨e
care: to take care of (2) erledigen
career (6) die Karriere, -n
careful(ly) (2) vorsichtig
to cash a check (6) einen Scheck
  ein•lösen
catalogue (6) der Katalog, -e
to catch a cold (17) sich (acc.) erkälten
chance (6) die Chance, -n
cheap (16) billig
check (8) der Scheck, -s

chess (18) das Schach
child (5) das Kind, -er
child prodigy (20) das Wunderkind, -er
to clarify (18) klären
class: German class (7) die Deutschstunde, -n
to close (4) zu•machen
coach (5) der Trainer, —
coffee (7) der Kaffee; to make coffee (10)
  Kaffee kochen
coincidence (20) der Zufall, ¨e
color (10) die Farbe, -n
combination (14) die Kombination, -en
to come along (12) mit•kommen, kam mit, ist
  mitgekommen
to come in (2) herein•kommen, kam herein, ist
  hereingekommen
comfortable (10) bequem
commercial (radio, television) (5) die Werbesendung, -en
complicated (10) kompliziert
compliment (6) das Kompliment, -e
composition (10) der Aufsatz, ¨e
compromise: to make a compromise (12) einen
  Kompromiß schließen, schloß, geschlossen
to concentrate on (17) sich (acc.) konzentrieren
  auf (acc.)
concerned: as far as I am concerned (7) meinetwegen
concert (7) das Konzert, -e
to congratulate on (8) gratulieren zu (dat.)
consequence (12) die Folge, -n
contract (4) der Vertrag, ¨e
to contradict (12) widersprechen (widerspricht),
  widersprach, widersprochen (dat.)
contrary: on the contrary (4) im Gegenteil
to convince (12) überzeugen
to cook (17) kochen; to do one's own cooking
  selbst kochen
cookie (4) das Plätzchen, —
corner (7) die Ecke, -n
to cost (16) kosten
courage (12) der Mut
crazy (8) verrückt; to be crazy about verrückt
  sein auf (acc.); to drive crazy (16) verrückt
  machen
cruel (6) grausam
crummy (12) mies
to cry (20) weinen
curiosity (13) die Neugierde; to die of curiosity
  vor Neugierde sterben (stirbt), starb, ist gestorben
customer (5) der Kunde (weak), -n

dangerous (12) gefährlich
to dare (12) wagen
darling (8) der Liebling, -e (*male or female*)
date (5) das Datum, die Daten
daughter (5) die Tochter, ¨
day (11) der Tag, -e
to deal with, be about (7) handeln von (*dat.*)
dean (5) der Dekan, -e
to defend oneself (17) sich (*acc.*) verteidigen
dentist (7) Zahnarzt, ¨e
department store (7) das Warenhaus, ¨er
desk (3) der Schreibtisch, -e
destiny, fate (8) das Schicksal, -e
detail (16) Einzelheit, -en
to develop (20) entwickeln
to die (13) sterben (stirbt), starb, ist gestorben;
  to die of fear vor Angst sterben
diet: to be on a diet (4) eine Schlankheitskur
  machen
director (5) der Direktor, -en
to disappoint (4) enttäuschen
disco (7) die Disko, -s
dishes: to do the dishes (12) das Geschirr
  spülen
to disturb (2) stören
to do (3) tun, tat, getan
dog (7) der Hund, -e
dormitory (2) das Studentenheim, -e
drama (5) das Drama, die Dramen
dream (6) Traum, ¨e
to drink (4) trinken, trank, getrunken
to drive (2) fahren (fährt), fuhr, ist gefahren
driver's license (6) der Führerschein, -e
to drop a course (16) mit einem Kurs auf•
  hören
to dry-clean (20) reinigen; **to have
  something dry-cleaned** etwas reinigen
  lassen
dumb (10) dumm
during (7) während (*gen.*)

early (10) früh; **at the earliest** frühestens
easy (12) leicht
to eat out (17) essen gehen, ging, ist gegangen
egotistical (10) egoistisch
embarrassing (16) peinlich
to embrace, hug (17) umarmen
employee (9) der Angestellte (*adj. noun*)
end (5) das Ende, -n
enemy (6) der Feind, -e
engaged (8) verlobt; **to be engaged to** verlobt
  sein mit (*dat.*)

enough (1) genug
to be enthusiastic about (8) begeistert sein
  von (*dat.*)
to envy (2) beneiden
error (20) der Irrtum, ¨er
evening (11) der Abend, -e
every (6) jeder, jedes, jede
exam (3) die Prüfung, -en; **to pass the exam**
  die Prüfung bestehen, bestand, bestanden;
  to flunk the exam in der Prüfung durch•
  fallen (fällt durch), fiel durch, ist durchgefallen
except (7) außer (*dat.*)
excuse, pretext (20) die Ausrede, -n
to excuse (2) entschuldigen
to expect (12) erwarten
expensive (13) teuer
to exploit (18) aus•nutzen
extremely (10) äußerst

to be fair (2) fair sein
faith (5) der Glaube (*weak; gen.* -ns), -en
faithful (12) treu
fall (11) der Herbst, -e
to fall asleep (14) ein•schlafen (schläft ein),
  schlief ein, ist eingeschlafen
family (8) die Familie, -n
famous (9) berühmt
fast (10) schnell; **to be fast** (*clock*) (11) vor•
  gehen, ging vor, ist vorgegangen
fat (12) dick
father (7) der Vater, ¨
favor: to ask for a favor (12) um einen Gefallen bitten, bat, gebeten
to feel like (12) Lust haben zu (*dat.*)
a few (9) ein paar
fight, quarrel (12) der Streit
film (9) der Film, -e
to find (12) finden, fand, gefunden
to finish (*talking*) (20) aus•reden
fire: there is a fire (15) es brennt
floor (7) der Fußboden, ¨, *short:* der Boden, ¨
flower (8) die Blume, -n
to flunk: to flunk the exam (3) in der Prüfung
  durch•fallen (fällt durch), fiel durch, ist
  durchgefallen
flying saucer (20) die fliegende Untertasse, -n
folder (7) die Mappe, -n
to be fond of (20) gern haben
for (*prep.*) (7) für (*acc.*)
for (*coord. conj.*) (12) denn
foreigner (5) der Ausländer, —

to foresee (13) voraus•sehen (sieht voraus), sah voraus, vorausgesehen

to forget (2) vergessen (vergißt), vergaß, vergessen

Friday (11) Freitag, -e

friend (1) der Freund, -e; die Freundin, -nen

friendly (10) freundlich

from (7) aus (*dat.*) *or* von (*dat.*); **from ... to ...** (11) von ... bis ...

to gain weight (4) zu•nehmen (nimmt zu), nahm zu, zugenommen

garage (7) die Garage, -n

gentleman (5) der Herr (*weak*; -n) -en

to get, become (2, 3) werden (wird), wurde, ist geworden

to get, receive (2, 3) bekommen, bekam, bekommen

to get along with (12) aus•kommen, kam aus, ist ausgekommen mit (*dat.*)

to get one's Master's degree (12) den Magister machen

to get used *or* **accustomed to** (17) sich (*acc.*) gewöhnen an (*acc.*)

gift (8) das Geschenk, -e

girlfriend (1) die Freundin, -nen

to give up (12) auf•geben (gibt auf), gab auf, aufgegeben

glad (3) froh; **to be glad about** (8) froh sein über (*acc.*)

to go (2, 3) gehen, ging, ist gegangen; **to go back** (2, 3) zurück•gehen; **to go home** (2) nach Hause gehen; **to go into** (16) ein•gehen auf (*acc.*); **to go on foot** (13) zu Fuß gehen; **to go out** (13) aus•gehen; **to go wrong** (15) schief•gehen

good (3) gut

to gossip (4) klatschen

grade (4) die Note, -n

great (13) großartig

to grumble (4) knurren

haircut: to get a haircut (20) sich (*dat.*) die Haare schneiden lassen

hairdresser (14) der Friseur, -e

to hand in (4) ein•reichen

to handle (*treat*) (12) behandeln

to happen (3) passieren (ist)

to be happy about (8) glücklich sein über (*acc.*); (17) sich (*acc.*) freuen über (*acc.*)

hard, difficult (10) schwer; **the hardest thing** (10) das Schwerste

to hate (8) hassen

to have (2) haben (hat), hatte, gehabt

to have to (4) müssen (muß), mußte, gemußt

head: to lose one's head (6) den Kopf verlieren, verlor, verloren

to hear (14) hören

heart (5) das Herz (*weak*; *gen.* -ns), -en

help (8) die Hilfe, -n

to help (8) helfen (hilft), half, geholfen (*dat.*); **please help yourself** (17) bitte bedienen Sie sich

her (*poss.*) (6) ihr, ihre

hero (5) der Held (*weak*), -en

hint (5) der Tip, -s

his (*poss.*) (6) sein, seine

to hit the books (4) die Nase ins Buch stecken

hobby (5) das Hobby, -s

home: to be at home (1) zu Hause sein; **to go home** (2) nach Hause gehen; (14) **to stay at home** (14) zu Hause bleiben

hook (7) der Haken, —

hope (14) die Hoffnung; **to give up hope** die Hoffnung auf•geben (gibt auf), gab auf, aufgegeben

to hope (1) hoffen; **I hope** *or* **hopefully** hoffentlich

hot (9) heiß

hotel (5) das Hotel, -s

house (2) das Haus, ¨er

humid (12) feucht

hurry: to be in a hurry (2) es eilig haben

ID card (17) der Ausweis, -e

idea: to have no idea (2) keine Ahnung haben

if (12) wenn (*subj. conj.*)

to ignore (6) ignorieren

to imagine something (17) sich (*dat.*) etwas vorstellen

impolite (2) unhöflich

important (10) wichtig

to inherit (16) erben

insecure (10) unsicher

to improve, become better (6) besser werden (wird), wurde, ist geworden

in, into, to (7) in (*acc./dat.*)

information: to give information (9) Auskunft geben (gibt), gab, gegeben

in front of (7) vor (*acc./dat.*)

in spite of (7) trotz (*gen.*); **in spite of that** (8) trotzdem

instead (7) anstatt, statt (*gen.*); **instead of that** (8) statt dessen

insurance company (13) die Versicherungsgesellschaft, -en
to be interested in (17) sich (*acc.*) interessieren für (*acc.*)
interesting (9) interessant
to interrupt (14) unterbrechen (unterbricht), unterbrach, unterbrochen
invention (6) die Erfindung, -en
inventor (6) der Erfinder, —
to invite (2, 3) ein•laden (lädt ein), lud ein, eingeladen
its (*poss.*) (6) sein, seine *or* ihr, ihre

janitor (5) der Hausmeister, —
job (5) der Job, -s *or* die Stelle, -n
joke (8) der Witz, -e
just about: I was just about to ... (4) ich wollte gerade (eben) ...

to keep the promise (12) das Versprechen halten (hält), hielt, gehalten
key (3) der Schlüssel, —
to know (*something as a fact*) (3) wissen (weiß), wußte, gewußt; **Dr. know-it-all** (14) Dr Allwissend
to know (*be acquainted with*) (3) kennen, kannte, gekannt

lady (5) die Dame, -n
to land (3) landen (ist)
late (3) spät; **to be late** zu spät kommen, kam, ist gekommen; **at the latest** (10) spätestens
the latest (10) das Neu(e)ste
to laugh (2) lachen; **to laugh at** (3) aus•lachen *or* (8) lachen über (*acc.*)
lawyer (6) der Rechtsanwalt, ¨e; (14) die Rechtsanwältin, -nen
lazy (13) faul
lazybones (6) der Faulenzer, —; die Faulenzerin, -nen
to leave alone (20) in Ruhe lassen (läßt), ließ, gelassen
Lebanon (6) der Libanon
at least (10) mindestens
leather (7) das Leder
less (10) weniger
letter (8) der Brief, -e
library (7) die Bibliothek, -en
lie (20) die Lüge, -n
life (10) das Leben

to like (4) mögen; **I would like** ich möchte; (5) gefallen (gefällt), gefiel, gefallen (*dat.*); **like to do something** (20) etwas gern tun
likeable (20) sympathisch; **not likeable** unsympathisch
to listen (3) zu•hören
a little (10) etwas, ein wenig
to live (1) wohnen
logical (10) logisch
as long as (12) solange (*sub. conj.*)
to look at, take a look at (17) sich (*dat.*) etwas an•schauen *or* an•sehen (sieht an), sah an, angesehen
to look forward to (17) sich (*acc.*) freuen auf. (*acc.*)
to lose (3) verlieren, verlor, verloren
to lose weight (3) ab•nehmen (nimmt ab), nahm ab, abgenommen
to lose one's way (17) (*walking*) sich (*acc.*) verlaufen, verlief, verlaufen; (*driving*) sich (*acc.*) verfahren (verfährt), verfuhr, verfahren
a lot (3) viel
loud (14) laut
to be in love with (8) verliebt sein in (*acc.*)
love story (6) die Liebesgeschichte, -n
to be lucky (3) Glück haben, hatte, gehabt

machine (6) die Maschine, -n
to make (3) machen; **to make money** Geld verdienen
man (9) der Mann, ¨er
to manipulate (14) manipulieren
many a (6) mancher, manches, manche
matter (2) die Sache, -n
to marry, get married (13) heiraten
to be married to (8) verheiratet sein mit (*dat.*)
may, to be allowed to (4) dürfen (darf), durfte, gedurft
mayor (5) der Bürgermeister, —; die Bürgermeisterin, -nen
to mean (6) meinen
to meet (*for the first time*) (4) kennen•lernen
to memorize (18) auswendig lernen
message (17) die Nachricht, -en
mind: to lose one's mind (6) den Verstand verlieren, verlor, verloren
mistake (6) der Fehler, —
to be mistaken (17) sich (*acc.*) irren
modern languages (10) Neuere Sprachen
modesty (17) die Bescheidenheit
money (6) das Geld
Monday (11) der Montag, -e

month (11) der Monat, -e

mood: to be in a good/bad mood (1) gute/ schlechte Laune haben

more (10) mehr

morning (11) der Morgen; **late morning, fore-noon** der Vormittag, -e

most: at the most (10) höchstens

mostly, most of the time, usually (10) meistens, meist

motel (5) das Motel, -s

mother (7) die Mutter, ¨

to move to the country (13) aufs Land ziehen, zog, ist gezogen

movie (9) der Film, -e; **to go to the movies** (2) ins Kino gehen, ging, ist gegangen

movie theater (5) das Kino, -s

to mow (20) mähen; **to mow the lawn** (20) den Rasen mähen

mistake (9) der Fehler, —

museum (5) das Museum, die Museen

music (20) die Musik

must (4) müssen (muß), mußte, gemußt

must not (4) nicht dürfen (darf)

my (poss.) (6) mein, meine

name (5) der Name (weak; gen. -ns), -n

neat, orderly (10) ordentlich

necessary (2) nötig

neighbor (6) der Nachbar, -n; die Nachbarin, -nen

nervous (2) nervös; **to get nervous** (2, 3) nervös werden (wird), wurde, ist geworden

never (4) nie, noch nie

news (8) die Nachricht, -en

newspaper (20) die Zeitung, -en

newsstand (7) der Zeitungsstand, ¨-e

next to (7) neben (acc./dat.)

the next one (10) der Nächste; die Nächste (adj. noun)

night (11) (before bedtime) der Abend, -e; (after bedtime) die Nacht, ¨-e **tonight** heute abend; heute nacht

no, not a, not any (6) kein, keine

nobody (3) niemand; **nobody else** (15) niemand anders

noise (17) der Lärm

noon (11) der Mittag, -e

nosy (10) neugierig

not (1) nicht; **not yet** (8) noch nicht

nothing (12) nichts

to notice (3) merken

to notify (18) benachrichtigen

novel (5) der Roman, -e

nowhere, not anywhere (15) (motion to a place) nirgend(s)wohin; (place at which) nirgend(s)wo, nirgends

observation (12) die Bemerkung, -en

of, from (7) von (dat.)

of course (8) natürlich

offense: to take offense (2, 3) übel•nehmen (nimmt übel), nahm übel, übelgenommen

office (7) das Büro, -s

often (2) oft

on (7) (horizontal surface) auf (acc./dat.); (vertical surface) an (acc./dat.)

only (9) nur; **not only ... but also** (12) nicht nur ... sondern auch

opinion (7) die Meinung, -en; **in my opinion** meiner Meinung nach

or (6) oder

orange juice (10) der Orangensaft, ¨-e

our (poss.) (6) unser, uns(e)re

out of (7) aus (dat.)

to overlook (16) übersehen (übersieht), übersah, übersehen

overnight: to stay overnight (12) übernachten

to oversleep (14) verschlafen (verschläft), verschlief, verschlafen

over there (16) da drüben

to paint the house (20) das Haus streichen, strich, gestrichen

parents (10) die Eltern; **most parents** die meisten Eltern

to park (12) parken

party (5) die Party, -s

to pass the exam (3) die Prüfung bestehen, bestand, bestanden

patience (13) die Geduld

to pay (4) bezahlen

peace (5) der Friede (weak; gen. -ns)

people (5) die Leute

perhaps (1) vielleicht

permanent: to get a permanent (20) sich (dat.) eine Dauerwelle machen lassen

permission: to ask for permission (12) um Erlaubnis bitten

perseverance (13) die Ausdauer

petty (13) kleinlich

phone (7) das Telefon, -e

piano (6) das Klavier, -e; **to play the piano** Klavier spielen

to pick up (2) ab•holen; **to pick up the mail** (12) die Post ab•holen

picnic (18) das Picknick, -e or -s

pictures: to take pictures (8) Aufnahmen machen

pineapple punch (20) Ananasbowle

pity: it is a pity (4) es ist schade

to plan (12) vor•haben; **to have other plans** etwas anderes vor•haben

plane (3) das Flugzeug, -e

play (*stage*) (5) das Theaterstück, -e

please (2) bitte

poem (16) das Gedicht, -e

point (16) der Punkt, -e

policeman (5) der Polizist (*weak*), -en; **policewoman** die Polizistin, -nen

popular (20) beliebt

possible (1) möglich

to postpone (18) verschieben, verschob, verschoben

practical (10) praktisch

prejudice (13) das Vorurteil, -e

president (5) der Präsident (*weak*), -en

to pretend (14) so tun, als ob

pretty (10) hübsch

prize (14) der Preis, -e; **to win the first prize** den ersten Preis gewinnen

problem (4) das Problem, -e

project (8) das Projekt, -e

to promote (18) befördern

to propose (*marriage*) (18) einen Heiratsantrag machen

to protest (4) protestieren

to be proud of (8) stolz sein auf (*acc.*)

question (8) die Frage, -n

quiet (2) still

railway station (14) der Bahnhof, ¨-e

rain (7) der Regen

rainy weather (5) das Regenwetter

raise (*salary*) (12) die Gehaltserhöhung, -en; **to ask for a raise** (13) um eine Gehaltserhöhung bitten, bat, gebeten

to react to (8) reagieren auf (*acc.*)

real(ly) (12) wirklich

reason: for this/that reason (7) aus diesem Grund

receiver: to put down the receiver, to hang up (12) den Hörer auf•legen

to recognize (8) erkennen, erkannte, erkannt

record (6) die Schallplatte, -n or die Platte, -n

record player (6) der Plattenspieler, —

refrigerator (20) der Kühlschrank, ¨-e

to be related to (8) verwandt sein mit (*dat.*)

relative (15) der Verwandte (*adj. noun*)

reliable (12) zuverlässig

to remember (17) sich (*acc.*) erinnern an (*acc.*); **I don't remember** (3) ich weiß es nicht mehr

report card (8) das Zeugnis, -se

reporter (5) der Reporter, —; die Reporterin, -nen

to reprimand (10) tadeln

to resent (3) übel•nehmen (nimmt übel), nahm übel, übelgenommen

restaurant (5) das Restaurant, -s

to be right (2, 3) recht haben, hatte, gehabt

ring (6) der Ring, -e

river (7) der Fluß, ¨-sse

to room with (16) in einem Zimmer wohnen mit (*dat.*)

rumor (14) das Gerücht, -e

to run away (12) davon•laufen (läuft davon), lief davon, ist davongelaufen

same: the same (9) derselbe, dasselbe, dieselbe; **it's all the same to me** (15) es ist mir ganz gleich

to be satisfied or **content with** (8) zufrieden sein mit (*dat.*)

Saturday (11) der Sonnabend, -e or der Samstag, -e

to save (*money*) (12) sparen

to say (4) sagen

scholar (9) der or die Gelehrte (*adj. noun*)

scholarship (3) das Stipendium, die Stipendien; **to get a scholarship** ein Stipendium bekommen, bekam, bekommen

school (6) die Schule, -n

second-hand (9) gebraucht

secret (6) das Geheimnis, -se

to see (20) sehen (sieht), sah, gesehen

to sell (2) verkaufen

semester (5) das Semester, —

seminar paper (8) das Referat, -e (*oral presentation*)

to send (6) schicken

to set the clock (11) die Uhr stellen

shall (4) sollen

to shave (17) sich (*acc.*) rasieren

shocked (3) schockiert

shoe (10) der Schuh, -e

short (*a person's height*) (10) klein

to show (6) zeigen

shrimp (20) die Krabbe, -n

shy (14) schüchtern

sick (6) krank

to sign (4) unterschreiben, unterschrieb, unterschrieben

silent: to remain silent (12) schweigen, schwieg, geschwiegen

simple (4) einfach

since (prep.) (7) seit (dat.)

since (sub. conj.) (12) (referring to time) seit, seitdem; (stating reason) da

since then (18) seitdem

to be single (13) ledig sein

sister (8) die Schwester, -n

to sit down (17) sich (acc.) setzen

to skip class (2) schwänzen

to sleep (2, 3) schlafen (schläft), schlief, geschlafen

slim (10) schlank

sloppy (10) liederlich

slow (10) langsam; **to be slow** (clock) (11) nach•gehen, ging nach, ist nachgegangen

to smoke (13) rauchen

so that, in order that (12) damit (sub. conj.)

soccer field (7) der Fußballplatz, ˙-e; **soccer game** das Fußballspiel, -e; **soccer player** (5) der Fußballspieler, —

to solve the problem (12) das Problem lösen

solution (10) die Lösung, -en

some (9) einige; etwas

somebody (15) jemand; **somebody else** jemand anders

somehow or other (15) irgendwie

something (9) etwas; **something or other** (15) irgend etwas

some time or other (15) irgendwann

somewhere, anywhere (15) (motion to a place) irgendwohin; (place at which) irgendwo

son (5) der Sohn, ˙-e

soon (14) bald; **as soon as** (12) sobald (sub. conj.)

Spanish (7) spanisch

to speak (14) sprechen (spricht), sprach, gesprochen

speech: to make a speech (19) eine Rede halten (hält), hielt, gehalten

to spend money (10) Geld aus•geben (gibt aus), gab aus, ausgegeben

sport: to do a lot of sport (12) viel Sport treiben, trieb, getrieben

spring (11) der Frühling, -e

stage fright (20) das Lampenfieber

stamp collection (7) die Briefmarkensammlung, -en

status symbol (6) das Statussymbol, -e

to stay (13) bleiben, blieb, ist geblieben; **to stay a little longer** etwas länger bleiben; **to stay fit** fit bleiben (12)

to stop, end, cease (2) auf•hören, Schluß machen

story (5) die Geschichte, -n

to straighten up (3) auf•räumen

strict (10) streng

strike (18) der Streik, -s

stubborn (4) stur

student (6) der Student (weak), -en; die Studentin, -nen

to study for an exam (4) für eine Prüfung lernen

stupid (9) dumm

subway: to go by subway (6) mit der U-Bahn fahren

success (6) der Erfolg, -e

such a (6) solcher, solches, solche or solch ein, solch eine or so ein, so eine

suggestion (6) der Vorschlag, ˙-e

suitcase (8) der Koffer, —

summer (11) der Sommer, —

Sunday (11) der Sonntag, -e

to be supposed to (4) sollen (soll), sollte, gesollt

surprise (6) die Überraschung, -en

Switzerland (6) die Schweiz

table (7) der Tisch, -e

to take along (12) mit•nehmen (nimmt mit), nahm mit, mitgenommen

to take care of (2) erledigen

to take seriously (12) ernst nehmen (nimmt), nahm, genommen

to talk of or **about** (8) sprechen (spricht), sprach, gesprochen von (dat.); **to talk with** or **to** sprechen mit (dat.)

tall (a person's height) (10) groß

to taste (10) schmecken

teacher (9) der Lehrer, —

telephone number (5) Telefonnummer, -n

television set (12) der Fernseher, —

to tell (3) sagen; (relate) (6) erzählen

temptation (4) die Versuchung, -en; **to lead into temptation** in Versuchung führen

tennis court (7) der Tennisplatz, ˙-e

tenor (20) der Tenor, ˙-e

term paper (4) die Semesterarbeit, -en

terrible (16) schrecklich
to thank for (7) danken für (*acc.*)
that (1) daß (*sub. conj.*)
that, those (6) jener, jenes, jene
their (*poss.*) (6) ihr, ihre
there is, there are (10) es gibt (*acc.*)
thing: the first thing (16) das erste; **the last thing** das letzte; **the only thing** das einzige; **many things** vieles
to think of *or* **about** (8) denken, dachte, gedacht an (*acc.*); (17) sich (*dat.*) etwas überlegen
this, these (6) dieser, dieses, diese
through (7) durch (*acc.*)
thunderstorm (7) das Gewitter, —
Thursday (11) der Donnerstag, -e
time: to be on time (16) pünktlich sein
title (5) der Titel, —
to (*prep.*) (7) zu (*dat.*); nach (*dat.*)
tolerant (1) tolerant
tomorrow (2) morgen
too (13) zu; **too bad** (3) schade
topic (5) das Thema, die Themen
torture (6) die Tortur, -en
train: to go by train (6) mit dem Zug *or* mit der Bahn fahren (fährt), fuhr, ist gefahren
to travel (3) reisen (ist)
traveler's check (6) der Reisescheck, -s
tree (7) der Baum, ̈-e
trip (17) die Reise, -n
trouble: to have trouble with (8) Schwierigkeiten haben mit (*dat.*)
true (3) wahr
to try (3) versuchen; **to try again** noch einmal versuchen
Tuesday (11) der Dienstag, -e
Turkey (6) die Türkei
to type (13) tippen
typewriter (13) die Schreibmaschine, -n

under (7) unter (*acc./dat.*)
to understand (3) verstehen, verstand, verstanden
unfortunately (18) leider
until (2, 12) bis
use: it's no use (12) es hat keinen Zweck

vacation (*from a job*) (12) der Urlaub, -e
very (10) sehr
village (7) das Dorf, ̈-er
violin (6) die Geige *or* die Violine; **to play the violin** Geige/Violine spielen

to visit (2) besuchen

to wait for (8) warten auf (*acc.*)
to want to (4) wollen (will), wollte, gewollt
to warn (4) warnen
warning (6) die Warnung, -en
to wash (*oneself*) (17) sich (*acc.*) waschen (wäscht), wusch, gewaschen; **to wash one's hands** sich (*dat.*) die Hände waschen; **to wash the windows** (20) die Fenster putzen
to watch television (4) fern•sehen (sieht fern), sah fern, ferngesehen
to wave (20) winken
weather (7) das Wetter; **in this weather** bei diesem Wetter
Wednesday (11) der Mittwoch, -e
week (11) die Woche, -n
weekend (11) das Wochenende, -n
what (2) was; **what a** (6) welch ein, eine; was für ein, eine; **what kind of** was für
when (12) wann, wenn, als
where (*at what place*) (1) wo; (*to what place*) (7) wohin
whether, if (1) ob
which (6) welcher, welches, welche
while (12) während (*sub. conj.*)
who (8) wer
why (1) warum
widow (6) Witwe, -n
wife (8) die Frau, -en
will power (10) die Willenskraft
to window-shop (17) sich (*dat.*) die Schaufenster an•sehen (sieht an), sah an, angesehen
windy (13) windig
winter (11) der Winter, —
with (7) mit (*dat.*)
without (7) ohne (*acc.*)
word of honor (6) das Ehrenwort
work (17) die Arbeit, -en
to work on (8) arbeiten an (*dat.*)
worker (5) der Arbeiter, —
world (7) die Welt, -en
worse: to get worse (4) schlechter werden (wird), wurde, ist geworden
worry (10) die Sorge, -n
wrong (14) falsch

year (11) das Jahr, -e
yesterday (11) gestern
young (9) jung
your (*poss.*) (6) dein, deine (*fam. sing.*); euer, eu(e)re (*fam. pl.*); Ihr, Ihre (*formal*)

INDEX